Cyclopedia of Magic

THE CUPS AND BALLS

Cyclopedia of Magic

BASED ON THE WRITINGS AND PERFORMANCES OF
Annemann, Blackstone, Cardini, de Biere, de Kolta, Devant, Downs, Erdnase, Farelli, Gibson, Goldin, Goldston, Herrmann, Hertz, Hilliard, Hoffmann, Houdini, Hugard, Kellar, Leipzig, the Maskelynes, Mulholland, Lang Neil, Okito, Robert-Houdin, Roterberg, Sachs, Thurston, and many others.

Henry Hay, Editor

SPECIAL CONTRIBUTIONS BY

Henry Blanchard, Louise Gifford, Frederick Little, Barrows Mussey, Doris Robbins, and Leo Rullman.

ILLUSTRATED WITH FORTY-TWO PHOTOGRAPHS BY AUDREY ALLEY,

PORTRAITS, AND OVER 350 LINE DRAWINGS

Dover Publications Inc., New York

Published in Canada by General Publishing Company, Ltd., 30 Lesmill Road, Don Mills, Toronto, Ontario.
Published in the United Kingdom by Constable and Company, Ltd., 10 Orange Street, London WC 2.

This Dover edition, first published in 1975, is an unabridged and unaltered republication of the work originally published by David McKay Company in 1949.

International Standard Book Number: 0-486-21808-2
Library of Congress Catalog Card Number: 74-27511

Manufactured in the United States of America
Dover Publications, Inc.
180 Varick Street
New York, N. Y. 10014

USER'S GUIDE

The prospective reader is entitled to know what this book attempts, and how it goes about it.

In the first place, it does *not* pretend to make magicians; it only steers the user to the classic and indispensable books that do make magicians—Hoffmann, Sachs, Downs, Hilliard, Devant, Hugard.

In the second place, neither novelty nor originality has been aimed at. The volume is frankly derivative; many of its articles have been extracted directly from standard works. "Latest novelties" of every kind, particularly the original specialties of professional conjurers now working, have been shunned. If such tricks are available at all, they can and should be bought through the authorized dealers.

The *Cyclopedia of Magic* does attempt to provide every learner, every performer, and every interested reader with a wide and solid background of magical knowledge. The whole repertory of standard modern magical effects has been explained and illustrated. The reader will be forearmed when a brother magician says, "You know the old . . . . trick," and will also find the supporting information that he needs in perfecting his own inventions.

The history of magic receives concise but comprehensive treatment.

To advanced performers the most valuable feature will be the subject articles on business methods, children's shows, the literature of magic, music, night-club shows, pantomime, programs, psychology, publicity, and stage settings. Several of these have been specially contributed by outstanding authorities in their own fields, and all are drawn from the best information on the subject.

The photographic plates by Audrey Alley are perhaps the most brilliant ever taken to illustrate magical manipulations.

Any book of this size must necessarily reflect less credit on the editor than on the contributors, living and dead.

The volume could never have been finished at all without the advice and active help of John Mulholland.

Audrey Alley, Henry Blanchard, Louise Gifford, Frederick Little, Barrows Mussey, Doris Robbins, the late lamented Leo Rullman, and James C. Wobensmith lend whatever special distinction the *Cyclopedia of Magic* can claim.

The staggering mass of routine editorial work fell on Ruth Mary Canedy.

The book is arranged alphabetically, with abundant cross-references to guide the user. All words printed in SMALL CAPITALS signify that further information is to be found under the heading so printed.

Many of the articles are signed with initials, which stand for the following writers:

A. R.	August Roterberg	*Card Tricks, How To Do Them*
B. M.	Barrows Mussey	*Magic*
C. B.	Charles Bertram	
C. L. N.	C. Lang Neil	*Modern Card Manipulation*
		The Modern Conjurer and Drawing-Room Entertainer
D. D.	David DEVANT	*Magic Made Easy*
		Our Magic (with N. M.)
E. J.	Eddie Joseph	*Magic and Mysteries of India*
E. S.	Ellis Stanyon	*Magic*
E. T. S.	Edwin T. Sachs	*Sleight-of-Hand*
H. H.	Henry Hay	*Learn Magic*
Houdini	Harry HOUDINI	*The Unmasking of Robert-Houdin*
H. T.	Howard THURSTON	*Tricks With Cards*
H. & A. W.	H. & A. Walker	*Secrets of Modern Conjuring*
		Up-to-date Conjuring
J. M.	John MULHOLLAND	
J. N. M.	John Nevil MASKELYNE	*Sharps and Flats*
L. H.	Professor Louis HOFFMANN	*Card Tricks*
		Later Magic
		Modern Magic
		More Magic
L. H. B.	Major L. H. Branson	*Indian Conjuring*
N. M.	Nevil MASKELYNE	*Our Magic* (with D. D.)
O. F.	Ottokar Fischer	*Illustrated Magic*
Okito	Okito (Theo BAMBERG)	*Quality Magic*
S. W. E.	S. W. Erdnase	*The Expert at the Card Table*
T. F.	Thomas Frost	*The Lives of the Conjurors*
T. N. D.	Thomas Nelson DOWNS	*The Art of Magic*
		Modern Coin Manipulation
V. F.	Victor Farelli	*Card Magic*
W. G.	Will Goldston	*Tricks of the Masters*

Permission to reprint from copyright works is gratefully acknowledged:

Abbott's Magic Novelty Company, *Magic and Mysteries of India*, by Eddie Joseph

A. S. Barnes and Company, Inc., *Magic*, by Barrows Mussey

Garden City Publishing Company, *Learn Magic*, by Henry Hay

The Macmillan Company, *Illustrated Magic*, by Ottokar Fischer

Valuable material has been made available from the enormous files of the Warshaw Collection of Business Americana.

For a general foundation in magic, the reader should begin with the articles on:

Apparatus, Ball manipulation, Billet- and message-reading, Black art, Business methods, Card manipulation, Card setups, Cards, key, Cards, one-way, pointer, divided, Children's shows, Chinese magic, Cigar manipulation, Coin manipulation, Comedy, Costume, Cups and balls, Divinations, Dollar-bill tricks, East Indian magic, Egg bag, Equivoques, Escapes and releases, Exposures, Fake, Forcing, Four-ace tricks, Gambling methods, Gimmick, Handkerchiefs prepared as vanishers, Hands, Hat tricks, History, Illusions, Impromptu effects, Invention, Levitations, Linking rings, Literature, Magical effects, Makeup, Mechanical decks, Mind-reading, Mirror principle, Miser's dream, Music, Night-club, Organizations, Pantomime, Patter, Plant, Practice, Presentation, Programs, Psychology, Publicity, Pulls, Rising Cards, Rope tricks, Routine, Servantes, Silent acts, Silk tricks, Slate tests, Sleight-of-hand, Stage settings, Spirit effects, String tricks, Sucker gags, Table tricks, Thimble tricks, Thread, Three-card tricks, Thumb tip, Thumb writer, Torn and restored paper, Tumblers, Vest-pocket magic, Volunteers, Wands, Watch tricks.

A

ACQUITMENT In BALL, COIN, and THIMBLE manipulation, any sleight for showing both hands empty when actually something is being concealed. The CHANGEOVER PALM is the most useful variety. Most acquitments are as labored as their name.

AERIAL MINT, AERIAL TREASURY (See under MISER'S DREAM)

AFGHAN BANDS Perhaps the most puzzling self-working effect in existence. An endless band or loop of cloth about four inches wide and three feet long is torn lengthwise, which naturally produces two loops. One of these loops is torn again, producing two loops, but they are interlinked. The other loop tears into a single cloth ring twice the length of the original.

The secret lies in the simple fact that a band of cloth or paper, if given one half-twist before the ends are fastened together, will automatically tear into linked rings. If given a full turn before fastening, it will tear into one long ring.

In the oldest form of the trick, three loops were in fact pinned together out of newspaper before the audience. The modern, immeasurably improved version was devised by the Philadelphia attorney, James C. Wobensmith (see INVENTION). The principle of the trick is exactly the same, only the single wide cloth band makes it possible to cut three slits lengthwise in one end of the band, so that the performer can start tearing easily. The center slit is long enough so that one half of the band can be given half a turn, the other half a full turn, before the ends of the cloth are pasted together. Tearing down the center slit, of course, simply produces two bands. *B. M.*

AMATEUR MAGICIANS In magic there is no hard-and-fast line between the amateurs and the professionals. Most professionals were once amateurs; and if performing for pay is the test, a good many enthusiastic middle-aged amateurs were once professionals.

From the very beginning of modern legerdemain, the best amateurs have been outstanding performers. A seventeenth-century Frenchman, Jean Cautares, who lived in the parish of St. Martin's in London, was described as having "the best hand and conveyance of any man that liveth this day." And only a few years ago the late Dr. Samuel Hooker built an act not one of whose secrets was ever solved by any of the great professional magicians whom he invited to see it. In fact magic owes many of its best effects to amateur magicians; the professionals, busy making a living, cannot always spend the time struggling toward perfection just for the love of it.

No one can estimate the number of practising amateur magicians. The members of the recognized magical societies alone number in thousands, and Professor Hoffmann's immortal *Modern Magic*, which converts nearly every reader to conjuring, has sold several thousand copies every year since its appearance in 1876.

Charles Dickens was an amateur performer; so was Lewis Carroll (Charles Lutwidge Dodgson, the author of *Alice in Wonderland*); so was King Edward VII; so is the Duke of Windsor. The late Hendrik Willem van Loon was an enthusiast. Fulton Oursler, Edgar Bergen, Chester Morris, Orson Welles, James Stewart, and Harold Lloyd are among the more celebrated living personages who spend their time on conjuring.

Many amateurs excel the average professional not only in invention but in dexterity; their weak point, comparatively speaking, is likely to be PRESENTATION. Showmanship, the art of pleasing the audience, is the one thing the professional lives by; the amateur can afford to please himself alone with difficult moves and devices that the audience never even sees. "Conjuring for conjurers" is a vice in a professional. In an amateur it is a vice only if he hopes to turn professional.

H. H.

AMBITIOUS CARD (See GENERAL CARD)

ANDERSON, JOHN HENRY (1814-1874) was born in Kincardine, Scotland, and started his professional career as an actor. He must have been a very poor one, too, for he states that he was once complimented by a manager for having brought bad acting to the height of perfection.

Anderson was first known as the Caledonian magician, then assumed the title of the Wizard of the North, which he said was bestowed on him by Sir Walter Scott.

He was the first great advertiser in the world of magic, and he left nothing undone that might boom attendance at his performances. He started newspapers, gave masked balls, and donated thousands of dollars to charities. He was known in every city of the world, and when so inclined, built his own theaters. He sold books on magic during his own performances, and would sell any trick he presented for a nominal sum.

His most unique advertising dodge was to offer $500 in gold as prizes for the best conundrums written by spectators during his performances. To make this scheme more effective, he carried with him his own printing press and set it up back of the scenes. While the performance was under way, the conundrums handed in by the spectators were printed, and after the performance anyone might buy a sheet of the questions and puns at the door. As everyone naturally wanted to see his conundrum in print, Anderson sold millions of these bits of paper. In 1852, while playing at Metropolitan Hall in New York City, he advertised his conundrum contest and sold his book of tricks, and such notables as Jenny Lind and General Kossuth entered conundrums.

He was among the first performers to expose the Davenport Brothers (see SPIRIT EFFECTS), whose spiritualistic tricks and rope-tying had astonished America. Directly on witnessing a performance and solving their methods, Anderson hurried back to England and exposed the tricks.

To sum up his history, he stands unique in the annals of magic as a doer of daring things. He rushed into print on the slightest pretext, was a hard fighter with his rivals and aired his quarrels in the press, and he was a game loser when trouble came his way. Not a brilliant actor or performer, he yet had the gift of securing excellent effects in his *mise en scène*. He made and lost several fortunes, generally recouping as quickly as he lost. He was burned out several times, the most notable fire being that of Covent Garden, London, in 1856. He was liked in spite of his eccentricities, but when he died his fortune was small.

Houdini

ANGLE-PROOF Said of an effect or device that can be used with spectators on all sides. A prime requisite for NIGHT-CLUB effects.

This rules out most palming, all BACK-PALMING, most methods of loading (see LOADS), nearly all SERVANTES, and, by extension, some effects that can be neither detected nor appreciated at all from the rear.

The BLACK ART table is angle-proof unless spectators are almost directly overhead.

ANIMALS "The rabbit out of the hat" has become synonymous with magic in the public mind. But the number of magicians who still use live rabbits and other animals is very small indeed. Nevertheless animal effects are always popular, especially with children.

The following hints for those who wish to use livestock are drawn largely from an article by George DeMott in *The Sphinx.*

In the first place, don't use livestock unless you like animals, and can get on with them. Neither you nor the animals can be happy and successful in your act otherwise. Make pets of your livestock if they will let you.

In the second place, cultivate the acquaintance of your veterinarian. No one short article can possibly deal with all the problems of keeping animals; the vet has the answers.

All living creatures need water. Even the milk-loving cat should have a dish of fresh drinking water constantly available. In addition, ducks need a tub of water for a bath at frequent intervals.

Furthermore, all animals need air. Make sure that all LOAD containers in your apparatus are well ventilated. Never leave animals waiting in a load any longer than you must; and even then, be sure they have enough air.

Animals also need exercise. If you have much livestock, DeMott suggests carrying a roll of chicken wire, which can be set up on edge to form a pen for small animals to run in.

As for specific animals:

Rabbits must never on any account be lifted by the ears; this injures them painfully. Pick them up by the scruff of the neck, and quickly support them with your other hand. They like a variety of food. Whole-grain oats, hay, carrots, apples, greens, and fresh grass in the summer are all good. They need a pinch of salt occasionally. Don't forget the drinking water. Doe rabbits (females) are smaller, better-tempered, and less restless than bucks (males). Baby rabbits are excellent if treated very gently. If a rabbit bites you, disinfect the bite immediately.

Poultry. Chickens and ducks eat such whole grains as corn and wheat, and also cracked mixed poultry feed. They depend on what grit they can pick up for digestion; you will need to buy cracked oyster shells at a feed store, and give it to them every day. Poultry should also have some greens occasionally. In summer they may be tethered outside by a string. Ducks in particular need bran middlings or some sort of meal stirred into a porridge with water. Don't forget the ducks' bath in addition to drinking water. Roosters are easily tamed and handsomer than hens for magical purposes. Female ducks, being smaller, fit into apparatus better than the drake.

Pigeons need both grain and oyster shells, and, like ducks, they should have a bath as well as drinking water available.

Guinea pigs can be treated about the same as rabbits. They may look dopey, but they need exercise.

Domestic cats. Very few performers have the patience or the personality to train cats. It can be done, however, and if you are among the skilful few, don't forget to give your cat a bunch of dry catnip occasionally during the winter.

Dogs. There is too much variety among breeds and individuals to give any rules. If you intend using a dog in your act, you have probably had one before as a pet.

Goldfish have been largely supplanted by carrot or manufactured dummies. Live ones must not be overfed, and they need air above the surface of the water they swim in.

There are preventive injections against distemper and certain other animal diseases. Consult your veterinarian about these. It is better to take a little trouble beforehand than to get attached to an animal and then lose it unnecessarily. *H. H.*

APPARATUS (See under: BLACK ART; BRADAWL; BREAKAWAY FAN; CARD BOX; CARD FRAME; CARD INDEX; CARD VANISHER; CHANGING BAG; CHING LING FOO WATER CAN; CIGARETTE MANIPULATION; COIN BOX; COIN TRAY; COINS, FOLDING; COINS, SHELL; DICE; DIE BOX; DIVINATIONS; DOVE PAN; DRAWER BOX; DROPPERS; DRUMHEAD TUBE; EGG BAG; ESCAPES; FAKE; FLASH PAPER; FLOWER PRODUCTIONS; FUNNEL; GIMMICK; HANDKERCHIEFS PREPARED AS VANISHERS; HAT LOADING; HOLDERS; HOOKS; HOULETTE; INVENTION; JAP BOX; LEVITATIONS; LINKING RINGS; LOTA; MECHANICAL DECKS; MIRROR PRINCIPLE; NEST OF BOXES; PISTOL; PRODUCTIONS; PULLS; SERVANTES; SILK TRICKS; SLATE TESTS; SPIDER; SPIRIT EFFECTS; TAMBOURINE; THREAD; THUMB TIP; THUMB WRITER; TUMBLERS; WANDS; WATCH TRICKS.

See also under individual tricks as BALL OF WOOL; BIRD CAGE; CAKE BAKED IN A HAT; CHINESE WANDS; CLOCK DIAL; EGG AND HANDKERCHIEF; FISH-CATCHING; FLAGSTAFF; GOLDFISH BOWLS; INEXHAUSTIBLE BOTTLE; JUMPING PEG; MULTIPLYING BILLIARD BALLS; ORGAN PIPES; PASSE-PASSE BOTTLE; PHANTOM TUBE; RATTLE BOX; RICE BOWLS; RISING CARDS; THIMBLE TRICKS; THREE-CARD TRICKS.)

ASSISTANTS (See VOLUNTEERS)

B

BACK-PALMING (See CARD MANIPULATION; COIN MANIPULATION)

BALL MANIPULATION (See also: HOLDERS; MULTIPLYING BILLIARD BALLS; SPONGE BALLS)

Palm. There are two methods of concealing a ball or egg in the hand. The first is what is known as palming, and consists of holding the object between the ball of the thumb and the raised part of the palm on the opposite side of the hand. (Fig. 1) The ball is held by a slight contraction of the muscles at the base of the thumb. To learn how to palm a ball in this way place the ball in the center of the open hand, with all the fingers wide apart, and try to grip the ball by moving the whole length of the thumb inward without bending any part of it. After considerable practice it will be found that a small object can be held in this way without moving any of the fingers to any appreciable extent, and the hand can be turned right over and held in any position without danger of dropping the object.

The next thing to acquire is the power of using the fingers freely by handling other things at the same time that the concealed object is palmed. As concealment is the sole reason for this sleight, it follows that the last part of the practice must be devoted to drilling oneself into always holding the hand in such a position that no one sees any part of the palmed article.

Another and easier way of concealing the ball in the hand is used in this combination; it is known as the *Finger Palm.*

The ball is held as in Fig. 2. Slightly bend the fingers of one hand and lay the ball in the hollow thus formed. Then bend the fingers just enough to grip the ball and turn the hand over afterward. Practice gripping the ball with the two middle fingers, leaving the other two free for such use as can be made of them without disclosing the presence of the concealed ball. They can be stretched out but cannot be spread wide apart.

N. M. & D. D.

The *Changeover Palm* lets you show both hands empty when you really have a ball palmed. It's very easy to do, but hard to work without giving a flash of the ball; so be careful if you want to use it.

Say the ball is palmed in your right hand. Hold your left hand up, palm

Fig. 1

Fig. 2

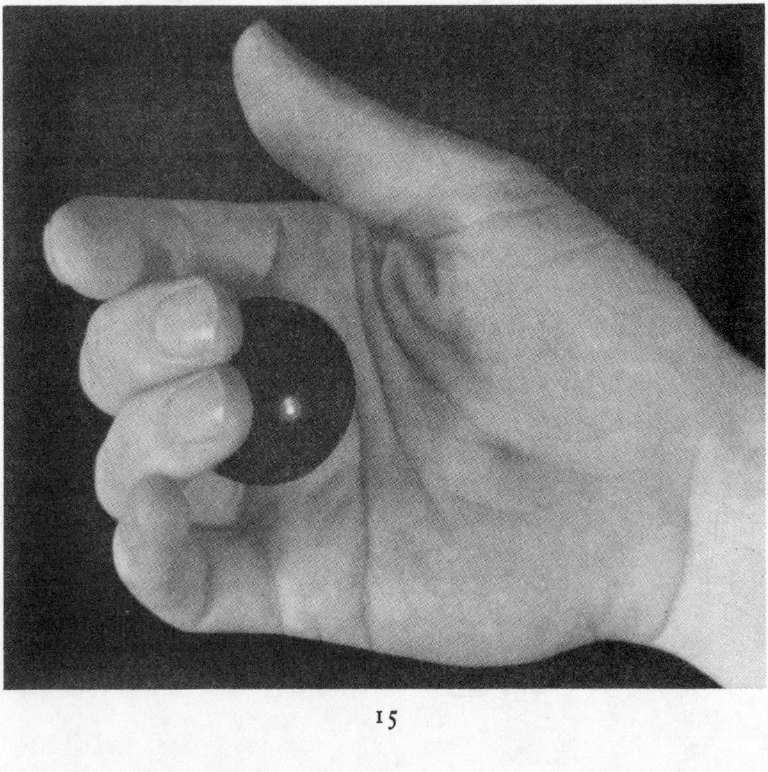

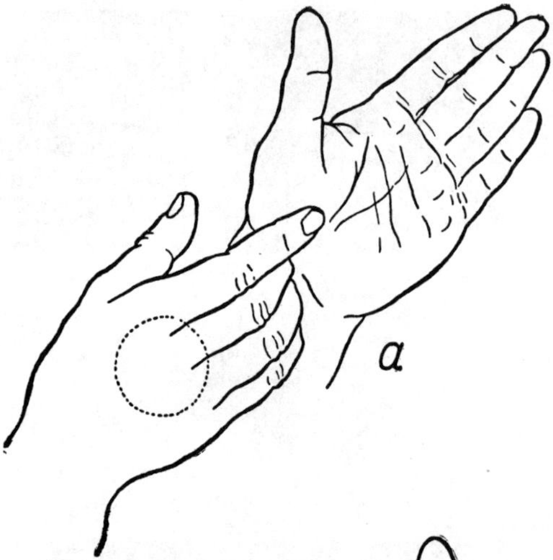

Fig. 1

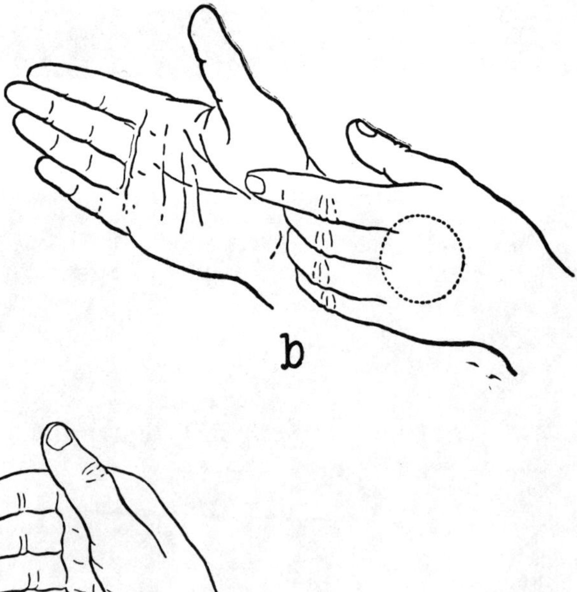

Fig. 2

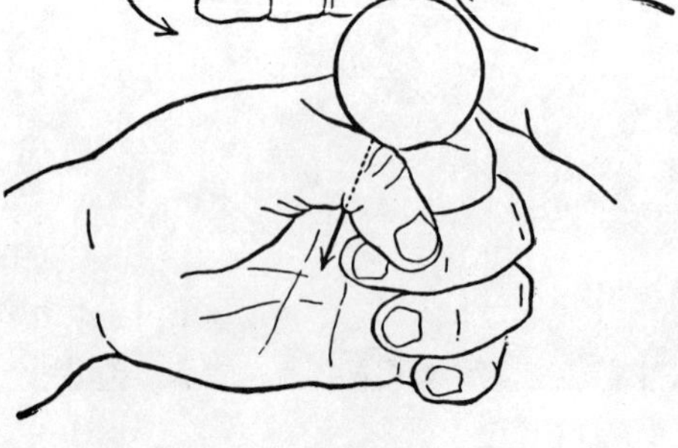

Fig. 3

to the audience. Your right forefinger, pointing, should about touch the heel of your left hand. (Fig. 1)

Swing over to show the palm of your right hand, pointing at it with the left forefinger. This brings both hands for a moment palm to palm. Roll the ball from your right palm over the heel of your left hand and up into your left palm, where you palm it again. (Fig. 2)

One thing besides the angles to watch out for is the movements of your thumbs. They may too easily seem to waggle as your hand shifts from empty to palming attitude.

The *Trap Pass* works like a magician's stage or table TRAP.

Close your left fist, and hold it out, thumb upward. Set a ball on the fist. Bring your right hand up in front of the ball, palm toward you, and close the fingers to carry off the ball. Just as your right hand seems to be taking it away, your left fist opens, lets it trickle down in, and palms it. (Fig. 3) Follow your right hand with your eyes, and don't move your left.

You can also approach the ball with your right hand from the left side, palm away from you, but this looks unnatural. *H. H.*

Pass with Palm. The ball is held on the open palm of the right hand. The left hand starts to pick it up, but the fingers do not close over it (although they appear to do so). Actually, as the hands are separated, the right is turned with its back to the audience to conceal the ball, which is palmed, while the fingers of the left are made to curl over an imaginary ball.

Pass with Finger Palm. The ball is held in the grip of the fingers, and the hand containing it is turned toward the open palm of the other hand as though dropping the ball into it. But the fingers do not relax; they retain the ball while the fingers of the other hand curl over as though they had really received it. Just before making this transfer the ball can be thrown up and caught in the hollowed fingers, or dropped from a position between the finger and thumb and apparently tossed into the other hand.

Pass by Combination Palm. In this the action of putting the ball into the opposite hand is simulated, whereas in the pass with palm the ball was apparently taken by the receiving hand and in the pass with finger palm it was dropped into the receiving hand.

The ball is held between finger and thumb of one hand, and as the hand travels toward the other the ball is dropped into the finger palm position and then transferred to the palm proper, while the fingers of both hands imitate the motions of giving and receiving the ball. *N. M. & D. D.*

Billiard-Ball Vanish. The ball is thrown into the air a few times and caught with both hands. (Fig. 1) The left hand is closed and held with its back to the audience, above the right hand, which pats it, turns around, showing the palm, and then turns again with its back to the audience. (Fig. 2) The left hand is then quickly opened and shown to be empty; the ball has vanished.

When the right hand has its back to the audience the ball is, of course, in the left hand, but it is held there outside the tips of the fingers. (Fig. 3) Now the right hand can palm away the ball easily as the closed left hand is turned around toward the audience. (Fig. 4)

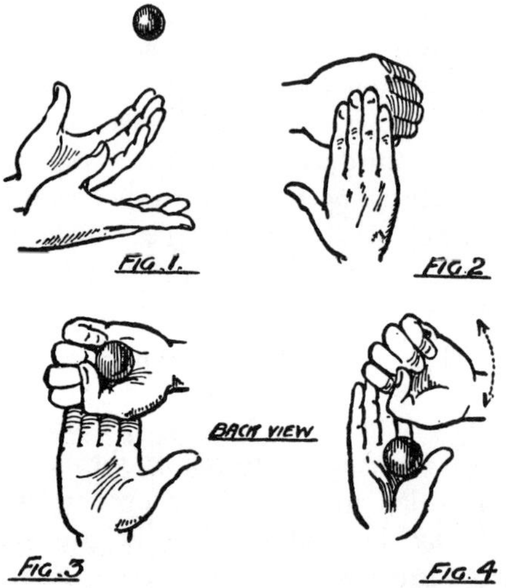

The deception is brought about by the fact that the fingers of the closed left hand do not move. In no other way can the sleight be performed successfully. *Okito*

The standard book on the subject, containing far more material than any one performer can use, is Burling Hull's *Expert Billiard Ball Manipulation.*

BALL OF WOOL An easy and effective way to end a money trick is to pass the marked coin into the center of a large ball of wool or worsted, the whole of which has to be unwound before the coin can be reached. The only apparatus necessary besides the wool (of which you must have enough for a good-sized ball), is a flat tin tube three or four inches long and just large enough to allow a coin to slip through it easily. It will be found a great advantage to have the edges of one end opened outward, as shown in Fig. 1. This not only facilitates the introduction of the coin, but also the withdrawal of the tube from the ball of wool, as the performer in this case has only to clip the tube between two fingers in order to get the necessary grip on it.

You prepare for the trick by winding the wool on one end of the tube in such a way that when the whole is wound into a ball, an inch or so of the tube will project from it. This you place out of sight.

Begin the trick by requesting someone to mark a coin, which you then SWITCH for a substitute; leave this substitute in the possession or in view of the spectators, while you get your ball of worsted from its hiding-place.

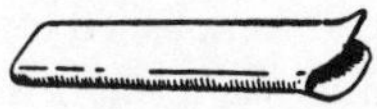

FIG. 1

Before producing it, you drop the genuine coin down the tube into the center of the ball, and withdraw the tube, giving the ball a squeeze to remove all traces of an opening. You then bring it forward and put it in a glass goblet or tumbler, which you hand to a spectator to hold. Taking the substitute coin, you announce that you will make it pass invisibly into the very center of the ball of wool, which you accordingly pretend to do. You then request a second spectator to take the loose end of the wool and unwind the ball; the coin then falls out into the goblet.

The only drawback to the trick is the tediousness of the process of unwinding. Some performers use a wheel made for this purpose, which materially shortens the operation.

Nowadays the coin is usually passed into a NEST OF BOXES at the center of the wool. *L. H.*

BAMBERGS, THE The family can boast of six generations of magicians.

The first of the family, Eliaser Bamberg (1760-1833), was born at Leyden. He won fame as a performer in pure sleight-of-hand, his favorite tricks being those with cards, coins, the CUPS AND BALLS, etc. In 1807 he was injured by an explosion on board a ship; his leg was broken and had to be amputated. After he had fitted himself out with a wooden leg he continued his professional work and used the wooden leg to good advantage as a secret SERVANTE, by means of which some very wonderful appearances and disappearances were effected.

David Leendert (1786-1869) became his father's assistant when he was nine years old, and, following his father's example, took up the study of pure sleight-of-hand, at which he quickly became expert. His performances enabled him to add to his father's fame, and he became a great favorite at court.

David's eldest son, Tobias Bamberg (1812-1870), upheld the family tradition and, being a very accomplished linguist, was able to patter equally well in French, German, English, and Dutch. He was appointed "court mechanician," but survived his father for only fifteen months.

D. L. BAMBERG

His only son, David Tobias Bamberg (born 1843), was appointed and brevetted "court mechanician" in 1870, and, being a very accomplished elocutionist and mimic as well as a very skilful magician, he soon added luster to the family name. He began his stage career as an actor, but in 1866 (at the age of 23) he made his debut in Rotterdam as a magician with great success. He was appointed royal conjuror to the court of Holland, and in 1886, gave two royal performances, one of which was specially prolonged for two hours.

In 1907, David Tobias Bamberg, together with his son "Okito," (Theo, born 1875), made a long tour, playing in Batavia, Java, Sumatra, Borneo, Guinea, Colombo, Ceylon, and other places. During this tour he offered a large reward to any fakir who would produce the famous INDIAN ROPE TRICK, but no one came forward to claim the prize.

FU MANCHU

Theo "Okito" Bamberg continued to assist his father until he decided to strike out for himself and appear as a Chinese magician. With this act he has toured nearly the whole of Europe, performing in nearly all the principal theaters with brilliant success.

Okito's son David (born 1904) has won success with a Chinese act under the name of Fu Manchu. He is enormously popular throughout Latin America (having starred, for instance, in Mexican moving pictures), and has also done well in Europe and the United States.

BELLACHINI Stage name of Samuel Berlach (1828-1885), a Galician Jew whose skill and showmanship made him famous in all the cities and courts of central Europe. One of his great features was the production of eggs from an assistant's mouth.

BILLET- AND MESSAGE-READING The effect of reading what is written on folded slips of paper, or billets, without unfolding the paper. Reading the contents of sealed envelopes is a closely related effect.

There are three main principles in use: the one-ahead gag; impressions; and (particularly in envelope tests) various forms of transparency.

The *one-ahead gag*, used in many branches of magic, consists in obtaining knowledge of one unit in a series—message, face-down playing-card, or whatever—, and keeping track of that unit. Another unit is picked up, and boldly "read" as being the one known to the performer. The performer then opens the billet or looks at the card to "verify" his reading. This gives him the "reading" for the next unit, and he thus goes on, keeping one ahead of the series, down to the last unit, for which he picks up the original known billet or card. The whole lot can then be given to the audience, having all been read correctly though not in the actual order.

Various methods are used to get knowledge of one unit. A PLANT may write a prearranged question; the performer may LOAD in one of his own; one card may be forced; and so forth. Either of the other main principles may be combined in this way with the one-ahead gag.

Impressions are obtained when the subject is writing a question. Various forms of writing pad and tablet have been contrived to hide a sheet of carbon paper. An ordinary scratch pad and a hard pencil will leave a clear impression on the second sheet of the pad unless the subject is careful. If a piece of paper has its back rubbed with a cake of dry soap, a sheet of glass (such as that over a framed portrait photograph, which is a natural and deceptive writing rest) will retain an impression that can be read only with the light falling at an angle. In fact there are many small variations of the impression principle.

Transparency of envelopes is produced in two ways: by rubbing the envelope with alcohol or cologne (usually kept in a small sponge), which makes the paper transparent until the alcohol evaporates; and by boldly cutting a window in the envelope, and arranging the ROUTINE so that no one ever thinks of examining the envelope. The most natural way is to use a stack of envelopes, only one or two having windows, and to burn envelope and question unopened after the reading.

"Living and dead tests" are a popular form of billet-reading, in which spectators write the names of deceased friends and living friends, and the performer sorts them out. The most elementary method is to tear strips off a sheet of paper, and simply ask spectators to write "dead" names on the top and bottom strips, each of which has one edge straight and one edge torn, while other spectators write "living" names on the strips that have both edges torn.

Many methods of billet- and message-reading are explained in David P. Abbott's *Behind the Scenes with the Mediums* and Theo Annemann's *Practical Mental Effects.* *H. H.*

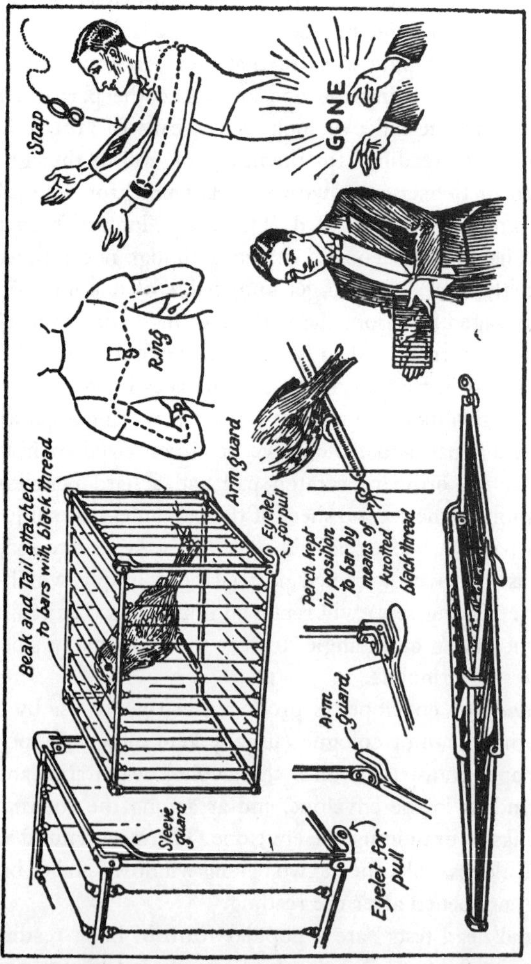

FIG. 1

BIRD-CAGE, VANISHING A trick that has made the reputations of perhaps more magicians than any other single one. Invented by DE KOLTA, it has been used with magnificent success by CARL HERTZ, BLACKSTONE, and MULHOLLAND.

The cage is rectangular, perhaps six inches high, six inches wide, and eight inches long; it is made of wire, on a frame of somewhat heavier metal rods. (Fig. 1) It often contains a bird–in the days of De Kolta and Hertz a live one, now almost always a dummy. The performer comes forward holding the cage by the ends between his flat palms. Some magicians invite a VOLUNTEER to put his palms on the top and bottom of the cage.

With no covering, the performer makes a tossing motion, and the cage vanishes instantly. He may remove his jacket, and allow himself to be searched, yet after a moment backstage he can repeat the trick.

The cage commonly used will, unless supported, collapse of its own weight, the bottom right rear and top left front corner pulling apart until the whole cage is drawn into a shuttle-shaped bundle not much more than two inches thick. A PULL is attached to the bottom right rear corner; when the performer actuates the pull by stretching his arms, the cage is drawn up the sleeve and between the shoulder blades, inside the waistcoat.

Despite Carl Hertz's demonstration to the contrary before a committee of Parliament, the bird is liable to be injured or killed, which has led to the use of the dummy. *H. H.*

BLACK ART In magic, the technical name for an optical principle and the tricks done by its aid. The principle is simply that dead black against dead black is invisible. All shadows are obliterated, and therefore the eye cannot distinguish the outline of any object masked in black. The most frequent use of this principle is the black THREAD. Another extension is to mask whatever must be hidden behind a piece of material that matches the backdrop (see STAGE SETTING).

At one time entire Black Art acts were presented, with assistants completely muffled in black velvet, or perhaps merely thrusting forward a black-gloved arm, to work the tricks. Nowadays, however, the Black Art table is almost the only surviving representative of the Black Art principle.

The *Black Art* table is one of the most valuable accessories that a conjurer can possess. It was the joint invention of ROBERT HELLER and Professor De Vere.

The table may be either of the "gipsy" form shown in Fig. 1, or mounted on a central pillar, as in Fig. 2. The first is perhaps slightly more portable, as it may be taken apart more easily for packing. In either case the table top is of wood, covered with black velvet, on which a geometrical pattern is embroidered in narrow silk braid of some bright color (preferably yellow). The pattern shown in Figs. 1 and 3 has been found to answer the

BLACK ART TABLES

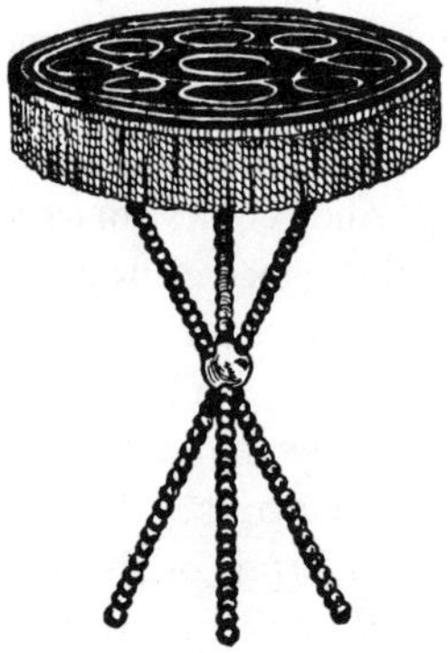

FIG. 1

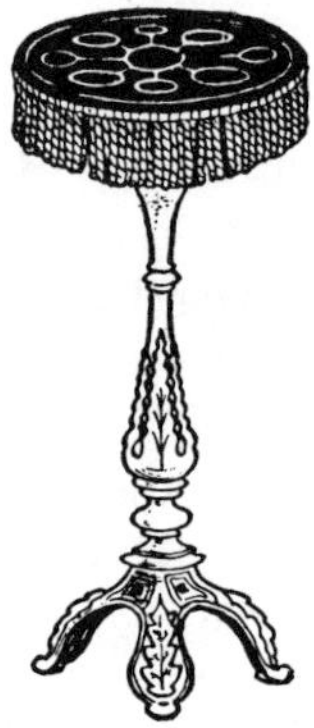

FIG. 2

purpose extremely well, while Figs. 4 and 5 show other designs, which may be useful by way of suggestion.

The performer may follow his own fancy, so long as the table top is broken up by intersecting lines into spaces of a convenient size and shape. In one or more of such spaces, the velvet and the wood beneath it are cut away just inside the braid, as shown by the darkened portions in the diagrams. A pocket of black velvet, about four inches deep, is then inserted into the space and its upper edges glued to the wood. Even at a short distance, the opening thus made is indistinguishable from the surface of the table in artificial light; the effect to the spectator is that the surface

FIG. 3

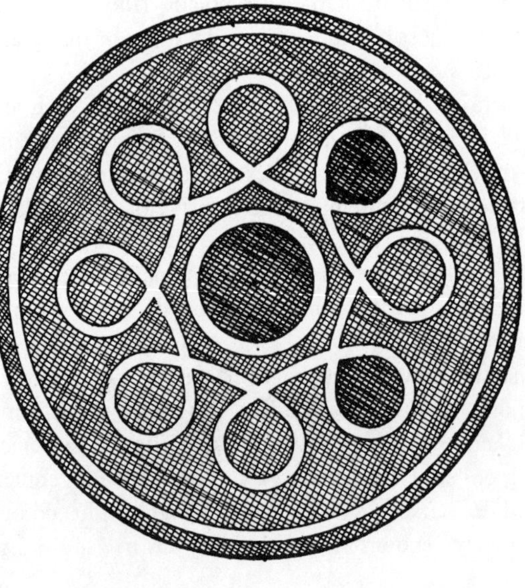

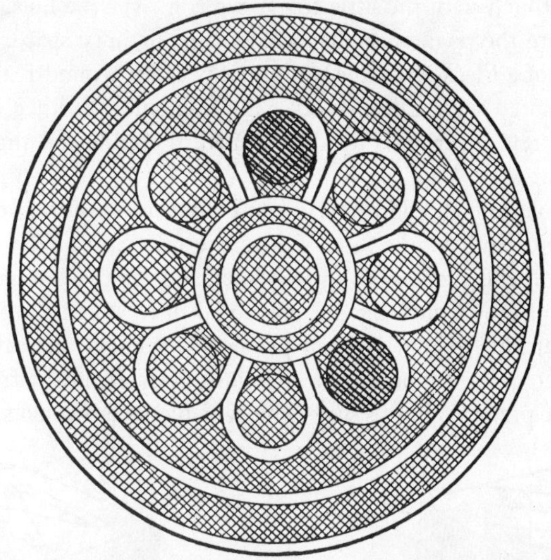

FIG. 4

is unbroken. A silk or woolen fringe about five inches wide around the edge of the table top prevents the pocket from being seen from below.

This provides the performer with one or more invisible holes in his table top. Suppose a billiard-ball is placed close to one of the openings. The performer ostensibly picks it up and comes forward with it. Just as the hand

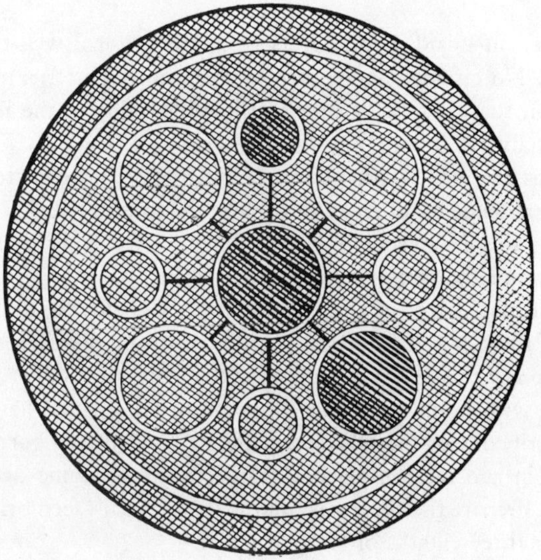

FIG. 5

reaches it, a touch with the little finger sends it over the hole, and it falls noiselessly into the pocket; the hand closes upon empty space. *L. H.*

Both sides of a *Black Art table* top, and especially around TRAPS or wells, should be painted with a dead-black paint containing neither varnish nor dryer. If the felt covering is torn or burned, the table top thus prepared will not show.

Felt for table tops should be shrunken before using. Wring out, in cold water, a white cloth of the same size as the felt. Spread the felt on the wet cloth; roll the two pieces up together and let the bundle stand for three hours, after which hang the felt up to dry. When the felt is quite dry, press out any wrinkles. If not properly shrunken, the action of the air or the glue will, in time, shrink the cloth away from the trap or well, and cloth not prepared in this way is more liable to show spots.

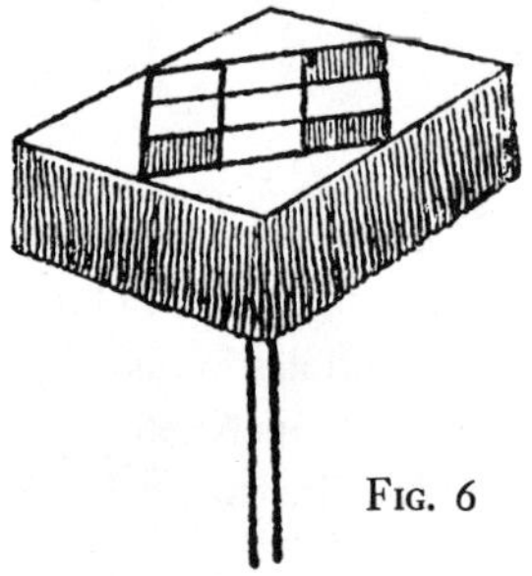

FIG. 6

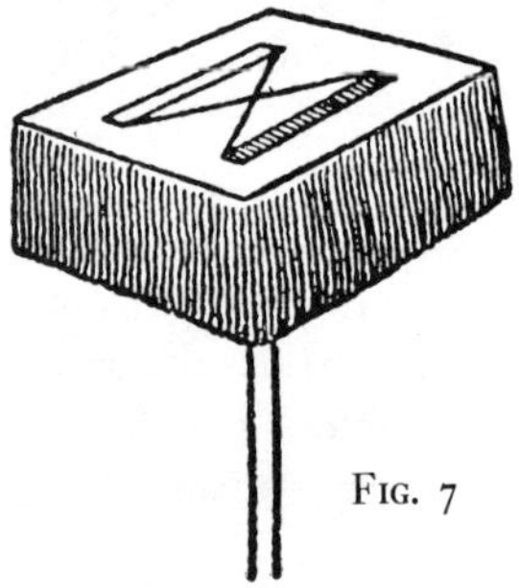

FIG. 7

The "Anderson Inlaid Top" differs from the original well-top table in two respects. No circular designs are used; circular patterns may lead to the impression that there is "a hole in the table," due to the natural idea that a hole is always round.

The designs are made with ribbon (Figs. 6 and 7), cemented into the felt top. The absence of all tacks and thick braid permits coins, cards, and larger objects to be moved into the well without picking them up. The shaded portion of the designs represent the wells.

Prepare the wood top of the desired size. Lay out the design on the wood with a scratch-awl, allowing for the width of the ribbon; then cut out the portion of the design intended for the well. Next cover the surface of the wood with liquid glue and apply black felt, which has been prepared as described. Cut the felt diagonally from corner to corner of each well, turn it in and tack in place. Again lay out the same design, using tailors' chalk. Prepare the ribbon as follows, using satin-faced bright yellow ribbon, about three-eighths of an inch wide.

Place the ribbon face down on a smooth surface; cut into narrow strips thin sheet rubber like that used by tailors (sometimes called "mending tissue"); lay the rubber on the ribbon and moisten at intervals of three or four inches. With a warm flatiron touch quickly one of the moistened spots on the rubber, and it will adhere to the ribbon. If the iron is too warm, or the motion of touching the ribbon is slow, the rubber will melt.

Prepare the necessary amount of ribbon in one piece, and trim off the surplus rubber at the edges. Lay the prepared ribbon between the chalk lines indicating the design on the table top; over it place a damp cloth and press with a flatiron which should be hot enough to make the cloth steam. The rubber now melts, immediately cementing the ribbon to the felt. Cut off the ribbon and repeat until the design is completed. Do not cut the ribbon in strips before applying, as it shrinks when steamed. *T. N. D.*

BLACKSTONE, HARRY Stage name of Harry Boughton (born in Chicago, 1885). He became interested in magic when he saw KELLAR's show in 1898. He is now perhaps the leading American performer who still carries a big show; his stage version of the DANCING HANDKERCHIEF is superb. His hobby is card manipulation.

BLINDFOLDS The effect of many tricks is greatly enhanced by having the performer blindfolded before he starts. The PUBLICITY effect known as the Blindfold Drive, wherein the performer, blindfolded, drives a car through the streets of a town, derives its sole virtue from the blindfold.

In general, even a careful normal blindfold will not prevent the magician from glancing down his nose enough to see what goes on close to him. By frowning deeply as the blindfold is put over your eyes, and then raising your eyebrows, you can shrug the bandage or folded handkerchief up enough to see nearly all you need to.

The other principle employed in fake blindfolds is to have the blindfold transparent over the eyes. The simplest method is to roll two diagonally opposite corners of an ordinary handkerchief inward until the handkerchief forms a long, narrow band with rolls at the top and bottom, but only a single thickness of cloth at the center, over the eyes.

One of several special blindfold methods in common use is given below.

To begin with, a pad of cotton wool is placed over the eyes. The pad is not prepared in any way, and anyone in the audience can test it. The pad is held in place by a folded bandage tied round the performer's head

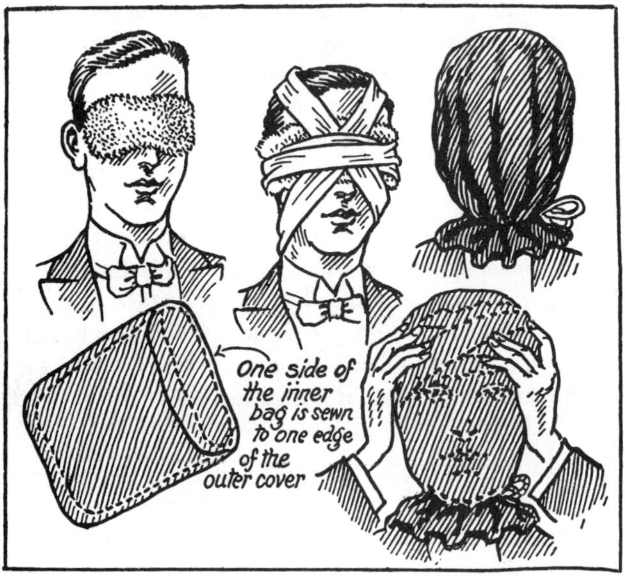
One side of
the inner
bag is sewn
to one edge
of the
outer cover

FIG. 1

(Fig. 1). Lastly, a black bag—which can also be tested by placing it over the head of a member of the audience, who will then be convinced that it is impossible to see through it—is placed over the performer's head; the strings of the bag are drawn round his neck and tied.

After all these preparations have been made, the performer is able to see quite easily.

The only faked article is the bag, which is really a double bag, one being inside the other. The tops of the two bags are sewn together on one side, but the other side is free. Faked stitching all around the bag gives the impression that the whole of the top is stitched.

When the performer puts the bag over the head of a member of the audience, he takes care to put the double side of the bag over the man's eyes, and the man cannot see through the bag. When the performer puts the bag over his own head, he has the single side over his face and, in getting the bag into position, he secretly pushes the whole of the cotton wool pad upward—a very easy thing to do. When taking off the bag, the performer has no difficulty in pulling the cotton wool pad into the right position again.

The cotton wool should be of the thick variety, about two and one-half inches wide, and cut into lengths not to cover the ears. The cotton wool is first put over the eyes; the cotton bandage covers the cotton wool, and is wound over the face both ways and completed as illustrated. Only one bandage is used.

This secret comes from Paul Graham. *W. G.*

BLITZ, SIGNOR ANTONIO (1810-1877) European magician and ventriloquist, was born probably in Germany or Holland, but possibly in England, and died in Philadelphia. He enjoyed great success with his full evening's show in many parts of the world, and spent most of his later years in this country, where he had at one time, he said, thirteen slavish imitators of his name and billing. His book, *Fifty Years in the Magic Circle*, is one of the liveliest of conjuring autobiographies, although—as so often in magicians' publicity—it is hard to tell how much of it is fact.

BOOK TEST *The Great Dictionary Trick* was invented by Mr. MASKELYNE, and when first produced made an immense sensation. A word is selected at random from a dictionary, in a manner that precludes all possibility of collusion; the magician then discovers the word and reveals his knowledge of it in some striking way. There does not appear to be even a loophole for deception left open, yet this surprising effect is produced by the simplest of means.

The properties for the trick consist of a dozen (or more if the audience is large) small, cheap, paper-bound dictionaries, unprepared, and one "special" one, prepared as later described; a small, thin paper-knife; a gross of counters, numbered consecutively from 1 upward, on a small plated salver, and eight or nine similar counters all bearing the same number, say "24." These last are placed until needed in the left POCHETTE, or in a clip under the left side of the vest.

For the preparation of the special dictionary twenty-eight to thirty ordinary dictionaries have to be sacrificed. These are unstitched and two consecutive leaves, say pages 37, 38, 39, 40, taken out from the middle portion of each. These are then pasted together in couples; page 37 of each pair against page 40 of the preceding pair. Against the foremost page 37 is pasted the first leaf, and against the ultimate page 40 the last leaf of the book, so as to secure a proper beginning and ending. The leaves thus pasted together should be dried in a press, and they must then be sewn together, in one of the original covers, by a bookbinder. (The mutilated copies should be carefully preserved, and utilized to make up other faked copies, as it would obviously be very unwise for the performer to use a dictionary opening at the same pages evening after evening.)

The dictionary thus made up will be externally just like the rest. It will have a correct first and last page, but wherever it is opened the pagination will be the same, that is, it will always open at pages 38, 39. This is placed at the bottom of the heap of unprepared dictionaries, as they lie on the performer's table.

The performer also has to prepare his own arms. On the left arm, just below the bend of the elbow, he writes, with red ink of good quality, or with slightly diluted crimson dye, the twenty-fourth word (or whatever the number intended to be FORCED) on page 39, the right-hand page of the faked dictionary. In the same way, he writes or gets somebody to write for him, on his right arm, the twenty-fourth word on the left-hand page (page 38).

Thus prepared, the performer is ready to show the trick. When distributing the dictionaries, which he does more particularly to those spectators in his own immediate neighborhood, he keeps the undermost (which is the faked one) to the last, and retains this in his own hand.

Then, producing the little paper-knife, say from his vest pocket, he asks some lady to thrust it between the pages. He leaves the book in her possession with the request that she will not open it just yet; this protects it from any inconvenient examination. The choice of right- or left-hand page makes no difference to him, except that if the *right*-hand page is chosen he will produce the word on his *left* arm, and vice versa.

The forcing of the number really presents no difficulty. Before picking up the tray of mixed counters from the table, the performer gets the forcing counters (those bearing the number 24) into his left hand. The tray in the same hand conceals the counters under the rim.

After inviting someone to take a handful of the visible counters, he puts the tray down, and borrows a hat. Receiving it in the right hand, he transfers it to the left, which grasps it with fingers inside and thumb outside. He takes back the handful of counters with the right hand, and apparently drops them into the hat; actually he retains them clipped against the lower joints of the two middle fingers and drops the forcing counters from the left hand into the hat. They are heard to fall, and no one is likely to suspect the substitution. It is, of course, now a certainty that the counter picked out of the hat will bear the number 24.

It only remains to explain how the performer can show his arm (right or left, as the case may be) without exhibiting the word written on it. The secret lies in the fact that he first exhibits the arm as shown in Fig. 1, when the writing is naturally concealed in the bend of the arm. He now lowers the arm vertically, apparently showing the opposite side of it. As a matter of fact, however, he gives it a half-turn at the same time, the effect being that it is *the same side* of the arm which is again exhibited, as in Fig. 2.

This audacious ruse is practically never detected. *L. H.*

FIG. 1

FIG. 2

Other methods are to use a special book with the same word at the same position on every page—if the given word is twenty-fifth on each page, the magician has only to force the number twenty-five; and to insert a card from the upper end of the book at the proper page; a spectator pushes a card in at random, and the performer manages to turn the book end for end, thus substituting his own card for the one inserted by the spectator.

Yet another method, recommended by HARRY BLACKSTONE, is to use an ordinary novel, and decide on some word that occurs frequently throughout. Three different stacks of colored cards are used—for instance, blue, white, and yellow.

The magician goes through the book, looking for the chosen word. Whenever he finds it, he writes on a card a number consisting of the page number immediately followed by the number of the word on the page.

Blue cards are used for single-digit page numbers; yellow cards for two-digit numbers: white cards for three-digit numbers.

There will thus be forty or fifty cards, all bearing different numbers.

The book is given to a spectator, along with the cards; he is asked to choose one card. Depending on the color, the performer tells him to use the first, first two, or first three numbers for the page, and the remaining figures for the position of the word.

The chosen word is revealed on the arm, by a SLATE, or by any other desired means. *H. H.*

BOSCO, BARTOLOMMEO (1790-1863) was perhaps the greatest magician Italy has produced. He was famous for his presentation of the CUPS AND BALLS, and invented, among other things, the sand CARD FRAME.

Bosco was not only a clever magician, but a man of many adventures, so that his life reads like a romance. This soldier of fortune was born in Turin, Italy, of a noble Piedmont family. From boyhood he showed great ability as a necromancer, but at the age of nineteen he was forced to serve under Napoleon I in the Russian campaign. He was a fusilier in the Eleventh Infantry, and at the battle of Borodino was injured in an engagement with Cossacks. Pierced by a lance, he lay upon the ground apparently dead.

A Cossack callously roamed among the dead and dying, rifling pockets and belts. When he came to Bosco, that youth feigned death, knowing that resistance meant a death wound. But while the Cossack robbed the Italian soldier, the latter stealthily raised his unwounded arm and by sleight-of-hand rifled the well-filled pockets of the Cossack.

Later Bosco was sent captive to Siberia, where he perfected his sleight-of-hand while amusing fellow-prisoners and jailers. In 1814 he was released and returned to his native land, where he studied medicine, but eventually decided to become a public entertainer.

He was not only a clever entertainer, but a good business man, and he planned each year on saving enough money to ensure a life of ease in his old age. But events intervened to ruin his plans. An illegitimate son, Eugene, became a heavy drag upon the retired magician, who was compelled to pay large sums to the young man to prevent his playing in either France or Germany or assuming the name of Bosco.

In the meantime, Bosco and his wife lived in poverty in Dresden, where the once brilliant conjurer died. *Houdini*

BOTTOMLESS GLASS (See under TUMBLERS)

BRADAWL or ICE PICK Often used in conjunction with the FUNNEL or the CHINESE WANDS. A curious effect may be obtained by piercing the nose of a VOLUNTEER with the magic bradawl. This appears to be an ordinary bradawl, but the blade is arranged so as to recede into the handle on the slightest pressure, again reappearing (forced forward by a spiral spring in the handle) as soon as the pressure is removed.

A duplicate bradawl of ordinary make is first handed out for examination; the trick bradawl being adroitly substituted, the performer proceeds to bore a hole with it through the nose of any juvenile volunteer who will submit to the operation. Holding a piece of cork on one side of the nose, he apparently thrusts the awl through the nose, the sinking of the blade into the handle exactly simulating the effect of a genuine perforation.

L. H.

BREAKAWAY FAN (See also: VOLUNTEERS) This appears to be a perfectly ordinary fan, as shown in Fig. 1. The performer closes it and hands it to a lady, inviting her to make use of it. She opens it, but it falls apart in her hands, and assumes the dislocated appearance shown in Fig. 2. The performer takes it from her, breathes upon it, and it becomes whole again.

The secret lies in the construction of the fan, which is strung so that when it is opened from *left to right* in the ordinary manner, it assumes the customary appearance of a respectable fan; when opened from *right to left*, however, it comes apart.

FIG. 1

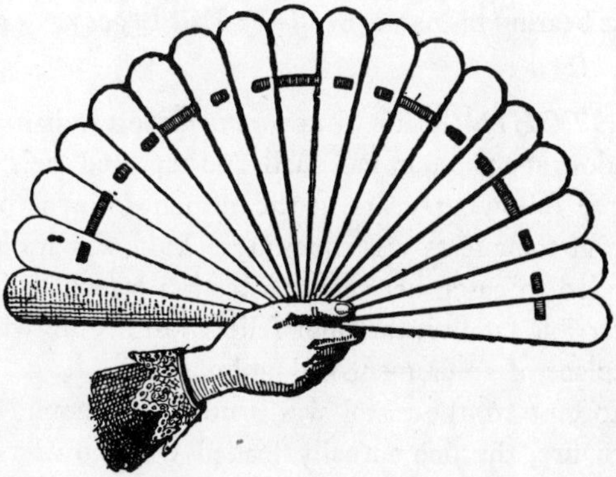

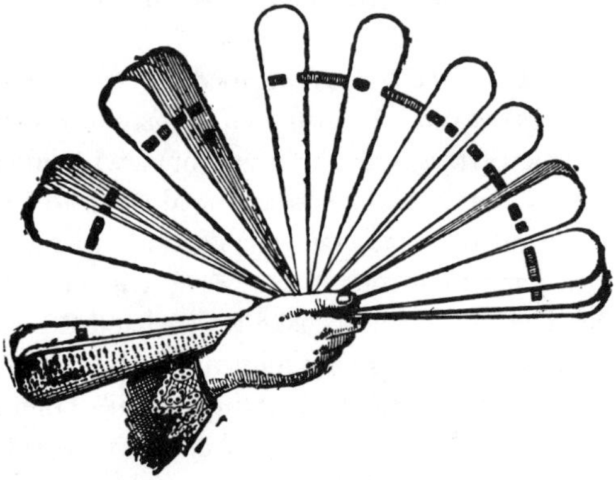

FIG. 2

By giving the fan a turn-over in the hand before opening it, the change is spontaneously effected, and the opening may always be in the same direction. This precaution is scarcely necessary, however, for the slight difference between opening from left to right and right to left is not likely to be noticed by anyone not in the secret. *L. H.*

BRESLAW (Apparently died 1783), German conjurer who moved to England at about the age of thirty-five, between 1760 and 1765, and became a very prominent figure in the earliest, outdoor period of modern magic (see HISTORY). He was a good showman and an accomplished SLEIGHT-OF-HAND performer, said by some to have been superior to FAWKES. He is remembered for a book of tricks bearing his name, *Breslaw's Last Legacy*.

BULLET-CATCHING In 1814 some clever Indian jugglers performed in London, at a room in Pall Mall, and repeated their performances during the three following years in the principal towns of the United Kingdom. One of their feats was the gun trick, in which one of the performers pretended to catch between his teeth a leaden bullet fired from a pistol. By a terrible fatality, the poor fellow lost his life while exhibiting this trick at a place of amusement in Dublin.

According to custom, the pistol was handed to a young gentleman in the audience to fire; the one actually loaded with powder and ball was inadvertently substituted for the weapon prepared for the trick. To the surprise and horror of all present, the bullet crashed through the head of the unfortunate conjurer, who fell dead upon the stage.

A similar catastrophe darkened the last years of the conjurer De Linsky, wno enjoyed a considerable repute on the continent. On the tenth of November, 1820, he gave a performance at Arnstadt, in the presence of the family of Prince Schwartzburg-Sondershausen, and wished to bring it off with as much *éclat* as possible.

Six soldiers were to fire with ball cartridges at the young wife of the conjurer; they had previously rehearsed the part, and had been instructed to bite off the bullet when biting the cartridge, and retain it in the mouth. This was trusting too much to untrained subordinates, and the result justified the apprehension of Madame Linsky, who is said to have been unwilling to perform the part assigned to her in the trick, and to have assented reluctantly to her husband's persuasion.

The soldiers, drawn up in a line in the presence of the spectators, presented their muskets at Madame Linsky and fired. For a moment she remained standing, but then sank down, exclaiming, "Dear husband, I am shot!" One of the soldiers had not bitten off the bullet, and it had passed through the abdomen of the unfortunate woman, who never spoke after she fell, and died on the second day after the accident. *T. F.*

In modern times CHUNG LING SOO is the most prominent performer to have lost his life by a hitch in the bullet-catching trick.

In the days of muzzle-loading firearms, the trick was performed by means of a metal tube, closed at one end, which fitted tightly over the ramrod used in loading the gun, and loosely inside the barrel. The gun was genuinely loaded with powder. Then the performer sneaked in the tube, open end upward, so that when the bullet was dropped in, it fell into the tube. A thrust of the ramrod picked up the tube and bullet together, enabling the performer's assistant to abstract the marked bullet and pass it to the performer for reproduction between his teeth, on a dinner-plate, or in some other manner.

With the use of modern breech-loading rifles, naturally new methods have become necessary. Sometimes a faked rifle is used, which fires a blank, leaving the cartridge with the marked bullet undisturbed; the performer catches a duplicate bullet, and SWITCHES it for the marked one, which an assistant has meanwhile removed from the cartridge.

When unprepared or borrowed army rifles are used, the performer switches the original cartridges for blanks.

BUSINESS METHODS (See also: PUBLICITY) There are bound to be as many ways of doing business as there are of doing magic. There are, however, a few general rules that deserve remembering. The professional will of course have developed his own methods; this article is addressed only to the semi-professional and the amateur who would like to develop an income from his hobby.

Free shows are legitimate and desirable if given for your own intimate friends or for organizations of which you are an active member. So are free charity shows provided you know that everyone else is also giving his services. Beyond this point, free shows merely destroy business that some professional may be depending on; furthermore, since people get such a show for nothing, they naturally decide that that must be what it is worth.

How much to charge is always a puzzle for the new magician. In the first place, remember that your time is worth something, and that any show takes more time than you spend on the stage. Naturally you would rather perform than not, or you wouldn't be a magician; but in a business way this fact is irrelevant. Even as a high school student you could be earning money some other way if you were not performing.

Once you have decided on a price, never reduce it. It is far better to give a show free than to become known as a person who can be beaten down. Furthermore, if you are competing with another magician or some comparable act for a particular job, don't try to get it by underbidding. The only thing you have to sell is the goodness of your entertainment; its cheapness will, in the long run, make prospective purchasers despise you.

It is a good idea to keep books on what you spend, as well as what you take in, through magic. You are required to keep records of your income for tax purposes—a requirement that cannot safely be neglected even by beginners. And you will be less inclined to think conjuring is a magic road to riches if you realize what you have spent on it. Furthermore, you can offset the expenses against the income on your tax return.

Sources of business must be found by each magician for himself. Schools, churches, and clubs are among the commonest employers of magicians. In large cities, business houses and conventions are another field. In small towns, with a big enough show, it may still be possible to hire a hall and charge admission.

It is a safe rule, once you have made a start in a particular field, to concentrate on that, and take other business only as it comes in. Your reputation spreads more quickly that way, and furthermore you have a known, concentrated group of new prospects to whom you can appeal by letter, telephone, or circular.

So long as you are arranging your own booking, your mailing list is your most valuable single business asset. Keep it up to date; be sure that all names are spelled correctly; make changes promptly.

When it comes to printed matter—letterheads, circulars, billheads, business cards—get the highest-priced help you can find. The best printer in town is none too good for you; if you know any advertising men, ask their advice. If you have any doubts of your own ability to write a good circular or a good letter asking for business, hire someone to do it for you; at the very least, get a high-school English teacher to pass on it.

Newspaper and magazine advertising is usually too expensive to pay new magicians; but small classified advertisements or "professional cards" may be possible in large towns if you know that they reach just the people you are looking for. A small ad on the society page, for instance, might bring you jobs at children's parties.

A booking agent will take many of these worries off your shoulders, but you must win a certain success on your own before any agent will handle your act. Here, too, only a good agent is good enough for you. Sign up with one you have confidence in, and leave him alone. He can make money only by doing his best for you; let it go at that.

One last rule, social as well as business: never knock another magician's act. In fact, if a dissatisfied employer complains in your presence, try to say something nice about the magician; one bad performer may give magic a black eye that you personally will suffer from. *H. H.*

C

CAKE BAKED IN A HAT This is an old and favorite hat trick. The necessary apparatus consists of two parts—first, a round tin pan *a* (Fig. 1), four inches deep and tapering from five inches at its greatest to four and a half inches at its smallest diameter. It is open at each end, but is divided into two parts by a horizontal partition at about two-thirds of its depth. Second, a larger tin *b*, five and a half inches deep, and shaped so as to fit somewhat tightly over the smaller tin.

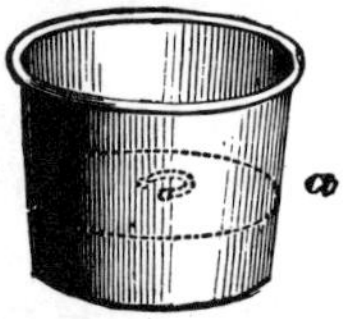

Fig. 1

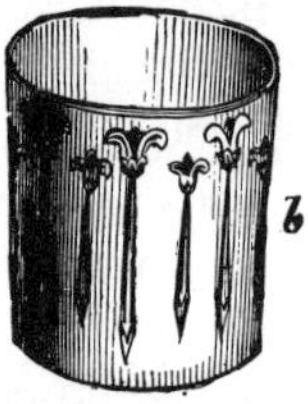

In the larger end of the latter is placed a hot cake or pudding, and in this condition it is placed on the SERVANTE of the table, projecting a little over the edge. The performer borrows a hat, and in passing behind his table, tips cake and tin together into it. The chances are that the tin will fall small end upward, (the opposite end being the heaviest); but if not, the performer turns the tin so as to bring it into that position.

Placing the hat mouth upward upon the table, he announces his intention of making a cake in it; for which purpose he takes, one by one, and mixes in the tin *b*, a quantity of flour, raisins, eggs, sugar, and the other ingredients for a cake, adding water enough to make the mixture into a thick batter. This he pours into the hat, holding the tin with both hands at first high above it, but gradually bringing it lower and lower until at last, as if draining the last drop of the mixture, he lowers the mouth of the tin right into the hat, and brings it well down over the smaller tin. On being raised again, it brings away within it the smaller tin and its liquid contents, the cake being left in the hat.

He next proceeds to bake the cake by moving the hat backward and forward at a short distance over the flame of a candle, and, after a sufficient interval, exhibits the result, which is cut up and handed around to the company for their approval.

As the batter around the sides of *b* is apt to cause *a* to stick pretty tightly into it, a folding ring is generally fixed inside *a*, in order to facilitate its removal after the close of the trick. *L. H.*

CARD BOX This is usually constructed of polished brass, the edges being ornamented with wire beading. Besides being ornamental, this beading is arranged so as to conceal entirely the secret of the box, which is just large enough to contain an ordinary playing-card.

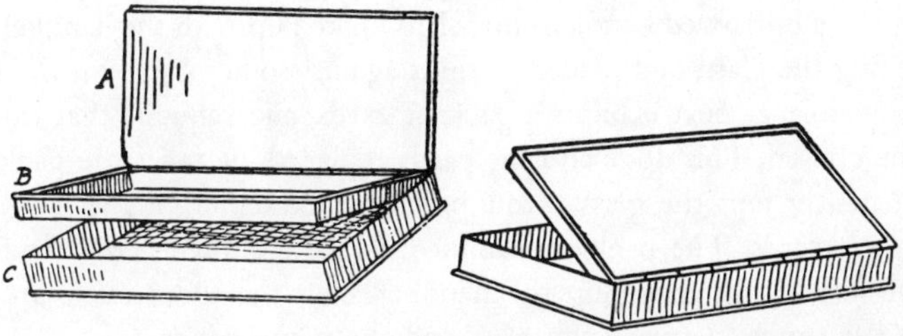

FIG. 1

The box is opened and a card placed inside, in full view of the audience. It is then closed and when, a second later, it is again opened, the card has disappeared—at any rate that is the effect of the trick. The secret, though ingenious, is very simple.

(Fig. 1) Between the lid, *a*, and the interior of the box, *c*, there is an intermediate tray, *b*. This tray can adapt itself either to *a* or *c* at the pleasure of the performer. When preparing the box for use, he fixes the tray *b* into *c* leaving *a* open. The box is then exhibited and a card placed inside. Showing the audience that the card is actually in the box and that there is no trickery about the matter, the performer closes *a*, the fastening being entirely concealed by the beading. When he again opens the box he lifts *a* and *b* together as in Fig. 1, the card lying concealed between them.

To prove that the box has absolutely nothing whatever to do with the matter the performer hands it around for examination. He knows that he is quite safe in doing so, because the separation of *a* from *b* demands not only knowledge of the secret, but the use of a special needle which is supplied with the box. *C. L. N.*

CARD FRAME (See also: CARD MANIPULATION) The oldest form of card frame is a picture-frame, supported on a brass pillar and enclosing a background of black cloth, on which borrowed articles are suddenly made to appear at a pistol shot. The articles have up to that point been hidden by a spring-blind of the same material as the background, which flies up and discloses them.

One frame is of plain gold bead, about twelve inches by ten, with a loose wooden back, kept in position by a cross-bar working on a pivot. The frame is glazed in the usual manner, and between the glass and the back lies a sheet of white paper, exactly filling the space.

The performer begins by calling attention to the frame, and takes it completely to pieces. Back, paper, and glass are successively taken out and replaced before the eyes of the company, the frame being laid for that purpose on a borrowed handkerchief. It is picked up with the handkerchief still veiling the glass, and placed upright against some object on the table.

The performer next exhibits a pack of cards, and requests that three of them be chosen. This done and the cards replaced, he takes the pack, and with it gently taps the glass through the handkerchief, at the same time riffling the cards. The pack is examined, and the chosen cards are found to have left it. On removing the handkerchief, the three cards are seen within the frame, between the glass and the white paper.

The secret lies in this apparently innocent sheet of paper, on one side of which are pasted, face outward, three cards, duplicates of those to be chosen. When the frame is first shown, the paper is turned with these cards *away* from the glass, showing only its blank side.

The performer begins by borrowing a handkerchief, which he lays flat on the table. He then unfastens the cross-bar and turns the whole contents of the frame, glass, paper, and back, out on the table beside the handkerchief, and on this latter lays the frame, now a mere skeleton, face downward.

He first replaces the glass. He next comes to the paper, but instead of turning it over, as would be necessary in order to replace it as before, simply lays it on the glass, bringing the "card" side *next* to the glass. The wooden back is then laid on the paper, and secured by the cross-bar. The frame is picked up with the handkerchief still concealing the glass, in order that the audience may not discover prematurely that the cards are already in position.

The three corresponding cards are FORCED and PALMED off by the performer after being returned to the pack, before he commands them to pass and calls attention to their disappearance.

In place of the paper with cards attached, a sheet of paper without any preparation may be used. Both sides can therefore be shown. The cards to be produced are palmed and introduced under cover of the sheet of paper while the frame is being reconstructed. This is a substantial improvement, but the trick remains open to the objection that from the moment of its reconstruction the frame must be kept covered, a considerable drawback to its effectiveness.

Another ingenious little piece of apparatus was the invention of the elder BOSCO. It consists of a little frame, about the same size as that last described, but with less bulky sides. The central space is just large enough to exhibit a playing-card, with a half-inch margin all around. At the outset this space is apparently occupied by coarse gray paper; but if the frame is held face downward for a few moments and again reversed, a card is seen to appear in its center. The frame can be opened at the back and the card removed.

The secret lies in the fact that there are in reality *two* glasses, with an interval of about an eighth of an inch between them. At one end of the frame is a receptacle filled with fine sand; if the frame is inverted, this runs into the space between the glasses, concealing the card which lies behind the inner glass. The appearance of the sand behind the glass is exactly that of coarse gray paper, and the back is lined with paper of exactly the same color and texture, a margin being visible around the card.

The frame is first shown with the card masked by the sand. The performer must, of course, divert attention from the fact that he turns the frame upside down, and occupy the minds of the audience during the few seconds necessary for the sand to trickle down into the secret reservoir.

Another type of frame (shown back and front in Fig. 1) measures five inches by four, the glass, or its visible portion, being about an inch smaller in each direction. It is backed by a thin slab of wood, held in position by a cross-bar working on a pivot at one of its sides, and fitting into a little wire staple on the opposite side. This slab, like the rear part of the frame, is stained a dull black. The apparatus is completed by a little piece of black silk, of the same width as the movable back, but about an inch longer. Three of its edges are left as cut, but the fourth, at one end, is pasted around a bit of stout string or wire, so that the piece of silk forms a sort of miniature blind, with lath at the bottom.

To prepare for the trick, the frame is laid face downward and the back removed. The piece of silk is laid upon the glass; the card, face downward,

FIG. 1

upon the silk; and the back over all, a small portion of the wired end of the silk hanging out between the lower end of the back and the frame. The back is purposely made a trifle short, leaving a little gap at the bottom, so that by taking hold of the stiffened end, the silk can be drawn out at pleasure. *L. H.*

CARD IN CIGARETTE One of the most popular modern tricks with a chosen card. A card is chosen, torn up, the pieces put in a CARD BOX, and one corner kept by the chooser. The magician meanwhile borrows a cigarette, but when he lights it, it refuses to draw. He pulls it apart, and finds inside the chosen card, rolled up tight, but lacking the corner held by the spectator. The card box contains nothing but a few grains of tobacco.

The preparation consists of tearing a corner off a card, and putting the corner in an accessible pocket; soaking the card in water until it can be rolled up and pushed into a cigarette or wrapped in a cigarette paper with a little tobacco stuffed in at the end. One compartment of the card box is loaded with a little shredded tobacco.

The performer FORCES a duplicate of the card in the cigarette. He borrows a cigarette, and SWITCHES it for the prepared one, which is easy, since no one knows why he wants it. The spectator who tears up the card drops the pieces in the card box; the performer, having stolen the previously prepared corner from his pocket, pretends to pick it out of the box and hand it to the spectator. The rest of the working will be obvious. *H. H.*

CARD INDEX This is the device used in the "Cards From Pocket" trick. The effect of this trick is that the pack is shuffled, split into halves, and one half is put into each trouser pocket. The magician promptly brings out any card named by the audience.

FIG. 1

The index can also be used for any other trick in which you must find (and, let us say, PALM) a given card or slip of paper on short notice. It consists simply of pieces of red manila board fastened together at the bottom and sides in such a way as to hold twenty-six cards in the pockets formed by the manila board. The cards are arranged in overlapping rows, each card projecting from its pocket. (Fig. 1) The cards are, of course, sorted and arranged into suits and sequences. With the index, any card can be found by touch with the fingering of not more than four cards.

In the Cards From Pocket trick, naturally the shuffled halves of the deck are left in the pockets, to be disposed of later.

CARDINI Stage name of Richard V. Pitchford, a former Welsh coal-miner who is perhaps the outstanding modern exponent of pure manipulation. His card-fanning, CIGARETTE and billiard-BALL MANIPULATION revived a type of act that had languished since the days of DOWNS AND THURSTON, and brought forth many very skilful imitators. According to JOHN MULHOLLAND, his "act is an example of the highest type of magician's pantomime."

CARD MANIPULATION *Back Palm.* The performer shows a card held between the thumb and first finger of either hand. A slight upward movement of the hand, and the card has vanished. The performer shows that the card is not concealed either in the palm or at the back of the hand.

A card is taken between the thumb and first finger as in Fig. 1, the hand and forearm make a slightly downward movement (about three to four inches) and then upward (eight to twelve inches), while the fingers manipulate the card as follows:

The thumb allows the card to fall somewhat across the back of the first, second, and third fingers, and the little finger comes up to the edge of the card as in Fig. 2.

The little finger grips the edge of the card between itself and the third finger, and the first finger is removed so that the thumb grips the opposite edge of the card between itself and second finger.

The first finger moves down the edge of the card and takes the place of the thumb in gripping the edge of the card against the second finger, which allows the thumb to move away. The fingers are extended and the back palm is now complete. (Fig. 3) The card has vanished, and the palm of the hand is seen empty.

To show the back of the hand, the hand is now turned over, the thumb coming over forward. While the hand is thus turning over forward, the following takes place: the fingers are closed to palm and the thumb grips the center of the edge of the card as in Fig. 4, allowing the four fingers to be opened outward until the first and little fingers grip the other end edges of the card against the two middle fingers as in Fig. 5, and upon the completion of the turn of the hand the back of the hand is shown.

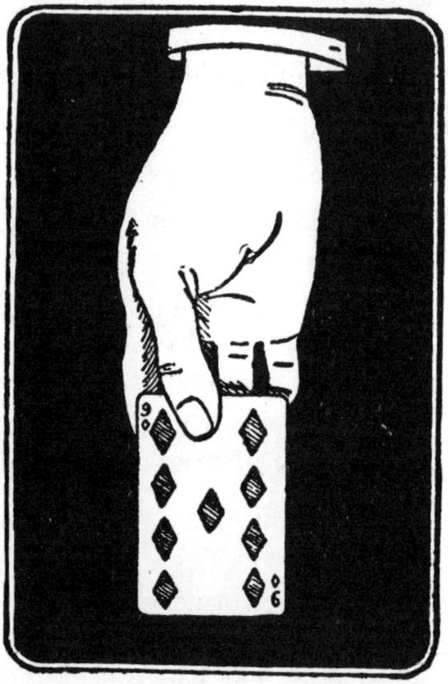

FIG. 1

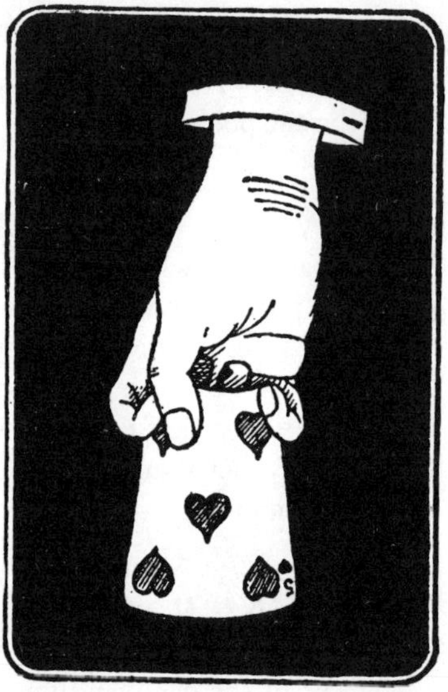

FIG. 2

CARD BACK-PALMING

FIG. 3

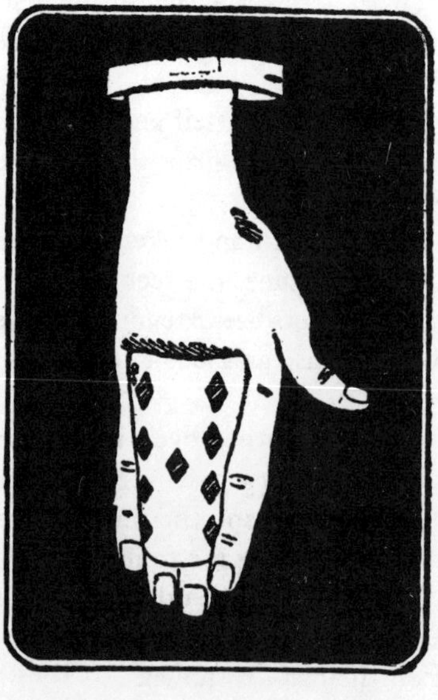

FIG. 4

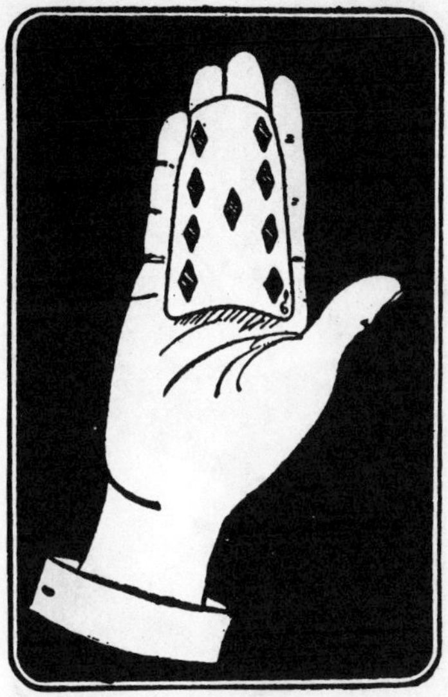

FIG. 5

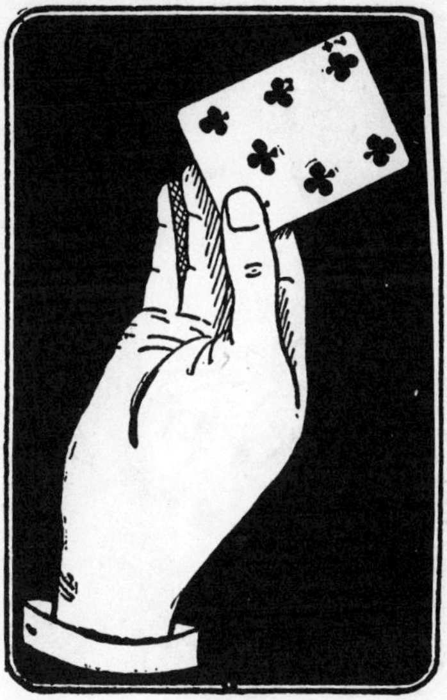

FIG. 6

To reverse the palm once more, in order to show the front of the hand empty, the hand is again turned over, and while turning the process is as follows: the fingers are closed, pushing the card back into its former position.

The sleight may be divided into three operations.

1. The back palm.
2. The recovery and front palm.
3. The reverse again to back.

To continue showing the back and front of the hand empty, parts 2 and 3 are repeated as often as the performer may desire. Both hands must be trained to work equally well, and then all sorts of effects may be obtained. For instance, the performer may commence with a card held in the right hand as in Fig. 1, the left showing its palm empty, a card being back-palmed.

The right hand back-palms its card simultaneously, and the left hand recovers its card. The left hand now back-palms it, and the right recovers its card, and so on, with variations according to each individual performer's ingenuity.

C. L. N.

Production from Back Palm. After the performer has vanished, say, five cards, by means of the back palm, and has shown both sides of the hands to be empty, he proceeds to reproduce the cards one by one at the fingertips, as in Fig. 6.

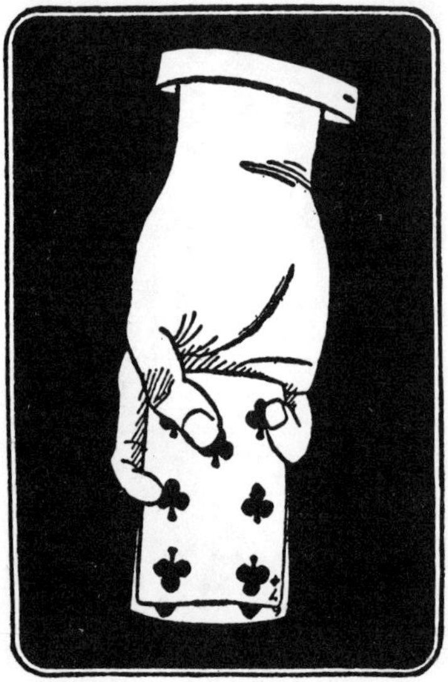

Fig. 7

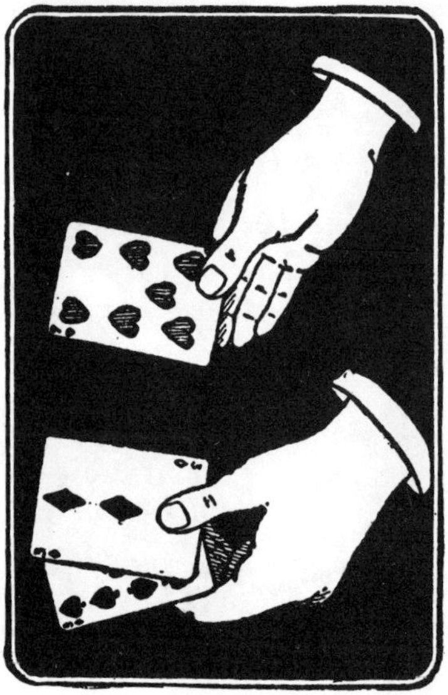

Fig. 8

Card Back-Palming

Fig. 9

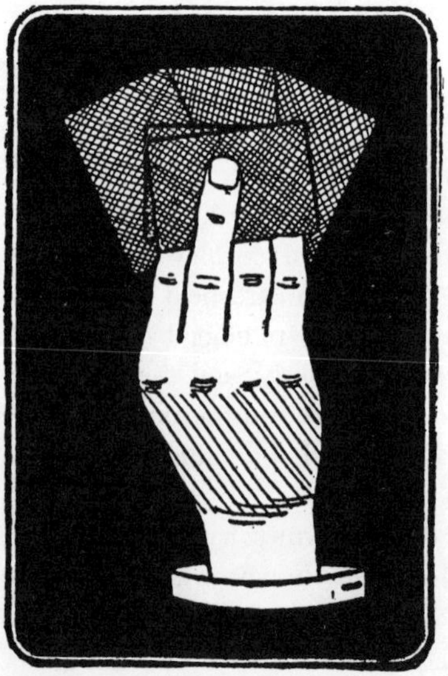

Fig. 10

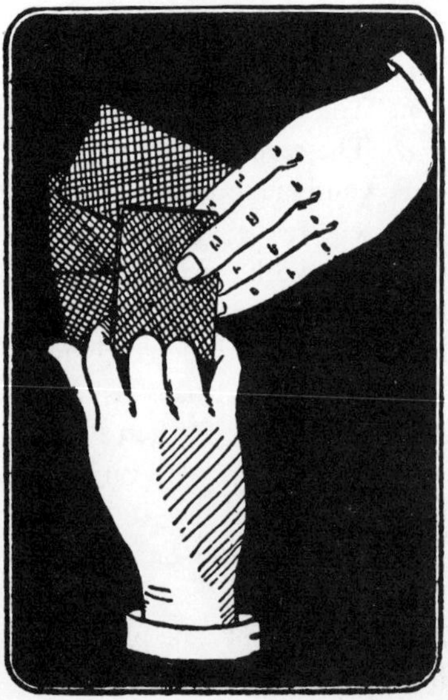

This is accomplished in the following manner: when it is desired to produce one card from the back of the hand, the thumb bends around to the upper corner of the nearest end of the outside card, springs it free of the forefinger, and literally pulls it away from the rest (Fig. 7), the first and fourth fingers aiding in its release by slightly relaxing their pressure. Once quite free from the back of the hand, the card is pushed by the thumb into the position depicted in Fig. 6. This must be done very slowly at first, but, of course, in the actual performance all the above movements must be made simultaneously. If this is done with a slight wave of the hand, it will appear to the audience that the performer actually caught the card from the air.

The effect of this trick can be further heightened if the performer, after having caught, say, three cards, shows his right hand to be absolutely empty, back and front, and the fingers spread wide apart.

As each card is produced at the right-hand fingertips, it is placed in the left hand. (Fig. 8 shows the exact position of both hands.) When the performer has caught the third card, in the act of placing it in the left hand, he secretly leaves the cards, still back-palmed, behind the three cards now in the left hand, gripped by the second finger. (Fig. 9 represents a back view showing the position of the hand and cards.)

The right hand is now shown empty, and the performer says, "No, nothing between the fingers. All we have here is three cards," meanwhile counting with the thumb of the right hand those in the left hand. Under cover of this movement the two hidden cards are again back-palmed in the right hand (Fig. 10), and produced at will. *H. T.*

Bottom Dealing. This art, although not the most difficult to attain, is perhaps the most highly prized accomplishment in the repertory of the gambler. The bottom is the most convenient place for retaining desirable cards during the shuffle or riffle, and perfection in dealing from that position largely eliminates the necessity of stocking, as the cards can be dealt at will, and consequently need not be run up in a certain order. As in many other feats, a thorough understanding of the exact manner in which it is performed will avoid the principal difficulties, and practice will soon do the rest.

Hold the deck in the left hand, resting one corner against the middle of the first joint of the second finger, the other corner of the same end in the second joint of the first finger, the first two joints of which rest idly along the end of the deck.

Press the deck outward as much as possible and rest the opposite inner end corner against the palm below the base of the thumb. Rest the thumb

FIG. 1

FIG. 2

on top of the deck, pointing toward the second fingertip, which just shows at the top of the corner. Bring up the little finger against the side, and the third finger midway between the second and little fingers. The deck is held in position principally by the corners, between the second finger and the palm below the base of the thumb. The little finger may aid in holding the deck, but it must be released when the bottom card is pushed out. (Fig. 1)

The second finger and thumb do the work. Draw back the thumb a little and push the top card over in the usual position to seize with the right hand for dealing. Then draw back the third finger until the tip rests against the edge of the bottom card. (This action is concealed by the overhanging card.) (Fig. 2) Press up and slightly inward against that card and push it out, at the same time releasing the little finger and holding the deck firmly between the second finger and the palm. If this is done properly it leaves the top and bottom cards in the same relative position, the top card effectively concealing the under one.

Now advance the right hand, apparently to take off the top card. (Fig. 3) Draw back the top card with the left thumb, and at the same instant seize the bottom card instead with the right thumb and second finger and deal it in the usual manner. (Fig. 4) With practice, this can be done so perfectly that the quickest eye cannot detect the ruse. The main thing is to understand the action thoroughly and hold the deck correctly.

FIG. 3

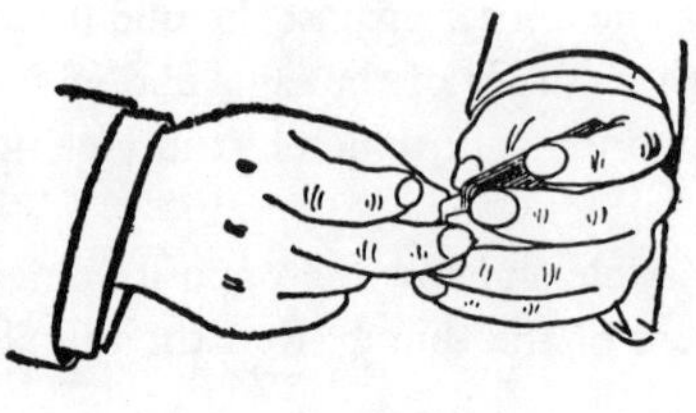

FIG. 4

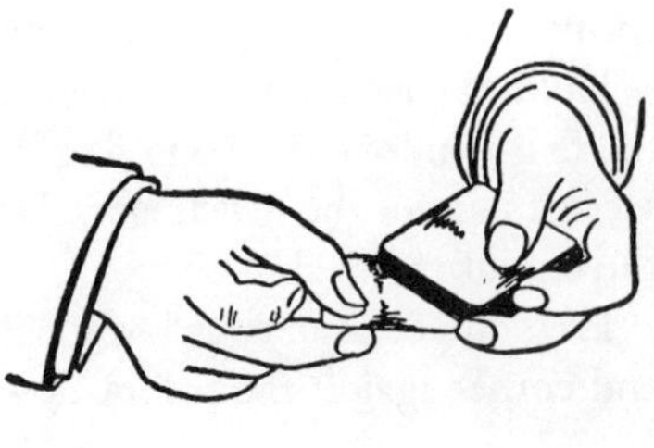

The position is an excellent one for ordinary dealing, and should never be changed. The corner pressed against the palm should be as far from the wrist as possible. Each time a card is pressed out from the bottom, the deck will have a tendency to slip toward the wrist, and must be held, or worked back into position again.

The left hand does nine-tenths of the work. After the hold is established, the main task is in acquiring facility to push out the bottom card with the second fingertip. The cards may come out in numbers, or appear to stick fast; but the process is very easy when the knack is once obtained. The second fingertip comes around the corner to the side, just barely enough to hold the deck in place, and when the third fingertip releases the bottom card from the hold of the second finger, it slips out quite freely. The thumb of the left hand plays a very important part in the blind, by drawing back the top card at the proper instant; and it is this action that makes the deal appear perfectly regular. The thumb movement is identically the same as in the true deal, and the drawing back of the top card is undetectable when properly and rapidly executed. A very slight up-and-down movement of the left hand as the cards are taken aids in concealing the action. Hoyle makes a point of instructing that a dealer should always keep the outer end of the deck, and the cards, as dealt, inclined toward the table. Following this rule tends to hide the work of the third finger in bottom dealing.

In another method of dealing, the deck is held in exactly the same manner as described for bottom dealing. The single-handed top deal is made by pushing over the top card with the thumb in the usual manner; then with a swing of the hand toward the player, the card is released by the thumb and slides off the deck over the table in the direction indicated. The *single-handed bottom deal* is made by first pushing over the top card as usual, then instead of pushing out the bottom card, as in the two-handed deal, it is sprung back a little by the third fingertip, and then suddenly sprung forward and out as the hand is swung in the direction of the player.

This bottom deal is really more deceptive than one which employs two hands because it appears so open, and the action is completely hidden by the natural swing of the hand necessarily made toward the player, to cause the card to slide in the proper direction. *S. W. E.*

Break. A space or division held in the deck. A break can be held firmly by a finger or thumb of either hand, and entirely concealed by the other fingers of the same hand. (Fig. 1 shows a little-finger break.) It is also the principal aid in the false riffles and cuts (see FALSE SHUFFLE).

When shuffling, it is held at the end by the right thumb. It is formed

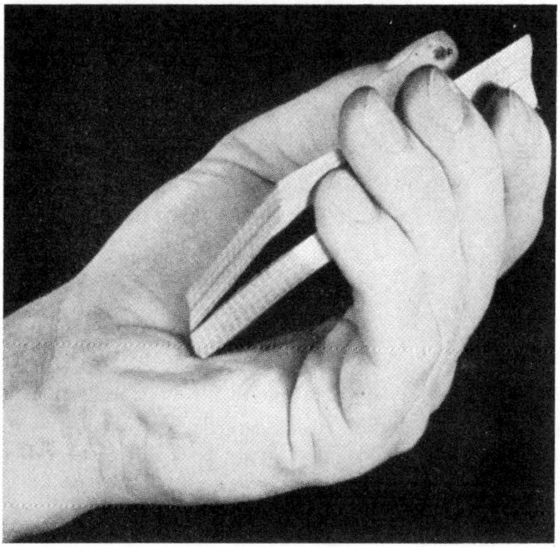

FIG. 1
LITTLE-FINGER
BREAK

under the in-jog when about to undercut for the shuffle, by pushing the in-jog card slightly upward with the right thumb, making a space of from an eighth to a quarter of an inch wide and holding the space, by squeezing the ends of the packet to be drawn out, between the thumb and the second and third fingers.

The use of the break during a shuffle makes it possible to throw any number of cards that are immediately above it, on one packet into the left hand, without disarranging their order. The break is used when not shuffling, to locate any particular card or position, and is infinitely superior to the common method of inserting the little finger. *S. W. E.*

A little-finger break, held with the left hand, is the method of location used when a spectator peeps at a card in the deck instead of making his selection from a fan. The SIDE-STEAL SHIFT usually follows.

Change, Top. Hold the deck in the left hand crosswise, face down, the thumb resting across the top. Hold the card to be exchanged in the right hand between the thumb and first fingertips, thumb on top, finger underneath. Now bring the hands together for an instant by an easy swing, both hands moving in the same general direction, but one hand faster than the other. As they meet, the left thumb pushes the top card slightly over the side, the right hand places its card on top and clips the protruding

Fig. 1
Top Change

card between the tips of the first and second fingers, carrying it off (Fig. 1), the left thumb retaining the now top card and sliding it back into position on the deck.

In theory, it would seem that this action would be very easily noticed, but in practice, it is almost impossible to detect, if cleverly performed. The general movement or swing of the hands is not stopped when the exchange is made, but is continued until they are separated again by some little distance; the swing should be taken naturally, with some ulterior motive, such as placing the card on the table or giving it to someone to hold. A slight turn of the body may bring the hands together easily. The swing may be made in any direction, in or out, up or down, to the right or left, one hand following or passing the other, but in no case stopping until well separated again.

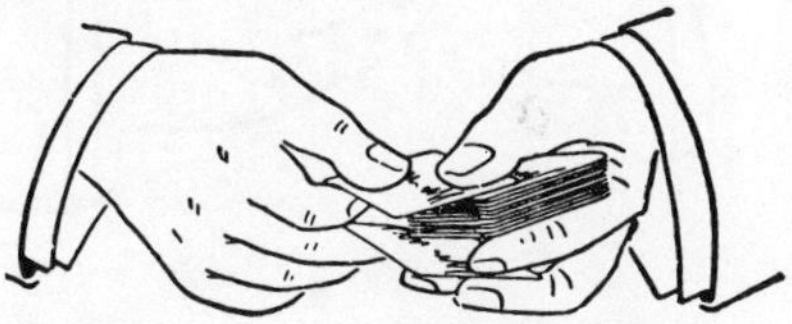

Fig. 2
Bottom Change

Change, Bottom. In this process the action is much the same, the difference being that the card in the right hand is passed to the bottom of the deck, the right hand carrying off the top card as before.

Hold the right-hand card between the thumb and the first and second fingertips, first finger on top. Hold the deck with the thumb and first finger, dropping the other fingers slightly to receive the right-hand card, drawing it back under the deck as the hands separate. The top card is pushed over as before and carried off by the right thumb and first finger. (Fig. 2) The swing of the hands is made in the same manner. The only difficulty in this change is getting the card fairly back under the deck with the left fingers.

Change, Double-Palm. This method may be employed to exchange one or several cards. The cards to be exchanged lie in a packet on the table face up. The other cards are secretly palmed face down in the left hand. The left hand now picks up the packet on the table by the sides, between the thumb and second and third fingertips, and transfers the packet to the right hand. As the left hand turns palm up, the right hand palms the packet just picked up and seizes the packet in the left palm by the sides, carrying it slowly and openly away, and the left hand is seen empty. (Fig. 3)

As the right hand palms the upper cards, the left first finger curls up under the palmed cards, bending them upward, thus enabling the right hand to seize them easier and also effectually taking out the crimp or bend that may have been caused while so closely palmed.

The only objectionable feature of this change is that the right hand carries the packet away by the sides, while it may have been noticed that the packet first in view was seized by the ends. But this is a splendid change for many purposes.

FIG. 3

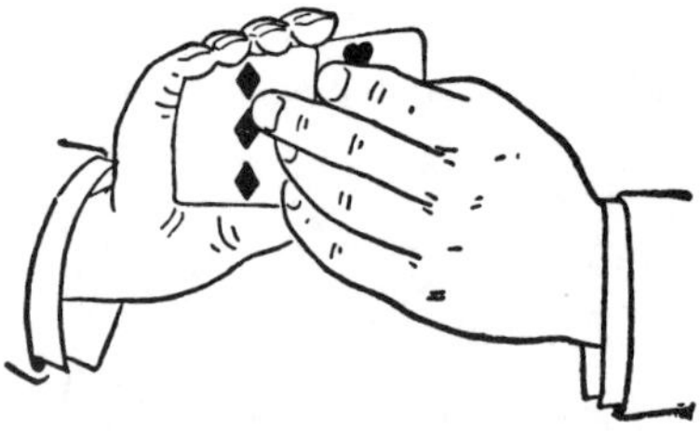

FIG. 4

Change, Palm. The two cards to be exchanged are held in the right hand by the ends between the second and third fingertips and the thumb, and close together, so that when shown to the audience they appear as one. The right hand is now turned palm down and the left hand apparently takes the card that was exposed, laying it on the table, but in reality takes the second card, leaving the other one palmed in the right hand. This is done by seizing both cards between the left thumb and second and third fingers, and drawing out the upper one with the thumb and pressing the lower one up into the right palm with the left fingers as the top one is drawn off. (Fig. 4)

This change is one of the simplest and easiest feats in the whole range of card sleights, and yet one of the most useful and undetectable. The action should be performed in about the same time and manner that would ordinarily be taken in transferring a card from one hand to the other.

S. W. E.

FIG. 1

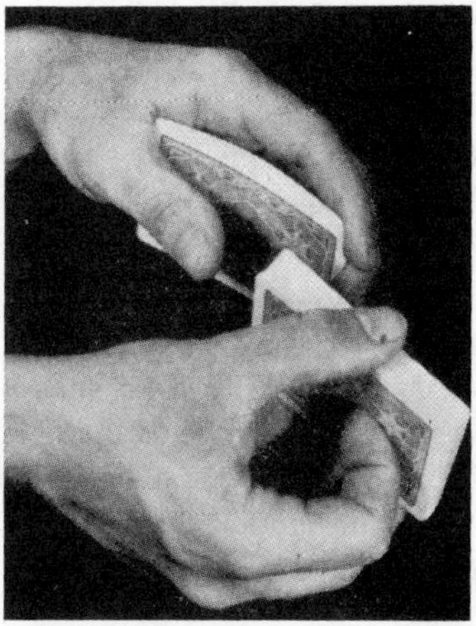

FIG. 2

Color Change: The Clip. A novel sleight, by which the front card of the pack, which is held in the right hand, is mysteriously transformed into another card. This change takes place under cover of the left hand, which is shown to be empty before being placed over the cards, and also after the transformation has taken place.

The pack is held in a perpendicular position between the thumb and middle finger of the right hand. The fingers of the left hand are momentarily placed over the cards, the thumb resting on the back of the pack. As this hand is taken away with a slight downward movement, the rear card of the pack is carried along with it (Fig. 1), being clipped between the root of the thumb and that of the first finger.

As the front card of the pack is still in its place, no one will attach any suspicion to this movement. The left hand is then, a moment later, replaced on the pack (Fig. 2), and this time leaves the palmed card on top of the latter. The hand is then removed and the transformation of the front card is seen to have taken place. *A. R.*

Color Change: Slip-Slide. The right hand holds the wrong card, which has just been exhibited; the left hand holds the deck between the thumb and second, third and little fingers at the sides, first finger at end, the back of the deck to the palm and the selected card on the bottom. The deck is inverted or the hand turned palm down, so that the bottom card cannot be seen.

The right hand now openly places the wrong card on the bottom of the deck and carelessly shows the palm empty. Then the tips of the right-hand fingers are placed against the bottom of the deck, both hands turning it up in view, showing the wrong card that was just placed there. But as the deck is turned up, the right fingertips push the wrong card up against the left first finger, about one inch, so that the right palm a little below the base of the fingers may be pressed against the selected card, which is the next one.

This card is drawn down slowly by pressing against it, the downward movement being apparently to give the company a full view of the wrong card. (Fig. 3) When the ends of the two cards pass each other the lower card is tilted on top and the right palm again covers the whole deck, carrying the selected card along, and the left first finger presses the wrong card back into position. This very effective sleight may be performed rapidly or slowly, as the operator fancies.

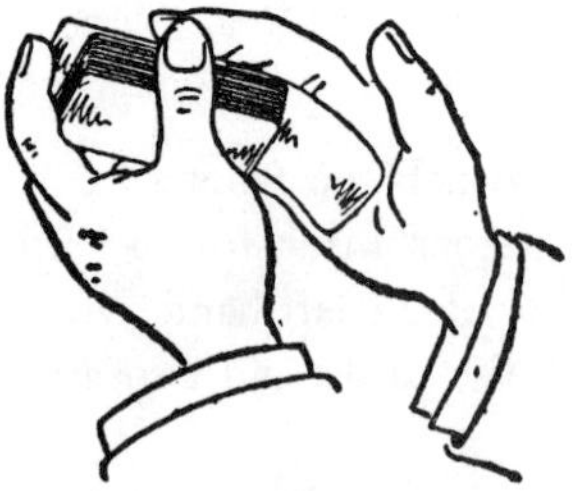

FIG. 3

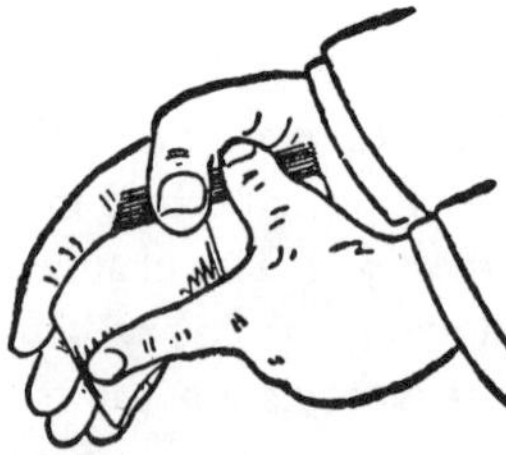

FIG. 4

Color Change: Forefinger Steal. Hold the deck in the left hand, between the thumb and second, third and little fingers, at sides, first fingertip against the back near the end, and the back, or top card, the selected card; the wrong card being on the bottom, or placed there and held in full view. To make the transformation bring the right hand over the deck with the four fingertips against the end. Slide or push the selected card with the first fingertip up against the right-hand finger ends, drawing the deck down toward the wrist until it clears the lower end of the selected card, which is pressed into the right palm by the left first finger. (Fig. 4) Then slide the deck back to its first position. This sleight may be made in an instant and the action is fully covered.

Color Change: Little-Finger Steal. Hold the deck in the left hand by the ends, between the tips of the thumb and second and third fingers, the first finger resting against the side and the little fingertip against the bottom, close to the corner, the face of the deck to the company and the finger end down.

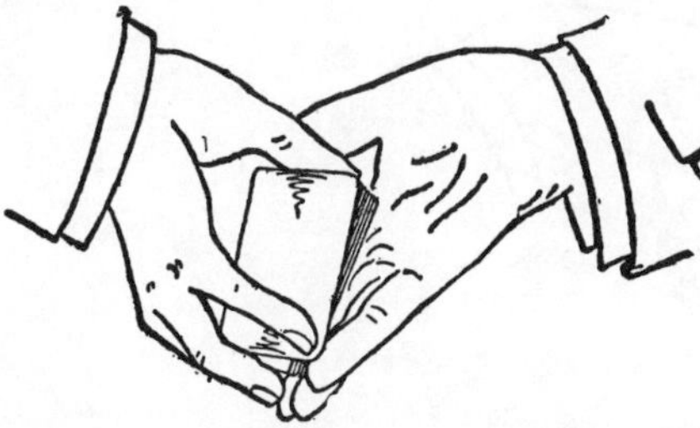

Fig. 5

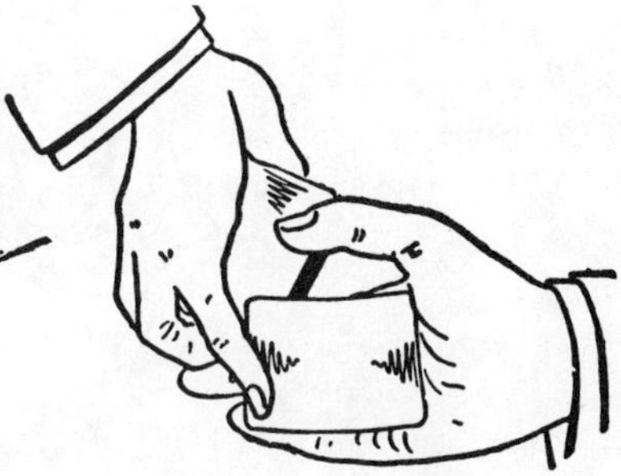

Fig. 6

Bring the right hand forward so that the little-fingertips meet at the corner of the deck, the palm partly facing the company, and showing the hand empty, the wrists being about six inches apart. Now, with the left little-fingertip push the corner of the lower card slightly over the side, and clip it with the right little-fingertip, so that it is firmly held between the two tips (Fig. 5), and press it down against the left third finger, turning the right hand over and moving the upper end of the deck to the left at the same time.

This action will cause the lower card to swing out at the upper end, and it is caught and palmed by the right hand as the hand turns over. The left little finger is extended as the turn is made, pressing the card firmly against the right fingers. (Fig. 6)

Now the right hand immediately seizes the deck close to the lower end, and the left hand releasing it, is shown empty. Then the left hand again seizes the deck, but this time by the sides, with the little finger against the lower end. The right hand is now released and passed rapidly downward over the deck, leaving the palmed card on top, and the right hand is shown empty. The left little finger at the end aids the replacing by catching the palmed card as the right hand is drawn down.

Of course, the performer makes the movements of passing the deck from hand to hand and showing the hands empty, ostensibly to prove that no palming takes place. The act of palming, if cleverly performed, is absolutely undetectable; the right hand turns over just in time and sufficiently to cover the card coming out, but not obstructing the continued view of the face of the deck. The actual palm can be made as rapidly as desired and without a sound. *S. W. E.*

FIG. 1
CRIMP

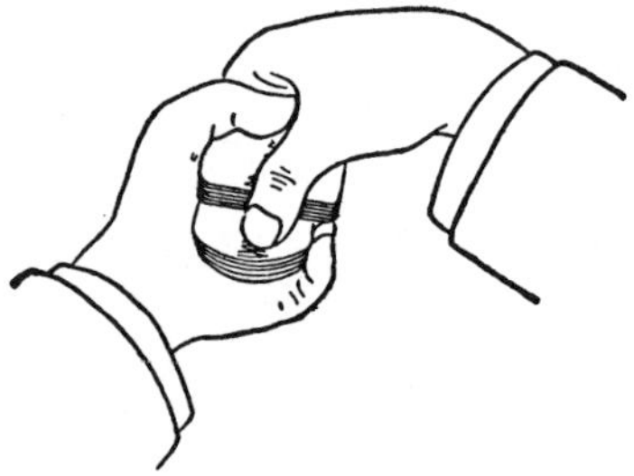

Crimp, or Bridge. This is a method used by both magicians and gamblers to mark a specific location in the pack. Gamblers depend on it to help or make another player cut to the prearranged stock. Magicians use it in such effects as the TRANSFIXED PACK.

The earlier form of the bridge was crosswise. The back is bent sharply downward over the left first finger, which lies across the middle; then the upper half is bent back against the left thumb. Making the SHIFT leaves the two halves of the pack with an elliptical opening between.

The lengthwise crimp is much more used by gamblers, and also by modern magicians; it is less noticeable than the crosswise bridge. The simplest way to make it is merely to BREAK the pack at the desired point, and then with the left fingers to push in sharply against the right-hand edge of the lower half, bending the center downward. (Fig. 1) This avoids both the double motion and the shift.

Double Lift. A sleight for showing the top two (or three or four) cards of the pack as one card. There are various methods, but all require that the two cards be separated somehow from the pack. The simplest is to hold the pack in dealing position in the left hand, cover the cards with the right as if preparing for the SHIFT, and pick up the near end edges of the cards to be lifted, one at a time, with the right thumb; the left little finger then holds a BREAK, and the right hand either picks the cards off without changing position, or grabs them by the lower right-hand corner between thumb and forefinger. An entire chapter is devoted to lifts in Hugard and Braue, *Expert Card Technique*.

False Count. The purpose of this sleight is to make it appear that the performer has more cards than he actually holds. The cards are held as if to deal, and the cards drawn off with the right thumb, one at a time, with a kind of snapping noise as each card is removed, one snap being made with the right thumb on the edge of the other cards without removing one. This is not distinguishable when counting quickly and evenly.

False Shuffle, Overhand: Glossary.

Stock: That portion of the deck that contains certain cards placed in some particular order for dealing; or certain desirable cards placed at the top or bottom of the deck.

Run: To draw off one card at a time during the process of the hand shuffle. There is little or no difficulty in acquiring perfect ability to run the whole deck through in this manner with the utmost rapidity. The left thumb presses lightly on the top card, the right hand alone making the movement necessary to shuffle.

FIG. 1
IN-JOG

Jog: A card protruding a little from any part of the deck, about a quarter of an inch, to fix the location of a particular card or cards. While shuffling, if the top card is to be jogged, it is pushed over the little finger end of the deck by the left thumb, the little finger preventing more than one card from moving. (Fig 1) If the first card is to be jogged, that is, the first card in the right hand, it is done by shifting the right hand slightly toward either end of the left-hand packet during the shuffle, so that the first card drawn off by the left thumb will protrude a little over the end of the left-hand packet.

In-jog: The card protruding over the little finger of the left hand.

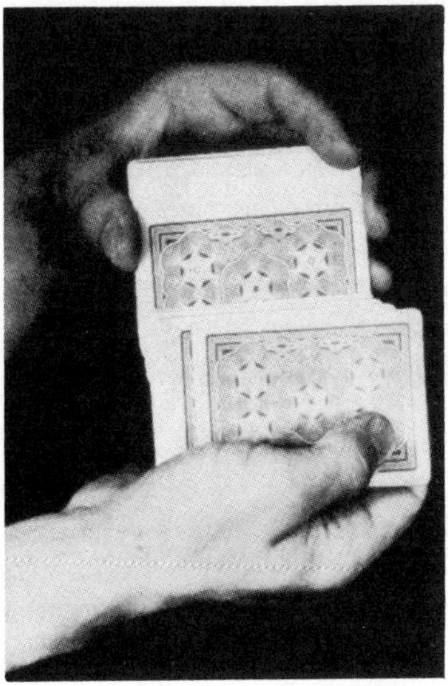

FIG. 2

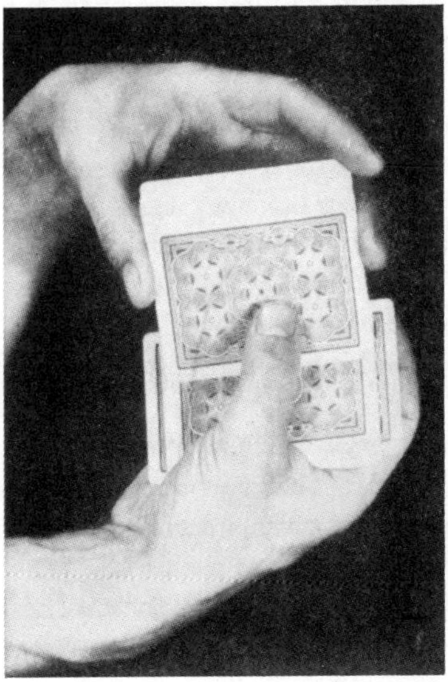

FIG. 3

Out-jog: The card protruding over the first finger of the left hand. (Fig. 2) (Fig. 3 shows an in- and an out-jog in combination.) The hands are reversed in the photographs.

Throw: To pass from the right hand to the left, during a shuffle, a certain number of cards in one packet, thereby retaining their order. A throw may be required at the beginning, during the process, or at the end of a shuffle; and the packet to be thrown may be located by the jog, or break, or by both.

Culls: The desired cards. To cull is the act of selecting one or more desired cards, and may consist simply in making the selection as discreetly as possible while gathering up the cards for the deal, or it may be the operation of a much more obscure and apparently impossible feat—that of gathering the desired cards rapidly and easily, from various positions in the deck, to the bottom, during the process of a shuffle that appears perfectly natural and regular.

Blind: Any method of shuffling, riffling, cutting or culling, designed to appear regular, but actually retaining, or arranging, some preconceived order.

Uppercut: To take or draw off a packet from the top of the deck.

Undercut: To draw out a packet from the bottom of the deck, during the process of a shuffle. (Fig. 4 shows the act of undercutting to an in-jog.)

Run Cut: To draw off several or many small packets from the top of the deck.

Top Card: The card on top of the packet held in the left hand, or the original top card of the full deck, which is about to be shuffled.

False Shuffle Overhand: Stock Shuffle. The method in common use by expert players is to draw the particular cards from the bottom, in the following manner:

Seize the deck at the ends, between the second finger and thumb of the right hand in the usual manner for shuffling, the first finger resting on the side. Run several cards into the left hand, but well down into the palm, so that the second and third fingers protrude to the first joints from underneath. Then when the right hand has made the next downward motion, instead of drawing off the top card with the left thumb, press the left second and third fingertips against the bottom card and let it slide into the left hand, drawing it into position on the other cards with the left thumb as the right hand is raised. (Fig. 5)

The right hand aids the left fingers by pressing the deck against them and drawing up more horizontally. Then run one card less than the number of players and again draw one from the bottom, and so on until the stock is complete. The left thumb goes through the same motion when the under card is drawn, but merely slides across the top card without disturbing it.

When the last card has been drawn from the bottom, run as many cards as there are players between the dealer and the player for whom the bottom cards are intended, out-jog the next card and shuffle off the balance. Then under-cut to out-jog and throw on top. *S. W. E.*

False Shuffle Overhand. The objects of false shuffling are to retain a top stock, that is, to retain in the same order the upper portion of the deck which has been prearranged for dealing; or to retain a bottom stock, which

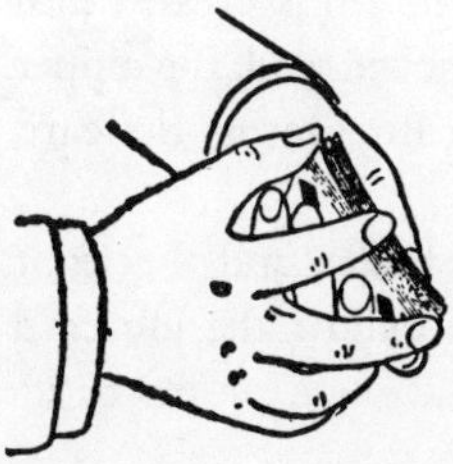

FIG. 4

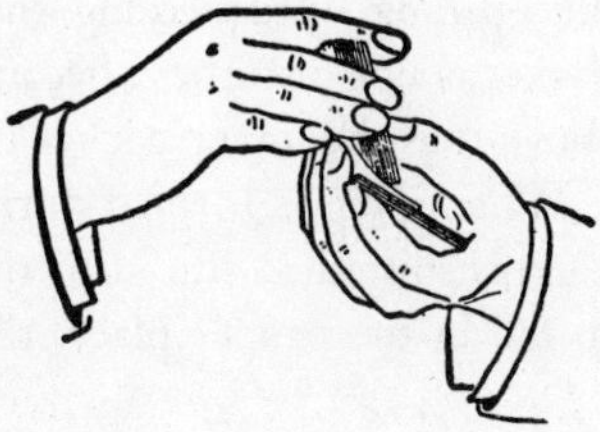

FIG. 5

usually consists of certain desired cards placed together at the bottom, to be taken from that position at will, during the deal, by bottom dealing; or to retain the whole deck in a certain order, which is rarely attempted, though quite possible. Under the respective headings of "Stock" and "Cull," it will be learned how the false shuffle runs up the cards in any desired order, and gathers certain cards from any position to the bottom; but the several methods of retaining the top and bottom stocks are treated separately.

False Shuffle Overhand: To Retain Top Stock and Shuffle Whole Deck. Undercut about three-quarters of the deck, in-jog first card and shuffle off. Undercut again about three-quarters of deck, forming BREAK at in-jog, shuffle off to break and throw the balance on top. This blind apparently shuffles the entire deck, but really leaves the top portion in the original order.

There should be no difficulty in forming the break. The right thumb presses slightly upward on the in-jog card when seizing the under portion, and the space created is held by squeezing the ends. This should be done altogether by touch, although the operator might glance at it without being noticed. It is practically impossible for a spectator to see it unless he is directly behind the performer. When shuffling off to the break, the right hand holds the cards firmly and the right thumb gives the warning by the sense of touch when the break is reached. If desired, the right hand may shuffle off, quite carelessly, several cards at a time and throw the last lot up to the break, by slightly decreasing the pressure on the ends. Above all, a uniformity of time and action must be maintained, although it is not at all essential to the blind to shuffle rapidly.

False Shuffle Overhand: To Retain Bottom Stock and Shuffle Whole Deck. Undercut about three-quarters of the deck and shuffle off about two-thirds, then in-jog one card and throw the balance on top. Undercut to and include in-jog card, and shuffle off.

This blind retains the bottom stock and apparently shuffles the whole deck. The only difficulty in the action is in including the jog card in the second undercut. The jog card is pulled back by the thumb, creating a space above it; then as the undercut is made, the thumb tip is pressed into the opening by squeezing the ends of the under packet, and the upper packet is not disturbed, because the thumbnail slips easily across the card above it as the lower packet is drawn out.

When a jog is formed during the process of any shuffle, and the right hand is shifted a little in or out as the case may be, to allow the jog card to fall in the proper place, the right hand does not at once return to its former position, but gradually works back as the shuffle progresses. This leaves the cards in the left hand a little irregular at the ends, and effectively conceals the fact that any one card is purposely protruding. The ablest shuffler cannot keep his cards quite even, and the irregularity appears even more natural than if in perfect order.

False Shuffle Overhand: To Retain Whole Deck. Retaining the whole deck in a prearranged order is seldom or never attempted, or even desired, at the card table. But the conjurer performs many very interesting tricks through such an arrangement; therefore it is necessary to provide a false shuffle that will not disturb any part of the deck.

Hold the deck in the left hand, crosswise, in the customary manner for the hand shuffle. Undercut with the right hand about three-quarters of the deck, and bring it down in the usual way of shuffling on top of the packet in the left hand, dropping a small packet from the top. Now, in raising the right hand again, still in the ordinary manner, seize the lower packet that was first left in the left hand between the right third finger and thumb, bringing it up with the rest of the cards; the packet that was dropped from the top now falls against the left fingers, concealing the fact that the under packet is withdrawn.

With the left fingers tilt the packet over against the left thumb, and drop another small packet from the top of the right-hand portion into the left hand between its packet and the fingers, still with the usual movement for shuffling. The left thumb now tilts the packet back on the other, and the right hand makes its customary movement downward, but this time drops the lower packet that is held between the third finger and thumb, by simply releasing the pressure of the third finger. Now the left-hand portion is again tilted against the thumb, the right hand dropping another packet from the top, then the left-hand packet is tilted back, and the right hand throws the balance on top. This process leaves the order the same, the deck having received but a simple cut.

The right hand makes five up-and-down movements in the ordinary or regular manner of shuffling, and without hesitating for an instant. The left fingers and thumb keep up the process of tilting its portion back and forth, allowing the right-hand packets to fall above and below it. The actions of the right hand in bringing up the first packet from the left hand, with the first upward movement, and in releasing it again on the third downward movement (instead of dropping a packet from the top) are undetectable if the shuffle is performed with some degree of rapidity and smoothness. It is not at all difficult, but some practice is necessary.

The method of shuffling over and under the left-hand packet is commonly employed, and incites no notice. The shuffle may be repeated as desired, and should be varied with an occasional cut.

False Shuffle, Riffle: To Retain Top Stock. Uppercut about half the deck with the right hand, and place two packets end to end on the table in the usual position for riffling. Seize both packets at the sides close to the adjoining ends between the third finger and thumb of each hand, and rest the hands on the outer ends of the packets. Raise the thumb corners, and at the same moment in-jog the top card of the left-hand packet by drawing it in a little over the left thumb, with the first finger of the left hand. The first and second fingers of the left hand conceal both the jog and the action.

Then begin to release, and spring or riffle into each other the ends of the lower cards with both thumbs, but more rapidly with the left thumb, so that the left packet, with the exception of the top card (which is retained on top of the left thumb) will have been riffled in before the right thumb has released the cards of the top stock. Continue the action with the right thumb until all are released, then release the last card held by the left thumb.

This action places one extra card on the original top stock. To square up in the ordinary manner would expose the fact that the upper portion had not been riffled. Drop the left thumb on the top card to hold the deck in position, and shift the left hand so that the edge of the palm will rest on the table at the end of the left packet and the second and third fingers come along the side. Then with the right hand in much the same position as the left, but held more openly, push the right packet in and square up.

Each time this riffle is made, it leaves an extra card on top, and the top stock is usually arranged to require two or three extra cards. But if not required the extra card is gotten rid of by one means or another.

This riffle is quite simple, and as easily executed as the true shuffle. There is no hesitation in the thumb action, although one moves more rapidly than the other. The movements are natural; the positions of the hands are regular; and even the manner of pushing in the cards is the customary one of many players.

But, as intimated, to retain the top stock in the riffle is the exception. In most instances, when the blind is used, it is to retain the bottom stock, and that process, which is next described, is even simpler and easier of execution, and more perfect in deception.

False Shuffle, Riffle: To Retain the Bottom Stock. Uppercut about half the deck with the right hand, and place the two packets end to end in position for the riffle. Seize both packets at the sides close to the adjoining ends between the second finger and thumb of each hand, the third and little fingers curled in, with the first joints resting on top of the packets. Raise the thumb corners and release the bottom stock first with the left thumb, then continue the action with both thumbs until all the cards are riffled in. Push both packets together in the ordinary manner and square up.

There is no need to cover the bottom stock when squaring up; unless it is very large, it is not noticeable, and more than half a dozen cards are rarely held there. However, the same plan used to conceal the top stock may be adopted if desired.

Perhaps a simpler way to perform the blind is to leave the bottom stock on the table without riffling it at all, and the left thumb to pick up the cards above it. The right thumb, of course, picks up the entire right packet. This method prevents any possible difference in the sound of the riffle, though when cleverly performed it is imperceptible to the ear.

This riffle can be varied by drawing out the bottom half with the right hand and leaving, or first releasing, the bottom stock with the right thumb. However, all blind riffling should be occasionally alternated with blind cuts, and when the action is gracefully executed without either haste or hesitation, it is absolutely impossible for any eye to follow the action or detect the ruse.

In performing the Top Stock Riffle, the use of the third fingers and the positions of the hands and other fingers are very important, as concealment is an essential of the blind. But in the Bottom Stock Riffle, especially when the stock is small, the action of not interlacing the bottom cards is not perceptible, and the handling of the deck should be as open and artistic as possible; hence the use of the second fingers and the curled-up positions of the third and little fingers.

The blind process of riffling the two packets truly together, and squaring up in a slightly diagonal position, then withdrawing the packets, throwing the original top one on top again; or pushing the two packets completely through in the diagonal position, leaving the order of the whole deck the same, is quite possible, but very difficult to perform perfectly.

False Shuffle, Twist-Out Riffle. This false shuffle will require considerable practice to perform nicely, but it is worth it.

Seize the deck with both hands, face down, second and third fingers at one side, thumbs at the opposite side, little fingers at opposite ends, held somewhat under the deck, and first fingers curled in with tips on top. The second fingers touch each other at the middle of the side, and the thumbs touch at opposite side. Each hand occupies identically the same position.

Now divide the pack with the thumbs and draw off the upper portion with the right hand; place the inner corners of the outer ends together so that the two packets form a sharp angle, but the right-hand packet about half an inch further out. Now riffle or spring the corners of the left-hand packet into the right-hand packet, both thumbs springing the cards, but beginning with the left thumb and finishing with the right, so that the left hand holds several cards that are not interwoven at the bottom, and about half a dozen of the right-hand packet are still free on top.

Now shift the left hand slightly so that the four fingers lie across the bottom of its packet, and with the right thumb spread the top cards fan-wise over the left packet, at the same time bringing the inner ends of the two packets toward each other, twisting out the riffled upper corners and replacing the right-hand packet on top.

As the inner ends are brought together, the two packets are spread somewhat, and the right little and third fingers twist out the bottom card first, and bend it in on top of the left-hand packet slightly in advance of the rest. This prevents any of the other cards going wrong. The more fan-wise the packets are spread during the operation, the more perfect the blind.

The deck should be squared up rather slowly, the left thumb and fingers holding the deck with the cards in their irregular condition, the right hand being released and pushing or patting the cards into position. Care should be taken not to riffle the corners far into each other. The merest hold is sufficient, and in fact if the packets can be held under perfect control the cards need not be interlocked at all, and the difficulty of the twisting-out process is avoided. By slightly spreading the two packets as the springing or riffling of the sides is continued, the appearance of the corners being interlocked is perfectly maintained.

This shuffle can be performed very rapidly, and with perfect control of the cards, and it is an excellent one for conjuring, as these performers never riffle on the table. But it is difficult, and if the operator is not a skilful card handler he will find it quite a task even to riffle in the two packets—the simplest part of the operation.

When this riffle is alternated with the foregoing shuffle, it requires very close scrutiny to detect the fact that the operation is a blind.

Another form of the *Twist-Out* is to seize the deck with the thumbs and fingers at the ends instead of at the sides, the little fingers going under the sides, the positions being identical, only that the deck is turned endwise.

When the deck is separated into the two packets the thumbs riffle the inner corners together, the left fingers are shifted across the bottom, the right thumb spreads the top cards over the left-hand packet, and the right hand brings the outer ends of the two packets toward each other, twisting out the interlocked corners and placing the right-hand packet again on top in much the same manner. *S. W. E.*

Flourishes: Drop, One-Hand. Some performers regard this spectacular effect as the most sensational and difficult of all flourishes with cards. It will require many weeks of hard practice before it is mastered. The effect is shown in Fig. 1, below, left.

Hold the cards in the manner described under *Springing the Cards, Second Method.* Extend the arm in front of the body, straight from the shoulder. Now let the cards drop toward the floor, releasing them one at a time. The right hand moves slightly upward at the same time, say about five or six inches. When the last card has fallen, the right hand descends swiftly, catching the cards in its downward movement, and, if the flourish has been perfectly executed, the last card—or what was the first card released—will be caught as it is about to touch the floor.

The effect of this flourish is indescribable. There is a knack about releasing the cards that cannot be explained, but which will be acquired by practice. Failure will be the reward of the student for many weary days, and when he is about to give up in despair, the knack will suddenly be attained.

It is impossible for even the most expert performer to catch all the cards every time. On an average the flourish is executed perfectly perhaps once out of three times. As a rule the performer is successful in the first attempt. If this is the happy result during a public performance, it is wiser for him to rest on his laurels and resist the temptation to show his skill a

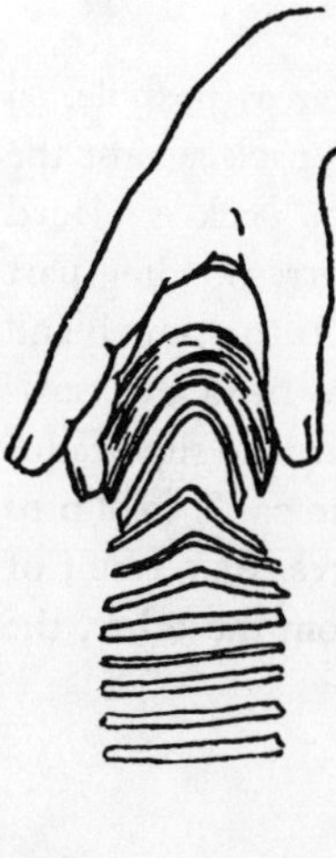

FIG. 1
ONE-HAND
DROP

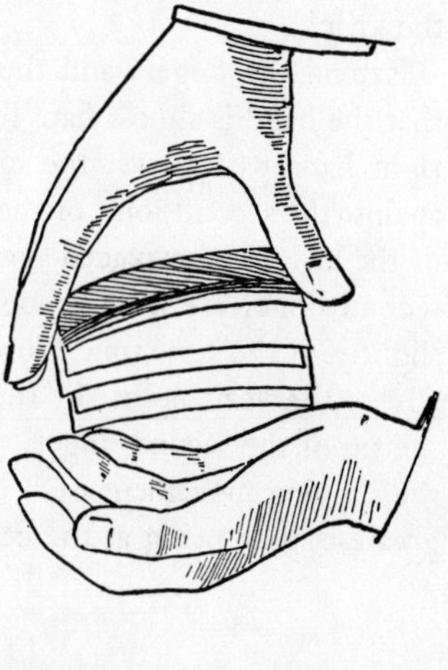

FIG. 1
SPRINGING
THE CARDS

second time. If, however, he is sufficiently expert in this kind of manipulation, he may respond to the encore with the following method:

The pack is held with the lower side parallel with the floor, as described under *Springing the Cards, Third Method.* The cards are dropped ribbon-wise, the faces toward the audience. The right hand catches the cards in much the same manner as described in the preceding sleight. This is even more brilliant in effect than the first method, and is correspondingly more difficult. *T. N. D.*

Flourishes: Springing the Cards.

First Method. Hold the pack firmly between the thumb and second finger of the right hand; and by bending the cards slightly *inward toward the palm* of the hand, increase the pressure, until at last the cards are forced to spring from the tip of the finger and escape from the hand as in Fig. 1, on the right at the bottom of the preceding page.

The left hand is held ready to receive them at a distance of about ten to twelve inches. This distance can (apparently) be considerably increased if, while the cards are being sprung, the performer describes an arc; or semicircle, with both arms. Although in describing the arc the relative distance remains the same, the audience imagine the cards to have been sprung over a gulf of quite two feet. Thick cards are the best, because they offer greater resistance, and consequently can be made to fly much farther than thin ones. *C. L. N.*

Second Method. It is very important that the student should understand at the beginning the principle of holding the pack; for upon his accuracy in this matter depends his success in the series of flourishes that follow. The exact method of holding the pack is difficult to describe, but if the reader will follow the directions with pack in hand he will soon acquire the knack.

Extend the fingers and thumb of the right hand as far as possible, so that the hand is almost flat. The left hand now places the pack against the right hand as follows: the middle of the top end of the pack is placed against the second joint of the second finger, while the corresponding part of the lower end is placed against the joint of the thumb. If the thumb and second finger are now brought slowly together, so as to bend the cards slightly, at the same time allowing the lower end of the cards to slip gradually to the very tip of the thumb, and the top end of the cards to slip to the tip of the second finger, the pack will describe a curve. As a result of the slipping movement each card is slightly separated from the other, the greatest space being at the center.

Now, instead of bending the fingers so sharply that the cards will shoot into the air, the pressure of the tips of the thumb and second finger should be gently relaxed, which allows the cards to fall (beginning with the bottom card), and at the same moment the right hand describes a rapid sweep upward, the left hand following at a distance of ten or twelve inches.

Just before making this upward sweep, the right hand is held about waist high, the left hand, palm upward, just below the right. As a matter of fact, a half-dozen cards actually fall from the right into the left hand before the right begins its upward sweep. After a little practice the student will be able to time the separation of the hands to a nicety. The hands should describe a sweep of at least two feet, and at the conclusion of the movement the left should be brought palm to palm with the right, the cards being instantly squared up. During the instant the cards are in the air there is an interval of about an eighth of an inch between cards, the effect being as if the performer were drawing out an accordion.

Third Method. This is perhaps more effective than the flourish just described. The cards are held in exactly the same manner, but the position of the hand is different. Instead of the pack being held so that the bottom card faces the floor, the right wrist is turned slightly so that the right side of the pack is parallel to the floor The left hand is held palm upward, and the lower side of the pack is allowed just to touch the extended fingers of the left.

The cards are now allowed to escape one by one, beginning with the front card, and at the instant the first card is released, the right hand moves upward in a straight line, to a distance of two feet or more. (Fig. 2) The effect is that of a ribbon of cards.

Fig. 2

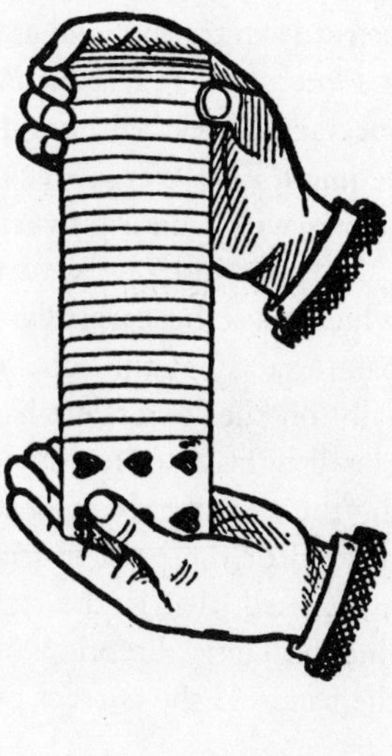

During the operation the left hand, palm upward, remains absolutely stationary. When the right hand reaches its highest point, it remains in that position for a fraction of a moment; then, while the cards remain like a ribbon in the air, the right hand swoops down, gathering the cards in its descent, the two hands come together with a sharp report, and the cards are squared.

Perfection in this sleight, which may be attained with reasonable practice, consists in the ribbon of cards being unbroken, and in the cards falling evenly into the left hand, so that when the right palm strikes the left the cards are squared. The reader is advised to practise only the releasing movement at first, the right hand remaining stationary. As perfection is acquired in this important movement, the right hand may be raised a few inches during the operation, increasing the distance gradually. Particular stress is laid upon the necessity of the right hand moving upward in a perfectly straight line; otherwise the ribbon of cards will not be even, which detracts from the effect.

Instead of holding the thumb and second finger of the right hand at the exact center of the two ends of the pack, the performer may find the flourish more easily acquired by placing the second finger at the upper right corner of the pack and the thumb at the corresponding upper left corner. This is a mere detail, however, and the student is advised to experiment with both positions, and to adopt the method that gives the best results.

Fourth Method. This is a variation of the preceding method. The effect is the same, but instead of the cards' being held endways between the thumb and second finger of the right hand, the pack is held sideways, so that in the upward movement the cards are ribboned lengthwise. As explained previously, the finger and thumb may grasp the pack at the middle or at the top. The student will find this variation much more difficult than the preceding method, as it requires assiduous practice to keep the ribbon from breaking. When this movement has been mastered, the reader will be ready to try his hand at the *One-Hand Drop*. *T. N. D.*

Flourishes: Tearing a Pack of Cards. There is no deception about this spectacular feat, although a certain knack in holding the cards must be acquired. To tear a deck of fifty-two playing-cards in two requires a strong wrist and a powerful grip.

There is just one way to hold the cards. The lower end of the pack, which must be carefully squared up, is laid across the ridge of the left palm exactly at the roots of the four fingers, the left thumb resting naturally on the lower left-hand side of the pack. The four fingers are now closed tightly on the lower end of the pack, which has the effect of pressing the pack firmly against the left palm. The right hand grasps the upper portion of the pack in exactly the same manner, except that the position is reversed; that is, the right thumb will be diametrically opposite the left thumb. These directions may be followed easily with a pack of cards in the hands. If the correct position is achieved it will be found that the cards are held as if in a vise. Everything is now ready for the exhibition of strength.

Twist the hands in opposite directions, the right hand turning to the right and the left hand to the left. Exert all your strength, and either your fingers or the deck will give way. At the outset you will find that the fingers cannot withstand the unusual strain, and for this reason it is wise to begin with thirty or thirty-five cards, gradually increasing the number until you can tear a bridge pack. Cheap cards are easier to tear than the calendered variety, and a brand-new pack is preferable to cards that are tough and leathery from much handling.

It is related of the late ALEXANDER HERRMANN that after a private performance before the late Czar Nicholas II, His Majesty, who was a very powerful man, undertook to show the magician a card feat that the latter could not imitate. He picked up a pack of cards and tore it into two pieces. "I am the only one in the world who can perform that feat," boastingly declared the Czar. Herrmann said nothing, but, picking up one of the halves of the deck, calmly tore it in two.

This feat looks very difficult, but is really little more so than the tearing of a whole pack. Were Nicholas alive, he would doubtless be amazed to learn that some performers actually tear two complete decks of cards, while Sandow is supposed to have put three decks together, ripping the unwieldy bunch asunder in the middle. An effective way of presenting this feat is to tear a new deck of cards, case, wrapper, and all. This is not much more difficult than tearing a pack, but the effect is greatly enhanced.

Most spectators are skeptical about the ability of the magician to tear a pack of cards, or doubt the genuineness of the feat. They give the absurd explanation that the pack is spread in such a manner that the cards are torn one at a time. The amateur performer will be repaid, therefore, by adding this feat to his repertory.

Flourishes: Throwing Cards. This is one of the oldest of the ornamental sleights. The regulation method is to hold the card lightly between the first and second fingers at the upper end. The hand should be curved toward the wrist and then straightened with a sudden jerk. In order to communicate a reverse movement to the card, the hand is jerked back toward the performer at the precise moment the card leaves the tips of the first and second fingers. Knack rather than strength is the secret of the sleight. The card can be thrown further if it is held between second and third, rather than first and second, fingers. This was HOWARD THURSTON's method.

A pretty variation of this sleight is supposed to be the invention of the French juggler and hand shadowist, Felicien Trewey.

Hold the pack in the left hand, as if for dealing, the thumb across the center of the top and the four fingers grasping the outer edge. Toss a card into the air, at any distance from ten to thirty feet, giving it a strong reverse twist, which causes the card to return toward the performer.

As the card falls, revolving rapidly in its flight, separate the pack at the outer edge with the four fingers of the left hand, by simply pressing the fingers downward. This leaves a wedge-shaped opening into which the card is allowed to fall. As the left hand is held high in the air, with the wedge-shaped opening toward the ceiling, the audience, of course, cannot see the break in the pack, and the sight of a card suddenly darting into the pack is pretty and effective. A skilled performer can propel a card a surprising distance over the heads of his audience, and cause it to return to his hand.

An effective variation is to throw a card high into the air, and, when it returns toward the performer, to seize a pair of scissors with the right hand and cut the whirling card in two. Before throwing the card, hold the scissors in the left hand, underneath the pack.

Another method is to toss the card into the air and, when it returns, gracefully catch it between the thumb and first finger of the right hand. This may be followed by a more elaborate and more difficult flourish.

Lay the pack on the table, taking two cards in the right hand and holding them as one. Now throw the double card into the air, giving it the reverse twist. The cards will remain together on their upward and outward movement, but the instant they begin their backward flight they will separate and whirl in different directions. With practice, the performer will be able to catch one card in the right and the other in the left hand.

T. N. D.

Flourishes: The Turnover. A favorite flourish with expert card manipulators is running the cards up the arm, from the fingertips to the elbow, and, by a slight contraction of the fingers of the left hand, causing the cards to turn over. It is an effective sleight, and not difficult, although some practice is necessary before the cards can be spread neatly and evenly along the arm.

The secret of this sleight is in holding the cards. The pack is bent slightly downward by the thumb and second finger of the right hand, the thumb at the lower end and the second finger at the upper end. Extend the left arm and hand, either palm upward or downward. Beginning at the very tips of the fingers of the left hand, the cards in the right hand are released, one at a time, the right hand at the same time sweeping up the left arm. It is important to remember that the cards are released by the fingers only.

This maneuver will leave the cards spread from the tips of the left fingers to the elbow, or even beyond it. As a matter of fact, the first card or two should overlap the left fingers about an inch. Now by quickly contracting the two middle fingers toward the palm, the whole row of cards will be reversed in a spectacular fashion.

There are several ways of terminating this flourish. One popular method consists in simply dropping the left arm to the side, the result being that the cards fall neatly into the left palm. Other performers reverse the cards in such a manner that instead of falling on the arm they drop into the right hand, which is held for this purpose just under the left elbow. In order to secure this pretty effect, the left forearm revolves slightly to the right at the very moment the cards are being reversed. This causes the cards to tumble like a waterfall into the right hand.

Another method is as follows: just as the cards, in the process of reversing, are about to fall on the arm, the right hand passing under the first falling card—that is, the card at the elbow, catches it on the extended right thumb. The right hand then sweeps toward the left palm, the result being that the cards are once more reversed and fall into the left hand, where they should immediately be squared, so that the flourish may be repeated if desired.

Another finish is to catch the falling cards at the elbow, on the right thumb, as just described, when the left forearm is allowed to drop from under the bridge of cards, all of which are caught by a swift forward dart of the right hand. The fact that the cards are lapped makes this move easy to accomplish.

Instead of the cards' being riffled on the left arm, they may be spread on the wand, or cane, held in the left hand. One end of the stick is held in the palm of the left hand by the third and fourth fingers. The first and second fingers are extended, serving as an additional support. The cards are held in the same position as for spreading the cards on the arm, but the work of releasing them is done by the thumb instead of the fingers.

Beginning at the inner end of the wand, the first three or four cards slipped by the thumb are gripped by the left thumb pressing them against the stick. It is now a simple matter to lap the cards to the end of the wand. The flourish may be terminated in two ways, either by throwing the lapped cards into the air and catching them in the right hand, after the manner just explained, or the stick may be tilted slightly upward, when the cards will slip back into the left hand. *T. N. D.*

Flourishes: Fanning. John Northern Hilliard described card fanning as the latest decorative feature in magic. Some performers have made whole acts out of fanning, much as they once did out of the back palm.

Exhibition fanning is difficult to learn, and almost impossible to teach; but the basic facts are as follows.

First, the cards should be thin, glossy, flexible bridge cards, brand new. One handling spoils them for further exhibition work.

Second, the performer's hands should be clean and dry. Perspiration must be wiped off before beginning.

Third, the cards should not be shuffled except for such a necessary purpose as making the giant fan. Some performers treat the cards with zinc stearate powder.

Two-handed "pressure" fans are essentially a form of *Springing the cards.* The cards are sprung slightly, escaping from the fingers only, not the thumb, around which the hands pivot. To make a right-handed forward fan, hold the pack in the right hand with the thumb at one end, the fingers at the other. The face of the pack is pressed lightly against the left first and second fingers; the right thumb touches the root of the left second finger. Thus the cards project well above the left hand, which is held flat.

Now the right fingers sweep around to the right, springing the cards gently as they go, while the left fingers are pivoted to the left. At the conclusion of the movement, the left thumb is brought down to hold the fan thus made. With practice, almost a complete circle of cards can be fanned.

A right-handed reverse fan is made with just the opposite motions. The right thumb touches the base of the left third finger instead of the second, and the cards project below the left third and fourth finger, instead of above the first and second. The right fingers are swept up and to the left, the left fingers swoop down and to the right. The result is a fan in which none of the cards except the front one show their faces at all. The whole pack can be displayed "blank" by hiding the front card.

One-handed fans depend not on springing, but on gentle friction. To make a right-handed forward fan, hold the pack by one end, the thumb at the front near the lower left-hand corner, all four fingers at the back. Push the thumb as nearly as possible straight to the right, the fingers straight to the left. Actually this results in a curving motion, but the fan will be wider and more even if a straight motion is attempted than if it be begun as a curve.

This is the only instruction that can be given for one-handed fanning; the rest depends on practice and good cards.

The Giant Fan is made by riffling the two halves of the pack part way together—with an eighth to a quarter of an inch of overlap—, and then fanning the pack. This is also done with two packs. The cards must be quite evenly interlaced; if they fall in bunches, the fan will be spoiled.

An effective flourish is to break a pack in halves as if for a riffle shuffle, then fan one half with each hand, and brush one fan down in front of the other, then up behind. The fans may be either interlaced, making a fancy shuffle, or smartly closed and slid together, which will serve for a false shuffle. *H. H.*

The Fan and Ruffle is simple but effective. It may be used as a flourish or fancy sleight, or may be employed effectively as a false shuffle.

The pack is held in dealing position in the left hand. The right hand is brought to the top of the deck, and the left thumb spreads the cards in the form of a fan, the thumb and fingers of the right hand assisting in the movement. The right and left hands are then separated, each hand holding a half of the fan of cards, the faces of the cards toward the audience.

The fan in the right hand is now brought directly in front of the cards in the left hand, so that the two fans touch. The performer sweeps the fan of cards in the right hand briskly across the face of the cards fanned in the left, the cards giving forth a sharp, crackling sound.

The instant the fan in the right hand is clear of the cards in the left hand, the two packets are brought together and squared up. These separate movements, which are rather difficult to describe, coalesce, so to speak, in actual practice, and the rapidity with which they are done deceives the audience into the belief that an intricate movement has been accomplished. It is rather discouraging to the clever manipulator of cards to discover that his most elaborate movements, demanding ineffable skill and adroitness, should elicit less enthusiastic comment and admiration than a simple movement like the fan and ruffle.

In another flourish, the performer fans a pack of cards in his left hand (a movement that will not be accomplished without some practice). He shows that his right hand is empty, back and front, and then produces a fan of cards from behind the right knee. This is how the flourish is accomplished:

In the preliminary handling of the pack the performer palms about a dozen cards in his right hand. He now fans the cards in the left hand, the right hand ostensibly assisting in the maneuver, but actually leaving the palmed packet behind the fan, securely gripped between the first and second fingers. The cards are held, of course, so that the fan conceals the packet (Fig. 1).

The proper position is to face the audience squarely, the left hand, palm outward, hanging in a line with the left knee. The right hand is thrust straight out from the body, fingers wide apart, and shown back and front, so as to convince the audience that nothing can possibly be concealed in the hand. The performer now strikes the faces of the fan with the tips of his right fingers, and repeats the movement on the back of the fan.

FIG. 1

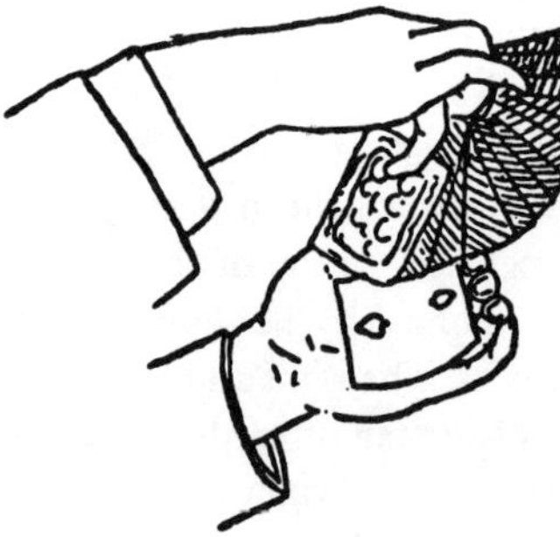

FIG. 2

As the right-hand fingers move back of the fan, the packet which is gripped between the first and second fingers of the left hand is palmed off in the right hand (Fig. 2). The instant the cards are palmed in the right hand, the left hand turns over so that the back of the fan is presented toward the audience. The right hand, containing the palmed cards, now strikes the back of the fan.

Once more the face of the fan is exhibited to the audience and is held, face outward, at the left knee. A slight wavy motion is made with the fan toward the right knee, and at the same moment the right hand produces, fanwise, the palmed cards from the right knee, the effect being that a portion of the cards in the left hand passed invisibly through the performer's knees and thence into his right hand. *T. N. D.*

Forcing. This is a method of compelling a person to draw such a card as you desire, although he is apparently allowed absolute freedom of choice. Your first step is to get sight of the bottom card, or, if you want to force a predetermined card, to get that card to the bottom.

Having done this, take the pack in the left hand, and insert the little finger half way down, in readiness to make the SHIFT. Make the shift, but, before uniting the two halves of the pack in their new position, again slip the little finger of the left hand between them. (The two halves will now be united at the end toward the spectators, but divided by the little finger at the end nearest to yourself; the original bottom card, which is the one you desire to force, is now the bottom of the top heap, resting on the little finger.)

Using both hands, with the thumbs above and the fingers below the pack, spread out the cards fanwise from left to right, at the same time offering them to the person who is to draw, and requesting him to select a card. Keep the little finger of the left hand still on the face of the card to be chosen, or you may now use, if more convenient, the same finger of the right hand, both being underneath the cards. As the person advances his hand to draw, move the cards onward with the thumb, so that the particular card shall reach his fingers just at the moment when he closes them in order to draw; and, if you have followed these directions properly, it is ten to one that he will draw the card you wish.

It may be imagined that forcing is a very difficult matter, requiring an extraordinary degree of dexterity, but this is by no means the case. The principal thing against which a beginner must guard is a tendency to offer the particular card a little *too soon*. When the cards are first presented to the drawer, the pack should be barely spread at all, and the card in question should be ten or fifteen cards away. The momentary hesitation of the drawer in making his choice will give time, by moving the cards quicker or slower, as necessary, to bring that card opposite his fingers at the right moment. *L. H.*

A lot of advice has been given in various works on the subject of card forcing, but it may all be summed up by saying that the whole secret consists in *timing*. That is to say, as the conjurer runs the cards in front of his victim, he should arrange matters so that the required card is in the correct position to be seized conveniently as the selector's hand reaches forward.

Closely allied to the subject of timing is that of *balance*. When about to force a card, the pack should be held fairly close to the body, *the weight of which should be on the left foot*, the right barely touching the ground.

The cards are run in the usual manner, and as the spectator's hand reaches forward to take a card, the body sways slightly, bringing the required card into a position from which it may easily be removed.

The point is that the movement of the body is imperceptible, whereas any change in the position of the hands would be noticed at once.

Experience alone will teach the novice how to select an easy victim. (See VOLUNTEERS)

In another method, the card to be forced must be placed on top of the lower half of the pack, the latter being CRIMPED thus: 

The pack is then thrown on the table, lengthwise, and with a sliding motion, the result being that the top card of the lower half is a trifle more exposed than the other cards. There is, therefore, every chance that it will be chosen by an unsophisticated spectator. *V. F.*

Thought Force. Forcing a person to think of a particular card may seem at first like an impossibility. Of course if the spectator were simply invited to think of a card, he would be very much more likely to think of a wrong card than of the right one, but simultaneously with the making of the request the conjurer rapidly spreads the cards before his eyes as if to assist his choice. If, among the cards displayed, the spectator gets a better view of one card than the rest, he is almost sure to think of that card.

The conjurer takes care that he does get such a view. Selecting a fairly conspicuous card, say a king or a queen, he places it at the bottom of the pack, and at the right moment brings it to the middle by the SHIFT, keeping the little finger in front of it. Holding the pack vertically, he then runs the cards rapidly over before the spectator's face, taking care that only half an inch or so of each is exposed, until he comes to the card to be forced.

When he reaches that card, say the queen of hearts, he takes care that a good three-quarters of its face is exposed (Fig. 1). He does not pause, but continues the movement with the rest of the cards, allowing a small portion of each to be seen, however. As the backs of the cards are toward the performer, and he appears quite indifferent in the matter, the spectator does not suspect the ruse, and in the majority of cases thinks of the precise card desired. A lady's choice is more apt to fall upon a king, and a man's upon a queen.

Sometimes the pack is arranged beforehand so that the card to be forced stands about seventh or eighth from the bottom (where the conjurer begins), all the other cards up to the fifteenth or sixteenth being *plain*

FIG. 1

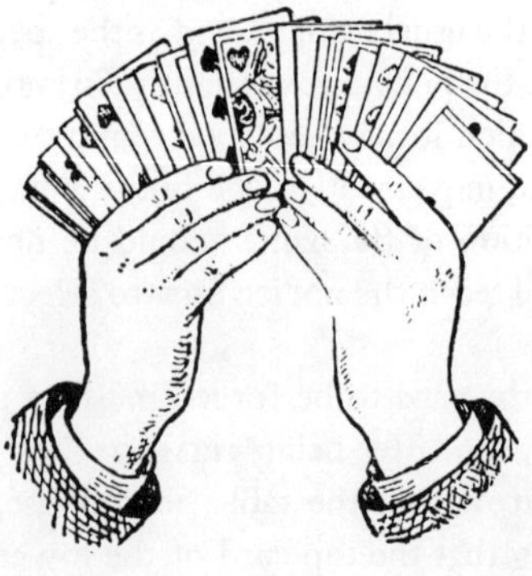

cards; this makes the face card stand out more conspicuously. This plan, however, is more likely to arouse suspicion.

Another method of forcing a person to think of a given card is to take the cards, after making the shift, but with the rear packet about half an inch higher than the other. Holding them vertically before the eyes of the spectator, clip them at top and bottom with the right hand, and bend their upper portions smartly backward, allowing them one by one to escape from the pressure. The step between the two portions of the pack will cause an inevitable pause between the first and second packets, and give the spectator the glimpse necessary to direct his thoughts to the desired card.

As soon as the process is complete, the shift is made again, bringing the card once more to the bottom, to be dealt with as necessary for the purpose of the trick. *L. H.*

In another version of the *Thought Force*, the conjurer places the pack behind his back, which he turns toward the spectators. Passing the cards from one hand to the other, he invites a spectator to think of one of them; then closing up the pack, and shuffling it, produces the selected card in any way that he sees fit.

As the conjurer rather rapidly passes the cards from one hand into the other, he keeps the attention of the spectator engaged by the remark: "As I pass these cards from one hand into the other, please think of one of the cards." The moment that he says "think," he stops for just an instant, fully exposing the face of the card that he is about to transfer, then actually placing it in the other hand and passing the remaining cards in rather quick succession on top of it. In almost every case the person will select the card at which the performer has made a brief stop; he did not know what the conjurer wished him to do until the latter came to the word "think," and it is almost impossible for him to select any of the following cards, because they are intentionally passed too quickly before his eyes.

The magician, who has slipped the little finger of the left hand above the forced card while transferring it to the other hand, closes up the pack, and in the act of turning around makes the shift, thereby bringing the card to the top of the pack.

In still another form, the performer advances toward a spectator and, holding the pack with the faces of the cards toward himself, causes them to spring (see FLOURISHES) from one hand to the other. At the same time he requests a spectator to think of any of the cards that he sees.

When about half the cards have been sprung, the performer stops for perhaps a quarter of a second, causing an extremely brief cessation of the springing and thus causing the last card that has been sprung to be more fully exposed than any of the others. The spectator readily grasps the chance offered to him and selects this card, which the performer, who quickly places his little finger over it, sees as well as he. The rest of the cards are then sprung on top of the others in the usual fashion, whereupon the pack is closed and the shift made. *A. R.*

FIG. 1

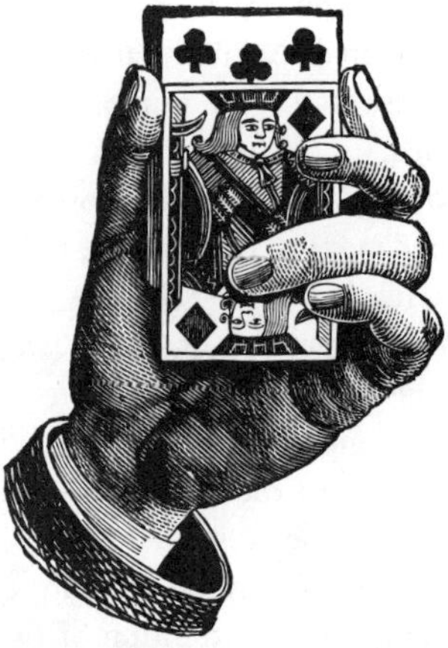

FIG. 2

Glide. The performer shows the bottom card, then dropping the pack into a horizontal position, face downward, he draws out, with the thumb and second finger of the other hand, apparently that card, but really the one next above it. This is done as follows:

Hold the pack upright in the left hand between the first finger and thumb, the back of the cards toward the palm, and the thumb and finger about the middle of each side of the pack. Let the third finger, which should be previously moistened, rest on the face of the cards. (Fig. 1) You will find that in this position, by moving the third finger, you can draw back the bottom card about an inch below the remaining cards, and thereby leave exposed a corresponding portion of the next card. (Fig. 2) This is the whole mechanism of the operation. You must, of course, take care, after showing the bottom card, to turn the pack downward before you slide back that card in order to draw the next card in its place.

Glimpse. The standard method of doing this sleight, whose purpose is to let the performer catch sight of a chosen card, without necessarily controlling it further, is to insert the left little finger under the chosen card. In the act of handing the cards to a spectator to shuffle, the performer slightly raises the upper one of the two packets, and thus obtains a rapid glimpse of the lowest card in the upper packet.

A more subtle method, used when the spectator peeps at a card in the pack instead of drawing one, is as follows. The pack is held in the left hand in dealing position, beveled to the right. As the spectator lifts up a corner of the pack to take a peep, the performer relaxes his hand, which opens a BREAK all along the right edge of the deck. A little-finger break is held.

The left fingers now bevel the pack to the left, at the same time that the hand turns its back upward. The result of this motion, combined with the little-finger break, is a step in the edge of the pack just at the heel of the hand, exposing the index of the chosen card. The right hand seizes the pack by the front end, and draws it forward, squaring it up again as it is handed out to be shuffled. The glimpse, of course, is made just as the right hand prepares to take the pack.

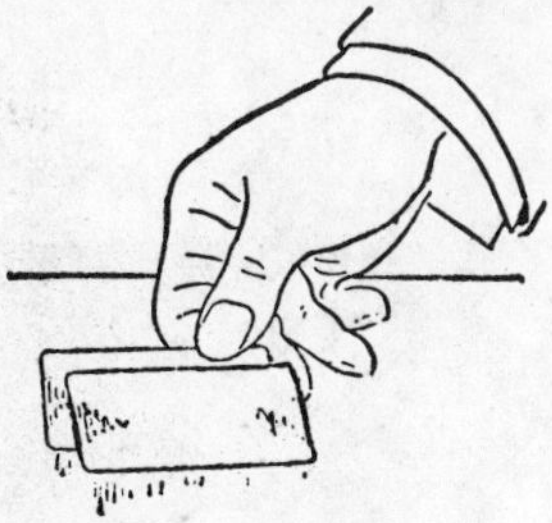

FIG. 1

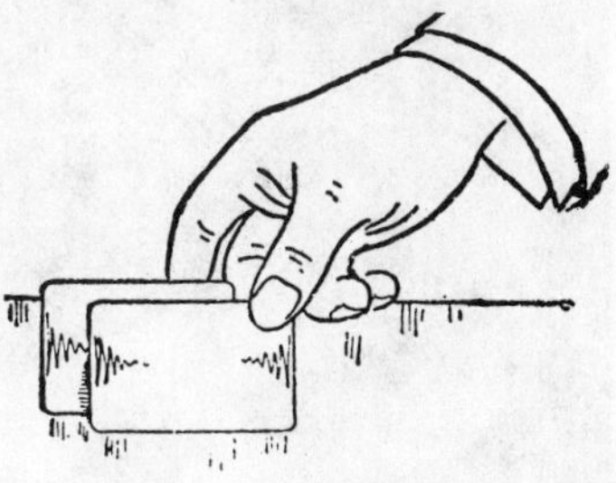

FIG. 2

Mexican Turnover. This sleight, a special form of CHANGE, was devised for the THREE-CARD TRICK, but can be put to other uses.

Hold the card in the right hand between the tips of thumb and first finger close to right inner end corner, thumb on top. Slide the free side of this card under the right side of the card on the table, until it is about two-thirds concealed, but half an inch exposed at the outer end. (Fig. 1) This will bring the upper, inner end corner of the table card against the tip of the second finger. Now shift the thumb to the corner of the table card, holding it against the second finger, carrying it to the left and turning over the lower card with the tip of the first finger. (Fig. 2)

Of course there is no hesitation in the action. The slipping of the hand card under the table card, and the turning over of the hand card, is done with one movement. The table card is not shown at this stage, but is slipped under the third card, and the exchange is again made in like manner. Then the last card is shown.

To perform this feat perfectly a cloth-covered table must be used. When the table is of polished wood the cards slip about, and it is much more difficult to slip the hand card into position under the other.

The only further advice is to avoid cards with white edges and to find a suitable cloth; then *always to use that identical cloth.* The sleight cannot be done perfectly except when the cloth employed is the performer's own property.

A piece of fairly well-worn green baize or billiard-table cloth is the ideal material. *S. W. E. & V. F.*

FIG. 1 PALMED CARD

Palm, Bottom. (See Fig. 1 for picture of card palmed.)

First Method. The pack is held in the left hand. The right hand approaches ostensibly to square the cards. The first finger of the left hand slides forward the bottom card (or cards) until its edge reaches the fleshy part of the first phalange of the fingers of the right hand.

The thumb and second, third, and fourth fingers of the left hand withdraw the remainder of the pack, the first finger pressing against the card which is left in the right hand until the instant the pack clears the inner end of it. The left with the pack moves away clear of the right hand, which must not move immediately on taking the card.

The effect is as though the right hand squared up the pack in the left, and the left then in a natural way removed the pack to proceed with whatever may be in progress at the moment. All that the audience see at the instant of palming is the back of the right hand, which is apparently squaring the pack.

This sleight is also used as the forefinger-steal COLOR CHANGE. *C. L. N.*

Second Method. Seize the deck with the right hand on top, between the first joints of the second and third fingers at one end, and the thumb at the other end; the fingers close together and the third finger and thumb close to each corner so as to expose as much of the deck as possible. Bring up the left hand and seize the deck from beneath at the right thumb end, between the first and second fingers, and the palm just under the second joint of the thumb, the thumb lying straight across the top close to the end. If this position is secured correctly, the tips of the left thumb and second finger touch the right thumb, as all three are at the same corner of the deck and almost the whole of the deck is exposed.

To palm, grip the bottom cards at the side of the corner with the tip of the left second finger, squeezing them in against the palm under the left thumb, and pull down over the end of the right thumb about a quarter of

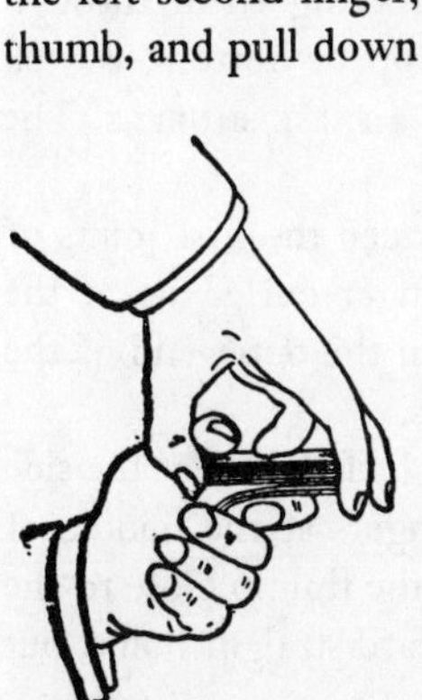

FIG. 2

BOTTOM PALM
SECOND METHOD

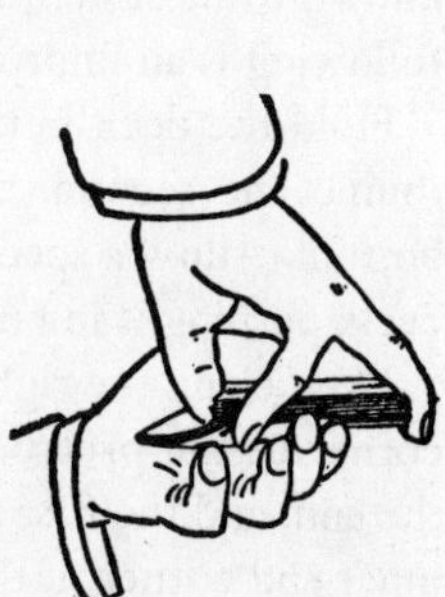

FIG. 3

an inch. (Fig. 2) This will cause the outer-end corner of the under cards to project a little at the side, under the right third finger.

Catch the projecting corner with the right little fingertip, pressing the cards firmly against the palm under the left thumb, and draw them in toward the right thumb—at the same time straightening out the left fingers—, until the under cards lie fairly along the palm. (Fig. 3) Slightly close left hand with the palmed cards, and turn partly over and inward as the right hand lays the deck on the table.

The entire action of this palm is extremely rapid, simple, easy and imperceptible. The only difficulty is in establishing the proper position for the left hand. To get this absolutely exact, palm half a dozen cards in the left hand in the most favorable position for holding and concealing. Then with one finger of the right hand press against the little-finger corner of the palmed cards, and—using the diagonal corner as a pivot—swing them out and over the first finger until the left second fingertip can be brought against the corner, and the left thumb lies across the end. Now, if the left thumb is raised and the balance of the deck is placed on top, the desired position is obtained.

After a shuffle, the position is taken quite naturally in squaring up by merely pushing the deck out of the left palm until the left thumb lies along the top close to the end.

This palm may be made without the aid of the right little finger. The positions of the hands are taken exactly as before, then the second left finger is dropped sufficiently to allow the little finger to take its place. The little finger then grips the corner and pulls the cards back to the left wrist until they lie along the left fingers as before.

Third Method: (The Diagonal Palm-Shift). The plan of having one or several selected cards inserted in the deck, then forcing them through slightly diagonally, and twisting them out to the top or bottom, is well known to most conjurers, and by some is treated as a FALSE SHUFFLE. The following is an improvement on this maneuver.

Hold the deck in the left hand, by the sides, between the first joints of thumb and second, third, and little fingers, first finger curled up at the bottom. Allow a spectator to insert a selected card in the outer end of the deck, pushing it in until about half an inch protrudes.

Now bring the right hand over the deck with the little finger at the side corner of the protruding card, second and third fingers at the middle of the end, and the first finger close to the end corner, the thumb close to the inner end corner of the deck. Apparently push the card straight home, but really push the protruding end with the right little finger, about a quarter of an inch to the left, so that the right first finger can push the tilted corner down the side of the deck, the card moving slightly diagonally, and the opposite corner just grazing the right thumb, and protruding about three-quarters of an inch. The left third and little fingers are released sufficiently to allow the card to protrude at the side. The left thumb now takes the place of the right first finger, pushing the corner flush with the side of the deck. (Fig. 4)

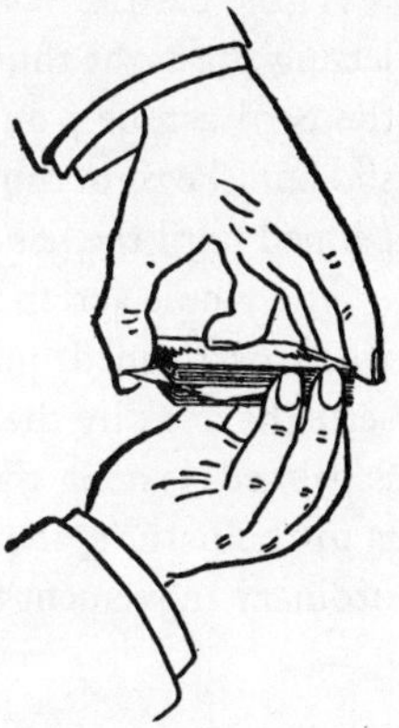

FIG. 4

The diagonal position of the selected card is now perfectly concealed, and the deck is held in a natural and regular manner. A little practice at the diagonal slide enables one to get the card in that position instantaneously. The next action is to palm the selected card in the left hand, as the right passes the deck to be shuffled.

With the left little finger against the side of the card, swing or turn it inward, using the right thumb as a pivot, straighten out the left first, second, and third fingers, catching the outer end as it turns, and at the same time sliding the pack outward and to the right; the left hand turns over and inward with the palmed card (Fig. 5), and the little finger slips to the end.

There should be no force or twist employed, the card running out as freely as though drawn. The card and the deck must continue on the same plane until quite free of each other. The left little finger may press the side of the card very slightly upward, so that as it is palmed it will bend into instead of away from the left hand.

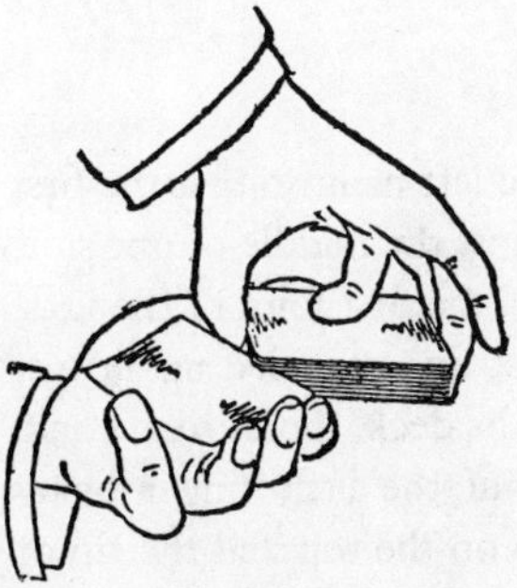

FIG. 5

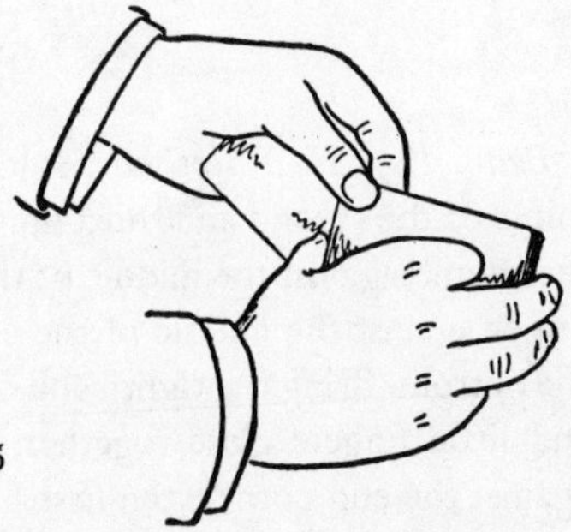

FIG. 6

As the card is being turned by the little finger, the left thumb is raised, letting the right thumb with the corner of the deck pass under it, so that the card can lie parallel with, but still above, the left palm. As the deck is slid out, the right thumb slides along the side of the card, and it is not actually palmed until the hands are almost free of each other.

The whole action may be made quick as a flash and without a sound, yet when performed quite slowly is still a perfect blind. The left hand may seize the deck by the corner, between the first finger and thumb, as the card is palmed, leaving the right hand free (Fig. 6); but the beauty of the shift is in the natural and simple manner of palming the selected card, by the ordinary movement the right hand makes in passing the deck to be shuffled.

S. W. E.

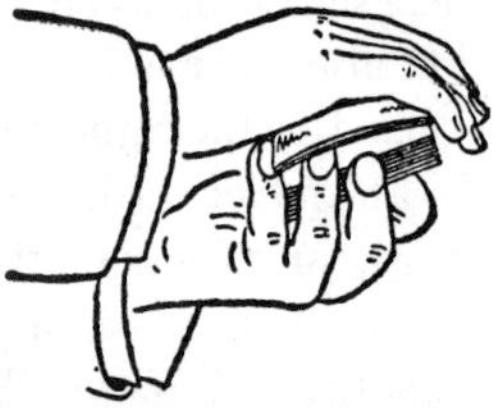

FIG. 2

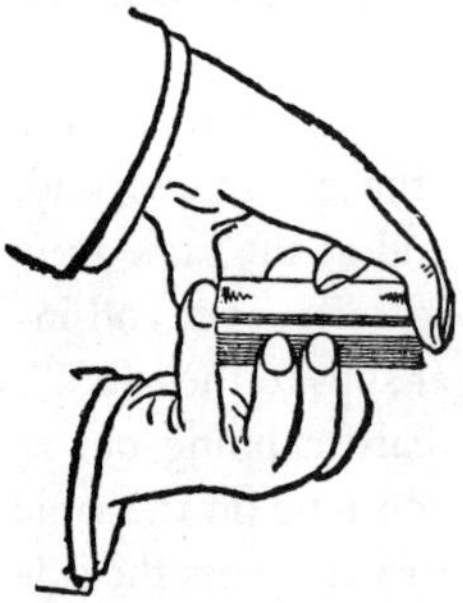

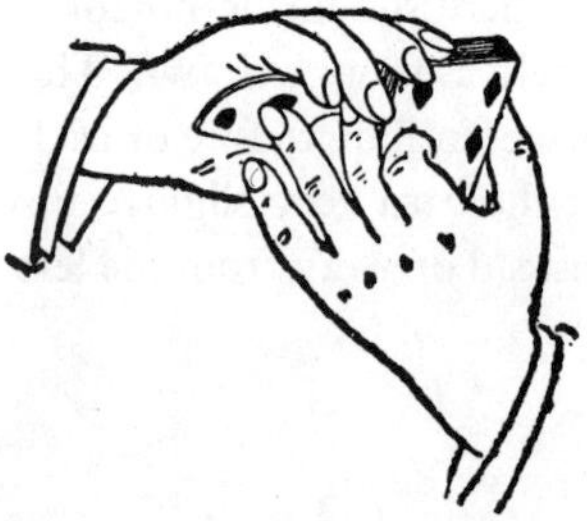

FIG. 3

FIG. 1

TOP PALM
FIRST METHOD

Palm, Top: First Method. Hold the deck in the left hand so that the first joints of the second and third fingers will be against the middle of one side, the thumb against the middle of the opposite side, the first joint of the little finger against the middle of the end, and the first finger curled up against the bottom. Bring the right hand over the top of the deck, the third, second, and little fingers close together, the first joint of the little finger being against the end corner, the first finger curled up on the top and the tip of the thumb resting idly at the end, above the left little finger.

To palm, press the right little finger, exactly at the first joint, firmly against the top cards, pull them up about half an inch at the corner, freeing them from the left second and third fingers, keeping the three right fingers (little, second, and third) perfectly straight. The cards to be palmed are now held firmly between the right little finger and the left little finger. (Fig. 1)

Straighten out the right first finger, swing the left little finger with the cards to be palmed free of the end of the deck, and press the cards into the right palm with the end of the left third finger. (Fig. 2) Draw the deck out about half way from under the right hand, and release the left hand entirely. (Fig. 3) Then the right drops the deck on the table to be cut. After the hands are in the first position, the whole process does not occupy half a second.

The deck should be kept in view as much as possible, and the right first finger is curled up on top for that purpose until the instant the palm is performed. The action of drawing the deck into view when the cards are palmed is made a part of the whole movement. *S. W. E.*

Second Method. In this method, supposed to have been used by BUATIER DE KOLTA, the pack is never touched with the right hand at all. The pack is held in the left hand, the cards to be palmed being divided off from the rest of the pack by the little finger, which is inserted there. They are kept down on the pack proper by pressure of the remaining fingers. As the right hand, under any plausible pretext, passes over the left, the pressure of the fingers

FIG. 4 TOP PALM, THIRD METHOD FIG. 5

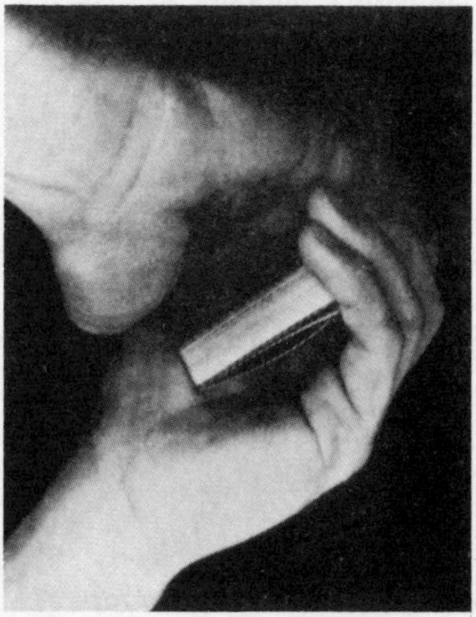

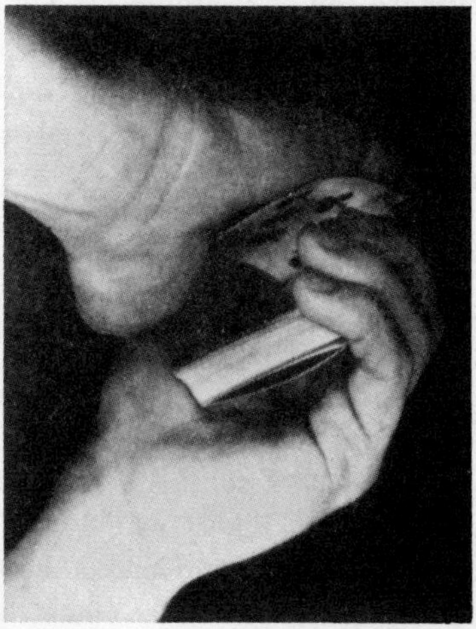

ceases, while at the same time the little finger tilts the first card lying above it upward, the cards are thereby rapidly and invisibly propelled into the right hand, which instantly palms them.

Third Method. Hold the deck in dealing position in the left hand, thumb out of the way along the left edge.

Bring the right hand forward, palm down, and press the right little-fingertip on the upper right corner of the top card. Push the right hand forward, carrying the top card with it for about a quarter of an inch; then push with the right little-fingertip. (Fig. 4)

This snaps the top card into the right palm. (Fig. 5) The right hand should then either begin squaring the deck, or remain still while the left hand carries the pack away. *H. H.*

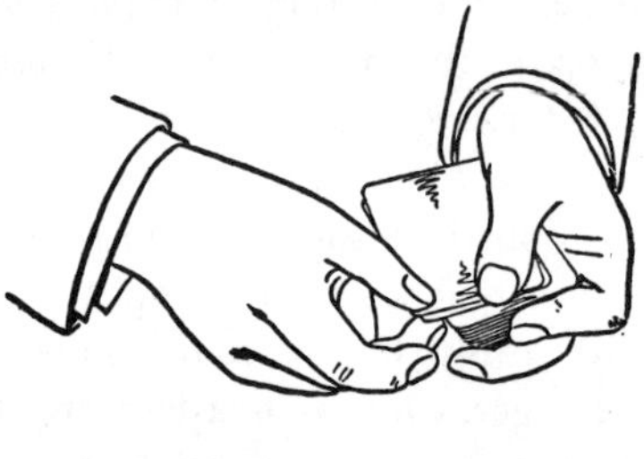

FIG. 1

Second Deal. As the term indicates, second dealing is the process of dealing the second card from the top. The deck is held by the left hand much the same as described for BOTTOM DEALING, the tip of the thumb being a little over the end of the top card. This position enables the thumb to come in contact with the second card by pushing the top card a trifle downward. To deal, the left thumb pushes the two cards over the side nearly together, the top card perhaps a little in advance, and the second card showing a little above it at the end.

The right hand seizes the second card by the exposed corner, the right thumb barely touching the edge, but the right second finger is well under the second card and helps to get it out by an upward pressure as the left thumb draws back the top card. (Fig. 1) Then the left thumb again comes in contact with the second card at the upper edge. The third fingertip prevents more than two cards from being pushed over the side.

The top card continues to move forward and back as the seconds are dealt, but the rapidity of the backward motion prevents the detection of the action. Properly executed, the appearance of the deal is perfectly regular. An expert can run the whole deck rapidly, and still retain the top card.

Another method of second dealing is to hold the cards loosely in the left hand, the left thumb pushing forward several at a time, each a little in advance of the other. As the right hand comes forward, the top card is drawn back and the second dealt. The left thumb uses some pressure in pushing the cards forward, but draws back the top card very lightly so as to have the second card protruding. The first method is decidedly the better, as it gives greater control of the cards, and there is less liability of the right hand seizing more than one.

There is a knack in seizing the second card. The second finger of the right hand comes in contact with it before the top card is drawn back, and gives it a slight pressure upward, thus helping to prevent going back with the top card. The right thumb may actually touch the top card as it is drawn back and the second dealt. The whole action of drawing back the top and dealing the second card takes place at the same instant.

Second dealing is as difficult a task as can be given in card handling, but once acquired it is easy to do. *S. W. E.*

Shift, Two-Handed. Hold the pack in the left hand as if about to deal, and open the cards at the middle, or at whatever part of the pack the shift is to be made, inserting the little finger of the left hand (Fig. 1).

Advance the right hand toward the pack, and while doing so open the left hand so that the cards will be open—at the top about an inch, at the bottom two inches. (The half of the pack above the little finger will be referred to as No. 1, and that below No. 2.)

This brings No. 1 half obliquely under the fingers of the right hand. The second, third, and little fingers must be kept close together, so as to form a screen. The *first* finger and thumb grasp No. 2 half at top and bottom of cards. The fingers of the left hand draw No. 1 half downward to clear No. 2 half (Fig. 2). At the same time the thumb of the left presses on the center of the top side of No. 2 half, which has the effect of turning it, the first finger and thumb of the right hand acting as pivots. This pressure raises the bottom side of No. 2 half, enabling No. 1 half to clear it easily. As soon as it is clear, the left fingers are closed up, bringing No. 1 half up underneath No. 2 half (Fig. 3). The fingers of both hands square up the cards, and the shift is finished.

This must be practised in front of a mirror, and all made to blend into one instantaneous movement, which must be quite noiseless and also quite unseen, the right hand being held all the while in such a position as to screen No. 1 half in its removal and replacement beneath No. 2 half.

This shift is the most important of all points to acquire to perfection, for

THE TWO-HANDED SHIFT

FIG. 1

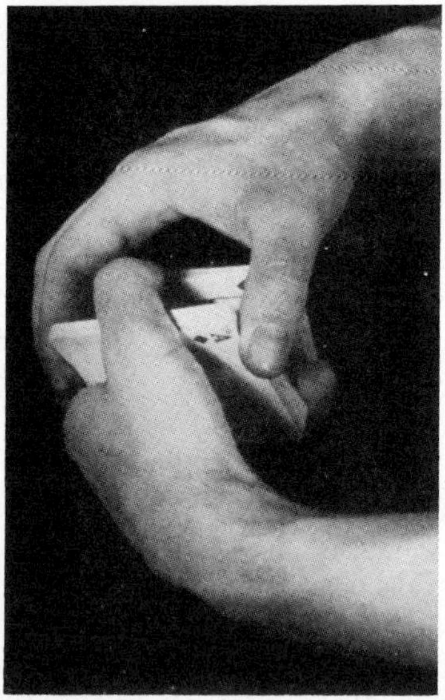

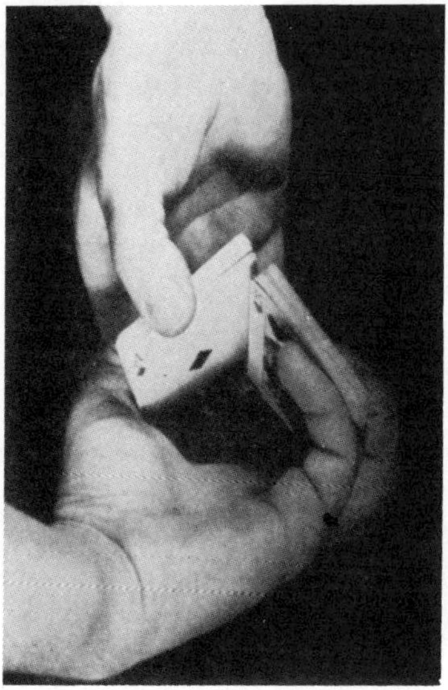

FIG. 2

FIG. 3

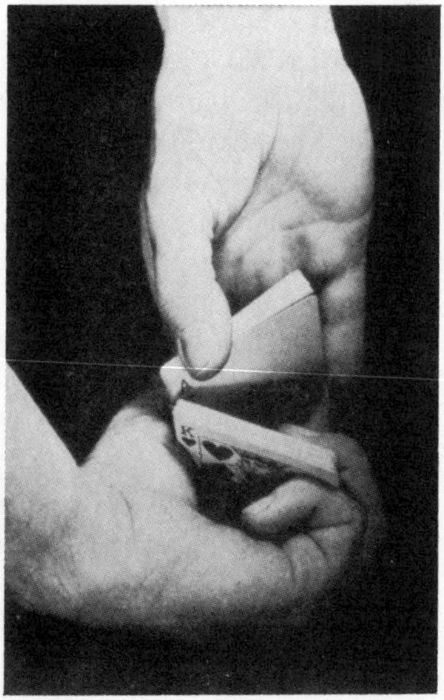

HERMANN SHIFT

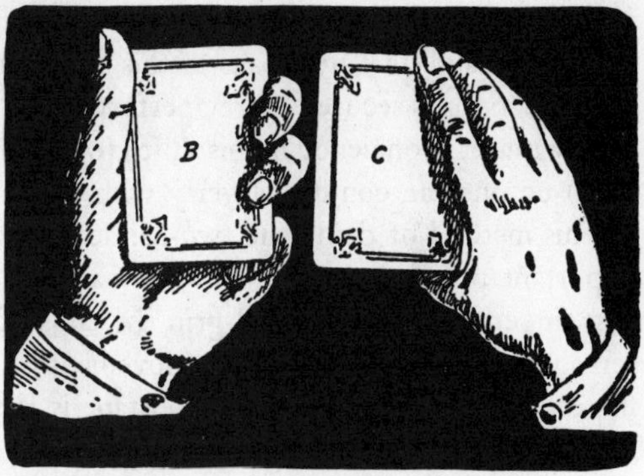

FIG. 1

FIG. 2

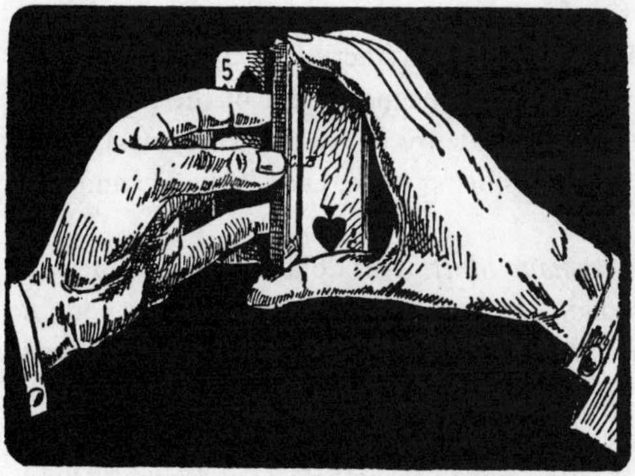

FIG. 3

it is the basis of, or is used in, almost every card trick which requires any sleight-of-hand. It is by means of this shift that any card placed in a pack by a spectator is secured by the performer, or a GLIMPSE of it obtained; in fact, without proficiency in this shift (for no other shift is absolutely necessary) no one can conjure cleverly with cards.

This method of doing the two-handed shift differs in several small but important points from the conventional way. By having the thumb and *first* finger of the right hand grip the ends of No. 2 half, a much better screen is obtained for the whole movement by the second, third, and little fingers being together; more important is the advice that No. 2 half is *levered up by the thumb of the left hand*, and *not* (as is sometimes advised) *raised by the second and third fingers and thumb* of the right hand, which necessitates a movement of the right hand.

The right hand comes to the pack ostensibly to square up the cards, and remains *dead still* as a screen for the operation of removal and replacing at the bottom of half No. 1, which is done in a fraction of a second by the left hand under cover of the right. The slight movement of the right hand (in order to raise No. 2 half) usually made by conjurers when making the shift, lets the audience see something is being done, even if they cannot see *what* it is. *C. B.*

Shift, Two-Handed: The Herrmann Shift. This double-handed shift was a favorite with ALEXANDER HERRMANN, who delighted to puzzle with it people versed in the usual sleights. It depends almost exclusively upon MISDIRECTION, and no change of the two halves of the pack can possibly be seen, no matter how closely the spectator watches for it.

The secret lies in the fact that the upper front half of the pack is held in an upright position. Behind this half, under cover of which the transposition of the two packets is made, the spectator is not allowed to see.

In the first position of the two packets, the lower, or rear, one is held in the left hand, the first joints of the second and third fingers at the side of the cards, while the first and little fingers lie curled up behind it. The upper, or front, packet is held in the right hand, in the position shown in Fig. 1, the thumb above, and the fingers below the cards, exposing as much of them as possible.

Both packets are held in a perpendicular position, being turned toward the spectators. Under cover of the upper packet, the lower is tilted downward and passed around the front of the upper (Fig. 2), being then placed on the latter.

After the reader has once understood the principle and purpose of the shift, he will find it very useful in cases where the spectator refuses to have his attention diverted by the performer's PATTER and rivets his eyes upon the conjurer's hands.

One excellent use to which this shift may be put is to convince the spectators that the selected card is neither at the top nor at the bottom of the pack. The card in this case occupies the top place; the regular double-handed shift is then made, whereby the card is brought to the middle of the pack, both packets being in readiness for the execution of the Herrmann Shift. After exhibiting the top card, the performer turns over the left hand, which holds the pack, and shows that the bottom card is not the chosen one either. In turning back the left hand to its original position, in which act it is assisted by the right, the Herrmann Shift is made and the desired card brought once more to the top of the pack. *A. R.*

Shift, One-Handed. In the old-fashioned method of making the one-handed shift, the pack is taken in the left hand and, with the thumb across the cards, opened bookwise at its outer edge. The second and third fingers are brought over, and the first and fourth under, the lower packet. (Fig. 3) The fingers are then extended until the inner edge of the lower packet just clears the outer edge of the upper, which falls below it, thereby effecting the desired transposition.

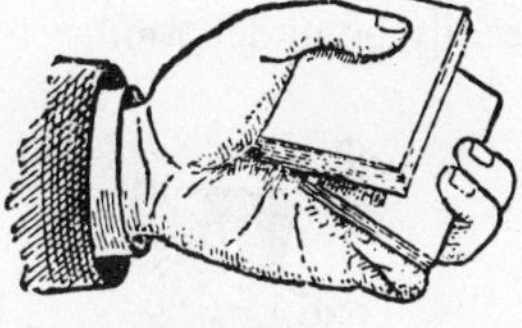

FIG. 3

A newer method is performed as follows: Take the cards in the left hand;

FIG. 4

FIG. 5

insert the third finger above the cards which are to be brought to the top (and which now form the lower half of the pack), and close the remaining three fingers on the top of the pack. Now extend the fingers, which will make the upper part of the pack describe a semicircle (Fig. 4), and at the same moment press downward with the thumb the left top corner of the lower packet. This will tilt up the opposite end of the lower packet, and give room, as you again close the fingers, for the upper packet to pass into the lower place. (Fig. 5)

To bring the original upper packet into the position which it occupies in Fig. 5, it is pressed slightly forward with the middle finger, and is thereby made to perform a semi-revolution, the third finger acting as a pivot. The packet is by this means turned over endways, that is, that end of the packet which was originally nearest to the performer is now farthest from him, and vice versa. If followed step by step *with the cards*, the movement will readily be understood.

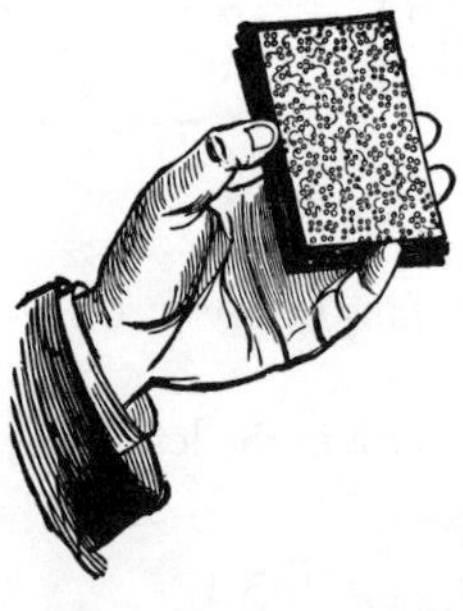

Fig. 6

Fig. 7

Shift, One-Handed: The Charlier Shift. The cards are taken in the left hand, supported by the tips of the second and third fingers and thumb (Fig. 6), the little finger taking up its position midway across the lower end of the cards, and the first finger remaining extended. The lower half of the pack is now allowed, by a slackening of the pressure of the thumb, to fall loose into the hand (Fig. 7).

The first finger then comes into play, and lifts the outer edge of the lower packet until it touches the ball of the thumb. (Fig. 8) The second and third fingers now relax their pressure, thereby allowing the outer edge of the upper packet to pass the edge of the lower packet (Fig. 9). The first finger is again extended, allowing the two halves of the pack to coalesce, and the pass is made. A backward or forward sweep of the arm will assist in covering the movement, which would be visible without such cover.

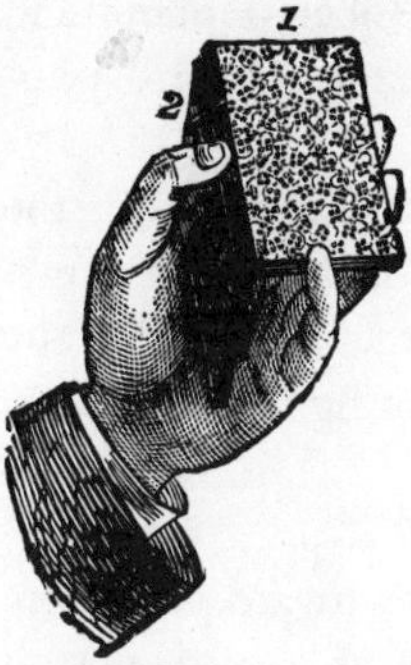

FIG. 8

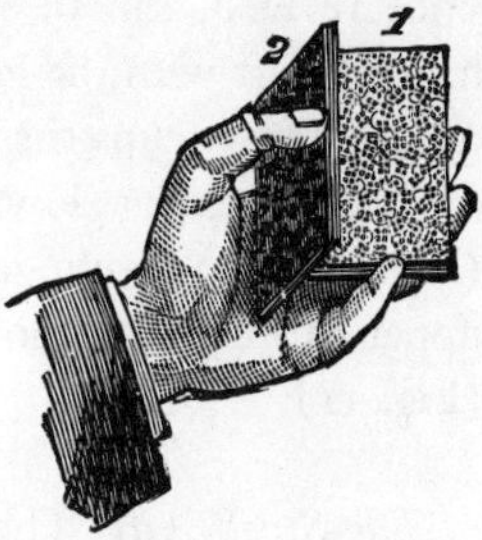

FIG. 9

The Charlier Shift is of constant utility. Among other things, it offers a ready and natural means of gaining possession of a drawn card. A card having been chosen, the performer offers the pack lying in the palm of his left hand, but as he does so, opens it bookwise with the thumb, thereby bringing it into the position shown in Fig. 6. The movement is so easy and natural that the drawer instinctively places the card in the opening. The pack is then closed, apparently with the card in the center, but in the act of closing it the shift is made, and the card lies on the top, to be dealt with at the performer's pleasure. *L. H.*

ROBERT-HOUDIN ONE-HANDED SHIFT (SEE NEXT PAGE)

FIG. 10

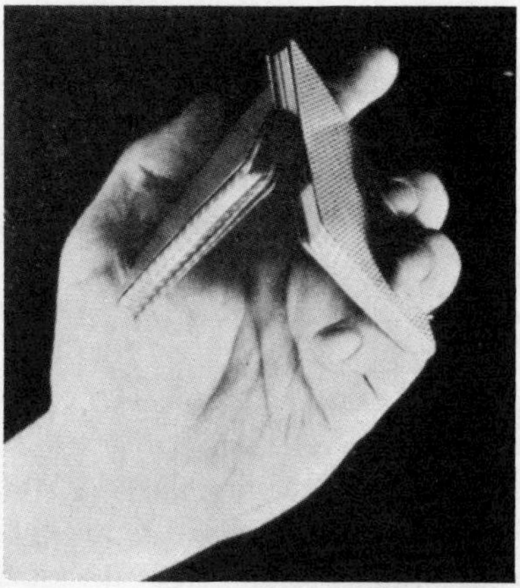

FIG. 11

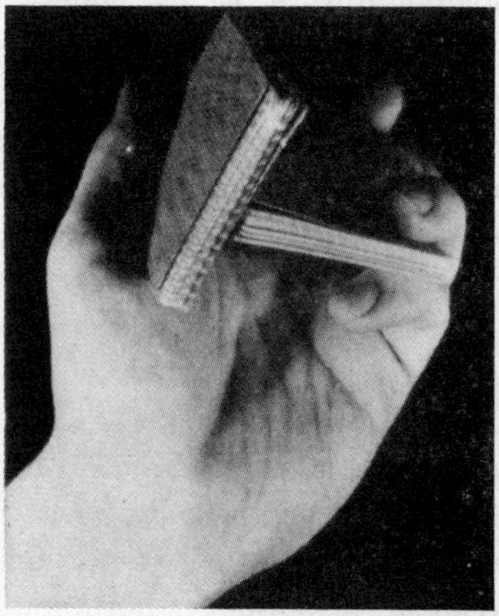

An extremely fast one-handed shift, described by Robert-Houdin and since revived, can be accomplished by simply doing the standard two-handed shift with the left hand alone.

The thumb clips the lower half near the upper left corner, and tilts the cards by pressing down. The fingers tip the top half and draw it down (Fig. 10); the forefinger serves as a dividing point in the middle until the upper half clears the lower, when the fingers close to bring it underneath. (Fig. 11)

Side-Steal Shift. The conjurer, holding the pack downward in his left hand, requests some member of the audience to look at a card—not to draw a card, or in any way disturb its position in the pack, but simply to lift slightly the upper right-hand corner of the pack and sight a card. During this operation the performer partly turns his back to the spectator, extending the left arm backward, in order that he may not catch a glimpse of the card.

After the card has been sighted, and the pack restored to its normal condition, the performer draws attention to the fact that the cards are squared up, and even allows the spectator to take the pack in his own hand and examine it. Nevertheless, the performer can instantly produce the chosen card in any manner he may choose.

The pack is held face downward in the left hand, in the usual manner of holding the cards for dealing, except that the four fingers on the outside press the pack rather firmly into the crotch of the thumb. The first joint of the first, second, third, and fourth fingers are pressed against the outer edge of the pack. The thumb extends slantingly across the top of the pack, pointing toward the first finger.

In this manner the cards are presented to the spectator, who is requested to lift the upper right-hand corner of the pack and remember one of the cards. The performer impresses rather strongly upon the spectator the importance of looking at only one card. While the spectator is engaged in this duty, the performer partially turns his body and head, so that he cannot possibly see the card sighted by the spectator, who, after making a mental note of the card, allows the upper portion of the pack to fall back into its original position.

If, however, the pack is held as directed, and a rather firm pressure maintained by the first and second fingers against the outer edge of the deck, it will be found that a small part of the fleshy tip of the first finger will be wedged between the two portions of the pack, forming a BREAK, the bottom card of the upper portion being the spectator's card. If, at the same time, the left thumb is pressed rather heavily on the top of the pack, this break will not be visible.

As you turn around and bring the hands together, the tip of the left first finger is inserted further into the break and then pushed upward and outward, forcing the chosen card (that is, the card at the bottom of the lower packet) outward until it extends about half an inch from the right side of the pack. The right hand, which covers the pack during this operation, grips the extended card between the first joint of the thumb (at the lower corner) and the second joint of the third finger (at the upper corner) (Fig. 1), and slips the card to the top of the pack. Deftly performed, with the back of the right hand toward the audience, the movement cannot be detected by the sharpest eye. *T. N. D.*

Most modern card workers hold a little-finger instead of a forefinger break, and slide the card out with first and second fingers together.

Slip. The slip is really a variant of the SHIFT, and is used to transfer a single card from the top of the pack to the bottom or middle. To transfer one from top to bottom, the procedure is exactly the same as for the shift, except that the little finger is not inserted, the pressure of the left fingertips sufficing to draw the card from the top of the pack.

To transfer a card from top to middle, as in FORCING, the pack is held in the left hand, with the fingertips pressed fairly firmly against the top card. The right hand lifts about half the pack and slides it to the left, but the left

FIG. 1 SIDE-STEAL SHIFT

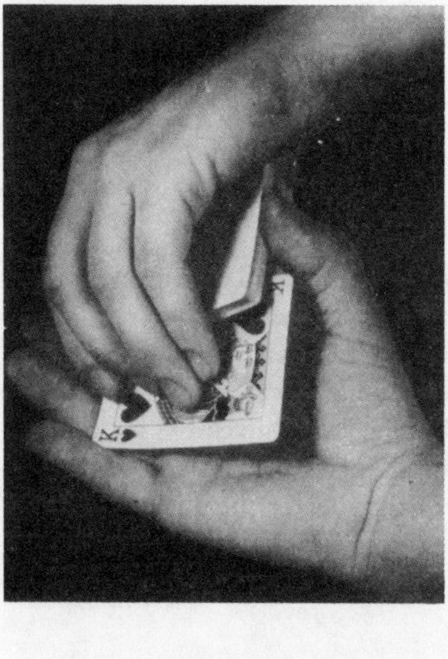

SLIP FIG. 1

fingers retain the top card (Fig. 1) which falls indetectably on the lower half.

In forcing, the right hand is held still, while the left hand slides down and out to the right, carrying the forced card along; the move serves ostensibly to hold out the lower half to the spectator, so that he may remove the top card and look at it. *O. F.*

Bibliography. The literature of card manipulation is enormous. Indispensable volumes are:

Blackstone	*Modern Card Tricks*
Downs	*The Art of Magic*
Erdnase	*The Expert at the Card Table*
Hilliard	*Greater Magic*
Hugard	*Encyclopedia of Card Tricks*
Hugard and Braue	*Expert Card Technique*
Merlin	*"And A Pack of Cards"*

CARD-MARKING (See also CARDS, KEY; GAMBLING METHODS) The systems of card-marking are as numerous as they are ingenious. They vary from a mark which covers the greater portion of the back of the card to a mark which is invisible. This latter may not appear to be of much use, but it must be borne in mind that the sharp is not restricted to the use of sight only.

All these various systems are capable of general classification under the following heads:

A. General principles of marking.
B. Marking by dot and puncture.
C. Cards marked in manufacture.
D. Shading and tint-marking.
E. Line and scroll work.
F. Cards marked while in play.

A. General principles of marking. Whatever method of marking may be adopted in the preparation of faked cards or "readers," however recondite that method may be, it is referable to one of two general principles; either each card has a distinctive mark placed in some convenient position, or the mark is similar in every case, the indication being given by the position which it occupies. Some systems are based upon a combination of the two principles; but all are developments of either one or the other. When the mark, whatever it may be, is placed at one end of the card, it is of course necessary to mark both ends.

The chief aim in marking, of course, is to produce work which is easily decipherable to the trained eye of the expert, but invisible to others. Many of the specimens given here have been submitted to experts who have been allowed to retain them as long as they pleased, and have been returned with the statement that to all appearances the cards have not been tampered with.

There is no difficulty in marking cards so as to arouse no suspicion. Anyone could invent a system which no one but himself could decipher, and which would defy detection. The only difficulty is to read the marks with speed and accuracy. The sharp who uses marked cards will contrive to work in those he has prepared when possible, but failing this, he is generally in a position to mark all the cards he wishes to know during the course of the game.

B. Marking by dot and puncture. The main outlines of this method will be understood from what has already been said. If the unglazed spots are represented by minute dots, the principle is practically the same. The only difference is in connection with marking by puncture. In this case the mark is made by pricking the face of the card with a very fine needle. This raises a minute point or burr upon the back, which can be detected by passing the thumb across the back of the card while dealing.

If a plate of metal the size of a playing-card is divided at each end into parallelograms, after the manner shown in Fig. 1, these divisions will represent the positions occupied by the puncture or dot in representing the various suits and values. A small hole being drilled in the center of each parallelogram, the plate will serve as a guide by which the cards may be pierced in the correct places.

The plate is laid upon the face of the card, and a fine needle is pricked through the proper hole, just far enough to raise the necessary projection on the back of the card. One point at each end, then, will serve to mark all the cards of a piquet pack. If cards lower than seven have to be marked, two points may be taken: for instance, a point in the top left-hand corner, together with one three divisions further to the right, will indicate the six of clubs. A point in the second space on the same line, with one in the fifth space, will represent the five of clubs, and so on.

This is a very good system of marking for many purposes. It takes only a short time to mark the whole pack; the marks are invisible, and will escape the closest scrutiny. But great practice is necessary to render the touch sufficiently acute, and the perception of the small differences sufficiently delicate, to read the marks with precision.

Another method whereby a single dot is made to represent both suit and value of any card is illustrated in Fig. 2. In almost every ornamental back,

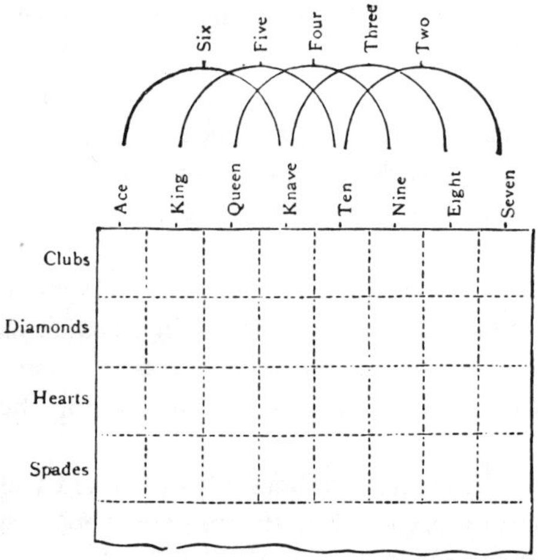

FIG. 1

there is some portion of the pattern which is more or less of a fan-shaped or radial design. If this should happen to contain thirteen divisions, nothing is easier than to assign to each one a value, and thus the entire suit is represented by merely varying the position of the dot. The suit is given by placing the dot nearer or farther from the center.

Fig. 2 illustrates this method in its simplest form. A dot placed outside the outline of the design stands for "spades," one just inside for "hearts," half way between the two lines for "diamonds," and close to the inner circle it means "clubs." The value or "size," as it is called, is shown by the radial line, opposite which the mark is placed. Having followed this ex-

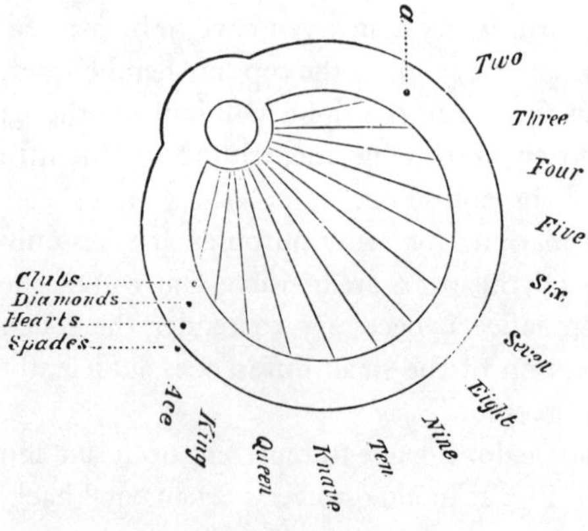

FIG. 2

FIG. 3

planation, the reader will see that the dot marked *a* represents the two of diamonds.

It frequently happens that there is no part of the pattern which contains thirteen divisions. Then, either more than one design must be used, or the form of the mark must be varied. If, for example, there are only six divisions available for the purpose, the six highest cards can be indicated by a dot, the six next in order by a small dash, and the last by a minute cross.

C. Cards marked in manufacture. It is obviously desirable to open a new pack of cards and find them marked ready for use. Fig. 3 is a reproduction of the first pattern ever supplied, ready marked, by the makers.

The distinctive marking was arranged by causing the end of the scroll, marked *a*, to assume various forms, and point in different directions.

This card did very well for a time, but the mark was very obtrusive and the pattern became obsolete.

The next improvement came with the introduction of the plaid-back cards, at one time largely used. It was soon discovered that these lent themselves readily to the purposes of falsification, and the result was the invention of a mark easy to read but not liable to detection. It is based partly upon modification of the pattern, and partly upon the position occupied by the mark.

This pattern is of especial value to the man who can SECOND-DEAL; by keeping the pack spread out a little, he can read off the values of the first four or five cards. That is the great advantage of having marks which come quite close to the edge.

Cards marked in printing have of late years been virtually abandoned, since they are readily detected, even by those who are utterly unable to discover the marks. In the first place, the ink with which the cards are printed is as a rule very inferior, and secondly, the ace of spades has no maker's name on it.

D. Shading and tint-marking. At the present time shading is principally confined to ornamental backs, and is effected by applying a faint wash of color to a farly large portion of the card. This color of course must be one which approximates the tint of the card, and must also be one which will dry without removing the glaze.

E. Line and scroll work. This is the kind of marking which is adopted by the most expert among card-sharpers. When well done it can hardly be detected even by another sharper.

This system may be summarized briefly as follows. Some convenient portion of the card-back is selected—a flower or some similar device in the pattern, for instance—and a shading consisting of very fine lines, in imitation of the normal shading of the pattern, is used, its position indicating the value of the card. A specially prepared "line-work fluid" is used, and the work is put on with a fine pen or, better still, a fine sable pencil. In using a pen there is always danger of scratching the enamel, but by the use of a "photographic sable" such as retouchers employ, this is obviated.

F. Cards marked while in play. Perhaps the most interesting system deals with the possibility of placing distinctive marks upon the cards during the game.

The earliest method appears to have been that of raising a slight burr on the edges of the cards with the thumbnail. This and other primitive methods alike have been superseded by others more scientific.

One of the simplest appliances is the "nail prick." This is simply a tiny piece of metal, with a point, which is held when in use under the thumbnail of the right hand. With this point the cards can be pricked without observation, in positions which will indicate suit and value.

Pricking the cards is a method chiefly employed by men who can deal seconds. The sharp will prick the corners of as many aces and face cards as happen to fall into his hands from time to time; while dealing, he can feel the little projections caused by the prick, and hold these cards back until he can deal them to himself. If he did this every time, he would win all the money sooner or later, but no sharp would arouse suspicion in this manner.

The most scientific method of pricking the cards is by means of an ingenious little appliance, known as the "poker-ring." This is an ordinary finger-ring, having attached to it on the under side a needle-point about one sixty-fourth of an inch long (Fig. 4). In the illustration, the length of the point is exaggerated.

As the cards are held in the hand, the corner of any one to be marked is simply pressed against the point with the thumb of either hand. Thus with one hand the sharp is enabled to mark any card he chooses without a single suspicious movement.

The greatest advance in this direction was made when the art of marking cards with shade-work was discovered. It was found that a little aniline color, taken on the tip of the finger, could be transferred to the back of a card, slightly deepening the tint in the spot to which it was applied. At first the color was derived from a piece of blue aniline pencil, on the point of which the finger was secretly rubbed. But soon a colored paste was concocted which would answer the purpose much better. A hole was made in a piece of cork, the cavity filled with the paste, and the cork was sewn inside the lower edge of the waistcoat, convenient to the hand. This idea has been improved to the form of appliances known as "shading boxes."

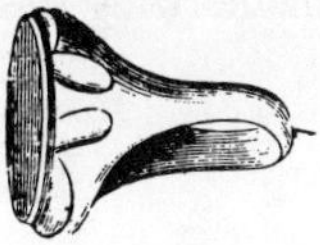

FIG. 4

FIG. 5

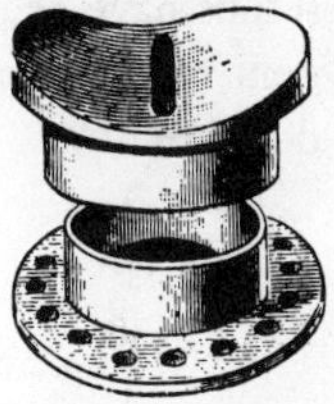

These implements of chicanery, of which Fig. 5 is an illustration, are little nickel-plated boxes, which are completely filled with the colored paste. In the center of the lid is a slot through which the color is pressed. The finger passes over this slot, taking up a little of the color. The base of the box is pierced around the circumference with small holes, for convenience in sewing it to the inside of the waistcoat or underneath the flap of a side pocket.

The boxes are generally used in pairs, one containing red composition and the other blue. With these two colors, almost every colored card can be marked. The paste for refilling the boxes is sold separately or may be made by the following recipe:

Olive oil, stearine, and camphor are melted, and mixed with aniline of the required hue. The mixture is then poured out on a level surface to cool. When cold it is worked up with the blade of a knife upon a sheet of white paper, to get rid of the superfluous oil. It is then ready for use.

Marking placed upon cards in this way can be removed instantly merely by rubbing the card upon the tablecloth. *J. N. M.*

CARD SETUPS (THE "ROSARY DECK") (See also SPELLING MASTER) Many ingenious effects are performed by arranging all or some of the cards in an order memorized by the performer. Convincing use of setups usually depends altogether on an effective FALSE SHUFFLE (see CARD MANIPULATION). The simplest arrangement, of course, is with each suit in numerical order, the way cards come new from the manufacturer.

The new pack makes possible a very striking poker trick: the performer deals six poker hands. The other five players get full houses, and stand pat; the performer, whose full house is the lowest of the six, retains the last card he dealt himself, discards four, and draws a straight flush. With a new pack, the only subterfuge necessary is to SHIFT or SLIP one card from the top to the bottom after dealing the second and fourth rounds.

The new-pack setup will not stand even a moment's inspection. Other setups have accordingly been devised in which no prearrangement is evident without some study. The most familiar is learned by memorizing this doggerel:

"Eight kings threatened to save
Ninety-five ladies for one sick knave."

The words obviously suggest the sequence, eight, king, three, ten, two, seven, nine, five, queen, four, ace, six, jack. The suits are alternated, red and black—say clubs, hearts, spades, diamonds, which is remembered by the order of consonants in the word CHaSeD. To arrange the pack, then, take in your left hand, face upward, the eight of clubs; on this put the king of hearts; on this the three of spades; then the ten of diamonds; and so on through the pack.

Obviously you can now tell, for instance, what any selected card is by merely glancing at the one above the place it was drawn from. Or if a row of cards are dealt out face down, and one is touched, you know what it is before the spectator does. *H. H.*

Another standard arrangement is the *Si Stebbins Setup.*

The cards should be laid out on the table in the order shown in Fig. 1.

AC	4S	7H	10D
KC	3S	6H	9D
QC	2S	5H	8D
JC	AS	4H	7D
10C	KS	3H	6D
9C	QS	2H	5D
8C	JS	AH	4D
7C	10S	KH	3D
6C	9S	QH	2D
5C	8S	JH	AD
4C	7S	10H	KD
3C	6S	9H	QD
2C	5S	8H	JD

Fig. 1

The second card (the four of spades) should now be placed on the first one (the ace of clubs), then the third one (the seven of hearts), and so on to the end.

It will be observed that each card is three higher than the one immediately behind it, the arrangement of the suits being: Clubs, spades, hearts, diamonds. The precise arrangement of the suits is practically immaterial, and it would, perhaps, be as well for the student to adopt a system of his own. The arrangement of the face cards is: Jack–11, queen–12, king–13, so that supposing the bottom card of the pack were the jack of clubs, the performer would instantly know that the next card beginning at the top of the pack was the ace of spades.

Finding the Card Named. The following explanation will require a little study, but if the rules are followed just as stated below, the student will soon comprehend the idea. It is the key to a great combination of card tricks.

FIG. 2

The card is named by the audience, the performer holding the pack so as to see at a glance, and note the last four cards, as seen in Fig. 2. These last four cards are: Ten of hearts, king of diamonds, three of clubs, and six of spades.

Suppose the card named is the three of spades. Now, according to table No. 1, you subtract the given card (three of spades) from the first card of the suit (six of spades), which leaves three. Next multiply by four–twelve; therefore, the three of spades is the twelfth card from the top.

Now cut the cards as near as possible to what you think is twelve. Should you cut at the eleventh card–which would be the king of clubs–you immediately know the card following a club is a spade, and if you cut at the king of clubs, the next card is three spots higher–the three of spades–so you open at the next card. Or, should you cut the pack at the thirteenth card, which in this case would be the six of hearts, you know a heart is preceded by a spade, and if you have the six of hearts, the card before it is the three of spades.

Table No. 1

The following table should be thoroughly learned and memorized.

Suppose the performer has effected the change of packs and is ready to find any given card in the pack; therefore he proceeds as follows:

Subtract the given card from the first card of the suit from the bottom of the pack. Now multiply it by four, and deduct the number of cards following the first card of the suit.

Refer again to Fig. 2.

Say the given card is the five of hearts, subtract five from the first card of the suit (which is the ten of hearts)–five.

Now multiply by four–twenty, less the number of cards before the first card of the suit from the bottom, which is three; three from twenty leaves seventeen. Therefore, the five of hearts is the seventeenth card from the top.

Table No. 2

If the card named is higher than the first card of the suit from the bottom, subtract the given card from thirteen.

Now add the number of the first card of the suit, then multiply by four, less the number of cards following the first card of the suit, and you will have the exact number of the given card from the top of the pack.

In Fig. 2 the last four cards are the ten of hearts, king of diamonds, three of clubs, and six of spades.

Say the five of clubs is named, the three of clubs being the first card of the suit.

As it is impossible to subtract five from three, you deduct it from thirteen (as explained in table No. 2), which leaves eight. Now add the number of the first card of the suit, which is three–eleven; multiply by four –forty-four, less the number of cards following the first card of the suit (one)–forty-three. Upon examination you will now find that the forty-third card is the five of clubs.

With a little careful practice the student will soon become familiar with the arrangement.

Mind-Reading With Cards. One or more cards should be selected by a spectator, and the pack laid on the table.

A lady or gentleman sitting on the opposite side of the room (without even as much as a look from the performer) immediately informs the drawer of the number and the names of the cards chosen.

This trick, which can, if desired, be presented as an exhibition of genuine mind-reading, will create a profound sensation.

The medium, or second party, to this experiment must be thoroughly acquainted with the order in which the pack is arranged, and should be seated on one side of the performer.

After the card or cards have been selected, the pack is cut, and the card that was above those selected brought to the bottom. In the act of laying the cards on the table, the bottom card is momentarily exposed to the view of the assistant, thus enabling him or her to name the one selected. This is easily accomplished when one thoroughly understands the arrangement of the pack as previously set out.

Naming Any Number of Chosen Cards. A spectator is asked to take out a few cards in a bunch–eight or nine, or in fact as many as he likes. The cut is made, the bottom card noted, and the performer is instantly able to name the chosen cards. When this has been done, if the cards are replaced on the bottom of the pack one by one in the order as chosen, the pack will still be in the correct condition for further tricks.

So as not to give any astute member of the audience a chance to observe that each card is three spots higher than the preceding one, it is advisable not to call them out in their exact order, when naming the cards selected.

H. T.

Nikola Setup. Probably the subtlest of all setups is the *Nikola card system,* which has no recurring regularities whatever except that every fourth card is a heart. The arrangement is arbitrary, and is learned by a mnemonic system.

This system, along with many good tricks using setups, is explained in Jean Hugard's *Encyclopedia of Card Tricks.*

CARDS, FLAP These cards change mechanically, without sleight-of-hand. To make them, two cards are split, the face being peeled off from the back after soaking. The two faces are glued together, back to back, for exactly half their length (or, alternatively, their width). Here they are folded in half away from each other, and one of the backs is pasted on to the two projecting half faces. This makes of the faces a flap that can be folded down either way, showing one card or the other at will. (Fig. 1)

For use in the RISING CARDS flap cards may be fitted with a rubber band that will snap the flap in one direction. The flap part is only half the length of the card, and works from side to side, not from end to end. (Fig. 2)

A mechanical pack has also been devised to make an endless series of COLOR CHANGES (see CARD MANIPULATION). Fig. 3 shows the construction.

FIG. 1

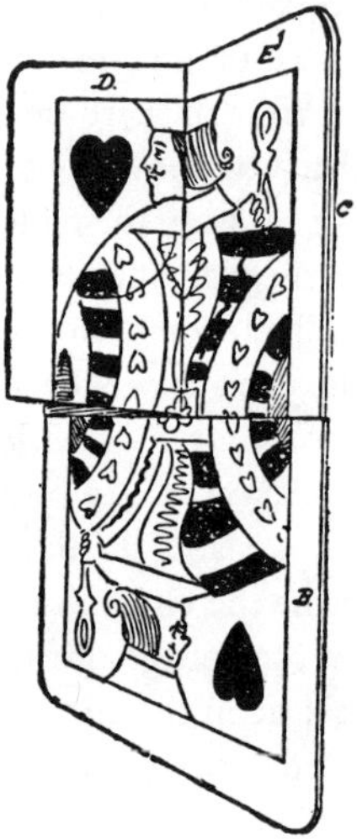

FIG. 2

FLAP CARDS
(see preceding page)

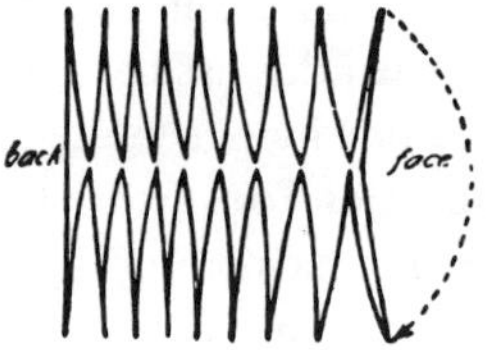

FIG. 3

CARDS, KEY Key or locator cards are used in various ways to assist in the discovery of a chosen card.

The key card may simply be known (as in the ancient trick of looking at the card above the one selected), or it may be marked or differentiated from the rest of the pack in a variety of ways. It may be CRIMPED, marked with a fingernail, or have one corner bent. (See CARD-MARKING.) Probably the oldest type of prepared card is the "long card," which may be either longer or wider than the rest of the deck. This enables the performer to cut by feel to the key card. The most practical way of preparing a long card is to use duplicate decks, and shave a tiny fraction of an inch off the end or side of one deck. Any card can then be removed from this pack, and its duplicate, from the untrimmed pack, will become the long card.

An improvement on the long card that will baffle the astutest eye is illustrated in Fig. 1.

To prepare the card, split it at one end and insert a small square piece cut from another card. Glue the card together and your fake, when dry, is ready for use. If you use a glazed card, the easiest way of splitting is to insert the end in warm water. The wetting will not injure the card, and as soon as it is dry the split portion may be glued together. For this purpose liquid glue is preferable to mucilage or paste.

The fake should not be large. Its greatest width, at the point where it leaves the card proper, should be three-sixteenths of an inch, and it should not extend more than one-eighth of an inch. The projection should be slightly rounded, as shown in the illustration. Instead of a duplicate piece of card, the fake may be made of very thin metal, preferably aluminum. A card thus prepared will last indefinitely. *T. N. D.*

FIG. 1 KEY CARD

The next step was the "short card," which may be short, narrow, or irregularly trimmed.

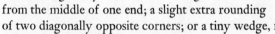

The irregularity can be a thin segment shaved from the middle of one end; a slight extra rounding of two diagonally opposite corners; or a tiny wedge, running from nothing at the lower right-hand corner to possibly a thirty-second of an inch at the left-hand corner.

With any of these cards, the performer has only to riffle the pack at the appropriate spot, and he can stop at the key card.

Another type of key that can be located by feel is the thick card. One method of manufacturing a thick card is to split an ordinary card, put a piece of thin silk between the layers, and glue all back together, pressing it hard and well.

Another way is to cut out the part of a face card within the border, and paste it securely in place on a duplicate.

The "detective card" of Leopold Figner was a nine of spades with extra pips carefully cut out and pasted over the upper left and lower right spots.

Other key cards can be detected by friction alone. These are divided fundamentally into "slick" and "rough" cards. J. N. Maskelyne gives their history as follows:

There are several methods of causing the cards to slip at any desired place. The earliest method of preparing a pack of cards consisted of nothing more than putting the pack in a damp place for some time previous to its use. This system had the further advantage that it was not even necessary to open the wrapper in which the cards came from the maker. When the cards had absorbed a certain amount of moisture, the low cards would slip much more easily than the face cards. The reason for this was that the glaze used in "bringing up the colors" of the inks used in printing contained a large proportion of hygroscopic or gummy matter, which softened upon becoming moist. The face cards, having a much greater part of their surface covered with the glaze than the others, were consequently more inclined to cling to the next card. Therefore the task of distinguishing them was not difficult.

Not satisfied with this somewhat uncertain method, however, the sharps set to work to improve on it. The next departure was to make the smooth cards smoother, and the rough ones more tenacious. Those cards which were required to slip were lightly rubbed over with soap, and those which had to cling were treated with a faint application of rosin. This principle is the basis of all the "new and improved" systems that have been put before the sharping public ever since. Either something is done to the cards to make them slip, or they are treated with something to keep them from slipping.

When the unglazed "steamboat" cards were much in use the "spermaceti" system worked well. The cards to be distinguished were prepared by rubbing their backs with hard spermaceti wax. They were then vigorously scoured with some soft material, until they had acquired a brilliant polish. Cards treated in this manner would be readily separable from the others in the pack. By pressing rather heavily on the top of the pack, and directing the pressure slightly to one side, it would be found that the pack divided at one of the prepared cards—the cards above the prepared one would cling together and slide off, leaving the doctored one at the top of the remainder.

With glazed cards, if they are required to slip, the backs are rubbed with a piece of waxed tissue paper, thus giving them an extra polish; but the better plan is to roughen the backs of all the others slightly. They may be "sanded" with fine emery-paper; any sandpaper would be too coarse, and produce scratches.

The cards may be made to cling by the application of very thin white varnish. This will make them stick slightly, so that by manipulating the pack as before directed in the case of the waxed cards, the slipping will occur at those cards whose backs have not been varnished.

A more recent way to make slick cards is by dabbing on floor wax or Simoniz with a ball of absorbent cotton.

Naturally, if the face of the card is slick, a slight downward and sliding motion of the left thumb will BREAK the pack and send the slick card to the bottom. If the back of the card is slick, it will cut to the top.

A still further ingenious dodge, apparently discovered by Ford Rogers, is to buy two packs, identical in size, back pattern, and color, but one pack ivory finish, the other air-cushion finish. An air-cushion card in an ivory deck will function satisfactorily as a slick card.

Among key cards located by sight, the "known card" has already been mentioned. A brand-new card in a matching deck that has been somewhat used will also serve as a locator.

The "inked card," inked for about half an inch along the side edges at the unindexed corners, can be located by a glance at the edge of the pack.

Some key cards may be actually FORCED on a spectator, who may then shuffle the pack indefinitely without stumping the performer. More generally, the performer will contrive to bring the card next to the chosen card, or—a most useful variant—to a known number of cards away from the chosen card.

Hilliard's *Greater Magic* gives extended treatment to key-card tricks.

H. H.

CARDS, ONE-WAY, POINTER, DIVIDED These terms describe three related systems of card location.

A *one-way deck* is a deck whose back pattern is not absolutely symmetrical. Most bridge cards use a picture of some kind, which makes a one-way back so obvious as to be unsafe for the card conjurer. Scroll designs are much the best, and of the many varieties in this category the "Angel Backs" are to be preferred. In all scroll designs there are more or less irregularities. These irregularities, of course, are imperceptible to the uninitiated; but when one knows where to look, the slight differences in the design are as plain as a moon in a cloudless sky. A glance at Fig. 1 will make this plain.

FIG. 1

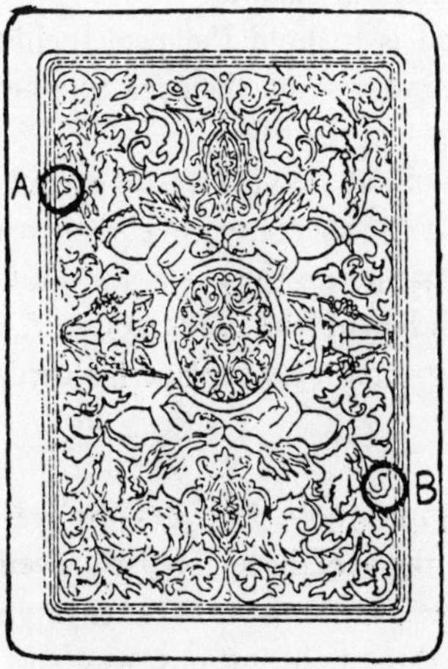

In the upper left-hand corner of the figure one of the small leaves is marked with a circle, at *a*. The leaf marked *b*, in the lower right-hand corner, diagonally opposite, is larger and of different shape. The difference in size and shape is very perceptible when attention is called to the irregularity; but a person might examine the card for months, if he did not know where to look, without observing the difference in design. On this slight irregularity depend all the tricks described in this section.

The pack should be arranged beforehand so that all the cards are in the position shown in Fig. 1, that is, with the small leaf in the upper left-hand corner. A little practice will enable the performer to keep the pack always arranged in this manner.

It is obvious that if a card is drawn and replaced in a reversed position, the card can be instantly located, no matter how much the pack is shuffled. The card thus reversed has the large leaf, *b*, at the upper left-hand corner, and is readily located by ruffling this corner with the left thumb. With a little practice the card can be located in a fraction of a second, when it is a simple matter to insert the little finger and bring the card to the top.

When the card is drawn, the performer must watch closely to see if the spectator reverses the card while it is in his hands. If the card is not reversed, the performer must reverse the pack. It will be found, in actual practice, that not once in a hundred times will a spectator reverse a card in his hands. It is not advisable to reverse the pack openly, for this might lead to the suspicion that the performer is using strippers. Simply give the pack a shuffle while the spectator is noting his card; during this operation the pack is reversed in the most natural manner.

One effective method is to hold the pack behind the back when the card is drawn. In wheeling around, the pack will be in the proper position for the return of the card.

The most effective method, however, is to spread the cards on the table. A card is selected, and if the spectator reverses it while in his hand request him to replace it; then gather up the cards and shuffle the pack. If he does not reverse the card, gather up the cards yourself, shuffle and reverse the pack, and request the spectator to replace his card, immediately offering the pack for shuffling. *T. N. D.*

Pointer cards are those whose face designs are not symmetrical: the seven of diamonds and the ace, three, five, six, seven, eight, and nine of all the other suits. The threes, for instance, have two pips one way and one the other way; the eights, three pointing one way and five the other. There are twenty-two pointer cards (twenty-three counting the joker), which is near enough a half for the purpose of most tricks.

Not only is it possible to detect one of the pointer cards if it is turned end for end among the rest, but a pointer card can be instantly sorted from among the non-pointers, or vice versa. If the pack is halved, and a pointer card selected and shuffled in among the non-pointer half, and the two halves are then riffled together, the one reversed pointer can still be located. The performer's own ingenuity will undoubtedly suggest many variations.

The *divided deck* is one in which the cards are segregated in two groups according to some principle of selection known only to the performer. The crudest and oldest method is to separate the pack into red and black cards; a card among those of the opposite color is then easily located.

The next step is to put hearts and spades in one group, diamonds and clubs in the other. This is good enough to fool the ordinary spectator. Or one may divide the deck into odd and even cards—twenty-eight odd, twenty-four even.

The final development of this principle is to sort the pack into odd hearts and spades and even diamonds and clubs in one part, even hearts and spades and odd diamonds and clubs in the other. This may seem like carrying complications too far, and indeed is probably seldom necessary, but with a little practice one learns to sort the cards in even this complicated division without hesitating.

Charles Jordan's *Thirty Card Mysteries* is a useful reference for this type of work. *H. H.*

CARDS UP THE SLEEVE (See also CARD MANIPULATION, CARD VANISHER)

Counting off twelve cards, the performer professes to make them pass one at a time from his left hand up his sleeve and into his right trouser pocket. The cards are heard to go. He first asks the audience to remember the names of the cards, and then, fanning the cards, passes them rapidly from left to right, counting quickly.

The audience show signs that they cannot possibly remember the names of all the cards, and the performer obligingly offers to count them again, this time more deliberately—"One, two, three, four, five," etc. When he arrives at six he inserts (of course unseen by the audience) the little finger of his left hand, and goes on counting up to twelve, saying, "Well, now you will remember at least a few of the cards sufficiently to know that I do not use a duplicate pack. Now, my trick is this: to pass these cards one at a time from my left hand, up my sleeve, along the invisible line of influence, into my pocket, which is quite empty." He pulls out the lining of his right trouser pocket, remarking, "You see my pocket is quite empty—which is nothing unusual."

While speaking, he holds the twelve cards in his left hand and allows the right hand to come to them once or twice, as though unconsciously, to square them up; each time as he removes it he allows the audience to see into the palm, being careful that the upward movement appears natural, and *not as though he were trying to show the palm empty*. At the fourth or fifth time he brings his right hand to the cards just as he is saying, "which is nothing unusual," and palms six cards in his right.

He removes the left with the other six to extended position, and lets it return, placing the six in his right again.

Then he takes the six into his left hand again, saying, "You will notice the cards pass one at a time up my sleeve," and holding out his right arm to its full extent he makes a riffle of the cards, at the same moment giving a delicate little pull with his right hand at his left sleeve at the elbow, and saying, "One card has already passed into my pocket."

Thrusting his right hand into the right trouser pocket, he pulls out one card and leaves five cards in his pocket. Throwing down one card on the table, he remarks, "Now I have eleven in my hand. Another the same way." He makes another riffle, and a second card is taken out of the pocket; "another," and a third card is removed, each time a riffle being made with the cards; "another," he puts his hand into his pocket, but withdraws it without the card. Remarking that "it did not squeak that time," he pulls the sleeve at the elbow, saying, "Ah, that's right! The card had caught at the elbow," and quickly pulls the card out of his pocket. Another riffle and the fifth card is removed.

"How many should I have in my hand?" (to someone in the audience). "Five from twelve—seven," he answers; and the performer says, "Thanks; the gentleman guessed right the first time." Then he counts them.

As the performer has only six cards in his hands, he makes a FALSE COUNT as he moves his right thumb downward, making it appear that seven cards are in the left hand instead of six.

The performer then asks two of the audience to hold his wrists, and, making the riffle, declares that a card has passed into his pocket. This is of course not believed, but the assistant on the right is told to put his hand into the performer's pocket without letting go of his wrist; he does so, and takes out the last of the six cards originally palmed. The performer immediately counts the cards in his left hand properly, and one is apparently found to have gone, as only six cards are there.

As the performer counts these six cards, he secretly introduces his little finger under the third card, ready for palming. Remarking that "every card in my hand goes in a similar manner," he palms three cards off, and takes them as before into his right pocket. Leaving two in his pocket and drawing out one, he says, "Here's the next—seven; leaving five in my hand."

The performer rapidly counts the remaining cards (really three), saying, "One, two, three, four, five," and making a false count as if five cards were there. "Now I will pass two cards together."

This time he makes two flips or riffles with the cards, remarking, "Two cards went that time"; and placing his right hand in his pocket produces them. "There are only three left now," he says, pretending to hear a remark from the audience. "That lady says, 'Wait until he comes to the last card, then we shall catch him.' Of course, the last card is the only one you see go." At that moment he takes the three cards into his right hand and BACK-PALMS them, showing the right hand empty.

Quickly he recovers them from behind the right knee, and apparently placing them in the left hand (really palming them in right), he turns the back of his left hand toward the audience. With a small rubbing movement the left hand is turned and shown empty, and the three cards taken from the right pocket.

It is absolutely essential to this trick that it should be slowly and nonchalantly performed. *The least hurried movement at any time when any cards are palmed in the right hand* will give the secret away. The amateur will find every temptation to hurry the cards into the pocket, as their abstraction is so barefaced that he is sure at first to feel that what he is doing will be seen by the audience. This idea must be absolutely disregarded, for it is only the natural slow and easy movement of the right hand at the time when it has cards palmed which gives the trick its finish and complete deception. *C. L. N.*

CARD THROUGH HANDKERCHIEF (See also CARD MANIPULATION) A member of the audience chooses any card from the pack and replaces it, laying the pack upon the handkerchief, into which it is entirely folded. The corners of the handkerchief are held, and the chosen card is shaken right through the center of the handkerchief.

The performer offers the pack of cards to someone, whom he asks to choose a card and show it to the company. He then takes the rest of the cards in his left hand, and requests that the chosen card be replaced, dividing the pack at about the middle by lifting off about half of the cards with the right hand. As the card is placed on the lower half, which is in his left hand, the little finger of that hand is inserted above it, and as the top half is placed upon it the two-handed SHIFT is made, and the chosen card is brought to the top of the pack.

The handkerchief is now picked up from the table (or one may be borrowed), and the assistant is asked to hold it for a moment. As if by an afterthought the performer says, "Oh, but perhaps you will be so good as to shuffle the cards," palming the chosen card and then handing out the pack with the right hand.

The handkerchief is taken back, shaken out, and held up with one hand at each of the top corners. The right hand is quickly placed under the handkerchief at about the center. The pack, which is now shuffled, is taken from the assistant with the left hand, and placed upon the handkerchief immediately over the chosen card, which is in the right hand underneath.

The handkerchief is now folded back over the cards: "We will cover the pack in the handkerchief—so." The left hand grasps the pack and also the card beneath, and the right hand gathers up the loose ends of the handkerchief, allowing the pack to fall gently into an upright position. A back view of the handkerchief and pack would show the chosen card partly covered by the folds of the handkerchief.

A pretense is made of drawing the card out by passing the left hand up and down in front of the handkerchief, saying, "You can see your card, can't you?" The assistant will reply in the negative, whereupon a slight shake of the handkerchief will bring the card down out of the fold, the performer exclaiming, "No! Why, there it is!"

If instead of allowing the assistant at the beginning of the trick to choose any card one has been FORCED on him, its name may be told. This adds a little effect when the hand is being passed in front and the performer says, "You can see your card, can't you?" He may point to the pack and say, "No! Why, I can; there it is. Look, the eight of diamonds," or as the case may be.

C. L. N.

CARD TRICKS (See under: BILLET- AND MESSAGE-READING; BLINDFOLDS; CARD BOX; CARD FRAME; CARD IN CIGARETTE; CARD INDEX; CARD MANIPULATION; CARD-MARKING; CARD SETUPS; CARD THROUGH HANDKERCHIEF; CARD VANISHER; CARDS, FLAP; CARDS, KEY; CARDS, ONE-WAY, POINTER, DIVIDED; CARDS UP THE SLEEVE; DIMINISHING CARDS; FORCING; FOUR-ACE TRICKS; GAMBLING METHODS; GENERAL CARD; MECHANICAL DECKS; MIND-READING; RISING CARDS; SERVANTES; SPELLING MASTER; THIRTY-CARD TRICK; THREE-CARD TRICKS; TRANSFIXED PACK; YOU DO AS I DO.)

CARD VANISHER For a few cards, see HOOK. To vanish an entire pack, there are several devices. One appliance is shown in Figs. 1 and 2. It is of tin, japanned black or flesh-color; its dimensions, at its open end, are

FIG. 1

FIG. 2

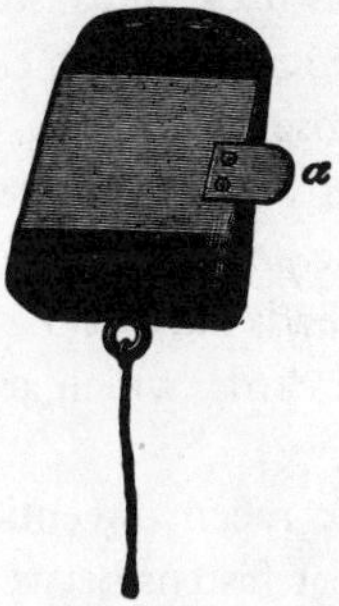

FIG. 3

such as to admit one end of a deck of cards. Just within the opening, riveted to back and front respectively, are a couple of steel tongues or springs, arranged to grip the cards firmly when in position, although they present no obstacle to their being inserted or withdrawn.

The opposite end of the card-case tapers to a point from which, secured by a knot within, comes a short piece of black silk cord. When the apparatus is in use, this is attached to a piece of stout elastic, which is made fast to a loop sewn to the back of the performer's vest, between the shoulders. The apparatus thus secured hangs inside the left sleeve, resting a few inches above the wrist when the arm is fully extended.

Holding the pack prominently forward in his right hand, the performer places the left hand on the hip, with a perfectly natural motion. The bending of the arm naturally shortens it, and allows the vanisher to drop into the left hand. Quickly securing it, he brings both hands together, and under pretense of simply pressing the cards, inserts one end of the pack into it. Thrusting his folded hands forward, he stretches the arms to their full extent, drawing taut the elastic, which being simultaneously released, draws the vanisher and its contents up the sleeve.

There is another form of vanisher, of French invention. This is a little clip made of two thin steel plates, japanned flesh color, and riveted to a solid piece of metal at their base, as shown in Fig. 3.

The "lips" of the two plates are rounded at the corners and slightly turned outward, one being made a little shorter than the other, the better to introduce the cards. There is a little thumbpiece *a*, riveted to the shorter plate, which is uppermost in use. This is a material aid in pressing the plates apart to insert the cards.

At the closed end of the clip there is a little loop or ring, attached to a piece of strong cord elastic. The elastic passes through a ring sewn to the performer's vest, at the edge of the armhole in front, and is thence carried behind his back and fastened to one of his waist buttons on the opposite side. The length of the elastic is arranged so as to draw the clip, when released, close up to the armhole. When required for use it is drawn down and secretly held in the left hand. Under cover of his patter, the performer inserts the ends of the cards into the clip, at the same time spreading the opposite ends fanwise. At the right moment he closes the fan and deftly releases the cards, which are forthwith drawn under the coat and up to the armhole. *L. H.*

A more recent invention is the *Top-It Vanisher*, a cloth bag or extra pocket that fastens between vest and coat. The opening is vertical. As the hand draws back to toss the deck away, the cards are dropped into the bag.

CARTER, CHARLES J. (1874-1936) An immensely successful American magician who began life as a "boy magician" touring Lyceum circuits, and traveled all over the world with a big, full-evening show. He died in Bombay on his travels.

CHANGEOVER PALM A sleight for transferring an object from one palm to the other while in each case showing the free hand empty. See BALL MANIPULATION and COIN MANIPULATION.

CHANGING BAG In appearance (Fig. 1) this is a bag about five inches across by seven deep, of velvet or plush, and mounted on a ring to which is attached a polished mahogany handle, about a foot long. The performer turns the bag inside out, revealing nothing but a very innocent-looking black lining. There is no sign of any inner pocket, or anything

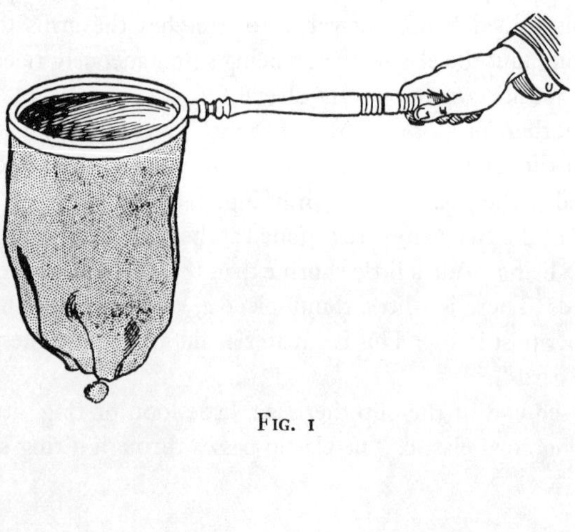

FIG. 1

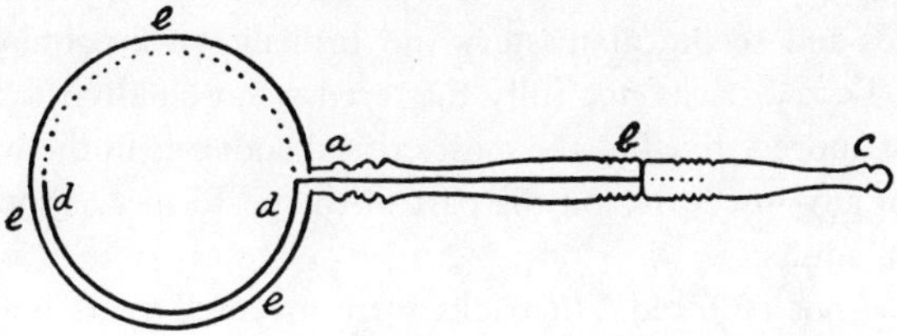

FIG. 2

else of a suspicious character; nevertheless, articles dropped into the bag are changed in a most mysterious way.

An inspection of Fig. 2 will reveal part of the secret. This lies mainly in the ring and handle, of which this diagram shows the construction.

The handle, *a b c*, is in two portions, that between points *a* and *b* being hollow. Through this portion passes a stiff wire rod, one end of which is firmly attached to the solid portion, *b c*, of the handle, and the other to one extremity of a half-ring *d d*, the other extremity of this half-ring being pivoted into the whole ring *e e e*, so that by twisting *b c* accordingly, this half-ring can be brought to either side.

The bag, besides its lining proper, has also a half or dividing lining, the upper edge of which is stitched to the half-ring. This, therefore, when turned to one side or the other, carries this inner lining with it, making it lie against the corresponding side of the bag.

Suppose a given article is privately placed in the bag, the half-ring being in the position shown in Fig. 2. A half-turn of *b c* causes the half-ring to perform a semi-revolution within the bag, shifting the false lining over to the opposite side, and shutting in the article just placed inside between the false and the true lining. The bag may now be turned inside out, and will appear to be empty. If some other article is borrowed and dropped in, and a half-turn in the reverse direction given to the handle, this last article is in turn shut in between the false and the true lining, and that first put in is revealed, one having apparently changed into the other. *L. H.*

CHILDREN'S SHOWS (See also: ANIMALS; COMEDY; MUSIC; PATTER; PRESENTATION; PROGRAMS; PSYCHOLOGY) Children through the age of eight accept magic as a reality; after that, they regard it as a game. Both attitudes demand that the performer be absolutely effortless in every trick he shows. If this is real magic, why must you hide the transformation under the handkerchief? If it is a contest of wits, why must you take unfair advantage?

That means technical simplicity—no precarious super-miracles to puzzle the initiated—and technical mastery—no brilliant back-palming that just *might* slip. To try tricks not fully mastered upon children is fatal. They are the most appreciative but the most critical audience in the world. They are aware of any insecurity on the part of the performer as soon as, if not sooner than, adults.

Novelty is not required. *All* tricks were invented years before any of your audience was born. You must surrender all pride as a magician, and be exclusively an entertainer.

Novelty is not required, but showiness is. Children have a roving eye, which must be caught and held with size, color, and motion—or, at the other extreme, with dainty doll-sized miniature props.

Animals fascinate children, appealing to their realistic sense, and they expect some livestock in a magic show.

Children always expect PRODUCTIONS to be distributed, and at least one distribution of loot is mandatory. Don't produce spring flowers that you can't give away unless later you are going to produce candy or throw out advertising cards.

If it is at all possible, have musical accompaniment.

So far as behavior is concerned, there are two methods of handling a juvenile audience. One way is to get down to their own level, and be one of them.

The other is to assume that they are at your own, adult level—not in tastes, perhaps, but in deportment.

The first way produces the more boisterous fun, but is far harder than it looks. Mere childishness on the performer's part only makes him contemptible in children's eyes, and results in pandemonium. The secret lies in a real sharing of children's *tastes*, not their behavior. The performer who can genuinely take the same noisy pleasure that his young spectators do in each new gush of water from the LOTA is on their level; the pleasure, not the noise, is what creates the juvenile atmosphere. In this atmosphere the magician naturally accepts some behavior—helpful shouts from the rear, grabs at the properties—that he will not put up with if he wants to create a decorous adult atmosphere.

Sometimes even a thoroughly happy juvenile audience begins to get out of hand. This must be stopped for the children's own sake, and the magician must momentarily drop his identification with the young audience. A very brief display of calm, cheerful, but firm authority will suffice. "That's enough; give someone else a chance to see," said crisply and with conviction, calms almost any tumult, without hurt feelings.

The adult atmosphere is largely self-explanatory. Performers who are naturally stiff and fastidious have no choice but this in giving children's shows; their only concession to the age of their audience is in the choice of PROGRAM. Usually such magicians will not want to specialize in children's shows, but they need to know how they can handle one if it is demanded of them.

The great weapon in creating an adult atmosphere is quiet, coupled with the *assumption* that the audience will behave itself. The noisier the children, the more softly the performer speaks; or he may work in complete silence.

Closely associated with this is the matter of COMEDY and PATTER. Comedy of situation appeals to children of all ages. Putting VOLUNTEERS in a ridiculous predicament always brings forth their laughs.

Patter comedy for children cannot be taught, but only learned. Children under eight have a special, rather rudimentary sense of humor that is a study in itself; at eight they begin to develop the word-humor that responds to comedy patter.

Fairy-story patter captures children through about eight years of age; after that they look down on it, and verbal comedy is more likely to succeed, since they have now ceased to accept magic as real, and consider it instead a sort of comic puzzle.

Variation in the program is essential. A juvenile audience needs to have its curiosity prickled, and continually to be given something fresh that keeps it in a state of expectant excitement. Not more than ten minutes must be given to any one particular kind of effect. Twenty-minute coin or billiard-ball acts will not do for children, though single simple coin and ball effects are ideal.

Sure-fire effects for children's shows are: AFGHAN BANDS; BALL OF WOOL; BRADAWL; BREAKAWAY FAN; CAKE BAKED IN A HAT; CARDS UP THE SLEEVE (typical of the very few card tricks that should be attempted); CHINESE WANDS; CHING LING FOO WATER CAN; CUPS AND BALLS (done smartly and not prolonged); DANCING HANDKERCHIEF; DIE BOX; DIMINISHING CARDS; DOVE PAN; EGG BAG; EGG AND HANDKERCHIEF; FISH CATCHING; FLAGSTAFF; FLOWER PRODUCTIONS; FUNNEL; GOLDFISH BOWLS; HAT LOADING; INEXHAUSTIBLE BOTTLE; KNOT THAT UNTIES ITSELF; LINKING RINGS; LOTA; MISER'S DREAM (some performers produce and distribute souvenir palming coins); MULTIPLYING BILLIARD BALLS; NEST OF BOXES; PASSE-PASSE BOTTLE; various PRODUCTIONS; RICE BOWLS; RING ON STICK; ROPE TRICKS; SHOWER OF SWEETS; SILK TRICKS; SPONGE BALLS; SUN AND MOON TRICK; THIMBLE TRICKS (if kept short and simple); THUMB TIE; TORN AND RESTORED PAPER; TURBAN CUT AND RESTORED.

Not more than one minute should elapse without some climax. Preparations must be short and simple, or else must have an element of comedy. No trick consuming more than five minutes altogether should ordinarily be used for children; it goes beyond the attention-span of the youngest spectators, and of course every audience must be judged by its lowest common denominator—the youngest, the slowest, the furthest away from the stage.

Tricks using volunteers are extremely popular with children. The superior and disdainful who are sure they are just as clever as you are can always be used to advantage. Left to themselves, they may upset the whole audience and crab the show; on the stage they are fair game for SUCKER GAGS and the butt of all the more embarrassing predicaments. Skill in segregating these disdainful youngsters can make or break a children's entertainer.

Shy children should never be forced to volunteer except when some individual reward is the result, or when no comedy role is intended.

One of the most important points for the children's entertainer to consider is his costume. Don't dress up as anything definite except a magician; whether Oriental or Occidental is your own choice. Such irrelevant costumes as clowns and cowboys are distracting, raising expectations that you cannot meet.

One of the best costumes, and one too seldom seen, is an old-fashioned dress suit complete with high collar, heavy watch chain, carnation, white gloves at least for the entrance, and above all a neatly waxed and curled mustache. A prop mustache is quite as good as a real one, and is very nearly essential to complete the child's image of an old-fashioned magic man.

Every performer who hopes to make a career of children's shows must thoroughly study *The Child From Five to Ten*, by Arnold Gesell and Frances Ilg.

Doris E. Robbins
Principal, Academy School
West Brattleboro, Vermont

CHINESE MAGIC According to John Mulholland, probably the best-informed magical traveler, the Chinese are the finest magicians of the East, closely followed by the Japanese; the East Indians make a rather poor third. This opinion applies to the national *magic* of the three countries; individual *magicians* have no fixed nationality.

MISDIRECTION is the strong point in Chinese magic; conjurers are apprenticed to the trade at five years of age, and begin acrobatics and juggling before they advance to conjuring.

A number of real Chinese tricks have been successfully transplanted to the West: the LINKING RINGS and the GOLDFISH BOWL production are the best known. These effects were introduced to the western repertory by PHILIPPE.

The greatest Chinese performer to visit America was CHING LING FOO, who set a vogue for Chinese acts that still continues. He repopularized the goldfish bowl among Occidental magicians. CHUNG LING SOO was his outstanding imitator. Okito and Dr. Fu Manchu (see BAMBERGS) may perhaps also be counted among his followers.

Long Tack Sam is a modern Chinese who carries on the national tradition of combining magic with juggling and acrobatics. He has truly Chinese cleverness in all three.

In attempting a Chinese act, or even a single Chinese trick, the western magician must learn to distinguish between Oriental splendor of trappings and the mere gaudiness, disfigured by pretended ideographs in gold paint, that is usually found in "Chinese" apparatus bought from dealers. This does not mean that Occidental tricks cannot be successfully dressed up as Chinese magic; they certainly can, and indeed Chinese magicians from time to time have borrowed European magic for themselves. *H. H.*

CHINESE WANDS (See also BRADAWL) Apparatus, sometimes called the *Pillars of Solomon*, for apparently uniting a piece of cut string. It consists of two slips of wood, each about four inches long by five-eighths of an inch square, laid side by side. At about an inch from one end of each, a transverse hole is bored; a string which is passed through both holes may be drawn backward and forward from side to side. (Fig. 1) The apparatus having been shown in this condition, the performer passes a knife between the two slips, apparently cutting the string; but the string is still drawn backward and forward through the holes, as sound as ever.

The secret lies in the fact that the string does not actually go straight through the two slips of wood from side to side. Instead of passing straight through, as it appears to do when the two pillars are laid side by side (the condition in which they are first exhibited to the spectators), it passes down the length of the first pillar, out at the bottom, and into the second pillar, where it passes upward and emerges at the top, outside. (Fig. 2) The passing of the knife does not therefore affect the string in the least.

It is obvious that in this form of the apparatus the two pillars, being joined by the cords at the bottom, cannot be completely separated, and the fact of their always being kept close together at the lower end is enough to betray to an acute observer the principle of the trick.

In an improved form, the two pillars are held wide apart, one in each hand, after the apparent cutting of the cord, and yet when they are again

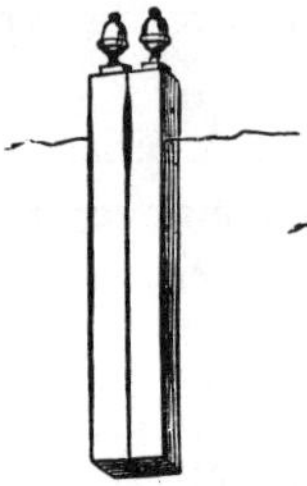

FIG. 1

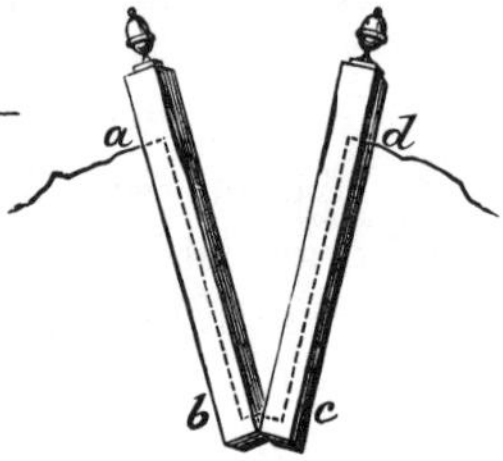

FIG. 2

placed side by side, the string runs backward and forward as merrily as ever. In this case, the pillars are as shown in Fig. 3. They are about six inches long, and have at each end a ball or knob of about an inch and a quarter in diameter, flattened on one face so that the pillars can be laid closely side by side.

The cord, as in the former case, passes down the first pillar from *a* to *b*, but instead of going out at *b*, it is rolled around a little pulley working in the lower knob of that pillar. (Fig. 4 gives a sectional view of the lower portion of each pillar.) A similar cord is passed down from *d* to *c* in the second pillar, and is there rolled around a second pulley, but in the opposite direction to that of the first cord, so that if both pulleys move in the same direction, the cord on one will be wound, and the cord on the other unwound. Each pulley is of one piece with its axis, the axis of one terminating in a little square tenon or nut, and that of the other in a corresponding mortise or hollow, so that when the two pillars are placed side by side, their axes fit into each other, and whichever of the two pulleys is set in motion, the like movement is communicated to the other.

A very short piece (perhaps an eighth of an inch long) of similar cord is glued into a little hole on the flat side of each of the upper knobs, exactly opposite the points *a* and *b;* these greatly heighten the appearance of reality upon the apparent cutting of the cord.

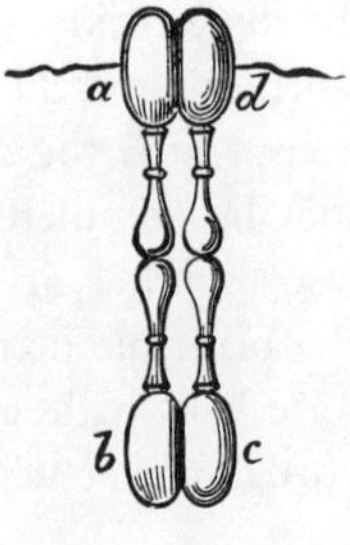

FIG. 3

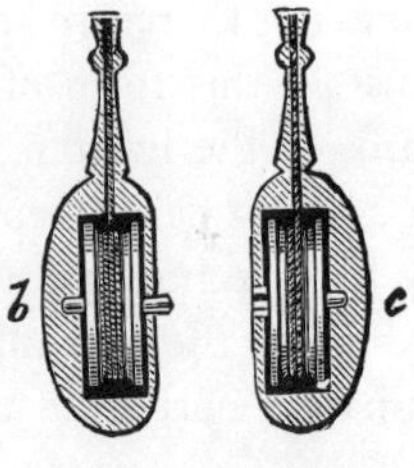

FIG. 4

Some little fun may be created by placing the upper knobs of the pillars pincer-fashion, one on each side of a person's nose, the cord being thus apparently made to run right through the nose. *L. H.*

The trick in its above form is never seen any more, having been replaced by a simpler and even more ingenious device. The two sticks are now made tubular—preferably of bamboo, but nowadays more often of red enameled metal—, and have no interconnection whatever. Each stick has a hole bored from side to side at the top, and through it runs a cord with a button at the top and a tassel at the bottom. The cords run perfectly freely through the holes; they can be drawn up by the button, and allowed to fall back of their own weight. Yet when the magician draws up one button, it is the other tassel that rises. When he drops the button he is pulling on, the cord falls through, and that tassel descends full length. He next pulls up on the other button, drawing the string out, whereupon the other, unconnected tassel rises. The effect is worked as a SUCKER GAG until the audience begins to clamor that the string goes down around the bottom of the sticks. Then they are separated, and the incongruous shortening and lengthening of the strings continues undisturbed.

The secret is that each stick contains a small lead weight with a pulley at the top, through which the string runs. When the weight is drawn up to the top by the tightening of the string, and the stick held level, the string can be pulled up and dropped without interference. If the stick be tipped, however, the weight slides down, taking the string with it, and pulling up the tassel.

The trick is an extremely clever one, but requires a good ROUTINE and good comedy PRESENTATION to carry it off. *H. H.*

CHING LING FOO Stage name of Chee Ling Qua (1854-1918), the greatest CHINESE MAGICIAN of modern times to tour the Occident. His stage magic was superb, his close-up work even better. His passion for detail carried him to great lengths. For instance, the goldfish bowls he produced were originally hidden between his knees under his flowing mandarin gown. This required him to walk on the stage with the pompous, straddling gait not uncommon among prosperous Chinese. Never, indoors or out, day or night, did he walk with any other stride. It might have exposed his fish-bowl trick. He used to say that no one could be a really good magician with less than forty years' practice.

CHING LING FOO WATER CAN A can that can be used to produce or vanish water. It is usually about four inches in diameter, and a foot high, tapering inward toward the top, with the mouth flared for about an inch. Inside, extending downward for about half the depth from the mouth, is a secret compartment formed by the flat side wall. This chamber is open at the lower end, closed at the top of the can, whose inside is painted black to conceal the irregular shape.

If the can is tipped over with the chamber on its lower side, a pint or so of water is retained, and the can may be twirled around on the end of the wand. By turning the chamber uppermost in tipping over the can, one pours out the water.

CHOPPER EFFECTS A class of small illusions and pocket tricks using a sort of wooden pillory with one or more holes, through which a sharp steel blade slides from top to bottom. Its action is exactly that of a guillotine. The blade is first used to cut up a carrot, proving that it is sharp and solid. Then the blade and the top of the pillory are removed, allowing an assistant or a VOLUNTEER to put either his head or a wrist (or, in the pocket version, a finger) through the hole. The top is replaced, followed by the blade, which is forced down, apparently cutting the volunteer in two.

The pillory is unprepared, but the blade, mounted in a wooden frame, is actually double—two thin blades lying together. The front blade is only half the width of the frame it is mounted in, and slides freely up and down in it. The rear blade is full width and fixed, but has a large piece scooped out in the middle where the neck-hole of the pillory is.

A catch keeps the two blades firmly together while the carrot is being sliced. The performer undoes the catch when he takes out the blade. This allows the front blade to slide upward in the frame when the assistant's neck stops it. The real blade does not touch the assistant's neck, being cut out at that point, but it can be seen descending through holes on each side of the main hole in the pillory. *H. H.*

CHUNG LING SOO Stage name of William Ellsworth Campbell (1861-1918), an American magician who won international fame as a Chinese after the success of CHING LING FOO. Originally a bookseller under the name of Campbell, he changed his name to Robinson. He served as an assistant to ALEXANDER HERRMANN and HARRY KELLAR, and then branched out for himself with a Chinese act. He met his death owing to a mysterious malfunctioning of the gun in the BULLET-CATCHING trick.

CIGAR MANIPULATION (See also WANDS) Wooden dummy cigars for manipulation purposes can be had at magic shops, but they are not a convincing imitation. It is also possible to prepare a real cigar by forcing half of a safety match into the point, and then wrapping the cigar spirally with pasted-down brown paper. It is probably better, however, to work cigar tricks entirely impromptu. If cigars are to be produced in quantity, they will have to be distributed to the audience, and cannot be prepared in any case.

The chief sleights applicable wholly to cigars are described below.

First Method. The cigar is held vertically on the left palm, being supported at the pointed end by the middle finger of the right hand (Fig. 1). The hands are brought together and the left hand is closed, as though it contained the cigar. (See left hand in Fig. 2) The cigar is really palmed in the right hand by being held between the tip of the middle finger of the right hand and the palm. (See right hand in Fig. 3.) The left hand is opened quickly and shown to be empty, and the cigar is produced from the knee. (Fig. 4)

Second Method. The left hand is held with the back of the hand toward the audience and the fingers, close together, pointing upward. (Fig. 5) The right hand apparently pushes the cigar (pointed end downward) into the left hand. (Fig. 6) When the cigar is out of sight the right hand presses on the end and so causes it to swing up into the right hand (Fig. 7). The left hand is closed as though it contained the cigar, but the cigar is really palmed along the middle finger of the right hand (Fig. 8). The left hand

FIG. 1

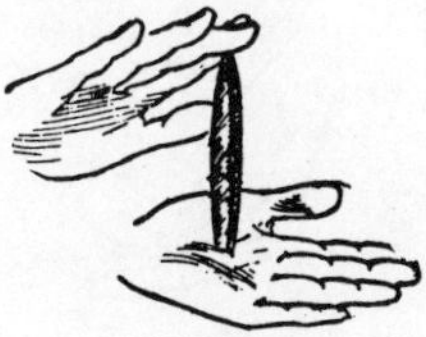

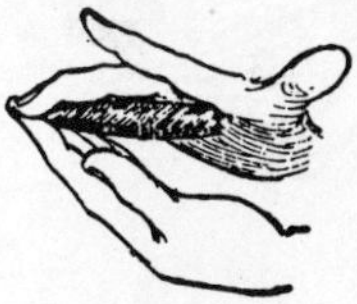

FIG. 2

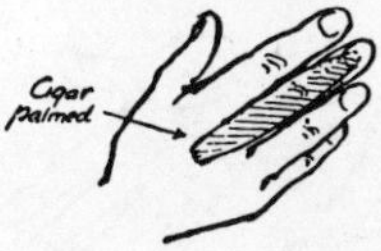

FIG. 3

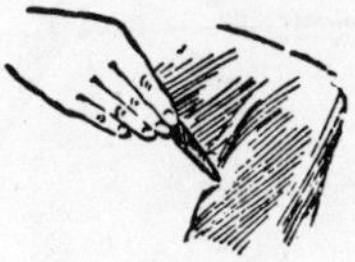

FIG. 4

Fig. 6

Fig. 5

Fig. 7

Fig. 8

Fig. 9

Cigar Manipulation

Fig. 10

Fig. 11

Fig. 13

Fig. 12

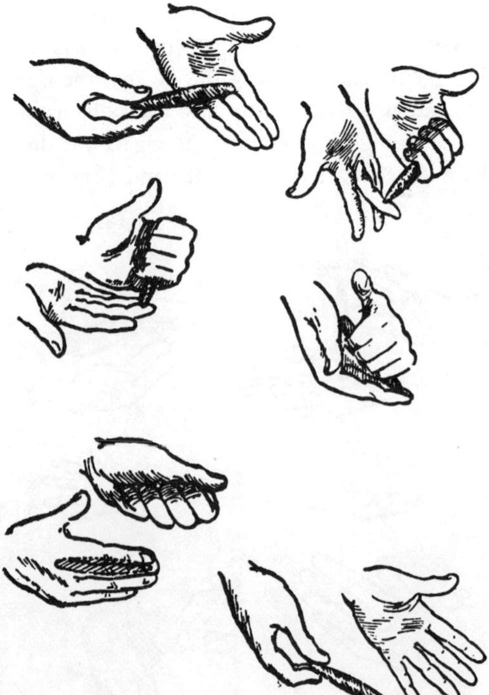

is opened and shown empty and the right hand produces the cigar from the sleeve (Fig. 9).

A cigar placed in the left hand instantly disappears; it is reproduced by the right hand.

Hold the top of the cigar by the thumb and the first finger of the right hand and place it on the palm of the left hand (Fig. 10). Close the left hand and, with the middle finger of the right hand, push the cigar into the left hand; at the same time the left hand is turned over (Figs. 11 and 12). Open the left hand and show that the cigar has vanished; reproduce it with the right hand.

When the cigar is pushed into the closed left hand, that hand is turned over and the cigar is levered out into the right hand (Fig. 13). The back of the left hand is now toward the audience and the cigar is palmed in the right hand, ready for reproduction. *Okito*

CIGARETTE MANIPULATION Both the manipulation and the concealment of unlighted cigarettes differ radically from methods with lighted cigarettes. The success of CARDINI and his followers has made lighted cigarettes the overwhelming favorites. The sleights here described, therefore, are those that can be done with cigarettes lighted or unlighted.

For the same reason, the *cigarette dropper*, a device worn under the vest or coat, which delivers one cigarette after another upon pressure from outside, has gone somewhat out of fashion.

Quite deceptive dummy "lighted" cigarettes are available from magic dealers, and can be effectively combined with real, burning butts in an act.

The *thumb palm* is the one important hold for a cigarette. Fig. 1 shows this perfectly. If the cigarette has been smoked part way down, there is very little danger of the burning tip's touching the inside of fingers or palm.

The *tip-tilt pass*, originally devised for unlighted cigarettes, is easily adapted to a burning one. The cigarette is held near the lighted end between left first and second fingers, with the thumb at the other end. The right hand is cupped to receive the cigarette (Fig. 2). The left hand then turns over to drop the cigarette into the right hand, but actually presses it near the outer end against the right second finger, tilting it back into a position where the left hand can thumb-palm it (Fig. 3). The right hand closes and moves away (Fig. 4).

The *poke-through vanish* simulates the movements used with a THUMB TIP or PULL. The left hand is closed into a loose fist. The right hand pokes the cigarette, lighted end first, through the circle of the left forefinger and thumb. The right thumb pokes the cigarette all the way into the left fist,

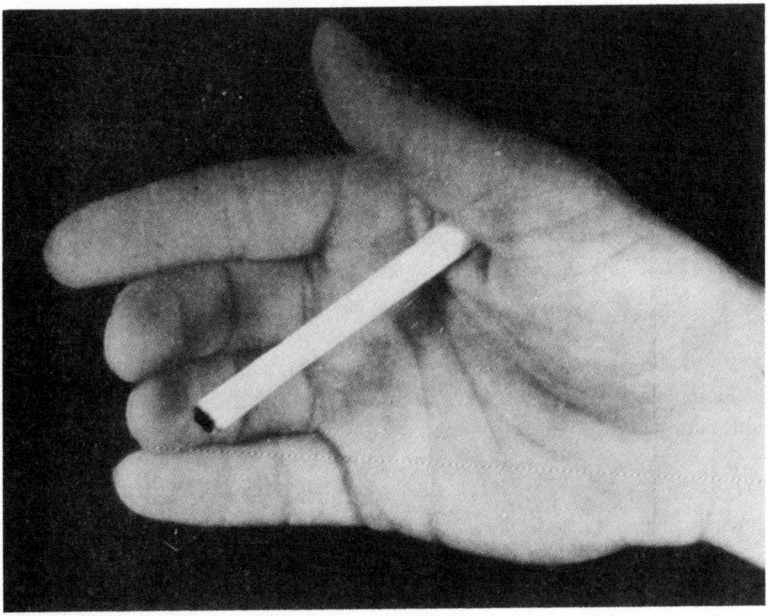

Fig. 1

and the cigarette vanishes. The start of the move is shown in Fig. 5. As the cigarette is pushed further in, the right first and second fingers come forward and conceal it (Fig. 6). The right fingers then carry away the cigarette, and thumb-palm it as the left fist moves away (Fig. 7).

Tonguing a cigarette is a vital maneuver in production routines. The cigarette must be smoked down to about a third of its original length. It can then be caught between the lower lip and the under side of the tongue tip, and tilted upward and backward until it lies inside the mouth, the lighted end to the rear, and the mouth is closed. The tongue is kept slightly hollowed so that it shall not be burned. The use of this move will be obvious: the cigarette may be either "removed," thrown on the floor, and stepped on (actually being tongued), and then reproduced by reversing the tonguing motion, or it may be tongued when the performer exhibits a previously thumb-palmed cigarette stolen from a HOLDER.

A *cigarette pull* is a small metal tube with a flat spring inside, whose pressure holds the cigarette; the closed lower end is attached to a piece of black elastic. The free end of the elastic is fastened up the sleeve or under

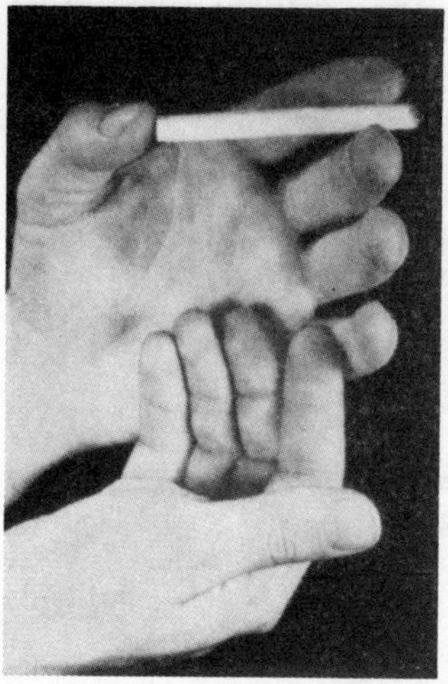

FIG. 2

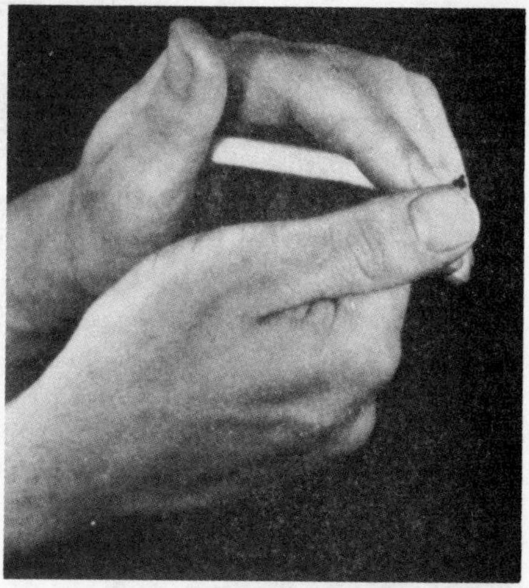

FIG. 3

FIG. 4

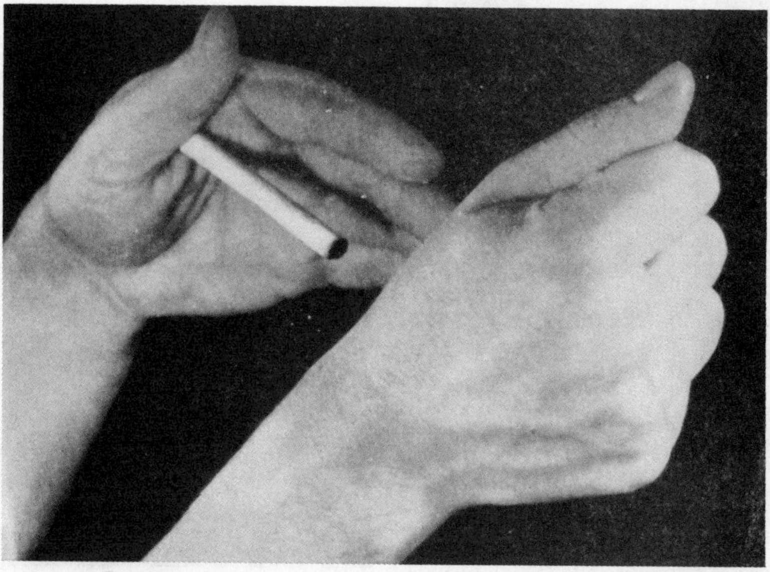

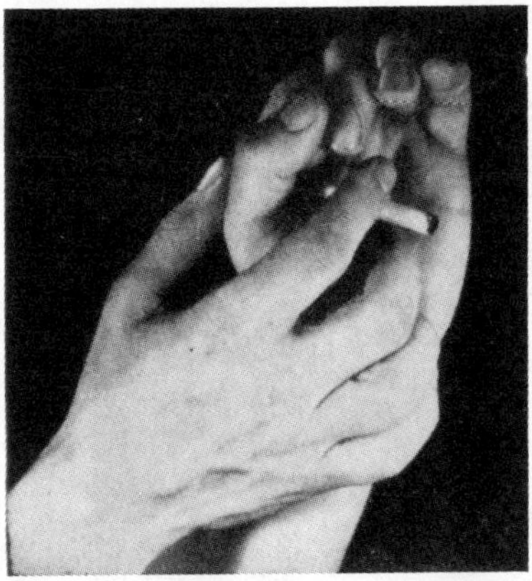

Fig. 6

Fig. 5

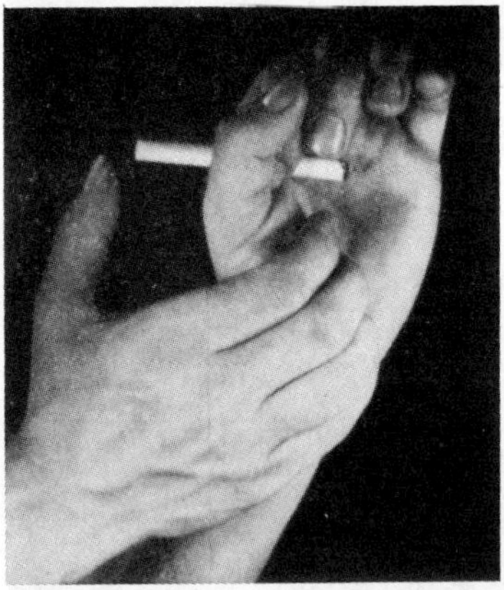

Fig. 7

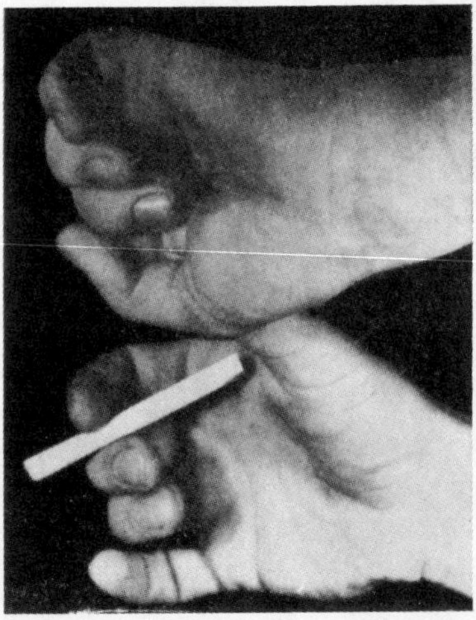

the coat, and the device is used like all other PULLS to vanish a burning cigarette from the fist. *H. H.*

One of the most effective of all the modern tricks is the production of a number of lighted cigarettes. The accompanying illustrations show a method of performing the trick.

Five lighted cigarettes are placed in a perforated metal GIMMICK which is pinned on to the performer's trousers; the fake is covered by the waist-

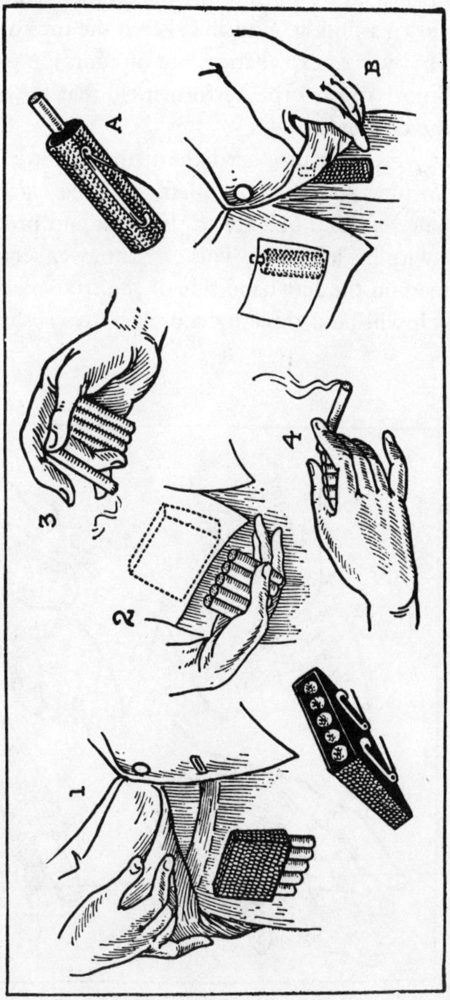

coat, and there is just enough spring in the fake to hold the cigarettes securely. The lighted ends of the cigarettes are at the top. (Fig. 1)

The performer points upward into the air with his left forefinger, as though he could see something there. The eyes of the audience turn in the same direction. The performer turns slightly to the right, and with one movement, shown in Fig. 2, gets all the cigarettes from the tank into his right hand. Fig. 3 shows how they are held there and how each is produced singly; of course, by this time, the performer has turned around to the left, so that the back of the right hand faces the audience. The production is easily managed by putting the middle finger under a cigarette, when it can be shown as in Fig. 4. In this sketch the tops of the other cigarettes are shown by way of explanation, but of course in practice the hand is turned a little more toward the performer, so that the audience do not see the tops of the cigarettes.

When the performer has produced the fifth cigarette, he takes a few puffs and then, turning slightly to the left, puts the cigarette on an ash-tray. He then swings around quickly to the right and produces one more lighted cigarette with his left hand. This cigarette was secretly taken from a small fake pinned on the left-hand side of the trousers (Figs. A and B).

A "tank" which will hold three lighted cigarettes is shown in Fig. 5.

W. G.

FIG. 5

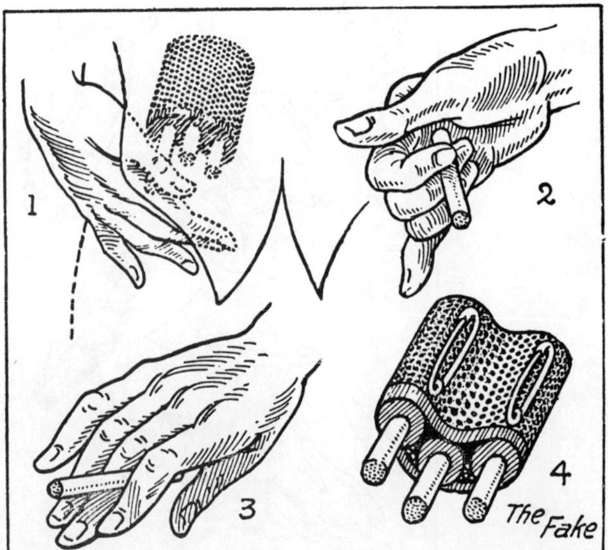

It is more usual among good performers to STEAL cigarettes from holders one at a time, producing them with alternate hands.

Cigarette tricks are treated in Hilliard's *Greater Magic* and Hugard's *Modern Magic Manual*, and a full ROUTINE is given by Keith Clark in *Celebrated Cigarettes*.

CLOCK DIAL The mysterious clock is a trick as old as the obedient-card trick, if not older. The hands will point to a figure, move with rapidity, or as slowly as possible, or in time to music. In fact the performer has full control of the hands—he can make them do his bidding. It is sometimes used for FORCING.

Before electricity was introduced, magnets were employed; but the earliest method was to make use of THREAD wound about the spindle of the clock hand, and because of its simplicity that method is still the best.

The clock has a transparent face, such as you see in any jewelry shop. Some magicians utilize only one hand, which permits the easy use of electricity or magnet, while others employ two and even three hands. When more than one hand is used, the hours and minutes are indicated simultaneously and, if cards are pasted on the clock face, the largest hand is used to find the chosen cards. The clock can be purchased from any reliable dealer of conjuring apparatus.

The clock may be placed on a pedestal, in an upright position, or hung in midair on two ribbons or strings. It can be hung on a stand made for the purpose, or it can be swung in a frame. It is usually placed in the position best suited to the method of working.

When the clock is taken off the hook or the stand on which it is placed, and handed to one of the spectators to hold, the latter places the hand on the pin in the center of the glass face, and revolves it. The arrow or hand is worked by a counterweight, controlled by the performer, who has it fixed before he hands it to the innocent spectator.

For a clock worked by counterweight, the hand of thin brass is prepared in the center, where there is a weight of peculiar shape, which has a small pin at the thin or tapering end. This pin is fixed permanently to the weight and can be revolved about the small plate on which it is riveted. There is a hole in the exact center of this plate. All this is covered with a brass cap. To make the arrow point to any given number, you simply move the weight with your thumb. The pin clicks and allows you to feel it as it moves from one hole to another.

With very little practice you can move this weight, while in the act of handing it to someone to place on the center of the clock face; and when spun, the weight will land on the bottom of its own accord, causing the hand to point where it is forced by the law of gravity. The plate on which the weight is fastened is grooved or milled, so that it answers to the slightest movement of your thumb.

When the clock is on the stage and the hand is moved simply by the command of the performer or audience, it is manipulated by an assistant behind the scenes, either by the aid of electricity or by an endless thread, which is wrapped about the spindle and which runs through the two ribbons or strings that hold the clock in midair. Some conjurers work the clock so as to make a combination trick, first by having it worked by the concealed confederate, then taking the clock off the stand and bringing it down in the midst of the audience. For this trick you can use only one hand.

Houdini

COILS (See also TAMBOURINE) Rolls of paper ribbon for PRODUCTION. According to their size and purpose they are called Mouth, Hat, or TAMBOURINE coils.

COIN BOX, OKITO A shallow, cylindrical metal box big enough to hold a half-dollar not too snugly, with a simple lid that fits over the top. The basis of the trick is that the box is a perfect cylinder, and the cover fits over top or bottom equally well. The box is laid on the open fingers of the left hand, and a coin or coins dropped in. The right hand makes a move to put the cover on the box, but in the process the left fingers close enough to flip the box over, so that the cover goes on the bottom. A sidewise shake rattles the coin against the sides of the box. The turnover movement is repeated as the top is removed to show the box empty. Sometimes a card is slid underneath, and the coin drops through box and card.

The Brema coin box is identical in principle.

COIN-CATCHING (See under MISER'S DREAM)

COIN IN HANDKERCHIEF, or DISSOLVING COIN This familiar trick is the best-known example of the transparency principle in GIMMICKS. A coin, held under a handkerchief by a spectator, and dropped into a glass of water, vanishes when the handkerchief is removed.

The secret is that the performer substitutes for the coin a glass disk, which feels like a coin through the handkerchief, but is invisible in the water as it lies at the bottom of the glass.

To get the best possible effect, the disk should be ground slightly hollow on both sides, creating a suction, and the glass used should have a bottom exactly the size of the disk. The water can then be poured out, and the disk, still invisible, will stick in the glass.

The same principle has been used with a glass half-shell for a billiard-ball, and with a transparent "penetrating thimble" that is passed through a handkerchief.

COIN MANIPULATION *Back Palm.* If the reader desires to excel in this particular sleight, he should first of all select a coin which best suits his fingers. The smaller the coin used, the more difficult it is to carry out the trick successfully. It is therefore advisable to start with a large coin, say a silver dollar, and follow this up gradually with smaller coins until you find one which exactly suits the width of your fingers.

To begin the trick, the coin is placed on the front of the hand, gripped between the tips of the first and fourth fingers (Fig. 1). Now draw down the two middle fingers until the points rest behind the coin at its lower end. If you exert with these two fingers a slight pressure on the lower part of the coin, it revolves between the first and fourth fingers (Fig. 2); next extend carefully the two middle fingers, which stretch out in front of the coin (Fig. 3 gives a back view), now held in the same position as at first, except that it is at the back instead of the front of the hand. The coin is now quite invisible and appears to have vanished.

To cover this movement, which should be executed with lightning-like rapidity, the performer makes a short movement with the hand as if about to throw the coin away. The slight movement facilitates the deception to a great extent. To make the coin reappear, the above movements are simply reversed. This novel movement should be practised by both hands, so that each can perform it with equal freedom and ease. With considerable practice this can be accomplished with more than one coin.

When the coin has been reversed to the back of the hand, as in Fig. 4, the little finger moves away from the coin, which is left gripped between the first and second fingers. Next, the fingers are bent round toward the palm, and with the assistance of the second and third fingers the coin is transferred to the palm of the hand (Fig. 5), thereby allowing the performer to show the back of the hand with all the fingers and thumb extended (Fig. 6).

The coin is picked up with the two middle fingers and replaced between the first and second fingers, being exactly the reverse of the previous move, enabling the front of the hand to be shown. By next placing the third

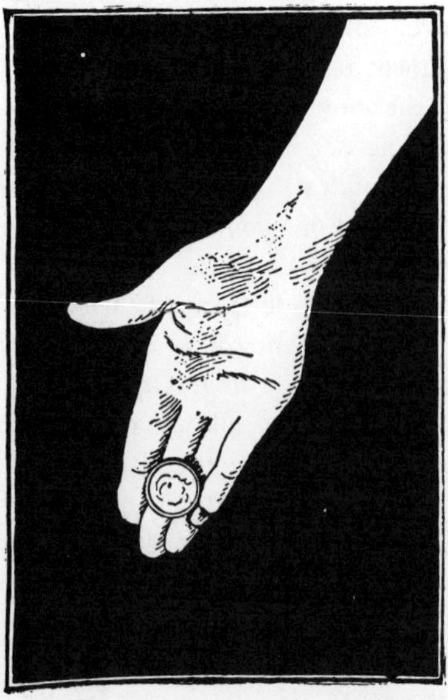

FIG. 1

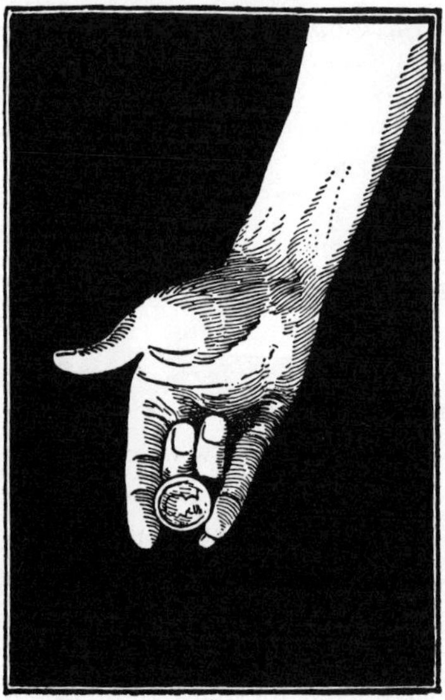

FIG. 2

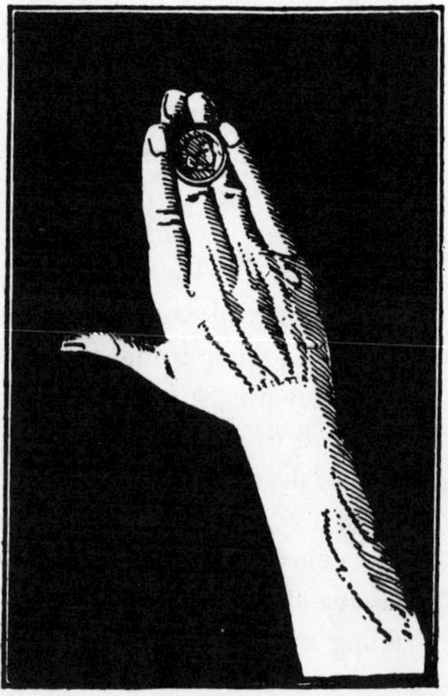

FIG. 3

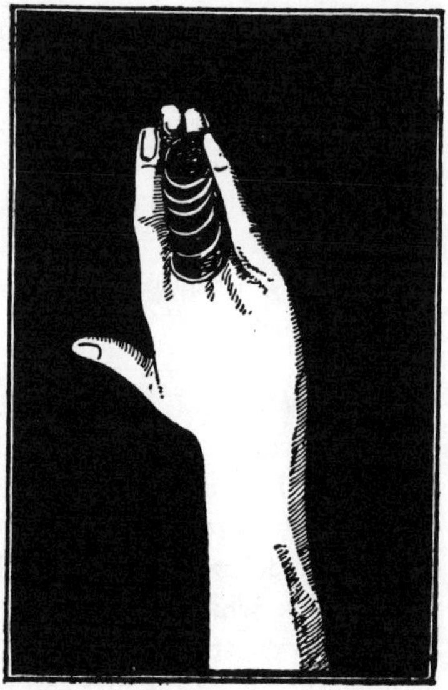

FIG. 4

Fig. 5

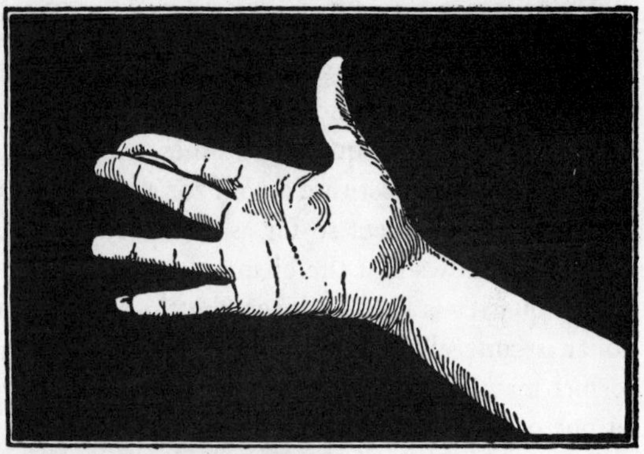

Fig. 6

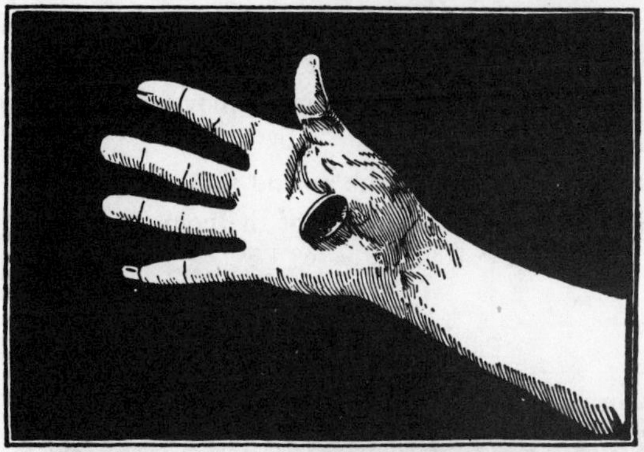

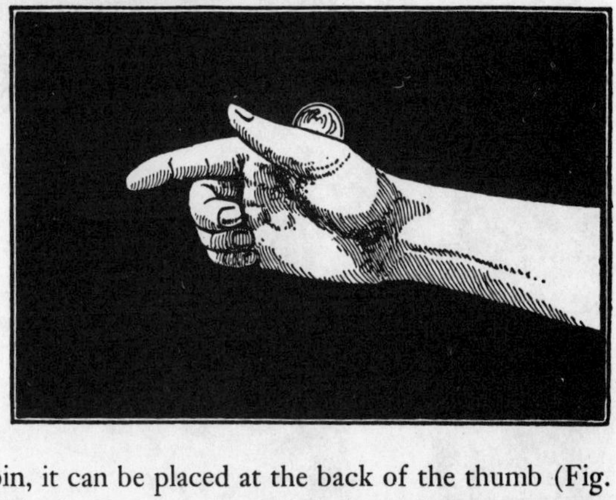

Fig. 7

finger up behind the coin, it can be placed at the back of the thumb (Fig. 7), where it lies gripped in the fleshy part, so that the performer can now show the front of the hand empty, but with the fingers extended. The hand is now closed, the coin being allowed to drop in, and then opened, whereupon the coin is produced. *T. N. D.*

Change. A quarter is shown to the audience, and held in their sight between the first finger and thumb. The hand makes a slight upward movement, whereupon the quarter vanishes, and in its place is seen a silver dollar.

When used to substitute a coin for a borrowed one in the course of any trick there is no effect so far as the spectators are concerned, as only the performer knows that the change has been made.

The quarter is held between the tip of the first finger and thumb; the dollar is concealed in the bend of the second and third fingers. The performer may borrow the quarter; if he used his own he should take care to let one or two people handle it, to show that it is not a trick coin.

This done, the hand is held so that the audience can see that it is actually empty. Attention should not be called to this beyond the statement, "This is an ordinary quarter, which I shall change into a coin of another value." The hand is then given a slight upward or sideways movement, during which the change is made as follows:

With the thumb press the quarter on to the second finger, at the same moment withdrawing the first finger to the edge of the coin (Fig. 1).

FIG. 1

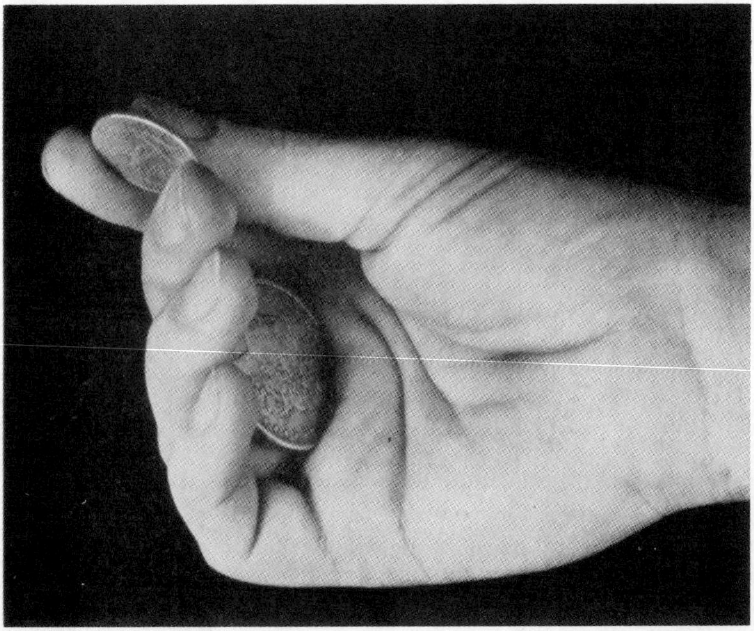

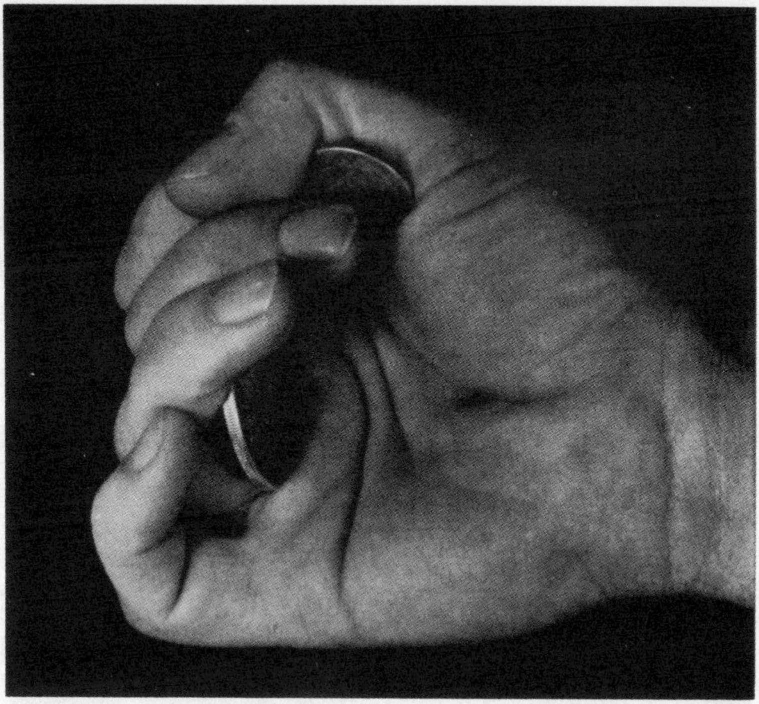

FIG. 2, Above Below, FIG. 3

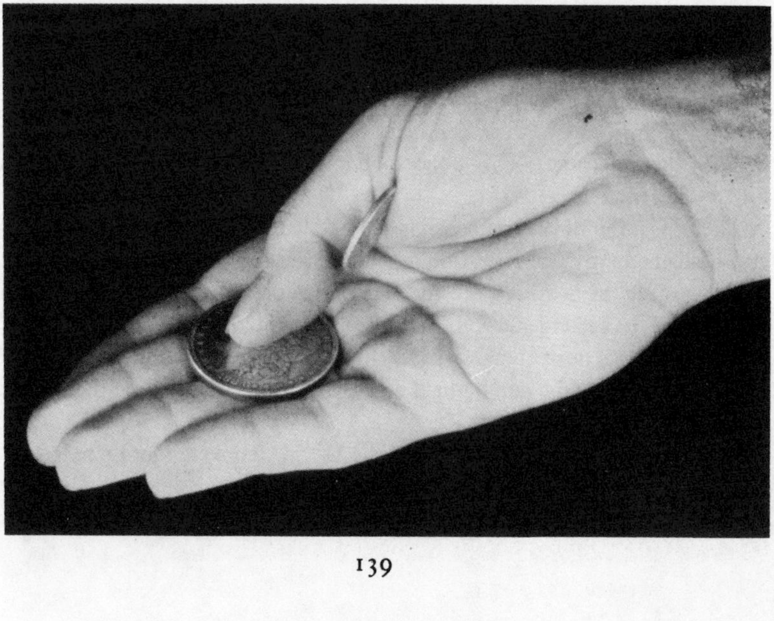

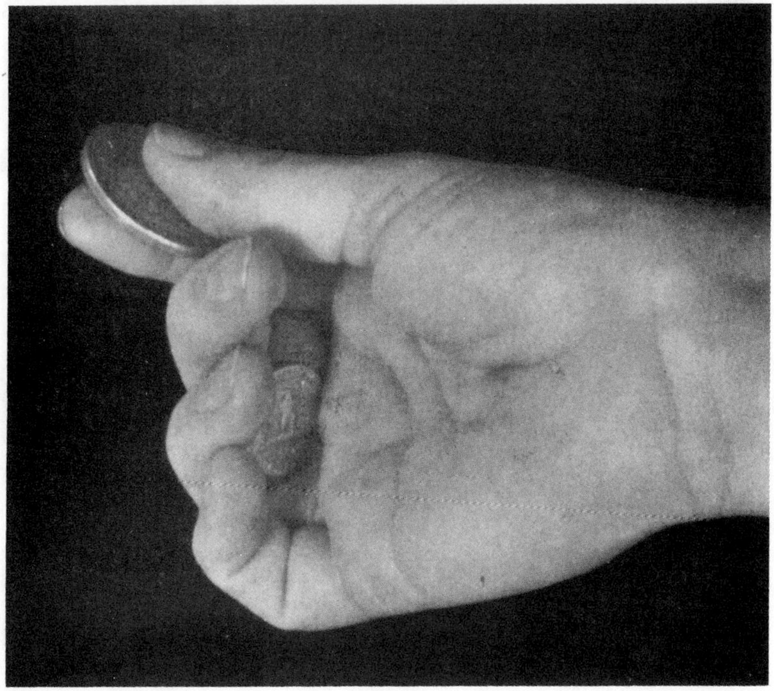

FIG. 4

Now the first finger slides the quarter to the root of the thumb, where it is gripped between this and the first joint (Fig. 2).

Next slightly extend the second and third fingers, thereby releasing their grip on the dollar; at the same moment lower the thumb until its tip rests on the dollar (Fig. 3).

Then the point of the thumb presses the dollar to the tip of the first finger and holds it there. The act of doing this causes the quarter to be released, whereupon it turns over on to its edge and slides into the place, between the bend of the second and third fingers, just vacated by the dollar (Fig. 4).

The change is now complete, and the dollar is exhibited in place of the quarter. This should again be held so that the audience can see the empty palm.

These movements, if practised, will be found to dovetail into one instantaneous motion. *C. L. N.*

FIG. 1

Fold, Handkerchief: First Method. Holding the coin upright between the fingers and thumb of the left hand, throw the handkerchief fairly over it. Having shown that it is covered, remark, "Perhaps you think I have changed the coin, but I have not."

With the right hand palm upward, take the coin through the handkerchief (as shown in Fig. 1), between the first and second fingers of that hand. For a moment let go with the left hand (but without removing it from under the handkerchief). Turn over the right hand toward yourself, and again seize the coin with the left hand; but this time nip the opposite edge of the coin to that which it first held, through the double thickness of the handkerchief.

Remove the right hand from the coin; with it raise the outer edge of the handkerchief and show the coin, as in Fig. 2. Then let both edges of the handkerchief fall. Apparently the coin is underneath, and in the center of the handkerchief; actually, it is outside, lying in a slight fold on the side away from the spectators.

Second Method. Spread the handkerchief over your left hand and count four coins one by one upon it; then giving a glance around at the company, you say, "You have all seen that the four coins are wrapped in the handkerchief," or make any other remark in order to draw the general attention as a sharp, quick remark almost always will, to your face and away from your hands.

At the same moment you move the left thumb over the face of the coins, thereby covering them with a fold of the handkerchief, and seize them, through the fold thus made, between the thumb and fingers of the right hand (Fig. 3), immediately withdrawing the left hand. The coins will now be held in the right hand, the handkerchief hanging down loosely around them. To anyone who has not watched your movements with more than ordinary vigilance, it will appear that the coins are within and under the handkerchief, although actually they are wrapped in an external fold.

L. H.

FIG. 2

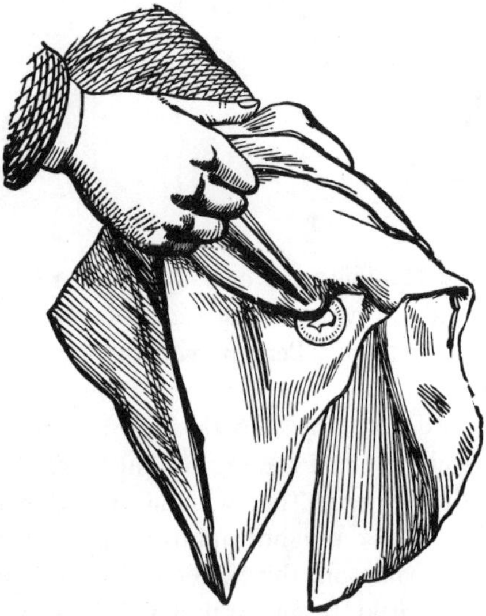

FIG. 3

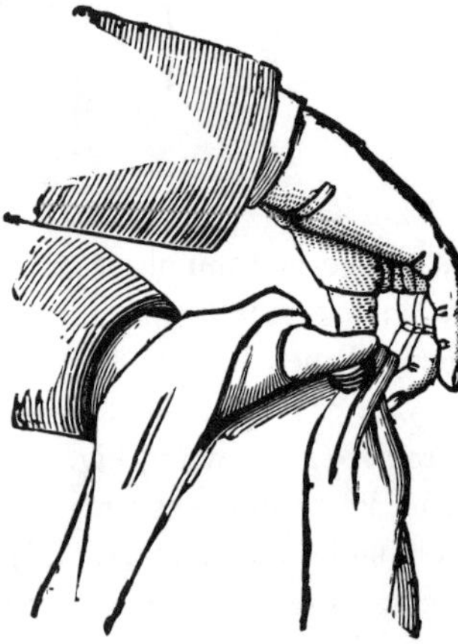

Fold, Paper: First Method. Wrap up a coin carefully in an ordinary piece of paper. The coin is obviously there; it rings when you bang it on the table; its shape is visible through the paper. And then you touch a match to the paper, which burns to a crisp. The coin is gone.

The trick is in how you wrap the coin. If you follow directions with a piece of paper in your hands, you should have no difficulty in understanding the method.

You want a piece of tolerably stiff paper (letterhead paper is fine) about six inches square; this you fold in two, but not in equal halves; one part should be about an inch wider (measured from crease to edge) than the other. The wider part we will call A, the narrower, B.

Put the coin in the fold, approximately at the middle.

Now the natural way to fold would be over upon B. But that is the trick; you fold the paper approximately in thirds, the coin being enclosed in the middle third, by turning the open ends of your first fold *back upon* A.

This leaves the extra inch of A sticking up, as it were, from within a surrounding sheath of B. Now if you were to turn this inch over on B, the coin would still be shut in on all four sides.

But again you turn it back on A, and thus the coin is enclosed on only three sides. When you tip the package open-side down, the coin will slide out into your hand.

Before you do this, you should press the paper around the coin, so that the visible impression remains; then take the packet by the open side in your right hand, and bang it on the table, to convince people by the sound that the coin is still there. Now take the packet by the opposite side with your left hand, letting the coin slide quietly out into your right. Reaching into your pocket for a match to light the paper, you leave the coin behind.

B. M.

Second Method. The paper should be square, moderately stiff, and about four times the diameter of the coin each way. Place the coin in the center, and fold down each side over it, showing at each stage that the coin is still there. Two sides having been folded, take the paper and coin upright in the right hand. Fold over the upper end, at the same time allowing the coin to slide down into the lower. Fold this latter over with the coin in it, and give the whole thing to someone to hold. The paper still contains the coin, but instead of being in the middle, as the spectators suppose, it is really in the outer fold, where you can let it slide out into your hand at pleasure.

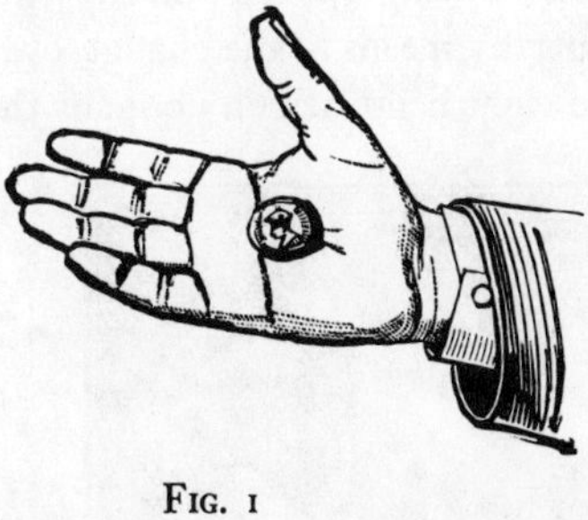

FIG. 1

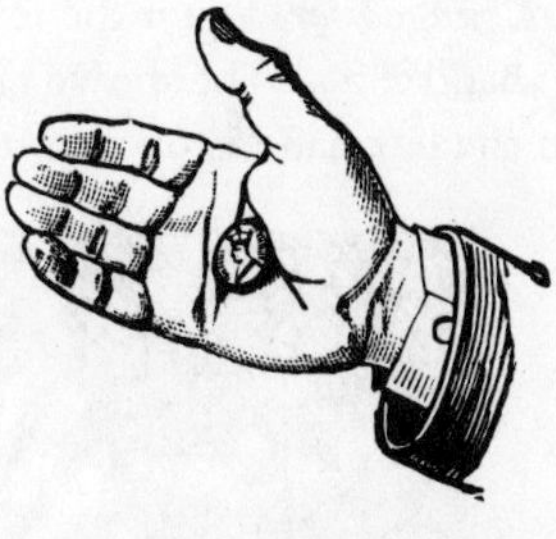

FIG. 2

Palm. The first faculty which the novice must seek to acquire is that of palming—that is, secretly holding an object in the open hand by the contraction of the palm. To acquire this power, take a half-dollar, and lay it on the palm of the open hand. (Fig. 1) Now close the hand very slightly, and if you have placed the coin on the right spot (which a few trials will quickly indicate), the contraction of the palm around its edges will hold it securely (Fig. 2), and you may move the hand and arm in any direction without fear of dropping it.

You should next accustom yourself to using the hand and fingers easily and naturally, while still holding the coin as described. A very little practice will enable you to do do this. You must bear in mind while practicing always to keep the inside of the palm either downward or toward your own body, as any reverse movement would expose the concealed coin. When you are able to hold the coin comfortably in the right hand, practice in like manner with the left, after which you may substitute for the coin a watch, an egg, or a small lemon—all these being articles of frequent use in conjuring. *L. H.*

Palm, Edge. This method of palming, introduced by NELSON DOWNS, revolutionized coin manipulation. It is exactly like the regular or flat palm except that the coin stands out from the palm at about the same angle that the thumb makes with the hand; that is, it lies in the plane of the thumb. (See *Back-Palm*, Fig. 6) It is the only way of palming or reproducing coins noiselessly one at a time, and the only possible method for the CHANGE-OVER PALM. The coins are added or withdrawn at the bottom of the stack—the side away from the palm. The third finger slides the coin, while the second either clips it or steadies the upper edge, as the momentary need may be.

Palm, Changeover. Upon the left hand being opened and shown empty, the right hand can also be shown empty by means of the change-over palm.

When the left hand is opened, the right hand, which contains the coins

FIG. 1

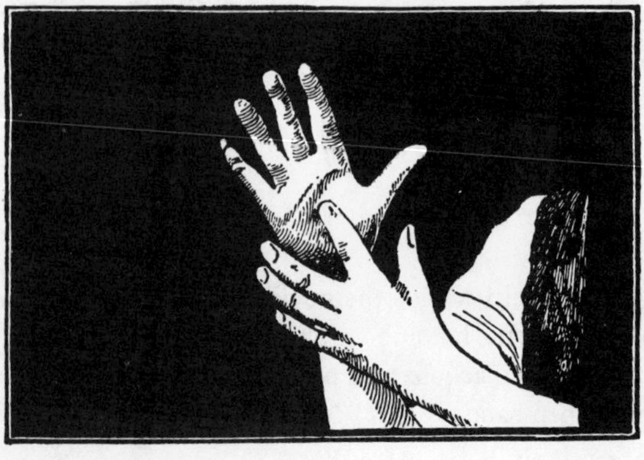

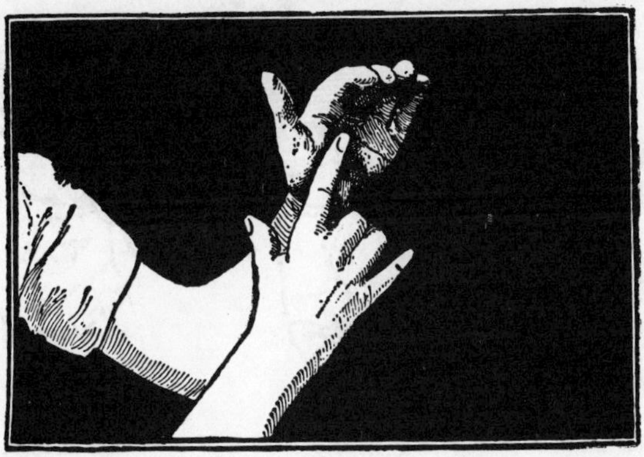

FIG. 2

palmed, is brought face to face with the left one, and the coins transferred to the palm of the left hand, which is immediately turned round (under cover of the right) to show (apparently) that there is nothing at the back, and then the right hand can be shown empty back and front (Fig. 1). The left hand is next turned around under cover of the right hand, and the coins re-palmed in the right (Fig. 2).

This is an exceedingly difficult sleight, and requires a considerable amount of delicacy in manipulating. It is very desirable to have the coins all of the same size and thickness, otherwise one or more may slide out from the rest in the act of transference. T. N. D.

Palm, Finger. Take the coin in the open right hand, letting it lie across the lower joints of the second and third fingers. Make the motion of transferring the coin to the left hand, but as the right hand turns over in transit, slightly bend the two fingers above mentioned, a very trifling contraction serving to hold the coin. The fore- and little fingers should remain extended, though not too stiffly. This position of the hand seems so easy and careless that not one person in a hundred will suspect that the coin remains in the hand.

Palm, Thumb. Take the coin by the edge between the first and third fingers of the right hand, the sides of those fingers pressing against the edges of the coin, and the middle finger steadying it from behind (Fig. 1). Carry the right hand toward the left, and at the same time move the thumb swiftly over the face of the coin until the top joint just passes its outer edge (Fig. 2); then bend the thumb, and the coin will be found to be securely nipped between that joint and the junction of the thumb with the hand (Fig. 3).

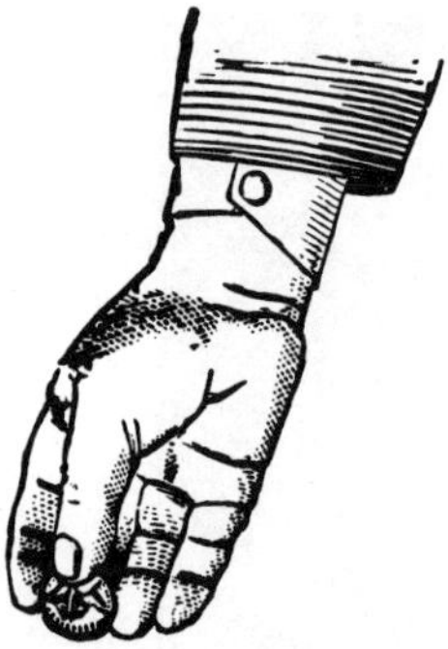

FIG. 1

FIG. 2

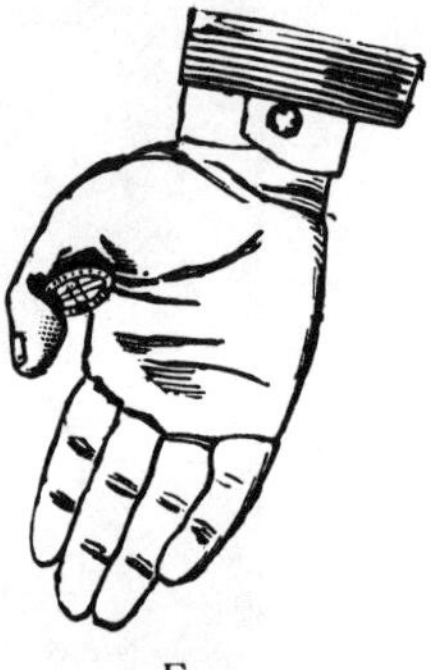

FIG. 3

As in the last case, the left hand must be closed the moment the right hand touches it; and the right must then be held with the thumb bent slightly inward toward the palm, so that the coin may be shielded from the view of the spectators. This is an especially quick method of palming, and if properly executed the illusion is perfect. *L. H.*

FIG. 1

FIG. 2

Palm, Thumb, Edge. The hand is shown empty, back and front, the fingers wide apart, and yet a dozen or more coins are produced, one at a time, or in a fan, at the fingertips.

At the outset a dozen coins are edge-palmed. The hand holding the coins—the right hand—is lowered, the stack is dropped to the third joints of the fingers, when it is crotched between the thumb and first finger, as shown in Fig. 1. (Of course the hand is not held so that the coins are visible, as depicted in the illustration, which shows the exact method of holding the coins.) In the actual presentation of the trick, the hand is held as in Fig. 2, the palm toward the audience. The hand may now be shown back and front and the fingers separated, without any risk of exposing the coins.

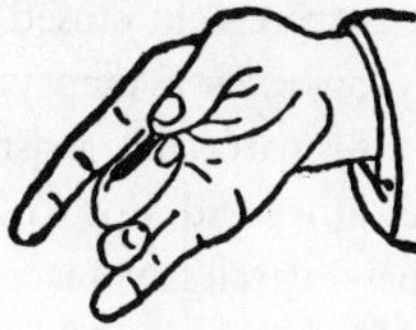

FIG. 3

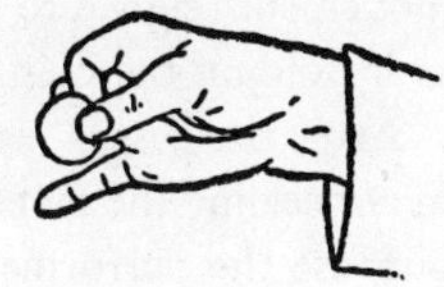

FIG. 4

To produce the coins, one at a time, at the fingertips, the bottom coin is slipped out by the second finger (Fig. 3), and is caught by the tips of the first finger and thumb (Fig. 4).

T. N. D.

Pass. Being thoroughly master of simple PALMING, you may proceed to the study of the various passes. All passes have the same object: the apparent transfer of an article from one hand to the other, though the article really remains in the hand which it has apparently just left. As the same movement frequently repeated would cause suspicion, and possibly detection, it is desirable to acquire different ways of effecting this object.

Take the coin in the right hand, between the second and third fingers and the thumb (Fig. 5), letting it really be supported by the fingers and only steadied by the thumb. Now move the thumb out of the way, and close the second and third fingers, with the coin balanced on them, into the palm. (Fig. 6) If the coin was placed right in the first instance, you will find that this motion puts it precisely in the position above described as the proper one for palming; and on again extending the fingers, the coin is left palmed.

When you can do this easily with the hand at rest, you must practice doing the same thing with the right hand in motion toward the left, which should meet it open, but should close the moment that the fingers of the right hand touch its palm, as though upon the coin, which you have by this

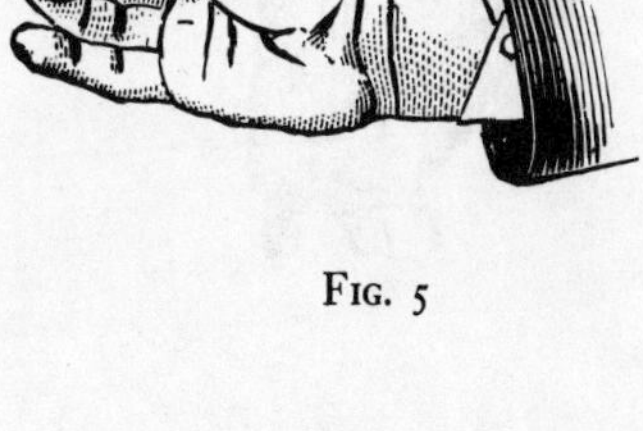

FIG. 5

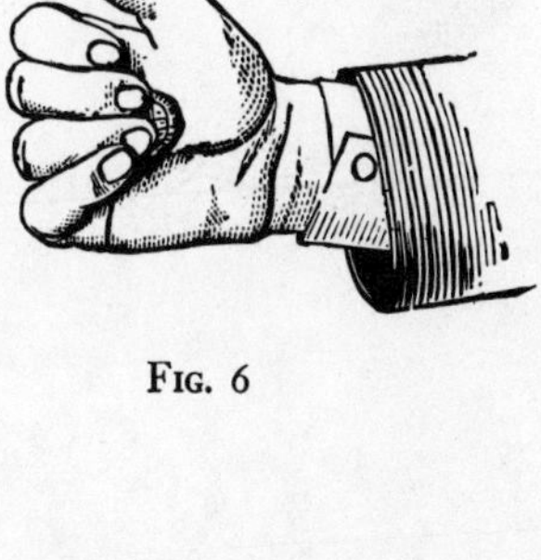

FIG. 6

movement feigned to transfer to it. The left hand must then remain closed, as if holding the coin, and the right hand hang loosely open, as if empty.

After the pass is made, a judicious use of the wand will materially assist in concealing the fact that the object still remains in the right hand. For this purpose the performer should, before beginning the pass, carelessly place the wand under either arm, as though merely to leave his hands free. Immediately after the pass is made the right hand should, with a sort of back-handed movement, which under the circumstances is perfectly natural, grasp the wand, draw it from under the arm, and thenceforth retain it until an opportunity occurs of disposing of the coin as may be necessary. The position of the fingers in the act of holding the wand is such as to mask the concealed coin effectively, while the hand appears perfectly easy and natural. The same expedient may be employed with equal advantage in the remaining passes.

In another modification of the pass, the coin is held as in Fig. 7, between the thumb and first and second fingers of the left hand. You then make the movement of taking it between the same fingers of the other hand, which for that purpose makes a kind of "swoop" down upon it, the back of the hand being kept toward the spectators. At the moment when the coin is covered by the fingers of the right hand, it is allowed to slip gently down into the palm of the left, and the right is instantly elevated as if containing it. *L. H.*

FIG. 7

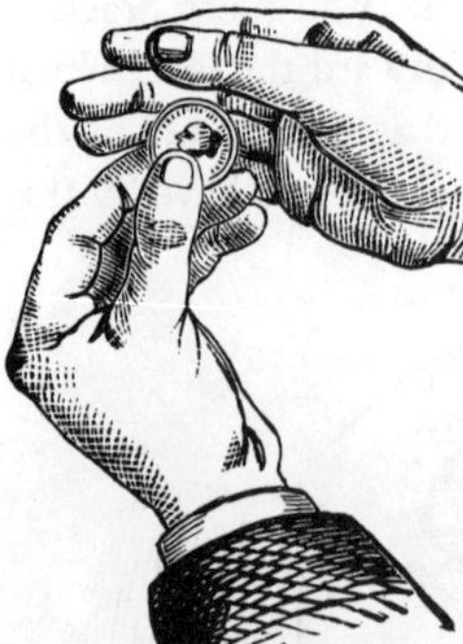

FIG. 8

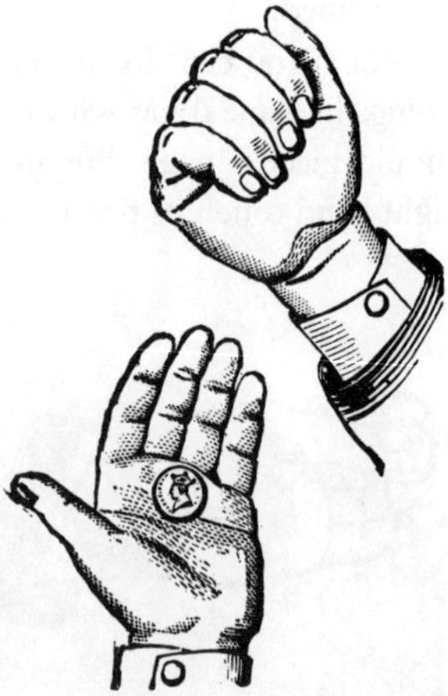

Pass, Click. The trick here described relies entirely on the above-named pass. Once acquired, it becomes most useful, and one of the most puzzling and deceptive sleights extant.

The method of performing it is as follows: Ten coins are borrowed and placed unmistakably in the left hand. Everyone is satisfied that the coins are really in the left hand, because they are heard to fall into it. The right hand now picks up an ordinary empty glass tumbler and the hands are held wide apart. The coins are commanded to pass *one at a time* from the closed left hand into the glass held in the right, which they proceed to do; each coin is distinctly seen and heard to fall into the tumbler.

After about eight coins have passed, the performer pretends to hear someone say that there are no coins in the left hand. He immediately opens the left hand and shows the two remaining coins. The hand is closed, and the two that are left pass singly into the glass held in the right, in the same manner as their predecessors.

To produce the above illusion it is necessary to study the illustrations. The coins are first placed in the right hand, as in Fig. 1, and the hand is then quickly turned over, the coins being apparently transferred to the left hand; actually the third and fourth fingers of the right hand arrest their fall (Fig. 2), (thereby creating a sound or *click* as if the coins had fallen into the left hand), and forthwith PALM them in the right hand. If the foregoing is tried once or twice it will be seen what a perfect illusion it produces. Now with the right hand (containing the palmed coins) pick up the tumbler. By slightly relaxing the muscles of the palm of the right hand, the coins are released one at a time and fall into the glass (Fig. 3).

A considerable amount of practice and delicacy of manipulation is essential to ensure the coins' dropping singly. The additional effect of being able to show two coins in the left hand, after eight have passed into the tumbler, is brought about by FINGER-PALMING in the left hand two dummy coins pivoted together, which can be spread apart to look like two coins. These are shown, and in the act of again closing the left hand, they are reverse-palmed, the fact that they are riveted together enabling this to be accomplished with ease.

Pass, Fan. The coins are held as in Fig. 1. The right fingers now allow the coins to slide down one after another with a jingle into the palm of the left hand, which forthwith closes up on them; but just as it does so the two middle fingers of the right hand grip the coins and immediately PALM them in the right hand. If this is carried out neatly, and under cover

CLICK PASS

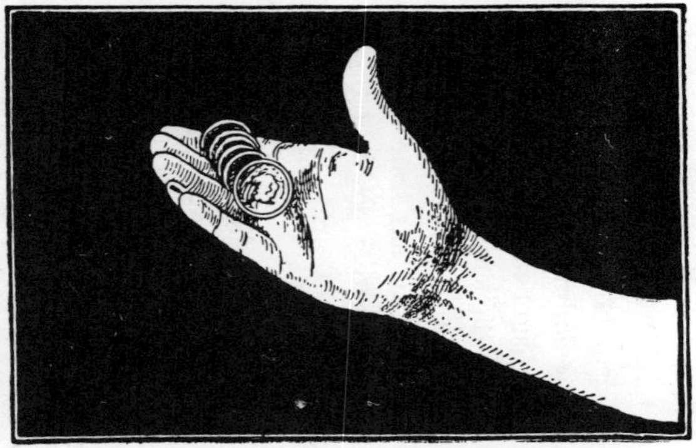

FIG. 1

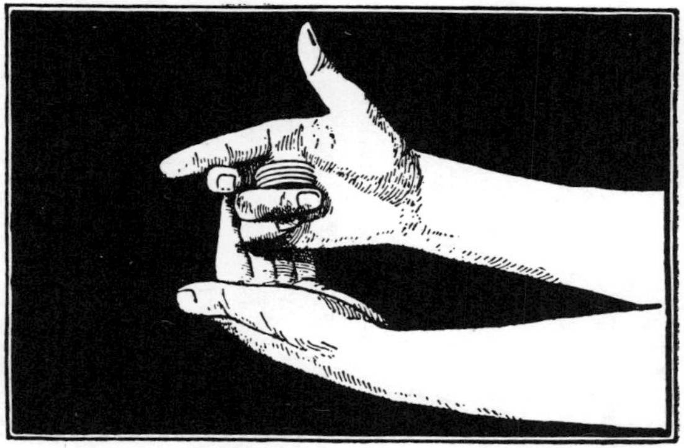

FIG. 2

(RIGHT) FAN PASS

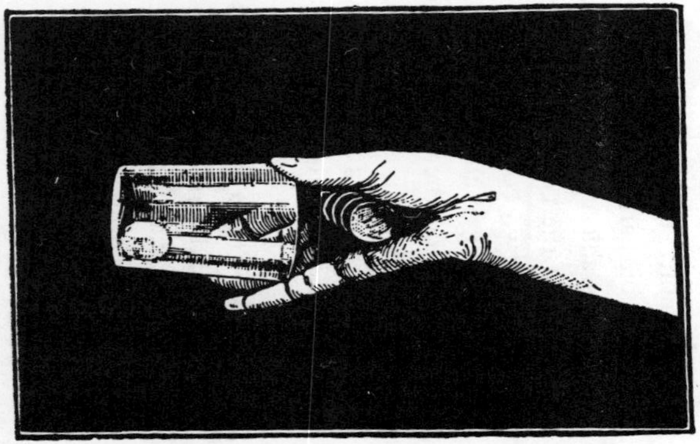

FIG. 3

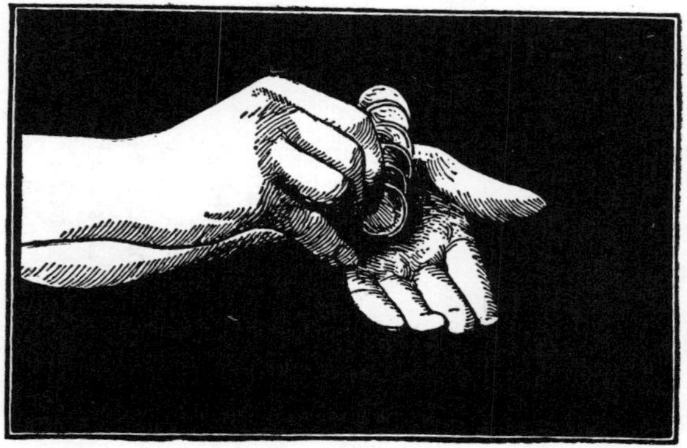

FIG. 1

of the movement of the left hand, the spectators will be absolutely convinced that the coins still remain in the left hand.

The foregoing is a very useful method of causing the disappearance of a number of coins after having produced them in a "fan."

Pass, Tourniquet. See *Tourniquet.*

FIG. 1

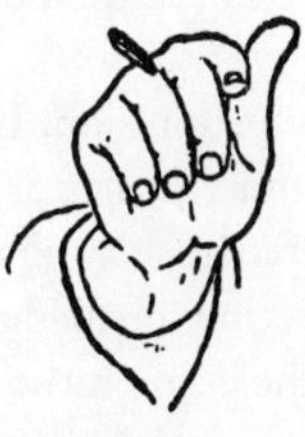

FIG. 2

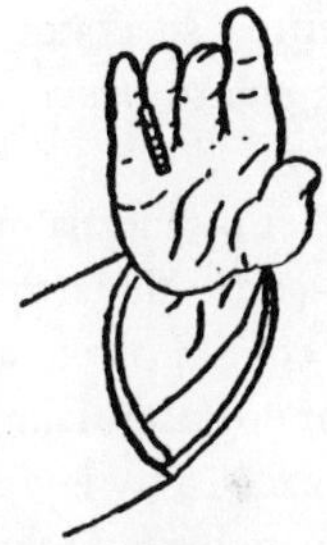

FIG. 3

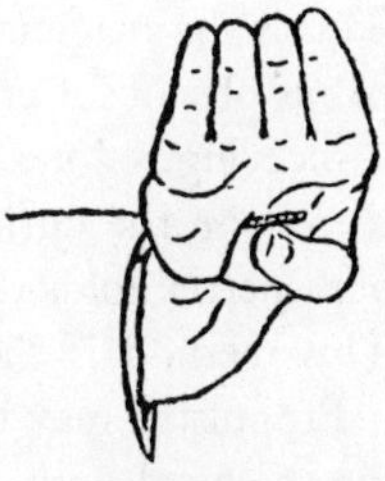

FIG. 4

Roll. This effective and difficult flourish will be appreciated by the reader who makes a specialty of coin manipulation. In effect a coin rolls or travels around the hand, from finger to finger. At the outset the coin is held between the thumb and the first finger near the base, as shown in Fig. 1. The coin is now allowed to fall over the top of the first finger and its opposite edge is caught between the first and second fingers at their roots; then it falls over the second finger and is caught between the second and third fingers. (Fig. 2)

Next the coin rolls over the third finger and is caught between the third and fourth fingers, and then allowed to slide down between the third and fourth fingers until it hangs underneath the fingers (Fig. 3).

For the sake of clearly illustrating the movement the coin is depicted hanging between the third and little fingers. In actual practice, however, the tip of the thumb keeps the coin from falling to the floor. The coin is then carried by the thumb, underneath the hand (Fig. 4), back to its original position, and the rolling movement over the top of the fingers is repeated.

At first these different movements will be slow and awkward, but as the student attains proficiency the coin will roll over the fingers rapidly and without a cessation of movement.

The manipulation is beautiful and effective, and is well worth the time spent in acquiring it. The illustrations show the fingers of the right hand manipulating the coin, but the left hand may be used if it comes more naturally to the student. A few performers are skilful enough to execute this flourish with both hands simultaneously, and the two coins rolling in opposite directions has an effect that must be seen to be appreciated.

T. N. D.

Sleeving. With a coin PALMED, the performer may find himself challenged by a sharp-witted spectator who says, "It's in the other hand." This is the magician's cue to *sleeve* the coin, and step forward with both palms obviously empty.

Sleeving is done either by inertia or by propulsion. If the coin is allowed to rest on the curled-under fingertips, and the arm is suddenly stretched out, inertia holds the coin in place, where the advancing sleeve catches it. This method is the more useful in meeting challenges.

Propulsion may be exerted by laying the coin on the fingertips, and closing the hand with a snap; by holding the coin between thumb and second finger, and actually snapping it up the sleeve; by putting the coin near the edge of the table, and pretending to pick it up, actually zipping it up the sleeve with a flick of the second finger; and, perhaps neatest of all, by holding the coin horizontally by opposite edges between the right thumb and forefinger, and pretending to take it in the left hand. As the left hand closes, the right thumb and forefinger suddenly press together, and squirt the coin up the *left* sleeve.

Proper sleeving is ANGLE-PROOF, which makes it a necessary accomplishment for the performer of TABLE TRICKS and for the NIGHT-CLUB table magician. *H. H.*

The performer spins a coin in the air and catches it in his right hand. He opens his hand and shows both sides of it quickly, with the fingers wide apart; the coin has vanished.

This is an easy sleight to do, but a difficult one to do well. After the performer has spun the coin into the air (Figs. 1 and 2), he turns his hands with the fingers pointing upward; as the coin falls apparently into the hand the fingers close over it (Fig. 3), but really permit it to drop down the sleeve. (Fig. 5) The hand can then be shown empty (Fig. 4). The learner must remember to keep the back of his hands toward the audience, and he must time the closing of the hand nicely. When this sleight is performed well it is very effective; it requires a good deal of practice. *Okito*

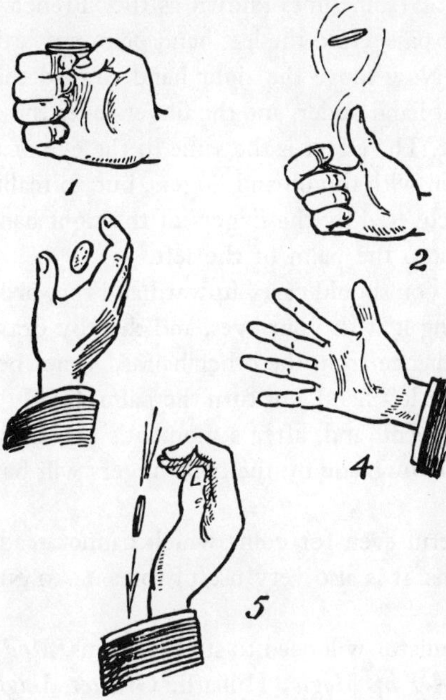

SLEEVE VANISH

THE TOURNIQUET

(see following page)

FIG. 2

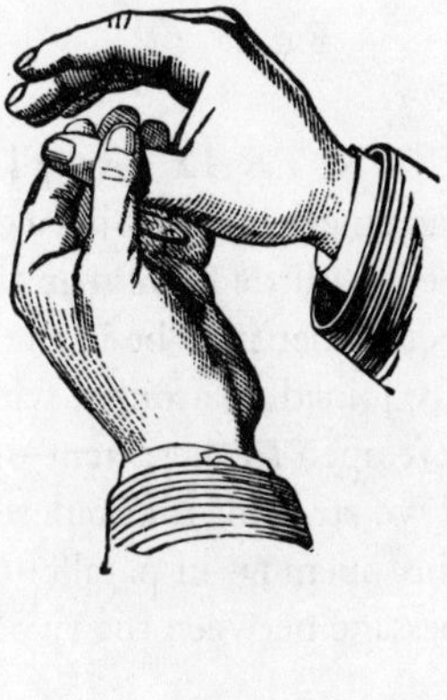

FIG. 1

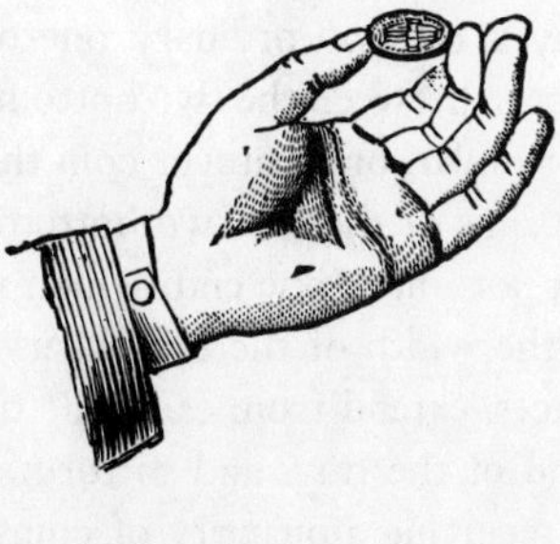

Tourniquet. This (sometimes known as the "French drop") is an easy yet most effective pass. Hold the left hand palm upward, with the coin as shown in Fig. 1. Now move the right hand toward the left, passing the thumb of the right hand under, and the fingers over the coin, closing them just as they pass it. The effect is the same to the eye of the spectator as if you seized the coin with thumb and fingers, but, in reality, at the moment when the coin is covered by the fingers of the right hand, you let it drop quietly (Fig. 2) into the palm of the left.

The right hand you should carry upward and forward after it leaves the left hand, following it with your eyes, and thereby drawing away the attention of the audience from the other hand. Do not be in any too great a hurry to drop the left hand, but turn the palm slightly toward you, with the fingers a little bent, and, after a moment's pause, let it fall gently to your side. The hollow made by the bent fingers will be sufficient to hold the coin.

This pass is useful even for coins which cannot readily be palmed by the ordinary means. It is also very useful for BALL MANIPULATION.

L. H.

The coin manipulator will need to study Downs, *Modern Coin Manipulation*, and *The Art of Magic*; Hilliard, *Greater Magic*; Hugard, *Coin Magic*; and Joseph, *Coin and Money Magic*.

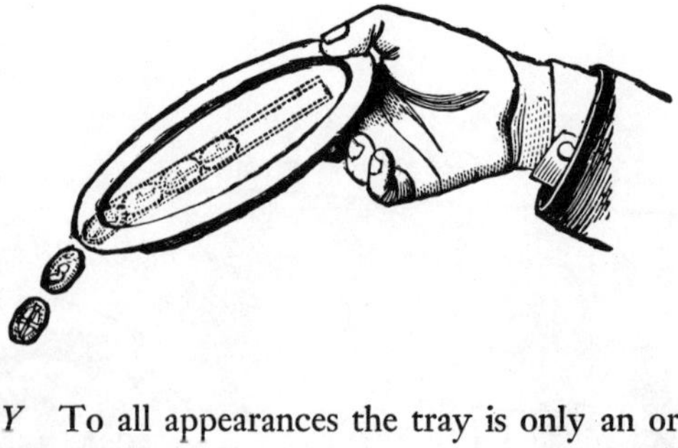

FIG. 1

COIN TRAY To all appearances the tray is only an ordinary one of japanned tin, but it has a double bottom, the space between the two bottoms being a little more than the thickness of a half-dollar, or whatever coin the performer may be in the habit of using. The rims of the the two bottoms are joined all around, with the exception of a portion at one end, which is left open to the extent of a little more than the width of the coin in use. Two strips of tin, soldered firmly in their places, extend from each side of this opening, in parallel lines, to the other end of the tray, and so form a passage between the two bottoms capable of receiving a quantity of coins, ranging in number according to the length of the tray or the will of the performer.

When the tray is tilted to any extent, the open end being the one that is depressed, the coins will naturally slide out one after another. (Fig. 1) If the space between the double bottoms is too deep, the rearmost coins will overlap those in front, and so cause an obstruction.

The tray is loaded with (say) five coins, and so brought on. About fifteen coins are then taken from the hat and placed on the tray, which is put into the hands of a spectator, who must be asked to rise for the purpose, and to keep very steady so as not to upset the coins. A boy's cap is then borrowed, and put into the hands of another spectator, who is placed close to and facing the holder of the tray. In the absence of a cap, a handkerchief held in the form of a bag will answer as well, if care is taken to arrange it so that none of the coins can escape and fall to the ground.

The performer retires to the stage and explains that, when he counts "three," the holder of the tray is to pour, as rapidly as he can, the fifteen coins into the cap, the holder of which is directed to close the cap the moment this is done. As the performer has taken care to place the tray in the assistant's hands with the opening away from him, it follows that, when the fifteen coins are poured from its surface into the cap, the five from the concealed receptacle will accompany them. A very distinct mark should be made on the tray so that the performer can readily distinguish one end from the other.

When the cap is closed, the performer counts five more coins into his hand, and "passes" them into the cap, the holder of which is then requested to count out the coins upon the plate, to prove that the number has been increased by five. All counting of coins should take place both before and afterward, or the audience may fail to perceive what has been done.

The trays sold at conjuring shops are nearly always round. This is a bad shape, as there is nothing to induce the holder of the tray to tilt it as the performer desires. When it is oval, it is only natural to pour the coins off the narrow end. It is also impossible to notice from any distance whether a round tray has been shifted, accidentally or otherwise. A couple of inches' difference will cause the trick to fail, for the coins will not pour out.

E. T. S.

COIN TRICKS (See under: BALL OF WOOL; COIN BOX, OKITO; COIN IN HANDKERCHIEF; COIN MANIPULATION; COIN TRAY; COINS, FOLDING; COINS, SHELL; DIVINATIONS; DROPPERS; HOLDERS; HOOKS; MISER'S DREAM; NEST OF BOXES; SPIDER; SYMPATHETIC COINS; TUMBLERS; WANDS.)

COINS, FOLDING The coin, say a penny, is placed on a lathe, and a deep groove cut all around its outer edge. This done, the coin is cut into three parts, of equal width. The three parts are now joined together again by means of a tiny india-rubber ring, inserted into the groove, and so encircling the coin. (The diameter of the india-rubber ring before extension should be about one-third that of the coin. If larger, the parts of the coin will not be drawn taut. The india-rubber ring will require frequent renewal.)

The coin thus reconstructed will fold into one-third of its diameter, and in its folded condition may be passed into a narrow-necked bottle, but again expands and resumes its shape the moment it has passed the neck. If well made, the cuts in the coin are scarcely perceptible, and if the bottle is shaken a little as it is passed before the eyes of the audience, there is little fear of their detecting that the penny is not an ordinary coin.

L. H.

COINS, SHELL The shell coin (say a half-dollar) is of special construction: it actually consists of two half-dollars. One of them is hollowed out on one side, so as to leave a mere shell. The other is simply reduced a little in circumference, so as to fit easily within the first, in which condition the two look like only one coin.

Some little practice is necessary in order to manipulate the shell coin neatly. It should be taken, as shown in Fig. 1, between the first and third fingers, the shell portion being toward the spectators, and the thumb supporting the solid coin from behind. By relaxing the pressure of the thumb and at the same time tilting the double coin a little, the solid coin falls back on the thumb as shown in Fig. 2, from which position it may be brought into view to right or left as may be necessary. Even when both hands are used, the developing process is still the same.

The shell coin may also be used for a form of the "head-or-tails" trick. The solid coin is in this case double-headed, that is, assuming that the shell coin represents a tail, the solid will show a head on each side, or vice versa. The solid coin is spun in the air and caught by the performer, who im-

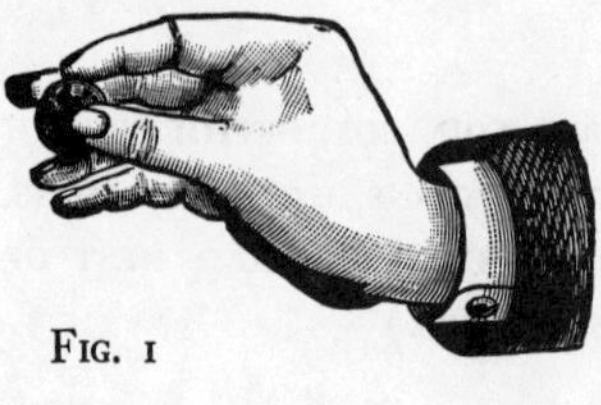

FIG. 1

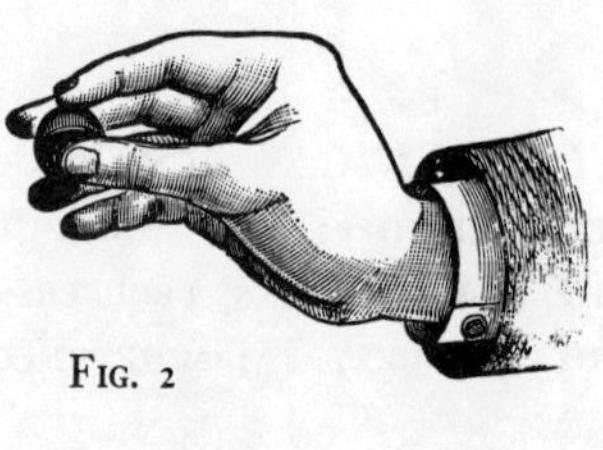

FIG. 2

mediately claps his opposite hand over it, in the customary manner. This other hand, however, contains the shell coin, which was held breadthwise between the first and fourth fingers, and which is thus brought over the solid coin.

The opposite party is now invited to call. If he calls heads, the coin is exhibited with the shell over it, when it will of course represent tails. If he calls tails, the shell is lifted off by the first and fourth fingers as before, and the solid coin exhibited; a very proper illustration (from the sharper's point of view) of the old saying, literally true in such cases, "Heads I win, tails you lose." *L. H.*

A method of doing the SYMPATHETIC COINS with the help of a shell is described in Hilliard's *Greater Magic.* Many other ingenious shell ROUTINES have been devised by various performers, and the reader can probably develop his own.

The most popular pocket form of shell coin is the *penny and dime trick*, in which the penny is a shell, and the dime is silver on one side, but has the face of a cent soldered to the back, so that when it is fitted in place the cent can be all but handed for examination.

COINS TO GLASS (See under COIN MANIPULATION: PASS, CLICK)

COMEDY (See also CHILDREN'S SHOWS; PANTOMIME; PATTER; PRESENTATION; PSYCHOLOGY; SUCKER GAGS; WATCH TRICKS)

Comedy cannot perhaps profitably be written about, but it is something that the magician must certainly think about. Al Baker, probably America's most truly gifted comic magician, likes to tell about a man who billed himself as "Magician and Entertainer." When he had finished his act, the chairman of the entertainment committee said, "Well, that part was fine. Now how about the entertainment?"

It is not strictly necessary to have any humor at all in a fairly short magic act; but the whole tendency of modern public entertainment is very strongly toward comedy.

Besides, the simple pleasure of an audience in a good trick often expresses itself in laughter. MIND-READING, SPIRIT EFFECTS, and to some extent ESCAPES follow different rules, but straightforward conjuring usually has something intrinsically comic about it.

There are three chief kinds of innate comedy in tricks; irrelevance, petty misfortune, and repetition.

The CHINESE WANDS are comically irrelevant; people laugh automatically because when you pull up one string, it is the *other* tassel that rises.

The SUN AND MOON TRICK is inherently funny because people enjoy the small misfortunes of the assistant and the owner of the handkerchief (but they would stop laughing if the damage were not repaired, and they would not *start* laughing unless they thought it was going to be).

They laugh harder and harder at the repeating three SPONGE BALL and pocket routine, because the simple repetition of a small effect grows funny with time.

All three of these tricks are humorous in themselves; two of them can be very successfully done in dumbshow. (See PANTOMIME; SILENT ACTS) One basic point about good comedy magic is that it must not depend *solely* upon PATTER for its comedy. Ready-made comic patter is almost never comic except (occasionally) in the mouth of its originator.

This is not to say that patter, as well as tricks, cannot be inherently funny. You are strongly urged to read Max Eastman's *Enjoyment of Laughter*, a lively analysis of the whole structure of humor. The following are his "Ten Commandments of the Comic Arts," with a magician's interpretation of what he means by them.

1. *Be interesting*. In other words, give your gags a build-up. Don't spring them until you have said enough to interest the audience in that particular subject. Don't jump people's attention around *at the start*.

2. *Be unimpassioned*. This does not mean that you cannot be absorbed in the drama of your story; it means that you must not involve the feelings and beliefs of your audience too deeply. No jokes about religion, no tricks with dead animals.

3. *Be effortless*. Any sign of toil, says Eastman, destroys the playful spirit that all comedy demands in the listener. "Effortlessness" requires years of effort to escape from involved patter, the labored introduction, the "Which reminds me," the "On my way here this evening, I . . ."

4. *Remember the difference between cracking practical jokes and conveying ludicrous impressions*. By "practical jokes" he means the humor that starts off in one direction, and then dodges, or deliberately disappoints you. His kind of practical jokes must begin plausibly, and collapse suddenly. In a manner of speaking, SUCKER GAGS are practical jokes; so, again, are the Chinese Wands; whereas the MISER'S DREAM conveys a cumulative ludicrous impression, with no plausibility, and no sudden collapse.

5. *Be plausible*. "By plausibility," says Eastman himself, "I mean successfully leading a person on." This is the very essence of all conjuring, and no more need be said about it. The Miser's Dream is not plausible in plot, but the motions of catching coins and tossing them into the hat must be so.

6. *Be sudden.* This is a general statement of the magical rule that you must never tell the audience what you are about to do. In jokes, don't telegraph the punch.

7. *Be neat.* An extension of rule three: the point must be right at hand, with no explaining needed. Eight out of ten mathematical tricks are not neat, and the spectator is too weary by the time of the climax to feel any surprise.

8. *Be right with your timing.* In its way the most important rule of all, and the hardest to explain. You must not rush either your trick or your joke so that people don't take it in; once they have taken it in, you must not dawdle and bore them. And when your effect is over, you must give them time to appreciate it, yet you must not drag on into a stage wait.

9. *Give good measure of serious satisfaction.* By this, Eastman intends to denounce the "anything-for-a-gag" attitude. There should be a little sense somewhere underlying even the most total nonsense. The Miser's Dream is total nonsense, but love of money is not; to do the same trick with thimbles, catching far more than you could put on your fingers, would be stupidly senseless.

10. *Redeem all serious disappointments.* In its crudest application to magic, this means that you must do something nice at the end for a VOLUNTEER assistant whom you have made ridiculous. When THURSTON used to wrap up a live rabbit for a little girl to take home, he was skirting a double disappointment: the child's parents did not want to to take care of any rabbits in a small apartment; yet when the rabbit vanished, that was a disappointment for the little girl. And when the package turned into a box of candy, both disappointments were redeemed. *H. H.*

COMMITTEES (See VOLUNTEERS)

COMTE, LOUIS CHRISTIAN EMMANUEL APPOLLINAIRE (1788-1859) Among the most distinguished early French magicians. He was highly praised by ROBERT-HOUDIN, and had many performances for royalty and upper nobility.

CONFEDERATES (See PLANTS)

COSTUME (See also CHILDREN'S SHOWS) The costume *de rigueur* of the magician of the past has been ordinary evening dress. The effect of the feats performed is greatly heightened by the close fit and comparative scantiness of such a costume, which appears to allow no space for secret pockets or other place of concealment. Actually, however, the magician is provided with two special pockets, known as *profondes*, placed in the tails of his dress-coat. Each is from four to six inches in depth and seven in width, and the opening, which is across the inside of the coat-tail, slanting slightly downward from the center to the side, is, like the SERVANTE, so placed as to be just level with the knuckles of the performer, as his hand hangs by his side.

He can thus, by the mere action of dropping either hand to his side, let fall any article instantly into the profonde on that side, or take anything out in the same manner. The action is so natural that it may be used under the very eyes of the audience, at very small risk of their observing it; and if the performer at the same moment slightly turns his other side to the spectators, he may be perfectly secure from detection.

Some performers have also a couple of *pochettes* (small pockets) made in the trousers, one behind each thigh. These are generally used for purposes of PRODUCTION only, the profondes being still employed for getting rid of any article, which, indeed, is their primary purpose, for they were originally made too deep (hence their name) to get articles out of them easily.

Many performers also have a spacious pocket, opening perpendicularly, inside the breast of the coat, under each arm, for the purpose of LOADING, that is, bringing a rabbit, or other article, into a hat, etc. Other pockets may be added, as the fancy or invention of the performer may dictate; but the above are those generally used.

It will also be found convenient to have an elastic band, about an inch wide, stitched around the lower edge of the waistcoat on the inside. When the waistcoat is worn, the band makes it press tightly around the waist, and any object of moderate size—a card, or a pack of cards, a handkerchief, etc.—may be slipped under it without danger of falling. Used in conjunction with the pockets before described, this elastic waistband affords a means of instantaneously effecting changes of articles too large to be palmed with safety; one hand drops the genuine article into the profonde on that side, while the other draws the prepared substitute from under the waistband, a very slight turn of the body, toward the table or otherwise, sufficing to cover the movement.

The accompanying diagrams illustrate some of the ways in which the conjurer's costume may be adapted to his art.

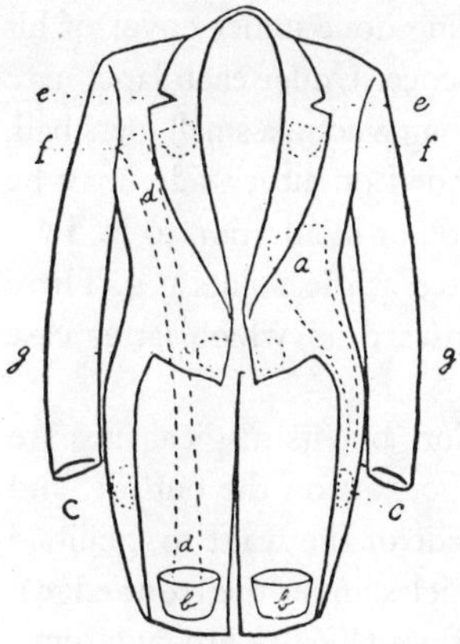

Fig. 1

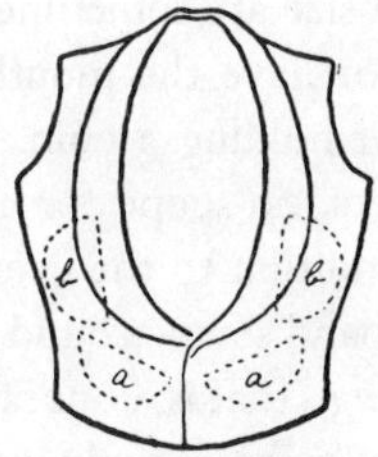

Fig. 2

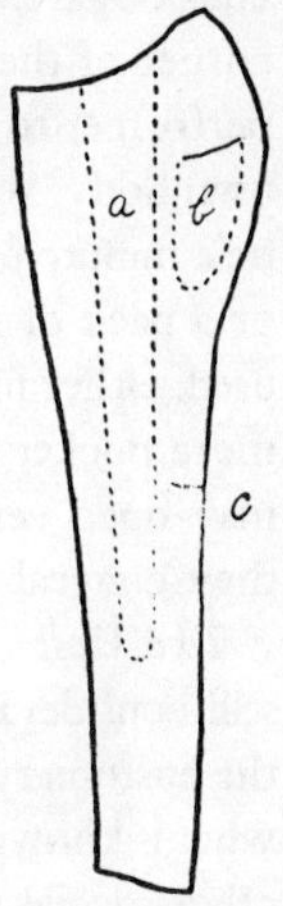

Fig. 3

The Coat. Every conjurer is familiar with the ordinary loading-pocket within the breast of the coat. Fig. 1 (*a*) shows another form. The pocket (which may be duplicated on the opposite side) is in this case made to extend downward to the waist, or even further, tapering as it goes. Its object is to hold a folding bouquet, a plume of feathers, or some other article of greater length than breadth. In some cases the mouth of the pocket is enlarged by laying it open down one side for a few inches, to facilitate the production of the object. The usual profondes are shown at *b b*, and *c c* are pochettes (of rather doubtful utility) under the tail of the coat, one on each side, and having vertical openings. In addition to these are the regular tail-pockets, opening on the outside and used without disguise for the ordinary purposes of pockets.

The letters *d d* represent a special pocket, opening under the armpit, a little above the breast pocket, and continued downward through the whole length of the coat, being in fact a mere tube of silk, discharging at the bottom into the profonde, so that any object of suitable size and weight, say a watch, placed ostensibly in the breast pocket, at once secretly slips down into the profonde. Some performers have the upper openings of these pockets made on the outside of the coat, under the armpits, the article being in this case secretly slipped into the pocket under cover of the act of drawing back the coat sleeve.

Even the coat collar has its magical uses. The outer edge of the upper part (the portion which goes around the neck) is sewn to the coat, forming a tubular pocket designed for the reception of a silk handkerchief. The ends *e e*, are open, and an inch length of black silk THREAD, attached to the corner of the handkerchief, with a black bead at the free end, enables the performer to draw it out when desired, this being done under cover of his own body, while his back is turned to the audience. Under each lapel may be a minute pochette, *f f*, very handy for receiving a coin, a small glass ball, or a pack of DIMINISHING CARDS. A clip, suspended on either side, may be used, either in substitution for the little pochette, or in addition to it. Two more pockets of small size are sometimes inserted at the points *g g*. These may open vertically, or have the mouth downward, in which latter case they conceal a clip for holding a coin.

The Vest. This offers less scope for adaptation, but its magical uses are still considerable. In addition to the everyday pockets on the outside, and the customary elastic band sewn around the inside of the waist to facilitate what is known as *vesting* (that is, concealing articles under the front edge), other special pockets may be introduced. Thus *a a* (Fig. 2) are two semicircular pockets just within the breast, adapted for the reception of small fishbowls or the like. Outside, at the back, on a flap suspended from the waist, may be a couple of similar pockets. Inside the breast are two smaller pockets, *b b*, opening vertically. (Similar pockets may be placed outside, but in such case the opening is brought somewhat nearer to the armpit.) And in front, just inside and above the waistband, may hang two or more clips for the reception of cards or coins.

The Trousers. These naturally have their share in the general deception. A leather sheath (Fig. 3), *a*, down either leg, provides a resting-place for the staff of a flag, a Japanese sunshade, or other lengthy object. A loose-mouthed pocket, *b*, on either hip, placed somewhat farther forward than the customary pistol-pocket, forms a capital receptacle for articles to be vanished. Some performers use a single pocket, about nine inches in width and seven in depth, lying over the central portion of the loins, with a vertical opening on each side. A pocket of this kind will be found extremely useful for many tricks. For card-conjuring, this may be replaced by a couple of oblong pockets, opening vertically at the side, and designed each to hold a prepared pack of cards in a horizontal position, about an inch of the cards projecting.

Further, the outer seam down either leg, a little above the knee, is frequently opened for about an inch in two or three places; the openings (which are invisible when the performer stands up) are in fact the mouths of tiny pockets designed for the reception of small silk handkerchiefs to be produced when needed. A couple of rubber bands, attached inside the trouser-leg, just above the shoe, may form a temporary resting-place for half-a-dozen playing cards, to be "passed" there in the course of a performance à la THURSTON.

The reader is doubtless already acquainted with the pochettes located behind the leg at *c*, these having formed part of the equipment of the conjurer ever since the days of ROBERT-HOUDIN. They may be larger or smaller, according to the particular purpose they are intended to serve, and it is feasible (and sometimes very useful) to have a small pocket sewn on the outside of a larger one. *L. H.*

Exotic Costumes–Chinese, East Indian, Egyptian–, if worn at all, should be authentic. Books on costume and travel will help you out if you are uncertain.

The modern tendency is more and more to abandon even the formality of a dinner jacket, and to perform in ordinary street clothes. This means pretty much the end of special pockets and "body work."

JOHN MULHOLLAND points out that almost any STEAL from a normal pocket can be made unnoticed by putting both hands in corresponding pockets simultaneously.

COSTUME TRUNK TRICK (see next page)

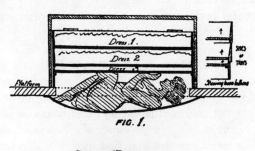

FIG. 1.

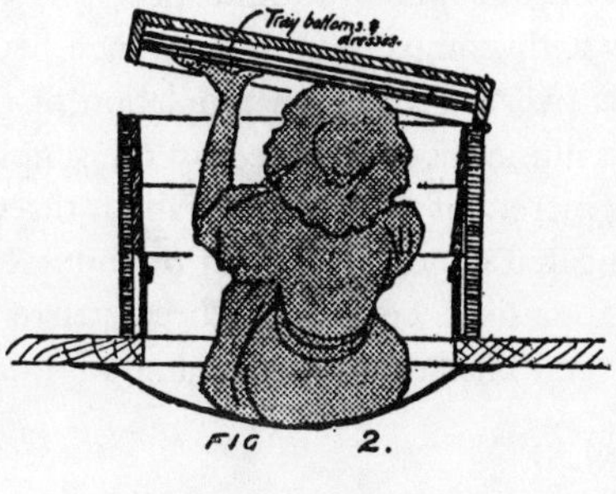

FIG 2.

COSTUME TRUNK TRICK This has the appearance of the ordinary wardrobe trunk except that in this case the frame has no bottom, being merely a shell and a loose lid. There are three trays for dresses, which after the body is removed are openly displayed on a thin platform upon which the trunk is placed.

The costumes are exhibited and a member of the audience is requested to select one printed card from a number shown with different names of costumes, and call out the name of the costume (which of course is FORCED). This done, the trays are stacked, the box dropped over, and the lid placed on the lot.

Almost immediately a lady jumps out of the trunk dressed in the very costume chosen by the member of the audience.

The secret lies in the platform upon which the trunk is exhibited. This has a top surface very much in excess of the size of the trunk, and although very thin it sags in the center, as shown in Figs. 1 and 2. Two of the trays are removable, but the third (the bottom one) is permanently fixed in position in the center of the platform. The lady is hidden by the costumes carelessly laid in it, part of her bulk being in the tray and part concealed by the sag in the bottom of the stand. *W. G.*

CULPITT, FRED. (died 1944) A noted British performer and inventor. The DOLL'S HOUSE illusion was one of his many creations. Some good judges rated his influence on other magicians as high as that of DAVID DEVANT. He was a successful performer as well as a great inventor–two qualities that do not often go together in magic.

CUPS AND BALLS This subject may be said to be the groundwork of all legerdemain, as it is supposed to be the very earliest form in which sleight-of-hand was exhibited. It is well worth the attention of the student of modern magic, not only as affording an excellent course of training in digital dexterity, but as being, in the hands of an adept, most striking in effect. It is by no means uncommon to find spectators who have received more elaborate feats with comparative indifference becoming interested, and even enthusiastic, over a brilliant manipulation of the cups and balls.

The prestige of the illusion is heightened by the simplicity of the appliances used, consisting merely of three tin cups about three inches high, each in the form of a truncated cone, with a rim or shoulder around the base the ordinary wand, four little cork balls, three-quarters of an inch or a little less in diameter and blackened in the flame of a candle, three larger balls of about an inch and a quarter in diameter, and four more of such a size as to just fill the goblet. These last are generally stuffed with hair and covered with cloth. The number of balls may vary according to the particular passes which the performer desires to exhibit.

The whole art of cup-and-ball conjuring resolves itself into two elements —the exhibition of a ball under a cup where a moment previously there was nothing, and the disappearance of a ball from beneath a cup under which the audience have just seen it (or believe that they have seen it) placed. The routine is as follows:

A cup is lifted, to show that there is nothing beneath it, and again replaced, mouth downward, on the table. A ball is taken in the right hand, transferred to the left, and ordered to pass under the cup. The hand is opened; the ball has vanished, and is found beneath the cup.

Again, the ball, first exhibited in the right hand, is openly transferred, either directly under the cup or first to the left hand, and thence to the cup. Everyone having seen it placed beneath the cup, it is now commanded to depart; on again lifting the cup, it is found to have vanished. These simple elements are capable of numerous and surprising combinations.

The sleight-of-hand requisite for the cups and balls is technically divisible into four different acts or movements: 1. To palm the ball. 2. To reproduce the palmed ball at the end of the fingertips. 3. To introduce the palmed ball secretly under the cup. 4. To simulate the action of placing the ball under the cup.

1. *To Palm the Ball: First Method.* We use the generic term "palm" for the sake of convenience, though in this first method the ball is really concealed between the second and third fingers, and not in the palm.

Take the ball between the first finger and thumb of the right hand (Fig. 1); bend the fingers slightly, and at the same moment roll the ball with the thumb across the first and second fingers (Fig. 2), until it rests between the second and third fingers, which should slightly separate to receive it, again closing as it is safely lodged. The ball will now be as shown in Fig. 3, and it will be found that the hand can be opened or closed with perfect freedom and, indeed, be used in any manner without being in the least hampered by its presence.

The student should practice palming the ball in this manner both in the act of (apparently) transferring the ball to the left hand, and in that of (apparently) placing it under a cup lifted by the left hand for that purpose.

Second Method. The second method is to actually palm the ball, in the same manner as a coin. (See COIN MANIPULATION) For this purpose the ball is, as before, taken between the first finger and thumb of the right hand,

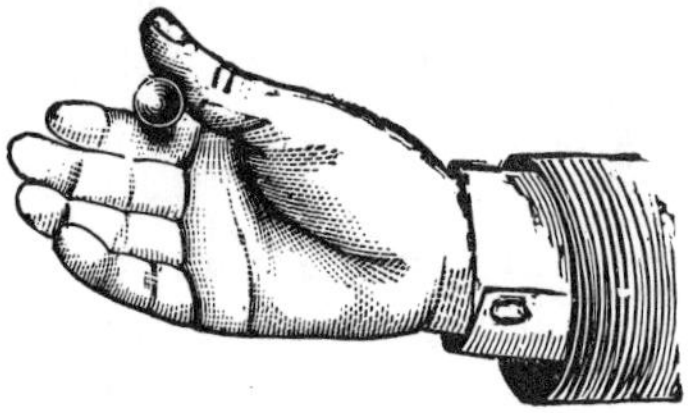

Fig. 1

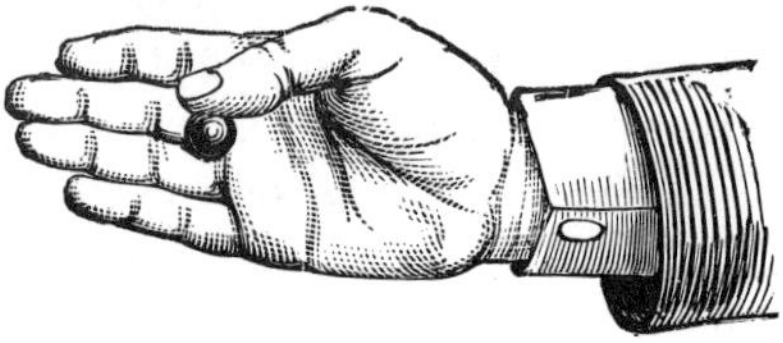

Fig. 2

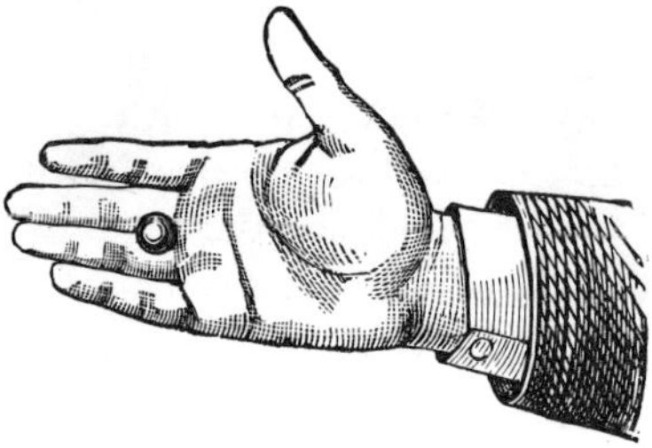

Fig. 3

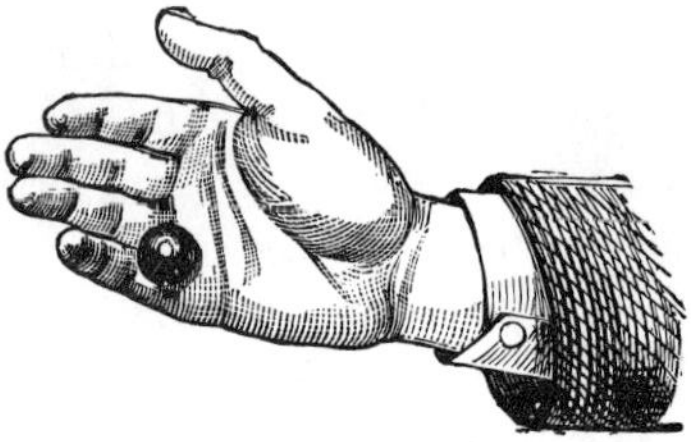

Fig. 4

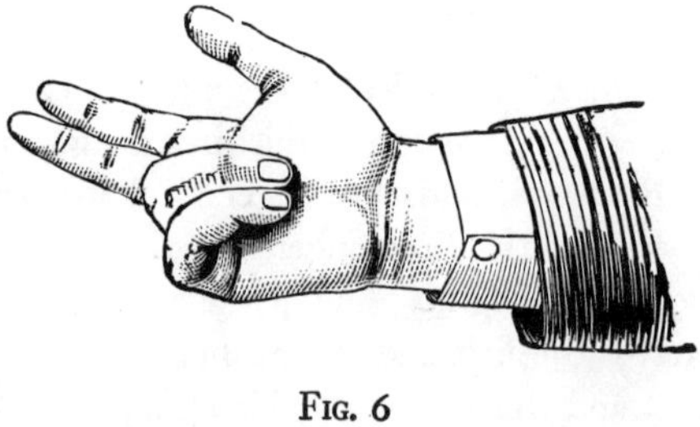

Fig. 6

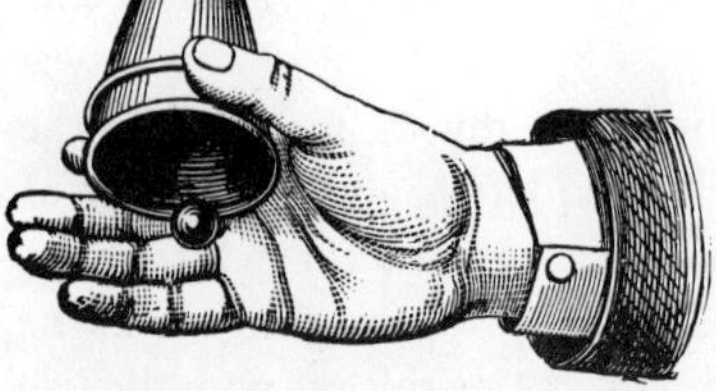

Fig. 7

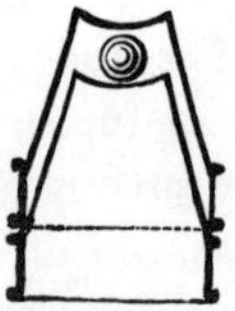

Fig. 8

but is made by the thumb to roll between the tips of the third and fourth fingers, which immediately close into the palm and, again opening, leave the ball behind them. With a little practice, two balls in succession may be palmed in this way, and then a third by the first method.

Third Method. The third method is that which was adopted by the celebrated BOSCO, a most accomplished performer with the cup and balls. Being accustomed to use balls of a larger size than those above described, and therefore too bulky to palm by the first method, he used to hold them by means of a slight contraction of the little finger. (Fig. 4) The necessary movement of the fingers to place the ball in position is nearly the same as by the first method.

Fig. 5 represents the form and arrangement of the cups, balls, (large and small), and table which Bosco was in the habit of using.

Of the five cups placed on the table, three have no special preparation, but the other two are arranged, the one to let fall or cause the appearance of three *muscades,* the other to take them away. The right-hand cup is fitted internally with a considerable number of needles placed vertically, and adapted so as to stick into and carry away the balls, when they are covered with this particular cup. At the bottom of the other cup is a chamber of such a size as to hold three *muscades.* On touching a little projecting stud on the outside, a flap closing this compartment drops and lets the *muscades* fall.

2. *To Reproduce the Palmed Ball at the End of the Fingers.* If the ball was palmed by the first or third method, it is simply rolled back to the fingertips with the ball of the thumb, exactly reversing the process by which it was palmed. But if the ball was palmed by the second method, it is not get-at-able by the ball of the thumb for the time being. In this case the first step is to close the third and fourth fingers upon the ball (Fig. 6), and therewith roll it to the position shown in Fig. 4, when the thumb can reach it, and roll it to the fingertips in the manner just described.

3. *To Introduce the Palmed Ball Secretly under the Cup.* This is always done in the act of raising the cup (with the right hand), for the ostensible purpose of showing that there is nothing underneath it. The chief thing to be attended to is the position of the right hand (in which we are supposing a ball to be palmed by one or another of the methods above mentioned) in raising the cup. This should be done with the hand spread almost flat upon the table, and grasping the cup as low down as possible, between the thumb and the lowest joint of the forefinger.

In the act of raising the cup, the fingers naturally assume the position shown in Fig. 7, whereby the ball is brought close to, and slightly under, the edge of the cup. If the ball is palmed by the first method, all that is necessary in order to release it is a slight backward movement of the second, and a forward movement of the third finger, made just before the cup again touches the table. This will be found to drop the ball immediately under the cup. If the ball is palmed by the third method, its introduction under the cup is a still easier matter, as by the act of raising the cup it is brought directly underneath it, and is released by the mere act of straightening the third and fourth fingers. If the ball is palmed by the second method, it becomes necessary, before taking hold of the cup, to close the third and fourth fingers slightly (Fig. 6), and bring the ball to the position shown in Fig. 4. From this point the operation is the same as if the ball had been originally palmed by the third method.

It is sometimes necessary to introduce a ball between two cups. It will be remembered that each cup is made with a cylindrical rim or shoulder, so that when two cups are placed one upon the other (Fig. 8), there may be a space between them sufficient to receive a ball or balls. To facilitate the introduction of the ball, the top of each cup is made not flat, but concave.

To introduce a ball between two cups, the performer, having the ball ready palmed in his right hand, takes up a cup in the same hand, and with it covers the second cup, at the same moment introducing the ball beneath it in the ordinary manner, but with the addition of a little upward jerk, easily acquired with a little practice. The ball is thereby thrown to the top of the uppermost cup, and, in again falling, is received by the concave top of the lowermost cup.

4. *To Simulate the Action of Placing a Ball under a Cup.* This may be done in two ways. The first is to raise the cup with the left hand, apparently placing the ball underneath it with the right, but really palming it. Care must be taken that the edge of the cup touches the table at the very moment that the fingers of the right hand are removed.

The second and more common method is apparently to transfer the ball to the left hand, palming it in transit; then bringing the closed left hand close to the cup on the table, raise the cup with the other hand, and immediately replace it with a sort of scraping movement across the fingers of the now opening left hand.

When the student has thoroughly mastered the various operations, he will have little to learn except the combination of the various passes, simply a mattter of memory. There are, however, one or two subordinate sleights with which he should make himself acquainted before proceeding to exhibit his dexterity publicly.

To Produce a Ball from the Wand. The WAND is supposed to be the reservoir from which the magician produces his store of balls, and into which they vanish when no longer needed. The method of production is as follows: The performer, holding the wand in his left hand, and drawing attention to it by some remark as to its mysterious powers, secretly takes with his right hand, from the SERVANTE or elsewhere, a ball which he immediately palms (preferably by the first method).

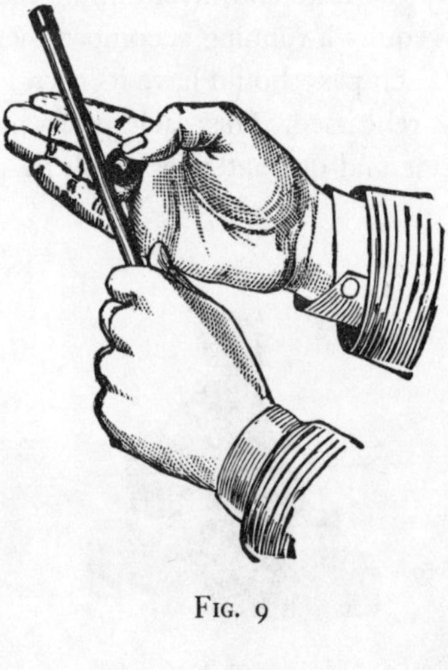

FIG. 9

Daintily holding the wand by either end with the left hand, in such a manner as to show that the hand is otherwise empty, he slides the thumb and fingers of the right hand (the back of which is naturally toward the audience) lightly to the opposite end, at the same moment rolling the ball with the thumb to the ends of the fingers, as already described (Fig. 9). The ball thus comes in sight just as the hand leaves the wand, giving the effect that the ball is squeezed out of the wand by some mysterious process.

To Return a Ball into the Wand. This is the converse of the process just described. Taking the wand in the left hand, as before, and the ball between the thumb and second joint of the forefinger of the opposite hand, the performer lays the end of the wand across the tips of the fingers, and draws the hand gently downward along it, at the same time palming the ball by the first method.

To Pass One Cup Through Another. This is an effective sleight, and by no means difficult. Taking onc of the cups, mouth upward, in the left hand, and holding another in a similar position in the right hand, about a foot above it, the performer drops the right-hand cup smartly into that in the left hand (which latter should be held very lightly). If this is neatly done, the lower cup will be knocked out of the hand by the concussion, while the upper one will be caught and held in its place; the effect to the eye of the spectator being as if the upper cup had passed through the other. The lower cup may either be allowed to fall on the ground or table, or may be caught by the right hand in its fall.

The successive appearances and disappearances of the balls underneath the cups are known as passes; the particular combination of such passes should be governed by the taste and invention of the performer.

The cups and balls require a running accompaniment of talk, even more than most conjuring. Each pass should have its own PATTER, carefully prepared and frequently rehearsed. This each performer must arrange for himself, to suit the style and character in which he performs. *L. H.*

FIG. 10

FIG. 11

In the East Indian version (Fig. 10), the cup is turned out of wood, and shaped like an ordinary wine glass (Fig. 11). There is a short stem at the bottom of the cup terminating in a knob. The measurement from the mouth of the cup to the knob is slightly under 3 inches, the stem under 1 inch, the diameter of the mouth slightly over 2 inches, and the depth of the bow 1 1/2 inches. Their "undersize" construction calls for more accurate judgment in manipulation, since it is far easier to LOAD a large cup than a small one.

The balls are made of cloth and are about 3/4 inches in size. Several of these are used. The wand completes the equipment.

A ball is palmed in the right hand. The performer lifts a cup between his first and second fingertips, a few inches off the ground (Fig. 12); in lowering his hand to replace the cup, he moves the palm forward, which brings the ball directly under the mouth of the cup. Continuing the movement, he lowers the cup, with the ball underneath. The ball is not dropped and then covered, but is actually carried down within the cup. This requires faultless judgment and coordination.

To show a cup empty when there is actually a ball under it, the ball must, of course, be lifted with the cup. In this case the cup is again held

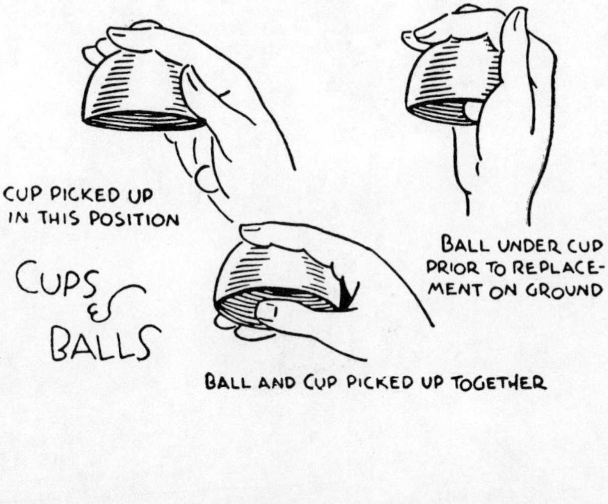

FIG. 12

between the tips of the first two fingers, but in raising it off the ground the thumb enters the mouth and presses the ball against the side of the cup. The moment the cup is raised, the thumb enters, and the mouth of the cup is turned away slightly so that no one can see inside, and then replaced.

For the ordinary pass, a ball, before vanishing, is shown on the palm of the right hand. The third finger presses on it, not so much to facilitate the palm, as to make it felt that the ball needs support. The right hand pretends to drop the ball in the left hand; at the same time the third finger moves out. This creates the impression that the ball has actually been dropped. The ball is held palmed and the left fingers close over the empty hand. *E. J.*

There is a whole literature dealing with the cups and balls. Lang Neil and ROBERT-HOUDIN (*Secrets of Conjuring and Magic*) give classical versions. Modern treatments are in Hilliard, *Greater Magic;* L. L. Ireland, *Cups and Balls;* Eddie Joseph, *A Practical Lesson in Cups and Balls*, *Advanced Lessons in Cups and Balls*, *The Last Word On Cups and Balls.*

D

DANCING HANDKERCHIEF In the stage form of this trick a black silk THREAD is used: it crosses the stage from side to side, lying until needed on the floor. During the performance of the trick each end is held by an assistant.

The handkerchief may be a borrowed one, but should be fairly large. At the beginning it is laid upon the performer's table, behind which he passes while the thread is still on the floor. The moment he has done so, the thread is raised horizontally to the height of a foot or so above the table. Standing behind it, he begins to prepare the handkerchief, the first step being to tie a small knot in each of two diagonally opposite corners. He then ties a loose *double* knot in one of the other corners (the object of tying twice over being to take up a larger portion of the handkerchief). This knot is tied around the horizontal thread. Finally, he tucks the fourth corner into the knot last made, the result being a grotesque sort of puppet, with head and arms complete.

The assistants at the wings slacken the thread the moment the principal knot is tied, and then move forward as far as circumstances permit, so that the threat, when taut, will clear the table. When the figure is complete, the performer begins to make mesmeric passes over it, announcing that he intends to make it dance. At this point, a simultaneous pull, followed by an immediate slackening of the thread, jerks the handkerchief off the table on to the floor. "Oh! you want to escape, do you? But you won't. If you won't dance on the table you shall do so on the floor," says the performer. As he says this, he moves forward and steps over the thread, so as to get in front of it. He waves his wand horizontally over the handkerchief, and after a few moments it is seen to be slightly agitated. Presently it begins to stand erect, and finally to dance after a fashion, actuated by the thread in the hands of the assistants, who should have practiced their task, as considerable skill is required to perform it properly.

An additional effect may be got by placing a chair over the handkerchief while it is still dancing. This, of course, makes no difference to its performance, while it effectively destroys the idea which naturally occurs to the minds of most spectators, that the dancing figure is manipulated by a thread from above. The possibility of using a horizontal thread is much less likely to suggest itself.

When the dance has lasted long enough, the performer picks up the handkerchief and brings it forward, still knotted, and, if borrowed, returns it to the owner. First, however, one of the assistants releases his end of the thread, which is then rapidly drawn away through the knot by the other, leaving no trace of the *modus operandi.* *L. H.*

HARRY BLACKSTONE does this trick better than any other performer living or dead.

DE KOLTA, JOSEPH BUATIER (1845-1903), was born apparently at Lyons, France. He was one of the most prolific innovators and inventors in the history of magic. He introduced spring FLOWERS, is credited with having been the first to show a billiard-ball trick, and invented many ILLUSIONS, of which the Vanishing Lady, the Cocoon, the BIRD-CAGE vanish, and the Expanding Die are perhaps the most famous.

Although he seems to have been a Frenchman (he occasionally claimed Hungarian birth, taking the name of de Kolta from his wife), his greatest success was in England and America.

DEVANT, DAVID Stage name of David Wighton (1868-1941). Probably the greatest English performer of modern times. He was associated for many years with the MASKELYNE family in St. George's Hall, a variety theater on whose program magic always predominated. Here he was constantly ready to help on and train the new magical generation, which partly explains his all-pervasive influence on British conjuring.

His many inventions and his books are also among the best of their kind. He invented the first THIMBLE trick, and his devising of the DYE TUBE opened the way to the fantastic modern development of SILK TRICKS.

His graceful, witty PATTER and PRESENTATION were almost in a class by themselves, doing much to lift the whole level of his contemporaries. He collaborated with his partner, John Nevil Maskelyne, on *Our Magic*, the greatest textbook of magical theory yet written.

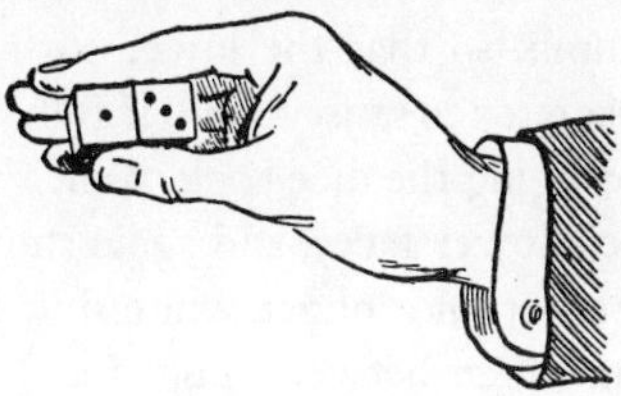

Fig. 1

DICE (See also DIE BOX; GAMBLING METHODS)

Changing Dice. The performer, holding the dice as shown in Fig. 1, first exhibits the upper faces, and then (by raising the hand) the lower; then changes the latter, professedly by rubbing with the forefinger of the opposite hand, but actually by a slight upward movement of the thumb, compelling the dice to describe a half-turn on their own axis, under cover of lifting the arm for the second time.

This trick can be improved by changing the lower faces of the dice during the *first* upward movement of the arm, and bringing them back to their normal position as the hand descends. When the lower faces of the dice are exhibited for the second time, they simply retain their position; as no further movement is required, the performer may even allow his wrist to be held, and his right hand to remain perfectly motionless, while he passes the forefinger over the faces of the dice to change them.

Of course an expert in the use of dice would know that the upper and lower faces of a properly made die invariably amount to seven, and might call attention to the fact that those first shown as the points of the lower face are not quite as they ought to be. However, so few people are experts in this particular that any fear of objection on this score may be safely disregarded.

Another variation is to suppress the points of the dice altogether, but to have them specially colored, three of the sides (one of them being at right angles with the other two) white, say, and the other black. The working is practically the same as in the other case.

Suppose the cubes, colored in this way, are taken between the finger and the thumb as in Fig. 1. The exact placing, however, is a matter of importance. They must be arranged (for this particular purpose) so that the sides next to the thumb are black, as also the two lower and the two end surfaces. Under these conditions, the performer lowers his hand and shows that the upper surfaces are white.

He raises it to show the lower faces, but in so doing makes the upward half-turn with the thumb, so that the lower surfaces appear white also. Having allowed the spectator to satisfy himself fully on this point, he lowers the hand once more, bringing the dice back to their normal position; passes the forefinger over their lower faces; and again shows them *without* making the turn, when they are no longer white, but black.

Again, take the same dice between finger and thumb, but placed so that the innermost of the two has one of its black sides at the top, one to the front, and the other in contact with the second die. The white faces of the latter should be on the top, next to the finger and next to the other die.

As before, the performer shows the upper faces, pointing out that the white face is nearest the tips of the fingers. He then (making the turn) shows that in the case of the lower faces the white face is likewise outermost. When he again shows the lower surfaces, without the turn, they are found to have changed places, although the upper surfaces remain as before.

In another form of the trick, each die used has five sides white and one black. When taken between the finger and thumb the black sides are undermost, but after having shown the upper surfaces, the performer, in the act of raising the hand to show the under sides, makes the dice describe the usual half-turn, so that the sides actually shown are white. In again lowering the hand he brings the dice back to their original position. Drawing the finger across the under surfaces, he raises the hand *without* making the turning movement. The dice are thus shown in their original position, the lower faces now being black. When he desires the black to disappear he lowers them once more, and on again raising them does so with the turning movement as at first.

To produce the maximum effect in this case, the performer should provide himself with two pairs of cubes, one pair being white all over. These are handed for examination, and when returned are taken back with the left hand, and apparently transferred to the right, in which the trick dice are already hidden. Those are then placed in position and the trick worked as above. As the whole attention of the spectators is given to the right hand, there is nothing to prevent the plain dice from remaining FINGER-PALMED in the left hand and again being substituted for the others at the conclusion of the trick. *L. H.*

Die Through Hat. The effect of this trick is that a solid die—about two and a half inches square—is brought forward and a skeleton frame and a little stand are shown to the audience. The audience actually see the die on all sides, and it is then put into the frame or case. The case is now taken off the stand and a hat is borrowed. A handkerchief is placed over the case and die and the whole is put on the stand on top of the hat. At the word of command, however, the handkerchief is removed and the die is seen to have vanished from the case and to have found its way under the hat.

FIG. 1

FIG. 2

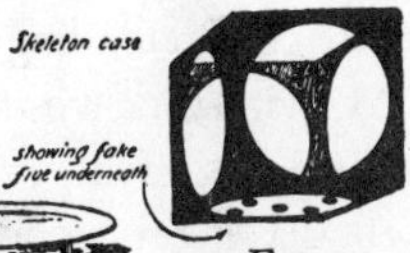

FIG. 3

The stand (Fig. 2) is made of tin and painted black. The skeleton case is made of tin, and is perfectly open on all sides, but the bottom has a piece of paper representing the five fixed on the inside, so that if this is turned toward the audience it will appear that the solid die is there with the five facing them. The back of this paper is painted black, so that when the skeleton case is turned over on the stand it cannot be noticed. (Fig. 3)

Have the skeleton case on the stand, with the fake five at the bottom, and put the solid die in the case, with the five toward the front. Show the die in the case on all sides, and put it back on the stand, covering it with a handkerchief.

Next borrow a hat, and under cover of it lift the handkerchief and case; give the case a turn to bring the fake five to the front, and allow the solid die to slip out on the table. The hat screens this movement.

Place the skeleton case and the handkerchief together with the stand on the top of the hat, and lift the handkerchief a little so that the audience can apparently see the die still there. Take the opportunity while adjusting the handkerchief to give the case another turn toward the audience. This will bring the prepared side of the die flat against the stand. Give the password, lift the handkerchief, and the die will appear to have passed from the skeleton case underneath the hat. Put the case on the stand immediately, so that the audience will not notice that it is faked. *H. & A. W.*

DIE BOX, SLIDING Perhaps the most typical and elaborate of all SUCKER GAGS. The box is oblong, divided by a center partition into two compartments, capable of exactly containing a painted wooden die three inches square. Each compartment has a hinged door on the front, and another on the top. The bottom of the box has a hidden channel in it, running lengthwise, with a weight that can be secured or allowed to slide back and forth by pressure on a hidden spring.

When the die is first shown, it is covered with a tin shell that lacks two adjacent sides; otherwise, it is painted outside to resemble the die, inside to resemble one of the compartments of the box. The performer explains that he is going to pass the die from the box into a borrowed hat. As he says this, he lowers die and shell into the hat, leaves the die behind, and brings the shell back. Pretending it is the die, he puts it into one compartment of the box, with the two missing sides of the shell corresponding to the top and front doors. He then releases the slider, and tilts the box, which makes a loud click as if the wooden die had slid from one compartment to the other. He opens the doors of the upper compartment, and shows it empty. He next closes the doors, tilts the box the other way (with a loud click), and shows the other compartment empty. This is continued as long as the audience will fall for it, and finally all four doors are opened, the box is shown empty, and the die removed from the hat.

An improvement is to make the front doors double, with a hinged lining, painted like one face of the die, which can be left closed when the actual door is opened, thus showing the die in place. A further development allows the magician to produce a lemon or a billiard ball in place of the vanished die in the box. *H. H.*

DIMINISHING CARDS (See also CARD MANIPULATION: FLOURISHES, FANNING) The CARDS UP THE SLEEVE forms a natural introduction to the feat of the diminishing cards, the performer offering to explain "how it's done."

The illusion in ROBERT-HOUDIN's day was produced entirely by the skill of the performer, who showed an increased or diminished amount of the surface of the cards. Placing an ace at the bottom and spreading the cards fanwise, he showed first that they were of ordinary size. Closing the fan, he made believe to stretch the cards by pulling them strongly in the direction of their longer diameter; then he again spread them fanwise, allowing them to project a little further from the hand, and boldly asserting that they had grown larger, which, from the greater amount of surface exhibited, really appeared to be the case. This was repeated, the cards being made to project yet a little more from the hand. The fan again being closed, the performer, giving the cards a squeeze, and again spreading them as at first, showed that they had returned to their original dimensions.

Once more the fan was closed, and pressure again applied. The cards were spread again, but this time only a very little way, and mostly covered by the fingers, in which condition they appeared to have diminished to much less than their normal size. An ace was put at the bottom, as the size of the pattern on the face of the cards would otherwise tend to destroy the illusion.

The trick as above described is really illusive in competent hands, but its effect is uncertain. To remove all possible question, a graduated series of packs is now used.

The series usually sold consists of the ordinary-sized pack (No. 1), and about a dozen cards of exactly half the size, secured together by a rivet at one corner. The first card of this pack (No. 2) is a full-sized card folding in half. On the back of each card of this pack is pasted a still smaller card, and the set is completed by a quite miniature pack (No. 3) of cards not exceeding an inch in length, likewise fastened together by a rivet, or in some cases with a simple loop of silk thread. The pattern of the cards, back and front, should correspond in design throughout the series.

Pack No. 2, with the full-sized card extended, and with two or three loose cards of the same size lying on its face, is secretly substituted at the right moment for the ordinary pack previously in use. The loose full-sized cards are handed to the audience, or carelessly shown and thrown on the table ostensibly to prove that they are ordinary cards; then the performer, under pretense of squeezing the pack, folds down the one full-sized card, and spreads pack No. 2 as far as the rivet will permit.

Another squeeze, under cover of which the pack is turned around, showing the still smaller cards on the reverse side. Another squeeze, and pack No. 2 is palmed off altogether, pack No. 3 being shown in its place. No. 2 is dropped into a pocket, or on the SERVANTE, and the performer, holding pack No. 3 between the second finger and thumb of the left hand, takes it (apparently) in the right, and vanishes it altogether.

In a later version of the trick, the folding card is done away with, and packs No. 2 and 3 are not riveted, having no speciality except size. They usually consist of about a dozen cards each, and are placed in readiness under the waistband or in the *pochettes*. The trick is worked as follows:

The performer takes a dozen or so of the full-sized cards, and makes believe to reduce them in size, after Robert-Houdin's fashion. While attention is being called to their apparent decrease in size he gets into his left hand, and PALMS, pack No. 2. Once more professing to squeeze the full-sized cards, he palms them in his right hand, and shows pack No. 2 in their place, repeating the process again with No. 3. The palmed larger cards can in each case be got rid of while taking a full-sized card from the table to stick into the fan for comparison.

In this case Robert-Houdin's method may be employed with perfect safety for the first stage of the diminution, because when the cards are unmistakably reduced in size at the next stage, any doubt in the minds of the spectators is set at rest. *L. H.*

DIVINATIONS A class of effects in which the performer discovers which one of several almost similar objects the audience has concealed, or what order they have been arranged in. The most important principles used are discussed below.

One is a revival, in improved form, of a trick which was familiar to our great-grandfathers. A little oblong box contains four wooden or cardboard slabs, exactly fitting it. Each of these bears a numeral, as shown in Fig. 1.

The length and width of the box are such that it has exactly room for the four slabs. A rebate on the under side of each block, corresponding with a fillet extending along the interior of the box, ensures that no block can be inserted in any position, save with the number right side up, but the four can be inserted in any order at pleasure, allowing of twenty-four different combinations.

The box is handed to some member of the company, with a request that he arrange the blocks in any order he wishes. Meanwhile, a little tube of brass or pasteboard, about one inch long by one and one-quarter in diameter, is handed out for examination. Sometimes this tube has a lens at one end, after the manner of a watchmaker's eyeglass; sometimes it is open from end to end, and sometimes closed. Whichever pattern is adopted, the result is the same.

The box may be locked, tied, and sealed, but the performer, using the little tube as an eyeglass, and applying it at regular intervals along the lid, reads off with unfailing accuracy the number formed by the four blocks within; this may be repeated any number of times.

The secret of the trick lies in an ingenious application of the familiar scientific principle that the needle of a magnetic compass, when placed over a magnet of greater power, will lie parallel to the larger magnet, but with its poles in the reverse direction, that is, north on south and vice versa. Each of the four blocks has imbedded in it a minute bar-magnet (consisting of an inch of watch-spring strongly magnetized), but in a different position. (Fig. 2.)

The little tube which was handed for examination is SWITCHED by the performer for another, in which the place of the lens is occupied by a small

(Fig. 1)

(Fig. 2)

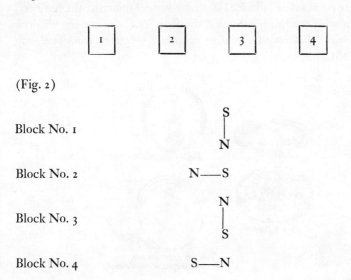

Block No. 1	S (top) — N (bottom)
Block No. 2	N—S
Block No. 3	N (top) — S (bottom)
Block No. 4	S—N

magnetic compass. This being applied (outside the lid of the box) over the position of either of the blocks, the needle will at once point in the direction of the *south* pole of the concealed bar. Thus, if it point vertically upward, the performer will know that the block beneath is the 1. If it point to the right, the 2; if downward, the 3; if to the left, the 4. It is therefore an easy matter to determine the number formed by the concealed blocks. When the trick is over, the unprepared tube is again substituted, and the whole handed for examination. *L. H.*

In a newer and simpler version the flat slab has a different color on each side, making a total of eight possible colors. The top of the box is paneled, with a piece of raised trim running along the middle of the panel. The panel is made to slide when this raised trim is pushed toward the front, exposing four small holes through which the performer can see the colors of the slabs. A stiff spring pushes the panel back into place.

Another principle much used in divination effects involves weighting the objects. The *Mummy Case*, for example, is a miniature coffin with a rounded bottom, and will take any one of three miniature mummies, each differently decorated, but apparently otherwise just like the others. One mummy is unprepared; the second is weighted at the head; the third, at the feet. If the case is put down on the table, it rocks and balances when the unprepared mummy is inside. With the second mummy, the head end goes down; with the third, naturally, the foot. The mummy shape is one of several ways that may be used to prevent a spectator from reversing the concealed object.

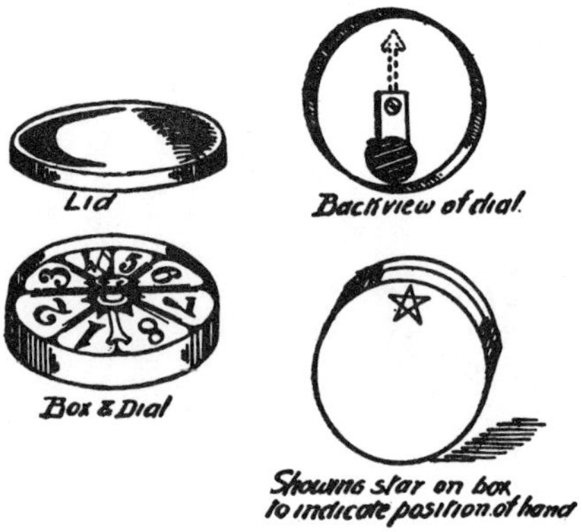

FIG. 3

A different use of weighting is the *Divining Dial*. This is a sort of simplified hunting-case watch, a flat, cylindrical box with a revolving pointer inside, which may be set to point at numbers, or at different-colored spots, around the dial. The lid is closed, and the performer immediately tells which way the pointer is pointing. Between the dial and the bottom of the case is a small counterweight attached to the spindle on which the pointer turns. On the outside bottom of the box, near the edge, is engraved a star, apparently a mere ornament, which gives the pointer a fixed point of reference. The case is tipped on edge, and rolled or allowed to turn until the weight is downward; this tells the performer how the pointer has been set. (Fig. 3)

The dial effect is sometimes shown with an unprepared hunting-case watch; this requires considerable practice, because the conjurer simply learns to open and shut the case with one swift motion as he lifts the watch to his forehead; he thus catches a flash of the time the watch is set at.

A relatively new principle in divination effects is the use of luminous paint. Such paint is not inherently luminous, but absorbs any light it is exposed to, and then slowly gives it off in the dark. For magical purposes, a surface is coated with luminous paint—a card, the back of a small round mirror, or the like. The audience may, for instance, be requested to lay their choice of a dime, quarter, or half-dollar on the card while the performer is absent. They then remove the coin, but the performer can tell which one was used. He has only to hold the card under his coat, or in comparable darkness, and he can see a dark spot the size of the coin standing out against the glowing background. *H. H.*

In another trick the performer hands out three little cardboard lids for examination. He then turns his back for a moment while a spectator puts a coin under any one of the three on the table. The lids can be moved around to any position, but the conjurer can immediately point out where the coin is.

The apparatus can be made easily. Three ordinary pill-box lids a little larger than the coin will do. The sets supplied by magical dealers nest into one another for convenience.

Prepare the coin by cutting a little nick in the edge, and insert a fine hair about two inches long, afterward hammering the coin gently to secure the hair tightly. The hair gives the clue to the trick. Nobody is likely to notice it on the coin, especially if you have a newspaper on the table. When the covers are in position, you have only to see which cover the hair protrudes from to locate the coin.

If you are going to repeat the trick, it is as well to take note, while your back is turned, of any mirrors or pictures in the room, as these may reflect what is happening on the table.

The Four Colored Plugs. The plugs are really pieces of wood about three inches long, and colored red, white, blue, and green respectively. They are given to a spectator, together with a nickel-plated case just big enough to hold one, and he is asked to place one plug in the case and put the other three in his pocket so that they will be out of sight. You can instantly tell which plug is in the case.

To perform this little trick, the colors should be memorized in the following order: red, blue, white, green.

The first two plugs are a sixteenth of an inch shorter than the other two, so that if either the red or the blue plug is in the case, the lid will fit right down to a line engraved on the outside of the case. If either the white or the green plug is in the case, however, the lid will not shut right down, and remains a little way above the mark. In addition, the blue and green plugs have a weight inside, which can be heard to rattle when the box is given a slight shake.

When the case is handed to you, ask the audience to concentrate on it. A quick glance at the lid will tell you whether the plug belongs to the first or second pair. Give the case a shake in putting it on the table, and if the plug rattles you know that it is either the blue or the green.

This little summary gives the complete order:

Red Plug: Lid fits right down; plug does not rattle.

Blue Plug: Lid fits right down; plug rattles.

White Plug: Lid fits higher up; plug does not rattle.

Green Plug: Lid fits higher up; plug rattles.

The audience must not notice you jerk the case as you put it down, but this is quite easily avoided.

The Cryptic Die. In this effective little trick, the die, which measures some three-quarters of an inch, is quite unprepared. It is handed out for examination, together with its celluloid case, which is just large enough to contain the die. The person examining the apparatus is requested to place the die in the box with any side that he desires uppermost. The case is then handed to the performer, who, after demonstrating that it is impossible to see the die, instantly tells the number of dots at the top.

Although the box will bear examination, it is peculiar in one point: the material used for the bottom is slightly thinner than the rest of the box, and therefore partially transparent. When the die is inside the box there is a space of about an eighth of an inch between this and the top of the lid. If a spectator turns the box over to examine it, the die will drop down inside, and thus cannot be seen through the bottom.

When the performer takes the box, he tilts it over with the bottom toward him to prove without calling special attention to it that the die inside cannot be seen. This movement tilts the die away from the spectator and toward the performer, and he is able to ascertain the number of spots on the bottom of the die. The spectator, of course, cannot see the die from his position.

When the number on the bottom of the die is known, it is an easy matter to calculate the number of spots on the top, as all dice are marked so that the numbers on opposite sides total seven. If, therefore, the bottom shows 4 the top would be 3; if 1, the top is 6, and so on. *H. & A. W.*

DOEBLER, LUDWIG LEOPOLD (or LOUIS) (1801-1864), Austrian magician. He and HOFZINSER were the greatest Austria has produced. He started life as a metal-engraver, then became a conjurer, and toured the continent, England, and Ireland with enormous success. He gave royal command performances, and amassed such a fortune that he retired permanently in 1847. A street in Vienna is named after him.

DOLLAR-BILL TRICKS (See also TORN AND RESTORED PAPER) A banknote is borrowed, and the performer proceeds to tear it into a number of pieces. These are rolled into a ball, and after a mystic pass or two the pellet is unrolled and the banknote is found to have been magically restored. The performer offers to repeat the trick, and does so with even more startling effect.

A duplicate bill is used for the second demonstration, but in the first part of the experiment *only one banknote is used.*

The performer has a banknote of his own—say a dollar bill—loosely crumpled into a ball and concealed under a fold of the sleeve at the left elbow. He borrows a dollar bill, selecting a note that is neither too old or too new—a bill of medium freshness and stiffness, and resembling as closely as possible the duplicate bill. The borrowed bill must not be frayed or torn on the edges.

Having borrowed the proper banknote, the performer holds it in his left hand, taking especial pains to show that his hands are otherwise empty, although he does not verbally call attention to this fact. The banknote must be held in the left hand precisely as follows: the note is held at the upper edge, the face of the bill toward the performer, between the first joints of the thumb and the first finger. If properly held, the tip of the thumb should exactly cover the letter "S" in the word "States," and the tip of the first finger will cover the final "E" in the word "Certificate" on the back of the bill. The upper left-hand corner of the bill will be wedged in the crotch of the thumb.

The right hand now grasps the bill at the opposite upper edge, between the thumb and the first finger. In order to attain the exact position, the tip of the right thumb should cover the words "States" and "America," on the front of the bill, while the first joint of the first finger completely covers the word "Silver" on the back of the bill. If the student will follow these directions with a banknote in his hand, he will instantly ascertain the exact position.

The right fingers now make a quick, sweeping movement toward the palm of the left hand, the upper edge of the bill slipping between the thumb and first finger, producing a noise that is an exact imitation of the tearing of paper. The movement must be quickly made, and the thumb and the finger should press rather tightly on the bill. At first the student will be loath to exert sufficient pressure, fearing to tear the bill; but if the upper edge of the bill is neither torn nor frayed there is no danger of such an accident. The paper used for banknotes is tough and strong.

After the right hand makes the swoop to the palm of the left, the right end of the bill lies naturally along the fleshy part of the left thumb extending toward the wrist. The second, third and little fingers of the left hand hold it in this position. Properly done, the noise and appearance of the folded bill produce a startling illusion, and the spectator who loaned the banknote will be willing to take his oath that his property will have to be sent to the Treasury Department for redemption.

The performer does not pause long enough for the spectators to cogitate on the matter, however. The right hand is held as if containing a part of the bill—that is to say, the back is toward the audience and the tip of the thumb presses tightly against the bunched tips of the four fingers, imitating as closely as possible the action of holding a piece of the banknote. The right hand now apparently places the torn pieces of banknote on the supposed half in the left hand, and it is on the naturalness of this movement that much of the illusion depends. The fingers of the left hand are opened, of course, so as to receive the torn half. The student should practise this movement in front of a mirror until he is able to deceive himself into the belief that he really places the torn half of the banknote in his left hand.

At this stage of the trick the banknote is folded in two. The right hand does not pause after apparently placing the torn piece in the left, but immediately grasps the doubled bill at the upper right-hand corner, and repeats the tearing movement. This is accomplished in the same manner as before except that in this instance there is but half the surface to operate on. Accordingly the right thumb and forefinger clip the bill at the lower right-hand corner, and move as before toward the left palm, producing the tearing noise. The second and third fingers of the left hand immediately close on the triangularly folded bill, which leaves only a small portion of the banknote exposed in the left hand. The effect is that you have actually quartered the bill.

As before, the right hand simulates the action of holding a portion of the mutilated bill, and the same motion of apparently placing the torn portion on to the pieces in the left hand is repeated, this time the fingers of the right hand coming down on the folded bill with a smart slap, the noise assisting materially in the illusion. The banknote is now bunched in a sort of ball. A portion of the ball is grasped between the thumb and the tips of the first and second fingers of the right hand, and the bill is twisted back and forth, the performer apparently exerting much strength to tear the bunch of supposed pieces. Finally, after an extra strong tug and wrench, the right hand flies away from the left, the tightly pressing fingers and thumb producing a sound as of tearing.

The supposedly torn portion in the right hand is immediately slapped upon the bunch held between the left thumb and the first and second fingers, and the two supposed portions are rolled together into a ball. This ball, which is about the size of a marble, is now held in the left hand between the thumb and tips of the fingers. If the movements have been neatly and smartly done, the audience will be convinced that the ball is composed of the fragments of a once-perfect bill.

The performer makes two or three mystic passes over the pellet, breathes on it, and unrolls it in a restored condition, during which operation he takes especial pains to show that no duplicate bill is concealed in his hands.

The trick, however, is not finished. The performer repeats the trick exactly as described—that is, the first three tearing movements. The banknote is now bunched in the fingers of the left hand. The fingers of the left hand, still holding the bill, grasp the right sleeve at the bend of the elbow and pull the sleeve up. The right hand does the same for the left sleeve, at the same time obtaining possession of the duplicate bill, which is placed *behind* the larger bunch in the left hand. Both bills are squeezed together so as to appear as one. The right hand grasps the duplicate bill and the left hand holds the borrowed bill. The performer now operates on the bunched bill, working the fingers back and forth, making it appear as if he were exerting every ounce of strength in his hands. In reality the two bills are pressed tightly together.

Suddenly, with a movement as if twisting the bill in two, the fingers are wrenched apart, the right hand carrying away the duplicate bill and the left hand holding the borrowed bill, the rubbing of one ball against the other producing a loud tearing noise. The tightly bunched condition of the banknotes and their jagged edges absolutely convince the spectators that you have destroyed the bill.

The performer now apparently rolls the two bills into one, really palming the duplicate bill in the right hand. He hands the other bill to a spectator, requesting him to breathe on the pellet and to unroll it. During this operation all eyes are naturally on the spectator, which gives the performer ample opportunity to get rid of the duplicate bill.

Another effective impromptu trick, which naturally follows the experiment just described, produces the following effect: a borrowed banknote—any denomination—is marked with the initials of the owner and wrapped in a handkerchief. A borrowed and examined lemon is placed under a tumbler. The banknote is commanded to leave the handkerchief, and is found inside the lemon.

The only property required for this trick is an ordinary handkerchief, in one corner of which is sewn a tightly rolled piece of paper to represent a tightly folded banknote. This handkerchief is carried in any convenient pocket. Borrow a lemon, or allow a lemon of your own to be examined, and while the examination is going on, borrow a banknote.

Request the lender to mark the note with his initials, and while he is thus engaged take back the lemon, and with the thumbnail cut through the skin at one end. This small slit will allow you to poke your forefinger into the lemon. Care should be taken not to make the hole too large. Request the spectator to fold the bill in half; to fold it again in half; to fold this quarter in half; to fold this eighth in half; to fold this piece again in half, and roll it up, when it will resemble the size and shape of the paper concealed in the corner of the handkerchief.

While holding the lemon in the left hand (the end with the hole toward the palm), take out the handkerchief, show it on both sides, and throw it over the left palm—covering both the hand and the lemon.

The handkerchief should be arranged so that the right-hand corner (the one nearest the body) is the one that conceals the folded piece of paper. Taking the folded and rolled banknote from the spectator, you apparently place it in the center of the handkerchief; actually, however, you fold in the corner of the handkerchief containing the piece of paper. While the right hand is under the handkerchief, the borrowed banknote is pushed well into the lemon. In actual practice these two separate movements blend into one and occupy but a fraction of a second.

The handkerchief is immediately handed to someone to hold, and as the spectator grasps what he thinks is the borrowed banknote, no suspicion is aroused. No one will suspect that the lemon has been tampered with.

The lemon is now placed on the table and covered with a tumbler. Taking hold of one corner of the handkerchief, you request the spectator to drop the banknote at the word "three." "One, two, three!" The bill disappears; you divide the lemon in half, and, separating the two halves, reveal the banknote sticking in the upper half. This half is handed to a spectator, who removes and identifies the banknote. For obvious reasons the other half of the lemon is not handed for examination. It is either pocketed or thrown on the table.

There is another method of doing the trick which, while just as effective, is not quite so clean in workmanship. In this method two lemons are employed. One has a slit in the side, near the center. This lemon is in the right coat pocket at the beginning of the trick. An unprepared lemon is shown and then placed in the same pocket. A bill is borrowed and apparently wrapped in a handkerchief, as described in the first method.

Hand the handkerchief to someone to hold, and take the faked lemon out of the pocket, at the same time inserting the bill. Lay the lemon on the table—slit side away from the audience—and vanish the bill. Cut the lemon, beginning on the side opposite the slit and finishing with the knife in the slit. Allow a spectator to remove the top half and take out the bill. The only advantage that this method has over the first one is that both halves of the lemon may be examined. *T. N. D.*

DOLL'S HOUSE An illusion invented by FREDERICK CULPITT. A two-story doll's house standing on a four-legged table is shown, and turned completely around. The front end of the house opens, showing the interior with a second floor and some doll furniture. These are removed, leaving the house quite empty. The front end is closed, house and table turned around again, and then the roof opens, and a woman steps out.

The inside back of the house is false, being set about a foot from the outside back. There is also considerable room between the inside bottom floor of the house and the bottom of the table, which has a wooden apron like any kitchen table. The woman sits with her body between the false and true end of the house, and her legs in the box of the table. The false back folds forward to lie flat on the floor. The woman has only to push it forward, stand up, and push up the roof.

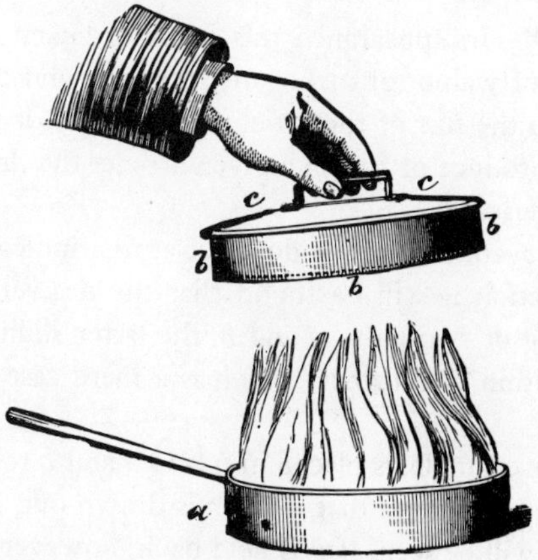

FIG. 1

DOVE PAN A shallow pan of brass or tin, about ten inches in diameter by two and a half in depth. Within this is an inner pan, also of brass or tin, fitting tightly within it, but about half an inch less in depth. The lid is made with a very deep rim or shoulder all around, and just fits within the lining, although less tightly than the latter fits within the pan. (See Fig. 1, in which *a* represents the pan, *b* the lining, and *c* the lid.)

Three doves may be put in *b*, which is then covered with *c* (the two together having the appearance of a simple cover).

The performer makes an "omelet," breaking eggs into *a*, and claps on the cover. When the cover is again removed, the lining remains in the pan, concealing the omelet beneath it, and revealing the doves.

DOWNS, THOMAS NELSON (1867-1938). The creator of coin manipulation as a separate branch of magic, and one of the greatest sleight-of-hand performers of all time. He was born and brought up in Marshalltown, Iowa, where he became a railway telegrapher. Hours of toying with the money in the change drawer gave him incredible skill at palming, and he developed the modern back palm with coins (see COIN MANIPULATION). He was a suberb showman, famous almost throughout the civilized world as "The King of Koins," and amassed a fortune so shrewdly that he was able to retire quite early in his career, and devote the last quarter-century of his life to his hobby, which was magic and magicians. The book written for him by John Northern Hilliard, *The Art of Magic*, remains one of the finest manuals of sleight-of-hand in existence.

DRAWER-BOX In appearance this is an ordinary drawer, with an outer box or case of walnut or mahogany (Fig. 1), and of various dimensions, according to the size of the articles with which it is intended to be used. Its use is to produce or vanish a given article; the drawer will appear full or empty at pleasure.

Even when removed, the drawer does not at first indicate any speciality. On closer examination it will be found that the drawer is really double (Fig. 2), consisting of two parts, *a* and *b*, the latter sliding backward and forward freely within the former, which is a mere case or shell, open at one end.

If an orange, for example, is placed in *b*, and *a* and *b* together are placed in the outer case, it is obvious that when *a* is drawn out, *b* will come with it, and the orange will be seen. If *b* is held back, however, *a* will be drawn out alone, and the drawer will apparently be empty.

The outer case has a groove or mortise cut in its under surface (Fig. 3), along which lies a spring or tongue of wood, fixed by a screw at one end, the free end being provided with a catch *c*, which, upon pressure, is forced through an opening in the bottom of the outer case, and made to sink into a little notch in the bottom of *b*, being withdrawn again by the

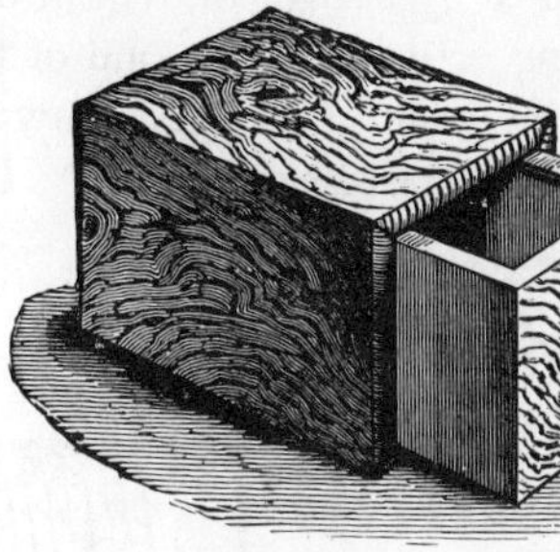

FIG. 1

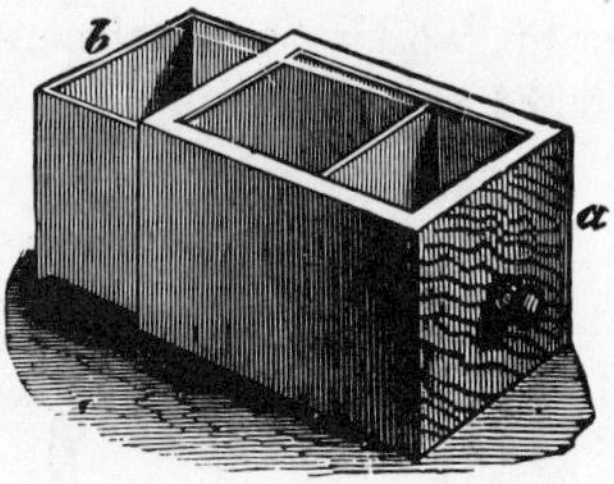

FIG. 2

action of the spring as soon as the pressure is removed. The bottom of the outer case is covered with velvet, ostensibly as a finish, but really to conceal the wooden tongue.

When it is desired to draw out *a* without *b*, the apparatus is held as in Fig. 3, and a gentle pressure is applied by the finger through the velvet upon the free end of the wooden tongue, thus forcing the catch upward, and keeping *b* back. If *a* is drawn out without this pressure, *b* will come with it. The upper edge of *a* is turned over all around, so that the casual observer is not likely to detect any difference in the thickness of the sides of the drawer, whether it is drawn out with or without its inner casing.

In some drawer-boxes *b* may be bolted to *a* at pleasure, and the two may be thus handed out for examination with little chance of their being de-

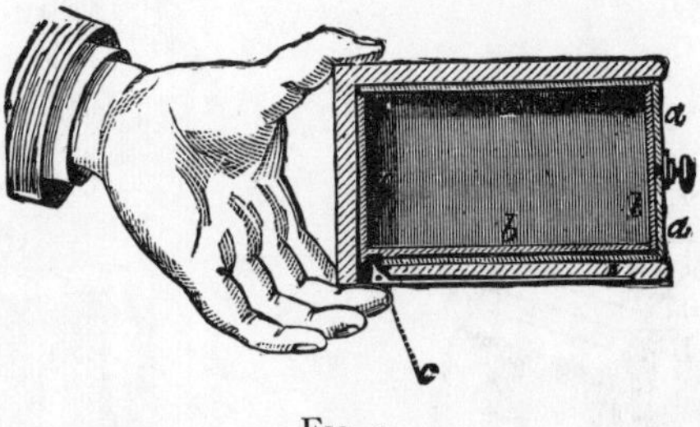

FIG. 3

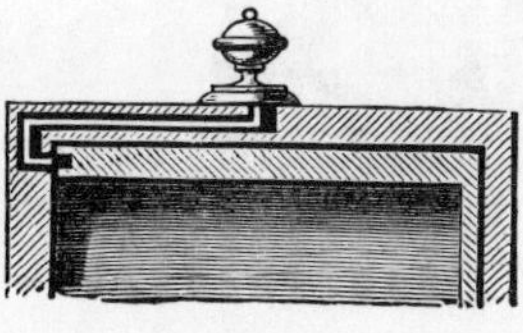

FIG. 4

FIG. 5

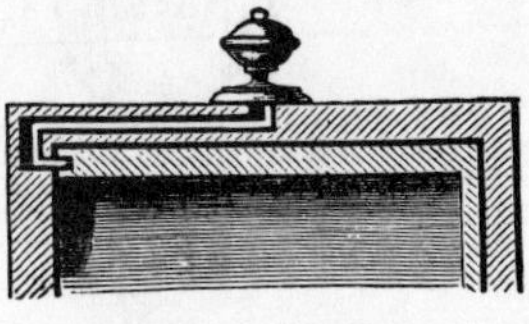

tected. The bolting and unbolting is effected by a slight movement up or down of the knob in front, thereby raising or depressing a kind of hook of bent tin, working in the thickness of the front of *a*. Fig. 4 shows this hook raised and unhooked, Fig. 5 shows it depressed and hooked. *L. H.*

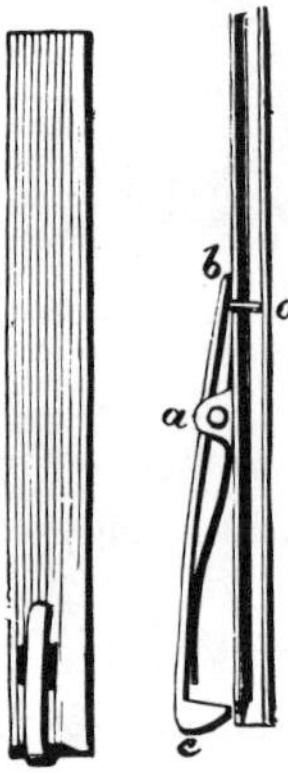

FIG. 1

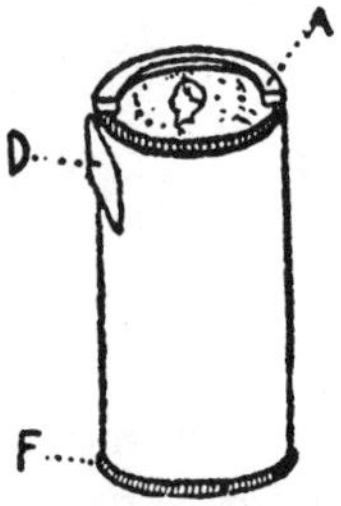

FIG. 2

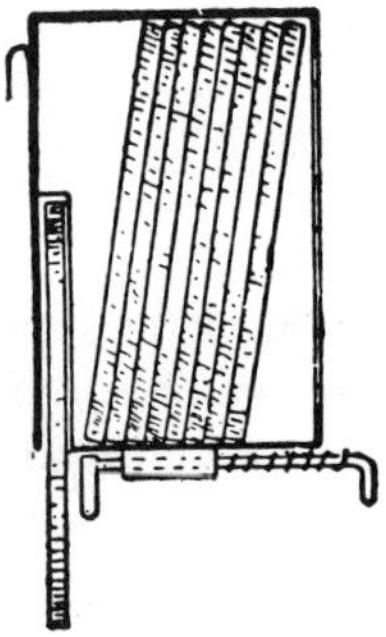

FIG. 3

DROPPERS (See also HOLDERS) Droppers are devices usually worn about the clothing, generally under the vest or coat, from which the performer can STEAL small objects, either in a bunch or successively.

Coin droppers are the most numerous. Those illustrated will deliver coins

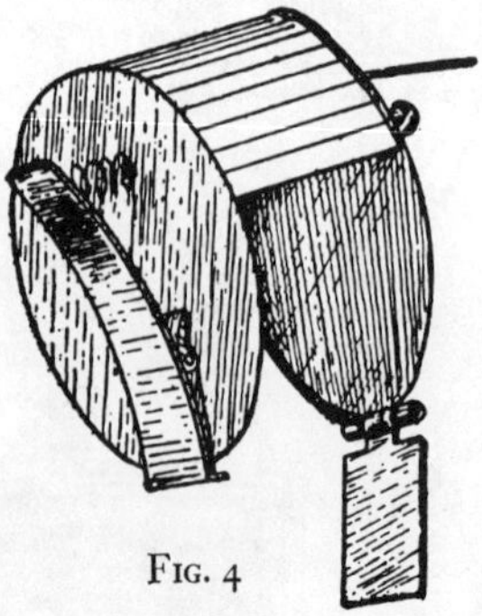

FIG. 4

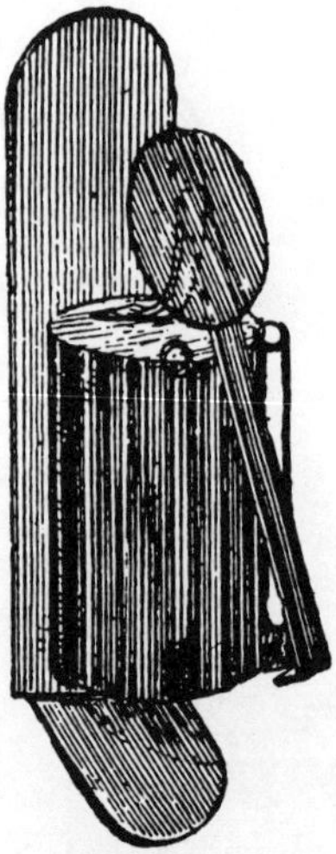

one after another from under the vest (Fig. 1); singly from the hand, for the MISER'S DREAM (Fig. 2); singly, by tilting the hat in the Miser's Dream, for which it is hooked to the sweatband (Fig. 3); and in a stack from under the vest (Fig. 4).

Cigarette droppers have now largely given way to holders or "tanks" (see CIGARETTE MANIPULATION), which allow the cigarettes to be produced lighted. Dummy lighted cigarettes are still sometimes used in the droppers, which work on the same principle as the first type of coin holder above.

H. H.

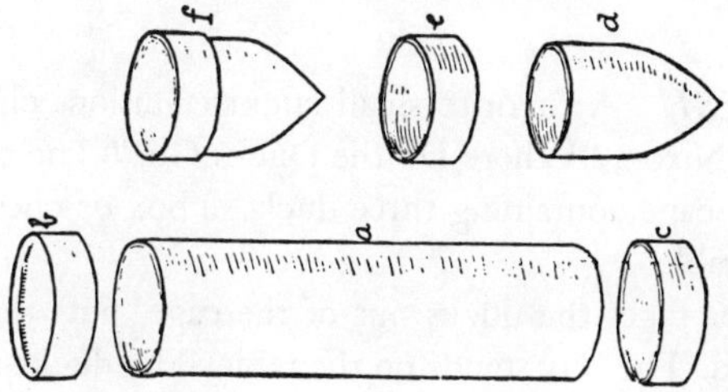

FIG. 1

DRUMHEAD TUBE This ostensibly consists merely of a brass tube, polished or nickel-plated, five inches long by one and a half in diameter (*a*, Fig. 1), and a couple of flat metal rings, *b*, *c*, fitting easily over it. A book of cigarette-papers, about two inches wide, completes the visible apparatus.

The performer hands the empty tube to one of the spectators, who is invited to place one of the cigarette-papers over one end, and to secure it by forcing one of the rings over it. It is then passed to someone else, and the opposite end is treated in the same way, the tube thus forming a sort of miniature drum, with tissue-paper ends.

The little drum being returned to the performer, he places it in the hands of a third spectator for safe-keeping. Taking a small silk handkerchief, he vanishes it; then, taking back the little drum, he breaks the paper at one end, and the handkerchief is found inside.

The secret lies in the use, unknown to the spectators, of the little appliance marked *d* in the diagram. This is a metal tube, one end of which is normally open. The opposite end is closed, tapering down to a fairly sharp-pointed cone. This is prepared by packing a duplicate handkerchief into it, after which the open end is closed with another cigarette-paper, which is kept in position by a third ring, *e*, passed over it. The upper edge of *e* curls over slightly to the outside, the appearance of the two in combination being as *f*, and the two together being of such a diameter as to just fit within *a*.

When the newly made "drum" is handed to the performer he has this PALMED in his left hand, point outward. He takes back the drum with his right, and holds it horizontally between the hands while he asks who will volunteer to take charge of it. In that moment he presses the fake into the end of the drum, the conical point forcing its way through the original paper. When it is fully home it leaves the appearance of the drum exactly as before, though it is now loaded with the duplicate handkerchief.

L. H.

DUCK VANISH A favorite small SUCKER illusion, christened by its inventor, W. J. Nixon, "Where Do the Ducks Go?" The equipment consists of a wicker cage containing three ducks; a box or chest; and a rather heavily draped table.

The performer takes the ducks out of the cage, puts them in the box, and closes the lid. The box stands on the table. The ducks vanish, and the performer quickly takes the box apart, showing all the parts separately. The audience suspects the table, and indeed when the cloth is removed, white feathers are sticking out below.

The feathers turn out to be part of a fan, and the performer fans himself, then takes the top off the table. The ducks are completely gone.

Part of the top to the wicker cage will sink down on pressure. The lid of the box has a cloth bag underneath, into which the ducks are pushed when they go into the box.

The performer then casually takes off the top of the box, and lays it flat on top of the cage. The bag of ducks pushes down the movable part of the cage lid, and is hidden from the spectators by a wicker panel woven around the top of the cage.

The rest of the effect, naturally, is pure build-up.

DYE TUBE (See under SILK TRICKS)

E

EAST INDIAN MAGIC Traditionally the most fabulous of all conjuring is that performed by the East Indian fakirs. The INDIAN ROPE TRICK, the INDIAN BASKET TRICK, the INDIAN MANGO TRICK, and LEVITATION have been described again and again, in the most startling terms, by travelers and mystery-lovers during the past century and a quarter. It must be a very young magician indeed who has not been asked by his friends about the "Hindu magicians." The word *fakir* in India is applied to religious ascetics, not magicians.

Of the tricks actually performed by the Indians, the smaller ones—the diving duck in a bowl of water, the dry-sands trick, the cups and balls, the potsherd trick (a mark made on a pottery fragment reappears on a spectator's palm)—are the best from a magician's standpoint. The manipulation is superb, and offsets the inherent shortcomings of the tricks themselves. The bigger and more gory effects are often poor conjuring, but invariably splendid acting.

As a badge of office the magicians use, not the gentlemanly wand of the West, but a small drum with two leather clappers fastened by thongs to the side, so that if the drum is shaken, the clappers rapidly swing to and fro, striking both heads of the drum. The gourd flute (used also by snake-charmers) serves for atmosphere, MISDIRECTION, and distraction. The East Indians, who generally travel in troupes rather than singly, are uninhibited in chanting, wailing, drum-beating, and generally carrying on; they rely for their effects, John Mulholland explains, on "deadening the attention of the spectators." For the Western spectator, furthermore, this noisy to-do lends an exotic atmosphere to the whole show. Deadening the attention, however, is more limited in its application than misdirection; hence East Indian magic is not equal to CHINESE MAGIC.

In such tricks as the CUPS AND BALLS, the performer's posture, squatting on the bare ground, while it seems to make his work more difficult, actually renders it largely ANGLE-PROOF. And the variety of colleagues, assistants, and costumes, gives considerable play to STEALS and LOADS.

Eddie Joseph's *Magic and Mysteries of India* is an excellent and enlightening treatment of the subject. *H. H.*

EGG AND HANDKERCHIEF For this capital feat, generally identified with the name of COLONEL STODARE, the following are required: a glass goblet, two small handkerchiefs (generally of plain crimson silk, and about sixteen inches square), a larger silk handkerchief—to which is attached, by a silk THREAD about four inches long, a blown eggshell—and a hollow celluloid egg, with an oval opening on one side of it measuring about an inch and a half by one inch, or a little more.

The performer comes forward, having in his right hand the goblet and one of the red silk handkerchiefs. The larger silk handkerchief is thrown with apparent carelessness over the other hand, and upon it rests the blown egg, placed so that the thread is out of sight; beneath the egg, concealed in a fold of the handkerchief, lies the second red handkerchief, rolled up as tightly as possible. The hollow egg is, meanwhile, placed in the left-hand secret pocket of the performer.

He passes quickly in front of the audience, as though tendering the articles for examination (taking care, however, to keep his right arm advanced toward the spectators, so that the glass and small silk handkerchief will bear the brunt of inspection), and finally places the glass and small handkerchief on a table or chair in full view.

He places the egg in the glass, and covers it with the handkerchief, in one movement, for as the egg is already lying on the handkerchief, a mere turn of the wrist places the egg in the glass, and at the same time lets the handkerchief fall over it; and at the same time the smaller handkerchief, which was concealed in the larger, is released, and falls into the glass with the egg.

"You have all seen me place the egg in the glass" (at the same time shaking the glass, to show by the sound that the egg is still there), "which I will not touch again. I shall now take this small handkerchief" (the one which has remained on the table), "and standing as far as possible away, I shall command the handkerchief to dissolve and pass into the glass, and the egg which is now in the glass to come into my hands."

So saying, he holds up the handkerchief in such a way as to show indirectly that he has nothing else in his hands. Taking a few steps, as though merely to get further from the glass, and holding the handkerchief hanging down between the finger and thumb of the right hand, he drops the other hand to his side, and secretly takes from his pocket the hollow egg, which he PALMS, keeping the opening outward.

Standing with his left side toward the spectators, he then joins his open hands (Fig. 1), the handkerchief hanging down between them. Requesting the audience to watch him closely, so that they may be sure there is no

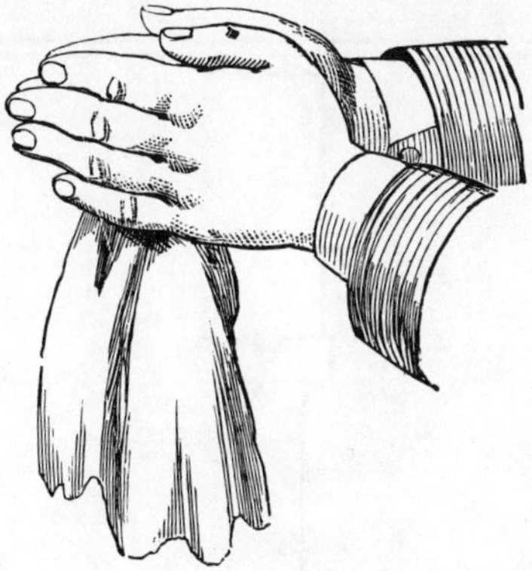

FIG. 1

deception, he begins to wave his joined hands slowly up and down, the second and third fingers of the right hand (which is away from the audience) meanwhile gradually working the handkerchief into the hollow of the egg. Every now and then he pauses to show that the handkerchief is gradually diminishing, and at last when it is wholly worked into the egg, opens his hands and shows the egg lying in his palm, taking care, of course, that the opening is undermost. To all appearances, the handkerchief has changed into an egg.

He puts the egg, still with the opening downward, on the table, and taking hold with the finger and thumb of the handkerchief which covers the glass, lifts it daintily up, carrying with it, concealed in its folds, the eggshell attached thereto, and leaving the duplicate red handkerchief lying in the glass. *L. H.*

A favorite combination trick is that in which an ordinary egg, marked with a pencil, and dropped into a glass and covered with a paper cylinder, changes places with a handkerchief held in the performer's hands. The usual method of accomplishing this effect is by means of a BOTTOMLESS TUMBLER.

The bottomless glass is retained in this method, but it is used in conjunction with a dainty and ingenious piece of apparatus—the miniature table or "handkerchief pedestal" illustrated in Fig. 2. This table, nickel-plated throughout except for the top, which is covered with figured felt, is sixteen inches in height, and the base and top measure five inches in diameter. The standard is composed of two parts. The lower part, nine

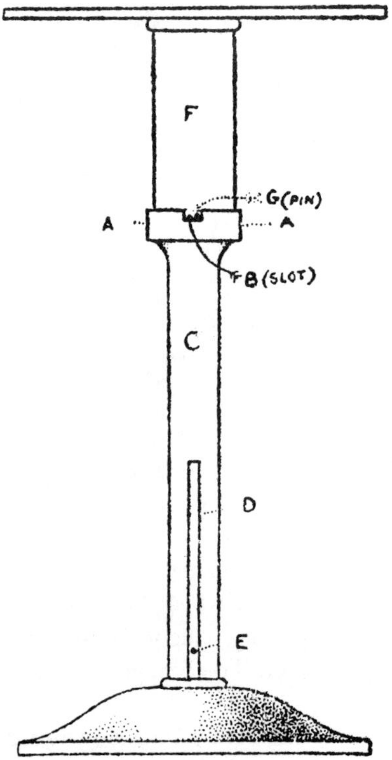

FIG. 2

inches long, is made of half-inch tubing, to the top of which is soldered a cup-shaped attachment (*a* in Fig. 2) made of metal one-twelfth of an inch thick. The diameter of this flaring cup at the top is one and one-twelfth inches. The cup, bulging in this way, provides an inside collar or rim, about one-eighth of an inch wide.

One side of the cup is slotted for a bayonet catch (*b* in Fig. 2). Fitted inside the tube *c* is a piston seven and one-half inches long, the top of which normally rests inside cup *a*. A slot two and a half inches long is cut in one side of the tubing (shown at *d*), and by means of a small projecting stud *e* the piston may be raised. The upper part of the leg or standard *f* is made of tubing a trifle less than an inch in diameter, and is just large enough to fit snugly in the cup *a*, a small pin *g* being soldered to the lower end of the tube which fits in slot *b*. This part of the leg is permanently attached to the under side of the table top, being threaded into a metal plate which is fastened by screws to the wood.

The table top is sawed out of quarter-inch stuff, painted black on the under side, and the top is covered with the very best quality of figured felt. A black felt with green figures gives the best results. A circular hole corresponding to the diameter of the metal tube is cut through the top. The felt is cut to correspond with the hole in the table top, except that the circular piece is not entirely removed, a hinge of cloth being left so that the small circular piece of felt forms a flap which covers the hole. As the felt is figured, the line of this cloth trap cannot be seen at a distance of three feet.

To prepare for the trick the two parts are fitted together, as in Fig. 2, a small silk handkerchief is pushed into the upper part *f*, and the felt flap is smoothed down flush with the top. The apparatus thus loaded should stand on one of the regular tables. A duplicate handkerchief lies on the table beside the little stand.

In presenting the trick, an examined and marked egg is covered with a large handkerchief. In the act of placing the covered glass on the little stand the egg is allowed to fall into the palm of the left hand. This hand adjusts the handkerchief, which should be large enough to fall down as far as the slot *d*, and at the same time the right hand moves the stud upward, the piston forcing the concealed handkerchief into the glass.

Taking the duplicate handkerchief from the table, and holding it in the left hand so that the egg is concealed, the performer announces that he will pass it into the glass. Placing the two hands together and standing with the left side to the audience, he moves his arms up and down, and under cover of this movement works the handkerchief into the fingers of his left hand, the egg eventually becoming visible. The egg is then transferred to the right hand and passed to the audience for examination.

The left hand, in which the small silk handkerchief is concealed, whips the large handkerchief off the glass, and in laying the handkerchief cover on the table, the palmed handkerchief is dropped into a SERVANTE, or simply hidden under the larger handkerchief. The left hand now jerks the small silk handkerchief out of the glass, and with a synchronal movement the right hand carries the glass away. The glass is not lifted from the table, but is taken off with a sliding movement so that the bottom edge will level the felt flap flush with the top. This flap, of course ,was raised by the action of the handkerchief being pushed by the piston into the glass, and as it is not heavy enough to fall back by itself, the sliding movement of the glass is an important detail. *T. N. D.*

Another popular modern egg and handkerchief trick falls in the class of SUCKER GAGS. The performer merely transforms a handkerchief into an egg. He then explains that it is done with a hollow egg, demonstrating as he speaks. In the end, however, he breaks the egg into a tumbler, showing that it is real, and the handkerchief has vanished. To perform this effect an oval bit of cloth to match the handkerchief is glued on a fresh egg, and at the appropriate moment the fresh egg is substituted by palming (see BALL MANIPULATION) for the hollow egg with the handkerchief stuffed inside, which is simulated by the patch on the fresh egg.

DE BIERE'S EGG BAG

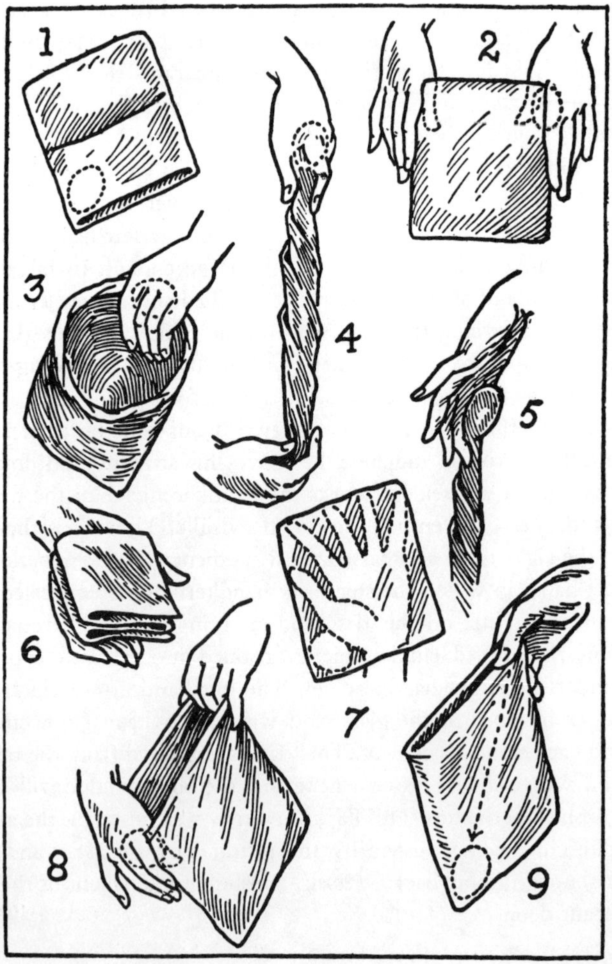

EGG BAG The egg bag is about eight inches deep and six in breadth, and made of alpaca or some opaque material. Its only peculiarity is that one of its sides is double, the stuff being folded down inward from the mouth of the bag to about two-thirds of its depth, and stitched at the sides, but left open at its lower edge. The effect of this arrangement is to make a sort of pocket, mouth downward, inside the bag.

If any small article, such as an egg, is placed inside the bag, and the bag turned upside down, the article will not fall out, but will fall into the pocket, which, in the reversed position of the bag, will be mouth upward. This will enable you to conceal the presence of any article in the bag, as you may turn it upside down and even inside out without any fear of the article's falling; and so long as you take care to keep the pocket side of the bag toward yourself, the spectators have no reason to suspect that the bag is not empty.

The uses to which this little bag may be put are various. Among others, it is available either to produce or cause the disappearance of an egg, and may thus, in combination with other apparatus, be made useful for many tricks.

The performer comes forward, having in his hand the bag, in which a small egg is placed beforehand. He turns the bag upside down and inside out, thus proving to all appearance that it is perfectly empty. Holding the bag for a moment with his teeth, he pulls back his coat cuffs, to prove that he has nothing concealed there, taking care as he does so to show clearly that his hands are empty.

Taking the bag in his left hand, and imitating (if he can) the clucking of a hen, he dips his right hand into it, and produces an egg (or rather *the* egg). This he places in his mouth, letting everyone see that he does so; then making a gesture of swallowing, he again dips his hand in the bag and produces a second egg, of which he disposes in the same way, repeating the operation until a dozen or more have apparently been produced and swallowed.

The egg, though actually placed in the mouth, is instantly pushed out again with the tongue under cover of the hand, and PALMED, making it very simple to produce (apparently) another egg from the bag. If neatly performed, this trick produces a complete illusion. *L. H.*

De Biere's egg bag was the ordinary one, with the secret pocket about half way on one side of the bag, but de Biere always made his own bags, for he knew the importance of having the right material–neither too thick nor too thin–and of having the pocket neatly made; a pocket slightly too large might have been dangerous, but as he always worked the trick rather quickly and had to get at the egg without the slightest fumbling, it was important that the pocket should not be too small.

In shape de Biere's bag differed slightly from the one generally used. He made his bag so that he could easily show it as a circular bag (Fig. 3).

He had another good reason for making his bags himself. Sometimes, when performing on the stage, he would begin the trick by tossing out the bag for inspection by his audience. The bag given out was, of course, an ordinary bag, but an exact copy, in shape, size, and material, of the bag which he actually used in the trick. The exchange was made when he took off his coat; the bag which the audience had examined was left in the sleeve of the coat.

The illustrations show the position of the egg at various stages in the trick. In Fig. 1 the egg is in the pocket, with the bag turned inside out. Fig. 2 shows how the egg was held at the top of the pocket when a member of the audience was asked to put his hand in the bag and satisfy himself that it was empty; and Fig. 7 shows how and why the hand failed to discover the presence of the egg.

Figs. 4 and 5 show the position of the egg when the bag was being twisted up to convince the audience that it was empty, and Fig. 3 shows the bag in its normal state but with the egg concealed by the magician's fingers. In Fig. 6 the bag is folded up flat on the hand, and Figs. 8 and 9 show how the bag could be shown empty to a member of the audience and yet, a fraction of a second later, the magician could dip his hand into the bag and take out the egg without hesitation.

The trick is more difficult when a blown egg is used because it is much lighter than an imitation egg, and, of course, one has to be more gentle with a blown egg than with one that cannot be broken. *W. G.*

Most present-day performers use a SUCKER routine in which they explain and demonstrate how the egg is sneaked out of the bag in the right hand (see EXPOSURES), put in the trousers pocket, and then sneaked back in. The second time that the conjurer goes through the motion, he leaves the egg in the secret pocket of the bag, holds his hand half-closed to simulate the egg, and pretends to put the egg in his pocket. He then has a spectator hold his wrists, with instructions to stop him if he tries to reach for his pocket. Of course the egg reappears in the bag nevertheless.

EQUIVOQUES ("CONJURER'S CHOICE") According to the dictionary, an equivoque is an "ambiguity." Magicians apply the word to the simplest form of FORCE.

The oldest equivoque known to magic is the "right-or-left" force. The magician has two objects on his table, behind which he stands, facing the audience. He offers the choice of the two objects, right or left. But he does not say whether it is his right or the audience's right. Suppose he wants to force the object on his own right. If the audience shouts "right," he puts out his right hand, and takes it. If they call, "left," he says, "The one on your left?" He still takes the one at his own right.

Another standard equivoque is "take-it-or-leave-it." In the case of two objects, the performer simply asks a spectator to touch one. If he touches the object to be forced, the magician picks it up and uses it; if the other, the magician says, "All right, we'll put that aside." To force one of four, the magician asks the spectator to touch two, forces the proper two, and then forces the proper one of those. *H. H.*

ESCAPES AND RELEASES Although the two terms are often used to mean the same thing, there is a distinction: an *escape* is an effect, an item in a program; a *release* is a method, which may be used to perform an escape, but also to conceal the performer's part in some trick, such as spirit manifestations in a cabinet. Releases are reversible: the performer can fasten himself up again. (See SPIRIT EFFECTS)

The classes of escape likely to be used by the ordinary magician are three: ties; handcuffs and the like; bags, boxes, and containers.

Typical rope ties and releases follow.

The Jacoby Rope Tie. The performer takes two strong cords or tapes (tapes are preferable in a drawing-room performance), each about two yards long. He places the middle of one cord on the extended wrist of the right hand, so that the ends hang down. The cord is now tied around the wrist by a committee from the audience (see VOLUNTEERS), the knot coming on the inside of the wrist. As many knots may be tied as the committee desire, and the knots may be sewed or sealed with wax. The other wrist is then tied in the same manner.

The performer now places the left hand, as far as he can reach, under his right armpit; then he places the right arm *over the left elbow*, extending the right hand under the left armpit. The cords hanging down from each wrist are brought together at the performer's back and tied into a secure knot, which may also be sealed.

The performer seats himself on a chair (preferably a Vienna bentwood chair, or one with a straight rail at the top), and the double tapes are tied to the top rail of the chair near the post on the right side. The ends are either sealed to a card or tied to a bunch of keys. The method of tying the performer bears a slight resemblance to a straitjacket, and the performer may enhance the effect by calling attention to this fact, and also to the utter impossibility of his moving any portion of the arms or hands.

The rest of the body is now tied to the chair—that is, the waist and the feet are securely fastened. These last ties have no significance, as the performer desires only the use of his arms. A screen is placed around the performer (Jacoby was carried into a cabinet), or he can be left on one side of a double room closed from view by a curtain.

As soon as this is done, the performer leans back a little, sitting as far toward the front of the chair as possible. He pushes the left hand as far as he can under the right armpit; this allows the right arm a little play, and with the right thumb he seizes the double cord extending from the right wrist and lifts it over his elbow and head. He now sits around a little toward the right and clasps his hands together several times. Then he quickly seizes the double cord with his right thumb and lifts it back again over his head and arm, assuming his former position. The committee may now examine everything.

A borrowed watch or ring is now laid upon the performer's right knee, and the cabinet is again closed, or the curtain drawn. The performer brings his right arm over as before and sits around to the right. He pushes the ring, or the ring of the watch, over the loop formed by the double cord hanging between the right wrist and the rail of the chair, and seizing the loop by his right hand pushes it (without twisting it) under the tie around the left wrist from the rear out (that is, from the cuff toward the fingers); he then pulls the loop over the tips of the fingers.

Drawing it entirely over the left hand, passing it under the tie on the upper part of his wrist, he pulls it back over his left hand again. Then he brings the double cord hanging from the right wrist to the front again, passing it over the head and left elbow, thus assuming the exact position in which he was tied. If the directions have been carefully followed, the ring or watch will be tied in a knot at the back of the chair.

The committee now make an examination, and the members are requested to remove the ring, a task they will soon give up. To remove the ring from the cords, a reverse process is employed. The directions may seem complicated at first reading; but if each move is followed with the materials in hand (an assistant doing the tying and reading the description), the knack of the Jacoby rope tie will soon be acquired.

The Jacoby rope tie may be used for almost all the so-called spiritualistic tests, such as spirit writing on slates, cutting out paper patterns, driving nails into a board, playing musical instruments, ringing bells, thumping a tambourine. Jacoby's final test was to invite one of the audience to sit in the cabinet with him. The spectator was blindfolded, and when the curtains were thrust aside, the spectator's vest was discovered turned inside out.

In another method the performer hands out for examination a fifty-foot line, preferably a new clothesline, and offers himself to be bound up in any manner the audience sees fit, stipulating, however, that they begin at one end of the rope and finish at the other. This is one of the chief points of the trick; it is almost impossible to tie anyone tight with this amount of line.

While the committee from the audience are tying you, slightly contract the muscles. Do this in such a way that it will not be noticed by the audience, but rather contract the muscles of that part of the body that the rope is being fastened to. By the expansion of the lungs and stiffening of the limbs, the rope can be kept apparently tight. Stand as stiffly as possible, placing the hands or arms wherever required, and allow them to be tied together at the sides, behind the back, or in front. The committee has to use one end of the rope; threading it through each knot and loop will soon tire them, and they will begin winding the rope around the body.

As soon as the rope is all wound and tied around you, request that you be carried to your cabinet, or behind a screen. Next comes the work of releasing yourself, which, after two or three attempts, you will be able to accomplish in the incredibly short time of two minutes.

To begin with, draw in the breath, and shrink the body as much as possible. This allows you to see any slack loops or looseness in the coils. In nine cases out of ten you can release your hands first. If you cannot, shake the loose coils around on your body, and begin to work them loose. Free the hands as soon as possible, or one hand. If the rope is around your neck release yourself here, and remove your coat (never be tied without it). This move practically places you in a position to remove the rest of the rope that is attached to your body and legs.

A good plan to work in connection with this tie is to force one of the hands to be tied first. This is accomplished by having a common slip knot in one end of the rope. Present the wrist to be tied first; then if bothered at all in trying to release yourself, get possession of a small sharp knife from your person and cut the rope at the slip knot; this gives you one free hand to work with. As soon as the rope is off and clear, make a duplicate knot in the end of the rope and conceal the small piece of rope you have cut off.

T. N. D.

Handcuff escape methods can be no more than hinted at within the compass of this book. Starting at the bottom of the scale, there are prepared cuffs that will open to a sharp pull, or on being struck smartly against something hard. Hinged irons may have removable hinge-bolts. Some ratchet handcuffs, adjustable to the size of the prisoner's wrist, can be opened by driving a strip of thin steel along the inside of the cuff, forcing back the ratchet catch or bolt, and allowing the cuff to slide open.

More frequently the lock of the handcuff must be picked, and the performer's part is twofold: hiding a selection of skeleton keys and picklocks where the committee from the audience will not find them; and quickly choosing and employing the right key when the moment comes.

Developing a handcuff act is a lifetime job, and no more than a bare outline has been attempted here.

Sack escapes are an easy and popular form of effect; there are several methods. In all of them the performer is tied up in a large sack having a drawstring at the mouth. The drawstring is tied, and often sealed. The performer quickly gets out without disturbing the fastenings.

One way is to lay open the inside of the hem through which the drawstring runs for an inch or two. When the magician gets inside the sack, he grabs the drawstring through this opening, and pulls down a couple of feet of slack, so that escape is a very easy matter.

Another method requires duplicate sacks, one being concealed in the performer's clothes at the start of the trick. He gets into the other sack; his assistant gathers up the mouth over his head, at which he pokes the mouth of the duplicate up through. A number of handkerchiefs are tied tight around the neck of the sack. The assistant takes care that these hide, but do not permanently stop, the mouth of the outer sack. Once hidden behind the screen, the conjurer can step right out of the sack, which he hides, and come forward with the duplicate, whose mouth is genuinely bound, tied, and sealed.

A third method is for the performer to carry a small, hard bolster an inch and a half thick by six inches long. Just as the audience starts tying the mouth of the sack, he jams this bolster up among the folds; by withdrawing it, he can get room to work his hand through the opening, and reach the cords outside. The bolster method will also work with a large paper bag. *H. H.*

The Mail Bag. A committee from the audience examines the mail bag carefully, inside and out, and finds it perfect in every respect, with no opening except at the top, which can be securely fastened.

The bag is made of leather and canvas, and is almost air tight. The canvas part of the bag is sewed by machine to make it strong; the leather part is sewed and riveted to the canvas.

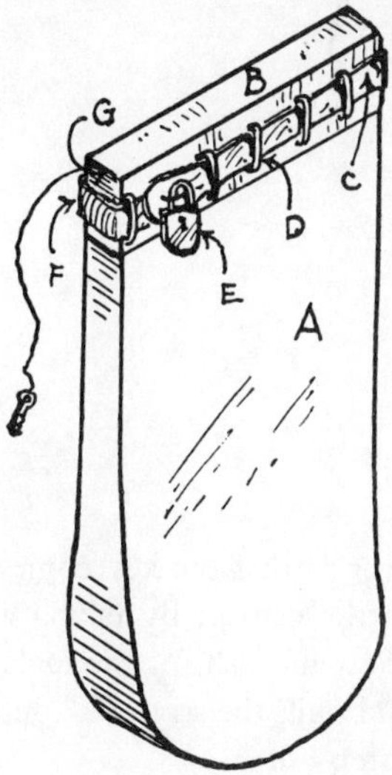

FIG. 1

FIG. 2

Fig. 1 shows the type and appearance of the bag to be used. "A" shows the canvas part of the bag, made large enough for the performer to move around inside. "B" shows the leather part of the bag, which lifts back to allow entrance to the bag. "C" is the leather strap which passes through the hasps to fasten the leather top in place, "D" indicates the hasps themselves, and "E" is the lock. (If a lock is used which has the keyhole on the bottom, the escape can be made much quicker and easier.) "F" is a small strap used to help close the opening on the end so that the performer cannot pass his hand out while he is inside, and "G" is a small opening between the bag and the flap.

Fig. 2 shows the appearance of the bag when it is opened, ready for the performer to step in.

The performer must have a duplicate key for the lock. This key is fastened to a string (Fig. 3), and the other end of the string tied inside the clothing, so that it cannot be lost during the act. The performer now steps into the bag, and is locked in securely, after which the cabinet is placed around him.

He takes out his key (making sure that it is securely tied to his clothing), and pushes it out through the small opening between the bag and the flap

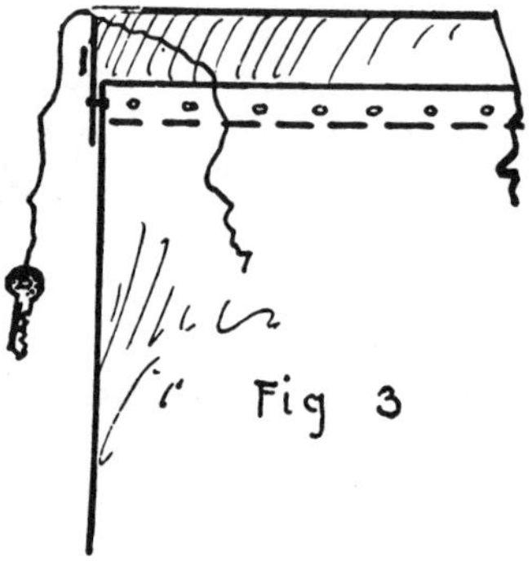

(Fig. 1). After the key is pushed out, he leans over so that the key comes on the upper side and its weight holds it against the canvas. By taking a fold of the canvas in his hand, he can grasp the key and fish for the lock. He inserts and turns the key, removes the lock, and pulls the strap "C" out from the hasps. Then he can open the flap and step out.

The bag now has to be closed and locked exactly as it was with the performer inside; the keys are concealed, the assistant signaled, and the cabinet removed, showing the audience the bag and performer just as they were at the beginning of the act.

The straitjacket escape, a standard feature among specialists, is a perfectly genuine exhibition of strength and skill. The hands must be forced over the head, as in the Jacoby Rope Tie; once that is accomplished (which may take many minutes if the jacket has been properly put on) the various straps and buckles can be undone by the teeth and hands, working through the canvas.

Escape from a Paper Cylinder. The performer brings forward, and has examined, a large paper cylinder open at both ends, half-a-dozen shoestrings, and a stick of sealing-wax. The cylinder, which is made of stout wrapping-paper, is then marked in any manner the audience wishes, and the performer is assisted into it; both ends are tied with the shoestrings and the knots are sealed.

The performer in his paper prison is then carried into his cabinet or behind a screen, and in a few minutes appears carrying the paper cylinder which is again examined without his means of exit being discovered.

To effect the escape, the performer has concealed in his clothing a pocket knife with one of the blades ground down as thin as possible, also a razor-like edge. As soon as he is in his cabinet, he gets possession of this knife, and placing one of the mouths of the cylinder flat on the floor, he feels for the strings and makes a clean cut about three-quarters of an inch long in the paper, and also through one of the strings. This enables him to pull the other portion of the strings to the opening thus formed and sever them, allowing him to make his escape.

He now quickly folds up the mouth of the cylinder in exactly the same shape as at first, and ties it with duplicate strings in the same manner as the committee from the audience did. He procures from his pocket a small bottle of alcohol and a cork with a piece of lamp-wick threaded through it. The cork is removed from the bottle and the cork with wick inserted and lighted. A similar piece of sealing-wax is now brought into play and the knots sealed as before, the complete operation lasting only a few minutes. Care must be taken to cover the cut in the paper with one of the folds, or better still, seal at this place. *T. N. D.*

Escapes from nailed-up packing cases were a sensational feature in HOUDINI's programs. Some performers fake the case, but this is hard to do in a way that will stand much examination. To escape from an unprepared case, the performer may carry in his clothes a three-part, demountable metal GIMMICK that works on the principle of a screw-jack. The gimmick is braced between top and bottom of the case, and the middle, being turned round and round, screws the ends outward until they simply force the top off the case by drawing the nails.

FIG. 4

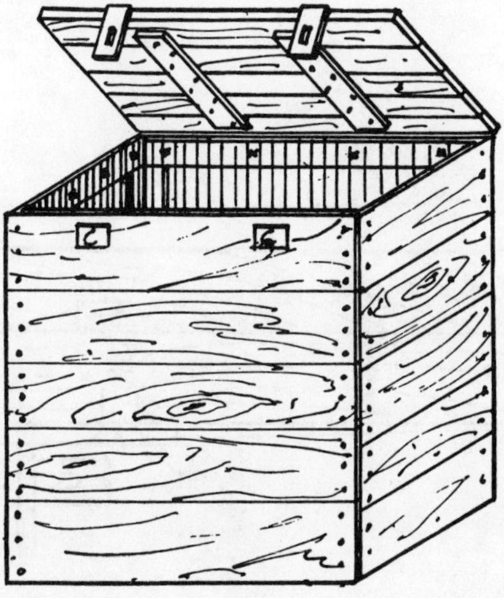

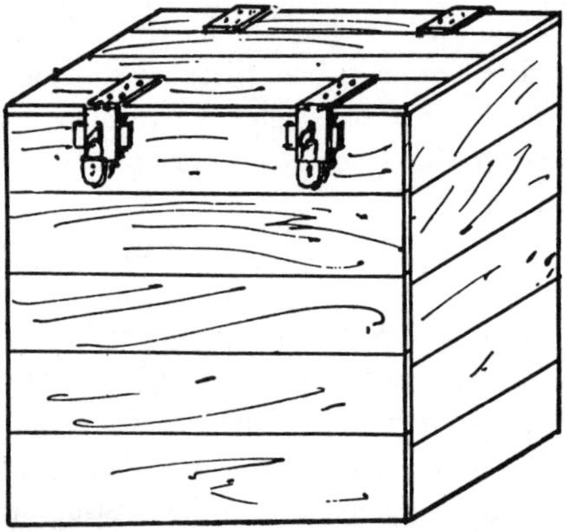

FIG. 5

When a prepared case is used, it should be large enough to hold the performer easily, about three feet each way. It is made of 7/8-inch white pine boards with all joints matched, and is strongly nailed and fitted with stout hinges and hasps, which are fastened with padlocks.

A committee is allowed to examine the box and to use their own padlocks in fastening the hasps. The performer is placed in the case, the cover is closed and locked, and the cabinet placed over it. Within a short time the escape is made, the canopy removed, and the packing case shown to the audience, still locked as at first.

FIG. 6

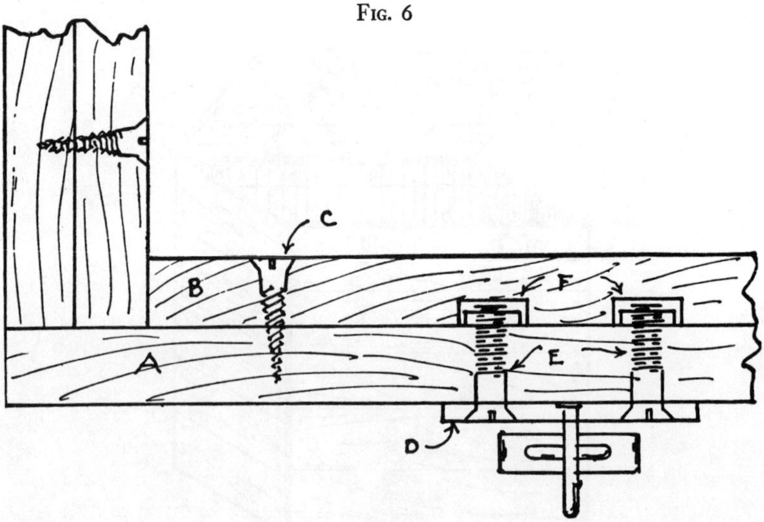

Fig. 4 shows the packing case as it appears open at the beginning of the act. Fig. 5 shows the case closed after the performer has been placed in it, and the padlocks in position. Fig. 6 shows the section of the case wherein the trick lies. This is a section through the front corner of the case, looking down. "A" is the front board of the case on which the locks are placed, "B" the cleat which runs entirely around the top of the case, inside, as shown in the open view in Fig. 4. The cleat is fastened with screws all around, one of which is shown in "C," Fig. 6. There are three screws in each cleat. "D" is the hasp that holds the lock and cover in place, held on by the screws "E." These are really machine screws, but they have heads like ordinary wood screws. They are fastened on with nuts on the inside of the front boards; the front cleat has counter-sunk holes "F," so as to fit over these nuts and lie close to the case.

After the performer is in the box and the cabinet in place, he takes a small screwdriver which he has concealed about him, removes the three screws from the front cleat, ("C," Fig. 6) and takes off the cleat. This allows him to get at the nuts, four in each hasp, which he now removes.

Then he can push out the machine screws "E," which will free the locks from the front of the case. This allows the cover to lift up so that he can step out.

He now takes the locks off the hasp and puts the hasps back in place, fastening them on again with the little nuts. The cleat "B" is fastened on again with the screws "C." The cover is now closed, the padlocks (which have been opened with duplicate keys) sprung in place on the hasps, and the case is locked as at first, showing no signs of having been tampered with.

Siberian Chain Release. A steel chain and padlock are given out for examination. This examination can be as thorough as desired, as neither the chain nor the padlock is faked in any way. The performer's wrists are chained together as tightly as possible and the padlock fixed; but in less time than it takes to tell, the performer's wrists are free and the chain and padlock are once more handed out for examination.

The secret of the trick lies in the way the chain is put on. The chain is provided with two rings (Fig. 7), which make it possible to have a small amount of slack between the wrists without the audience being aware of the fact.

Take the chain in the left hand and thread the end through the top ring, making a loop. Put the right hand through this loop and pull the chain together over the wrist tightly, but take special care that the ring on the end of the chain is on the top of your hand when the hand is held in a

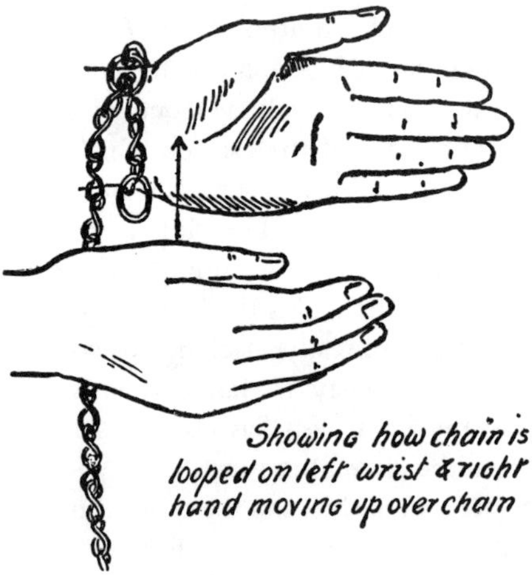
Showing how chain is
looped on left wrist & right
hand moving up over chain

FIG. 7

perpendicular position, and the second ring at the bottom. It will now be seen that the chain is hanging down over the top ring.

Press the wrists together tightly and ask a member of the audience to bring the chain around the left wrist underneath, across the top of both wrists, and through the ring which is hanging underneath the right wrist. The chain can now be brought back as far as it will go, and padlocked. When these movements are completed, it will be found that there is more than an inch of slack chain between the wrists, and it is the work of a second to release the wrists. *H. & A. W.*

EVERYBODY'S CARD (See GENERAL CARD)

EXPOSURES All magicians, and a good many other people in the entertainment world, denounce the exposure of conjuring secrets to the general public; but there is no general agreement whatever about what constitutes exposure.

The individual performer will soon learn that he is very foolish if he explains his own tricks, even good-naturedly after a private performance. SUCKER GAGS are, of course, an exception, but one to be carefully treated. In the "explanation" of the EGG BAG routine, for instance, some magicians unthinkingly display the egg palmed, instead of holding it clumsily; this is a grave mistake.

For one magician publicly to explain another's tricks is always unforgivable, and usually the height of folly as well, since it harms the business of magic and invites reprisals.

Publications are the real area of disagreement. Articles in periodicals explaining tricks or ILLUSIONS performed on the professional stage are pretty generally condemned. Nevertheless some explanations raise the performer in the eyes of the public by emphasizing his skill rather than the childish simplicity of the trick. To explain some SLEIGHT-OF-HAND tricks is only to enhance them. And the competent explanation of parlor tricks may launch new magicians, widening the interested, intelligent audience for magic.

Books present an insoluble problem. The Society of American Magicians does its utmost to prevent the writing and publication of books that retail for less than two dollars a copy. The theory is that the high price will limit the circulation, and thus the damage, of exposure. But the simple price criterion rules out *Modern Magic*, *The Expert at the Card Table*, and other magical classics that have made magicians by the thousands, while it lets in several books that do no more than hastily explain, with pictures, stage illusions that the reader might otherwise have enjoyed seeing performed.

The nature and purpose of a magic book would seem to be a much safer guide. The author is certainly exposing if he merely outlines the mechanics of a trick. If he makes some honest effort to teach performance, then he may be expected rather to bring new recruits to the art. The growth in magic directly traceable to the writings of Professor Hoffmann, Edwin Sachs, C. Lang Neil, and Hatton and Plate is beyond all calculation.

B. M.

F

FAKE In magic, a container or dummy prepared in some manner unknown to the audience.

Some writers distinguish between fakes, which are seen but not understood by the spectator, and GIMMICKS, which are not seen.

On this principle, a die shell (see DICE) or billiard-ball shell (see MULTIPLYING BILLIARD BALLS) is a fake, while a Stillwell ball (see SILK TRICKS) is a gimmick.

FAKIRS (See EAST INDIAN MAGIC)

FAWKES, ISAAC (died 1731), English conjurer, the best-remembered of the early fair and outdoor performers (see HISTORY). The EGG BAG was one of his big features. He accumulated the then ample fortune of £10,000 entirely by his work at the fairs. His son Fawkes the Younger succeeded him, and succeeded also to his partnership with the Pinchbeck family, the eminent mechanicians.

FINALE (See PROGRAMS)

FISH-CATCHING A trick introduced with great effect by CHUNG LING SOO: the hook of a fishing-rod was baited; the line whipped through the air, and a goldfish appeared on the hook. Several goldfish in succession were produced and put into a bowl of water, where they swam around.

Two FAKES are used: the bait and the rod. The bait is so constructed that on a sharp jerk it releases a cloth dummy goldfish much bulkier than itself. The handle of the rod contains a number of live goldfish, packed in wet cotton wool, which can be stolen one after another by giving a part turn to the handle. The performer steals a real fish, substitutes it for the dummy in removing the latter from the hook, puts the live fish in the bowl, and drops the dummy in the bait-box while getting fresh bait. *H. H.*

FLAGSTAFF Large silk flags used to be produced without staves; but up-to-date performers now produce each flag on a rigid staff, in some instances six feet long, or even more.

The secret lies in the fact that the staves are made on the telescopic principle, so that when closed they occupy a comparatively small space.

The staff for a flag three feet square is, when extended, a little over four feet long. The telescope consists of five brass tubes, sliding one over the other. Four of these are each ten inches long; the fifth and innermost is thirteen inches long, surmounted at the top by a brass knob. This inner tube (Fig. 1) terminates at its opposite end in a little conical stud which catches in a wire-loop at the bottom when the telescope is closed, but is released when desired by pressure on the thumb-piece shown at the side. The object of this arrangement is to prevent the tube's opening out prematurely.

To make it extend itself, the performer grasps the outer tube at the bottom, presses the thumb-piece, and gives the tube a semicircular swing with

FIG. 1, TOP BOTTOM, FIG. 2

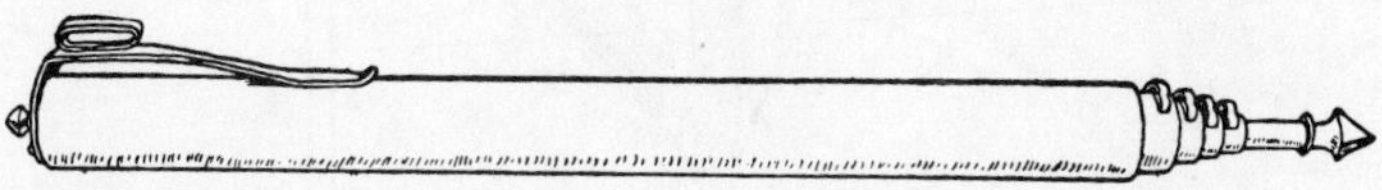

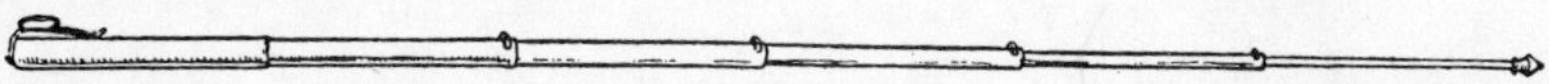

his arm. Centrifugal force causes each of the inner tubes to fly out to its full extent, and the staff assumes the appearance shown in Fig. 2.

Each of the tubes is made slightly smaller at its upper end and larger at its lower end. This difference is not perceptible, but it serves the double purpose of preventing the sections from coming apart and of keeping the staff extended after it has been developed; the base of each tube wedges itself into the upper end of the next The staff may be left standing upright after production.

At the upper end of the smallest tube there is a minute hole, and at the upper end of each of the next four tubes a little eyelet. To these one edge of the flag is fastened, the final result, when the flag is unfurled, being as shown in Fig. 3.

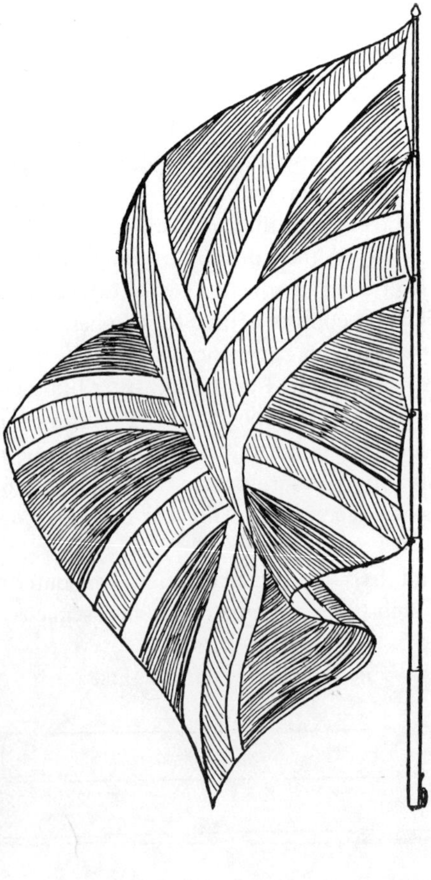

FIG. 3

To prepare the flag thus mounted for use in the trick, the telescope arrangement is closed, and the flag is folded in accordion pleats, first lengthwise, then crosswise, until it forms a small and compact package.

Thus arranged, flag and staff are placed in an appropriately shaped breast-pocket inside the coat. Reaching into this with the opposite hand, under cover of the flags already produced, and taking a firm hold of what may be called the handle end of the staff, the performer brings it out with a semicircular outward swing, when flag and staff at once expand to their full dimensions. Where two flags are to be produced, both breast pockets are loaded, the right hand producing the left-hand flag, and vice versa.

L. H.

FLASH PAPER Tissue paper chemically treated so that it disappears instantly, with a bright flash, when set fire to. It is most often used to "wrap up" small objects that are to vanish sensationally and be rediscovered elsewhere. (See COIN MANIPULATION: FOLD, PAPER)

Flash paper can be bought from all magic dealers, which is much the best procedure unless you need large quantities, and are used to handling dangerous chemicals.

It can, however, be prepared as follows: take four parts of concentrated sulphuric acid, and pour it very slowly into five parts of fuming nitric acid (specific gravity 1.52). Always pour the sulphuric into the nitric, stirring with a glass rod as you do so This mixture must then be covered to keep out moisture, and allowed to stand for twenty-four hours. Press down sheets of white tissue paper into a glass dish of the mixture, using the rod. Put the paper in one sheet at a time, soak it for about ten minutes, and then put it under a large stream of running cold water. Unless the paper is well washed, it will heat up and spoil. The paper must then be kept in a dish with water running through it (the volume need not be quite so large) for not less than two hours. Keep them there until a piece of blue litmus paper, dipped into the water, shows that there is no acid left.

Finally the sheets of tissue must be dried between sheets of blotting paper. Complete drying may take nearly a week. *H. H.*

FLOATING BALL; FLOATING LADY; FLOATING MATCH; FLOATING WAND (See under LEVITATIONS)

FLOWER IN BUTTONHOLE A good OPENING EFFECT. Through the center of an artificial rose or carnation, without stalk, a short piece (about ten inches) of thin black elastic is passed, and secured by a knot on the inside of the flower. The other end is passed through the buttonhole, from the outside, and then through an eyelet-hole made for the purpose in the breast of the coat, directly under the buttonhole. The extreme end is looped over a button sewn on the vest near the waistband. The tension of the elastic draws the flower close against the buttonhole, but allows it to be pulled out several inches.

Before coming forward to perform the trick, the conjurer draws the rose away from the buttonhole and places it under his left armpit, holding it in place by keeping his arm close to his side. When he waves his wand, he makes the first motion facing to the right, the second facing the audience, and the third facing slightly to the left, at the same time striking the buttonhole with the wand and throwing up his left arm. The flower, released from under his arm, instantly springs to the buttonhole. *L. H.*

FLOWER PRODUCTIONS So far as the audience are concerned, there are two kinds of flower production: growth (a variant of the INDIAN MANGO TRICK), and simple PRODUCTION.

Probably the earliest Occidental flower-growth trick was what Robert-Houdin described as "a mysterious orange-tree, on which flowers and fruit burst into life at the request of the ladies. As a finale, a handkerchief I borrowed was conveyed into an orange purposely left on the tree. This opened and displayed the handkerchief, which two butterflies took by the corners and unfolded before the spectators." The effect, which was more of a mechanical automaton than a trick in the modern sense, has been traced by HARRY HOUDINI through the programs of ISAAC FAWKES in 1730, Christopher Pinchbeck, Sr., PINETTI, ROBERT-HOUDIN, and others. The tree was artificial, and the flowers and fruit were made to grow by revolving hemispherical screens of leaves that concealed them at the start.

When word of the Indian Mango Trick reached the West, Occidental magicians began devising means to produce whole plants from nothing. HARRY KELLAR grew rose-bushes in pots that stood on small tables. He would cover the pot with a tall metal cylinder, and when the cylinder was lifted, the rose-bush had appeared. The bushes (real ones) stood to begin with on SERVANTES behind the tables that supported the pots, and Kellar contrived to lower the covers over the bushes and carry them away so that they could be set on the pots when he put the covers over.

Kellar's version is seldom if ever seen any more, partly because the MISDIRECTION required is very difficult, and partly because the tables must be draped nearly to the stage if a bush of any size is to be produced.

One method of eliminating the STEAL from the servante was to use a cover with a thick double wall, inside which was compressed a tall bouquet of feather flowers. Feather flowers are bright-colored objects made specifically for magicians, and sold by all magic dealers; they are sometimes attached to weighted darts, so that they may be tossed out to stand upright all over the stage. They have come in for a good deal of well-deserved condemnation because they are so obviously compressible, and do not look at all like real flowers besides.

The simple production, as opposed to growth, of flowers may have begun with the old trick of hiding a small bouquet, stems outward, in the sleeve, and withdrawing it under cover of a handkerchief. A standard version is the following:

One illusion of the eminent magician, BUATIER DE KOLTA, consisted of the production from a sheet of paper, freely shown on both sides and then rolled into a cone, of a quantity of paper flowers of all sizes and colors.

The main secret of the trick lies in the ingenious construction of the flowers. They are made as follows: the first step is to cut off a number of pieces of green tissue paper (not too thin) of the shape shown at *a* in Fig. 1. The extreme length of each is about four and one-half inches, and its greatest width an inch and three-quarters. Next should be cut out double the number of mixed colors, red, yellow, blue, pink, mauve, and white. These should be of the shape shown at *b* in the same figure. They may be of the same width as the green leaves, but are only one and three-quarters inches long.

The next step is to provide the necessary springs to make the flowers

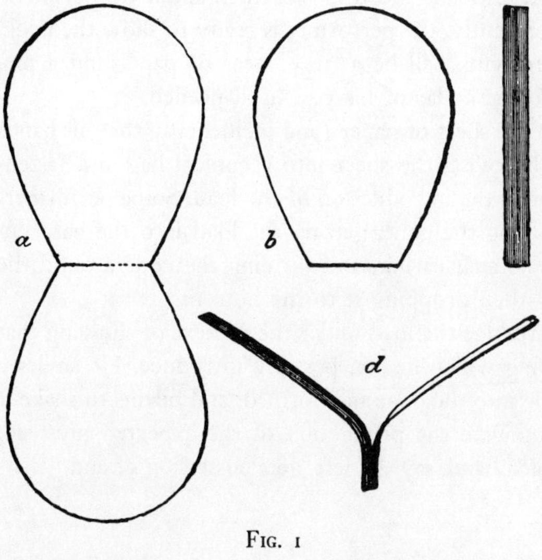

FIG. 1

FIG. 2

expand. These are made by cutting a sheet of rolled steel or hardened brass, the thickness of brown paper, into strips two inches long and a little less than a quarter of an inch wide; each strip must then again be cut down its center to within three-eighths of an inch of the opposite end (*c*), and the two portions then bent apart as *d* in the same figure.

Taking one of the green papers, fold it across the middle, and placing one of the steel springs between, secure it with strong paste to the center of the leaf, pasting a strip of the same paper, three-eighths of an inch wide, over it to conceal the spring. Lay these aside to dry; meanwhile taking pairs of the smallest pieces of paper (each pair of the same color), paste two of their edges together, and let them dry. This done, take one of these, and inserting it in the opening of one of the green papers, paste the free edges to the corresponding edges of this latter. The effect will now be as shown in Fig. 2. By pressing the sides together, the flower may be made perfectly flat, though it instantly expands again as soon as the pressure is removed. The flowers may also be purchased from a conjuring shop.

Having provided himself with a couple of hundred of the flowers, the performer should divide this quantity into (say) three LOADS. Taking the flowers one by one between finger and thumb, he presses each flat on its predecessor; when he has thus dealt with a sufficient quantity, he secures them between two slips of stiffish cardboard, three by two inches, with an elastic band passed around these in the direction of their greater length. When the ends of the cardboard are pressed, they separate in the middle, freeing the flowers at once.

When he has prepared his loads and disposed them about his person so that he can get at them instantly, the performer is ready to show the trick. His only further requirements will be a large sheet of paper and a pin, which he may stick into the collar of his vest until needed.

Showing both sides of the sheet of paper (and incidentally that his hands are otherwise empty), he twists the sheet into a conical bag and fastens it with the pin. Next comes the introduction of the load. Some performers do this in the act of making the cone, getting the load into the hat (say from the waistband) a moment earlier, and forming the cone around the hand which contains it—then dropping it to the bottom.

Another plan is to introduce the load under the pretext of showing that the performer has nothing which he can possibly introduce. He smiles a self-satisfied sort of smile into the cone just formed, and begins to shake it a little, as though to stimulate the production of the expected mystery; meanwhile the unoccupied hand, say the left, gets possession of and PALMS the load.

He shows the interior of the cone; then in order to show the right hand free he transfers the cone to the left, grasping it with the fingers inside, and thereby introducing the load. Having shown the right hand empty, he again takes the cone in the right hand, grasping it by the smaller end, and shows his left hand in the same way. The load meanwhile slides gently down to the bottom, and the trick is practically done.

The right hand grasps the cone outside the load, and prevents its too rapid development. The left hand dips into the cone, and under pretense of taking out the first one or two flowers, frees the remainder, and arranges them for subsequent production. As the performer diminishes the pressure of the encircling hand, the flowers naturally expand, and seem to well up spontaneously to the mouth of the cone, from which they are shaken into any convenient receptacle. The production should not be too rapid, as the effect of quantity is enhanced by a discreet amount of deliberation.

The production of a second load is an easy matter; since the general attention has been drawn to the gush of flowers from the mouth of the cone, the performer has ample opportunity to palm and introduce a further supply.

For the third load, however, the method of production should be varied. Getting the load into the palm of his left hand, and shaking out the last remaining flowers from the cone, the performer should remove the pin and open out the paper. Then spreading the paper over his right hand, he should bring the left hand violently down on its center, as if crushing the paper, and twist it into a crumpled ball, the load just introduced being of course in the center.

He crumples and knocks about the ball of paper thus produced, as though merely to carry still greater conviction to the minds of the audience that it contains nothing. When he has maltreated it sufficiently, he again unfolds the paper with due precaution, and again a gush of flowers comes welling from it—this last effect being, to most spectators, the most surprising of any. *L. H.*

FORCING (See also CARD MANIPULATION; CLOCK DIAL; EQUIVOQUES; MECHANICAL DECKS; PSYCHOLOGY)

The magical term for compelling a spectator to choose a known object from among a number of them, though he believes he has had freedom of selection.

Most methods of forcing depend on the principle of offering a spectator a choice among a number of objects—cards, billets, or numbered counters—that he supposes to be all different, but that are in fact all alike. Very often the objects will be shown all different, and then SWITCHED. Numbered counters, for instance, can be dropped into a CHANGING BAG, and thus secretly replaced with counters all bearing the same number.

One of the most familiar BILLET-READING methods is for the performer to write down on slips of paper the names or words suggested by the audience. Actually he writes the same word every time, and promptly destroys the rest of the billets after one has been chosen.

Other, less reliable methods of forcing depend on PSYCHOLOGY. It is a fact, for instance, that a person standing at one end of a row of five objects will usually pick the second one from his end. If a choice of certain numbers is offered, for instance five to ten or ten to twenty, certain ones will be picked more often than not (in this case, seven and fifteen).

The psychological and the manipulative forces are used almost entirely in card tricks. (See CARD MANIPULATION)

There are also various mathematical methods of forcing some particular number. For instance, you have someone write down his own telephone number; add two zeroes; subtract the telephone number; add up the digits of the answer. The result of that addition will always be eighteen, twenty-seven, or thirty-six. If in turn you add those digits, the answer is always nine.

The subject is very thoroughly covered in the late Theo Annemann's *202 Methods of Forcing.* *H. H.*

FOUR-ACE TRICKS (See also CARD MANIPULATION) The four-ace trick naturally has been improved upon since its invention, although the principle remains unchanged—the dispersing of the aces and their subsequent assemblage. Every performer, of course, has his own particular method of accomplishing this effect, in which he employs his pet passes and favorite moves; but the following methods are among the best known.

Charles Bertram's Method. The performer asks the assistance of a member of the audience. The four aces are taken out of the pack and placed on the top. The assistant deals the four aces separately on to the table, and upon each ace deals three other cards. He then chooses three of the heaps, which are placed in the pack, leaving one ace with the three indifferent cards on top of it on the table. He places his hand firmly over these, while the performer, taking the pack in his hand, makes a little "flip" with the cards, and draws from beneath the assistant's arm the three indifferent cards. The performer makes two more "flips" in rapid succession, and informs the assistant that he now has the four aces all beneath this hand. The assistant raises his hand and sees the four aces; on hearing that the three indifferent cards have passed into his pocket, he puts in his hand and finds them there.

Request someone to come and assist you, and while receiving him on your left, pick up your pack and PALM four cards. Place the pack on the table, saying, "Please give me the four aces out of the pack, and satisfy yourself that it is an ordinary pack of playing-cards, containing no more than four aces."

Being on your left, he will probably advance his right hand to take the pack, whereupon you arrest his arm with your left hand, and at the same time dive your right (containing the four palmed cards) into his inner or outer breast pocket, where you leave three of the cards, draw out one, and place it in the pack, remarking, "You really must not take any of my cards away like this without my asking you to. Perhaps you will lay the four aces on the table, and let me know whether there are any more aces in the pack."

The assistant will of course answer that there are no more than four aces, and as he lays these on the table you take the rest of the cards, and, placing them on the table, ask him now to place the four aces on top of the pack. This done, you take up the pack in the right hand, and secretly inserting the little finger of the left hand in the center of the cards, swing the left hand up with the pack and make the "flip," thus raising a suspicion in his mind as to what you may have done.

You mock-innocently ask, "Where are the four aces?" Your assistant will probably say, "At the bottom," or, "In the middle of the pack." If so, show him that they are on the top. Should he say, "On the top," make the SHIFT, keeping the little finger on the aces, and show him that they are gone.

Make the shift again, bringing the aces to the top. Tap the pack with your wand, and tell him, "A touch of the wand immediately restores the aces." Make another and louder "flip" than before, and deal the four aces face downward on the table, saying, in a confident yet suspicious manner, "The four aces are there now, aren't they?" He will probably say, "No, I don't think they are," in which case you show that the aces are there, turning them up one by one on the table.

Palm off three cards, and place the pack on the table, asking your assistant to put the four aces on top. Then take the pack with your right hand, placing the three palmed cards on top.

Count one, two, three, four cards, keeping the pack in position as though for dealing, and show them, of course only allowing the ace to be seen, saying, "Yes, you have placed the aces fairly on top of the pack this time."

Hand him the pack into his left hand, and tell him to deal the four aces in a row upon the table, face downward. As he moves his right hand to the pack, you place your left hand gently and persuasively on his arm just above the wrist, and guide each card down to the table, saying as you do so, "One here, and one here, and one here, and the fourth here."

As the fourth card (an ace) is laid down, you quickly turn it up, giving the audience a sight of it, and say, "Upon this ace put three cards." He does so, you again guiding his arm, as the three cards are the other three aces and must not be seen.

As soon as the three aces are safely upon the fourth ace, you stop guiding his hand. "And three on the next ace," you say, "and three on the next. You may take them from any part of the pack you choose" (as now it does not matter). "And now three upon the last ace. You see I do not even touch the pack. Now will you please place the pack on the table and tell the audience what you have done? You have placed four aces on the table, and upon each ace you have placed three cards. Is that right?" He will of course agree.

Hand him the wand and request him to touch two of the heaps. If he touches heaps one and two (the heaps are numbered in the order the cards were laid on the table), take them and place them in the pack.

Should he, however, touch heap number four and another, then you remove the two heaps which he did *not* touch and put them into the pack, saying, "You choose those, then I will take these," so leaving number four and another on the table.

Ask the assistant to touch one more heap. If he touches number four, remove the other, saying, "Then I will take this." If he touches the other, remove it all the same into the pack, so that in any event number four is left on the table.

You pick up the pack and say, "Having had a perfectly free choice, you have now left me one ace and three small cards. Will you please put your hand firmly on this remaining ace and the three indifferent cards? My trick is this: I shall, against your will, make you raise your hand from the table, and in that instant I shall take from you the three indifferent cards and give you the three aces from the pack instead."

As you speak, palm three cards, and running your hand up his arm produce the three cards from underneath his elbow. Put them on the pack, saying, "Here I have the three indifferent cards. Now to give you the three aces." Take the pack in your left hand; run it down his arm, making the "flip" loudly as you do so, and say, "That gives you the three aces."

Give a sharp upward movement with the pack, making the "flip" again in the direction of his pocket, where you first left the three cards at the beginning of the trick. Then with one movement spread the pack face upward on the table, exclaiming, "And the three indifferent cards I pass into your pocket. Please see if you have the aces, and if so, show them to the audience. And now to conclude, will you please give me the three cards from your pocket? Perhaps they are in this one" (point with the wand to a pocket where they are not. He feels for them and says "No"); "perhaps this pocket" (pointing to another where they are not. He looks again and says "No"); "perhaps here" (pointing to the pocket they *are* in, and he draws them out). *C. L. N.*

Second Method. The four aces are placed on top of the pack by a spectator. The conjurer shifts three to the bottom, and deals an ace and three indifferent cards, separately, on the table. The three indifferent cards are dealt on each supposed ace. The three aces at the bottom are shifted to the top, and the performer takes up four cards, holding them so as to appear as one card. He picks up two or three other cards in the same hand, as if he were looking for some particular card; then he replaces the cards on top of the pack and deals the three aces on the ace on the table. If this is done carelessly, the spectators will be convinced that he has dealt three indifferent cards on the ace, and the subsequent assemblage of the aces will have the desired effect.

Third Method. The feature of this method is that the four aces are laid face upward on the table, three indifferent cards being dealt, also face upward, on each ace. This is a beautiful and mystifying trick, admirably adapted for a stage performance.

Prepare six aces (two hearts, two clubs, and two diamonds) by splitting them and gluing indifferent cards to their backs. The ace of spades is not prepared. Place three of the prepared aces on the bottom of the pack, indifferent side down. Then place nine miscellaneous cards underneath, and under these place the other prepared aces (ace side down) and leave the unprepared ace of spades at the bottom of the deck.

In presenting the trick, the performer deals the aces (the ones at the bottom of the pack, of course) face upward on the table, placing them side by side, the ace of spades occupying the last position. Now deal three cards face upward on each ace, which operation gets rid of the nine indifferent cards originally placed between the two sets of prepared aces. The three prepared aces, the indifferent side face up, are dealt on the unprepared ace of spades.

Pick up each packet, and spread the cards, showing one ace and three cards. In closing the packets, turn over the ace under cover of the indifferent cards. When you exhibit the packet with the ace of spades on the back, bring this unprepared ace to the front and turn the three cards under cover of the ace. The aces are now with the ace of spades, and there are no aces in the other piles. By the familiar system of elimination the spade pile is forced, and the remaining packets are returned to the pack. The pack is handed to a spectator, the three aces commanded to join the ace of spades on the table and the three indifferent cards to return to the pack. After the magic formula has been pronounced, this transposition is found to have taken place. Although there are three prepared cards in the pack, the performer need have no hesitation about inviting a spectator to look through the pack in order to convince himself that the aces are really gone. He will never think of looking at the backs of the cards.

In order to make the trick suitable to the stage the performer utilizes a small triangular-shaped contrivance covered with black velvet. It stands on the performer's table, and the cards are laid against the outer face so that they are always in full view of the spectators.

Fourth Method. This method is adapted to a small audience, and is excellent for IMPROMPTU work. Four aces are shown; each one is marked by a spectator; and they are then laid face downward on the table, side by side, three odd cards being dealt on each ace. As usual the four aces assemble in one heap.

The basis of this trick is the old and familiar sleight known as the TOP CHANGE. Lay the four aces on the table, face downward. Hold the pack in the left hand, and with the left thumb push three cards over the edge in readiness for the change. With the other hand pick up one of the aces and hand it to a spectator with the request that he mark it.

Take back the card in the right hand, and, sliding this card under another ace, pick up this second ace and also offer it to be marked. This card is taken back in the right hand, on top of the first ace, and the two, held together as one card, are slipped under another ace. This third ace is offered to another spectator to mark, and is received back in the right hand on top of the other two aces. The three aces in the right hand, held as one card, are now slipped under the fourth ace, which is likewise held out to a spectator.

While the fourth ace is being marked, the performer exchanges the three aces in the right hand for the three indifferent cards on the top of the deck. This sleight is accomplished as he turns to lay the pack on the table. Take back the fourth ace in the left hand, on which you immediately drop the three indifferent cards from the right hand. You now have a packet of four cards, one an ace (at the bottom) and three indifferent cards.

Hold this packet so that the ace is visible, although not verbally calling attention to the card. Place the four cards face downward on the table as usual, and deal three indifferent cards on each supposed ace, and the three aces on top of the ace. The trick is then brought to the familiar conclusion, the four aces assembling in one packet. This is a fine sleight-of-hand experiment, and the reader is strongly advised to add it to his repertory, for it is convenient at times to have more than one method of accomplishing this popular effect.

Fifth Method. Offer the four aces to a spectator with the request that they be marked, after which he is directed to place the ace of spades on the bottom of the pack and the ace of hearts on top, the performer holding the pack in his own hand. The performer makes the TWO-HANDED SHIFT, thus bringing the ace of spades and ace of hearts to the center, and, lifting up the ace of hearts, he inserts the little finger between it and the lower part of the pack. Opening the pack at this BREAK, the performer requests the spectator to place the ace of clubs and the ace of diamonds in the center of the pack. When this is done, drop the ace of hearts on the two aces just replaced in the pack and, closing up the cards, insert the little finger between the ace of hearts and the ace of spades.

Now make the shift, with an exaggerated move of the arms, so as to attract attention. This shift brings the ace of spades back to the bottom of the pack and the ace of hearts to its original position on the top. All is the same as before except that under the ace of hearts, at the top, are the ace of clubs and the ace of diamonds.

The chances are that if the shift is made in the manner suggested someone in the audience will remark that the aces have been juggled away, or at least there will be suggestive smiles on the faces of the spectators. Ask the audience to name the position of the different aces. They will probably answer that the ace of spades *was* on the bottom, that the ace of hearts *was* on the top, and that the ace of diamonds and the ace of clubs *were* in the center. "Correct," replies the conjurer, turning over the pack so as to show the ace of spades. "The ace of spades *is* on the bottom, and (turning up top card) the ace of hearts *is* on the top, just as they were placed by this gentleman (indicating the spectator). And the other two aces are in the center of the pack." The conjurer does not offer to show that the ace of clubs and the ace of diamonds are in that position; the other two aces are in their original position, and the spectators are satisfied that everything is as it should be.

The performer now shifts the two bottom cards to the top, so that the ace of spades is the second card from the top. "Would you believe," observes the conjurer, "that I could make the four aces fly from this pack? Really, it is a very simple matter. I have only to click the pack four times like this (clicking the lower corner of the pack with the little finger of the left hand) and the cards obey. See!" He shows that the ace of spades has left the bottom of the pack, and by turning up the indifferent card on top, shows that the ace of hearts has also obeyed his command.

Now comes the boldest and yet the most successful and convincing move of the whole trick. Observing that the ace of clubs and the ace of diamonds have also left the pack, the performer deliberately spreads the cards, one by one with the left thumb, face upward, before the eyes of one of the spectators. At the outset the cards are spread slowly, the movement being accelerated after the center of the pack has been reached, while toward the last the cards are spread briskly.

At the same time the performer holds the cards nearer to the face of the spectator, so that when the end of the pack is reached the cards are so close to the spectator's eyes that he is not able to see that the last six cards (four of them aces) are not spread at all, but are held as one card.

The performer does not give the spectator any time to reflect. Turning abruptly, he repeats the operation before the eyes of a second spectator. A third demonstration is not necessary, as the audience is convinced by this time that the aces really have left the pack.

Now for the reappearance of the wandering aces. The performer gets rid of the top card either by the shift or a FALSE SHUFFLE; he holds the pack in the left hand, the face of the cards toward the audience. The position of the pack is much the same as in the first position for executing the CHARLIER ONE-HANDED SHIFT, with the single exception that the left thumb, instead of resting on the upper edge of the deck, extends over the face of the bottom card, as in the conventional dealing position.

The right hand now grasps the pack at the lower ends, between the thumb and first finger. The back of the right hand is toward the audience, but the bottom card of the pack is not for an instant hidden from the eyes of the spectators. The ostensible reason why the right hand approaches the pack is to square up the cards; but the real reason is to obtain possession of the top card of the deck (the ace of spades). This is accomplished by the four fingers of the left hand pushing the top card downward until it is in a position to be palmed by the right hand. This operation is invisible, as the sliding of the card is masked by the right hand. A trial before a mirror will convince the conjurer of the practicability of this move.

The right hand is now moved away from the left, and is then suddenly brought palm down on the face of the pack with a resounding slap, the right hand being immediately drawn back. The effect to the audience is that simultaneously with the noise the ace of spades appears on the face of the pack. The sudden and mysterious appearance of the card has a bewildering effect.

The reader is advised to produce the other aces by means of the various methods for producing what is known as the COLOR CHANGE. If he has faith in his skill he may produce the last ace in the same manner as he did the first.

Sixth Method. This effect differs radically from the conventional four-ace trick, but in good hands it forms a satisfactory and mystifying experiment.

The performer secures the assistance of two spectators. A pack of cards is handed to them with a request to remove the four aces and the four kings and, if they so desire, to mark them. Two ordinary envelopes are examined; one is marked "Kings," the other "Aces," *in large letters.* The performer takes the envelope marked "Aces" and in it places the four aces, in full view of the spectators, seals it, and hands it to one of the assistants. In like manner he places the kings in the other envelope, which is held by the second assistant. A little PATTER, and the assistants are requested to open the envelopes, when it is found that the aces and kings have changed places.

A duplicate ace and king must be prepared by gluing to their backs cloth of the same color as that on the performer's table, preferably black or dark green. The prepared cards are on the table. In addition to the faked cards, an ordinary pack of cards, two envelopes, and a lead pencil are used.

After the assistants have removed and marked the aces and kings, hand them the envelopes. While they are examining them, take back the cards. Get the ace and king corresponding to the faked cards to the front of their respective piles, taking especial pains that the audience shall notice the card at the bottom of these piles.

Now lay the two piles of cards on the table, putting the pile of aces on the faked king and vice versa. Now call for the envelope marked "Aces"; take up the kings with the faked ace in front, and apparently place them in the envelope. In reality, after showing the ace at the bottom, the cards are turned with their backs to the spectators, and the four kings alone go into the envelope, the faked card slipping down behind on the outside. As soon as the fake is safely out of sight behind the envelope, bend back the flap so that the audience can see that the four cards, which they imagine to be the aces, are really placed inside the envelope. The faked card is held behind the envelope with the thumb of the left hand, and is palmed in that hand in the act of raising the envelope to the lips to moisten the gum on the flap.

The envelope is then handed back to one of the assistants, and the performer has an opportunity to dispose of the palmed card. The movements are then repeated with the other cards; a little patter follows; and the assistants are requested to open the envelopes, when the cards are found to have changed places.

The weak point in this trick is the repetition of the movements. The performer can avoid this by laying down the envelope first used, ostensibly to pull back his sleeves a little, but really to dispose of the faked card without palming. He is then able, in sealing the envelope, indirectly to call the attention of the audience to the fact that his hands are empty, which makes it easier to palm the second cloth-covered card without detection.

T. N. D.

Seventh Method. First pick out and exhibit on the table the four aces, and request someone to replace them on the pack, when you place three other cards secretly upon them. This you may either do by bringing three cards from the bottom by the shift, or you may, while the company's attention is occupied in examining the aces, palm three cards from the top in the right hand and, after the aces are replaced on the top, simply cover them with that hand, thereby bringing the three palmed cards upon them.

You next take off and hold up to the audience the four top cards, being the three indifferent cards with an ace at the bottom. You cannot, of course, exhibit them fanwise, or the deception would be detected at once; but the spectators, seeing an ace at the bottom and having no particular reason to suspect otherwise, naturally believe that the cards you hold are really the four aces. Laying the four cards on the table, you distribute them, as in the last trick, in different parts of the pack, taking care, however, that the last card (the genuine ace), is placed among the three already at the top.

You now invite someone to cut. When he has done so, you take up the two halves, in their transposed position, in the left hand, at the same time slipping the little finger of that hand between them. The four aces are now, of course, upon the top of the lower packet. You then announce, "I am now about to order the four aces, which you have seen so well divided, to come together again. Would you like them to appear on the top, at the bottom, or in the middle of the pack?" If the answer is, "In the middle," you have only to withdraw the little finger, and invite the company to examine the pack to see that they are already so placed. If the answer is, "On the top," you make the shift to bring them there.

To produce them at the bottom is rather more difficult, and unless you are pretty confident as to your neatness of manipulation, it will be well to limit the choice to "top" or "middle." In order to be able to bring the four aces to the bottom you must, in picking up the cards after the cut, push forward a little with the left thumb the four top cards of the lower packet, and slip the little finger below and the third finger above them, so as to be able to make the shift above or below those four cards as occasion may require.

If you are required to bring those four cards to the top, you must withdraw the little finger (thereby joining those cards to the upper cards of the lower packet) and make the pass with the aid of the third finger instead of the fourth. If, on the contrary, you desire to produce the four aces at the bottom, you simply withdraw the third finger, thereby leaving the aces at the bottom of the upper packet, when the shift will bring them to the bottom of the pack.

Eighth Method. This version may be made to follow many other card tricks. To perform it, the first essential is the possession of a pack of cards similar in size and pattern to that you have in general use, but consisting of aces only.

You must have these cards close at hand, in such a position as to enable you to add them instantly, and without attracting observation, to the pack you have been using. You may place your pack of aces on the SERVANTE, or in one of your pochettes. In either case, you will have little difficulty in reaching them at the right moment, and placing them on the top of the ordinary pack, holding the whole in your left hand, but keeping the little finger between.

Having done this, you say to the person assisting you, "You appear to be fond of aces, sir. How many would you like?" He is fully convinced, having previously examined the pack, that you have only the ordinary four; but, from a desire to put your powers to an extreme test, he may possibly name a larger number—say, seven. "Seven!" you reply; "that is rather unreasonable, seeing there are only four in the pack. However, we will make some more. Will you oblige me by blowing upon the pack?" which you hold just under his nose for that purpose.

He does so, and you deliberately count off and give to him the seven top cards, which all prove to be aces. You then say, "Perhaps you would like some more. You have only to blow again. How many will you have?" He again blows on the pack, and you give him the number desired.

While he is examining them, you cover the pack for a moment with your right hand, and palm a dozen or so of the remaining aces. Then remarking, "You blew a little too hard that time. You blew a lot of aces into your waistcoat," you thrust your hand into the breast of his waistcoat, and bring out three or four of the palmed cards, leaving the remainder inside; then pull out two or three more, dropping them on the floor, so as to scatter them about and make them appear as numerous as possible.

You then say, "There seem to be a good many more there yet. Perhaps you will take them out yourself." While he is doing so, you palm in your right hand all the remaining aces.

When he professes to have taken them all out, you say, "Are you quite sure that you have no more aces about you? You blew very hard, you know. I really think you must have some more. Will you allow me?" Then, standing on his right, you place your right hand just below his eyes, and spring the remaining aces from it (see CARD MANIPULATION: FLOURISHES), the effect being exactly as if a shower of cards flew from his nose. *L. H.*

FOX, IMRO Stage name of Isidor Fuchs (1852-1910), a former German cook who became celebrated as the comedy magician member of the "Triple Alliance," whose other members were SERVAIS LEROY and FREDERICK EUGENE POWELL.

FRENCH DROP (See under TOURNIQUET)

FRIKELL, WILJALBA (1818-1903) German conjurer, the first to perform in ordinary evening dress instead of the previously customary flowing robes, and the leader in simplifying stage settings and apparatus. (See HISTORY) Frikell cleaned up his stage so that it looked like a drawing room of the period, and wore ordinary evening dress. He relied on skill, not on bulky apparatus.

According to Thomas Frost, Frikell was born in Finland, educated at Munich, and traveled successfully throughout eastern and southern Europe, Turkey, Egypt, and India.

FUNNEL A little appliance which may be incidentally introduced with good effect in the course of any liquid trick. It is a tin funnel, made double throughout, with a space of half an inch or so between its inner and outer sides. It is, in fact, a funnel within a funnel, joined at the upper edges. (Fig. 1) It has an airhole *a*, generally on the under side of the handle.

When required for use, the hidden space is filled with wine. The simplest way of doing this is to stop the spout of the funnel with the finger, and then to fill it with wine, which seeking its own level, will gradually rise to the same height in the outer space as it stands at inside the funnel. This must, of course, be done with the air-hole open. When the space is filled, the air-hole is stopped, and the wine remaining inside the funnel allowed to run out. The funnel will now appear perfectly empty, and may be used as a funnel in the ordinary way.

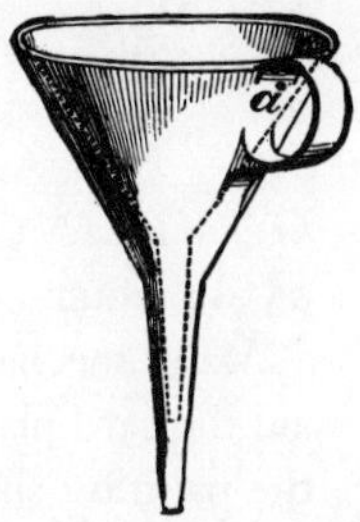

FIG. 1

The method of using the funnel is somewhat after the following manner, subject of course to variation.

A spectator is invited to take a glass of wine. When he has drunk it, the performer asks a second spectator whether he would like a glass also. The reply is pretty sure to be in the affirmative, but the performer pretends to find, when about to oblige him, that his store is exhausted. He begins to apologize for the supposed disappointment, but as if suddenly bethinking himself, says, "However, you shan't be disappointed. Suppose we take back the wine this young gentleman has drunk. I don't suppose it will be any the worse. Let me see, where is my magic funnel. Oh, here it is. Let us make sure first that it is quite clean."

He pours water through it, and then holds it up to the light in such a manner that the audience can see right through, thus indirectly showing them that it is empty. "Now, sir" (addressing the youngster who has drunk the glass of wine), "I am going to take back that glass of wine. Be kind enough to bend your elbow, and hold it over the mouth of the funnel, so. And you, sir" (addressing the expectant), "perhaps you will be kind enough to take this young gentleman's other arm, and work it gently up and down. In fact, we are going to transform him into a pump. Now, sir." The performer holds the glass under the funnel, and as soon as the pretended pumping begins, opens the air-hole, when the wine runs into the glass, and is handed to the second young gentleman as a reward for his exertions.

Acted with spirit, this little interlude is sure of an uproarious reception from the juvenile portion of the audience, particularly if the performer possesses the magic BRADAWL, and makes use of it to bore a small hole in the victim's elbow before beginning to pump the wine from it. *L. H.*

G

GAMBLING METHODS (See also CARD MANIPULATION; SHELL GAME; THREE-CARD TRICKS)

Many mechanical contrivances termed hold-outs have been invented to aid the card player. A sleeve machine which passes the cards into and from the palm by spreading the knees may be worth from seventy-five dollars to several hundred dollars. In almost all cases where hold-outs are used, the principal skill possessed by the player is that of working his apparatus perfectly and secreting the extra cards while in his hands; but to employ a machine successfully requires considerable address, and especially nerve. These devices can be purchased from the dealers in "club-room articles," but the expert professional disdains their assistance. They are cumbersome, unnecessary, and a constant menace to his reputation.

Marked cards, generally known as "readers," can be distinguished by the backs as readily as by the faces when the key is known. Printed cards are manufactured, but these are rarely used by professionals. The usual plan is to mark the standard decks by hand. (See CARD MARKING)

Nearly all standard cards are red or blue. Marking inks absolutely indistinguishable from the printer's ink can be obtained from any of the dealers. Cards of intricate design are best adapted for the purpose. Each card is marked at both ends, so as to be read in any position. The peculiarity of the figures or design across the end is first closely considered, and twelve fairly distinct points, or dots or dashes, are noted and located.

Then the four aces are laid out, and with a fine pen the first point located is shortened barely enough to notice. The point is white and the background red or blue, the color of the ink used; and the slightest shortening of a single point or the obliteration of a single dot on a card is undetectable unless it is known.

The four aces are treated in this manner, then turned end for end, and the operation repeated. Then the kings are doctored, the second point located being shortened in this instance. Then the four queens at the third point, and so on throughout the deck for the twelve values, the absence of any mark denoting the deuce.

Now the suits are marked. Three additional points are located, possibly close to one corner. The first point is marked, say, for diamonds, the second for clubs, the third for hearts, and spades left unmarked. Thus the operator, by noting the location of the two blockouts, can name the cards at a glance as they are dealt.

Combination systems lessen the number of points to be located. The design of the particular deck will suggest whether a dot, line, or blockout, would be least noticeable. It is seldom that two operators work alike. Cleverly done, it is almost impossible to detect. Most of the supply houses keep a skilled operator constantly employed, and will mark any deck to order for about one dollar.

Some players make a practice of marking cards during the process of the game. As desirable cards come into the player's possession, they are creased or indented at certain locations with the fingernail or thumbnail, which is kept pointed for the purpose; and in the course of an hour, the principal cards can be readily distinguished. Another plan is to darken the edges with different prepared inks that are conveniently adjusted in pads. These maneuvers, while making nothing sure in a given instance, always net the operator a favorable percentage in the long run.

The cold deck is a prearranged pack that is introduced at an opportune moment. The cards are not marked, but two or more hands are set up ready for dealing. The name is probably derived from the fact that the deck must await its opportunity. Little skill is required in making the exchange. It is almost invariably done quite openly, and in company where the attendants and players are in collusion. In most gaming rooms the decks are exchanged every hour or less. Sometimes the players will call for a new deck, but usually the exchange is made at the instance of the management.

When the cold deck is sprung, a FALSE SHUFFLE is made by the dealer, a blind cut by an ally, and the hands fall in the desired order. Of course an exchange may be made by sleight-of-hand, but the player who can accomplish this feat successfully is generally well versed in the higher orders of card-table artifice, and will dispense with such makeshifts as cold decks or any kind of prepared cards.

When two card experts work together, their difficulties are greatly lessened. The opportunities of securing the desirable cards before the shuffle are doubled. If they understand each other perfectly they can often arrange one or two hands ready for dealing, and find little trouble in getting several desirable cards together while apparently gathering up the deck in the most careless manner. If sitting together so that one cuts on the other's deal, the possibilities become so great that ordinary chances will be taken in perhaps nineteen deals out of twenty. Two or three coups in the course of an evening will not flush the quarry, and are quite sufficient to answer all purposes.

Advantages without dexterity can be taken in almost any card game when two or more players are in collusion, by the use of any secret code of signals that will disclose the hand of each to the others. For instance, in Poker the ally holding the best cards will be the only one to stay, thus playing the best hand of the allies against the rest; quite sufficient advantage to give a large percentage in favor of the combination. Again, the allies may resort to crossfiring, by each raising until the other players drop out. There are hundreds of small but ultimately certain advantages to be gained in this manner, if collusion is not suspected. No single player can defeat a combination, even when the cards are not manipulated.

As the reader obtains an understanding of the art of advantage playing, it will be seen that the old-fashioned or hand shuffle gives the greater possibilities for running up hands, selecting desirable cards, and PALMING.

While the riffle cannot be employed for arranging the cards, it is equally well adapted for retaining the top or bottom portion, or even the whole deck, in any prearranged order; and the blind riffle can be performed just as perfectly as the false shuffle. A clever bottom dealer will usually employ the riffle, as he rarely takes the trouble of running up a hand. His purpose in that respect is sufficiently answered by keeping the desired cards at the bottom. If he has an ally to blind cut, everything goes well, but if playing alone, he must either palm the bottom cards for the cut or make a SHIFT afterward.

The shift is very rarely attempted in any kind of knowing company, and it is awkward to make a palm when the riffle is used. The deck must be tilted on its side, and while the movement may pass as an effort at squaring up, it is not quite regular. The hand shuffle avoids the difficulty, as the deck is held naturally in easy position for palming, and not an instant is lost during the operation.

The hand shuffle is almost ideal for stocking and culling.

The first acquirement of the professional player is proficiency at false shuffling and cutting. Perfection in performing the false shuffle, whether the old-fashioned hand shuffle or the riffle supplemented by a thorough knowledge of blind cutting, makes it impossible for the smartest card handler living to determine whether the procedure is true or blind. Sight has absolutely nothing to do with the action, and the expert might perform the work just as well if he were blindfolded.

The inviolable rule of the professional is uniformity of action. Any departure from his customary manner of holding, shuffling, cutting or dealing the cards may be noticed, and is consequently avoided. The player who uses the old-fashioned hand shuffle will never resort to the table riffle in the same company, and vice versa. The manner of holding the deck will always be the same, whether the action is to be true or blind. In dealing, one particular position for the left-hand fingers is always adhered to, and the action of the right hand in taking off the cards and the time or rapidity of the dealing is made as uniform as possible. In cutting the rule holds good, and the true cut is made with the same movements as the blind. Whether the procedure is true or blind, the same apparent action is maintained throughout.

The deportment of the successful card player must be as finished as his skill. A quiet, unostentatious demeanor and gentlemanly reserve are best calculated to answer his purpose, especially the entire suppression of emotion over gains or losses. Without ability to control his feelings, the advantage player is without advantage. Ability in card handling does not necessarily ensure success; boldness and nerve are also absolutely essential. The greater the emergency, or the greater the stakes, the greater the nerve required.

S. W. E.

There are some tricks and dodges which are practised by even the most high-class cheats. The rule is, however, that mere sleight-of-hand is to a great extent obsolete; at least, among those who seek to swindle really good card-players. The methods of legerdemain are more widely known than formerly, and this fact tends to operate very largely to the detriment of the sharp.

In card games especially there is always a risk in resorting to manipulation. There is the ever-present possibility of someone among the cheat's antagonists having sufficient knowledge to detect him in his manipulation of the cards. He is haunted by the fear that sharp eyes are watching his every movement, and he knows that he can accomplish nothing in this way without some movement which a trained eye would instantly detect.

As a professional sharp remarked to a young friend, to whom he was giving lessons in the art of cheating: "The best gamblers play with fair cards only; and, by being wonderfully keen card-players, make their brains win, instead of cheating with the pack. They play in secret partnership, and are invincible, as they know all the various swindles and so can protect themselves from being cheated. The most successful men are among this class, although nearly all of them can do the finest work with a pack of cards.

"The next-best class are those who play marked cards well, many of them using cards that no one not acquainted with the work could find out in a lifetime. These men, if they can only get their own cards into a game, are sure to win.

"Then, after these, come the class of 'second dealers,' 'bottom dealers,' and men who habitually do work with the pack to win. *These men always get caught in the long run.*"

It is possible to obviate to a great extent the necessity for marked cards by the use of certain little instruments of precision known familiarly as "shiners."

The sharp of long ago was content to rely upon a small circular drop of wine, or whatever he happened to be drinking, carefully spilled on the table directly in front of him. The faces of the cards held over this drop would be reflected from its surface, for the information of the sharp who was dealing them.

Times have advanced since then, however; the reflector is no longer a makeshift; it is a well-constructed instrument, both optically and mechanically, costing from two and a half to twenty-five dollars.

The table reflector is designed for the purpose of being attached to the card table during the game. Another very efficient form of reflector is one so constructed as to be adaptable to the interior of a pipe-bowl. It consists of a small convex mirror, similar to the one used in the table reflector, which is cemented to a piece of cork shaped to fit inside the bowl of an ordinary briar-root pipe. (Fig. 1)

Among the various forms in which reflectors are supplied, there are some attached to coins and rouleaux of coins of various values. Also there are some so constructed as to be attached to a pile of banknotes.

FIG. 1

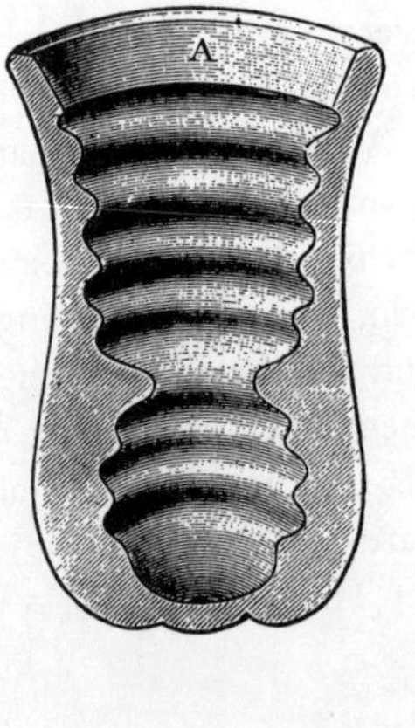

FIG. 2

Broadly speaking, cheating at dice may be classed under two heads—the manipulation of genuine dice, and the employment of unfair ones. From this it will be gathered that loaded dice are by no means necessary to the sharp who has made this line of business his specialty.

Cheating with fair dice is known as "securing," and consists of a plan of retaining certain dice. One is held against the inside edge of the box, while the other is allowed to fall freely into it. In this way one of the dice is not shaken at all, and falls on the table in the same position as it previously occupied. In order that this may be accomplished satisfactorily, it is necessary to use a suitable dice-box.

The dice-box referred to is simply the usual form, with the interior corrugated to ensure the thorough turning about of the dice. The only preparation is that the flat inside rim or lip, marked "A" in Fig. 2, is roughened by rubbing it with coarse glass paper. This gives it a kind of tooth, which prevents the dice from slipping when they are "secured" against it.

A box of this kind being at hand, nothing further in the way of apparatus is required for the operation of securing. All else depends entirely upon practice. As the dice are taken from the table, one of them is secured, and the others are thrown into the box. An expert will use three dice, securing one and letting the others go, but it requires some skill to pick up three dice in the proper manner without fear of dropping them all. Therefore a novice will use only two. The process is carried out as follows:

The dice are laid on the table, side by side. The one farthest from the operator is placed with the ace uppermost, consequently the six is on the face which lies on the table. This is the die which is about to be secured. The first two fingers of the right hand are now laid flat on the dice, and between these two fingers the dice are taken up by their right-hand edges. (Fig. 3)

They are now pushed well home by the thumb. (Fig. 4) The die nearest the operator is allowed to fall into the dice-box, while the other is retained. (Fig. 5)

The box is next taken in the right hand, the fingers lying flat over the mouth of it, and the thumb holding it at the bottom. (Fig. 6)

In the act of closing the fingers of the right hand over the box, the die which has been retained is firmly pressed between the second finger and the inside edge of the box. In this position it is completely hidden by the forefinger, and is held there while the box is shaken. If the forefinger were raised, the die would appear situated in the manner shown in Fig. 7.

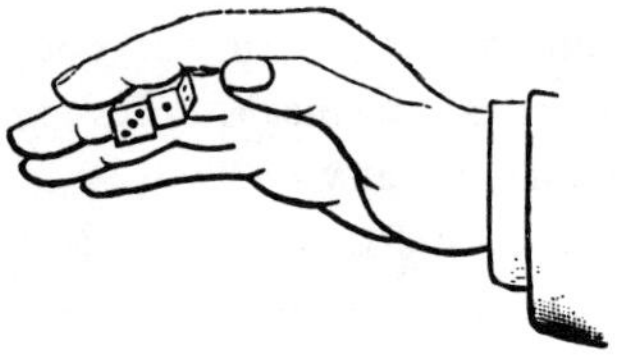

FIG. 3

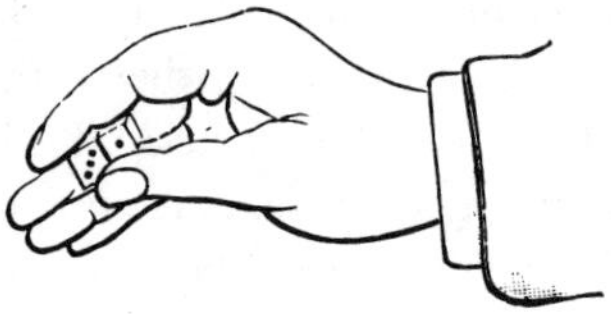

FIG. 4

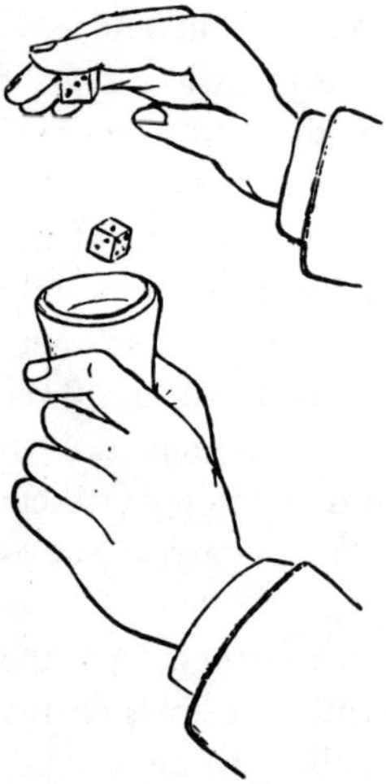

FIG. 5

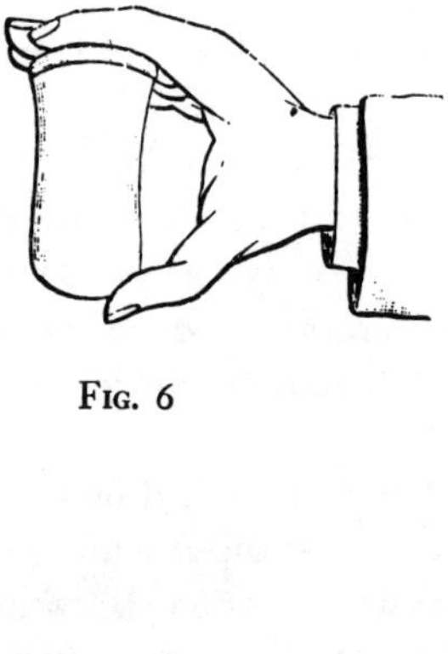

FIG. 6

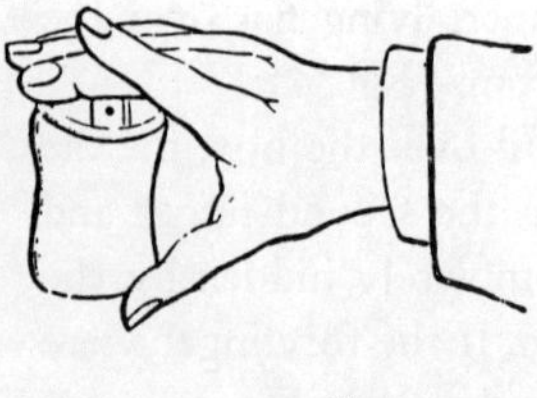

FIG. 7

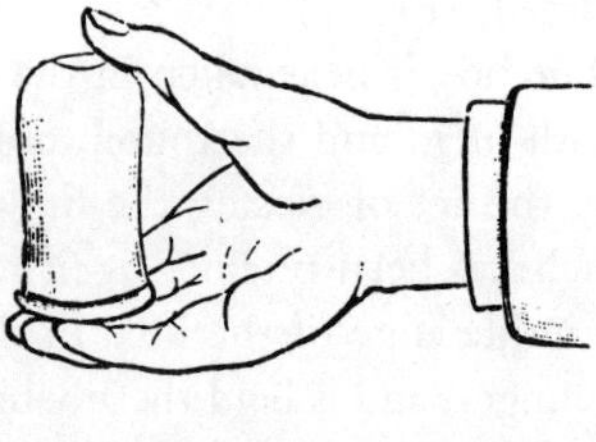

FIG. 8

The sharp, however, is particularly careful *not* to raise his forefinger. The box is now shaken, and of course the die which is not secured is heard to rattle within it. Finally, the hand is turned around so that the mouth of the box is downward and the backs of the fingers rest upon the table (Fig. 8).

After the box has thus been turned upside down, then comes the crucial point of the whole operation. If the fingers are not carefully removed, the secured die will not fall upon the face intended. The proper method of "boxing" the dice upon the table is to remove the fingers in the following order. First, the second and third fingers are opened, allowing the loose die to fall upon the table. Then the first and second fingers are gently opened, easing the secured die into position. Last, the forefinger is moved to the edge of the box, at the same time withdrawing the second finger entirely, and the box is let down over the two dice. It is immediately lifted up and the score is recorded.

There is nothing at all suspicious in any of these movements; they are quite usual, or appear so when quickly performed, the only difference between the genuine shake and the false being the retention of the one die. Of course, the entire operation should occupy the least possible time, the hands being kept somewhat low and the dupe seated upon the right-hand side of the operator.

The secured die naturally falls with the six uppermost, while the loose one cannot show less than one. Therefore the sharp cannot throw less than seven with two dice. That is the lowest score possible for him to make, while the dupe may throw only two. Now, in an infinite number of throws with two dice, seven is the number of pips which will be the average for each throw.

Sometimes, of course, only two pips will be thrown; sometimes both sixes will come uppermost, making twelve pips together. But with one die secured in such a manner as to fall six, the average of an infinite number of throws is necessarily very much increased, because it is impossible to throw less than seven. The chances of the two players bear no comparison, and the dupe is bound to be beaten. For instance, the chances of throwing twelve by the player who secures one die are as one to six—that is to say, they are six to one against him, while the chances against the player who goes to work fairly are *thirty-five to one*. This will serve to give the reader some idea of the value of one secured die out of two in use.

J. N. M.

Readers interested in faked dice are referred to *Scarne on Dice*.

GARTER TRICK (See under STRING TRICKS)

GENERAL CARD The name for an entire group of ROUTINES, usually but not always performed with a chosen card, whereby the entire pack seems to be made up of one card. In the end, the pack is handed out, and this card is the only one missing. The performer then takes it from his pocket.

It is also known as the Ambitious Card, and Everybody's Card.

No routine will be given here, since each performer has his own tried and true method. Some FORCE the card, and work with duplicates; others have a card freely drawn, then force it on several spectators in succession, apparently putting all the chosen cards on the table one after another, but actually putting down indifferent cards by the top or bottom CHANGE. DOUBLE LIFTS, SHIFT, and SIDE STEAL can be combined to show that the top, second, middle, and bottom card are all identical.

The trick requires great skill and smoothness of manipulation, but is hard to beat for effect.

GIMMICK A small secret device or secret preparation that makes a trick work; hence, by extension, the secret of a trick as distinguished from its effect. Prepared articles are "gimmicked" or "gaffed."

A distinction may be drawn between gimmicks and FAKES in that gimmicks are never seen by the audience, whereas fakes are merely not understood.

GOLDFISH BOWLS The performer comes forward with a shawl in his hand, which he spreads and exhibits on both sides, to show (as is really the case) that there is no preparation about it. The spectators being satisfied on this point, he swings the shawl about, finally throwing it over his left shoulder and arm, the arm being held square before him. The arm now gradually sinks down, and the form of some solid object is seen defined beneath the shawl, which, when removed, reveals a glass bowl brimming with water and with goldfish swimming about in it. This is repeated a second and a third time, the performer sometimes discarding the shawl, and borrowing a pocket-handkerchief among the audience for the production of the last bowl.

The bowls used are saucer-shaped, measuring six to eight inches in diameter, and one and a half to two inches in depth. Each is closed by an india-rubber cover. Thus secured, they are concealed about the person of the performer. The precise method of concealment varies a little: where three bowls are to be produced, one is generally carried beneath the coat-tails, in a sort of bag open at the sides, suspended from the waist, and the other two in pockets, opening perpendicularly, inside the breast of the coat or waistcoat, one on each side.

Sometimes, by way of variation, bowls of fire are produced. The bowls are in this case of thin brass. They have no covers, but the inflammable material (tow moistened with alcohol) is kept in position by wires crossing the bowl at about half its depth, and is ignited by a wax match, struck

FIG. 1 GOLDFISH BOWL (see next page)

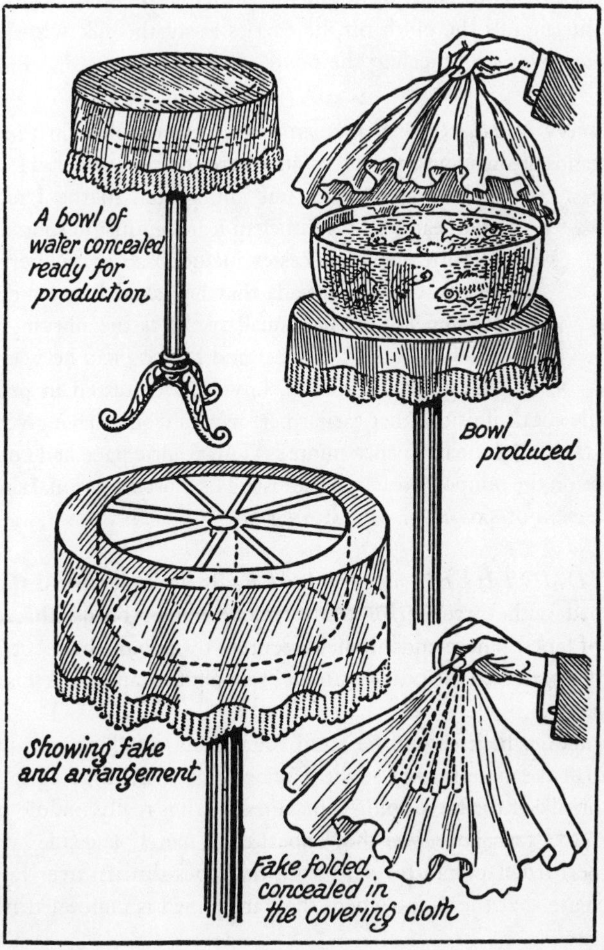

against the inside of the bowl under cover of the shawl and immediately dropped into the bowl, when the contents instantly burst into flames. Some bowls have a mechanical arrangement for igniting the tow. *L. H.*

A modern method of producing larger and deeper bowls depends on the table shown in Fig. 1. The performer carries a wet sponge where he can get at it with his right hand; the cloth is spread over the bent left arm, and the performer seems to catch a bowl. A quick squeeze of the sponge gives a convincing imitation of water spilling from a bowl. The performer then seems to set the bowl on a small side table.

Actually, of course, the bowl is already on the table, covered with silk stretched on a wire FAKE made on the principle of umbrella ribs. When the conjurer pulls the cloth off, he carries away the silk with it, and the wire fake collapses, revealing the bowl.

GOLDIN, HORACE Stage name of Hyman Goldstein (1873-1939), an outstanding illusionist as well as an all-around performer. He was born in Russian Poland, but immigrated to the United States at an early age, and began learning magic soon afterward. His European successes included so many performances before crowned heads that he called himself the "Royal Illusionist"; at such small tricks as the untying handkerchiefs (see SILK TRICKS) and the EGG BAG he was a master. His great innovation, however, consisted in producing a vaudeville act of illusions that earlier performers would have given an hour and a half to, all done in twenty minutes. This frantic pace had considerable influence on the tempo of other illusionists. His most sensational single effect was a version of SAWING A WOMAN IN TWO.

GRANDMOTHER'S NECKLACE In its older form this trick is performed with three perforated wooden balls or beads, threaded on a couple of tapes, whose ends are held securely by two of the spectators. The problem is to detach the beads without breaking the tapes, and this is done as follows:

The tapes, which should be from four to six feet long, are previously doubled in the middle, and slightly joined at the bend of each with fine cotton or silk of the same color. The tapes are thus really middle to middle, although to a casual observer they appear to be merely laid side by side.

The performer comes forward with the tapes thrown over his left arm (taking care that the point where they are joined is concealed next to his body), and with the beads in his hands. These are mere wooden balls from one to two inches in diameter and perforated to admit the tapes.

He hands the balls out for examination; when they are returned, he threads them one after another on the tapes, which he holds in a loop so that the balls will sink down to the middle and cover the joining. Next he requests two spectators to come forward and hold the tapes; he hands two ends to one and two to the other. Each person believes that he holds one end of each tape, though actually each has both ends of the same tape.

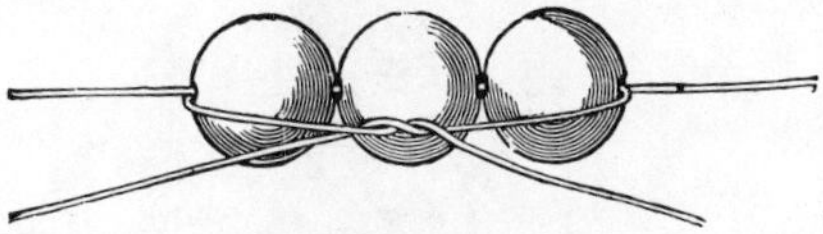

FIG. 1

The performer takes from each spectator one of the ends which he holds, and crossing the tapes in the manner shown in Fig. 1, gives to each the end which the other previously held. Holding a hat below the balls, he requests each person to pull smartly at the word "three." The word of command is given and, the thread breaking, the balls fall into the hat, although the ends of the tapes still remain in the hands of the holders.

An improved version uses six balls, three red and three black. The red balls having been first threaded on the tapes, and the two ends crossed and returned to the holders in the manner already described, the black balls are in turn threaded on the tapes at either end, and the performer, holding the hat underneath, says, "Which will you have, the red balls or the black?"

Whichever the answer, the result is the same, for only the red balls can come off the tapes, the black remaining; but in either case the performer can satisfy the choice which has been made. If the red balls were chosen, he says when they fall, "You chose the red, and your commands have been obeyed." If, on the other hand, the black were chosen, he says, "You prefer the black? Then I will take the red," which he does.

The audience, having heard the choice freely offered, believe that the performer was able to take off or leave on the tape whichever group of balls he pleased. *L. H.*

This principle is used for many similar effects, such as the *Ropes and Rings,* which replace the tapes and beads, and are hidden by running the ropes through the sleeves of a borrowed coat.

Or the performer doubles two strings and hangs them side by side over a stick. He puts a borrowed ring over each double strand, then makes a simple knot with the two strands, then puts on more rings, another simple knot, and finally crosses one string each from the two strands. When the stick is pulled out, the rings fall off.

GROWTH OF FLOWERS (See under FLOWER PRODUCTIONS)

GYNGELL (died 1833), English showman and conjurer at fairs. He started performing in 1788. He gave a very varied show, almost a circus, employing all the members of his family. He inherited the entire show of a man named Flockton, who was a poor magician and turned that part of the show over to Gyngell.

Gyngell was the last great representative of the itinerant, outdoor stage in magic (see HISTORY).

H

HANDKERCHIEF PEDESTAL (See under EGG AND HANDKERCHIEF)

HANDKERCHIEF TRICKS (See under SILK TRICKS)

HANDKERCHIEFS PREPARED AS VANISHERS One prepared handkerchief is for vanishing a coin. It is an ordinary handkerchief of silk or cotton, in one corner of which, in a little pocket, is sewn a coin or any substitute which, felt through the substance of the handkerchief, appears to be such a coin.

The method of using it is very simple. Holding the handkerchief by the corner where the coin is, and letting it hang loosely down, the performer borrows a similar coin; after carelessly shaking out the handkerchief to show that all is fair, he apparently places the borrowed coin in the center (underneath), and gives the handkerchief to someone to hold. In reality, he has only wrapped up the corner containing the substitute coin, and retains the genuine one for his own purposes.

When it is desirable to make it appear that the coin has left the handkerchief, he simply takes it from the person holding it, and gives it a shake, at the same moment rapidly running the edges of the handkerchief through his hands, until the corner containing the coin comes into one or the other of them.

Another version really does cause the disappearance of any article placed under it, and is available to vanish not only a coin, but a card, an egg, a watch, or any other article of moderate size. It consists of *two* handkerchiefs, of the same pattern, stitched together all around the edges, with a slit of about four inches long cut in the middle of one of them. The whole space between the two handkerchiefs thus forms a kind of pocket, of which the slit is the only opening.

In shaking or otherwise manipulating the handkerchief, the performer takes care always to keep the side with the slit away from the spectators, to whom the handkerchief appears to be merely the ordinary article. When he desires by its means to cause the disappearance of anything, he carelessly throws the handkerchief over the article, at the same time secretly passing the latter through the slit in the under side, and hands it thus covered to someone to hold. Then, taking the handkerchief in one corner, he requests him to let go, when the object is retained in the space between the two handkerchiefs, appearing to have vanished into empty air.

The *Die-Vanishing Handkerchief* is colored, and prepared as follows: Five square pieces of stout pasteboard, each a shade larger than one side of the solid die, are joined together with hinges of tape or cloth, in the form shown by the dotted lines in Fig. 1. The center piece *a* is attached to the middle of the handkerchief, the others being allowed to hang loose upon their respective hinges. A second handkerchief of similar pattern is then laid upon the first, and the edges of the two are stitched together all around.

The performer exhibits the die, and places it on the table. Spreading the prepared handkerchief beside it, he places the die on the center of the handkerchief, and gathering up the four corners of the latter, lifts it, bag-fashion, with his left hand, the four loose flaps of pasteboard naturally folding themselves up around the die. He now takes it with his right hand, clipping the solid die within the pasteboard, and turns the whole over as in Fig. 2, thus bringing the die uppermost, with the folds of the handkerchief hanging down around it.

Next he takes in the left hand a borrowed hat, holding it up for a moment to show that it is empty. Then, turning it mouth upward, he remarks, "I will place the die here in the hat." Suiting the action to the word, he lowers his hand into the hat, but, as if suddenly bethinking himself, he

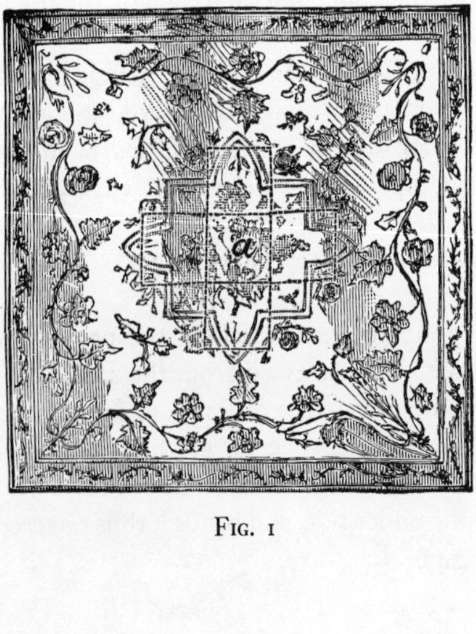

FIG. 1

FIG. 2

says, "No! I won't use the hat at all. Perhaps someone will kindly hold the die." In withdrawing his hand, however, he relaxes the pressure of his fingers, thereby leaving the solid die in the hat, though as the folded pasteboard retains its cubical shape, he gives the handkerchief in charge to one of the spectators, who is directed to hold it in like manner. The hat he places carelessly on the table.

He commands the die to pass from the handkerchief. The person holding the handkerchief is asked if he felt it depart, but he naturally maintains that it is still in the handkerchief. "You are mistaken," says the performer; "what you see is merely the ghost of the die still clinging to the handkerchief. Allow me!" and taking one corner he requests the owner to drop the handkerchief, which he then shakes out, exhibiting both sides to show that the die has vanished.

L. H.

The first cloth to vanish a glass of water simply consisted of two cloths sewn together with a piece of cardboard, the size of the top of the water tumbler to be vanished, sewn in the center. The first improvement on this old idea was a disk of celluloid in place of cardboard, and as the celluloid was transparent, the cloth could be held in front of a lighted candle without betraying the secret.

Next came a disk of celluloid with a tiny hole in the center (Fig. 1). There was also a thin metal rod, pointed at both ends, sewn into the cloth; the ends of the rod protruded at the holes *C* and *C* in the diagram. Having covered the glass with the cloth and got the disk over the top of the glass, the performer allowed the glass to drop into a well in the table. He then

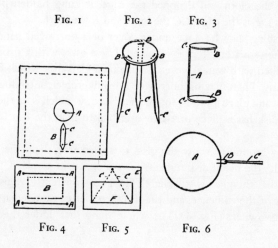

FIG. 1

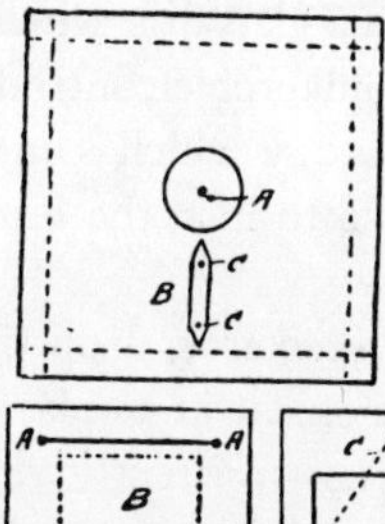

FIG. 2

FIG. 3

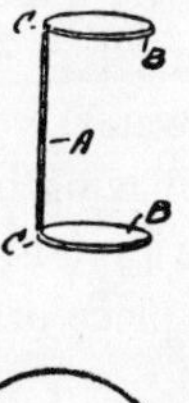

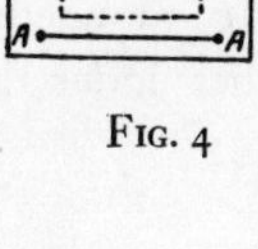

FIG. 4

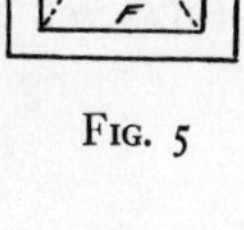

FIG. 5

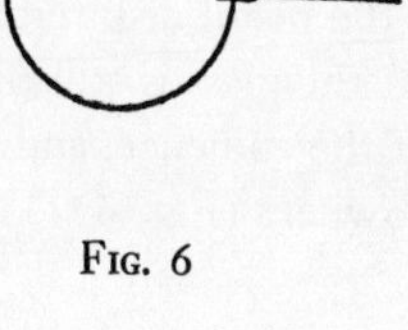

FIG. 6

secretly inserted one end of the rod into the hole in the celluloid disk while he was removing the cloth from the table. He put it down on another table or a chair, and secretly stuck the other end of the rod into the wood. The audience could apparently see the glass still under the cloth, because the rod was the same height as the glass. The vanish was then very mysterious.

A further improvement was to attach three little legs to the disk, which, in this case, was made of thin metal (Fig. 2). These legs were pointed and hinged at the points marked *B* in the diagram. The whole FAKE could be sewn between a double cloth and, of course, after the glass had been secretly removed, the legs of the fake were allowed to drop and the fake, covered with the cloth, was stood on another table. The glass was apparently there.

This idea was improved again by using two wire rings hinged to a thin strip of metal (Fig. 3). When the magician wished to put his cloth into action, he merely folded the rings down, and the stops–shown at *C* in the diagram–kept them at right angles. When the cloth was picked up, the lower ring dropped down by its own weight.

A cloth for vanishing a BIRD-CAGE has two threads sewn by their ends to it. The threads are parallel (Fig. 4). By pushing the thumbs and first fingers between the two threads and the cloth, the conjurer is able to make the cloth taut, and he thus conveys the idea that the bird-cage is still there. The inventor of this cloth had a strong black loop of thread fastened on the bottom of the cage, and when he put the cage on the table, he secretly hooked the loop on the tablecloth. Thus, when he picked up the cage covered by the cloth and dropped the cage, it hung hidden behind the table (Fig. 5). *F* is the cage, *CC* the loop, and *E* the cloth.

The vanishing may be done under cover of a borrowed handkerchief, and so a much greater effect is obtained. Use a glass with a ground edge. After it is filled with water, secretly PALM on a glass disk which fits snugly over the glass. Then, having borrowed a handkerchief, introduce a metal disk under it and place it on the top of the glass disk which is on the tumbler. The metal disk has a piece of elastic attached to it in the usual way, like a PULL.

In turning around to show the glass to a spectator, drop the glass into the profonde; the metal disk remains for a moment in its place, giving the impression that the glass is still there. The glass apparently vanishes while in the midst of the audience, and the handkerchief can immediately be returned to its owner. (Fig. 6) The whole thing flies under the coat.

Okito

HANDS The magician's hands are his one priceless asset, and also his trademark. They need almost no care to do their work, but remember that they are looked at even more intently than the performer's face. In any regular performance there can be no excuse for dirty hands, soiled cuffs, or cracked or dirty fingernails. A manicure before every date is a good investment. (See MAKE-UP)

It is popularly supposed that magic requires large hands or long fingers, but the magic student will soon learn that this is not so. The hands of NELSON DOWNS were rather on the small side; many fine manipulators are unfortunate enough to have blunt, ugly hands, which are redeemed by the grace and deftness of their employment. Any normal hand, and some that have been mutilated, will serve for magic.

Performers with very dry skin may find trouble in PALMING unless they rub their hands with some lotion containing lanolin.

Naturally moist hands must be dried before working.

To keep your hands looking their best, wear gloves in the winter, and work gloves whenever you are doing rough or dirty work.

Some manipulators advocate special exercises to develop coordination and suppleness of fingers; others, including the editor of this volume, consider these a waste of time, since the special skill required for each trick can be learned only by practising that particular trick. (See PRACTICE AND REHEARSAL)

H. H.

HAT TRICK (See also LOAD) The production of articles from an empty silk hat is an ancient trick, brought to its greatest perfection by Joseph Michael Hartz (1836-1903), whose act is described below.

The appearance of the stage at the rise of the curtain was as shown in Fig. 1. There was a small center table, placed well forward, though the performer carefully avoided passing behind it at any stage of the trick. The only other furniture consisted of a little round table, used from time

FIG. 1

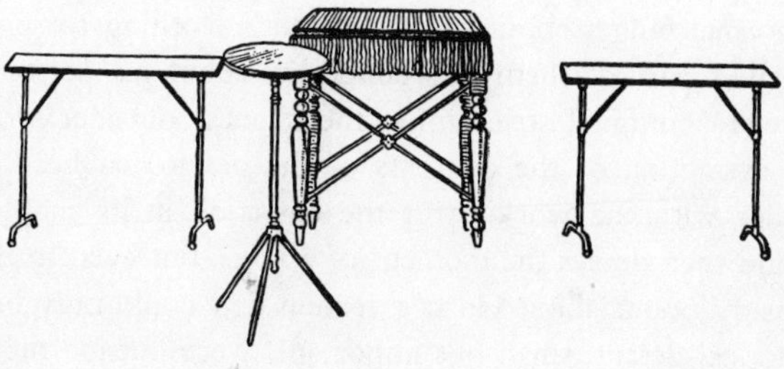

to time to rest *the* hat upon, and a couple of side tables three feet long, but only six inches wide. The center table had a shallow fringe around it, but these had none, and their tops (which were of white enamelled iron) were only half an inch thick.

On the center table lay a folded piece of green baize and a pile of some half-dozen cardboard mats. On the little round table, which had a plain wooden top without fringe, was a square woolen cover, and beside this a block of blackened wood, about four and a half inches in length by two in width and one in thickness, curved inward and padded along one of its longer edges. Its opposite edge was shaped to fit into a mortise cut in the table top. When so fixed, the block formed a rest for the hat, to prevent its rolling off the table when laid on its side. With these exceptions, all was bare; there was not even a flower-pot to relieve the general nakedness.

Under these difficult conditions the performer, borrowing a hat, and showing it absolutely empty, produced from it in succession, a number of silk handkerchiefs–not the flimsy twelve-inch squares which figure so largely in present-day magic, but honest bandannas of respectable size–; ten silver-plated pint goblets and a wig; seven cigar-boxes, of the size to take fifty cigars; ten more goblets; a square silver cage containing a canary; and a shower of playing-cards, in itself enough to fill half a dozen hats. Next, a hundred yards or so of sash-ribbon, four inches wide; seven lanterns, with colored glass sides, each containing a lighted candle; and last, a doll representing a life-sized Japanese baby, and a lady's crinolette or "dress improver." This, in the days when actual crinoline was worn, was a complete skeleton petticoat of the kind then used.

The production of the whole occupied twenty-two minutes; the performer never left the stage once during the whole of that time. The articles as they were produced were deposited on one or another of the tables, every available inch of space being occupied by them at the close of the trick.

Where did the articles come from, and how did they get into the hat? The ordinary spectator could not make even a guess at the answer. There were no abnormal bulges about the performer's clothing to suggest that even the smallest part of them was concealed about his person; and his movements were confined strictly (so the keenest outsider would have said) to the extraction of the contents of the bewitched headgear. The expert, familiar with the working of the hat trick in its simpler forms, might now and then detect the moment of a LOAD, but even to the expert there were many points about Hartz's version that could only be guessed at. Some practical details, small but important, were outside the range of guess altogether.

The articles used in the act were as follows:

The center table. The top consisted of a couple of pine boards, two and a half feet long by nine inches wide, and not quite an inch thick, hinged on the under side so as to fold together for packing. When opened out for use, each end rested on a cross-piece, eighteen inches long by two inches wide, through which the legs were screwed into metal plates, one at each corner. The legs were rather long, the total height of the table being just three feet. The cover, which was of box shape, so as to drop over the top, was of black calico, trimmed with plain black woolen fringe six inches wide. The upper edge of this fringe was level with the table top, the calico falling down behind it.

At a later period a narrow shelf was added for the accommodation of the champagne bottles which thenceforth formed part of the production. This extended across the back of the table at a height of five inches. It was supported at each end by a piece of strap-iron, bent into a suitable shape, and fitting into a metal socket. Later still, at the back of this shelf, a red plush curtain, nine inches deep, was fastened. This served as an effective background for the bottles, and also prevented their accidentally falling off to the rear. Behind this again, in the center, rose a brass upright supporting a small oblong bracket, which at one period served as a resting-place for a skull, which was made to rise automatically from the hat; when this item was abandoned in favor of other effects, the bracket held the last produced of the lanterns. (Fig. 2 shows the appearance of the table in its amended condition.)

Two of the most important loads were obtained from the front of the center table. The doll (with which the crinolette was tied up in a compressed condition) was suspended under the table near the left-hand corner. (Where *right* or *left* is mentioned, the side answering to that description from the *spectator's* point of view is intended.) It hung by a loop, which was passed over the outer end of a small bolt, of the kind known to mechanics as a "necked" bolt. This was kept fastened until the last moment, and was drawn back by a cord terminating in a ring on the surface of the table, just in time to release the load for use. The portion of the table cover which hung down in front of the load was slit vertically, to allow it to be taken out.

Near the opposite corner of the table top was an oblong wooden box or case, open at the end facing the spectators, for the reception of the bird-cage, one of the later additions to the trick. This was about seven inches high by five inches wide by four and a half inches deep. Its sides were rigid, but the bottom could be pushed up to within an inch and a half of the top, the space left vacant below it accommodating fifteen packs

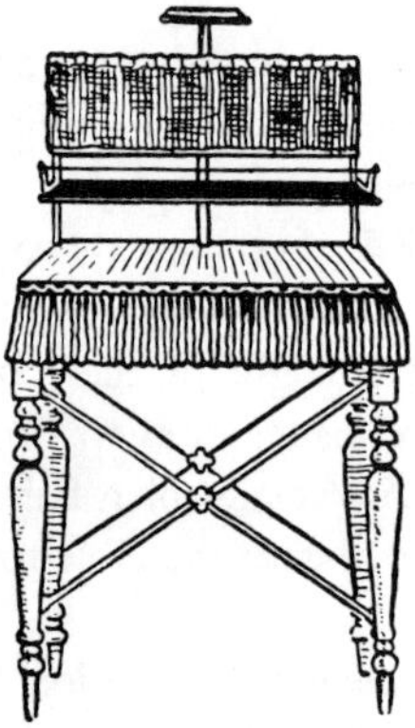

FIG. 2

FIG. 3

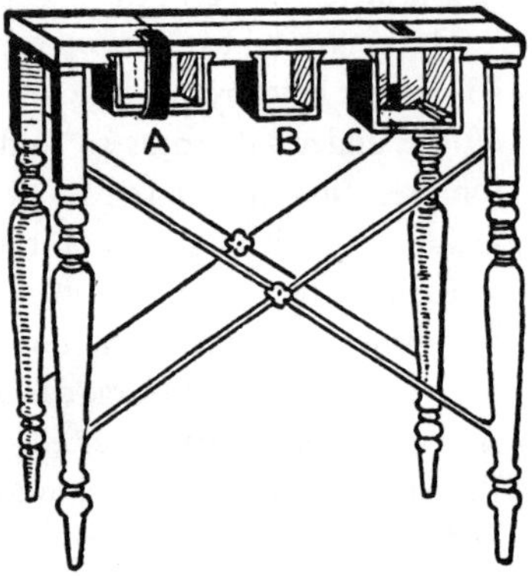

of cards. These were arranged, one upon another, in two columns, with a blackened tin plate at the bottom. A piece of black braid tied around the cage held everything securely.

The cage, thus loaded, with a living canary in the upper portion, lay on its side, bottom outward, in the wooden case mentioned above (*C* in Fig. 3), a flap being cut behind the fringe to let it slide out. Cut in the table top, just above the medial line of the cage, was a vertical opening, six inches long and finger-wide, terminating at its outer end just short of the front edge of the table. In the table cover was a corresponding slit.

The only specialities of the little round table were the space cut in the top to receive the hat-rest, and a pin-point projecting from the edge which in use was turned toward the audience.

The two side tables were absolutely devoid of mechanism or preparation. At a later period in the history of the trick, a circular bracket, supported by a light wire arch, was added over the center of each. To the under side of one of them, midway, a hook was added.

The seven lanterns were circular, with dome tops, and fitted one inside another, the outermost measuring six inches in height by five in diameter. The framework was of metal, the sides professedly of glass, but actually of colored mica. One side of each lantern was open; when the lanterns were nested, the openings coincided, giving access to all the interiors simultaneously. All except the innermost were bottomless; the sockets for the candles (of the miniature sort used for Christmas trees) were in each case carried on a short wire arm. The outermost lantern had on one side of its opening a tube holding a match. The wicks of the candles had been moistened with turpentine, so that all seven could be lighted at once, merely by passing the match over them. Each lantern had a circular opening at the top, beside which was a ring, which folded down flat.

The seven nested lanterns were deposited, upside down, in a pocket made across one corner of a small square table cover—a duplicate of the one already mentioned as lying on the round table at the beginning. This was placed on a chair just behind one of the wings until needed. The pocket, which corresponded in shape with the inverted lanterns, had an opening at its smaller end, through which the performer could take hold of the rings above mentioned. The lanterns were held firmly together by a piece of braid tied around the bases of the rings.

The handkerchiefs used had no speciality except that they were slightly graduated in size, ranging from twenty-four to thirty inches square. They were laid one upon another, the largest at the bottom, then folded in quarters and twisted into a convenient shape; then they were placed in the performer's left coatsleeve, just above the cuff, the centers outward.

The cigar boxes were of pasteboard covered with paper grained in imitation of wood, and were constructed with the ends folding inward, allowing the box to collapse until the proper moment, when a pull upon a loop of narrow ribbon expanded it to its full dimensions. Seven of these, pressed flat and held together by a piece of braid, were stowed under the left breast of the performer's coat.

The ribbons, rolled and packed into an open-mouthed bag or pocket of green baize, just large enough to contain them, were laid at the beginning just behind the large piece of similar baize already mentioned as lying folded upon the center table. When, at a later stage of the trick, this was picked up to be spread on the floor, the roll of ribbons was deftly transferred to the inside of the wig, and placed with it upon one of the side tables.

The goblets were of burnished nickel; each had a wire rim to facilitate its separation from the rest. A couple of loads of these, each ten in number, were packed in black calico bags and carried by the performer in pockets shaped to receive them, one behind each trouser leg, in the position usually occupied by a pochette. These pockets were made specially strong, and lined with silk to minimize friction. The wig was stowed away in the innermost of the set of goblets to be produced first.

The hat used, though professedly borrowed, was actually the performer's own property, as a hat of large size was essential.

Hartz's first proceeding was to take the cover off the little table, shaking it out carelessly to show that there was nothing in it. Then, as if merely to get rid of it, he stepped aside and made a pretended attempt to hang it on a projection of the wing. It fell to the floor, and was picked up and drawn out of sight by the hand of an unseen assistant, who then pushed a chair into view, and laid the cover (really the other one with the pocket containing the lanterns) upon it. Meanwhile, Hartz returned to the little table, and casually showing the hat-rest, fixed it openly in the space prepared for it in the table top.

"Borrowing" a hat, he showed, first, that it was unmistakably empty. Resting it on the little round table, he then proceeded to turn up the leather lining, and in doing so drew down into it from his sleeve the bundle of handkerchiefs. Professing to find the hat rather shallow, he proceeded to look into the cause, which he found to be the presence of the handkerchiefs. These he did not at once completely remove, but drew out portions of them so as to hang over the brim of the hat in all directions. Under cover of these and of the hat itself, he got the cigar boxes from under his coat with his right hand, and after holding them behind the hat for a moment or two, loaded them in. Changing his position so that his left side should be to the rear, he got the nest of goblets from the pocket on that side, let them rest temporarily behind the hat, and presently, under cover of the continued production of the handkerchiefs, loaded them in also. The handkerchiefs, as finally drawn out, were laid across one of the side tables, hanging down more or less from it.

The next item to be produced was the wig, which had been stowed in the nest of goblets. Next followed the goblets themselves, which were ranged along one of the side tables. The production of these was single-handed, the hat being held in one hand and the goblets taken out with the other.

Next came the cigar-boxes. Hartz later discarded these, so that he could truthfully state that not a single collapsible article was used in the trick.

A movement toward the center table enabled the performer to load into the hat the second set of goblets, which he placed on this table. (After the colored goblets had been added to the trick, these were placed upon the side tables, and the metal goblets wholly upon the center table.) In order to make room for them, he took up the piece of green baize lying on that table, and moved it aside, in so doing transferring the roll of ribbons from it into the wig, which lay close beside it.

Midway in the production of the goblets he appeared to notice that the nap of the hat was ruffled. He picked up the wig and smoothed the hat with it, introducing the roll of ribbons under cover of this very natural action.

Finding, apparently, that two or three more goblets still remained in the hat, he made further room for them on the table by removing the green baize altogether, and spreading it on the stage in readiness for the subsequent production of the cards.

He then returned to the table and placed on it the remaining goblets. The placing of the last one brought his right hand (the hat being held in the left) just over the pile of mats. He picked these up, and showing each as he did so, laid them on different parts of the table. In picking up the mats (which were laid just over the bird-cage), the performer's middle finger, dipping down through the slot in the table, pushed the bird-cage into the hat, held in readiness to receive it. The action was so easy and so well disguised that even a spectator who knew the manner and the precise moment of the load, could not claim to have actually *seen* the operation.

The cage and bird were produced next. The braid being untied, the mere act of lifting the cage out of the hat caused the bottom to sink by its own weight into its proper position, carrying down with it the perch and seed trough; the cards remained in the hat. The cage might now be handed around for inspection, as it was perfectly rigid on all sides except the bottom.

Next the performer held the hat in both hands and shook the cards out, scattering them on the outspread baize, where they appeared equivalent to many times the bulk of the hat.

The roll of ribbons which had been introduced into the hat just before the cage load were now paid out yard by yard on to the little round table, and as they appeared likely to increase indefinitely, it became necessary to provide for their accommodation.

For that purpose the performer fetched the table cover from the chair at the wing and laid it over the table with the pocket containing the lanterns on the side away from the spectators, who naturally assumed it to be the unprepared one they had previously seen. The little point in the edge of the table caught the cloth and prevented its being dragged off by the weight of the lanterns.

When the ribbons had all been brought out, the performer gathered up the cloth by the four corners, and made a pretended attempt to put the whole back into the hat. He naturally failed to do so, as the ribbons alone, in their unrolled condition, formed a mass about five times as big as the hat; but under cover of the make-believe attempt he took hold of the rings of the lanterns (through the hole in the pocket) and gently lowered them into the hat. The next step was to light them by means of the match provided for that purpose, after which they were produced one by one and deposited on the center table, on the mats placed in readiness to receive them.

The putting down of the last lantern brought the performer's hand to the corner of the table underneath which were the Japanese doll and crinolette. In depositing the lantern he drew back the bolt, pushing the hat forward for a moment under the overhanging fringe. In drawing it back again the load was brought away within it. The doll was produced in due course, and the production of the crinolette brought the trick to an end.

Even in its earlier form, as above described, the trick was sufficiently astonishing. But Hartz was never content with doing well if it was possible to do better, and he was always on the lookout for some further element of mystery. His first improvement was the substitution for the doll of a human skull, which rose automatically from the hat, the performer standing at a distance from it, and taking no part whatever in the operation.

A papier mache skull was suspended with the crinolette under that portion of the table where the doll had formerly been, and was introduced into the hat in the same way. After the load, the performer placed the hat on the little round table, and moved away from it to another part of the stage. Presently an uncanny grating sound called attention to the hat. Rising by slow degrees, the skull came into view, as shown in Fig. 4. The performer took it out and placed it on a raised bracket over the center table. The production of the crinolette followed, and concluded the trick.

The automatic rising of the skull was managed in a very ingenious way. Fixed to the inside of the crown at the top, and ending in an oblong metal base about four by six inches at the bottom, was a rack and pinion arrangement having an upward and downward movement of four inches. The

FIG. 4

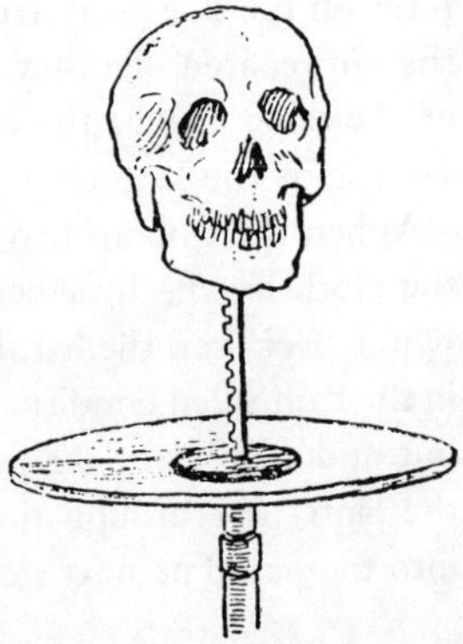

FIG. 5

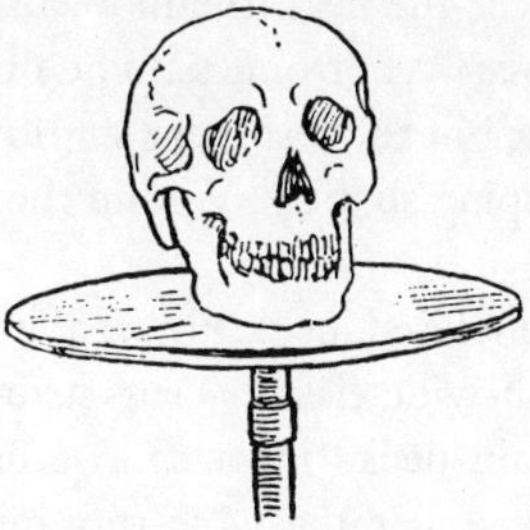

FIG. 6

pinion connected with a spring-barrel which forced it normally upward, into the position shown in Fig. 5. The skull, however, yielded to gentle downward pressure, and when it had reached its lowest point, as in Fig. 6, could be arrested there by pressing back a lever. Under these circumstances, the base was not noticeable, and it was in this condition that the skull was loaded into the hat. A brass eyelet, close to the end of the lever, served to suspend it under the center table until needed.

Once the skull was in the hat, a forward push of the lever started the rising movement. Before taking it out of the hat, Hartz pressed the skull down again to its lowest point, preventing it from rising again by pushing the lever back to its original position. In placing it on the bracket above the table, he took care to handle it so that the base should not be seen.

A further improvement was the production (in addition to the metal goblets) of eighteen red and green goblets, supposedly of glass. Twenty metal goblets were still produced, but a smaller-sized set was used, the whole twenty now forming a single load. These were carried in the pocket behind the thigh on the left side. The transparent goblets were made of colored celluloid.

This set of eighteen goblets was placed in the pocket behind the right thigh, and were loaded into the hat as the second set of metal goblets had formerly been. The wig was now placed in the innermost of these, with a second half-dozen silk handkerchiefs packed in on top of it, which were also produced in the course of the trick.

The production of ten apparently full pint champagne bottles was a still later addition. They were of thin copper, colored with a brownish-green lacquer, which, by artificial light, gave them the appearance of glass. They were duly labeled, and had the usual gold foil around their necks, but they were made corkless, the neck tapering gently right up to the mouth. The supposed cork was in reality a metal cap, molded to the proper shape, wired and gilded, and slipped over the neck the moment before production.

The bottles were necessarily bottomless. The outer one of the nest was in other respects complete, but the rest were slit down one side from top to bottom, the edges overlapping slightly. Within the cavity of the innermost were the "corks."

The set of bottles was enclosed, necks inward, in a tapering bag of black calico, with a piece of inch-wide elastic across its broader end. Thus enveloped, it was inserted, again necks inward, in a narrow, open-ended box (B in Fig. 3) immediately under the table top, midway between the two front legs. A ring, attached to a thin cord, was slipped over the smaller end of the bag. From this ring the cord passed outward over the front edge of the table top, and then (through a hole made for that purpose) back to its under side; then again through a pulley and a couple of brass eyelets to the right side of the table, hanging down in a loop midway between the two legs. After putting the last of the metal goblets upon the table, Hartz gave this loop a pull, drawing the ring forward and shooting the bottles into the hat.

Both hands were needed to separate and cork the bottles and produce them from the hat. The hat was laid on its side on the round table, with its crown toward the spectators, the performer standing behind it, and the hat-rest keeping it in position.

The last and crowning improvement was an alteration in the FINALE. The crinolette was discarded, the concluding effect being the production in quick succession, and without any intermediate load, of a handsome blue porcelain bowl, spherical in shape; a bowl similar in shape, but of clear glass, with goldfish swimming in it; and an elegant circular bird-cage, containing a live bird. Each of the three objects was of such a size as to fill the hat completely.

This cage was of silver-plated metal, and of a construction familiar to conjurers; the bottom slid up to within about an inch of the top, in the center of which was a circular door, working on a pivot, for the insertion of the bird. When the bottom was pushed up, the side wires (each pair forming a loop like an elongated hairpin) folded inward upon it.

In this condition (in which it was only an inch and a half deep) the cage was placed in a shallow box, open at the end facing the audience, in the position formerly occupied by the doll load. The act of pushing it in from the front took up the slack of a piece of black webbing, which crossed the mouth of the box in a vertical direction from its under side. From this webbing a cord was carried along a groove over the top of the table beneath the cover, and brought out at the back just beside the left leg. A pull upon this, immediately after the placing of the last lantern, drew the webbing taut again, and so pushed the cage forward into the hat.

A glance at Fig. 3 will show the construction of the table, as adapted to this later phase of the trick: *A* represents the receptacle for the cage, with the webbing (drawn taut) that brings it forward; *B* the resting-place of the champagne bottles; and *C* containing the square cage and the cards.

The production of the two bowls was the most ingenious part of the trick. The supposed porcelain bowl was actually of metal; it was bottomless, and constructed so that its lower half would easily open outward, although it was normally kept closed by very weak springs. The glass bowl, which was just a shade smaller, was inserted into the metal one from below, and the two were suspended under the left side of the table, midway between the two legs on that side.

The bowls were held together by a shallow black calico bag covering the lower half of the outer one, and kept taut by a strap of broad elastic, buttoned over the top. The lip of the metal bowl, which curved outward, was then passed over two flat little metal hooks, which were screwed to the under surface of the table. A wooden stop prevented the bowl from being pushed in too far.

After the performer had placed the last lantern and was moving away from the table, he pretended to notice that one of the lanterns was out of line with the rest. He stepped back to rectify this, and as he did so with the right hand, the left, under cover of his body, passed the hat for an instant under that side of the table, raised it under the two bowls, and drew them away within it.

The act of lifting the blue bowl out of the hat caused its movable sections to spread apart (leaving behind it the glass bowl, pulled through by its own weight), closing again the moment it was clear. The blue bowl having

FIG. 7

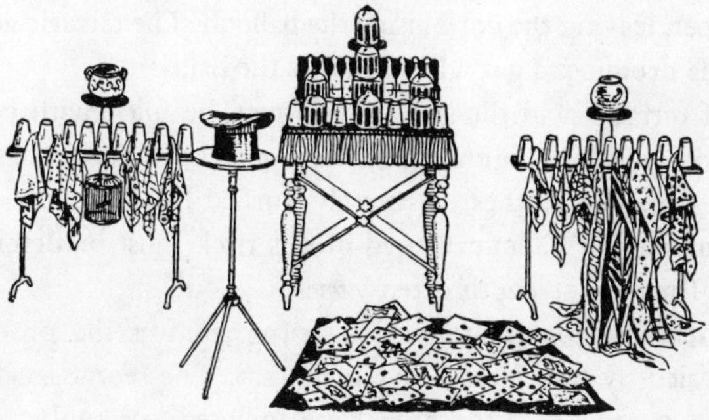

been exhibited and placed on its bracket, the glass one was next produced, the unmistakable "no preparation" of this one naturally inducing the belief that the blue bowl was equally free from deception.

The two bowls were placed one on each of the brackets over the two side tables. The production of the second cage followed. This was suspended from the hook under one of the side tables, and made a brilliant finish to the trick, the final appearance of the stage being as shown in Fig. 7.

L. H.

The production of inflated balloons is unquestionably the most brilliant of all hat tricks. HOWARD THURSTON introduced the trick into this country, inflating the balloons with a gas that carried the globes to the dome of the theater.

The method used by Mr. Thurston was ingenious and scientific, but the apparatus was decidedly cumbersome and impractical for anything but stage work. The interior arrangement of the hat was mechanically intricate, and the balloons were inflated by gas drawn from a tank in the wings. The gas was forced through a tube under the stage, to which the performer made connection by means of a heel plate. A rubber tube passed up the performer's trousers, up his back and down his sleeve, and was connected at will with the inflating apparatus inside the hat.

The simplest, safest and best of the many methods of inflating the balloons is as follows: Take a small glass medicine vial, about two inches long and three-quarters of an inch in diameter. Fill this flask with a solution of tartaric acid and cork it with a rubber stopper. Place a small quantity of bicarbonate of soda inside the balloon, and in its mouth insert the small flask half way, tying a string around the balloon to hold the bottle firmly in place.

A half-dozen balloons arranged in this way are loaded into a hat—preferably an opera hat—and to produce them it is necessary only to pull out the rubber stopper, leaving the cork inside the balloon. The tartaric acid mixing with the soda produces a gas which inflates the balloon.

Instead of tartaric acid the small bottle may be filled with commercial sulphuric acid, but the conjurer must use extreme caution in handling this chemical or damaged clothes or severely burned hands will be the result. The exact amount of chemicals used in this trick must be determined by experiment, for their strength often varies.

A novel feature from Harry Stork's program was the production of piping hot fried oysters from a borrowed hat. The secret is simple. The oysters—each impaled on a toothpick—are enclosed in a rubber bag which retains the heat for about an hour. If a longer time must elapse before producing them, the oysters may be kept warm on a hot tin behind the scenes until the performer is ready for them. *T. N. D.*

HEIMBURGER, ALEXANDER (1818-1909) German stage performer, billed as Alexander the Conjurer. He toured North and South America with enormous success, performed at the White House for President Polk (the first magician, and one of few, ever to appear there), declined an engagement with P. T. Barnum lest he damage his own prestige, mystified Samuel F. B. Morse, of telegraphic fame, with his "spirit bell" trick, and amassed such a fortune that he got into fashionable society in his native Germany, and retired from magic.

HELLER, ROBERT Stage name of William Henry Palmer (about 1826-1878), English stage conjurer, mind-reader, and musician. He started in life as a very promising music student, attending two conservatories and winning scholarships. He also learned magic when very young, and became so fascinated by it that he launched himself as a professional. He began by slavishly copying ROBERT-HOUDIN, even adopting his first name, dyeing his hair, and talking with a French accent. The act was a failure, so he took it to America, and failed again. He settled as a music teacher in Washington, D. C.

When he returned to magic he did a show that was truly his own, including SECOND SIGHT, piano-playing, and automaton puppets. In consequence he was a great success all over the United States, Great Britain, much of Europe, China, Malaysia, Java, Ceylon, India, and Egypt. He was the first performer in the United States to attract society to his shows. *J. M.*

HERRMANN A family of four magicians, two of them among the greatest in all magical history. *Samuel Herrmann*, the first of the name, was a German physician who performed as a hobby.

C. HERRMANN

Carl Herrmann (1816-1887), Samuel's eldest son, made a great name for himself throughout Europe. In a subsequent agreement, he and his brother Alexander divided the hemispheres between them, he taking the eastern, Alexander the western, so that Carl (also called Compars) never afterward appeared in the Americas. He did, however, compete successfully with ROBERT-HOUDIN in England.

Alexander Herrmann (1843-1896), known to generations of Americans as Herrmann the Great, was Carl Herrmann's youngest brother When Alexander was eleven, old Samuel objected to having more than one magician in the family; Alexander ran away to join Carl, and traveled all over Europe with him for three years. At the age of fourteen, Alexander set up for himself, making his debut before the Queen of Spain at Madrid. Throughout North and South America Alexander Herrmann's wit, Mephistophelian looks (originally copied from Carl), and grand style became almost as legendary as his superb sleight-of-hand. He and ROBERT HELLER were the leaders in raising magicians out of the mountebank and sideshow class. (See HISTORY) Herrmann made magic the best type of family entertainment; in showmanship, iron nerve, and charm he has never been surpassed.

A. HERRMANN

L. HERRMANN

When Alexander Herrmann died, his widow Adelaide continued to perform, and employed his nephew, *Leon Herrmann*, the fourth of the name, to work with her. He looked very much like his uncles, and so was often confused with them, but he lacked their ability, and did not long continue with Mme. Herrmann.

HERTZ, CARL Stage name of Laib Morgenstern (1869-1924), a successful performer and inventor who was born in San Francisco, and made his name in England. He appeared before a committee of the House of Commons to refute charges of cruelty to animals in the performance of the BIRD-CAGE vanish. He showed the trick, and was lucky enough on this occasion to have the canary escape unharmed. He first became interested in magic through seeing ALEXANDER HERRMANN's show. In later life he emphasized the invention and performance of ILLUSIONS.

HISTORY (See also: ANDERSON; BAMBERGS; BELLACHINI; BLACKSTONE; BLITZ; BOSCO; BRESLAW; CARDINI; CARTER; CHINESE MAGIC; CHING LING FOO; CHUNG LING SOO; COMTE; CULPITT; DE KOLTA; DEVANT; DOEBLER; DOWNS; EAST INDIAN MAGIC; FAWKES; FOX; FRIKELL; GOLDIN; GYNGELL; HARTZ; HEIMBURGER; HELLER; HERRMANN; HERTZ; HOFFMANN; HOFZINSER; HOUDINI; KELLAR; LAFAYETTE; LAURANT; LEIPZIG; LEROY; MASKELYNES; MULHOLLAND; NICOLA; PHILIPPE; PINETTI; POWELL; ROBERT-HOUDIN; ROBIN; SELBIT; STODARE; THURSTON; TORRINI; VAN HOVEN; WILLIAMS; WYMAN)

The history of legerdemain (conjuring with no tinge of the occult) falls into three periods. One period overlaps another in respect to both performers and tricks; yet the divisions are fairly clear.

The first period begins in a small way before recorded history, and tapers off into the succeeding period during the eighteenth century. In this first stage, the performers were mountebanks, itinerant showmen who worked alongside of jugglers, contortionists, and story-tellers outdoors or in booths at fairs, or perhaps on special occasions in the great halls of the nobility. The great characteristic and universal trick was the CUPS AND BALLS; magicians habitually wore an apron forming a large pocket in front of their thighs, which served both as stowage for small apparatus and as a combination SERVANTE and PROFONDE. The modern German word for conjuring is still *Taschenspielerei*, pocket-play. FAWKES and GYNGELL are almost the only two names now remembered from that period. The conjurers of the time were still strongly suspected of dealing in witchcraft and trading with the devil; they could not safely have exhibited some of the better modern effects, even if they had known them.

The second great period began about the middle of the eighteenth century, and straggled to an end in the second half of the nineteenth. In this stage, magic was allied to mechanics. The *boîte à confrère*, a center table draped to the floor to hide an assistant who worked TRAPS and pistons, was in general use. The conjurer wore flowing robes; his platform was covered with heavy, bulky apparatus, much of it worked by hidden manpower; and writing, dancing, and musical automata (some genuine, some operated by human agency) were the conjurer's showpieces. Magicians doffed the pocket apron, came in out of their booths and street-corner pitches, and began hiring theaters for a full evening's show. The audience was perhaps quite as much impressed by the sheer splendor of the magician's stage setting and paraphernalia as by the tricks themselves.

PHILIPPE (the first to introduce Eastern magic to the Western repertory on a large scale), and JOHN HENRY ANDERSON, the pioneer in modern publicity and advertising ballyhoo, were the outstanding figures of this period, partly because they rose above some of its grosser crudities.

ROBERT-HOUDIN began his career in this second, mechanical phase of conjuring, and played some part in the transition to modern times. He learned his art, furthermore, from TORRINI, who represented the earliest, itinerant type of conjurer.

The first halting steps toward the modern style of magic were taken by FRIKELL, ably seconded by Robert-Houdin. Frikell worked on a clear stage, abandoning the clumsy mechanical contraptions of his immediate predecessors. Robert-Houdin followed this improvement, and formulated once and for all the modern definition of a prestidigitator: "A conjurer is an actor playing the part of a magician."

Modern magic, though it has profited by its earlier association with both street showmanship and mechanics, is now fundamentally a branch of practical PSYCHOLOGY. The public, habituated to scientific marvels no whit less surprising than anything the conjurer can show, will not be impressed by a chess-playing doll. And since the human hand is far slower than the eye, mere juggling will not suffice to deceive.

In the modern period, magic has grown too far for any one performer to master it all, and this in turn has created specialists—illusionists, like KELLAR and GOLDIN; specialized manipulators like DOWNS and CARDINI; escape artists, beginning with HOUDINI; mind-readers, and many others.

The growth of magic as a hobby for AMATEUR MAGICIANS falls overwhelmingly within the last period, and largely within the twentieth century. *B. M.*

HOFFMANN, PROFESSOR LOUIS Stage and pen-name of Angelo John Lewis, M.A. (1839-1920), the greatest writer on magic who ever lived. He first took an interest in magic at ten years old, after seeing the show of a Professor James Taylor. As an undergraduate at Oxford he saw JOHN HENRY ANDERSON.

For some time after his university days he was a London barrister, and then deserted the law for journalism. He was an author, critic, editor, and translator for nearly fifty years, during which time he wrote *Modern Magic*, *More Magic*, *Later Magic*, and several lesser conjuring books, translated ROBERT-HOUDIN's books on magic and gambling, wrote several volumes on sports and games, and revised Hoyle. He was on the staff of the London *Saturday Review* for many years. He often gave magic shows, but apparently always as an amateur, for charity.

He was not distinguished as a performer, but his books marked an epoch in magic LITERATURE, and undoubtedly made more magicians than any other one cause in the history of the art. Hoffmann had the priceless ability to teach his reader magic, instead of just explaining it. *J. M. & H. H.*

HOFZINSER, JOHANN NEPOMUK (1806-1875) Perhaps the most brilliant inventor among Austrian magicians. He introduced the roller-curtain CARD FRAME, double-faced cards, the counter-weighted CLOCK DIAL, and many brilliant effects still in use by men clever enough to do them. He specialized in card work, but was also skilful in other branches of small magic.

Ottokar Fischer's book, *J. N. Hofzinser Kartenkuenste*, translated by S. H. Sharpe as *J. N. Hofzinser's Card Conjuring*, is the best single reference on his work.

HOLDERS (See also CIGARETTE MANIPULATION; DROPPERS; HOOKS; THIMBLE TRICKS)

Holders, like DROPPERS, are devices usually worn under the clothes to keep some small article in readiness for a STEAL. They differ from droppers in that the object must be pulled away instead of being released automatically.

Holders for special purposes are discussed under CIGARETTE MANIPULATION and THIMBLE TRICKS.

Ball and egg holders are usually made as shown in Figs. 1 and 2. A third variety was described by its inventor, NELSON DOWNS, as "in reality a long cloth tube stitched down the inside of the coat. The diameter of this tube is just large enough to hold comfortably a billiard ball. Around the lower end is sewed an elastic which keeps the balls from falling through, but which allows of a ball being pressed out by the fingers of the left hand."

FIG. 1

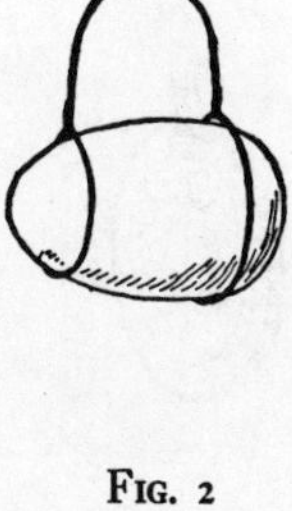

FIG. 2

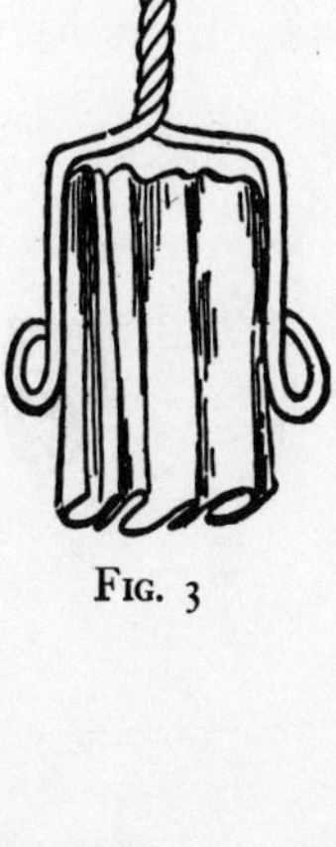

FIG. 3

Coin holders are usually of the dropper type, though a holder for a single coin may be improvised from two linked paper clips or an excelsior clip (see HOOKS).

Card holders for supplying a steal (as distinguished from CARD INDEXES) are also likely to be improvised clips.

Handkerchief holders may well be home-made out of insulated wire, as in Fig. 3.

H. H.

HOOKS A needle-point soldered near the edge of a coin, handkerchief hand-box (see SILK TRICKS), or other small piece of apparatus, at an angle pointing toward the center, will serve to attach the object temporarily to the performer's clothes, hand, or any other convenient place.

The Excelsior clip is one of the smallest pieces of apparatus which can be used by the conjurer, but its usefulness is out of all proportion to its size. It is a minute spring clip, of steel, with the outer portion of one of its longer arms bent over into the form of a hook and sharpened to a point, so that it can be hooked on to any portion of the clothing (Fig. 1). It is only half an inch long, and three-eighths of an inch wide. The clip, however, opens widely enough to take in the edge of a coin (as in Fig. 2), and on the other hand closes with so firm a grip that it will hold a card, or even a slip of paper securely.

The possible uses of this little clip are many. For instance, it may be hooked, holding a coin, inside the vest, just above the waistband, or underneath the lapel of the coat. Under the vest a little higher up, it will hold a card, or half a dozen cards, ready for production when necessary. By its aid a coin may be hung on one finger at the back of the hand, and so vanished, or may be temporarily suspended on the back of a VOLUNTEER assistant, to be reproduced, apparently from nowhere, a moment later. Or again the performer may ask a volunteer assistant to shuffle the pack thoroughly. When it is returned, he remarks that that was a good enough shuffle for a

FIG. 1

FIG. 2

FIG. 3

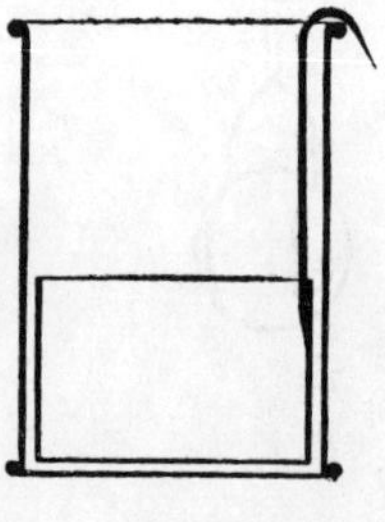

beginner, but if the gentleman had been a poker-player, he would have kept back a few cards under his knee, so! Whereupon he passes his empty hand under his own knee and produces a straight flush, or some similarly staggering combination. The explanation is, of course, that the cards in question were suspended in the clip behind the leg, the performer taking care to keep full face to the company until he has produced them.

These are but a few of the possible uses of the Excelsior, which has two secondary advantages: first, it is so small that if accidentally dropped on the floor it causes no sound and attracts no attention; and secondly, its price is so nominal that the performer can use, or lose, half a dozen without feeling any the poorer. *L. H.*

A longer hook is sometimes attached to a small cylindrical cup, which is secretly introduced into a metal cup or tube. A small article dropped into the cup is then vanished by catching the hook on the sleeve. Fig. 3 shows a coin-vanishing cup; a handkerchief-vanishing tube is made on just the same principle.

HOUDINI, HARRY Stage name of Ehrich Weisz (1874-1926), the greatest performer of ESCAPES and probably the most skilful PUBLICITY-getter in the history of magic. The son of a rabbi, brought up in Appleton, Wisconsin, he began practising magic and escapes as a boy, and traveled with circuses and carnivals before he was out of his teens.

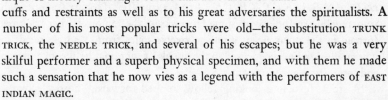

He learned to lend an atmosphere of sensation to every trick he did, and developed among other things the technique of money challenges to the manufacturers of handcuffs and restraints as well as to his great adversaries the spiritualists. A number of his most popular tricks were old—the substitution TRUNK TRICK, the NEEDLE TRICK, and several of his escapes; but he was a very skilful performer and a superb physical specimen, and with them he made such a sensation that he now vies as a legend with the performers of EAST INDIAN MAGIC.

He was an avid collector and student of magical history; his book, *The Unmasking of Robert-Houdin*, was epoch-making despite its obvious faults of temper and emphasis.

Houdini, by Harold Kellock, is the standard biography. *B. M.*

HOULETTE (See under RISING CARDS)

I

ILLUSIONS Large, stage tricks, usually those involving a person or large animal. BLACKSTONE's Vanishing Horse is an illusion; the VANISHING BIRD-CAGE is not.

(See also BLACKSTONE; CHOPPER EFFECTS; CHUNG LING SOO; COSTUME TRUNK TRICK; DEKOLTA; DEVANT; DOLL'S HOUSE; DUCK VANISH; GOLDIN; HERRMANN; HERTZ; HOUDINI; KELLAR; LAFAYETTE; LEROY; LEVITATIONS; MASKELYNES; MERRY WIDOW; SAWING A WOMAN IN TWO; SELBIT; SILENT ACTS; STAGE SETTINGS; STODARE; THURSTON; TRUNK TRICK; WALKING THROUGH A BRICK WALL.)

IMPROMPTU EFFECTS (See under PROGRAMS; PUBLICITY; TABLE TRICKS; VEST-POCKET MAGIC; BILLET- AND MESSAGE-READING; CARD MANIPULATION; CARD THROUGH HANDKERCHIEF; CARDS, ONE-WAY, POINTER, DIVIDED; CIGAR MANIPULATION; CIGARETTE MANIPULATION; COIN BOX; COIN MANIPULATION; COINS, SHELL; DICE; FOUR-ACE TRICK; GENERAL CARD; JUMPING PEG; MIND-READING; MUSCLE-READING; RATTLE BARS; RING ON STICK; SILK knots; SLEEVE, up his; SPONGE BALLS; STRING TRICKS; SYMPATHETIC COINS; THIRTY-CARD TRICK; THREE-CARD TRICK; THUMB WRITER; TRANSFIXED PACK.)

In addition to the standard works, the following books contain good impromptu material: David Devant, *Magic Made Easy;* Jean Hugard, *Encyclopedia of Card Tricks;* Jean Hugard and Frederick Braue, *Expert Card Technique;* Barrows Mussey, *Magic.*

INDIAN BASKET TRICK In 1832, the Rev. Hobart Caunter, who was traveling in India with some friends, saw the famous basket trick performed in the open air, at a village twelve miles from Madras; regarding it as an illusion unprecedented in the annals of juggling, he wrote a graphic and interesting account of it.

"A stout, ferocious-looking fellow stepped forward," he says, "with a common wicker basket of the country, which he begged we would carefully examine. This we accordingly did; it was of the slightest texture, and admitted the light through a thousand apertures. Under this fragile covering he placed a child about eight years old, an interesting little girl, habited in the only garb which nature had provided for her, perfect of frame and elastic of limb—a model for a cherub, and scarcely darker than a child of southern France. When she was properly secured, the man, with a lowering aspect, asked her some question, which she instantly answered, and as the thing was done within a few feet from the spot on which we were seated, the voice appeared to come so distinctly from the basket, that I felt at once satisfied there was no deception.

"They held a conversation for some moments, when the juggler, almost with a scream of passion, threatened to kill her. There was a stern reality in the whole scene which was perfectly dismaying; it was acted to the life, but terrible to see and hear. The child was heard to beg for mercy, when the juggler seized a sword, placed his foot on the frail wicker covering under which his supposed victim was so piteously supplicating his forbearance, and to my absolute consternation and horror, plunged it through, withdrawing it several times, and repeating the plunge with all the blind ferocity of an excited demon. By this time his countenance exhibited an expression fearfully indicative of the most frantic of human passions. The shrieks of the child were so real and distracting that they almost curdled for a few moments the whole mass of my blood; my first impulse was to rush upon the monster, and fell him to the earth; but he was armed and I defenseless. I looked at my companions—they appeared to be pale and paralyzed with terror; and yet these feelings were somewhat neutralized by the consciousness that the man could not dare to commit a deliberate murder in the broad eye of day, and before so many witnesses; still the whole thing was appalling.

"The blood ran in streams from the basket; the child was heard to struggle under it; her groans fell horridly upon the ear; her struggles smote painfully upon the heart. The former were gradually subdued into a faint moan, and the latter into a slight rustling sound; we seemed to hear the last convulsive gasp which was to set her innocent soul free from the gored body, when to our inexpressible astonishment and relief, after muttering a few cabalistic words, the juggler took up the basket; but no child was to be seen. The spot was indeed dyed with blood; but there were no mortal remains, and, after a few moments of undissembled wonder, we perceived the little object of our alarm coming toward us from among the crowd. She advanced and saluted us, holding out her hand for our donations, which we bestowed with hearty good-will; she received them with a most graceful salaam, and the party left us, well satisfied with our more than expected gratuity. What rendered the deception the more extraordinary was that the man stood aloof from the crowd during the whole performance—there was not a person within several feet of him." *T. F.*

The method of performing this trick which has been handed down through generations of Hindus, is as follows: The boy subject is firmly tied in a net, having had his big toes and thumbs fastened down with bandages. Then, with many a grunt and a groan, he is lifted into the basket.

The boy, however, pretends that the basket is too small, so he is really seated on one side and keeps his back in the air. This is done to give the appearance eventually that it was impossible for him to crouch down or around the basket. The lid of the basket is placed on his back, and a large sheet thrown over the entire apparatus, concealing from the audience every movement made by the subject.

The magician and his assistant begin their yells, groans, and incantations, and strike the basket with swords or canes. Gradually the cover of the basket sinks until the basket seems empty. The fakir takes off the cover of the basket, but leaves the sheet over it. Then he jumps into the presumably empty basket, stamps all around, and takes out the net, in which are found the turban worn by the subject and the thumb tie. To prove further that the basket is empty, the fakir seats himself in it. The lid of the basket is now replaced, the sheet taken off, and the basket tied up.

During all this time the subject, who is something of a contortionist, is wriggling about on the bottom of the basket, keeping out of reach of the sword, and often guiding its thrusts, as every movement on the part of the fakir has been carefully thought out and rehearsed in advance.

By this time the fakir has convinced the audience that the basket is empty. True, he has not allowed any spectators to come too near him or the basket, nor has any hand but his touched it, but his clever acting almost persuades even the skeptical onlooker that the basket is empty.

With the lid of the basket replaced, this time over the sheet, he resumes his weird incantations. The basket begins to rock, the subject gradually raises himself inside the basket, and when the noise is at its height, he straightens up in the basket and raises it with his back as far as it will go, making it appear as if he had returned to an empty basket in his original position.

Sometimes the trick is varied: instead of the subject's being found in his original position, he is seen running toward the crowd as from a distance. This is accomplished by having two subjects, one in the basket, and one hidden on the outskirts of the crowd, who are doubles or at least who show a marked resemblance and are dressed exactly alike. *Houdini*

INDIAN MANGO TRICK The Indian conjurer, sitting on the ground, heaps up some earth in front of him. He wets this until it has the consistency of mud. He then places in this little mound a mango stone and covers the whole with a cloth.

He plays his flute for a few moments, and then takes away the cloth; the heap is found to be as before. He takes the lid of his basket, and covering it with the cloth, places it over the heap of mud, propping up with a little piece of stick the end toward him. More flute-playing. He takes away the lid and cloth, but with no result, so he puts back the covering.

After a certain amount of manipulation, during which the rustling of leaves is heard, he lifts up the covering, and shows a small plant. He waters it, adjusts its leaves, and again goes through the same performance as before. Each time that he takes away the basket cover the tree has grown larger.

The making of the loose earth into a mound is necessary so that the bits of branches stuck into it from time to time will stand upright. When the performer takes the basket lid away, he picks up with the cloth a small bundle by his side which contains a small piece of a mango twig with two or three leaves upon it. Under cover of the replaced lid he unwraps the bundle, gets out the twig, and sticks it into the mud heap, pressing it down firmly so that it stands erect and appears to have grown there.

He plays a little music, and then takes away the lid, carrying with it the empty rag that contained the twig. He puts the lid on the ground and so gets rid of the rag.

While the audience are showing their surprise at the development of the twig, he picks up still another larger bundle containing a still larger mango branch. He replaces the lid; under cover of it he unfolds the bundle, gets out the branch, adds it to the twig already in the mud heap, and makes all secure by pressing down the mud again.

Finally he plants in the same way the branch, which has possibly two mangoes on it. When the trick has been completed, the conjurer sweeps the branches, earth, and all away in one destructive swoop which does not allow his audience to ascertain whether the tree had any roots.

Occasionally, instead of the basket lid, the magician uses three sticks together in the form of a tripod over which he places his cloth. *L. H. B.*

INDIAN ROPE TRICK Probably the most famous single trick (or, more properly, ILLUSION) ever heard of. Not the most famous trick "in existence," because there is no concrete evidence of any sort to show that it has ever been performed, and the most tempting offers have failed to lure forward any East Indian magician who would attempt it.

In brief, the effect is supposed to be that the magician throws a coil of rope into the air, where it remains upright. An assistant shins up and disappears at the top, followed by the performer himself, who then throws down the severed, bleeding members of his assistant. The performer reappears, slides down the rope, and reassembles and restores the assistant.

The best explanation of the story is offered by JOHN MULHOLLAND, who has traced it to a Chinese fairy story very closely resembling our own *Jack and the Beanstalk*.

A few attempts by THURSTON and others to show the effect on the Occidental stage must be put down as lamentable exhibitions. *B. M.*

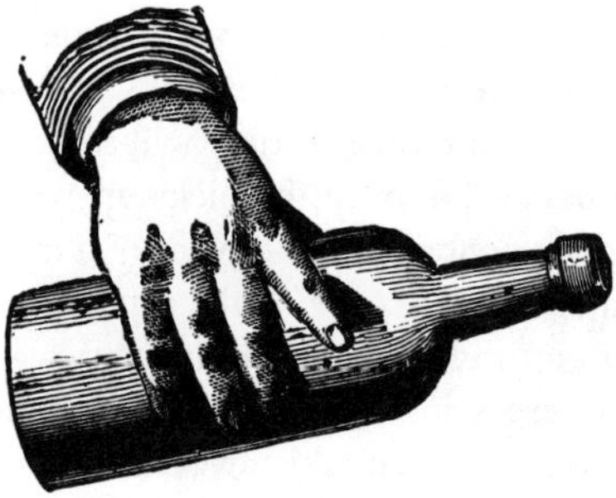

FIG. 1

INEXHAUSTIBLE BOTTLE Although it appears to be an ordinary glass bottle, the inexhaustible bottle is in reality of tin, painted black. Internally it is divided into three, four, or five separate compartments, ranged around a central space, and each tapering to a narrow-mouthed tube, which terminates about an inch from the top of the bottle. A small pinhole is drilled through the outer surface of the bottle into each compartment, the holes being placed so that when the bottle is grasped by the hand in the ordinary way (Fig. 1), each hole may be covered by one or another of the fingers or the thumb. The central space is left empty, but the surrounding compartments are filled by means of a funnel with a very tapering nozzle, with the wines or liquids expected to be most in demand, or to which it is intended to limit the spectators' choice. A tray full of glasses, made especially of very thick glass so as to appear to contain more than they actually do, completes the apparatus.

The performer brings on the magic bottle, followed by an attendant bearing the tray of glasses. He begins by openly pouring water into the bottle and out again, so as to raise the inference indirectly that the bottle must be perfectly empty. The water actually passes into the center space only, and thence runs out again as soon as the bottle is tilted. The fingers, meanwhile, are tightly pressed on the different holes and, thus excluding the air, effectually prevent any premature flow of wine from the various compartments.

The performer, still holding the bottle mouth downward, says, "You observe, ladies and gentlemen, that the bottle is now perfectly empty, and yet I shall compel it to refill itself for your benefit." He then, addressing various individuals, asks each whether he prefers port, sherry, gin, etc., and when the answer is given, has only to raise the finger stopping the air-hole of that particular compartment to cause the liquid named to flow from the bottle, stopping as soon as the finger is again pressed on the hole.

In order to prevent confusion, it is a good plan to place the liquors in the bottle in alphabetical order, beginning at the hole stopped by the thumb. Some performers increase the variety of the liquors produced by placing beforehand in certain of the glasses a few drops of different flavoring essences. By this means a compartment filled with plain spirits of wine may be made to do duty for brandy, whisky, etc., at pleasure, according to the glass into which the liquid is poured.

Where the trick is performed before a very large audience, a single bottle would not contain sufficient liquor to answer all the demands upon it. In this case it is necessary to change the bottle, sometimes more than once in the course of the trick. *L. H.*

Various improvements have been made in the inexhaustible bottle trick. For instance, after the bottle has yielded its various liquors, it is broken, and from the bottle the performer produces some borrowed article which has been vanished in a previous trick and then apparently forgotten. This may have been a ring, glove, or handkerchief, which will be discovered tied around the neck of a small guinea-pig or dove taken from the broken bottle.

This is accomplished by having the bottle especially constructed. Its compartments end a few inches above the bottom of the bottle; the portion below has a wavy or cracked appearance, and is made to slip on and off. The conjurer goes through the motions of actually breaking the bottle by tapping it near the bottom with a small hammer or wand, and the appearance of the guinea-pig or lost article causes surprise, so that the pretended breaking of the bottle passes unnoticed.

This bottle can be genuine, with no loose bottom at all, and a small article can be inserted, but this makes a great deal of trouble, and the effect is not greatly increased.

Many names have been given to this trick. The old-time magicians who remained for months in one theater had to change their programs frequently, so for one night they would present the bottle without breaking it, and on the next they would break the bottle, so as to vary the trick.

This bottle trick originated in "The Inexhaustible Barrel." The first trace of this wonderful barrel is found in "Hocus Pocus, Jr., the Anatomie of Legerdemain," written by Henry Dean in 1635 (Second Edition). On page 21 is described a barrel with a single spout, from which can be drawn three different kinds of liquors. This was worked precisely on the same principle as was the inexhaustible bottle trick centuries later, by shutting up the air-holes of compartments from which liquors were not flowing.

Houdini

The trick has had a big revival of late years as a NIGHT-CLUB effect. A cocktail-shaker or teakettle generally replaces the venerable bottle, and most of the flavors are produced by essences in the glasses. One performer billed as "Think-a-Drink Hoffman" has made an entire act of the trick.

INVENTION (See also MAGICAL EFFECTS) Invention is the life blood of magic, as PRESENTATION is the flesh and bones. A magician need not be an inventor in order to succeed, but without inventions magic would eventually wear out and die.

The thing most to be striven for in a magical invention is satisfactory novelty of effect; next to this comes novelty of method.

Since an invention essentially comprises some definite element of novelty, not merely in conception, but in the practical application of a specific principle, it is quite easy to indicate certain sources from which inventions may be derived.

Inventive genius depends primarily upon a faculty for exercising the imagination upon possible *combinations* hitherto unknown. But inventors are not necessarily born; they can also be made. The man who wants to invent, but does not know how, can learn to invent, if he will but take the trouble. So long as a man has sufficient imagination to form some idea of what would be the immediate result, for example, if it were known for certain that the world would come to an end tomorrow, he has an inventor's chief qualification. The man who has no imagination cannot expect to gain the power of foreseeing possibilities and anticipating results, without which no invention can be made.

In the training of an inventor, then, the first essential is cultivation of imagination. The man of imagination is one who exercises his brains upon problems relating to work which he himself intends to carry through, when those problems have been mentally solved. That is the kind of imagination an inventor wants.

The faculty next in importance is observation. Inspirations seldom come to those who do not look for them. Equally there is little use in looking unless one knows where and how to look. Therefore, it is necessary that an inventor's power of observation be well trained, not only in looking out for inspirations, but also in recognizing the channels through which inspiration may possibly come.

One of the most extraordinary facts concerning invention is the evolution of conceptions in unbroken sequence. The inventor begins working out a certain problem he has conceived; and, as he proceeds, there grow out of his work suggestions which may lead to many new inventions. Each of these may lead to further inspirations; and so on.

As a general rule, inventions are not derived from accidental ideas, happy thoughts, or heaven-born revelations. Inventors are always on the lookout for sources of inspiration, and always endeavoring to imagine novel combinations and novel applications of familiar devices. When an inventor finds some detail lacking which known methods cannot supply, he is led to seek out in imagination a new method—even a new principle—that will fulfill his requirements.

Having a definite aim in view and the ability to imagine possible means of achieving that aim, the chances are a hundred to one that he finds what he wants. Thus, an inventor's work consists in laborious effort devoted to the building up, mainly from fragments of existing knowledge, of complete structures which possess the element of novelty in some form. For this reason the art of invention is capable of being learned. A wide field exists for those who, without special gifts, are willing to do their best toward inventing things for themselves.

In magic, as in all other directions, the chief source from which inventors derive their inspirations is the work already done. But this is where one wants to know where and how to search. It is useless to read magical works, or inspect magical devices, and then confine one's attention to what has been read or seen. One must not look at just what is directly in view; one must look all around it, above it and beyond it.

The greatest aid to success is a complete understanding of the subject; in any technical subject, a complete understanding cannot possibly be possessed by anyone who lacks theoretical knowledge. The theory of magic is comparatively simple. It is, however, nonetheless important on that account. Its very simplicity renders a lack of knowledge the less excusable on the part of those who ought to possess it. And, seeing how useful that knowledge becomes, when one is seeking for novel suggestions and inspirations, the magician who neglects this branch of his subject must be accounted blind to his own interests.

MAGICAL TECHNICS

Manipulative Magic

CLASS OR TYPE	PRINCIPLE OR METHOD
Prearrangement	Collusion Disposition Preparation
Concealment	Covering Disposal Retaining
Interposition	Loading Duplication Substitution
False Handling	Forcing Securing Transposition

Mental Magic

CLASS OR TYPE	PRINCIPLE OR METHOD
Thought Transference	Code Work Secret Speech Secret Conveyance of Documents Duplicate Reading
Memorization	Artificial Memory Counting Down
Divination	Clairvoyance Discovery Prediction

Physical Magic

CLASS OR TYPE	PRINCIPLE OR METHOD
Mechanical	Outer Casing Concealed Access Secret Cavity or Receptacle Diverse Formation Double Facing Concealed Mechanism or Motive Power Concealed Connection Invisible Suspension
Optical	Mirror Masking Reflected Images Transparent Reflectors Lantern Projection Background Work Chiaroscuro
Acoustic	Misdirection by Sound Conveyance of Sound Disguise by Sound
Electrical	Conveyance of Motive Power through Supports Trigger action by Current Ignition Electro-telegraphy and Telephony
Chemical	Apparent Transformation of Substance Ignition Change of Color by Chemical Reaction Invisible Writing
Molecular	Change of state, from solid to liquid, from either to gaseous, or vice versa Change of color, properties, or dimensions by variation in temperature, pressure, etc.

N. M. & D. D.

Once an invention has been made, the inventor may wish to protect it legally. The following material is condensed, by gracious permission of the author, from a series of articles by James C. Wobensmith, originally published in *The Sphinx.*

Lawful monopolies of three forms are recognized in this country: first, those arising under the patent laws; second, those arising under the copyright laws; and third, those arising under the law of unfair competition, of which the law of trademarks forms a part.

The real meat of the law of patents is found in Sec. 4886 of the Revised Statutes, as follows: "Any person who has invented or discovered any new and useful art, machine, manufacture, or composition of matter, or any new and useful improvements thereof, not known or used by others in this country, before his invention or discovery thereof, and not patented or described in any printed publication in this or any foreign country, before his invention or discovery thereof, or more than one year prior to his application, and not in public use or on sale in this country for more than one year prior to his application, unless the same is proved to have been abandoned, may, upon payment of the fees required by law, and other due proceeding had, obtain a patent therefor."

We first consider who may secure a patent. No distinction is made as to age or citizenship. Patents are frequently obtained by minors, although in disposing of their rights under a patent they suffer the usual disabilities of minors in making valid contracts. Patents are granted to aliens, resident or nonresident; their citizenship has merely to be stated in the application.

An essential requirement peculiar to American law is that the person obtaining the patent must be the original inventor, or his assignee. The application must be made and sworn to by the actual inventor; or in case of his death between the time of the invention and the patent application, or of insanity, by his legal representative.

We next consider what may be patented. The statute provides for four separate classes: a new and useful art, a machine, a manufacture, and a composition of matter.

Patents falling into the category of an art are more commonly known as "process" or "method" patents. Included in this classs are cases where the invention resides in a series of steps that bring about a physical change of the material operated on.

The great bulk of patents falls within the statutory class of machines—in patent parlance any assembly of relatively movable co-operating parts that bring about a useful result. The flat model Brema CARD BOX is a machine from the patent standpoint; so is a series of elements not necessarily having any direct physical connection, such as the parts of game apparatus, provided there is a co-action of some sort among the parts.

"Manufacture" in the language of the Patent Office means any single unitary structure of a novel character, capable of a useful purpose. The term includes almost any physical structure that cannot be termed a machine.

Patents on compositions of matter relate to mixtures of substance by means of which new and unexpected results are obtained. The result in each case must be one which arises out of the admixture, rather than the mere addition of the expected actions of the individual components. Such patents are usually difficult to secure, because it is almost always possible to find prior compositions in which the constituents are used for analogous purposes.

In applying for a patent, it is necessary to specify which of the four classes an invention falls into.

The next requirement is that the invention must not have been known or used by others in this country before the applicant invented it. A mere abandoned experiment, however, will not defeat the patent; the prior knowledge and use must have been of a character that added to the sum total of human knowledge. Prior knowledge and use without publication in a foreign country will not defeat a patent in the United States.

If the idea has been patented or described in print *anywhere* before the invention, however, or more than one year before the patent application, the right to a patent is forever gone. A single public use more than one year before the application is filed will defeat the patent.

It is always advisable to get an application in promptly, because in cases where conflicting inventors are in the patent office at the same time, the first applicant has a tremendous advantage.

The last provision is "payment of the fees required by law, and other due proceeding had." As patent application papers are exceedingly technical, it is advisable, and the Patent Office recommends, that they be prepared by a competent attorney. The choice of an attorney should be carefully made; it is most important to have a lawyer who is capable of understanding the invention. Avoid those who advertise flamboyantly or seem to offer to work for ridiculously low fees.

A patent application comprises a petition, an oath, a specification, and usually drawings. The petition is a purely formal paper. The oath requires the applicant to make affidavit that he is the actual inventor; the form of the affidavit is prescribed by the Patent Office rules.

The specification and drawings determine the extent of protection afforded by the patent. The breadth of the patent can be no greater than that of the disclosure; in the preparation of magical patent applications, therefore, difficulties are sometimes encountered in determining just what should be disclosed. When we come to large stage illusions, considerable thought must be given to what should be shown and what left out.

The drawings of the patent application are not required to be working drawings; they are of the type that lies between working drawings and sketchy illustrations. They should be clear enough to illustrate the point of the invention without requiring too much reference to the specification.

The most important part of a patent application is the claims, which conclude the specification. Here the several elements that make up the invention are tersely recited; it matters little how much the drawings and the body of the specification disclose, if the claims are not broad enough in their language to cover the idea to be protected.

In submitting an idea to a patent solicitor, the inventor should point out wherein he believes the novelty resides, and also what parts of the apparatus have been used before in other arrangements. This is particularly important in applications relating to magical apparatus. Otherwise the inventor may find himself with a patent covering merely the old features of the invention, which an informed opponent can easily pull apart in court.

After the application is signed and sworn to by the inventor, the papers are forwarded to the Patent Office with the fees. The application is then classified, and referred to the proper examining division of the Patent Office.

The application is either allowed or rejected; very few applications are allowed as originally filed. If rejected, the application may be amended. By way of successive rejections and amendments the application is rendered acceptable to both the examiner and the applicant's attorney, or else finally rejected. After allowance a final fee must be paid to the Patent Office to secure the patent.

Copyright protection secures for a limited time to "authors" the exclusive right to their "writings." This provision has been stretched to cover many things that are not strictly writings; on the other hand, it does not cover several subjects that it is commonly supposed to. Titles and names cannot be copyrighted; if entitled to trade-mark protection, they fall under the law of unfair competition. Neither can a sleight-of-hand performance, as such, be copyrighted, although the patter can.

All printed literary works are copyrightable as "books," whether published in ordinary book form or as pamphlets, leaflets, cards, or even single pages. The direction sheet accompanying a piece of magical apparatus can be copyrighted as a book; so can advertising circulars or folders containing printed information.

The procedure in copyrighting a book or periodical is very simple, and should be taken care of through the publisher or printer—who should not, however, be allowed to overlook it.

Lectures and similar productions prepared for oral delivery and not printed for publication can be copyrighted. This classification includes magicians' original patter. It is necessary merely to deposit in the copyright office one complete copy of the work, which may be in typewritten form, together with the application form properly filled out, and a fee of $1.00.

Another classification is dramatic and dramatico-musical compositions, which are put together for production and not for publication. This will serve to protect dramatic sketches employing magical features, although the protection does not extend to particular stage settings, mechanical devices, or "stage business."

The copyright law cannot be used to cover things that fall under the patent laws. For instance, a trick in a copyrighted book may be freely manufactured and sold by anyone who chooses, unless the trick has also been patented.

The law of unfair competition is considerably trickier than patent or copyright law, and cannot be explored without the help of a competent attorney. Since it is of interest chiefly to magic dealers and a few professional performers, it is not dealt with here.

J

JAP BOX The Jap box is apparently a plain wooden box, of walnut, mahogany, or rosewood, in length from twelve to twenty inches and in depth and width from nine to fifteen inches. Whatever its dimensions, its width and depth, exclusive of the lid, must be alike. To prove that it is without preparation within, the performer turns it over on the table toward the spectators and, lifting the lid, shows that it is perfectly empty. Again he closes it, and, turning it right side up, opens it once more and instantly proceeds to take from it a variety of different articles. At any moment the box is again turned over toward the audience and shown to be empty; but it is no sooner replaced than the performer again starts taking from it toys, bonbons, etc., the supply being many times larger than could possibly be contained at one time in the box.

The bottom *a b* of the box (Fig. 1) is movable, working on a hinge *b* extending along its front. When the box is turned over to the front, this bottom piece does not turn over with it, but remains flat upon the table as before. A piece of wood *b c*, of exactly similar size and shape, is glued to *a b* at right angles. When the box stands right side up, this piece lies flat against the front of the box, whose upper edge is made with a slight return, so as to conceal it. When the box is turned over to the front, this piece, like the

FIG. 1

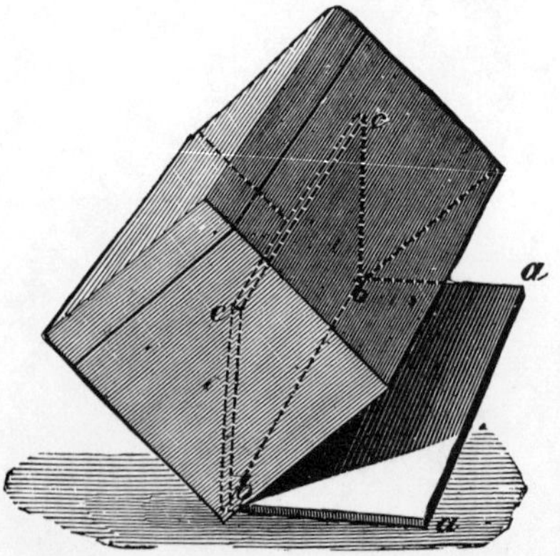

FIG. 2

bottom, retains its position, while any object which had previously been placed in the box remains undisturbed, but hidden by this latter piece. (Figs. 1 and 2) It is, of course, necessary that such object should be of a size which will not overpass the arc which the edge of the box describes in its change of position, and the length from *b* to *c* must be exactly the same as that from *a* to *b*.

Any number of objects, not exceeding the limits mentioned, may be placed in the box, which, being then turned over, can be shown apparently empty. When the box has been replaced in its normal position, the articles are again within it, and can be produced at will. Each time that the performer turns the box over to show that it is empty, he takes a fresh supply of articles from the SERVANTE or from his pockets, and places it upon *a b*, to be produced as soon as the box is right side up again. This gives the effect of inexhaustibility.

The hinge at *b* is made to act freely, so that the weight of the bottom will hold it in position when the box is turned over. Some boxes are made with a catch or pin at some part of *a*, to prevent *a b* from falling prematurely while the box is being placed on the table, or while the performer shows that the box is without preparation, inside and out. This, however, the performer may safely do, even without the use of any catch or fastening, by taking care to grasp the box by its front edge, with his fingers inside it. The fingers will thus press *b c* closely against the front of the box, preventing *a b* from shifting its position.

The box is, of course, in the case supposed, really empty. The performer therefore has to make an opportunity for introducing into it the necessary articles; this he may do by remarking as he replaces it on his table, "You are satisfied by this time that there is nothing in this box, but I will show you once more that it is absolutely empty." He turns it over and once more shows the interior, at the same time placing on *a b* whatever article he intends to produce.

Another form of the same apparatus has an additional element of mystery, produced by the use of a box within a box. The inner box is an ordinary inexhaustible box, as described, but made with a flat wooden lid instead of the hollow or box lid used in the older form of the trick. The outer box just fits over the inner, and is, in fact, a mere cover for it, being an ordinary wooden box, except that it has no front. The two are brought on one inside the other.

The performer begins by taking the smaller box (already filled with the objects to be produced) completely out of the larger, which he shows to

FIG. 3

be absolutely empty. He then places the two boxes together (Fig. 3), turning over the smaller box to show its interior. After this has been done, the smaller box is tilted back to its normal position within the larger, the lid of the larger being slightly lifted to allow it to pass; then both lids are opened together, to begin the production of the contents.

The function of the larger box is merely to act as a screen to the rear part of the smaller, when turned over toward the audience. The only advantage of this over the ordinary box is that it is ANGLE-PROOF, but this advantage is counterbalanced by the drawback that nothing can be produced except what was originally in the box, nor can the smaller box be carried around and shown empty. This, however, may be met by beginning the trick with the two boxes together and then, after having brought out all of the original contents, offering (for the pretended purpose of heightening the effect) to continue the trick without the aid of the outer box. The inner box may then be replenished from behind in the same way as the ordinary inexhaustible box.

The inexhaustible box is frequently made the vehicle for those distributions of bonbons, toys, etc., which to the juvenile mind form an attractive feature of a magical performance. (See CHILDREN'S SHOWS) It is also available for the production of flowers, balls, goblets, bird-cages, and the miscellaneous articles generally associated with HAT TRICKS.

JUMPING PEG This is the typical effect among a whole series of small tricks depending on a double turnover move. The move is also used in a modified form with DICE.

The jumping peg is pushed into one of three holes bored through a small wooden paddle or pencil. It is put in the middle hole, and the paddle is shown from both sides; then the peg instantly jumps to one of the end holes.

The secret of the paddle is that only two, adjacent, holes go clear through. Toward the handle end on one side, and toward the outer end on the other, is a hole burned part way through.

Accordingly, from one side of the paddle the peg will seem to be in the middle hole; from the other side, in an end hole.

The double turnover move serves to hide this fact. The two sides of the paddle can be successively shown by a forward-and-back swing of the wrist. In addition, the paddle or pencil can be spun over an extra half-turn by rolling it between forefinger and thumb.

By a combination of both movements, the same side of the paddle will be shown over and over again, although apparently the audience is seeing alternate sides. Obviously, then, the peg can be shown at will in a middle or an end hole, simply by making or omitting the extra half-turn with the fingers.

The same principle is used for an after-dinner trick with a silver table knife and six little bits of wet paper napkin or newspaper. The wet bits are stuck at regular intervals on both sides of the knife blade, and are thus the equivalent of the holes in the paddle.

The paper bits are removed a pair at a time until the knife is bare, and they then suddenly reappear; or they may jump, multiply, or form some other combination. The pairs of spots are apparently pulled off between forefinger and thumb, but actually only the upper bit, under the thumb, is removed. The double turnover makes it look as if one spot were gone from each side.

Another variation of the jumping-peg principle is the *Spot Sticks*. These are two or three small, short, flat sticks. Paper matches will serve. They are marked with a combination of spots or colored patches, which appear, disappear, and change at will from one or both sides of the sticks.

The sticks are first held parallel, flat side uppermost, by the opposite ends between left thumb and forefinger. That is, the fingers press against the ends, and the flat sides are fully exposed.

The right thumb and forefinger then nip the sticks crosswise, and turn them over, end for end. The left hand resumes its hold.

The extra half-turn is of course added by rolling the right thumb and forefinger as the hand is turned over. The further working of the Spot Sticks will be obvious from what has gone before. *H. H.*

K

KELLAR, HARRY Stage name of Harold Keller (1849-1922), American illusionist. He carried a full evening's show, and was the most famous American performer between the time of HERRMANN and that of THURSTON, who bought and carried on Kellar's show.

Kellar hardly attempted sleight-of-hand, and was not distinguished for inventiveness; he owed his fame to personality, showmanship, and the prodigious care he took with every detail of his act. If he so much as stepped off on the wrong foot in going onstage, he would return and start over. He changed his name so that people should not think he was trading on that of ROBERT HELLER. William E. Robinson (later famous as CHUNG LING SOO) was one of his assistants. Throughout his life he was ready to help and encourage his fellow magicians, and he will always be kindly remembered in the art.

KELLAR TIE Probably the quickest rope release (see ESCAPES AND RELEASES) in general use. It is performed with a three-foot length of clothesline or sash cord, which, if new, should be soaked in water to soften it. The rope is hung by the center over your right wrist, and tied on the inside of the wrist in a square knot. The left wrist is laid upon the right wrist, behind your back, and apparently made fast in exactly the same way, with a square knot over the exposed inside, or pulse, of the wrist.

Actually, as the right hand goes behind your back, the fingers catch the upper piece of rope near the knot, and pick up a loop of slack, which they press against the heel of the hand for the brief moment before the left wrist is laid on top to cover the loop. If the hands are now clamped firmly together, the volunteer assistant can pull quite hard in tying the second square knot without dislodging the slack. Yet the hands can be instantly separated, and as quickly brought together, the tie seemingly as tight as ever. *B. M.*

KNOT THAT UNTIES ITSELF (See under SILK TRICKS)

L

LAFAYETTE Stage name of Siegmund Neuburger (1872-1911), a brilliant illusionist of German birth, who was, however, always considered an American. His stage-settings and music were memorable for their splendor, and authorities have said that his showmanship, onstage or off, was beyond that of any other magician. He died an untimely death trying to rescue a favorite animal from a theater fire in Edinburgh.

LAURANT, EUGENE Stage name of Eugene Greenleaf (1875-1944), the leading American performer on the Chautauqua platform. He also appeared in vaudeville and with a full show. Fulton Oursler described him as a great master of MISDIRECTION.

LEIPZIG, NATE Stage name of Nathan Leipziger (1873-1939), probably the greatest American master of close-up sleight-of-hand. He began life as an optometrist in Detroit, then went into vaudeville, touring America, Europe and Africa with a card, coin, and thimble act; but his greatest success came in later life as a private entertainer. At TABLE TRICKS he has never been equalled; his CARD MANIPULATION has become legendary. He is largely responsible for the popularity of the SIDE-STEAL pass among skilled card-workers.

LEROY, (JEAN HENRI) SERVAIS (born 18), Belgian illusionist, spent most of his professional life in the United States. LeRoy was a skilful performer of magic large and small, and distinguished as an inventor. His best-known creation was Asrah, the favorite modern form of the Floating Lady illusion (see LEVITATIONS).

He taught his wife, whose stage name was Talma, to do a coin act that NELSON DOWNS called the best among all his imitators. The act of "LeRoy, Talma, and Bosco" (the name given to whatever comic performer they had with them) traveled widely and with success.

Just before the turn of the century LeRoy joined with IMRO FOX and FREDERICK EUGENE POWELL in an act called "The Triple Alliance."

FIG. 1

LEVITATIONS (See also RISING CARDS, SPIRIT EFFECTS, WANDS)

Levitations are tricks that apparently defy gravity. Magically speaking, they can be divided into effects where the person or object floats free in the air and effects where it clings to the hand of the performer.

Of the first class, the various forms of *Floating Lady* are perhaps the oldest as well as the most sensational. The trick apparently began among the East Indians, who would show a performer seated cross-legged in mid-air, his elbow alone supported by a stick. (Fig. 1) The history of improvements on the effect has been the history of efforts to do away with the supporting stick. The MIRROR PRINCIPLE has been called into play, along with other, cruder methods of hiding the support. The most perfect modern method, invented by SERVAIS LEROY, was called Asrah.

The Floating Lady. A table is first brought on the stage and a lady is introduced. She is then laid on the table and apparently put into a trance. A white sheet is then placed over her and she is commanded to rise. She rises very slowly, until eventually she attains a height of about seven feet from the ground.

The performer now holds the corner of the sheet and commands her to vanish, at the same time pulling the sheet away quickly; much to the surprise of the audience the lady has disappeared completely.

The table is a special one with a large trap running the whole length of it; at the beginning of the trick the lady drops through the trap, which automatically closes. A wire FAKE made to shape is levitated in her place. This fake is usually covered with the same material as the backdrop, so that it will not be noticeable even from a comparatively short distance. The fake is attached to a crank, which in turn is operated from the back of the stage, and is arranged so that the fake will move upward, forward, backward, or downward.

FIG. 2

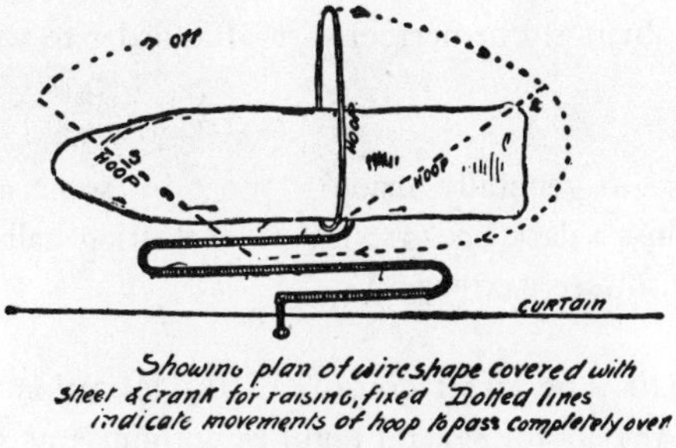

Showing plan of wire shape covered with sheet & crank for raising, fixed. Dotted lines indicate movements of hoop to pass completely over

Showing hoop being passed over frame covered with sheet

FIG. 3

At the beginning, the fake is resting against the back curtain in a convenient position. The table is brought on and turned around once or twice without calling any special attention to it. The lady is then introduced and after being "mesmerized" is laid on the table directly over the trap and covered with a large sheet. While this is being adjusted, the performer and his assistant place the fake in position. As soon as this sheet is laid over her, she sinks through the trap, which at once assumes its former position.

The performer now commands the lady to rise; this is the signal for the operator behind the scenes to start work. The fake is levitated only a foot or so to start with, and while the attention of the audience is fixed on this an assistant comes on and removes the table to the wings. This move is not likely to arouse suspicion in the average audience because, in the first place, they assume the lady to be in the air, and secondly, their attention is taken up by the actual levitation in progress.

The fake is taken up gradually, and then the performer passes a hoop over it, apparently demonstrating the impossibility of any connection. Figures 2 and 3 show how this is accomplished.

After this has been done the performer adopts a dramatic attitude, and after saying, "Are you ready?" quickly pulls the sheet away. This, of course, leaves the covered wire fake suspended in mid-air, but as it is covered with the same material as the back curtain, it cannot be seen.

The fake must obviously be perfectly rigid in order to work the illusion successfully. *H. & A. W.*

Smaller objects are generally made to float by some arrangement of black THREAD against a dark background. The floating ball was brilliantly performed by Okito (see BAMBERGS).

The Floating Ball. The effect consists of the levitation of a large ball which remains in the air for several minutes without any apparent means of support. The ball will rise or fall, or move in any direction, at the will of the performer, and a wooden hoop can be passed over it to prove the absence of any threads or wires.

Despite this, however, the bare outline of the secret can be given in three words—black silk thread. The trick is, therefore, not suitable for a small room, and if worked on a stage the help of an intelligent assistant is desirable. The background, of course, should be of some dark material so that the thread will be invisible.

One end of the thread is made into a running loop, which is placed around the performer's shoulder. The other end is either fastened to the wall on one side of the stage about seven feet from the floor, or else held by the assistant behind the scenes, who can manipulate it as required.

The ball is hollow—it would break the thread if it were too heavy—and has a small hook fastened to it. The diameter of the ball should be about eight inches.

The hoop is an ordinary wooden one, which you place over your head before the thread is put on, so that when the hoop is taken off it is already over the thread.

You are now ready to begin. Show the ball, and make a few passes over it as if mesmerizing it. In doing this, hook it on the thread, but do not take the hands away for a minute or so. You have meanwhile stepped back so that the thread is taut. Continue moving your hands around the ball all the time.

Now gradually move forward; the ball will, of course, run down the thread until it is some distance from you. A slight movement of the body, which looks quite natural if you move your hands dramatically, will make the ball rise or fall, and by moving backward or forward you can regulate the distance of the ball from yourself. It is important that all your movements should be slow and natural, as you appear to be merely following the ball or controlling it from a distance. Bring it near to you again, and keep it stationary while you pass the hoop over it; then hold the hoop still and let the ball run through it. By careful manipulation you can make the ball drop into a hat placed on a chair.

You then secretly disengage it from the thread, make your bow to the audience, and retire with the ball in your hand. *H. & A. W.*

Other floating articles are the glass of milk, popularized by BLACKSTONE, in which the thread generally runs through two holes drilled near opposite sides of the glass, and the electric light bulb.

A different form of support is used in the floating match, a VEST-POCKET effect. A wooden match is lighted and stood on end on top of a small matchbox. After one or two attempts it stays upright, and then rises an inch or two in the air. The GIMMICK is not thread, but a piece of very fine black wire, just strong enough to support a match without bending. One end of the wire is sharpened to a point; just below the point, the wire bends at a right angle, then in perhaps half an inch it bends at another right angle, in the opposite direction, so that the sharpened point and the main shaft of the wire are parallel. The lower end is twisted into a loop big enough for the little finger.

The matchbox is held horizontal by its "striking" edges between thumb and forefinger. The little finger is caught in the loop of the gimmick, and the bend hooks over the top of the matchbox, so that the sharp point goes straight up. When the match is finally balanced erect, naturally it is forced down on the point. Moving the little finger upward "levitates" the match.

The other class of levitation, which might perhaps be called adhesion, is performed with such objects as WANDS, cigars, and walking-sticks. A variety of gimmicks have been made for the purpose, most of them attachable in some way to the object to be levitated, and provided with a pair of small wire points about an inch and a half apart that can be clipped between the fingers.

Often a better method is to use a loop of black thread fastened to some part of the clothing, and so adjusted that the article can be slipped into the loop, and held there by pressure from the extended hand or finger.

A walking-stick with a crook for a handle will cling to the almost perpendicular palm if balanced correctly and turned with the crook slightly toward the hand; this gives the stick a tendency to roll up the palm.

Small objects like cigars and cards can be stuck to the hands with various unnoticeable adhesive substances, such as Seccotine; magic dealers have proprietary compounds for the purpose.

LINKING RINGS The first genuine Chinese trick (adopted by PHILLIPPE) to win lasting Western popularity. A number of separate steel or electroplated rings are shown, examined by several members of the audience, and found to be quite solid rings, without any joints or openings. The performer, nevertheless, proceeds to link them together, right under the eyes of the spectators. Chains are formed, and rings linked and unlinked at a touch of the wand or a breath of a spectator upon the spot where they join. Finally the performer makes a number of figures with them.

Ten large steel or electroplated rings are needed. Four are separate solid rings, two are linked together, three are linked together, one is a ring with an opening which allows others to be linked into it.

Lay the rings in a heap on your table as follows: at the bottom the three rings, upon them the open ring (with the opening toward the back of the table so that when you come to pick up this ring you can do so with your finger and thumb over the opening, without so much as glancing down to find the spot), upon this the two rings, and the four loose ones on top.

Pick up all the rings in the left hand, without disturbing the order in which you laid them down. Hand one of the loose rings to someone, then another, a third, and the fourth. These will be the four loose ones which were arranged on top, and will be the first four as you now hold the bundle in your left hand and take them one by one with the right hand. It is absolutely essential that you should take them naturally and readily, *without looking to see which you give*, as the slightest suspicion of choosing which to give ruins the trick irrevocably.

You now ask any spectator who is examining one of the rings to assist you; you hand him a second ring, which you take from one of the other spectators, who has satisfied himself that there is no trick in the ring. Your assistant now has two loose rings, and there are two more in the audience, which will probably be passed from hand to hand, assuring everyone of the genuineness of the rings.

Lay the rest upon your table, taking the next two rings (the two linked together); do not show that they are joined, but swing them back and forth, asking your assistant to do the same with his. Let one of your rings fall; of course it will drop to a hanging position through the other as if you had just joined them. Your assistant, if he follows instructions literally, will drop one of his on the floor; perhaps he will be vainly trying to push one through the other.

In any case walk over to him, picking up—with your finger and thumb concealing the opening—the open ring, which is the next on top of those on the table. Take his two loose ones and join one of them on to your open ring, bringing them together as before, swinging them just as you did the two joined ones, and allowing the loose ring to fall to a hanging position. Pick up the second loose ring you took from your assistant, swing it against the open ring, and as you slip it through the opening, draw it up into a three-ring chain (open ring in center).

Walk to a lady or child in the audience, saying, "These rings, once they are joined, can only be taken apart by being kissed or touched by the magic wand. Would you mind kissing them apart for me?" Place the rings close below the lady's mouth; bring the finger and thumb holding the top ring close to the finger and thumb covering the opening in the open ring, and slip off the top ring (Fig. 1), at the same time making a sound as of kissing. Hand the loose ring to the lady, and take the other two to another member of the audience, saying, "Perhaps you will blow these apart"; disjoin them as before.

Go back to your table with the open ring in your hand and lay it down, at the same time picking up the three joined rings, but without showing that they are joined. Make a swinging movement or two with them as though you were joining them as you did the others, and allow first one to fall, then the second, creating the impression of having joined them into a string of three. Hang them over your left arm at the elbow; go to the assistant and take the two joined rings he is holding; pick up your open ring and join it on (always making the same swinging movement with the rings, as though necessary to the joining). This gives you two sets of three, one over the left arm and one in the right hand, the open ring being at the top of this latter set.

Swing and disjoin the open ring from the others in the right-hand chain; place these on the table, retaining the open ring, and join it to the top ring of the three fixed ones from the left arm. This gives you a chain of four.

Say, "I will now make a few figures with these rings. My first will be a stirrup."

To make this, give the top ring a sharp twist to the left, which will swing all the others around if they are hanging clear of your body. When they have swung around as far as they will go, take up the bottom ring with the left hand and slip it through the open ring, at the same instant giving a jerk forward to all the rings, so that they fall into the form of a stirrup.

Draw up the bottom ring which you last slipped through the open ring and disjoin it, so reverting to the straight chain of four, and announce, "My next will be a garden seat."

Bring up the bottom ring again and pass it through the open ring, the latter being straight and the bottom ring at a right angle to it (Fig. 2). Reach between the two middle rings, and pull the bottom ring up and forward into the position of Fig. 3.

Announce, "My next will be a school globe." While you speak, let go with your left hand and swing the rings forward by your right, still holding the finger and thumb over the open ring. At the moment that the lowest ring swings forward, catch hold of the bottom part of it and bring it up sharply to the right hand (Fig. 4), grasping it and the open ring together, thus forming Fig. 5. Give the wrist a sharp turn or two in either direction, so making the figure appear more like a globe than if held still.

The grasp of the right hand on the rings must be *very firm*, or the succeeding figures will fall to pieces. Announce the next as the lotus blossom.

To make this, with the fingers of the left hand press apart the two rings which meet at the top of the "globe." When you have pressed them about five inches apart, remove your left hand, and you will find that by gradual-

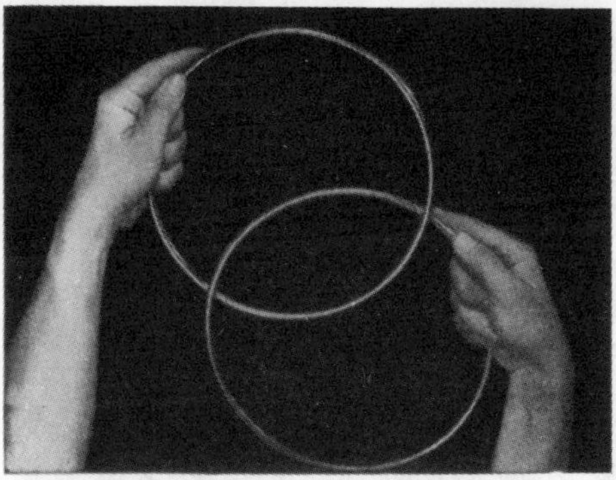

FIG. 1

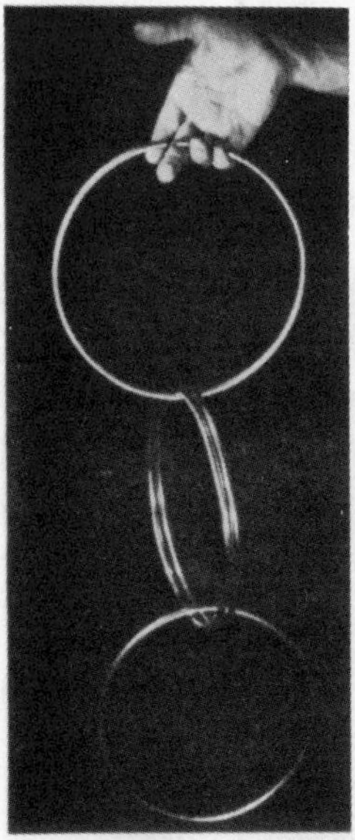

FIG. 2

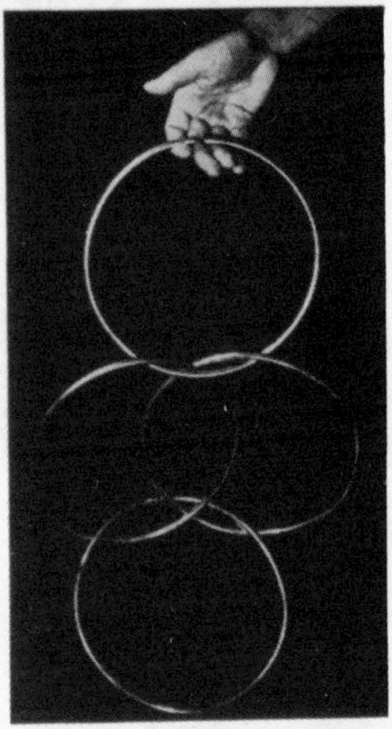

FIG. 3

FIG. 4

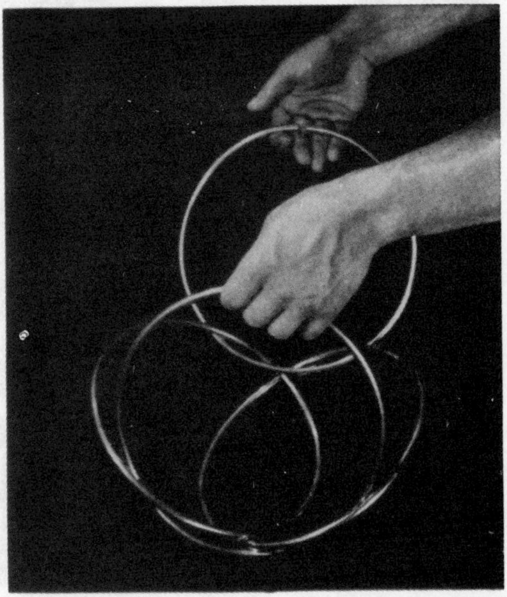

FIG. 5

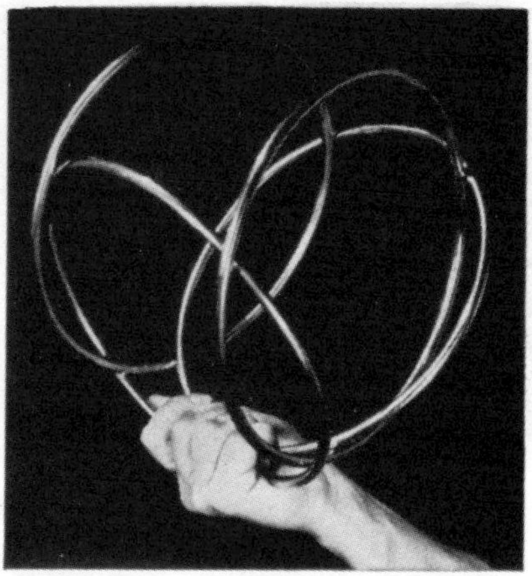

FIG. 6

FIG. 7

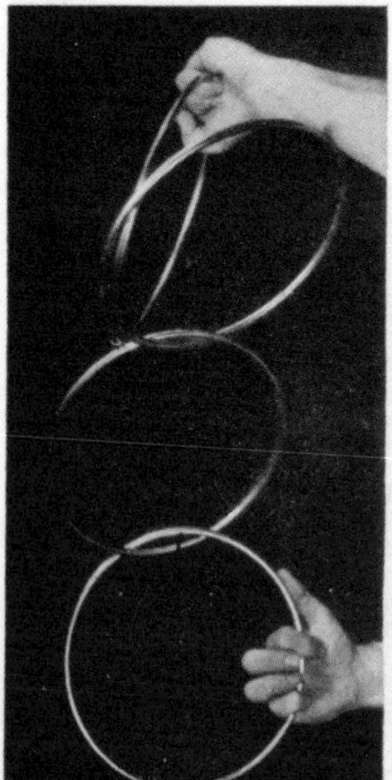

FIG. 8

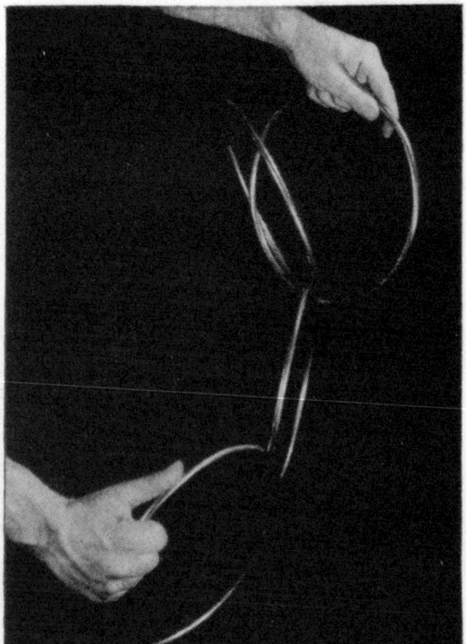

ly relaxing the grip of your right hand—very gradually it must be—the rings will open themselves out to the position shown in Fig. 6.

While the rings are opening, you say, "Notice the bud opening."

Relax the grip gradually until the rings bend right back toward your arm, but be very careful not to lose *control* of them, as if you do the whole figure falls to pieces.

Now announce, "The next figure will be a portrait frame for four photographs."

Give the hand a sharp jerk backward (practice will accustom one to know how sharp a jerk), and the rings will come into the position of a four-leaf clover.

You then say, "My last figure will be the ace of clubs," and as you speak, sharply pull over the top ring of the portrait frame, and it will fall down to rest on your hand.

Now quickly unhook the bottom ring of the chain, which has remained linked into the open ring since you hooked it there to make the garden seat. *C. L. N.*

Get the straight chain of four into your left hand, with the open ring at the bottom, the cut covered by your right hand. Twist the key ring around to the left so that all the rings turn around in that direction. Then give one further twist to the left. This will make the next to the top ring rise and lie over against the top ring (Fig. 7).

Relax your grip of the rings slightly, and the second ring will flop down again (Fig. 8). This will be immediately followed by the third ring (Fig. 9), and you can allow the key ring to fall over, and unhook it. A few trials will show you the total effect, which is that one ring passes straight down the chain until it falls off.

Methods of linking and unlinking the key ring and another ring should be carefully practised.

One way is to hold the solid ring upright in the left hand, and strike the key ring crosswise against the top of it. After two or three blows, the key ring passes through as in Fig. 10.

To unlink the rings in the same fashion, strike the key ring against the *bottom* of the solid ring (Fig. 11). After two or three attempts the solid ring is passed through the cut.

The most deceptive way to link the rings is to hold one in each hand as in Fig. 1, and slide the key ring straight down and straight up. As the solid ring passes the cut, the right forefinger pushes it through. Neither ring should be turned or "hooked."

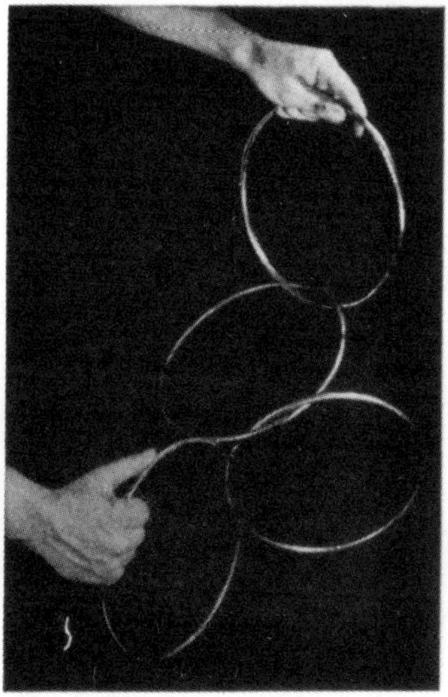

Fig. 9

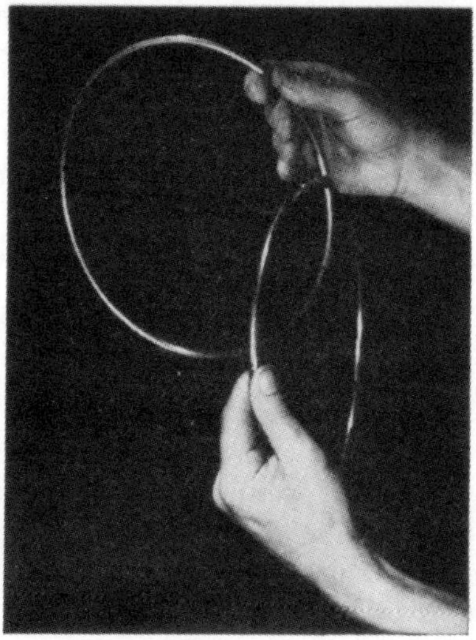

Fig. 10

Fig. 11

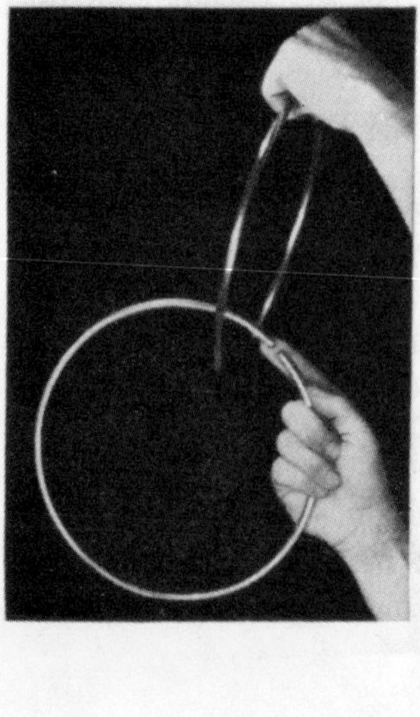

Fig. 12

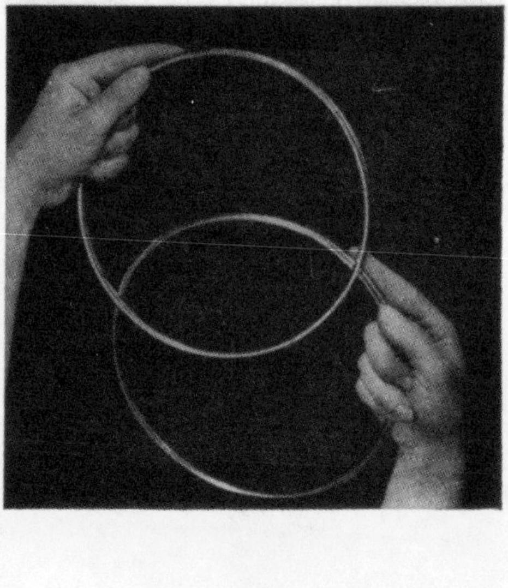

The rings are separated by simply reversing the motion (Fig. 12).

Slip off the three fixed rings, and collect all your rings from the audience and the two fixed ones from your table, all the while jumbling the lot about between your hands, making a considerable clatter; in reality be passing all the rings, fixed and loose, one after the other through the open ring, finally giving them a spin around as they hang from the open ring. Lay them aside and proceed to the next trick.

LITERATURE OF MAGIC The story of magic, in so far as conjurers' secrets are concerned, is shrouded in antiquity. The first book of which we have record is Reginald Scot's *Discouverie of Witchcraft*, 1584, of which very few copies are to be found. This volume, which tends to expose the fallacies of the belief in Witchcraft, ran counter to the opinion of James I, who described it as a heresy and ordered all copies burned by the common hangman. As always, a few copies escaped this fate and are now highly prized by the owners. A second edition is dated 1651 and a third was published in 1665. It was again reprinted in 1886, this time in a limited edition of 250 copies, and finally another edition appeared in 1930. In a long chapter, with illustrations, are described many "conveiences" of the traveling mountebank of that day, a number of which, in modified form, are still being presented by our contemporary magicians. The fact that exposures of conjurers' secrets were frowned upon even in that day explains the regret expressed by Scot when he wrote . . ."being sorry that it falleth to my lot, to lay open the secrets of this mysterie, to the hindrance of such poor men as live thereby; whose dooings herein are not onelie tollerable, but greatlie commendable, so they abuse not the name of God . . . but alwaies acknowledge wherein the art consisteth. . . ."

The second book on the subject, so far as we know, is *The Art of Juggling, or Legerdemaine*, 1612 (another edition 1614). This is really the first book devoted principally to magicians' tricks. It is of the greatest rarity and, so far as our researches have gone, there appear to be fewer than six copies. The authorship is masked under the pseudonym of "S. R.," which has resulted in considerable discussion as to the possibility of the author's having been Samuel Rowlands. The book is printed in black letter and is without illustration.

Following this in chronological order is *Hocus Pokus Junior*, 1634. This edition is also *rarissime*, only a very few copies being known. The second edition appeared in 1635 and a third in 1654, which latter two are to be found in several of the leading magical collections. The latest edition of which we have knowledge is the 13th, dated 1697. A German translation of 1667 appeared in smaller format.

From that date forward appeared many booklets and brochures on this subject. Most of these, because of their ephemeral character, are almost as hard to come by as the "Big Three" just described. The bibliophile will recognize many of the titles, but for the general practitioner they have little value. To name but a few, we find

The Castel of Memorie
Ady, *A Candle in the Dark*, 1656
White, *A rich Cabinet, with Variety of Inventions*, 1668
Hill, *Natural and Artificial Conclusions*, 1670
Snow, *Apopiroscopy*, 1702
Neve, *Hocus Pokus, the Cabinet of Legerdemain Curiosities Broke Open*, 1721
Round About Our Coal Fire, *ca.* 1740
Dean, *The Whole Art of Legerdemain, or Hocus Pokus in Perfection*, 1722
Pinetti, *Physical Amusements and Diverting Experiments*, 1784
Breslaw's *Last Legacy*, 1784
Gale's *Cabinet of Knowledge*, 1796
Astley, *Natural Magic*, 1785

Early American imprints are fewer in number and later in date, but many are exceedingly scarce. So far as our researches go, the City of Brotherly Love cradled the first book of magicians' secrets approximately 150 years ago. In 1795 appeared a little brochure entitled *The Whole Art of Legerdemain*, now practically worth its weight in gold. Some ten years later (1805) a Boston publisher issued *The Expositor; or Many Mysteries Unravelled*, by William Frederick Pinchbeck. The title suggests that the book sought to explain *A Few of the Most Wonderful Feats Performed by the Art of Legerdemain*. Again, from a Philadelphia press came *Hocus Pokus, or the Art of Conjuring Made Easy*, in 1827. Next we have *Ventriloquism Explained and Jugglers' Tricks and Legerdemain Exposed*, Amherst, 1834. At about the same time (1835) was issued a little book, *The Humorous Magician Unmasked*, by Engstrom. A rare American imprint is *The Wizard*, Chillicothe, Ohio, 1848.

In 1850 Wyman the Wizard sponsored a little booklet entitled *Wyman's Hand-Book of Magic*, also published in Philadelphia. A later edition appeared in New York in 1851. Still another scarce title sponsored by Wyman, but written by E. Mason, appeared in 1860 under the title *Ventriloquism Made Easy; also an Exposure of Magic and the Second-Sight Mystery*. And finally, from Hinsdale, New Hampshire, came, in 1865, *Prestidigita-*

tion or Magic Made Easy. For the most part these were innocuous publications dealing in fantastic explanations of impracticable tricks. One doubts if any valuable secrets of the magician's art were disclosed thereby.

A most necessary adjunct for the collector of magical literature are the bibliographies, of which, unfortunately, very few are available. An even approximately complete bibliography of the subject is not yet on the horizon, but of those now in print the following may be cited: beginning with a German imprint is Gräsze, *Bibliotheca Magia et Pneumatica*, Leipzig, 1843, covering the subjects of conjuring, pneumatics, automata, black magic, folk lore, superstition, and general occulta. Half a century later we find Burlingame's *Bibliotheca Magica, a Classified List of Important Works on Natural and Occult Magic, Conjuring and Amusements*, Chicago, 1898. In the present century there is, first, the splendid work compiled by Frederic Jessel, *A Bibliography of Works in English on Playing Cards and Gaming*, London, 1905. This comprehensive work includes many conjuring publications. Also there is *The Bibliography of Conjuring and Kindred Deceptions*, by Clarke and Blind, London, 1920, which carries several thousand entries of books, pamphlets and magazines dealing with the subject.

Again, in a foreign language, is a list of French publications compiled by Theodore Ruegg, with the title *Bibliographie de la Prestidigitation française Ancienne et Moderne*, published at Dijon in 1931. A more comprehensive bibliography of French works is in course of preparation. The National Laboratory of Psychical Research, of London, published in 1929, as Part II of Volume I, Proceedings, *A Short-Title Catalogue of Works on Psychic Research, Spiritualism, Magic, Psychology, Legerdemain and Other Methods of Deception*, compiled by Harry Price, Honorary Director, containing some 6000 titles, and later followed by a Supplement with another 3000 entries. And finally the reader is referred to Ellis Stanyon's *Bibliography of Conjuring*, London, 1899, which carries references to many of the more rare titles of this subject.

The literature of conjuring has a very wide scope. No bibliography to date can be said to cover the subject adequately. This is, in part, due to the fact that much of this literature is transitory in character and make-up. The cheap pamphlet of today is thrown away and forgotten in a few years, and the bibliographer compiling a list of publications of even twenty years ago is often dependent upon the memory of others for his data.

Modern magic, or conjuring, as we understand it today, is so pregnant with PSYCHOLOGY that a reference to this phase of the art is deemed essential. All the masters of the art, and every successful amateur presenting a conjuring program, are familiar with this fact and cultivate it carefully. To quote but a few lines from Max Dessoir, the well-known psychologist: "What makes prestidigitation the art of deception is not the technical outward appearance, but the psychological kernel. The ingenious use of certain soul faculties weighs incomparably heavier than all dexterity and machinery." And so it is thought well to include here a short list of titles of "the science of the human mind."

We begin with Dr. Max Dessoir's *Psychology of the Art of Conjuring*, Chicago, 1897, included as an introduction to Burlingame's *Herrmann the Magician*, Chicago, 1897. Also we find Alfred Binet's *Psychologie de la Prestidigitation*, Paris, 1894; Norman Triplett's *The Psychology of Conjuring Deceptions* (American Journal of Psychology, Vol. XI, 1900); J. E. Coover's *Legerdemain Explained* (*Delineator*, Jan. 1921); James Sully's *Illusions: A Psychological Study*, London, 1905; and Dr. Douglas Kelley's *Conjuring as an Asset to Occupational Therapy* (Occupational Therapy and Rehabilitation, Vol. 19, April, 1940). A careful reading of ROBERT-HOUDIN's *The Secrets of Conjuring and Magic*, 1878, will afford much practical information.

The art of the conjurer is well represented in periodical literature. During the past fifty years many such magazines have come and gone. Only a comparative few survived the mortality of these ephemeral publications, but their number is augmented from time to time by new efforts to interest the enthusiast in the latest devices and the current gossip of the Magical Rialto. The earliest periodical publication in this country was *Mahatma*, first issued in 1895, but since defunct, which ran to nine volumes. This was a monthly publication.

Of current magazines in the United States, the oldest is *The Sphinx*, also a monthly, which began life in Chicago, moved to Kansas City, Missouri, and is now being published in New York City. It was founded in 1902, and is now in its 45th year of continuous publication. It was followed in chronological order by *The Linking Ring* (Kenton, Ohio, 1923), *The Dragon* (Illinois, 1932), *Genii* (Los Angeles, 1936), *Tops* (Colon, Michigan, 1936), *The Phoenix* (New York, 1942), *Hugard's Magic Monthly* (Brooklyn, 1943), and *The Conjurors' Magazine* (New York, 1945).

Other countries have a similar record, periodicals in their respective languages having been issued in England, Germany, France, Italy, Hungary Poland, Spain, Austria, Belgium, Portugal, Russia, Norway, Canada, Australia and Brazil. Practically all of these magazines carry dealers' advertisements offering books, GIMMICKS, and magical apparatus for sale.

The question of what should constitute a "five-foot shelf" of magical literature is somewhat controversial, depending upon the individual attitude toward the subject. Magic today is highly specialized, and the respective devotees of illusion magic, mental effects, card tricks, manipulative magic, or historical and biographical subjects may have varying opinions on the question. However, except in the case of the merest tyro, the following titles would, in our opinion, offer the most "meat" to one desiring to obtain a working knowledge of the subject: Robert-Houdin, *The Secrets of Conjuring and Magic;* Professor Hoffmann, *Modern Magic;* Edwin Sachs, *Sleight of Hand;* Camille Gaultier, *La Prestidigitation sans Appareils* (translated into English under the title *Magic Without Apparatus*); Maskelyne and Devant, *Our Magic;* Hatton and Plate, *Magicians' Tricks;* Triplett, *The Psychology of Conjuring Deceptions;* Wraxall (trans.), *Memoirs of Robert-Houdin;* Annemann, *Practical Mental Effects;* Dr. Tarbell, *The Tarbell Course in Magic;* Hilliard, *Greater Magic;* and Erdnase, *The Expert at the Card Table*. In addition there are many other excellent treatises specializing in sleights with small objects that might be accorded space on such a shelf, but in the main the titles mentioned provide a wide range of reading which will be helpful to the amateur and professional alike.

Collectors of magical literature are a law unto themselves. To begin with, they are all bargain hunters! Quite recently a collector wrote he had acquired the Glasgow edition of Dean's *The Whole Art of Legerdemain; or, Hocus Pokus in Perfection*, 1806 (13th), for the nominal price of one dollar! The thrill that comes with finding a scarce item at such a price is comparable only to that of the poker player who completes an inside straight in the draw. It accounts somewhat for the fact that few collectors care to purchase a more or less complete library as such. The excitement of the search and the joy of finding a book you long have sought is sufficient reward for your patience.

> "How pure the joy when first my hands unfold
> The small, rare volume black with tarnished gold."
> (*Bibliomania*, John Ferriar)

It is easy to understand.

One collector is enamored of first editions and association copies. First editions have been called "a madness." Well, perhaps. Still, a first is more desirable. And autographed copies of Anderson, Blitz, Chung Ling Soo, Devant, Downs, Hoffmann, Houdini, Kellar, Maskelyne, Pinetti, Robert-

Houdin, Thurston et al., add materially to the value of a collection. Some collectors want only titles in English, while others collect in all languages. Still others want every edition of certain books of certain authors. A few are interested in fine bindings and invest considerable sums in leather and gilt. Naturally collectors prefer their copies in good condition, but this can be carried to extremes, as for example in the case of a collector who once wrote he desired only immaculate copies, his object being to have his volumes make a nice showing in his bookcase. Necessarily he missed many of the rare items generally found in the libraries of great collectors.

Collectors are not necessarily confined to conjurers. Many who toil in office or laboratory are enamored of this habit, and the avidity and assiduity with which they apply themselves to the furtherance of their hobby are interesting to behold. There are numerous large collections in this country and abroad. While making no attempt to settle a controversial issue, it may be stated that on this side the palm must go to the libraries accumulated by John Mulholland, C. A. George Newmann, Earl Rybolt (recently sold), and H. Adrian Smith. The famous Houdini Collection, given at the time of his death to the Library of Congress, while extensive, does not rank in scope or detail with the above-mentioned four.

The collecting of books is a hobby exemplifying many virtues—in particular, patience, discrimination, and energy. Owing to the foresight of certain present-day publishers, magical literature is now being accorded the respectful attention of bibliographers, and is taking its proper place in the writings of the day. *Leo Rullman*

LOAD To introduce an article or bundle secretly into some container such as a hat or box, usually with the purpose of producing the article afterward by magic; to prepare a container beforehand with its secret contents. (See HAT TRICK) Prepared or "restored" substitutes for decks of cards, smashed watches, etc., are also loaded into the place where they ultimately reappear.

A load is what the magician secretly introduces by loading. Loads are often classified by where they are stolen from: body loads, from the magician's clothing; table loads; chair loads; SERVANTE loads.

LOADING POCKET (See under COSTUME)

LOTA A metal vessel for the magical production of liquids. *Lota* is the Hindustani word for the common small brass or copper water-jar of India. The form shown in Fig. 1 is that used by the East Indian magicians, from whom the rest of the world has borrowed it.

In use, the Lota is completely filled with water, center and secret compartments as well. The water is poured out of the center, and the Lota set down until the water in center and secret compartments has flowed to the same level. The center compartment is emptied again, the vessel set aside, and so on.

Fig. 1

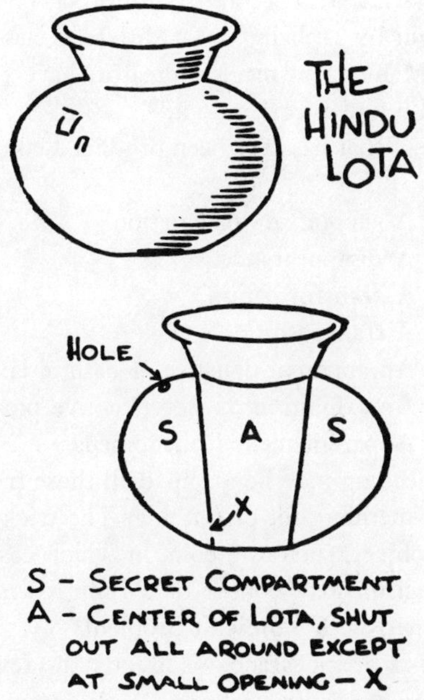

M

MAGICAL EFFECTS (See also INVENTION) The would-be inventor of tricks must begin by realizing what different classes of effect he can hope to produce. Many great magical creators have reiterated, "Give me a good *effect*, and I'll find a way to do it."

Any magical effect that has ever been produced comes under one of the following headings:

1. A PRODUCTION or creation.
2. A disappearance.
3. A transformation.
4. A transposition.
5. An apparent defiance of natural laws.
6. An exhibition of secret motive power.
7. Apparent mental phenomena.

Under the first heading may be grouped all those tricks in which a performer produces something out of nothing. The trick may be performed with a very small object, such as a coin, in which case the trick is fairly easy; or the production may consist of a full-grown woman, when the conjurer is confronted with a difficult problem.

The second class—a disappearance—is exactly the reverse of the first.

In the third group are those tricks in which one object changes to another under conditions which apparently preclude any possibility of such a change occurring.

Tricks of transposing an object from one place to another are perhaps a little complicated to perform, and consequently are not so often included in the programs of amateurs. The simplest of them is the old trick of asking two people to count a certain number of coins or cards, and to hold them in the hand. The trick consists in making the two sets of coins or cards change places.

Tricks which involve an apparent defiance of natural laws are always very effective. The famous ILLUSION of cutting a man's head off is an excellent example of tricks that come under this heading.

The "secret motive power" tricks are such as the RISING CARDS and the animated walking-stick.

Lastly come the tricks in which the performer apparently gives a marvelous exhibition of thought-reading in some form. These tricks are always popular with amateurs, because they can be learned comparatively easily, and can always be trusted to entertain a drawing-room audience.

The most successful tricks presented by public performers will usually include two or three of the above effects. A really good combination, in which the performer leads from one effect to another in a natural way, and surrounds the whole trick with appropriate PATTER, is really the outcome of a great deal of hard work and thought. *D. D.*

MAKEUP The amateur appearing informally in ordinary room lighting will probably not want to use makeup at all. Makeup is desirable, however, and for some complexions a necessity in ambitious performances behind the footlights.

Try to get the best expert advice you can, for instance from local amateur or college theatrical directors.

In addition (or instead if such help is not available), study the standard text, *Stage Makeup*, by Richard Corson, which gives complete directions for every variety of makeup, including HANDS, with many illustrations and a color chart.

MASKELYNES, THE Family of English conjurers and mechanicians, the first being John Nevil Maskelyne (1839-1917), who began life like ROBERT-HOUDIN, as a watchmaker. He first became active in magic through a demonstration, given with his friend George A. Cooke, exposing the SPIRIT EFFECTS of the Davenport Brothers. Maskelyne and Cooke eventually opened the Egyptian Hall, a theater where they and other magicians and vaudevillians gave regular daily performances for years. Maskelyne's own contribution lay chiefly in the real and pretended automatic figures that he constructed (see HISTORY), and in the business management of the concern. Cooke's name in the firm was succeeded by that of DAVID DEVANT, who became a partner (which Cooke never was). At the Egyptian Hall and its successor, St. George's Hall, the Maskelyne family carried on the show for more than fifty thousand performances.

JOHN NEVIL MASKELYNE

Maskelyne's son Nevil Maskelyne (1863-1924) carried on his father's business, and, like him, left the actual performing to his partner Devant. Nevil's sons Clive, Noel, and Jasper Maskelyne came out before the footlights themselves. Clive died, Noel retired, but Jasper continued active after St. George's Hall was closed by World War II, and is still working.

MECHANICAL DECKS (See also CARDS, KEY; RISING CARDS)

A *stripper* pack consists of cards all of which are a shade wider at one end than the other. (See Fig. 1, in which, however, the actual difference of width is exaggerated in order to make the shape of the card clear to the eye.)

When two cards shaped as above are placed one upon another, but in opposite directions, the effect is as in Fig. 2. If the whole pack is at the outset placed with all the cards alike (that is, with their ends tapering in the same direction), a card reversed and returned to the pack with its wide end corresponding with the narrow ends of the other cards becomes a long card. By offering the pack for a person to draw a card, and turning the pack around before the card is replaced, you cause that card to become reversed, and you will be able to find it again in an instant, however thoroughly the cards may be shuffled.

FIG. 1

FIG. 2

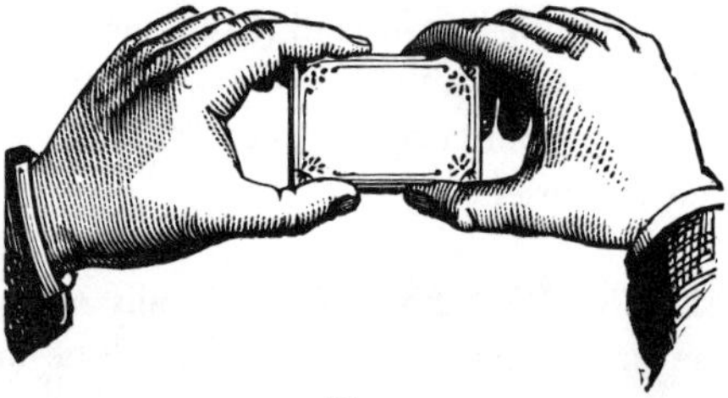

FIG. 3

If the pack is arranged beforehand with the narrow ends of all the red cards in one direction and those of the black cards in the other direction, you may, by grasping the pack between the finger and thumb at each end (Fig. 3), and drawing the hands apart, separate the black cards from the red at a single stroke; or, by preparing the pack accordingly, you may divide the face cards from the plain cards in the same way. Many other tricks may be performed with a pack of this kind. *L. H.*

End strippers are tapered along the ends instead of the sides, and will often fool someone who is looking for the regular variety.

"*Cornered*" cards are another variety of stripper. The preparation consists of shaving off one corner of the pack, to the extent of about the thickness of a dime. If any card be turned end for end in such a pack, its corner will project beyond the blunted corner of the remaining cards, and will be easily distinguishable by touch.

Forcing Decks. As even the most accomplished performer cannot always be certain of FORCING a single card, another expedient may be used in order to ensure success. This is made absolutely certain by the use of what is called a forcing pack—that is, a pack in which all the cards are alike. Thus, if the jack of hearts is the card to be drawn, the whole pack will consist of jacks of hearts, and the drawer may therefore do his utmost to exercise a free choice, but the card which he draws will certainly be the jack of hearts.

Where more than one card is to be drawn, as, for instance, in the RISING CARDS trick, the pack may consist of groups of two or more particular cards. Thus, one third may be jacks of hearts, one third aces of diamonds, and the remaining third sevens of clubs—the cards of each kind being together. With the aid of such a pack, it will require very little skill to ensure one of each sort being drawn.

Instead of keeping the cards of each description together, a series of three cards, sixteen times repeated, may be used thus: jack, seven, queen; jack, seven, queen; and so on to the end.

The performer comes forward shuffling these cards, but in such a way as to leave them in the same order (see FALSE SHUFFLE). He then places the cards on a tray, asks a spectator to cut them where he pleases, and then to take the three top cards, retaining one for himself, and handing the two others to his neighbors. He is of course bound to have one of each kind, but the proceeding looks so fair that not one person in a thousand will suspect that the selection has been governed by anything but chance.

L. H.

The *Svengali pack* is probably the most ingenious forcing deck in existence. Half the pack consists of different, unprepared cards. The other half are all alike, and all trimmed a tiny fraction of an inch shorter than the unprepared cards. The pack is arranged with an unprepared card on the bottom, a short card above it, another unprepared card, and so on alternately. If the pack is riffled before the eyes of a spectator, he sees only the twenty-six different unprepared cards. But if it is riffled, and he is asked to insert a finger or pencil in the pack, he is bound to do so above one of the force cards. The Svengali pack may be riffle shuffled without serious harm to its working.

The *Mene Tekel* or *self-shifting pack* is a variant of the short-card forcing principle. In this deck the cards must be arranged in pairs, the short card in each case being a duplicate of the normal card. Each short card goes above its unprepared mate. The pack is shown all different by riffling. When a pencil is inserted during a riffle, it necessarily goes above a card whose duplicate is immediately beneath it. By cutting the lower half of the deck to the top, the performer immediately puts the duplicate on top (whence the name of "self-shifting"). Obviously the Mene Tekel pack cannot be genuinely shuffled.

To spring the cards from one hand to the other is a feat that demands considerable practice. The ingenuity of some performers has produced mechanical packs of cards, whereby a similar effect may be produced at much less expenditure of personal dexterity. Such packs vary somewhat in arrangement.

The earliest, mentioned by ROBERT-HOUDIN, had the ends of each card glued, to a depth of about half an inch, to the cards next preceding and following it. Thus the top card would be glued to the bottom of the second card, the second to the top of the third, the third to the bottom of the fourth, and so on throughout, so that the whole, when drawn apart, formed a zigzag, although when pressed together there was no difference in appearance from an ordinary pack.

The cards thus prepared could be drawn apart three feet or more; with the aid of such a pack, substituted when necessary for the ordinary pack previously in use, the springing from hand to hand could be very neatly simulated.

A pack arranged in this way could obviously only be opened in one direction; the packs now used for the same purpose are usually strung together with a double line of narrow white silk ribbon, allowing about half an inch of play between each pair of cards, and arranged so that they lap over enough to hide the ribbon.

The pack first described can be riffled, and might be made available for an independent trick, as follows: The pack should be made up with black and red cards alternating, so that one side of the zigzag will be all black, the other side all red cards. When this pack had been substituted for the ordinary pack already in use, the performer would say, "Now, ladies and gentlemen, I will make these cards either all black or all red, at your pleasure." Riffling the cards, he would show that they were (say) all red, while by turning the pack around endwise and repeating the movement, they would be seen to be all black. *L. H.*

Another form of mechanical deck for color changes will be found under CARDS, FLAP.

MENE TEKEL (See under MECHANICAL DECKS)

MERRY WIDOW Performed by CARL HERTZ. He showed the audience a small circular platform with a pole in the center, on which was hung a bathing-tent. (Fig. 1) The curtains were drawn for a moment, and then opened to show a tall lady wearing an enormous hat and carrying a long stick.

At the back of the platform was a hidden trap. When the curtains were drawn, it was an easy matter for the accomplice to come into the tent. The hat was hidden, all ready, in the top of the tent-canopy, and the stick was simply the tent-pole. The illusion was performed so quickly that audiences were left gasping.

FIG. 1

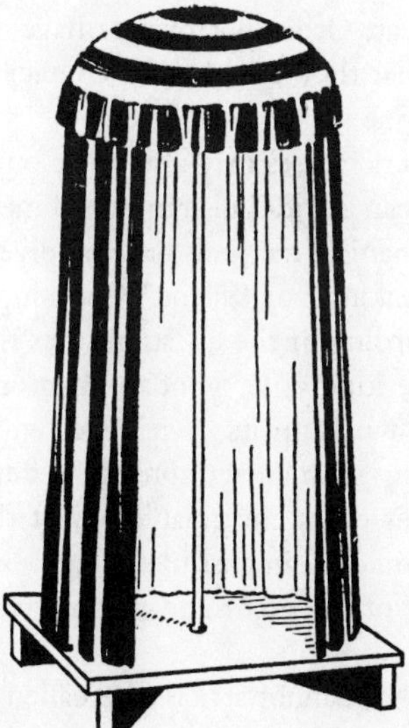

MIND-READING (See also BILLET- AND MESSAGE-READING; BLINDFOLDS; BOOK TEST; CARD SETUPS; DIVINATIONS; EQUIVOQUES; FORCING; HELLER; MUSCLE-READING; ROBERT-HOUDIN; SLATE TESTS; SPELLING MASTER; SPIRIT EFFECTS; THUMB WRITER)

Magical mind-reading falls into two main categories: (1) second sight, clairvoyance, or telepathy, in which two performers, usually a man and a woman, work as a team, and the woman on the stage, generally blindfolded, repeats information supposedly known only to the performer among the audience, such as the description of various borrowed objects; (2) "mentalism," in which a single performer discovers information supposedly known only to members of the audience. The two are often combined, as when a team does BILLET-READING, but the branches differ in method.

Teams must have some method of signaling. The methods are either mechanical or "codes." The first mechanical method, used by ROBERT HELLER and ROBERT-HOUDIN, was electrical. As the performer passed among the audience, borrowing articles for his partner on the stage to describe, his actions were followed through opera glasses by an assistant at a peephole in the wings. The assistant signaled to the "medium," who reclined on a sofa onstage, with an electrical buzzer to indicate the article in question. Sometimes the assistant would be planted in the audience, with the buzzer under the arm of his seat. Other performers have wired the entire auditorium in such a way that they could make contact through a metal plate in their heels, and send the signal themselves.

The assistant with opera glasses may also write on a blackboard offstage, but where the medium can see it. This requires some trick BLINDFOLD.

The most recent mechanical methods have involved small radio headsets.

Codes are either "speaking" or "silent." Speaking codes convey letters and numbers by the wording of the questions that the performer asks—for example, A: quickly, B: kindly, C: good, and so on down through zero: beside. Each team will work up its own code, which must be perfectly memorized. Skill in doing such an act consists in developing a vast system of abbreviations to cover every imaginable object that an audience might present; obviously it would be impossible to spell out each article a letter at a time by code. Some of the best mind-reading teams have cues running into many thousands.

A speaking method that cannot strictly be called a code is for the performer always to ask his question in the same words, such as "What's this?" The secret is that the performer and medium memorize a list of common articles sure to be found in any audience, and the performer then rushes around touching these objects *in the memorized order*. Some spoken signal is arranged to warn the medium to skip one item in case the performer cannot conveniently find it where he is.

A code that may be either speaking or silent is the "time," "counting," or "pulse" method. The signals are given by the interval of silence that elapses between questions, taps of pointer on blackboard, or the like. The performer and medium assiduously practise counting in unison at a set speed until they can unfailingly maintain that speed in their minds without counting aloud. In this way, obviously, the performer can signal numbers to the medium by the duration of his silence: both performer and medium will reach the same number at the same time. To signal letters quickly, the alphabet is broken up as in the diagram:

	1	2	3	4	5	6
1	A	F	K	P	U	V
2	B	G	L	Q	W	
3	C	H	M	R	X	
4	D	I	N	S	Y	
5	E	J	O	T	Z	

Each letter has two numbers, first the up-and-down number, then the crosswise number. E is 5–1, M is 3–3. V is merely 6.

Silent codes may be conveyed by the position of the head and eyes—face front, eyes right: 1; eyes left: 2; eyes up: 3; eyes down: 4; face tilted up: 5; tilted down; 6; face right: 7; face right and down: 8; face left: 9; left and down: 0.

Signals may also be given by the position of the right hand as it holds a card, program, or writing-pad. Hand at lower right corner of card, one finger underneath: 1; two fingers underneath: 2; and so on up to 4; hand at right center of card, one finger showing: 5; and so on up to 8; hand at upper right corner: 9; hand at top: 0; card in left hand: neutral position.

The variety of other possible code methods is infinite—far greater than the possible variety of effects. Hence freshness of PRESENTATION is much more necessary to a second-sight team than ingenuity of method.

One-man mentalism leans heavily on BILLET-READING.

The performer has also, however, all the wide resources of FORCING, card locations, and mathematics. MUSCLE-READING is another branch of the art.

In the presentation of mind-reading, every effort must be devoted to making people forget that the performer reads, not their thoughts, but their writing. Possibly the best way of doing this is by interspersing billet and card effects with tricks using a force, where in fact nothing need be written or touched.

In addition to the standard billet-reading methods, the mentalist may use various forms of reflector—for instance a reducing mirror, PALMED, and maneuvered to give a flash of what the spectator "subject" is writing (or more likely drawing); or a mirror or shiner used under cover of a writing-pad in the same way. Reading figures by the motion of the upper end of the subject's pencil as he writes is a knack that can be learned with practice, though of course it is not wholly dependable when the subject writes fast and small.

Many good mental effects are alleged *predictions* of what a spectator will choose or write. The magician usually writes his prediction, and puts it somewhere for safekeeping. Forces come into play heavily here, of course, but another versatile resource is for the performer secretly to write the chosen word or message *after* it has been selected, and then to make a SWITCH for the prediction that was held by or displayed to the audience at the start of the trick. Sometimes a pencil stub and small scratch pad in a trouser pocket will suffice; the THUMB WRITER is often used with blank cards; a form of CARD INDEX will hold a great variety of billets containing the appropriate prediction when the audience has a wide but not unlimited choice—say among names of famous authors.

The late Theo Annemann was probably the most ingenious and prolific inventor of mental magic in the history of the art, and his books, particularly *Practical Mental Effects*, are the indispensable basis for any study of modern mentalism. *H. H.*

MIRROR GLASS (See under TUMBLERS)

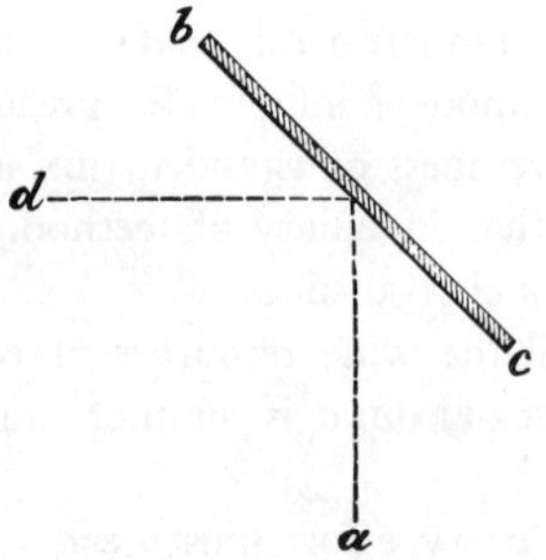

FIG. 1

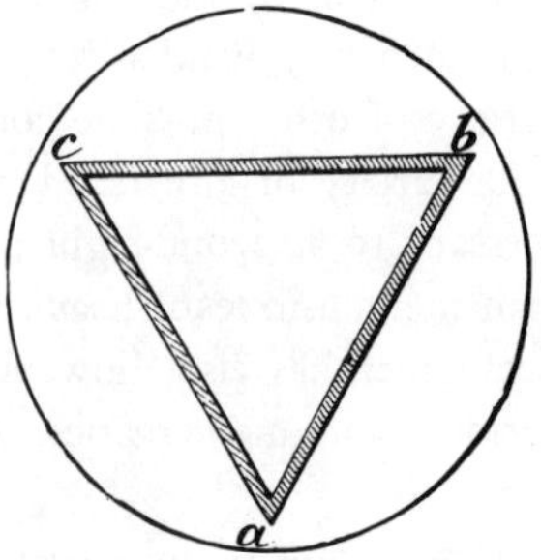

FIG. 2

MIRROR PRINCIPLE A frequent recourse in ILLUSIONS to hide a support or passage, for instance to a TRAP. It depends upon the well-known principle, common to optics as to mechanics, that "the angle of reflection is equal to the angle of incidence." Thus, if a person standing at the point *a*, in Fig. 1, looks into a mirror placed in the position indicated by the line *b c*, he will see reflected, not himself, but whatever object may be placed at the point *d*. By an ingenious application of this principle a looking-glass may be used to conceal a given object behind it, while at the same time an image reflected in the glass may be made to represent what would presumably be seen if no glass were there, and thus prevent the presence of the mirror from being suspected.

The basic requirement in using the mirror principle is that the sides and back of the stage or surroundings (*e.g.* the inside of a cabinet) be identical in appearance, so that the reflected sides are taken for the back (Fig. 2).

MISDIRECTION (See under PSYCHOLOGY)

MISER'S DREAM (See also COIN MANIPULATION) This is one of the immeasurably ancient, evergreen classics of magic, known under such various names as coin-catching, the aerial mint, the aerial treasury, the shower of money, and so forth. For the trick as done by its supreme exponent, NELSON DOWNS, the stage is devoid of any kind of furniture, with the exception of an ordinary property side table, which is totally unprepared. The performer enters and asks for the loan of a hat, which is then placed crown downward on the table.

The performer now turns up his sleeves to the elbow, and his hands are shown to be quite empty back and front with the fingers *wide apart*. The hat is now taken (without the slightest suspicious movement) in the left hand. The right hand makes a grab in the air, and there are two coins, which are placed in the hat. This is repeated until about twenty coins have been caught, but during the whole time the back and front and fingers of the right hand are shown to be absolutely empty, and not once do they approach the body.

By way of variation, a coin is sometimes passed through the side of the hat, being unmistakably heard to fall within; or a half-dollar is thrown in the air, completely vanishing, and the hat held out (a second or two afterward) to catch the coin, which is also heard to fall in. A coin is placed between the tips of the first and fourth fingers of the right hand, and pushed against the bottom of the hat, whereupon it instantly vanishes into the interior, making itself heard as it mingles with the other coins. The right hand now catches a dozen or twenty coins at once, dropping them all into the hat.

This is continued until an enormous number of half-dollars is collected.

Before going on the stage, the performer places twenty half-dollars in his right-hand waistcoat pocket, and fifteen in his right-hand trousers

FIG. 1

FIG. 2

pocket. A hat is borrowed, and, while taking it in his left hand, he palms in his right the coins from the waistcoat, and places them like a flash of lightning under the bent-over side of the rim on the outside of the hat (Fig. 1), which is placed with the same hand crown downward on the table.

If the coins have been placed neatly and properly on the rim, they will remain there when the hat is turned over; this is the most delicate part of the trick, as unless the performer is exceedingly careful some, or all, will fall as the hat is put on the table. With practice, however, this can be accomplished. [Downs generally used a dropper.]

The performer now casually turns up his sleeves. He takes up the hat with his left hand, the fingers of which get hold of the coins under cover of the rim. The hat is next passed into the right hand to show the left empty, and the artist will find with practice it is quite easy to pass the coins with the hat from hand to hand.

The hat is now taken by the edge nearest the audience, and, with the right hand, turned over so that the fingers of the left hand containing the twenty coins are brought into the inside of the hat (Fig. 2), in position for the money-catching. The right hand is now shown empty, and makes a grab in the air at an imaginary coin, immediately placing it (apparently) in the hat, where it is heard to fall; but, in reality, it is a coin dropped from the left hand. This is repeated, and, as the hand goes to the hat to make a pretense of dropping in a coin, two coins are quickly palmed in the right hand.

The performer looks in the air for more coins, and one of those palmed is now produced at the fingertips and visibly dropped into the hat. He now produces the second one, but instead of placing this in the hat, he drops one from the left hand at the same moment that the right approaches the top of the hat, thereby inducing the audience to believe that the visible coin was really placed in the hat. This is repeated as often as desired, and, by means of the "Continuous Front and Back Hand Palm" (see COIN MANIPULATION), the right hand can at any moment be shown apparently empty.

Additional effects can be produced according to the fancy of the performer. The apparent passing of a coin through the bottom of the hat never fails to bring forth applause. This is accomplished by holding the coin in the manner shown in Fig. 3. The BACK PALM is now made (Fig. 4), one coin being at the same time dropped from the left hand into the hat, creating the necessary jingle, and creating a perfect illusion.

A similar effect can be produced by holding the coin between the tips of the first three fingers and thumb and pretending to push it through the side of the hat. What really happens is that the coin is pushed by the hat down between the fingers (the back of the hand facing the audience) which hide

FIG. 3

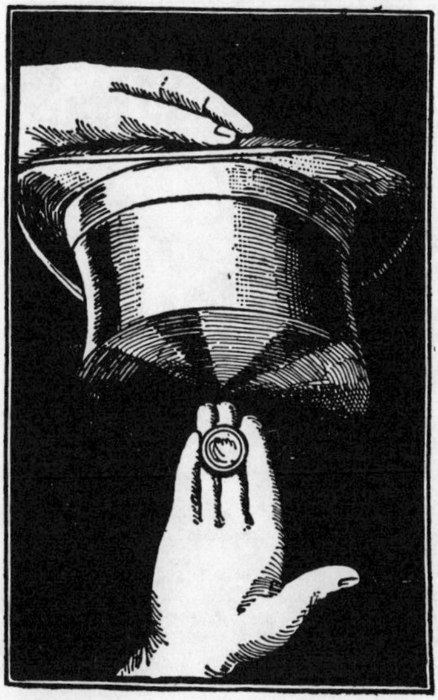

FIG. 4

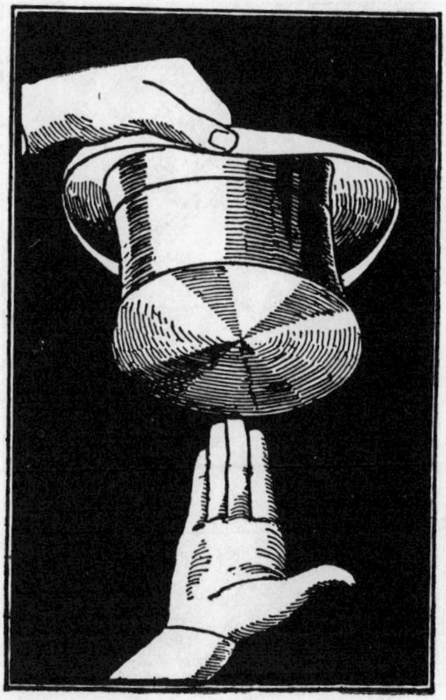

it, one, of course, being dropped by the left hand to create the necessary deception. It is as well to pay particular attention to these little moves, as they invariably create more furore than bigger and more difficult sleights.

A coin is now apparently thrown in the air, and caught in the hat a few seconds later. The coin is, of course, palmed in the act of throwing up the hand, and the hat is held out in the left hand as if waiting for the coin, which, at the right moment, is droppped from the left hand.

When the first load of coins is exhausted, the performer makes a bold move. He pretends to hear someone make a remark that he gets the coins from his pockets– "Which pocket?" he asks. "The left one?" and puts his left hand into the pocket. "No, the right one?" He now puts his right hand into the pocket, and forthwith palms fifteen coins previously placed there. "No, ladies and gentlemen, if I were to put my hands in my pockets, you would all see me. Please, see that my hands do not approach the body." Meanwhile, he has got the fifteen palmed coins on to the rim of the hat as explained at the beginning of this description. The hat can then, if desired, be placed on the table, crown downward, and the hands shown perfectly empty. The same process as before is now repeated.

If the above movements are executed with a certain amount of *sangfroid*, without hurrying to place the hands in the pockets, not one in a thousand

FIG. 5

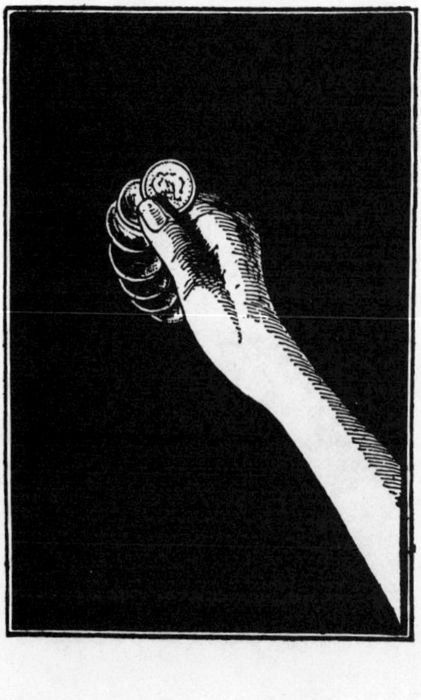

FIG. 6

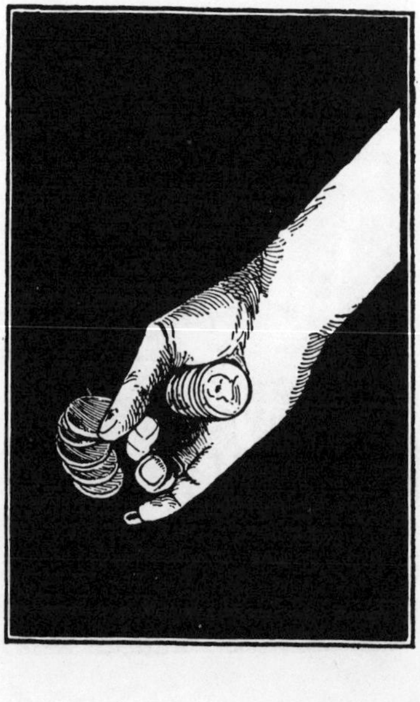

would guess that the performer was LOADING; the audience would never dream of such a bold deception.

When this last lot of coins becomes exhausted, another ruse is resorted to by the performer. His right hand dives into the hat and rattles the coins to show they are real ones, at the same time letting them pour in a shower from the hand into the hat. He repeats this once or twice, and then palms, say, a dozen, which, of course, enables him to go on catching them singly, or to make a grab in the air and produce the twelve in a fan (Fig. 5), with the remark that "When I desire more than one at a time I make this move."

The above can be repeated, if desired, but it will usually be found that thirty to forty coins will take some time to catch, provided the performer is not unduly quick about it. This must be avoided, and the artist must go about his business in an easy manner, without any jumps or jerks. To practise before a mirror is all very well, but before your friends is better, as they can give you hints as to mistakes which it is impossible for you to see yourself in a glass. *T. N. D.*

MULHOLLAND, JOHN (born in 1898). American magician, magic historian, collector, and traveler. Mulholland is an outstanding private and close-up performer, who also handles huge crowds well; at one time he was booked as a lecturer, merely showing tricks to illustrate an occasional point in his talk. HERRMANN and others in the late nineteenth century made magic socially respectable; Mulholland, and to a rather smaller extent HOUDINI, have made it intellectually respectable. Mulholland is outstanding for his inexhaustible knowledge of tricks, PRESENTATION, PSYCHOLOGY, PUBLICITY, HISTORY, and LITERATURE of magic; he is the editor of *The Sphinx*, the oldest and solidest magic magazine now being published, served as the consultant on conjuring to the *Encyclopedia Britannica* and the Merriam-Webster Dictionary, and is the only magician listed in *Who's Who in America*. He has written several books on the history and practice of magic. *H. H.*

MULTIPLYING BILLIARD BALLS (See also BALL MANIPULATION)

Effect: A solid "billiard ball" multiplies at your very fingertips into two, three, and finally four.

Properties: A set of three (or four) solid balls and a hollow half-SHELL.

Put one ball, with the shell over it, in your left trouser pocket; put the other two balls in your right trouser pocket.

PALM one ball from your right pocket. Produce the palmed ball. Make the PASS to your left hand, palming the ball in your right, and go through the performance of swallowing.

With your right forefinger, trace the "passage" of the ball down your throat and into your left trouser pocket.

Bring out the ball with the shell over it. Hold it between your thumb and forefinger, with the shell covering the front half. The ordinary pose is with your left hand held out shoulder-high, its back to the audience. For close-up work with people more or less around you, hold your hand, palm toward you, in front of your stomach.

Bring your second finger down across your thumb, push against the ball as it sits in the shell, and swing your finger back, rolling the ball over your forefinger, and displaying ball and shell side by side. (Fig. 1)

FIG. 1

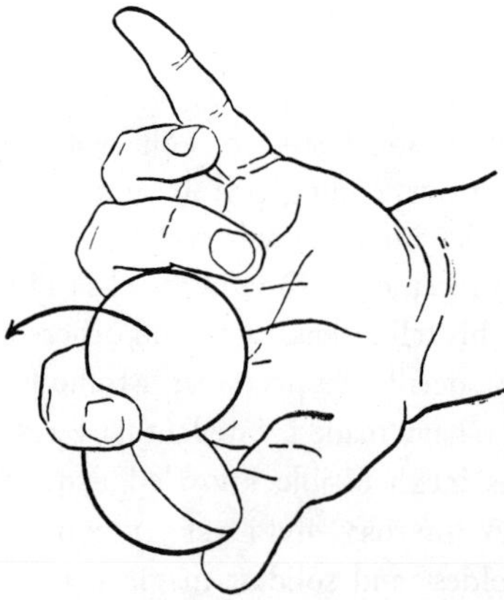

Get the palmed ball in your right hand into FINGER-PALM position. Come over with your right hand, and pick the solid ball from between left first and second fingers. With the same motion, slide the finger-palmed ball into the shell.

Knock the two balls together. Separate your hands, holding a ball in each. Put the ball from your right hand between your left *second* and *third* fingers.

Palm the last ball from your trouser pocket in your right hand. Roll the next ball out of the shell. Go through the same routine of sliding the finger-palmed ball from the right hand into the shell as you carry away the ball from between your first and second fingers. Knock all three balls together.

This time replace the ball from your right hand between your left *third* and *little* fingers.

Roll out the last ball from the shell. There you are, with four billiard balls in view, all five fingers occupied. If you simply want to stop with the four balls—a natural and effective ending—, you will need a fourth solid ball, which you can load into the shell.

Palm off the shell before you drop the four solid balls on the table or toss them to the audience. *H. H.*

MUSCLE-READING The first person to perform this apparent reading of the thoughts of others was the American pseudo-clairvoyant and mind-reader, Washington Irving Bishop, who attracted an enormous amount of attention. His sickly, nervous constitution lent color to the supposition, current in his time, that he possessed some intuitive power which enabled him to accomplish apparently impossible tasks.

But when Bishop died, barely 33 years old, his former assistant, Garner, under the name of Stuart Cumberland, performed the same experiments, but did them perhaps more perfectly than his late employer. He set half the world in an uproar, but people no longer believed that his work was supernormal, although the effect for years baffled all attempts at explanation. People outdid themselves in assumptions and suppositions which had some scientific foundation, but which did not get at the real root of the matter. There was a great deal of talk about muscle-reading, feeling of the pulse, and so on, which was all quite ridiculous, because the furious pace at which Cumberland dashed through his experiments left not the least chance for anything so minute and delicate as feeling of muscles or pulses.

The problem which made the reputation of Bishop and Cumberland was the "Pin Test."

In the absence of the performer a spectator hides a glass-headed pin in any part of the room, and returns to his seat. The performer, who may also be blindfolded if desired, comes in, takes the hand of the person who hid the pin, and asks the person to think intently of the place where the pin is to be found. Suddenly the performer, with his medium, begins to run; he runs hither and thither throughout the room, gradually getting nearer to the place where the pin is hidden, until at last he finds it.

A specimen of the class of experiments wherein the performer does something merely thought of by the spectators is the following: The conjurer is to go to a particular table, get a cigarette-case which is hidden under a napkin there, open the case, take out a cigarette, take the latter to the gentleman in the third seat of the sixth row, and put it in the gentleman's mouth.

The performer, who has meanwhile been in the next room, comes back, takes by the hand the person who set the task, and asks him to think intently of the successive steps involved. The magician then executes the task, step by step, as it is thought by the spectators.

The number and variety of such problems are unlimited, though they should for preference not be too extremely difficult in their details. Above all no action must be demanded in which the performer himself is concerned. Aside from this, however, the tasks or the actions to be done need not even be limited to the room where the performance is given; they may be spread throughout the whole house, or even to more distant places.

What then is the secret of these apparently supernormal performances?

The reader may be surprised to learn two things: first, that the performer has often until the very end no idea of what he is to do; second, that it is really not the performer, as one might think, but the assisting spectator, who does the mental work. As a matter of fact it is not the performer who leads the spectator, but the spectator who leads the performer. For this reason it is absolutely essential that the guide shall have a strong power of concentration.

It is the guide who, by his subconscious impulses, leads the performer step by step to the solution of the unknown problem. The art of the performer consists in reading these impulses aright. The guide must divide the task into sharply separated stages, and must give his mental commands to the performer accordingly. Furthermore he must always think "Right!" when the performer proceeds correctly, "Wrong!" when this is not the case. The practical application of these mental commands will be explained in dissecting the experiment with the cigarette-case.

All that the performer knows at the beginning of an experiment is that he must find a place, for the moment unknown to him, where something is supposed to be done. Thus his first task is to find the place. It would be inadvisable, especially in a large room, for the performer to rush aimlessly hither and thither until the guide gave him an impulse. So he mentally divides the room into two halves. He begins to hunt in one of these halves. If he receives no impulses from the guide, it is safe to assume that the other half is the one involved. This half is mentally halved again, and so on, always restricting the sphere of operations more and more, until a strong impulsive movement of the guide shows the performer that he is near the place he seeks. This mental subdividing is used not only for rooms, but for surfaces, walls, and even persons, which are regarded as surfaces; it is kept up until the smallest division leads to or near to the goal.

Now for the task. Supposing that the table on which the cigarette-case lies is at the rear against the left wall of the hall, as soon as the performer has taken the guide by the hand, the latter must think intently, "Go straight forward from here to the back wall!" The performer charges forward, pulling the guide with him, and then stops for a moment in the middle of the hall. Here he balances on his toes and leans uncertainly toward all four points of the compass, taking careful note of the least resistance he feels in any direction from the guide. As the guide's mental command is "Straight ahead," there will be no resistance in that direction; therefore the performer continues forward. On arriving at the wall, the guide must think, "Go left to the table." If the performer tries to go to the right, the guide must at once think "Wrong!" which immediately causes an impeding pressure in his hand, pushing the performer away from that direction. The latter then turns to the left, where he feels no resistance. When they get to the table, the guide mentally commands, "Stop! Pick up the napkin and take the cigarette-case." The performer at once recognizes that he has arrived at the prescribed place, and that something is to be done on or removed from the table.

In his mind he divides the table in two or four parts, and begins, with his free hand (the guide holds the other), to pick up and feel the objects lying in each quarter of the table, taking careful notice of any change in the pressure of the guide's hand. If, or as long as, the pressure remains the same, the correct object has been found. In the case of the napkin, a quiver, even if only a faint one, will be perceptible in the hand of the guide. Still the performer does not know whether the napkin may not be the object to be found. To determine this, he tries to leave the table, carrying the napkin with him. The guide at once thinks "Wrong!" and unconsciously resists the intended departure. This causes the performer to lay down the napkin; as the cigarette-case still remains, he can safely assume that this is the article in question.

Now begins a minute task requiring experience and skill. The guide of course thinks, "Open the case and take out a cigarette," but this thought causes no perceptible movement by which the performer may be guided. He has to resort to deduction, turning over in his mind every possible action which can be carried out with a cigarette-case and with the cigarettes themselves. Presence of mind and guesswork are extremely important at this stage. The most probable thing is that the case is to be opened and a cigarette removed, but the performer must keep an eye on other possibilities, and proceed accordingly.

Suppose the performer has fulfilled the mental command, and has taken a cigarette from the case, in which event he will feel the mental "Right!" of the guide. The next thing is to deduce what is to be done with the cigarette. The guide's mental command will be, "Go to the right from here," which can be done at once if the guidance is good; then, "Go up the aisle to the sixth row," which is also accomplished without difficulty. Here pretty much the only possibility is that of giving the cigarette to some person seated at the place. Performer and guide push into the row, fairly roughly; now the audience becomes an involuntary assistant. The person designated to receive the cigarette usually acts stiff and reserved, and this alone is enough to show that he has a part in the task. As the most natural thing to do is to put the cigarette between someone's lips, the performer tries to do so. Admiring exclamations are heard at once, whence the performer may conclude that his task is ended. Otherwise he would have to wait for further mental commands from the guide, to see whether he was not supposed to get matches from somewhere, or continue in some other way.

Of course practice is necessary in order to carry out this sort of telepathic experiment correctly and quickly. But the experiments can be practised and learned by *anyone* who is capable of grasping the motile impulses of the guide, so long as the guide can think logically and concentrate well.

Such experiments are often conducted without direct contact between guide and performer. In any case, the guide must follow at such a distance that a slight turn of the head will bring him into view. Here too the hesitations of the guide play the chief part. From a retarded step, a complete standstill, from toes turned to walk in another direction, from the whole attitude of the guide's body, including scarcely perceptible movements of body, legs, and arms, the experienced telepathist can almost always accomplish the tasks set for him.

As repeated seeking and finding would become monotonous in time, the tasks may be disguised in some more or less dramatic form, such as delivering correctly letters addressed to persons in the room. *O. F.*

MUSIC The importance of musical accompaniment is too little appreciated by any but a few professional conjurers. A SILENT ACT loses two-thirds of its effect, and is twice as hard to do, without music; nearly all magic is much the better for good accompaniment.

The following suggestions were made especially for this volume by Henry Blanchard, singer and musical authority.

Music is an invaluable factor in creating mood, upon which all successful magic rests. Not only the music itself, but the manner of its making, is vitally important to the performer. The accompanist—the maker of the music—ought to be on a par professionally and mentally with the performer, because so much of the merit of any performance is in the hands, and the quick brain of the accompanist, who—no matter how much rehearsing has been done—must interpret as he goes along, filling in breaks, supporting a build-up, interpolating both mood and music as the performance requires. There can never be a good performance of anything if the musicians are inferior to the magician. Further, success depends on the rapport between the performers; any kind of show can rehearse until the day of doom, with every beat and every measure marked, but the show itself will not turn out that way; and without flexibility on the part of the accompanist, quickness of uptake, the actual performance can fall apart.

Of course few amateurs can carry or rehearse with a regular accompanist. Those who do not will do well to buy some of the music listed below for use when a competent volunteer accompanist is available. Magicians who have a regular assistant may also manage with phonograph music from offstage, but its use must be as carefully rehearsed as any trick, and the assistant must play his part even more precisely than in pulling threads or making switches. Generally only part of a record will be used; the exact spots may be marked on the surface of the record with yellow crayon. Of course this is a poor substitute for the invaluable help of a real accompanist.

Music for the OPENING EFFECT should always be bright and gay. If this so-called overture fails to quicken the pulses of the audience, the show is dead before it begins. Popular songs are good—*Oh, What a Beautiful Morning;* the Toreador song from *Carmen;* the Grand March from *Aïda;* the march from *Tannhäuser;* Dvorak's *Humoresque;* such Cohan tunes as *Over There* and *Forty-five Minutes from Broadway;* the Strauss waltzes.

Manipulation of coins, thimbles, billiard balls, etc., is where the accompanist has to think, and make his fingers react automatically to what his brain foresees. Mere lists and practice can never be enough. Music in this part of the show should have the lulling effect (in the hypnotic sense) produced only by complete familiarity—the kind of music one sometimes hears as a radio background during light reading. Some suitable tunes are *The Blue Danube*, the *Emperor Waltz*, and any of the Strauss waltzes; *Beautiful Ohio;* the *Merry Widow Waltz; Anitra's Dance*, from Grieg;

The Sorcerer's Apprentice, by Dukas; Mendelssohn's *Spring Song* and *Spinning Song; Non Piu Andrai*, the aria from Mozart's *Marriage of Figaro.*

Suspense will have to be created by music tailor-made from parts of pieces like Rachmaninoff's *Prelude in C# Minor*, the opening of Beethoven's *Fifth Symphony*, and the overture to *Carmen*, which is a very rich source.

Suspense followed by a sudden climax has to be created in the same way. The overture to *William Tell* has a great variety of material–storm, calm, dawn, and so on–, which can be cut and repeated at will. The slow movement from Beethoven's *Sixth Symphony*, and, once more, *Carmen*, are an inexhaustible mine.

PRODUCTIONS, the reeling out of stuff by the yard, require music by the yard also: Chaminade's *Scarf Dance;* Chopin's *Minute Waltz;* Schumann's *Happy Farmer;* the First Movement of Mozart's *G Minor Symphony; Flight of the Bumblebee*, by Rimsky-Korsakoff.

Time-fillers, for use when a production of candy is being distributed, cards are being scaled into the balcony, or the magician is passing among the audience, should be tunes that can be whistled on one hearing: popular songs like *Home on the Range*, *Ol' Man River*, *Alexander's Rag-time Band;* patriotic tunes like *Yankee Doodle*; Strauss waltzes; Sousa marches; and the songs of Stephen Collins Foster, like *Oh Susannah* and *Camptown Races.*

Oriental music can be suggested by the use of tom-toms and flutes. The five-and-ten-cent stores have a usable supply of such instruments, and the tone quality need not be too fine in any case. Of actual tunes, *Orientale* by Cesar Cui, a piece of the same name by Amani, and *Song from the East*, by Cyril Scott, are appropriate.

For CHILDREN'S SHOWS, nursery tunes are very useful: *I Had a Little Nut Tree*, *London Bridge*, *The Farmer in the Dell*, *Row, Row, Row Your Boat*, *Mulberry Bush*, *Baa Baa Black Sheep*, *Mary Had a Little Lamb*, *Little Jack Horner*, *Humpty-Dumpty*, *Sur le Pont d'Avignon*, *Au Claire de la Lune*, *Little Boy Blue*, *Rockaby, Baby*, *Pop Goes the Weasel*, *Hickory Dickory Dock*, *The Bear Went over the Mountain*, *The King of France.*

Most music publishers have put out several volumes of theater music and collections of pieces for use in the movies. Such collections ought to be basic requirements for the conjurer. There is also an old volume called *Masterpieces of Piano Music* that contains nearly everything.

Manipulative ROUTINES, once the separate sleights have been learned, are best rehearsed to music, such as radio dance music. If secret moves are made in time with the music, they are much more likely to be detected than if they are slipped in *off the beat.*

N

NEEDLE TRICK Originally an EAST INDIAN effect, presented as a feat of skill: "threading beads on a horse-hair with the tongue." It was introduced to the western world by an East Indian performer named Ramo Samee, who visited the Occident and the United States in the early nineteenth century. Someone in America suggested to Ramo Samee that the trick would be more striking if done with needles. The most recent version discards the needles in favor of safety-razor blades, and only the other day a magic supply catalogue offered "stringing beads in the mouth" as a novelty.

The performer apparently swallows a number of needles, either singly or in a bunch, followed by a length of thread and a mouthful of water. The end of the thread reappears between the performer's lips, and is pulled out. The needles are threaded at intervals along the thread.

HOUDINI made a great feature of this trick, which he performed extremely well, with all his customary showmanship.

The secret is a SWITCH of the most elementary kind. A set of needles is threaded, and the needles tied on perhaps three to five inches apart. The most important point in working the trick is to bundle up this set of needles in such a way that they will come out easily, without having to roll, when the end of the thread is pulled. With care the thread can be successfully wound around the eye end of the bunch. This duplicate set is LOADED between the gum and the lower lip, or between jawbone and cheek; in either case, it will not interfere with talking. Some performers make this load just at the start of the trick; others follow Houdini's example, and carry the needles in place from the start of the show.

The separate needles and thread are, of course, tucked inside the unoccupied lip (upper or lower) by the tongue during the pretense of swallowing. Drinking the glass of water makes no difference in the working, but furnishes a sort of punctuation, and, the water being obviously swallowed, creates an inference that the needles were swallowed also, which greatly heightens the effect. Some performers steal the extra set of needles in the act.

The loose needles and thread should be got rid of as soon as possible; they may be stolen as the last of the threaded needles are withdrawn from the mouth. *H. H.*

NEST OF BOXES This consists of six or more circular wooden boxes, one within the other, the largest or outer box having much the appearance, but being nearly double the size, of an ordinary toothpowder box, and the smallest being just large enough to contain a coin. The series is so accurately made that, by arranging the boxes in order one within the other, and the lids in the same way, you may, by simply putting on all the lids together, close all the boxes at once, although they can only be opened one by one.

These are placed, the boxes together and the lids together, anywhere just out of sight of the audience. If on the table, they may be hidden by some bulkier article. Having secretly obtained possession of a coin, you seize the opportunity to drop it into the innermost box, and to put on all the lids at once. You then bring forward the nest of boxes (which the spectators naturally take to be only one box), and announce that the coin will pass at your command from the place in which it has been deposited into the box which you hold in your hand, and which you forthwith deliver to someone in the audience for safekeeping.

Touching both articles with the mystic wand, you invite inspection of the first to show that the money has disappeared, and then of the box, wherein it is to be found. The holder opens the box and finds another, and then another, and in the innermost of all the marked coin. Seeing how long the several boxes have taken to open, the spectators naturally infer that they must take as long to close, and are at a loss to imagine how, with the mere moment of time at your command, you could have managed to insert the coin, and close so many boxes.

If you wish to use the nest for a larger coin, you can make it available for that purpose by removing beforehand the smallest box. Nests of square boxes, with hinged lids and self-closing locks, are made, both in wood and tin, on the same principle. These are designed for larger articles, and vary greatly in size and price.

Another effect uses a borrowed watch (with possibly a ring or glove in addition), which is wrapped in paper and tied around with ribbon. The little packet thus made is loaded into the conjurer's PISTOL.

Presently he fires, taking as his mark a good-sized, elaborately-corded box, which has been in sight of the audience the whole evening, either standing on a side table, or (more frequently) suspended by a rope over the center of the stage. The box being lowered and the cord removed, it is found to be locked, but the key is speedily discovered in the possession of someone in the audience. The performer opens the box and takes from it another box of similar appearance, and corded in the same way. This also being opened, another box is produced. The precise number of series may vary, but it comes to an end with two boxes, locked but not corded. The innermost is handed to someone to open, and within it is found the packet containing the borrowed articles.

The key to the mystery lies in the fact that the smallest but one of the boxes is bottomless. Suppose that the series consists in all (as it most frequently does) of *four* boxes, of which the largest will be referred to as No. 1, and so on. The performer stands either behind or just beside his table, on the SERVANTE of which rests, open, the smallest box, No. 4 (which closes with a spring lock). The packet containing the watch is of course not actually placed in the pistol, but is deftly exchanged, at an earlier stage, for another of similar appearance. At the first convenient opportunity the performer drops the genuine packet into the box on the servante, and closes the lid.

When the performer, after firing, opens box No. 1 and takes out No. 2, he for a moment places the latter behind the former, which, however, he immediately afterward puts aside, or hands to his assistant. No. 2 is then pushed to the front of the table, to make room for No. 3, which in turn is placed for a moment behind No. 2. Before taking out No. 3, however, and while in the act of pushing forward No. 2, the performer brings up No. 4 with his disengaged hand from the servante, and places this behind No. 2. No. 3 (the bottomless box) is then lifted out of No. 2, and brought down over No. 4, which is eventually produced from it.

A second version requires three wooden boxes, of plain, thin pine put together with French nails, three at each corner, as in Fig. 1. The lids are

FIG. 1

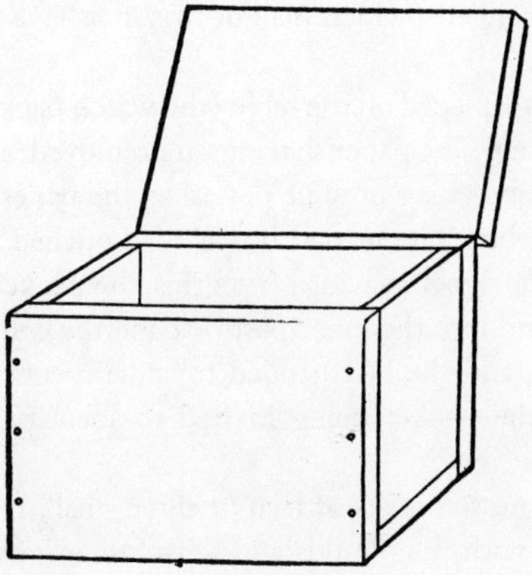

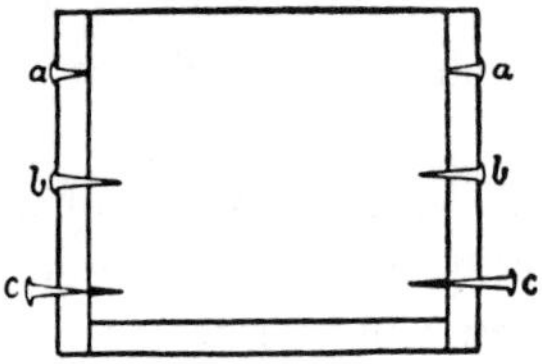

FIG. 2

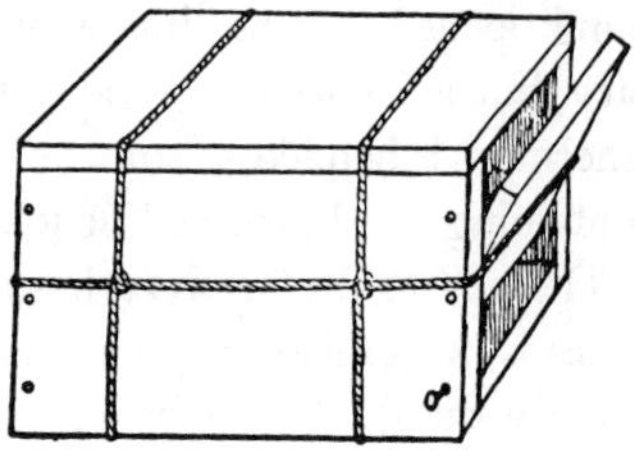

FIG. 3

mere flat pieces of wood. There is no speciality about either of the two larger boxes, but the third is a trick box, being a sort of rough imitation of the familiar watch box. It is four inches long, three wide, and two and a half deep. One end of it is FAKED, after the manner shown in Fig. 2.

The two upper nails, *a a*, are mere dummies, being just long enough to penetrate the sides, but not the end. The nails *c c* are a trifle longer, but fit loosely into their holes, so that they can be drawn out or pushed in at pleasure. When pressed in, they make all secure, but when drawn out, as in the illustration, they allow the end to work backward and forward on *b b*, which are nails of full length, and act as pivots. This box is partially filled with cotton-wool, and is tied up with tape and sealed, but it will be observed (Fig. 3) that the tape is passed around it after a special fashion, so as not to interfere with the opening of the end.

Thus arranged, this box is placed in the second, which is a good deal larger, the intervening space being loosely filled with paper shavings. This second box is tied up in the same way and placed in the third box, which again is a good bit larger, the intervening space being filled as before. The three boxes thus arranged (which may or may not have locks) are in view the whole evening.

The nest of boxes is placed on the table (the watch packet being deposited behind it) and opened. The paper shavings are removed, and the second box produced. The first box may now be put aside, the paper shavings masking the packet on the table. The second box is then opened, and, under cover of the removal of the paper shavings from this, the packet is deftly inserted through the open end into the innermost box and the end closed. The loose nails are pressed in, and the box handed to some spectator to open, those who had marked the packet being invited to identify their marks.

L. H.

The most recent nest consists of two or three small, rectangular, nickel-plated metal boxes with hinged lids and self-closing locks, which lock on being snapped shut. The boxes are generally employed for the BALL OF WOOL trick, and the necessity of unlocking them with a key adds a final surprise.

NICOLA, THE GREAT Stage name of William Mozart Nicol (1880-1946), American magician and illusionist, who at his death was described on good authority as the highest-salaried magician this country has ever produced. He toured the world with a full show, using many changes not only of scenery but of costume. He was one of the very few magicians who never on any account performed a trick that he had not legally acquired by either purchase or gift.

NIGHT-CLUB SHOWS After the decline of vaudeville, night-clubs became almost the only place where magicians could find steady employment with a short act.

Night-club shows are of two kinds: floor acts, which are a modified form of vaudeville; and table acts, in which the performer goes from one party to the next, doing TABLE TRICKS, and getting his pay directly from the patrons.

The requirements of all night-club work depend on the fact that none of the audience is in a mood to make any effort, and at least part of the audience will be somewhat drunk.

Therefore night-club magic must be fast in tempo, and it must require no concentration from the audience. In these respects CARDINI's is the ideal night-club floor act. The night-club floor act should not call for audience participation in any way more elaborate than the choice of a drink (see INEXHAUSTIBLE BOTTLE) or the cutting of a ROPE; the choice of cards, for instance, should be confined to table acts.

Only Cardini's great skill enables him to do his particular work despite the third essential requirement imposed by the average night-club layout: the act must be ANGLE-PROOF. This is true of both floor and table acts. BACK-PALMING and SERVANTES are practically ruled out; LOADS must be made with great care and discretion.

The tendency of magicians working a floor act is to forget that they are hired essentially as liquor salesmen; they are the entertainment that brings people into the place, but once the customers are inside, the magician must whiz through his act and get out of the way before he slows the flow of orders to the bar.

The night-club *table* magician has two special problems: an OPENING EFFECT that will catch people's attention and make him welcome at the tables; and a FINALE that will forcibly suggest financial contributions from the party. Jean Hugard's *Close-up Magic for the Night-Club Magician* offers suggestions for both categories. The magician can kill two birds with one stone by producing several real coins from the clothes of patrons at the table he has chosen to begin on (see MISER'S DREAM). The money is dropped carelessly on the table, which makes people realize that they are expected to add to the pile. Production of a WAND is another good opener. For a finale, Hugard strongly advises a trick with borrowed bills; some performers contrive to make it seem that the only gracious thing the patron can do is leave the bill with the magician.

Among the effects suitable for night-club work are: AFGHAN BANDS; BALL OF WOOL; BIRD-CAGE; BREAKAWAY FAN; CAKE BAKED IN A HAT; CARD IN CIGARETTE; CARDS UP THE SLEEVE (requires great care with angles); CHINESE WANDS; CIGAR tricks; CIGARETTE MANIPULATION; CUPS AND BALLS (for table acts only); DICE TRICKS; DIMINISHING CARDS; DOLLAR-BILL TRICKS; DOVE PAN; EGG BAG; FUNNEL; INEXHAUSTIBLE BOTTLE; JUMPING PEG effects; LINKING RINGS (floor acts only); LOTA; MISER'S DREAM; NEEDLE TRICK; NEST OF BOXES; ORGAN PIPES (floor acts only); PASSE-PASSE BOTTLE; RICE BOWLS; RING ON STICK; ROPE TRICKS; SILK TRICKS (when angle-proof); SPONGE BALLS (table acts only); SYMPATHETIC COINS; SYMPATHETIC SILKS; THIMBLE TRICKS (floor acts only); THUMB TIE; TORN AND RESTORED PAPER; TRANSFIXED PACK (table acts only); TURBAN CUT AND RESTORED; WATCH TRICKS (when angle proof). *H. H.*

O

ONE-AHEAD GAG (See under BILLET- AND MESSAGE-READING)

OPENING EFFECTS (See under PROGRAMS, NIGHT-CLUB SHOWS)

ORGANIZATIONS Magicians are far more clannish and fond of one another's society than any other class of entertainers. There is almost no town of any size in the United States without some organized or informal group of conjurers. These groups are often short-lived, but two of them are long-established, with local affiliates all over the country. The Society of American Magicians, having national headquarters in New York, is the older. Its branches are known as Assemblies. The International Brotherhood of Magicians (headquarters at Kenton, Ohio) has branches called Rings throughout the country, and publishes the monthly *Linking Ring* (see LITERATURE OF MAGIC). The I.B.M. admits somewhat younger members than the S.A.M. The New York City Knights of Magic is a local organization over twenty-five years old.

Many foreign nations have their own organizations, among the most prominent being the Magic Circle in England, the Syndicat des Artistes Prestidigitateurs in France, and (at any rate before the Second World War) the Magischer Zirkel in Germany. These organizations and others throughout the world issue their own publications.

Regular attendance at a magical club makes firm friendships and teaches the beginner much that he needs to know. On the other hand, the most ardent members often neglect PRESENTATION in favor of tricks, and fall into the habit of "conjuring for conjurers," to their own grave detriment as entertainers.

ORGAN PIPES This capital trick, known on the Continent by the more romantic title of "*Le Souper du Diable*," is the invention of an Austrian wizard named Antonio Molini.

The essential apparatus consists of six metal tubes, zinc, tin, or sheet brass, alike in length, but graduated in diameter so that the smallest passes easily through the next larger, and so on throughout. The metal may be either simply polished, or enameled to taste. For stage purposes, the tubes should

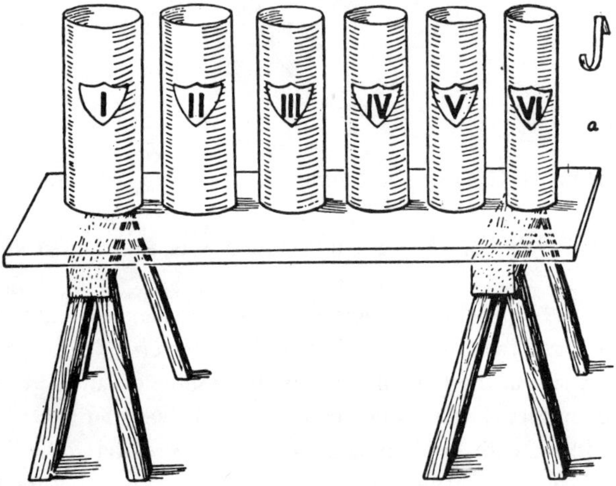

FIG. 1

be twelve to sixteen inches in height, and range downward from about six inches in diameter.

Each tube should have a number conspicuously painted on it, the largest being No. 1, the next No. 2, and so on. In the orthodox form of the trick these are arranged, as shown in Fig. 1, on a slab of plate glass, supported on low trestles. However, the performer may substitute for the glass slab a plain wooden plank, and for the trestles a couple of chairs. In either case, a plain wooden table, with seats for two persons, should stand close by.

The effect of the trick is as follows: The performer, having shown clearly that tube No. 1 is empty, proceeds to pass No. 2 through it, and then shows this also empty. No. 3 is then passed through No. 2, and No. 3 shown empty, and so on throughout. This done, the performer asks a couple of the spectators to step up on the stage, and join him at supper.

They take their seats at the table, and he produces from the empty tubes, first, a tablecloth, glasses, and plates; then a bottle of wine, a loaf (of the long Vienna shape), a sausage, eggs, a roast duck, and other eatables—in fact, all the materials for a complete meal, even to a vase of flowers to decorate the table.

The tubes are then nested, one within the other. The performer passes his arm through the innermost, makes his bow, and so carries them off the stage.

The secret lies mainly in a very ingenious method of LOADING the tubes, and of transferring the contents from one to another. The largest, No. 1, is empty at the beginning. The rest are all fully loaded, the contents being suspended from the upper edge of each tube by means of a hook, formed of a narrow strip of tin, bent into the shape shown at *a* in Fig. 1. The hook is bent at the top into an acute angle, while the lower bend is rounded. The load is in each case suspended from the lower arm of this hook by means of a loop of black THREAD, so that it will hang midway in the tube, or a little lower. There should be a clear space of two inches at the top. At the bottom, an inch or less may suffice.

One of the most important loads is the bottle of wine, which is a specially prepared article. It is a black bottle, of the shape used for Burgundy. The bottom is cut out, and a false bottom of tin cemented in below the neck, just far down enough to leave room for a couple of glassfuls of wine above it. Near the lower edge of the bottle is drilled a small hole, through which is passed the thread to form the loop, and by means of such loop the bottle is suspended, upside down, in tube No. 2. In the vacant space within the bottle are packed, also upside down, two small tumblers, one within the other, and, within these, other small articles, say, a mustard-pot and salt-cellar.

In tube No. 3 is suspended a tablecloth, rolled around a couple of table napkins and a like number of knives and forks, and held together by a couple of rubber bands, one at each end. In No. 4 may be a sausage, a Vienna loaf, and a net containing a couple of hard-boiled eggs. In No. 5, a roast duck or chicken, which *may* be the genuine article, though it is more frequently a papier-mâché imitation. In No. 6 is suspended, upside down, a vase of flowers, which may be arranged so as to expand freely when another rubber band, encircling them, is removed.

On his own person the performer conceals, under the vest on each side, a couple of small plates. These should be of enameled metal, to occupy less space.

When he reaches the appropriate stage of his discourse (which should be a little *before* he begins to call direct attention to the alleged emptiness of the tubes), the performer should take tube No. 1 in his hand and move it casually about so that everyone can see it is a plain, empty cylinder. He replaces this and lifts up No. 2, lowering it vertically into No. 1; when it is all the way down, he lifts No. 1 off again at the top. At the same time No. 1 lifts the hook off No. 2 on to its own upper edge, carrying away inside the parcel formerly suspended in No. 2, which can now be shown empty.

The same procedure is followed with the remaining tubes: No. 3 is lowered into No. 2, No. 2 is lifted off, No. 3 is shown empty, and so on. At the end No. 6 is left empty and all the other tubes are loaded, each with the original load of the next lower number.

Some practice will be needed to work this portion of the trick easily. The more quickly (without apparent haste) the operation is performed, the less time the audience has to realize that if the tubes were really empty, the obvious course would be to show them empty at the beginning, without passing one through another.

When he has completed this introductory process, the performer begins to lay his table, beginning with the production of the tablecloth. Drawing this out of the appropriate tube (privately removing the rubber bands), he notices with apparent surprise that there is something wrapped up inside, and he produces from the bundle the table napkins, knives, and forks. He lays these down temporarily on the table, shakes out the tablecloth, and produces from under it first one, and then the other pair of plates. The other requirements for the meal are produced from the remaining tubes.

The hooks and rubber rings are quietly pocketed, and the performer brings the trick to a conclusion by packing the six tubes one within the other.

L. H.

P

PALMING (See under: BALL MANIPULATION; CARD MANIPULATION; CIGAR MANIPULATION; CIGARETTE MANIPULATION; COIN MANIPULATION; CUPS AND BALLS; PSYCHOLOGY; SPIDER; SPONGE BALLS; THIMBLE TRICKS; WATCH TRICKS)

PANTOMIME (See also COMEDY; PSYCHOLOGY; SILENT ACTS) Pantomime as it concerns the magician is the art of acting, apart from the spoken word. It includes the performer's carriage or posture, gestures, and expression. It is utterly impossible to do magic without pantomime; SLEIGHT-OF-HAND *is* pantomime of a difficult order. Unfortunately it is all too easy to do magic without *good* pantomime.

Sleight-of-hand depends on skilled, well co-ordinated muscle control of the arms and hands. For dramatic pantomime this muscle control includes the whole body, legs, feet, trunk, head, as well as arms and hands. This co-ordinated, designed body or muscle control in pantomime is called *body mechanics*.

Besides body mechanics the magician and actor use what are called *stage mechanics and transitions*. The simplest of the three—body mechanics, stage mechanics, transitions—is stage mechanics.

Stage mechanics concerns going from front to back or across the platform or acting space. The new names for old friends are "upstage," "downstage," and "oblique." Years ago stage platforms were literally built on a slant, lowest near the audience, slanting upward toward the back or away from the audience. Although the stages are now built level, and the audience put on the slant, the terms of the past are still used. "Upstage" (u.s.) means away from the audience, up to the back. "Downstage" (d.s.) means down near the footlights or audience. In pantomime or stage directions *d.s.l.* means downstage left—left from the *performer; d.s.r.*, downstage right, right from the performer; *u.s.l.*, upstage left, etc.

A second and extremely important part of stage mechanics is the use of the *oblique*. When showing his empty palm the magician holds the palm at an angle visible to the audience sitting at the extreme left, full center, and extreme right. He is careful that neither shoulder hides arm or hand. He opens the upstage palm, points to the open palm with the downstage hand, keeping body facing front, shoulders on a line with the straight line of the platform opening. Often he moves s.r. to s.l., carefully keeping both shoulders visible to all the audience. This is using or moving on the oblique.

To practise moving on the oblique, walk across the stage to s.l. naturally. Keep this easy natural walk, going to s.r. turning the shoulders and head to the left as though talking to a person at extreme s.l. This will make a twist in the upper body. After practising in this extreme, modify the twist in the body just enough so that both shoulders stay visible to all the audience.

To acquire good body mechanics the use of observation and memory are important. In pantomime training many exercises are given to sharpen observation relating to how people walk, sit, react in everyday life. Everyone is familiar with the fact that feelings and body attitudes are closely connected. Body attitudes are made through feelings, and are shown through, and only through, muscle contractions, muscle extensions, or muscle release. Our vocabulary to describe the physical co-ordinations called posture, carriage or bearing consists of words for feelings. Posture is accepted as a symbol or indicator of an emotional condition. The words "dejected, elated, despairing, hopeful, joyous, sadly" bring to memory various and contrasting pictures of posture. Take weariness or dejection as an exercise. Carefully observe the muscle pulls or posture of a dejected or very weary person. Such a person is easy to find on any street. Also we may remember the pulls of a very weary unsuccessful walking jaunt. Observe carefully, remembering that the whole body, trunk, legs, and feet are included as well as the already skilled arms and hands of the magician. Practise this pattern of physical co-ordination with the entire body as carefully as a palming pattern or co-ordination for magic.

Good posture is accepted as an indication of well-being, of confidence, of success. It may be described as standing our full height, giving our lungs full breathing space, standing "tall," pushing the sky up from the soles of our feet through the *crown* of our head. Practise walking in this pattern of elation.

Besides walks resulting from states of feeling, there is what is known as a balanced walk. This walk too is colored by feelings; that is, a balanced walk may be dejected or elated, but under the sway of any feeling the walk will be graceful or balanced. Grace and economy of movement are synonymous.

In walking, economy of motion is grace. Tension has no part in economy. Tension is a tightening, a holding back; economy is a wise, easy, full distribution of energy *where* energy is needed for action.

To get a balanced walk try an exaggerated *un*balanced or *un*economical walk in this way. Stand with the feet wide apart as though walking two lines. To progress forward keeping this wide base the body is lurched first to one side, then to the other. Walk with this wide lurch several times around the room, then begin narrowing the base or getting the feet nearer each other; the lurching becomes less. Continue this narrowing of the base until the feet barely miss brushing as they pass forward. The lurching is gone, the walk is *almost in one tread*. This ALMOST IN ONE TREAD gives slenderness, grace, style to the body. To walk completely in one tread, like a tight-rope walker, becomes artificial and looks affected for any use other than a tight-rope. Try this from wide to narrow base before a mirror and judge the effect for yourself.

With this balanced walk practise the dejection and elation feeling patterns. Observe other muscle patterns, and practise them carefully and separately. For certain comic effects practise with the wide, lurching, uneconomical base.

Choice of a type character is one good way for starting a story. Possibly two of the best types to start with are a slightly intoxicated silk-hatted member of society suffering from hallucinations, and an irresponsible tramp carrying a torn and useless umbrella. Suppose the tramp is unhappy, wants to play a game of cards but has no cards. The memory of wanting something is familiar to all, wanting money but no money, wanting cards but no cards, just "wanting." Then suddenly from the blue our want is satisfied; we are happy, gay. Two different feelings, two different experiences, two different muscle co-ordinations are here, easily familiar to our memory as also familiar to the memory and experience of every audience. It is easy to remember seeing a character walking dejectedly, almost slinking past a cafeteria door, stopping, searching through his pockets, even turning a worn wallet upside down and shaking it, a sigh, then walking on in an unhappy or "wanting" condition. This is an incident in pantomime. Watching further this character with lowered head, slumped shoulders, dragging feet, we see him stop, examine a bright object. Suddenly his whole physical co-ordination changes. Quickly he moves to pick up the quarter—excitement, pleasure, head and shoulders higher; now with confidence he walks into the cafeteria. The complete happening is a story in dramatic pantomime.

Between these two feelings, as shown by changes in muscle co-ordination, is a place or *the* place where the change from one to the other is made. This place where the change takes place is called the *transition*. The drama is in the transition.

This transition must be slowed down many times slower than the change or transition in a real happening. The reason for this slowing down is that the eye of the observer watching from a distance may have full time to see physically and realize mentally what is happening. A transition for a dramatic story lets the audience see something is about to happen, see what does happen, see how and what makes the happening, and see the conclusion or result from this happening. The attention of the audience is kept on every obvious detail during the transition. It is often said that the best speech tells the audience what the speech will tell, tells, then tells what was told. This is another way of saying, at the transition let the audience see something is going to happen, let the audience see this happening, then let them see the result of the happening. The magician may need to practise the dramatic transition by suddenly stopping, staring at a place where nothing is, letting the audience see nothing is present, reaching for this nothing and finding a dollar in his hand, seeing this himself, letting the audience see this, *then* adjusting to the new situation, now a happy one. Putting the three parts together with an interesting stage line of movement, the result will be a convincing pantomime of a wanting character finding money and becoming a happy character.

To re-create the muscle pattern does not mean at all that the artist gets his personal feelings into a state. The artist uses his mechanics–good body mechanics, the skill to choose a posture design, then co-ordinates his muscles into this design. Observation, memory, and practise make it easy for an actor to co-ordinate impersonally for hope, joy, sadness, etc., one after the other.

When the whole body is co-ordinated for or in a chosen design the gesture continues in the pattern. Here again the body is free of tension, so the gesture will be easy and broad. Gesture on stage must be broader than in a room, for the simple reason that the gesture must be seen from a distance. When you beckon to a person at a distance you broaden, make larger, more open movements. The raised platform gives the performer distance from the audience. He must enlarge his gesture to reach the eye of the last seat in the most distant section of the house.

The audience follows the eye. The audience wants to see what the character is seeing. If the actor sees something, but his gaze becomes listless or moves on, the audience knows the object is of no value. The eye will reflect or mirror the body co-ordinations.

The mouth is used only in the extremes of emotion, the dropped jaw of final terror, etc. Such extremes are best left alone by the beginner. The easy relaxed face is best.

In really re-creating the posture patterns or muscle co-ordinations resulting from feeling, a *re-creation* rather than an *imitation* of the feeling is conveyed to the observer. This is the difference between the amateur and the artist. The amateur imitates or tries to *pretend;* the artist *re-creates the pattern.*

Louise Gifford
Officer of Instruction (Pantomime), Columbia University
Dance and pantomime director for Broadway productions of the Theater Guild, Brock Pemberton, and Winthrop Ames

PASSE-PASSE BOTTLE The performer has a bottle of beer, a tumbler, and two cardboard covers—which are in fact mere cardboard tubes, open at each end. Beer is poured from the bottle into the tumbler, and both articles are then placed upon the side tables, and each covered with a cover. After the performance of the usual magical passes, the covers are removed, when the glass and bottle are found to have changed places.

The following is the ingenious method by which the impossibility is apparently brought about. Have a tin bottle made, exactly in imitation of a beer bottle, between nine and ten inches high, and japanned so as to look like glass at a distance. The bottom of this bottle is open, but four inches from the lower edge is a tin partition, dividing the bottle horizontally into two compartments. The upper compartment is to hold the beer. Passing through its very center, and reaching to within half an inch of the top of the neck, is a tube about a third of an inch in diameter, or at any rate large enough to take a small funnel. By means of this tube communication is established with the lower open compartment.

Then have a second bottle made, also of tin, and japanned to match, just large enough to fit over the first one. This bottle has no interior whatever, and is in fact a mere shell. In height it need be only the merest trifle taller than the other, and should be as narrow as possible, compatible with an easy fit over the smaller bottle.

Each bottle should be decorated with a gaudy beer label, taken from a genuine bottle. The labels must of course be precisely alike, and if each has a piece accidentally (!) torn out of it, sufficiently large to be noticed by the spectators, so much the better. In the middle of the body of each bottle is cut a circular hole, nearly an inch in diameter, and fully two inches from the nearest edge of the label.

The two pasteboard covers may be of any length between twelve and fifteen inches. As these must be made to fit very closely over the bottles, without actually clinging to them, one will be larger than the other. Finally, two tumblers precisely alike will be wanted. They must not exceed four inches in height, or they will not go under the small bottle, on account of the partition there.

Behind the scenes the small bottle has its compartment filled with beer, and is then placed over one of the tumblers, the large shell-bottle being finally placed over both. By placing the middle finger through the holes in the bottles, pressure is brought to bear upon the tumbler, which in this way may be lifted with the bottles. The whole (looking to the audience merely like a single bottle) is thus brought on, and placed on the center table. The two covers are shown, the performer explaining that they are merely made to cover the bottle. Suiting the action to the word, he places the large cover over the bottle and at once withdraws it, nipping it near the botom so as to bring away the outer shell inside. With the other hand, the smaller cover is then placed over the smaller bottle and at once withdrawn. The company, knowing of only one bottle, will fancy they have seen both covers placed over it. The large cover, having the shell within it, must not be laid upon its side, but stood up alongside the empty one.

The performer now takes the smaller bottle in one hand—holding the tumbler beneath it as well, by means of a finger through the hole—and the visible tumbler in the other. Beer is poured out until the tumbler is filled. The performer now says that he does not want his glass too full, and, replacing the bottle on the table, places a small funnel in its mouth, taking care to insert it in the tube. Half the beer—neither more nor less—must now be poured into the funnel, and it of course finds its way into the tumbler beneath. The conjurer will have to experiment beforehand, so as to discover how much he must pour away, slight marks being made, with a diamond or file, for his guidance while exhibiting. It is highly essential that each glass contain precisely the same quantity.

The visible tumbler is now placed on one side table and covered with the large cover containing the shell. The small bottle is placed upon the other side table, with the tumbler still concealed under it, and covered with the small cover. By means of the wand, an imaginary exchange of the articles is now made, and the covers are lifted—that containing the shell lightly, so as to leave the shell behind, while that containing the bottle is gripped nearer the bottom, so as to lift that article with it, exposing the second tumbler.

The general method adopted in lifting the covers is to take them by the extreme top when the article contained is to be exhibited, and at the very bottom when it is to be carried away. These are certainly very safe methods; but they are unnecessarily so, and afford far too much clue to the spectators.

The variation between the positions of the hand need never exceed a couple of inches. The height of the upper edge of the body of the bottles may be indicated upon the outside of the cover. Half an inch below that line the performer has only to exert pressure to ensure the carrying away of the bottle or shell. A little above it he is clear of them, and need not fear carrying them away by mistake. A variation of two or three inches is a natural one, and unnoticeable.

The change made, the performer will of course offer to do it again, "in order to give everyone a chance of noticing how it is done." He may pretend to give his spectators some assistance by telling them, in confidence, that the tumblers and bottle really came out at the tops of the covers—his original statement, that the openings were there to prevent suspicion, being untrue, their real purpose being to afford easy exits and entrances for the articles. The articles then make a return to their original positions, after the covers have been replaced, the shell being carried away, and the bottle allowed to remain.

The feature of the trick, which completely mystifies the company, is the transposition of the beer-containing tumbler. The fact that the bottle has been nearly inverted in the act of pouring out the beer in the first instance precludes the idea that it could ever have been concealed in that. Although beer is mentioned here, claret or claret and water may be used, or any other showy liquid at hand. *E. T. S.*

PATTER (See also CHILDREN'S SHOWS; PRESENTATION; PSYCHOLOGY; SILENT ACTS) The question of patter is one that has caused a great deal of disagreement. Some performers have maintained that patter is all-important in the art of magic, while others have regarded it as entirely negligible. Obviously, both views cannot be right, and it is practically certain that neither is altogether correct, whatever may be said in its support. The fact is that patter is entirely essential in some cases and quite unnecessary in others.

Some well-known effects cannot possibly be performed as SILENT ACTS, while others, even though they might be given in silence, would suffer immeasurably. The former class comprises those in which the initial procedure requires explanation, either because members of the audience are required to assist the performer, or for various other reasons. The latter class consists of experiments involving extensive preparation, which might prove tedious if done in silence, and cases where some slight diversion of the spectators' attention is necessary. To dispense with patter, then, would be impossible in one case and unwise in the other.

The performer who confines himself to silent acts cuts himself adrift, artistically speaking, from a wide range of effects which would otherwise be available for his use. This in itself provides a strong argument in favor of patter, but it in no way proves that patter is indispensable to magic. It merely proves the value of speech on occasion.

There are, however, tricks which are more effectively done in silence, particularly those that require close attention from the audience. The introduction of patter here would be a distinct disadvantage.

A modern magician is an actor playing the part of a legendary magician, and whatever may be true of other actors is equally true of him. Since speech is highly important in other dramatic work, it is also important in magic.

Just as it is necessary to know when to use or discard patter, one must know what kind of patter to use when it is required, and what form of speech one is *capable* of adopting with proper effect. One may know what ought to be said, but unless one can say it properly, it will be better left unsaid. This requires the performer to make quite sure of his own ground, especially in relation to personal characteristics and ability. Unless he can carry out the proper method of procedure in a competent manner, it would be far better to adopt a less perfect method within the range of adequate performance.

Suppose a performer intends to present a magical item for which the best introduction would be a serious, well-written, and impressive address. The points he has to consider are these: can he be effectively serious and impressive, and can he write well enough to compose the address? If these achievements are well within his power, he need have no hesitation in going ahead. But if, in either respect, his personal limitations stand in the way of successful achievement, he should sacrifice something in procedure in order to bring the presentation within his ability.

In writing patter, of course, the performer may obtain assistance, but when it comes to public delivery, he must do the work himself. If he undertakes to give an impressive address, he should be an elocutionist. If the prevailing note is COMEDY, he should be a comedian. If what he has to say is pseudo-scientific, he should be at least something of a scientist. The complete magician would, of course, possess all such qualifications, but since the complete magician has yet to be born, everyone is compelled to sacrifice something of ambition, on account of his individual shortcomings.

With sufficient good sense, a magician may easily steer clear of the difficulties to which his personal limitations might otherwise lead him. The man who lacks education must be aware of that lack, and will take care to avoid mistakes in speaking. Since he cannot rely upon his own knowledge, he will obtain the advice and assistance of others who possess the education he has not acquired. The performer who keeps in constant view the deficiencies from which he suffers, and the need for overcoming them, can be as true an artist as though his education were of the best.

The man who has not learned to speak grammatically should not attempt to speak in public without first submitting the text of his speech to someone able to correct the mistakes he is bound to make. The man who has not learned French cannot expect to speak French without seeming ridiculous, even though he may have consulted someone who knows the language. The performer who does not understand elocution should not speak in public without having rehearsed before someone who can show him where he goes wrong. Above all, the performer whose accent is low class should *never* speak in public when circumstances render such an accent inappropriate.

When a performer trips over some obstacle which proper care would have enabled him to avoid, his reputation as an artist is bound to suffer. And since blunders in speech are the worst a performer can commit, they demand the utmost care in prevention. In every audience there will be people to whom errors in grammar or pronunciation will be distasteful, and who will regard the misuse of words as direct evidence of incompetency.

Every language abounds in "booby-traps" to catch the unwary or unskilled speaker, and every sensible man will take good care to avoid being caught. Unfortunately there are magicians who use terms they do not understand and words they cannot pronounce. The *artistes* who address educated people in such ruinous phrases are the men most likely to attach the highest importance to their own achievements as "perfeshnals," and to entertain the greatest contempt for the "amechure."

The performer who stands before educated people with the intention of addressing them in a favorable manner, must use the language that educated people speak, or else suffer ridicule and lose prestige. He should be master of his own language.

Another point to be considered concerns the practice of making contemptuous remarks about magic. A magical humorist can be funny without making fun of his art. If he says things which lower the public estimation of magic and magicians, he not only degrades himself and his performance, but reflects discredit upon the whole magical profession. Jokes in which magic is allied to humbug, swindling or chicanery of any kind can only serve to rank the magician among swindlers and impostors.

"Talking at" the audience is also an objectionable practice. People do not like to be talked at, whether they deserve it or not; in fact, the more they deserve it, the less they relish it. When, for example, a performer finds his audience undemonstrative, the very worst thing for him to do is to show resentment. The people in front of the footlights must, if possible, be led to forget their own concerns, and made to think only of the performance they are watching. If instead they are made to feel uncomfortable about what the performer thinks of them, spontaneous appreciation and enjoyment become impossible, and all chance of pleasure in the entertainment is destroyed, both for them and for him.

In the same way, references to the hypothetical poverty of magicians can only be detrimental; worse still are references to the possible poverty of spectators. It is bad enough to find a performer suggesting his own familiarity with the pawn-shop, but when such jokes are made at the expense of the audience, the fault is a thousand times more reprehensible. Such themes are not agreeable to anyone, and they add nothing to the general effect.

Remarks concerning the suitability of a performance to a juvenile audience are likewise objectionable. One often hears a magician make a sort of apology for introducing a certain item, on the ground that "so many young people are present." Could there be any readier method of bringing that item into contempt? Probably not. To present the thing as being especially suited to the mental capacity of children will suggest to the adults that what they are about to see is beneath their appreciation, and as to the children themselves, the result is even more disastrous.

Every child wishes to appear "grown up," and the mere fact of saying that a trick will appeal to children is enough to set every juvenile mind against it. Out of courtesy to his juniors, a child may be disposed to tolerate what pleases children; but he wants to believe that what pleases *him* really is something that is suited to the intelligence of his elders. To suggest that he requires children's fare is an insult to his understanding, and children understand a great deal more than their elders usually believe.

N. M. & D. D.

John Mulholland, in his useful little *The Art of Illusion*, says, "One last word about patter—always speak as if you were talking to the person farthest away. If you begin speaking directly to him you will find that you naturally will use sufficient volume to be heard. Listen to how loud you are speaking and then keep your voice that loud."

The whole subject of elocution and voice control deserves more attention than it gets from magicians. Study some standard book such as *The New Better Speech*, by Weaver, Borchers, and Woolbert. Learn to speak from your diaphragm instead of the back of your throat. One trick to help you enunciate is to hold a cork in your teeth, and then read aloud. Actors practise reciting the alphabet, putting into their voice successively the whole gamut of emotions.

It is an excellent idea to have a phonograph recording made of your voice while doing some short trick; this will probably show you many opportunities for improvement.

PENNY AND DIME TRICK (See under COINS, SHELL)

FIG. 1

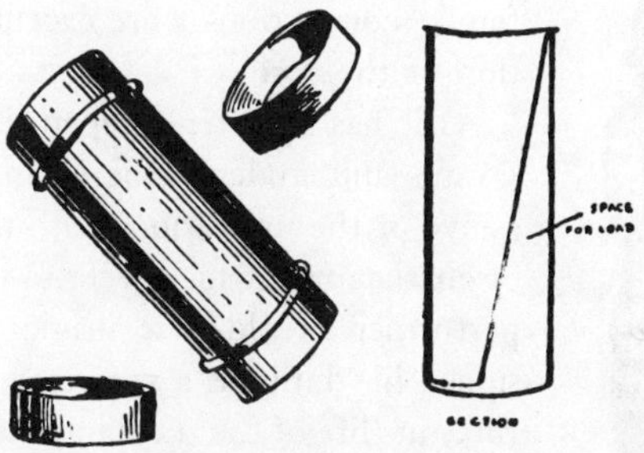

PHANTOM TUBE A PRODUCTION device, similar in effect to the DRUMHEAD TUBE. A metal tube is shown empty by being held up to the light; pieces of paper are fixed over the ends by means of rings; the paper at one end is broken, and silks or other LOADS are produced.

Inside the tube is a conical lining, tapering from the full size of the tube at one end to less than half the size at the other. (Fig. 1) The load goes between the tube and the lining. When the tube is held up with the big end toward the front, it merely seems longer than it should be to anyone looking through it, and this is never noticed. A second load can be produced by the drumhead method.

PHILLIPPE (or PHILIPPE) Stage name of Phillippe Talon (1802-1878), a French confectioner whose wanderings took him to Aberdeen. According to one story he there became acquainted with JOHN HENRY ANDERSON; at all events Aberdeen was where he launched himself as a magician. His great contribution to modern conjuring was the introduction of the LINKING RINGS, the GOLDFISH BOWLS, and other feats of CHINESE MAGIC, which he learned from a Chinese troupe in Dublin.

Frost says, in his *Lives of the Conjurors*, "Philippe did not make such a profuse display of glittering paraphernalia as Anderson did, but his deceptions were performed with the neatness and finish that distinguished DOEBLER's performances, and he was the first conjuror who exhibited with bare arms."

PILLARS OF SOLOMON (See under CHINESE WANDS)

PINETTI, GIUSEPPE, DE WILLEDAL (1750-1800) born in Orbitelle, a fortified town once claimed by Tuscany. What can be found regarding his early history goes to prove that his family connections were excellent and his education of the best.

As it has so often happened in the history of savants and students, there ran in Pinetti's blood a love of the mysterious with that peculiar strain of charlatanism which went to make up the clever performer in old-time magic. Evidently he resigned his duties as a professor for the more picturesque life of the traveling magician, and he was first heard from in this capacity in the French provinces in 1783. His fame quickly carried him to Paris, where in 1784 he appeared before the court of Louis XVI. His arrival was most opportune, for just then all Paris and, for that matter, all Europe had been aroused to a new interest in magic by Cagliostro.

From Paris he went to London, playing at the Haymarket and creating a sensation equal to that which he made in France. Later, he toured Germany, playing in Berlin and Hamburg. Next he went back to his native land, Italy, but later returned to Germany for a second engagement. In 1789 he appeared in Russia and never left that country. There he married a Russian girl, daughter of a carriage manufacturer. They had two children. Pinetti would have left enormous wealth, but in his later years he became interested in ballooning, the sensation of the hour, and spent his entire fortune on balloon experiments. He died in Bartichoff, Volhinie.

Pinetti was a man of rare inventive genius and almost reconstructed the art of conjuring, so numerous were his inventions. For half a century after his death his successors drew upon Pinetti's inventions and repertory for their programs.

Houdini

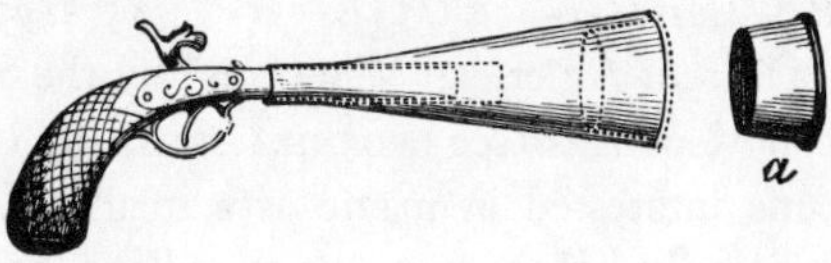

FIG. 1

According to the late Sydney W. Clarke, an authority on conjuring history, FAWKES dominated magic in the first half of the 18th century, and Pinetti dominated the second half.

PISTOL This consists of two parts, that is, an ordinary pocket-pistol, and a conical tin funnel, measuring about five inches across its widest diameter, and tapering down to a tube of such a size as to fit easily over the barrel of the pistol. (Fig. 1) This tube is continued inside the cone, and affords a free passage for the charge, which consists of powder only. Any object which is apparently to be fired from the pistol is pressed down between the outside of this tube and the inside of the tin cone, where it remains wholly unaffected by the explosion. The outside of the cone is nickeled, the tube and the rest of the interior always being black.

PLANT A confederate or stooge in the audience, put there either to hand in a prepared article (also known as a plant) when the performer asks to borrow something, or to play some prearranged part in a trick—writing a known question on a slip of paper for the ONE-AHEAD GAG, or conniving at some SWITCH that he is supposed to guard against, as in one version of SAWING A WOMAN IN TWO.

Magicians in general consider it beneath their dignity, if not downright unethical, to use plants. If magic is regarded as a battle of wits between performer and audience, a plant is certainly an unfair advantage. From the standpoint of sheer entertainment, plants are not quite so objectionable except that the audience feels peculiarly defrauded if the secret does happen to leak out.

Practically speaking, the need for a plant is about the worst technical drawback a trick can have; the usefulness of the effect is reduced to a fraction of what it would otherwise be.

On the other hand, some of the most successful professional magicians have used plants at times; in any given case, the performer will have to make his own decisions.

POCHETTE (See under COSTUME)

POWELL, FREDERICK EUGENE (1857-1938), American magician, chosen "Dean of American Magicians" by the Society of American Magicians (see ORGANIZATIONS) in his old age. He became interested in magic as a small boy, appeared professionally before he went to college, and then became a mathematics instructor at Virginia Military Institute. He later returned to magic, touring the United States, Canada, Mexico, Australia, and New Zealand. His great asset was his genial, polished stage presence. He was a member of the Triple Alliance (LEROY, FOX, and Powell).

PRACTICE AND REHEARSAL Nearly every sound writer on magic has emphasized the amount of practice necessary to make a magician. Magic books of another kind have boasted that they contained tricks which could be performed without practice. Modern educational psychologists have discovered that the truth lies between the extremes.

Unintelligent practice may simply form bad habits, and do more harm than good; but every amateur of a month's experience knows that showing a trick without practice is the sure road to disaster.

The editor of this volume prefers to distinguish between *practice* and *rehearsal.* Practice is purely manual, an exercise in some sleight or the operation of apparatus. Rehearsal is more largely mental—the planning, stage management, and PRESENTATION of a trick.

The first stage in either practice or rehearsal (and the one most generally neglected) is to gain a thorough understanding of what must be done. Must the top half of the pack be put underneath? Or the lower half on top? Or must the halves be turned face to face?

The next step, the vital one to the learner, is to understand *how* you will do it. Do you hold the coin between first and second fingers, or between second and third? Do you pull the end of the silk through the loop from behind or in front? This is the point where illustrations are of most value in a magic book. It is also, the psychologists have discovered, the point where wrong practice and bad habits generally start.

The simple class of trick that can be done "without practice" is in fact self-working once the instructions have been really grasped. But this must not lead you to attempt the trick without rehearsal.

Rehearsal starts where practice leaves off. Once you know how to work a trick, and have learned the necessary motions, you must begin the more important process of learning to perform it. You must memorize the prearrangement, the sequence of moves, the MISDIRECTION—in short, the

ROUTINE. You must combine your PATTER and the COMEDY, if there is any in the trick. And after the tricks and the routine have been mastered, you must rehearse an entire act or PROGRAM. This is not so much for the sake of the manipulation as to straighten you out in your stage-management—to teach you where things are and which way to turn at any given moment. You can spoil a perfectly done trick by searching for a LOAD or falling over your own feet.

The chief step in learning a trick, then, is to understand it and memorize it.

Perhaps the beginning magician will be surprised to know that actual practice can be overdone. Among the few things definitely known about the psychology of learning is that "motor learning"—practising motions—is most efficiently accomplished by frequent periods of practice with intervening rests. Even a rest of a minute or two every twenty minutes will speed your acquisition of a sleight. People differ in the length of time they can profitably practise without interruption; the one general point is, don't drive yourself. Jack Merlin, a great card manipulator, said in his invaluable book, ". . . *and a Pack of Cards*," "Practise is something I cannot resist. I practise because I enjoy it. When I force myself to it, I accomplish nothing. The proper method, especially for a beginner, is to take a sleight and dissect it. Take each phase of the move, and strive to accomplish the sleight with only such movement as is absolutely necessary and, at the same time, seek a plausible explanation to cover it." An English magician, Robertson-Keene, wrote, "There is such a thing as learning a thing too well. I have frequently back-palmed cards so continually that my grip and control of them were visibly lessened, and I have found that moderation is necessary in this, as in all things. Personally I do not care to practise anything when I have once learnt to do it to my satisfaction, as I find that public performance keeps me fit and practised enough."

Of course amateurs who give few shows do need to keep their hand in by playing with coins or cards.

"A plateau in the learning curve" is the psychologist's technical way of saying that during the process of learning anything you always reach a point where you seem to be making no progress. In learning a sleight, this "plateau" often comes at the point where you are trying to eliminate TALKING. At any rate, this discouraging stone wall is a recognized and inevitable step in whatever you learn, so don't let it stop you; it will be overcome quite suddenly.

"Dissecting" a sleight brings up the question of learning an action one part at a time. Some people learn better this way, some do not. The one general rule is that you should not practise the first part, then the first and second, then the first and second and third. This emphasizes the early stages far too much.

As is mentioned in the article on MUSIC, it is an excellent idea to practise manipulation to the radio, taking care to perform the secret moves off-beat.

The last step, after a trick has been well practised and well rehearsed, is to time it. In building a program, you absolutely must know how long each trick in your repertoire takes you to do.

The PALMING of coins and small objects can be practised at odd moments with your hand in a side coat pocket to forestall the inevitable dropping of the coin. *H. H.*

PRESENTATION (See also CHILDREN'S SHOWS; COMEDY; PATTER; PRACTICE; PROGRAMS; PSYCHOLOGY)

Rules of Presentation

1. Never set aside any accepted rule unless it is absolutely necessary to do so for some clearly defined reason.

2. Always endeavor to form an accurate conception of the point of view most likely to be adopted by a disinterested spectator.

3. Avoid complexity of procedure, and never tax either the patience or the memory of an audience.

4. Never produce two simultaneous effects, and let no effect be obscured by any subsidiary distraction.

5. Let each magical act represent a complete, distinct, and separate entity, comprising nothing beyond one continuous chain of essential details, leading to one definite effect.

6. Let every accessory and incidental detail be kept well within the picture and in harmony with the general impression which is intended to be conveyed.

7. Let nothing occur without an apparently substantial cause, and let every potential cause produce some apparently consequent effect.

8. Always remember that avoidable defects cannot be justified.

9. Always remember that a plea of justification is, ordinarily, an acknowledgment of error, and, consequently, demands every possible reparation.

10. Cut your coat according to your cloth, but spare no pains in the cutting, or your procedure cannot be justified.

11. Always remember that a notable surprise is incapable of repetition; and that the repetition of an effect, of any kind whatever, cannot create surprise.

12. A minor conception ordinarily demands the cumulative effect of repetition; a conception important in itself should, usually, create a distinct surprise.

13. The simultaneous presentation of two independent feats is permissible when one of them is associated with cumulative effect and the other results in a final surprise.

14. Unless good reason can be shown, never explain, *upon the stage*, precisely what you are about to accomplish.

15. When presenting an effect of pure transition, the first and most important essential is to avoid every possible cause of distraction.

16. When an effect of transition ends with a sudden revelation or surprise, the course of transition should usually be punctuated by actions or sounds leading up to and accentuating the final impression.

17. In every effect of pure transition, the beginning and end of the process involved should be distinctly indicated.

18. In each presentation, the procedure should lead up to a culminating point of interest, at which point the magical effect should be produced, and after which nothing magically interesting should occur.

19. When a presentation includes a series of effects, the final effect should represent the true climax, and the preceding effects the steps by which that climax is reached.

20. No magician should ever present in public any magical feat in which the procedure cannot be, or has not been, adapted to his own personal characteristics and abilities.

21. Never attempt in public anything that cannot be performed with the utmost ease in private.

22. Never present in public any performance which has not been most perfectly rehearsed, first in detail and, finally, as a whole.

Without adequate presentation there can be *no* art in magic. The final purpose of the art is the presentation of its effects; and until those effects are presented, the art itself cannot be perfected. Therefore, it is in this department of his art that the magician, as it were, puts the coping-stone upon the edifice erected by his skill and labor. On the manner in which that final work is carried out will depend the ultimate making or marring of the whole structure. Hence the supreme necessity, in connection with magical presentation, for obtaining a thorough knowledge of such general principles as may be derived from experience and logical reasoning.

The subject is admittedly one of extreme complexity, and simply bristles with controversial details. It can never be reduced to even the semblance of an exact science, but must be dealt with upon broad lines, capable of general application. Still, even when we confine our attention to simple generalities and allow a wide margin of elasticity in the few principles which may be established, there are many valuable truths to be ascertained by discussing the subject.

The personal characteristics of a performer should be considered carefully. A striking personality is an accidental advantage, and may be of great assistance in the practice of art; yet, in itself, it is not art, but chance. There are many performers who, without the possession of attractive personality or natural distinction, contrive to make their work effective in the highest degree—to hold the attention and gain the appreciation of their audiences, completely and invariably. Now that, clearly, *is* art.

On the other hand, there are men of charming personality who can never render their efforts convincing to an audience in spite of the natural advantages they possess. This indicates that striking personality alone is of little value.

In either case, there is just one thing lacking without which success is impossible—the knowledge of how to adapt personal qualifications to public service, that is, to present what is shown in a way that will appeal to the average spectator. An attractive personality is a good thing to possess; so, also, is technical ability. But neither of these good qualities, singly or in conjunction, will make the performer an artist. Something more is necessary: *he must understand the proper method of displaying his qualifications.*

The two prime factors in presentation, then, are personality and procedure, and upon their mutual adaptation to a definite purpose the artistic success of any performer must ultimately depend. They are both valuable factors, and usually they are variable within wide limits. The greater their variability, the wider will be the performer's range of efficiency, and the more numerous his opportunities for achieving success. This means that the higher a performer's ability as an actor, the greater will be his qualifications as a magician.

Conversely, the greater the diversity of procedure available in connection with a magical effect, the more readily may its presentation be made to harmonize with the personal characteristics of the performer. In this case the effect becomes more generally available to magicians as a body, because the procedure can easily be modified to suit various individualities.

However good an effect may be, and however desirable its inclusion in the performer's repertoire, he should reject it altogether if its presentation involves any essential feature which he cannot readily provide. If the necessary "business" includes either important details or general methods at variance with the artist's stage presence, mentality, or personal aptitude, he should throw aside all idea of attempting the presentation. Likewise, if an effect calls for any skill which the performer has not acquired, he should make good the deficiency before he tries the thing in public. If the acquisition of that essential skill is beyond his capability, he should sacrifice the production.

No two men are precisely alike in constitution or capability; therefore, no two men can exhibit any artistic accomplishment in identical manner and equally well. This is especially true in relation to magic. There is no valid reason why any man should form a mistaken estimate of his own capabilities, or experience a moment's doubt as to what he should or should not present in public.

Anything that cannot be done with facility cannot be done properly. Yet some magicians often disregard that fact. The spectacle of a performer attempting to present in public magical feats which obviously have not passed beyond the stage of difficulty in private practice, is by no means unusual.

An audience subjected to such an ordeal cannot fail to be either distressed or moved to sarcastic laughter. So far as the performer's success is concerned, it does not matter which of those two results is produced; both are equally disastrous. A magician should be able to make his audience think and feel as he chooses, not as accident may decide. He may excite laughter or arouse sympathy, but the impressions his spectators receive should be due to an interest in what he is presenting, and not to his own shortcomings. The audience should be made to laugh with him, not at him; to grieve in sympathy with his artistic suggestions, not in pity for his inartistic failures.

In connection with art of every kind, there are many things which are open to question. There is, however, one point upon which no question can be raised, and no dispute is possible: no one can achieve artistic success without great and persistent effort. Those who think otherwise, and act up to their convictions, are almost certain to fail. Year after year, such men come and go.

In magic, above all other arts, the phrase "all right on the night" has no place. Whatever is not entirely right before the night arrives will be found all wrong as sure as fate. It is an experience common to all magicians to find that, when producing a magical effect in public for the first time, everything that *can* go wrong *will* go wrong.

Speed in presentation is a most important point. Some performers can fill up two hours with half a dozen simple tricks. Others can rattle off a score of big effects in as many minutes. Each class of performer doubtless thinks his own method of presentation the best that can be devised. So it may be—for him.

Each particular method of presentation, in point of showmanship, has certain advantages. The rapid method undoubtedly has the advantage of giving the spectators plenty of magic for their money. The slow method, on the other hand, gives the performer ample opportunity for getting acquainted with his spectators and making them thoroughly interested in his work. In completely interesting and carrying conviction to the minds of his audience, a magician unquestionably fulfils the expectations of the public.

From an artistic standpoint, however, each of these methods has its disadvantage. The rapid method imposes so much strain on the attention of the audience that they cannot completely appreciate each effect, whereas the slow method does not sufficiently occupy the minds of the spectators. Both methods are lacking in certain artistic essentials.

Any presentation which leaves an impression of either indistinctness or over-elaboration has a very serious defect; the fact that a performance lacks one or another of the qualities which the public expects a public entertainment to possess is, in itself, sufficient to condemn the method of presentation adopted.

From a magical entertainer, the public expects two things—magic and entertainment. The man who gives the public plenty of magic, but serves it up in such hot haste that his audience has no time to digest it, merely surfeits the spectators with that particular requirement without satisfying their other expectations. He occupies their attention more than enough, but he does not entertain them as they rightly expect to be entertained. On the other hand, the performer who spins out his magical business displays a similar fault. The spectators may be greatly entertained by the performance, but when it is all over they will feel dissatisfied because they have not obtained what they paid their money to see. In such conditions the final effect is as incomplete and imperfect as when people have been allowed too little time for appreciation.

Then there seems to be little doubt as to the kind of standard to be adopted in this respect. The rapid method may suit some performers well, especially those who either lack repose or dispense with PATTER. The slow method may recommend itself to those whose strong point is either a "gift of gab" or a special ability in holding an audience. The question of personality must be allowed considerable weight in such questions.

The skilled magician who has no special ability as an entertainer is bound to rely for his ultimate success upon a rather rapid method of presentation. The man whose skill is that of an entertainer in the ordinary sense, rather than that of a specialist in magic, has to rely upon his general ability more than upon his magical effects. In his case, the comparatively slow method of presentation is essential to success.

A magical performance must contain sufficient magic to fulfil the expectations of the audience, and the audience must have time to understand, to consider, and to appreciate the successive items presented or the final impression will be confused and imperfect. True art and good policy alike point to the middle course as being best, and to the wisdom of keeping that course, so far as circumstances will permit. *N. M. & D. D.*

Dariel Fitzkee's *Showmanship for Magicians* deserves close attention by every ambitious performer.

PRODUCTIONS (See under: HAT TRICK; JAP BOX; ORGAN PIPES; PHANTOM TUBE; SHOWER OF SWEETS; SILK TRICKS; TAMBOURINE)

PROFONDE (See under COSTUME)

PROGRAMS (See also CHILDREN'S SHOWS; COMEDY; MUSIC; NIGHT-CLUB SHOWS; PRACTICE AND REHEARSAL; PRESENTATION; SILENT ACTS; STAGE SETTINGS; TABLE TRICKS; VEST-POCKET MAGIC)

The building of a program is more important to the performing magician than any one trick; yet it usually gets little attention from either performers or writers.

The *opening effect* must be carefully chosen, because it is the performer's introduction to his audience. It sets the tone for the whole act. The opening effect should be striking and quickly winning; no explanations or VOLUNTEERS must be used to delay it. A few of the good opening effects are: AFGHAN BANDS; BALL MANIPULATION, and the MULTIPLYING BILLIARD BALLS; Card FLOURISHES (see CARD MANIPULATION); CHINESE WANDS; CIGARETTE MANIPULATION; COIN MANIPULATION (but hardly the MISER'S DREAM, which takes the performer among the audience); FLOWER IN BUTTONHOLE; GOLDFISH BOWLS; LOTA (not an effect in itself); SILK TRICKS—bare-hand productions, knots, knot that unties itself—SYMPATHETIC SILKS, THIMBLE productions, and any small, quick production, but not large-scale productions, which should be saved for later in the act; ROPE TRICKS; TORN AND RESTORED PAPER; WAND from purse. For some acts and some audiences a quick SUCKER GAG that calls for no explanation is a good beginning. Quick vanishes are just as good as small productions.

In constructing the program, common sense should be used in avoiding effects that look too much alike—the cut and restored rope and TURBAN don't belong in the same show. In a card act, tricks calling for a card to be chosen should at least be alternated with effects that do not, such as the FOUR-ACE TRICK.

Common sense also requires that you adapt the size of the articles you use to the size of the audience. The people in the back row of a large audience cannot see such things as pennies, which may be the very staple of close-up work. With a large audience, you must talk louder, use bigger props, and *go slower* than with a few friends gathered around you.

For the performer's own benefit it is necessary to arrange the effects so that LOADS and GIMMICKS can be managed smoothly, not overcrowding SERVANTES and BLACK ART wells. For technical reasons, too, a single principle must not be overworked; one black art effect, one trick with a THREAD is enough in a short show. All of this positively must not, however, keep the whole program from building up to a climax. Each trick must in some way be a little better than the last.

Few amateurs will be doing a full evening's show, but in any case the advice of a professional, Fu Manchu (see BAMBERG) may be passed on. A full show requires an intermission. Fu Manchu believes that the next-to-closing effect in the first part should be something spectacular, something with box-office pull, which people will talk about during the intermission; it should be followed with something quick and flashy.

After the intermission, you have presumably established yourself on a friendly footing with the audience; this is a good time for something leisurely, such as a MIND-READING effect. From that point forward, however, the program must build up again, faster and faster, bigger and bigger, to close with a big bang.

Whether the show is a full evening or a five-minute IMPROMPTU series, the *finale* must be the most sensational thing you can do. A medium-sized show may close with one ILLUSION. A big production, leaving the stage piled high, is a good finish. For a manipulative routine, many of the same effects that are good to open with are also good to close with, if given a little more build-up—cigarette productions, vanishes that leave the stage clear, and the like. In short, the last effect must be something that justifies a *ta-da* from the orchestra.

There are two methods of passing from one trick to the next: having each effect merge into a new one, silks dyed and then changed into a billiard ball, which multiplies and changes into a card; and chopping off each trick at the end, and turning to the next with a fresh attack. A short act, particularly a silent one, favors the first procedure. In a long show it is, says Fu Manchu, "bad for balance." Although the stage wait after each trick of Professor Hoffmann's day has gone to well-deserved oblivion, the audience still needs some sort of breathing space, some punctuation in the show. The performer may lose a lot of his hard-earned applause if he slips imperceptibly from one good trick to the next.

So much for the choice of tricks in a program. Another important consideration is time—the time for each trick, and the length of the whole show. Putting aside the full evening, JOHN MULHOLLAND's rule is, "The larger the audience, the shorter the show." A scheduled platform appearance should seldom run over twenty minutes. Many excellent NIGHT-CLUB and vaudeville acts run only six or eight minutes; in night-clubs they can never run over fifteen minutes, and seldom over seven or eight.

As mentioned elsewhere, the final step in PRACTICE AND REHEARSAL should be the timing of each complete trick you learn. In the business of arranging programs, says Jasper MASKELYNE, "see that you time yourself properly. If you find that you can do six tricks in half an hour, do not include all six if you have to rush them. In calculating time, do not forget the moments spent in making your entrance, introducing the show and yourself, and making your exit. This may not take long, but the period it does take will probably preclude you from doing the sixth trick. On the other hand, always have another trick all ready in case you are allowed one encore. And in your programs add two or three items that can be used if you are asked to go on again, as sometimes happens at a dinner where you are given twelve minutes first and ten minutes later on if you are liked."

Even for offhand performance, Maskelyne suggests arranging all your tricks into set programs. The programs will be for different purposes—at the card table, dinner table, at a party with fifteen or twenty people, a formal act with the audience seated in rows; and they should be graded in length from five minutes to two hours. You can write out each program on a sheet from a loose-leaf notebook, and number them from 1 upward.

Each program sheet in your notebook should list not only the tricks, but all the necessary props and preparations, including the MUSIC if you have it. The short, impromptu acts, of course, you will soon memorize; indeed they are hardly more than ROUTINES; but anything requiring apparatus and preparation should be laid out in detail. Even though your ten-minute children's act is simply your fifteen-minute platform act with two tricks left out, you should type up a whole new program and prop list for each. Then you can decide on a show for a given purpose, and be all packed for it in a matter of minutes. There is no more helpful single short-cut you can take in your magical career.

Printed programs for distribution to the audience are less common than they used to be. If you have one, or if your tricks are being billed as part of an advertised show, try to pick names for the effects that will be attractive and tempting without betraying what is to happen. "The Twentieth-Century Handkerchief Trick" is a poor title because it does not tell enough to be tempting; "The Multiplying Billiard Balls" gives away too much, and may lead to detection.

This is a good place for a few remarks on the subject of novelties. Novelty of effect is always desirable in a trick; novelty of method is merely a private safeguard to the performer. But no kind of novelty is recommendation enough by itself. Building, rehearsing, and using a program is a long process that demands the best a magician has in him. A perfected program should never be upset to insert the latest novelty unless that novelty is manifestly better as a trick, and better suited to the performer and his program, than the effect it replaces.

Indeed the simple element of novelty *to the performer* should be almost wholly discounted. Novelty *to the audience* is important; but audiences as a whole have seen so few tricks that the RISING CARDS will be new to three spectators out of five. If you perform it well, it is intrinsically better than almost any card novelty you can buy. So try not to get tired of the good tricks simply because they are old to you.

This brings up an excellent. and neglected, source of program material: old books and magic magazines. Some of the very best tricks are slumbering forgotten in the pages of *Modern Magic*, Sachs's *Sleight-of-Hand*, and countless books of "parlor magic." On the radio, jokes from one to fifteen years of age are old; after that, they come out of hiding again. Tricks probably follow about the same cycle. That is one of the reasons why "latest novelties" have been eschewed in the present volume.

Max Holden's pamphlet, *Programmes of Famous Magicians*, will repay your study. *H. H.*

PSYCHOLOGY (See also COMEDY; FORCING; HISTORY; PRESENTATION)

So many different strands of psychology run through magic that it is impossible even to recognize them all, let alone list and expound them. In the conscious (or what should be conscious) exploitation of psychology by the conjurer, however, there are two main branches, each including various sub-branches.

The psychology of *deception* is what the magician calls *misdirection*—the quirks and tendencies of the human mind that make magic tricks possible at all. Probably the magician's chief reliance here is association. After two mental images have been presented together once or twice, the human mind automatically associates them: the sight of a knife-handle is immediately associated with the blade that goes with it; the sight of a tossing motion instantly provokes the image of a ball moving upward. Nearly all SLEIGHT-OF-HAND rests on this foundation: the magician makes a movement that produces, by association, the image of a familiar result; only he contrives in fact to bring about a result that is not normally associated with the original motion. Well-conceived APPARATUS relies heavily on association. A BIRD-CAGE is automatically associated with rigidity; the magician does far more harm than good if he describes the cage as solid, for he merely interferes with the process of association. Left alone, the audience will never dream that actually the bird-cage collapses. A hat is fundamentally a much better vehicle for PRODUCTIONS than any of the ingenious contraptions made for the purpose: hats have an association of simplicity, whereas the various boxes and tubes, being unfamiliar, have no association at all. Any article obviously made expressly for magicians is a puzzle more than a trick. Unless association says, "There's nothing wrong with this," the spectator must assume that there is something wrong, only he can't find it. The failure of association is the chief special difficulty in giving CHILDREN'S SHOWS: children have not yet learned to make the wide variety of quick associations necessary to adults.

The magician may also create his own associations. The RATTLE BARS are unfamiliar objects, but the performer soon builds up the association of "one bar, rattle, two bars, silent." Once this association has had time to sink in, he can lead the audience astray by picking up one of the silent bars, and producing the noise now associated with the rattling bar. Any series of unfamiliar objects or actions, if sufficiently prolonged, will build up an association that allows the magician to slip in a FAKE or a false move. *Consistency* is the best way of creating this association.

Closely related to association are the phenomena of *attention.* In the first place, normal attention has a narrow focus—one hand at a time, for instance, unless the observer is some distance off and both hands are moving. If attention is forcibly scattered, the only result is confusion. The focus of attention will move very quickly from one place to another, as in a tennis game or in throwing a coin from right to left hand; but at any given instant it is on one spot only. We have already seen how sleight-of-hand rests upon association; and association is what shifts the attention. Actually, of course, the attention of the audience is riveted, say, to the coin. Attention follows the spot where association says the coin is. Consciously or not, the successful performer picks a moment when attention has been forced away to palm the coin in his right hand; the association of "closed left fist, coin inside" makes the final disappearance a surprise.

An important form of association is that of time between cause and effect. The magician says "Pass!", and the audience (even though it really knows better) assumes that the bottle and glass changed places just then. Secret moves can be made with impunity by simply not competing for the spectator's attention—by acting before you tell him what you are going to do. It is even subtler, though less frequently practicable, to make the secret move *after* his attention has been disarmed, when association has led him to believe the trick is finished. "Catching" an object in your obviously empty fist, and then transferring it to the other hand, where it has been palmed all along, is an example of this.

Two other factors are important in the misleading of attention: imitation, and what may be called intensity. Imitation is thought by some psychologists to be a basic human instinct; at any rate it may be used in setting up a motor reflex. The prank of collecting a crowd on a street corner by simply standing and gazing upward is well known. Wherever the magician obviously looks, the audience will look also. Whether this is only a special form of association is not for a mere magician to decide, but the underlying fact is unquestionable, and is exploited by every magician half a dozen times in each trick he shows.

The principle of intensity simply means that the entire universe is competing constantly for the attention of every individual. Association is a sort of armor against this competition, because once association has pigeonholed a fact, the attention can move on. As John Mulholland points out in *The Art of Illusion*, the letters ELPO NITNAT SNOC challenge and defeat the attention: they are almost impossible to memorize. The same letters, reversed as CONSTANTINOPLE, are disposed of by association in a moment. The game of anagrams is the exact opposite of conjuring. It stimulates the player to spread his attention, to seek out new associations. Magic depends on restricting the spectator to the old associations, and preventing new ones.

Intensity seems to have been lost in the shuffle for a moment. We have seen that there is tremendous competition for a spectator's attention. Intensity is a method of winning this competition: the loudest noise, the fastest motion, the brightest color will capture the attention if given an even chance. The amateur magician finds this out when he learns to move his empty left fist away, and keep his right hand motionless with the palmed coin. The gesture of pointing focuses attention doubly, by intensity of motion and by imitation. To sum up, only two things can save any spectator from following the wrong hand in the coin pass when the performer looks, points, and moves his left hand. One thing is a definite knowledge of the trick, and the other is awkwardness in the performer—a clumsy, belated palm, or lack of conviction in his movements.

The psychology of memory. which is not quite so important to the magician, is a fusing of attention and association. You cannot remember an event correctly unless you have been paying attention in the first place, and have been able to form associations in the second. Remember the example of "Constantinople." This is why the layman's description of a trick he has seen is worthless. He almost never remembers *everything* he saw, and he *never* makes the correct associations, or else he would have seen through the trick. Furthermore, both association and intensity lead us to exaggerate in memory. Vanish four or five apples, and reproduce them from the air, and your average spectator will quite honestly remember that you caught a good half-bushel of apples from the air, and heaped them up on the stage.

Memory is purposive. Anything that strikes us as irrelevant we forget. This gives the magician a second line of defense, not so much in creating illusion as in evading detection. False starts, the conjurer's second thoughts, the times when Professor Hoffman tells you to say, "But stay! Perhaps you would rather I made it pass invisibly"—all these seem meaningless, and are forgotten, though really the key point of the trick is there.

This peculiarity of memory has been called a second line of defense, and (unlike the more direct misdirecting of attention) it can be overworked. One or two apparent failures, one or two "indicative gestures" are plenty in a short act. Otherwise they cease to be irrelevant, and the audience forms an association with them.

The other great branch of psychology necessary to the magician is covered at some length under PRESENTATION: the art of *pleasing* the audience with the tricks that misdirection has rendered puzzling. In this another aspect of attention plays its part: what psychologists call attention span. This means in theory that attention is limited in length as well as breadth; and in practice that you must give the audience frequent rests from close attention. Normal children must not be expected to keep their attention on one subject for more than perhaps five minutes at a time. If a child can, it is usually a sign of something wrong. The adult attention span, naturally, is longer, but the magician must never tax it, or even approach it. Magic, to be enjoyed, needs a cheerful, carefree spectator. Fatigue of his attention and the fatigue from an uncomfortable chair are equally disastrous to your show.

Therefore a trick that demands even a moderate span of attention must (to justify its existence) be a bigger and more striking effect than a trick that is over in a second. The INDIAN MANGO TRICK earns its time in a program; the RING ON STICK cannot be allowed to take half as long, though it is an excellent effect in its own class.

Physiological psychology—the mechanics of the five senses—is not so important in magic as one might suppose. The eye is difficult to deceive unless we include such extensions of optics as the MIRROR PRINCIPLE. The sense of touch may be misled by pressing a small, hard object like a coin into a spectator's palm, and making him close his hand quickly. It will be a second or two before the feeling of pressure wears off. Taste and smell seldom come into play in magic, and are deceived by magicians far less than by confectioners and perfumers.

Of all the senses, hearing is the most vulnerable to deception and the most useful to the magician. The important point is that hearing is not directional: your ears tell you only that a sound comes from roughly your right or your left, and nothing more, unless you turn your head and bring one ear to bear on a sound more strongly than the other. Ventriloquism is based wholly on this vagueness in the sense of hearing.

A special branch of magical psychology is psychological FORCING. A spectator asked to choose a number from one to ten picks seven more often than any other one number; asked to pick a number from ten to twenty, he is likely to say fifteen. Of five objects in a row stretching diagonally away from the spectator, he will generally take the second. People suddenly asked to name a color generally say red. Of three objects in a row, people usually pick the middle one, following the line of least resistance. If you step up before a good-sized audience, and ask them to call the name of a card, the chances are strongly in favor of at least one person's calling for the ace of hearts. This fact is exploited by steaming the stamp off a new pack of cards, removing the ace of hearts, and replacing the deck in its case with the stamp intact. The pack can be tossed to the audience before you start, and your own ingenuity is the only limit to the stunning effect you can create by producing the ace of hearts elsewhere.

In forcing one of two objects, you can often avoid resorting to EQUIVOQUES by remembering that the "force" position is at the end of the series: "Will you choose blue—or red?" The emphasis is on red. The eye of the Occidental spectator automatically travels from left to right, and comes to rest on the object at his right; if he is to see both, he must pass on from the left-hand one, and he will probably not make the extra effort to pass back again from right to left.

The psychology of COMEDY, so intimately related to magic tricks themselves, is treated under the appropriate heading. *H. H.*

PUBLICITY In purpose, publicity is advertising for the magician. In effect, it is better than any other form of advertising (see BUSINESS METHODS). In method, most magicians gravely misunderstand it, and thus fail to get it when they could.

Publicity depends directly on newspaper and magazine reporters and editors. Every magician, even the most resolutely amateur, should cultivate the friendship of journalists; this much is obvious. But friendship alone is not enough, and that is where most publicity-seekers (in the good sense) fall down. A newspaper man's living depends on his printing what his own particular readers want to read—what will interest, impress, or move them. It would be quite futile for him, even through friendship, to print something his audience did not care about; there would be no publicity, because his readers would merely skip it, and become non-readers.

The conjurer's problem, therefore, is to convince journalists, whether friends or strangers, that something about him is interesting to the reading public. Actually his tricks themselves are usually interesting if well described; but editors not unnaturally feel that such descriptions belong in the advertising pages. It is up to the magician to prove that they deserve better.

In doing this he has two main resources, of which the more important is a small stock of impressive, ever-ready tricks. They need not be genuinely impromptu, but should seem so; they should be better and bigger than the average vest-pocket trick. MIND-READING effects that can be shown quickly are very good (see Annemann's *Practical Mental Effects* for several beauties); so are quick, striking COIN MANIPULATIONS, DOLLAR-BILL TRICKS, the SYMPATHETIC COINS, a very, very few CARD TRICKS—anything that can be worked close-up without fear of detection, and that has no flavor of apparatus, preparation, or laboriousness. Tricks involving liquor are made to order for publicity of the more jovial sort, but not when you are trying to break into the *Temperance Advocate* or a strange small-town weekly.

The other help you have in convincing the editor that your tricks are news is action photographs. You should have several good ones, pictures that you yourself would stop to look at if they showed someone else, and you were not a magician. City papers like to have exclusive photographs; if you give the *Times* one picture, you should at least give the *Gazette* a different one.

Another way of breaking into the news, not directly by your tricks, is to learn a repertoire of good anecdotes about yourself. *Warning:* This does not mean lifting stories from the lives of Robert-Houdin, Herrmann, Signor Blitz, Houdini, and John Mulholland, or even from the best joke books. It means taking true stories of your own, and learning to tell them well (see COMEDY).

One inviolable rule in dealing with journalists: don't lie! Only the truth is good enough to print; if a newspaper takes your word for a falsehood once, it will be the last time.

An excellent hint for the publicity-seeker is to study a standard textbook of journalism. Learn how a newspaper is put together, and, above all, *what makes news.* Man-bites-dog is not reliable even as a rule of thumb, but local-names-and-addresses is. The mayor, bitten by a dog, will get more publicity than you do for biting one. Anything you can tie up to a prominent local institution or citizen will get you publicity; your triumphs or even your defeats in a town twenty miles away will not.

The same rule applies to public challenges and similar publicity dodges. (See SALTING) When they work, they work because the *local* police chief, the *local* box factory, the *local* spiritualists have been defied to do better than the police chief, the box factory, the spiritualists of some other city. Incidentally, they sometimes work partly because the magician spends a lot of money in paid advertising of his challenge. The friendly way is almost always the best way.

Procedure in dealing with the press must vary. of course, according to performer, place, and publication. As an advertised attraction in a town or small city, you may expect your employer, or perhaps your agent, to have sent out notices to the papers. You may be important enough to call up the important editors (inform yourself carefully about them before you start), and suggest that they send a reporter to see you. If you are polite, friendly, and unpretending, they probably will. Your publicity tricks and your anecdotes then come into play, along with exclusive copies of your photographs.

If the editor is very hard-boiled, ask for an appointment to call on him, but make it very plain that you want literally just five minutes of his time. Once again, don't lie. *Be ready to leave in five minutes.* If you have mastered the art of dealing with journalists, he will probably keep you there for an hour; but put it on him. Make a real effort to leave as soon as you have exchanged civilities and shown one trick. You are trying to advertise yourself not only as a magician but as a pleasant person to know. Overselling loses far more sales than underselling, no matter what your merchandise; and newspaper editors have more sales resistance to high-pressure methods than almost any class of men you can name.

Robert Bernhard's *Publicity for Magicians* has a lot of useful information.

H. H.

PULLS (See also BIRD-CAGE; CARD VANISHERS; CIGARETTE MANIPULATION; SILK TRICKS)

A pull is a device for the vanishing of a small object by drawing it up the performer's sleeve or under his coat. There are many varieties of pull.

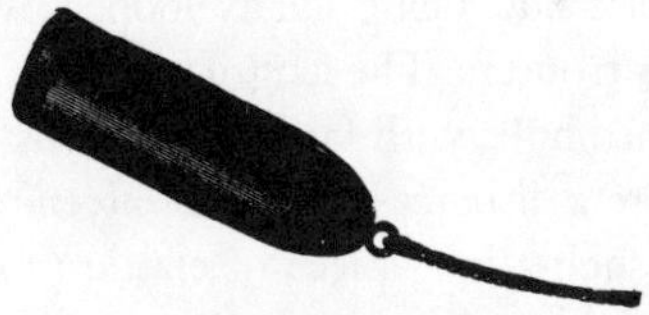

FIG. 1

One of the most perfect is known as the "Buatier Pull," after the ingenious performer who invented it. As applied to handkerchiefs, it consists of a cylindrical tin cup (Fig. 1), one to one and one-quarter inches in diameter, and two and one-half to three inches long, tapering at the closed end, and attached by the closed end to a silk cord, which passes up (say) the left sleeve, behind the back, and down the opposite sleeve of the performer, where it is made fast to the right wrist. The length of the cord is so adjusted that when the arms hang down at full length by the sides of the body, the tin cup lies about half way up the left forearm, though by bending the arms and slackening the cord, it may be brought into the hand at will.

When it is desired to use the Buatier pull to cause the disappearance of a handkerchief, the cup is got into the hand and PALMED, the performer standing (if the cup is in the *left sleeve*) with his left side toward the audience. Taking the handkerchief, he begins apparently to rub it between his hands, gradually working it into the cup with the second finger of his right hand, calling attention meanwhile to its gradual disappearance. When the whole of the handkerchief is safely stowed within the cup, he gives a forward lunge with both arms, at the same time relaxing his hold on the cup. The extension pulls the cord, and the cup is drawn up the sleeve, enabling the performer to show both hands completely empty.

The cup may be placed within either the right or left sleeve, as may suit the performer best; it may vary in shape or size, according to the object for which it is intended to be used. It was employed by its accomplished inventor (among other purposes) to cause the disappearance of a canary.

The aim of every true conjurer is to be able to produce the same effect by several different methods, so that, if foiled or suspected in the use of one of them, he may be able to fall back upon another.

To produce the bare-armed vanish, the tin cup is again called into use, but in a different way. The cord is in this case a piece of stout elastic, and passes through a small ring sewn to (say) the left armhole of the performer's vest. From there it passes behind his back (inside the vest), and around his waist on the opposite side, being finally looped over the central button of the waistband of his trousers. The length is arranged so that the cup will be drawn close to the armhole, with fairly strong tension, although it can be drawn out at pleasure to a distance of some eighteen to twenty inches from the body. The use of such a long piece of elastic (about three feet) is expressly designed for this purpose.

When the performer wishes to use the apparatus, he finds an opportunity to get the cup into his hand, and the rest is easy. The handkerchief is worked into the cup as described in the case of the sleeve fake. When it is all the way in, the performer makes a forward and backward movement of the hands; at the backward movement, he relaxes his hold of the cup, which flies under his coat lapel and up to the armhole, where it is effectively concealed.

The exact shape of the apparatus is a matter of taste. Its original shape was that of a tube, open at one end, but it is also made pear-shaped, with an oval opening at one side.

There is a trick involving the use of a spring pull, which secretly transfers a ring via the coat sleeves from the left hand into the right. This little contrivance is very useful.

Within a cylindrical bass drum (Fig. 2) is fixed a spring barrel, around which is coiled a catgut line, *a*, and which is wound up by drawing out this line. To one of the faces of the barrel is attached a ratchet wheel, between the teeth of which a pawl, attached to the upper end of the spring *b*, can be inserted, but is again withdrawn by pressing *e* (which is a movable arm, pivoted against the face of the drum) toward *b*. The outer end of *e* is wedge-

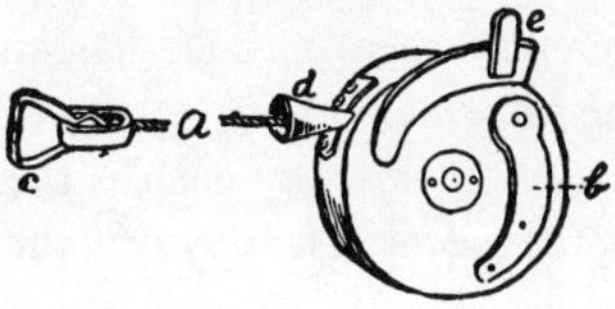

FIG. 2

shaped; when this is forced under the end of *b*, the pawl is lifted and the barrel released. To the free end of the gut line is attached a pair of spring nippers, *c*, which, when the apparatus is not in use, rest partially within the mouth of the funnel-shaped tube, *d*. A spring between the shorter arms of the nippers keeps their jaws closed so long as they are clear of the tube, but as soon as the shorter arms are drawn within, these are pressed together by the sides of the tube, and the jaws open.

The full length of the gut line is about five feet. It may be drawn out to this or any less extent, and fixed at that point by means of the pawl. The apparatus thus arranged is placed for use in the right trouser pocket. The line is carried across the back and down the left sleeve, the nippers hanging in the neighborhood of the wristband.

The performer desires, say, to vanish a silk handkerchief. He takes it by the center, letting the four corners hang down, and transfers it by the part he holds to the left hand. This hand meanwhile has got possession of the little nippers, and, by pressure on their shorter arms, has opened their jaws, between which he inserts the center of the handkerchief. The moment he releases the pressure of the fingers the jaws close, and the handkerchief is held securely.

The performer now places his right hand in the trouser pocket, and presses *e* under *b*, thereby withdrawing the pawl and causing the barrel to wind up the gut line. Meanwhile, standing with his left side toward the spectators, he slowly waves the left hand about, and while apparently merely gathering the handkerchief into the hand, allows it gradually to be drawn through the hand up the sleeve. As soon as it is quite free, the pull draws it across the back into the pocket. By elevating the arm, and so allowing the line to run freely, or by pressing the arm to the body, and thereby checking it, the speed at which the pull operates can be regulated at pleasure.

The performer continues the rubbing-away movement of his left hand for a moment or two after it is actually empty. Meanwhile the nippers have been pulled into the tube *d*, when the jaws open and release the handkerchief. The performer may then produce it from his pocket with his right hand, the left being shown empty.

The working of the trick in this way enables the conjurer to have the handkerchief marked by the spectators in any way they please, so as to prove that there is no substitution.

The apparatus may equally well be used to cause a ring to travel from one hand to the other.

The performer, with the apparatus in his right trouser pocket, and with the nippers secured between the fingers of his left hand or with their jaws closed on his shirt-cuff, borrows from different persons a couple of rings, the more exceptional in appearance the better. Showing a number of short ends of narrow ribbons of various colors, he invites a third person to choose one of them, and to tie the two rings together with it. Under pretense of examining the knot, he engages the ribbon in the little nippers, the cord, still slack, passing along the under side of his wrist.

With due precautions against any telltale exposure of the nippers, he shows the rings, held between the tips of his thumb and fingers. "However closely you may watch my hand, the rings will leave it and find their way into this pocket." He thrusts his right hand into his trouser pocket for a moment, as if merely to show which pocket he is referring to, and in that moment presses the little lever which releases the pull. He makes a rubbing movement with the fingers of his left hand, and under cover of this movement he lets the rings escape up his sleeve. A moment later he shows the hand empty, and produces the rings from the pocket on the opposite side.

Where the article vanished by the pull is not to be reproduced immediately, a different arrangement is sometimes adopted, the apparatus being attached by a belt to the performer's waist behind his back, underneath his coat; the mouth of the tube *d* is directed to the left armhole. The barrel is in this case started by means of a subsidiary pull, a piece of fine black cord attached to *e*, passing through a hole in the central screw, and finally brought around the right side and attached to one of the front suspender-buttons. By allowing the hand to rest for a moment on the hip (a perfectly natural position) the performer can get hold of the cord, tightening it slightly to start the pull. This arrangement allows the use of larger and stronger apparatus than could be used in the pocket.

Another excellent mechanical pull is practically identical in principle with the one just described, although different in many points of detail. Fig. 3 illustrates what may be called the front view, and Fig. 4 the back view, of the apparatus, which is of nickel-plated brass. The drum, clock-

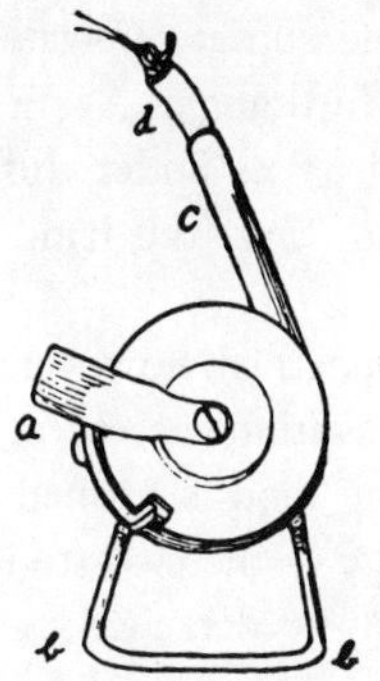

FIG. 3

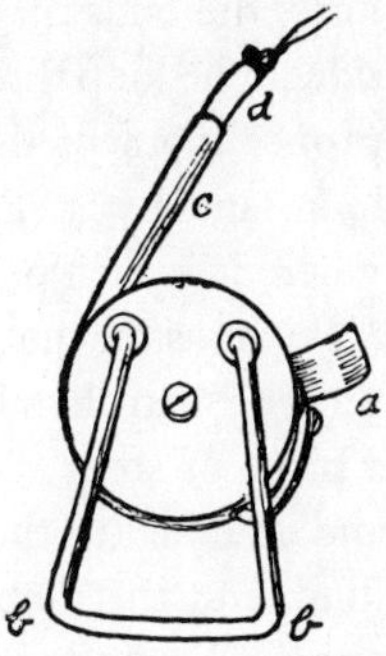

FIG. 4

barrel, cogwheel, and catch are retained, but the latter is withdrawn by pressure on a lever *a*, and the line is not of gut, but whipcord with a gut loop.

The vanisher is placed in position by means of a horseshoe-shaped wire loop *bb*, for the reception of which a special pocket is made in the vest, outside, close to the right armhole; the side shown in Fig. 4 is next to the body, and the lever *a* rests just within the armpit. In this position a very slight pressure of the arm against the body depresses the lever sufficiently to withdraw the catch and release the pull. The tube *c* comes just inside the sleeve, at the armhole; and the cord, which is in this case only about two feet long, passes, on leaving the tube, through an inch length of soft rubber *d*, which acts as a buffer on its return, the pull in this case being designed to act very rapidly. The spring is therefore made very strong, and brings back the cord with considerable force. The cord is knotted on the outside of the rubber, which breaks the violence of the shock.

The special object of this pull is to vanish a handkerchief instantly, though of course it may be used for other purposes. For this particular use, however, the nippers described in connection with the other pull are dispensed with, and replaced by a simple loop of thin gut, about six inches long. The handkerchief to be vanished is secretly passed through this to the middle, and doubled in half. If it is then held loosely in the hand and the pull is released, it flies up the sleeve with the rapidity of lightning.

There are one or two small modifications which may frequently be made with advantage in the direct or non-mechanical pull. In the case of the Buatier Pull, the cord was fastened by one end to the left wrist; it passed up the sleeve and ended in a little cylindrical cup, for the reception of the handkerchief or other article to be vanished. A valuable addition to this form of pull is a piece of flesh-colored silk thread, about twelve inches long, the ends of which are attached to the edges of the cup at opposite sides. The loop thus formed is passed over the second or third finger. At the proper moment the second finger of the opposite hand passes under this loop, and by a slight forward movement draws the cup into the hand, where it is then palmed for use as may be desired.

So far as the mere disappearance of handkerchiefs is concerned, however, the cup may be altogether dispensed with, the pull consisting merely of a piece of stout silk thread. At one end of this a running loop is formed. and attached to the right shirt-cuff. The cuff must be one of the two-stud kind, and the loop drawn over both studs so that it can be detached instantly. From the cuff the thread passes up the right sleeve, across the back next to the shirt, and out of the left armhole of the vest, the end being attached to the rear suspender-button on that side, but enough slack being left to form a short hanging loop just below the vest. Thus arranged, the thread creates no obstacle to the performer's movements.

When the pull is needed for use, the performer releases the running loop from the two studs with the opposite thumb, and passes it over the second and third fingers. In the course of his PATTER it is easy to pass the handkerchief as far as its center within the loop, after which the fingers are withdrawn, the handkerchief remaining in the hand. The thumb of the left hand is inserted in the bight of the silk thread on the opposite side; a quick downward movement draws it tight, and the handkerchief vanishes up the sleeve.

It will be found desirable to use the thread of two colors, flesh-color for the running loop, and black at the opposite end, joined at some intermediate point.

This appliance is frequently used in connection with the trick of vanishing a silk handkerchief from a glass lamp-chimney held between the two hands.

The running loop and stud arrangement is equally applicable to a rubber pull.

In another type of pull, a leather strap is buckled around the left arm, just above the elbow. On this runs a brass ring, to which is attached a piece of stout whipcord, two and a half feet long. At the free end of this is a loop of much finer cord, six inches long. These are "whipped" together so that there will be no knots to impede the perfect working of the pull.

The cord travels from the left arm across the back (outside the vest), and down the right sleeve. In order to keep the loop instantly available until wanted, and at the same time to leave his arms perfectly free, the performer may simply pass a spare handkerchief midway through the loop and allow it to be drawn up the sleeve. He has only to draw the handkerchief out of his sleeve (simultaneously passing the loop over his thumb), wipe his face with it, and place it in his pocket, to have the pull ready for action.

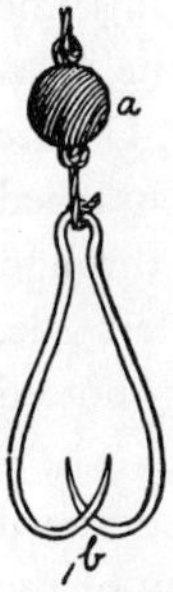

FIG. 5

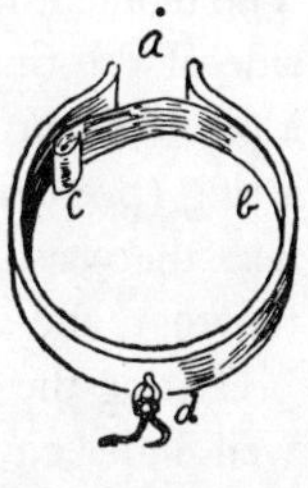

FIG. 6

Where in the course of a trick the performer desires openly to vanish a watch (either the original or a dummy which has temporarily represented it), this may be done neatly and effectively by means of a pull of silk elastic, one end being attached to the performer's vest, midway between the shoulders, and the other to a short piece of fine gut.

At the opposite end of this is a little wire clip with its points bent inward and crossing each other, as shown in Fig. 5. Just above the wire, secured by a knot above and below it, is a lead bullet *a*, with a hole through it. The length of the pull is adjusted so that the clip will lie normally midway up the forearm, or a little lower down.

When the arm is shortened by resting the hand on the hip, the appliance naturally falls lower and comes within reach of the hand, the bullet, which gives a better hold than the wire hook, being nipped between the finger and thumb. By passing the bow of the watch between the bent points of *b*, it is instantly and firmly secured. The watch is then professedly rubbed away to nothing between the hands, a sudden straightening of the arms, with simultaneous relaxation of the pressure of the hands, causing it to fly up the sleeve.

The performer should, of course, take the earliest available opportunity to retire and release the watch from its captivity, as its unexpected reappearance, dangling from the sleeve, would be distinctly objectionable.

Another appliance for the same purpose is known as the American vanisher. (Fig. 6) This is a flat metal ring one and one-half inches in diameter, and not unlike a key-ring, which indeed it resembles a good deal in principle.

At one part of its circumference it has a three-quarter inch opening *a*, the ends on either side being slightly curled back. Across this opening lies a piece of clock-spring, riveted at one end, *b*. The other end, *c*, is free, but presses firmly against the inner circumference of the ring.

If the bow of a watch is inserted in the opening and pressed against the spring, the end *c* gives way just enough to allow the passage of the bow. The moment it has passed *c*, it is securely threaded on to the ring. On the side of the ring opposite the opening is an eyelet, *d*. To this is attached a piece of cord elastic, the two ends of which are then threaded through a ring (preferably of ivory), sewn to the performer's vest on the left side, near the waist, and then carried to the opposite side of the body, knotted together, and slipped over one of the front suspender-buttons.

Getting the ring secretly into his left hand and keeping the elastic cord well under cover of his arm, the performer can easily slip the bow of the borrowed watch within the ring. Once secured, it is made, by extending the arms, to vanish under the coat, where it remains until the performer has an opportunity to leave the stage and remove it from the ring. *L. H.*

R

RAPPING HAND (See under SPIRIT EFFECTS)

RATTLE BARS (See under THREE-CARD TRICKS)

RATTLE BOX This useful and ingenious little piece of apparatus is an oblong mahogany box, with a sliding lid. Its dimensions are about three inches by two, and one inch in depth externally; internally it is only half that depth, and the end piece of the lid is of such depth as to be flush with the bottom. If a coin is placed in the box, and the box held in such a position as to slant downward to the opening, the coin will of its own weight fall into the hand that holds the box (Fig. 1), thus giving the performer possession of it without the knowledge of the audience.

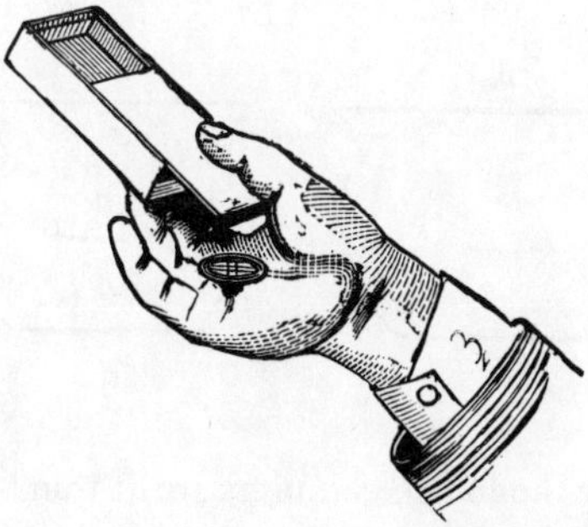

FIG. 1

Between the true and the false bottom of the box is placed a slip of zinc which, when the box is shaken laterally, moves from side to side, exactly simulating the sound of a coin shaken in the box. In its normal condition, however, this slip of zinc is held fast (and kept silent) by the action of a spring also placed between the two bottoms, but is released for the time being by pressure on a particular part of the outer bottom (the part in contact with the fingers in Fig. 1). A casual inspection of the box suggests nothing, except perhaps that its internal space is somewhat shallow in proportion to its external measurement.

The method of using it is as follows: the performer invites any person to mark a coin and place it in the box, which he holds for that purpose as shown in the illustration; the coin is thus no sooner placed in the box than it falls into his hand. Transferring the box to the other hand and pressing the spring, he shakes it to show by the sound that the coin is still there; then, leaving the box on the table, he prepares for the next phase of the trick by secretly placing the coin, which the audience believes to be still in the box, in any other place where he wishes it to be found, or makes such other disposition of it as may be necessary. Having done this, and having indicated the direction in which he is about to command the coin to pass, he once more shakes the box to show that the coin is still inside. Then, with the mystic word "Pass!" he opens the box, which is found empty, and shows that his commands have been obeyed. *L. H.*

REELS (See RISING CARDS)

RICE BOWLS This trick is popularly known by the name of the Chinese Rice Bowls, but this is a somewhat incorrect description. The trick in its original form is a specialty of EAST INDIAN conjurers.

FIG. 1

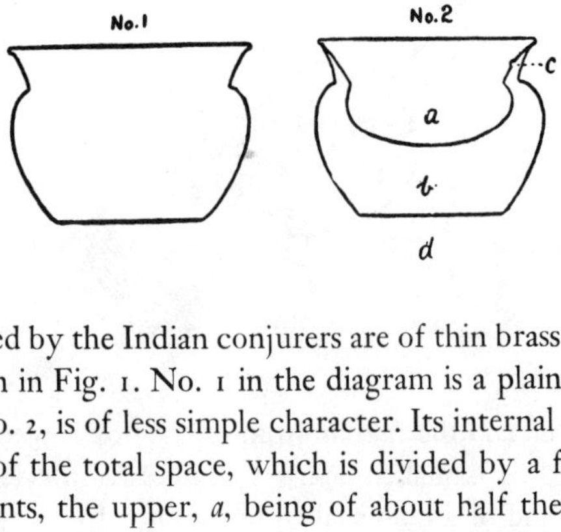

The bowls used by the Indian conjurers are of thin brass and of the shape shown in section in Fig. 1. No. 1 in the diagram is a plain, ordinary bowl; but the other, no. 2, is of less simple character. Its internal depth represents only one-third of the total space, which is divided by a false bottom into two compartments, the upper, *a*, being of about half the capacity of the lower, *b*. At the points *c* and *d* are minute holes. It is, in fact, a form of LOTA. The mouth of bowl No. 1 is a shade larger than that of No. 2, so that when turned mouth to mouth one shall slightly overlap the other; this prevents the liability to slip sideways which would arise if both were of exactly the same size.

In preparing for the trick, bowl No. 2 is immersed in a larger vessel of water until the compartment *b* has completely filled, the test of this being that air-bubbles cease to appear at the surface of the water. Before taking it out of the larger vessel, the operator closes the hole *c* by pressing a finger on it. He then takes the bowl out, holding it upside down, dries it inside and out with a cloth, and plugs the hole *d* with a pellet of soft wax. The finger may then be removed from *c*. If the bowl is properly filled, and the hole *d* duly plugged, there will be no escape of water, even though it remain inverted.

Having made these preparations beforehand, the performer comes forward with the two bowls on a tray. Both are turned upside down, one above the other: No. 1 is uppermost, as shown in Fig. 2. Putting down the tray, he takes the bowls, one in each hand, and clashes them together, mouth to mouth, after the manner of a pair of cymbals, producing the corresponding vibratory sound, although, actually, this is wholly produced by bowl No. 1, the liquid contents of No. 2 keeping that bowl practically silent. The spectators. seeing the bowls so freely handled, are convinced that they are empty; the more so because the performer, in the course of his manipulations, allows them a momentary glimpse of the interior of each. He may even, in a casual way, hand No. 1 for examination, meanwhile leaving No. 2 turned mouth downward on the table or tray.

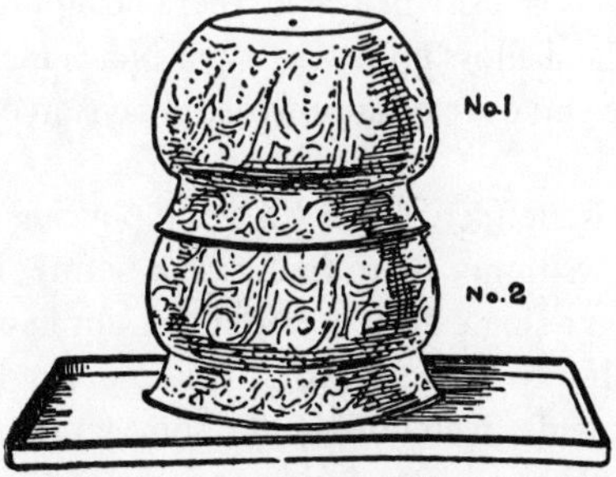

FIG. 2

Replacing No. 1, mouth upward, on the tray, he proceeds to fill it with rice. He levels the surface with his wand, or any other convenient instrument, and pours back any surplus rice from the tray into the receptacle from which it was taken. He then turns bowl No. 2 over bowl No. 1, mouth to mouth, and brings them forward between his hands, lifting No. 2 for a moment as he approaches the spectators, so that they may see for themselves that No. 1 is quite full of rice.

Again bringing the two bowls mouth to mouth, he returns to his table, and in the moment during which they are screened by his own body, reverses them so as to bring No. 1 uppermost, and places them thus reversed on the tray. With a wave of his wand he commands the rice to increase and multiply, and a moment later lifts the upper bowl and shows that it has done so. As the internal capacity of No. 2 (which is now underneath) is only about one-third that of No. 1, the rice naturally overflows, producing the effect that it has largely increased in quantity. The performer again levels it with his wand, letting the surplus rice fall on the tray.

Again he comes forward, holding in one hand No. 1, empty, and in the other No. 2, full of rice. In view of everyone, he inverts No. 1, and covers No. 2 with it. In returning to his table he once more reverses them, bringing No. 2 uppermost, and places them in that position on the tray. This done, he secretly removes the wax pellet from the air-hole *d*, whereupon the water begins to flow through the hole *c* into the lower bowl (No. 1). After allowing a sufficient interval, duly occupied by PATTER, for the water to pass from one vessel into the other, he lifts No. 2, and shows that the rice has apparently changed into water; for the former, being of the greater specific gravity, sinks to the bottom, while the two together just fill the bowl. As a proof of the genuineness of the transformation, he pours a portion of the water from No. 1 into No. 2, and back again.

Again he pours from No. 1 into No. 2, and this time purposely causes the water to overflow. This is easily managed, there being just twice as much as would suffice to fill the shallow upper cavity of No. 2. He places No. 1 upon the table, waves his wand over both bowls, and says, in commanding tones, "Stop!"

But the command is ineffectual. On his again pouring water from No. 1 into No. 2, it overflows rather more freely than before; and the performer explains that so long as a single drop of water remains in either of the bowls, the charm will probably continue to work. He accordingly pours the mixed rice and water (professedly water only) into some larger receptacle. Taking a cloth, he wipes each bowl dry, inside and out. He then inverts them, one upon the other, on the tray as before, and carries them off, or has them carried off by his assistant.

In an occidental version, often exhibited, the trick is performed with bowls prepared in such a way that no trace of preparation is left at the close of the trick. The material of the bowls in this case is glass which is milk-white and semi-opaque, or else aluminum. Their rims are ground perfectly flat, so as to fit exactly one upon the other. They should each be made with a foot, of the same shape as the bowls shown in Fig. 3, the projecting rim at the base enabling them to be handled more conveniently. With them is used a disk of clear glass or heavy clear plastic, edged with white enamel to make it more nearly match the bowls. This disk covers the bowl exactly.

FIG. 3

To prepare for the trick, one of the bowls is filled to the brim with water, and the brim itself moistened, after which the glass disk is laid upon it. The bowl may now be inverted without any fear of the water escaping, the glass plate being kept in position by atmospheric pressure. This bowl we will call No. 4, and the unprepared one No. 3. Both are turned upside down, and the two brought in side by side on the usual tray.

Picking up bowl No. 3, the performer shows that it is empty. He then fills it with rice, usually from a paper bag, and covers it with No. 4; then bringing forward the two together, he works the "turn-over" already described, as he replaces them on the tray. When the upper bowl is removed, there is the usual overflow of rice, the previous contents of No. 3 now lying on the surface of the glass plate. This is swept off, the empty bowl being used for this purpose, and No. 3 is replaced on No. 4, but this time there is no turn-over. At this point the performer, taking a glass tumbler, fills it with water and vanishes it by any of the familiar methods, at the same time commanding the water to pass into the covered bowl.

After a little more patter, No. 3 is lifted off, and with it the glass plate. These are laid upon the table, after which the bowl is restored to its normal position, and the performer brings it and the other bowl forward, one in each hand—No. 3 empty, No. 4 full of water. As a finish he pours the water (professedly that just before made to disappear) from bowl to bowl, but in this case without any increase of its quantity.

If the bowls are not too large (about six inches in diameter by three in depth will be found a convenient size), they may be held together between the fingers and thumbs of the two hands, and waved up and down, supposedly to assist the transformation in progress, and under cover of this movement they may be reversed without difficulty, even under the very noses of the spectators.

The glass plate is now usually made with a small lug at one point of its circumference. This in use is kept to the rear. When, after the rice has been exhibited, the performer again covers it with the empty bowl in order to level it (really sweeping it off altogether), he nips this lug between finger and thumb, and draws off bowl and plate together, laying them upon the table or tray. A moment later he lifts the inverted bowl and places it once more upon the lower bowl, before proceeding to show that the rice is transformed into water. The plate, meanwhile, is completely hidden by the rice.

The only weak point in the Indian original is the necessity of using a bowl which will not bear close inspection. But even in the case of a drawing-room show, in which the apparatus used by the performer is most exposed to inconvenient scrutiny, if the trick has been preceded by one or two others in which the appliances used have been left in the way of examination (this, by the way, is much better than offering them for that purpose), no one is at all likely to question the unpreparedness of the bowls. If, however, the performer feels any anxiety on this score, it is perfectly possible for him to start with two actually unprepared bowls, changing one of them, at the right moment, for the trick bowl. *L. H.*

RING The old conjuring word for making a secret substitution, perhaps shortened familiarly from "ring the changes." Now almost entirely superseded by SWITCH.

RING ON STICK A familiar trick that is a favorite of EAST INDIAN magicians. The performer either borrows or uses his own thin cane, and passes it around to his audience to show that it is devoid of all mechanism. He then borrows a wedding ring, which he also allows to be freely examined. He gets two members of the audience to hold the ends of the stick, each by one hand.

Then he proclaims that he proposes to pass the ring on to the middle of the stick without either assistant's letting go of his respective end of the cane. He takes the borrowed ring and wraps it up in the middle of a handkerchief, which he asks someone to hold and to feel the ring wrapped up in it. In order to let everyone know that the ring is really there, he takes the cane from his assistants and gives a tap on the ring.

He then gives the cane back to his assistants and requests the person holding the handkerchief to hold it over the middle of the cane. The performer holds the corner of the handkerchief and instructs the spectator to let go his hold at the count of three. The handkerchief is sharply pulled away and the borrowed ring is seen spinning on the middle of the cane.

The cane is an ordinary one, thin enough to pass easily through a wedding ring. The only prepared article is the handkerchief, in one corner of which is a duplicate wedding ring sewn into a small pocket. This ring does not have to be exactly like the one that is borrowed.

When the performer takes the borrowed ring to fold in the handkerchief, he folds the one that is already sewn in it, concealing the borrowed ring in his hand. When he takes the cane from his two assistants, he slides the borrowed ring on to the middle of it. He hands the cane back, but keeps his hand over the ring, concealing it until it is covered by the handkerchief.

When the handkerchief is pulled away, it takes with it the ring sewn into its corner; as it brushes the stick it makes the borrowed ring revolve as if it had just arrived in that position. *L. H. B.*

RISING CARDS This is one of the most effective of all card tricks, and certainly one of the oldest. Investigation, we believe, has disclosed the fact that the *modus operandi* of "the trick that mystified Herrmann" was known and practised in the middle of the seventeenth century. There is an old Dutch book on magic in which there is an illustration of the thread stretched between two doors.

Although there are many variations of the rising cards, the mechanical means of accomplishing the effect are limited. The favorite method of causing cards to rise is by the use of the black silk THREAD. The thread is operated in divers ways. Sometimes it is drawn by the performer himself, standing behind or beside his table; sometimes it is manipulated by a concealed assistant; or it may be operated by mechanical means.

One of the oldest methods was to have the thread attached to a small cylindrical weight within a pillar filled with sand. By moving a trigger at the foot of the pillar the sand was allowed to trickle slowly into a cavity in the base, and the weight, being deprived of its support, gradually sank down and pulled the thread.

Another method of drawing the thread is by a clockwork arrangement in a table. The most practical method, however, and the one commonly adopted, is to have the thread pulled by an assistant behind the scenes, or, in the case of a drawing-room performance, in the rear of a convenient screen. The most serious drawback to the mechanical methods of drawing the string is that the device will not always obey orders and is likely to go back on the performer in the midst of a trick. If the thread is pulled by an assistant, the performer may take his own time, and introduce many minor effects.

One of the finest performers of the rising cards was the late BUATIER DE KOLTA, who worked this trick in such a deceptive manner that even the most expert magicians were puzzled. Although he made the following method famous, the actual inventor was J. N. HOFZINSER.

The three cards destined to rise are threaded on the same general principle as all rising-card tricks—the thread passes under a duplicate of one FORCED card, over an indifferent card serving as a fulcrum, under another "force" card, over another indifferent card, etc.—but with a slight difference. Instead of the thread's being drawn *over* the top of each indifferent card, it is drawn through a tiny hole near the top of each indifferent card. The hole should be drilled in the exact center of the card and about an eighth of an inch from the upper edge. Arranged in this manner the glass or *houlette* containing the pack may be handed to the audience for examination without anyone being the wiser.

The free end of the silk is attached to one of the rear cards, which the performer rolls up into a little tube through which to blow at the cards in the houlette, such blowing being the ostensible motive to cause their ascent. This rear card is actually a double card: the edges of two cards are glued together around three sides, leaving the lower end open to form a sort of envelope or pocket. In this space the free end of the silk—two or three feet, as the case may be—is concealed. The end of the silk is of course permanently attached inside the double card. The thread should not be crowded into the double card in a helter-skelter manner, but should be neatly laid zigzag.

The working of the trick will now be obvious. The cards are threaded as described, the remainder of the silk being neatly laid in the double card. The arranged cards, face upward, are on the table, behind a handkerchief or some other object. The performer forces three duplicates. When these are replaced, the pack is shuffled by the audience.

Returning to the table, the performer drops the pack face upward on the arranged packet, at the same time taking up the glass and handkerchief. He wipes the glass in order to prove that it is unprepared. The cards are now dropped into the glass and the apparatus carried into the audience and freely exhibited. Owing to the fact that the thread does not pass *over the top* of the prepared cards, and that the free end is concealed inside the double card, there is absolutely no danger in handing the glass to a spectator for cursory examination.

The method of making the cards rise is simple. The conjurer simply removes the rear card—the double card containing the thread. As he removes the card, the thread is pulled out of the envelope. The performer rolls the card into a little tube, through which he blows toward the glass. The gradual withdrawal of the body, naturally bent in the act of blowing, draws the silk taut and produces the desired effect.

The use of a human hair instead of a thread permits having a member of the audience hold the glass while the cards ascend. In an artificial light and against a reasonably dark suit of clothes the hair is absolutely invisible. Care must be exercised in selecting a hair for this experiment. Some hairs are more brittle than others, and some have a betraying gleam. If a stout hair of a dull dark color is used, there is no danger of its being detected, even when the trick is performed directly under a strong light and in the midst of an audience.

DeKolta's New Rising Cards. Three cards are drawn from a pack, returned and the pack shuffled. The pack is dropped into a glass, which is placed either on a table or a chair. At the conjurer's word of command the three chosen cards rise, one at a time, from the glass, after which all the cards leave the tumbler, one at a time.

For this trick you need a pack of cards, a glass tumbler (preferably with a stem); and a reel of black silk thread.

Take a card in the left hand and the thread in the right. In beginning the threading process, leave a loose end of the thread, about twice the length of a card, hanging below what will be the bottom of the pack. Pass the thread *up* the back of this card (referred to as No. 1), *over* the *top* and down the face of the card.

Place the second card on the face of the first (the thread, of course, being between), and bring the thread up in front of the second card, passing it *over* the *top* of the two cards and *down behind the rear card.*

Place a third card at the rear (on top of the thread) and pass the thread *up this card*, over the top of the three cards, and down the front again. Put a fourth card in front, and pass the thread up and over the top of the four cards and down the rear card. Put a fifth card on the rear and continue passing the thread alternately back and front, over the top each time, until the whole pack, with the exception of one card, is threaded.

This last card, which should be a king of clubs or spades, has a slit in its lower edge. This slit should be large enough so that the thread may easily be drawn away and not pull the card with it. Pass the loose end of the thread, hanging below card No. 1 (in the center of the pack) toward the front of the pack, under this extra card, which is placed on the front, up over its face and down behind the extra card, and just through the slit, where it is knotted so that the thread cannot be drawn through. The last three cards threaded (not counting the extra card at the front) should be duplicates of the three that you are going to force.

The pack thus arranged is lying on the table behind a handkerchief or some convenient object. The free end of the thread passes to the concealed assistant. In order to make the cards rise the thread must be pulled perpendicularly or sideways; if perpendicularly, the glass may be stood on the seat of a chair, so that the thread, passing over the top of the chair, gives the necessary pull. If it is to be pulled sideways (at right angles to the glass), a small notch should be cut in the bottom of each card to keep the thread from slipping off.

The extra effort necessary to fix the last card is well worth the trouble. As the cards rise alternately from the back and the front of the pack, the spectators would soon suspect that the cards were fixed in some way. The extra card, however, masks the cards that rise from the front, as it is the last to leave the glass. Furthermore, without this extra card, one of the forced cards would have to be on the front of the pack, which would certainly detract from the effect of the trick. In this method, the extra card and card No. 1 leave the glass together, the extra card makes one revolution, and the thread is drawn away.

The performer forces three cards on the audience, duplicates of those arranged to rise first from the threaded pack. These cards are shuffled back into the pack, and in the act of exhibiting the goblet the unprepared pack is exchanged for the threaded pack. The prepared pack is dropped into the glass, and with the usual PATTER the three cards rise from the pack.

After the last drawn card has risen from the pack, the performer draws attention to the fact that only an ordinary glass and ordinary cards are used. To prove that there is no hocus-pocus about them, he commands them all to leave the glass, which they obligingly do.

Another pretty effect is to have four cards forced. Three of the cards rise, as described, and the performer proceeds to some other trick, apparently forgetting all about the fourth card. The spectators remind him that a fourth card was drawn; he feigns embarrassment, saying he had forgotten the card and fears it is hopelessly lost in the pack. He commands the cards to leave the glass; all of them fly out except one, which proves to be the selected card.

For this trick a slight variation in threading is necessary. If the ace of hearts, for example, is to remain in the glass, begin threading with that card. With the ace of hearts in the left hand, allow the loose end of the thread to hang down as before, although in this method a little more than the length of a card is required. Now pass the thread up the face of the ace of hearts, over the top of the card, down the back of the next card, and so on, until all the cards except the last, or extra card, are threaded. Place the extra card on the face of the pack as before, only this time with the slit edge at the top of the pack instead of at the bottom, as in the previous method. Pass the loose end of thread, hanging below the pack, toward the front of the cards; draw it up over the extra card and engage the end in the slit at the upper edge. If these directions are followed, every card will leave the glass except the ace of hearts.

Another method employs the familiar black thread stretched across the stage, just above the height of the performer's head.

In the wings, at each side, the thread passes over a pulley wheel, or through a round hook, and hangs down about four feet from this. At each end of the thread are attached small packets of cards—about a dozen—to act as counterweights. They keep the thread taut, but allow it to be drawn down easily and attached to a card which, when released, is drawn up by their weight. Most performers use prepared cards in this trick. That is, the cards that rise must have a sort of clip arrangement at the back in which to engage the thread. This method necessitates forcing duplicate cards, but obviates the difficulty by using an Excelsior Clip (see HOOKS).

Three cards are drawn by the audience, marked, and replaced singly in the deck. The cards are brought to the top by means of the SHIFT, and the pack is shuffled by the performer, leaving the selected cards on top. The clip is snapped on the first card. The performer draws down the thread, engages it under the little arm of the clip, and the card duly rises to the right hand, which removes the clip. The card can then be handed to a spectator, or scaled into the body of the theater.

Obviously this method is not applicable to the drawing-room, for at such close quarters the clip would be plainly visible to the spectators. The cards may be prepared so that the clip cannot be detected at a distance of even two feet. For every two cards prepared, another card must be sacrificed.

Cut with sharp scissors from the end of a card a piece resembling Fig. 1. This piece is glued to the back of a whole card in such a manner that point *a* (in the illustration) is free to form a sort of tongue under which to engage the thread. The entire pack is prepared in this manner. With the

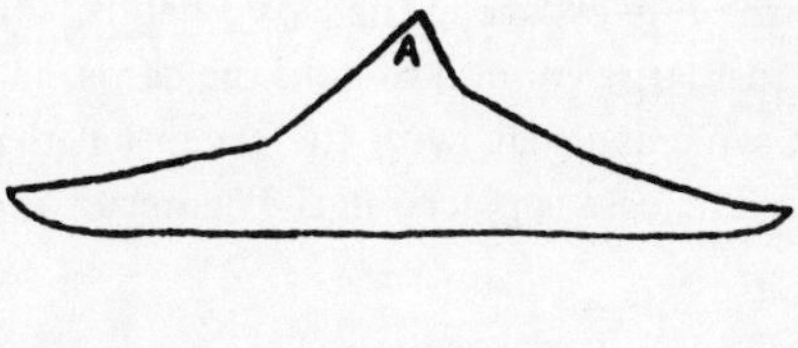

FIG. 1

cards thus prepared it is impossible to miss the horizontal thread, and if cards with a fancy pattern are used, they can almost be handed for examination.

One magician describes his method of performing this trick in the drawing-room as follows: "I carry with me two small, brass wheels with sharp points. Before the entertainment, these are pushed in the jamb at either side of an alcove or doorway, and my thread runs over these pulleys and across the door at a convenient height, the ends being properly weighted. In the center of the thread I put wax of a strong adhesive quality. When I get my cards (whether forced or not) I bring them to the top, get my thread while waving my hand, and press it with the open hand to the back of the card. Sometimes I miss it, but I have some good patter ready, and try it again."

Still another method does away with the services of an assistant. Three chosen cards are caused to rise from the pack in a tumbler or other receptacle. The three cards are, of course, forced, and the duplicate pack is arranged as usual, with the thread passing alternately under and over the cards. The thread passes down to the floor and is attached to a small disk. This disk is made of blackened cardboard or of leather, with a small tack stuck through it. (A dab of wax will do as well.) Now step on the disk, which will stick to your shoe, and a slight move of the foot will pull the thread, causing the cards to rise.

Another excellent method of performing the trick without the services of an assistant is to have a cap made to fit over the end of the wand, matching, of course, the genuine tip. Have the thread fastened to the duplicate cap, and lay it on the table. When ready to perform the trick, slip the cap on to the wand and proceed. Another clever method is to attach the thread to a handkerchief laid carelessly on the table. When about to perform the trick, simply pick up the handkerchief, wipe your hands, and thrust it into the breast pocket. An improvement is to have a hook on the end of the thread, in which case you can use any handkerchief.

One of the prettiest effects in the line of the rising cards is known to the profession as the "Obliging Bouquet." This was one of ALEXANDER HERRMANN's masterpieces.

The effect is this: a bouquet of real flowers is handed to a lady in the audience, and three or four cards are chosen from the pack. These cards are commanded to disappear. One by one they are then seen to rise from the bouquet while the flowers are in the lady's hands. The secret lies in the use of a metal case just large enough to hold the cards, and the arrangement of the cards is the same as usual, with the exception that a human hair is substituted for silk. The case is placed in the center of the bouquet, in such a position that it is not visible from the outside, yet allowing the cards to have free passage. The greatest care must be taken in arranging the case in the flowers, although the trick is not nearly so difficult as it seems. The essentials are nerve and audacity. *T. N. D.*

In most rising-card tricks, the card to rise must be forced, which is, to some extent, a drawback, and considerable ingenuity has been employed in order to overcome this difficulty. In what is known as Alberti's method, three cards are chosen (at pleasure), replaced in the center of the pack, and brought to the top by the shift.

The pack is then placed in a drinking-glass with perpendicular sides, and the performer, lifting it out again (with thumb and finger of right hand) in order to show all fair, takes the opportunity to press against the back of the rearmost card, at its upper end, a minute pellet of wax fixed to one end of a fine silk thread or hair, the opposite end of which is attached to a button of his coat or vest. He then drops the cards again into the glass, but the opposite way up, so that the pellet of wax is now at the bottom. The slightest increase of distance between the body and the glass causes a pull upon the thread, and compels the card to rise. The same process is repeated with the other cards which were chosen.

The *houlette* is a container for a pack of cards in the rising-card trick. There are scores of forms, some mechanical, some not.

One type is fastened to the performer's wand. It is of glass, set in a nickel-plated framework, with a socket attached to the metal bottom to allow it to be slipped on to the wand, as in Fig. 2, in which *a* represents the houlette, and *b* the wand. The wand is mechanical, having a sharp-pointed metal tongue, about two and a half inches long, projecting from its upper end and controlled by a slide within it. A minute oblong slot in the bottom of the houlette allows the point of the tongue to press against the back of the rearmost card, compelling it to rise.

Three cards are chosen, replaced, and brought to the top by the SHIFT. The pack is then placed in the houlette, which is fixed on top of the wand. The performer holds the wand upright in either hand, taking care that the cards lie well to the front of the case. When the card is ordered to rise, he pushes up, with his thumb or forefinger, the little projecting stud shown in the diagram. This lifts the tongue, which in turn pushes up the rearmost card. The card is removed from the case and thrown on the table; the tongue meanwhile is drawn down, to rise again a moment later and push up the next card.

FIG. 2

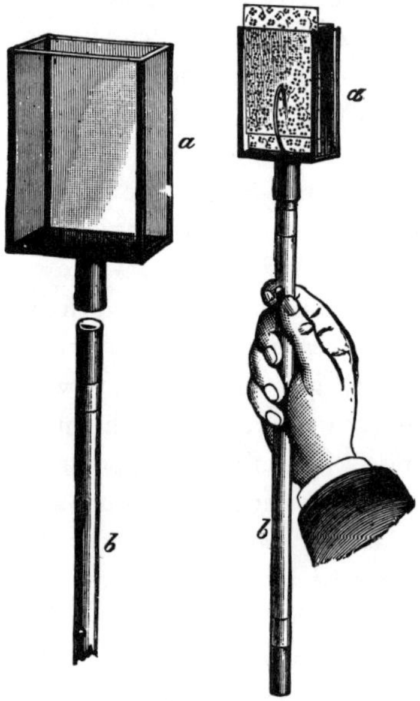

Another excellent method was adopted by Edwin T. Sachs. He used a metal houlette, painted black, with a cork plug below it, which is thrust into the neck of a newly opened bottle of wine. The houlette itself is an ordinary one, but on the table lies a silk THREAD, with a small button on the near end. This is dropped into the bottle just before the houlette is inserted, the pressure of the cork plug against the neck firmly holding the thread.

Three cards are drawn and retained by the drawers. The performer takes the remaining cards and places them in the houlette, drawing the silk thread across the top of them, from front to back. He now takes back the cards that have been drawn, and without looking at their faces thrusts them down one by one into the pack, the first near the front, the second and third a little further back. Each card carries down a portion of the slack of the thread with it.

To prevent the premature rising of the cards already placed, the performer places a finger on each, while he pushes down its successor. The opposite end of the thread travels behind the scenes in the ordinary way to the hand of an assistant; when it is pulled, the cards rise, of course in the opposite order to that in which they were inserted. They must therefore be called for accordingly.

In another form of the trick, the houlette is of glass, suspended from the ceiling by a couple of silk ribbons (some feet apart at the top) and set swinging by the performer. The cards rise as usual, notwithstanding the swinging movement of the case.

The secret lies in the fact that one of the ribbons is double; two ribbons have been sewn together at the edges so as to form a flat tube, through which the motive thread passes. The cards are arranged in the usual manner. *L. H.*

The *card reel* is a small round brass box similar to an ordinary tape measure, the place of the measure being taken by a black silk thread. To one side of the box is fastened a safety-pin, with which to fasten it to the performer's clothing; on the other side is a button which, when pressed, allows the thread to be drawn into the box by the internal spring.

This apparatus is pinned on to the top of the left side of the performer's trousers, just beneath the edge of the waistcoat.

At the end of the thread is a little hollow button of wood, into and slightly overlapping the hollow of which is pressed some conjurer's wax. This pellet of wax is stuck on to the back of the top waistcoat button, and some two and a half feet of slack thread is pulled out of the apparatus and allowed to hang loose.

Walking among the audience, the performer invites five persons to select a card each. This done, he collects the five cards, remembering the order of the people from whom he takes them back, and in turning and walking toward another member of the audience he exchanges these by dropping them into his right-hand PROFONDE (care being taken not to disarrange their order), and taking five others, hands them to the member of the audience together with the pack, requesting that they be shuffled into the pack. He then takes back the pack, and in walking back to the stage or table recovers the chosen five from the profonde and places them on top of the pack.

On reaching his position and turning around to face the audience once more, he removes the wax button from the waistcoat button and presses it against the back of the top card on the pack.

He now calls attention to the fact that the pack of cards is held quite isolated in the left hand, and the right hand is passed over and around the cards to show that no threads or wires are attached.

As the right hand passes underneath the cards it encounters the slack thread, which is allowed to pass between the first and second fingers, and is drawn up until the right hand is about the height of the face.

Turning to the person whose card he took back last, the performer inquires, "What was the name of the card you chose?" "Two of spades" (or whatever it was), is the reply. "Well, I will ask the two of spades to leave the pack and rise into my right hand."

While speaking, he presses his left elbow against the button on the apparatus, which allows the spring to draw in the thread; the card rises slowly to the right hand.

The pressure by the elbow on the button is stopped, and the right hand now brings down the card and places it in front of the rest in the left hand. Detaching the waxed button and affixing it once more at the back of the rearmost card, he turns toward the chooser of the card taken before the last to inquire the name of the card selected. Meanwhile the right hand is passed once more around the cards and brought up again to the previous position. While this is done the button must be pressed by the left elbow to allow the thread, which was drawn in at the rising of the previous card, to be drawn out again. The second card is commanded to leave the pack, and the operation is repeated until all five have risen.

This is THURSTON's own published method, but on the stage he used the horizontal thread described above. *C. L. N.*

J. N. Thornton's reel was an improvement on Thurston's: a small, round tin box, japanned black, of a size to fit easily in the vest pocket. Inside the box is a wooden windlass mounted on a spring. The thread is wound around the windlass, the free end passing through a hole in the side of the box and terminating in a small leather button coated with wax. The simple act of drawing out the thread winds up the windlass, by twisting the spring, and when the hold on the thread is released, the button flies back to the apparatus.

This apparatus works reasonably well when the conjurer is in a dress suit, and is performing at a comfortable distance from the audience; but no matter how fine the silk thread may be there is always danger of its being seen at close quarters, and the windlass will TALK in spite of all precautions.

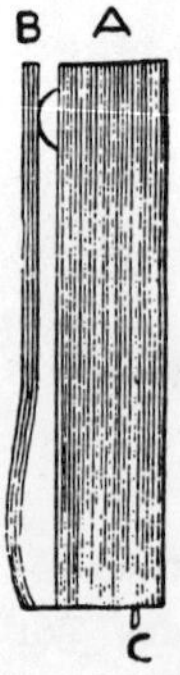

FIG. 3

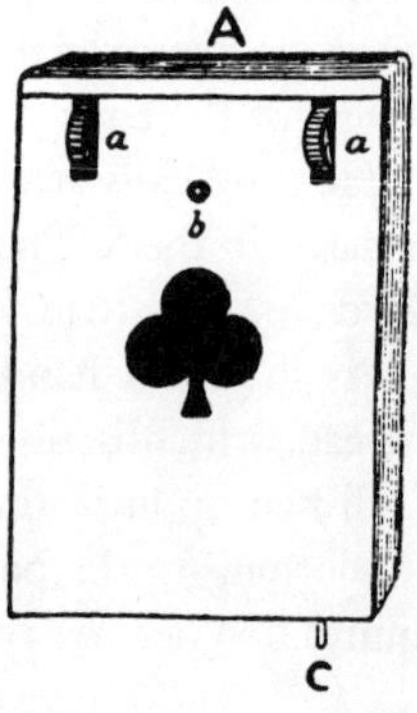

FIG. 4

The *clockwork pack* was invented by Joseph Michael Hartz, who also introduced the THUMB TIP. His pack is in two parts, *A* and *B* (Fig. 3), between which are inserted the cards intended to rise. The rear portion, *A*, consists of some forty-five cards pasted together, but having their central portions (except for the back and front cards) cut away to allow the necessary mechanism to be inserted. The front portion, *B*, consists of four cards, likewise pasted together, and made to bulge slightly forward a little below the center by means of a thin brass tongue two and a half inches long, glued vertically between them.

The only connection between *A* and *B* is by means of this tongue, which projects from the bottom of *B*, and is turned up square at its lower end so as to form a clip fitting into the lower part of *A*. Matters are arranged so that at this point *A* and *B* are a fraction of an inch apart, but at the top, for about one-third of its length, *B* presses slightly against *A*. By drawing *B* downward for a quarter of an inch the up-turned tongue can be withdrawn from *A*, and the two parts disconnected at pleasure.

The working mechanism is contained wholly within *A*, its only visible portions being two little rubber-covered wheels, *a a*, which project through slots cut in the foremost card, as shown in Fig. 4. The mechanism is not unlike that of a music box with the barrel and comb omitted. Two brass plates, the lower measuring three by one and three-quarters inches, the upper three inches by one inch, are held together, at a distance of three-eighths of an inch, by a pillar at each corner of the smaller one.

Between these two plates is fixed a spring-barrel, which is wound up like a watch; *b* in Fig. 4 indicates the hole for the key. The barrel is connected by an intermediate train with a contrate wheel (a wheel whose teeth lie parallel to its axis), which in turn is connected with the spindle on which the two little wheels *a a*, revolve. From about half the circumference of the contrate wheel the teeth are cut away.

When the mechanism is set in motion by upward pressure on a pin, *c*, projecting about a quarter of an inch from the bottom of the pack, the little wheels *a a* begin to revolve, rising to the front; and if three or four cards have previously been inserted between the two parts of the pack, the card for the time being in contact with *a a* will be forced slowly upward, except when the toothless portion of the contrate wheel comes into operation.

During this period, though the train is still running, no movement is communicated to the little wheels *a a*, which accordingly come to a temporary standstill. When the toothed portion of the contrate wheel is again reached, their movement recommences. The speed of the movement is controlled by a "fly" regulator, and the mechanism is so delicately adjusted that its working is inaudible, even at a distance of only three feet.

When the pack is in use, the upward pressure on the pin *c* is supplied by the weight of the pack itself. When it is desired to make the cards rise, the pack is placed in a holder (Fig. 5) just large enough to contain it. This has plate-glass sides and a metal bottom, to the under surface of which is soldered a socket to receive one end of a wooden rod, about a foot long, which serves as a handle to hold the apparatus aloft so that everyone may see it. (A plain glass goblet with upright sides makes an equally good holder.)

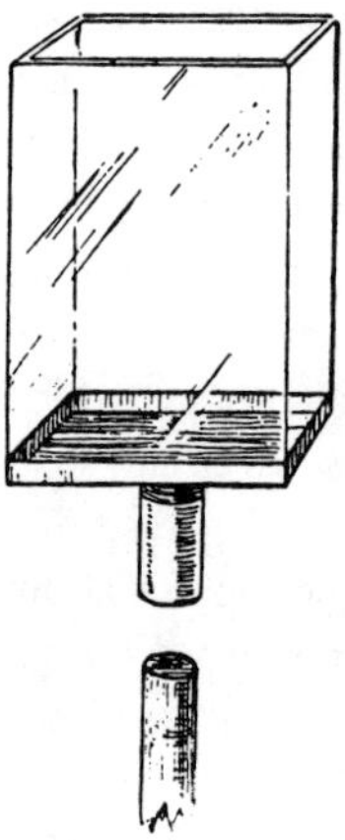

The removal of a portion of the teeth of the contrate wheel has as yet been unaccounted for. The object of this is to render the upward movement of the cards intermittent, and a little reflection will show the necessity of this. If it were not so, a second card would follow instantly upon the heels of the first, without waiting for invitation, and the theory of the trick—that the cards only rise at the performer's command—would be somewhat rudely disturbed. The brief interruption of the lifting movement after the appearance of a given card affords the performer just the time he requires to inquire the name of, and call for, the next one.

A similar stoppage likewise occurs midway during the upward progress of each card, but this heightens the effect; a partial rise, then a stoppage, and then a further rise being less suggestive of a mechanical force (and therefore more magical) than a continuous upward movement would be.

If the card which has risen is not removed at once, but is allowed to remain until the next has started on its upward course, the former will wobble about with a curious jumpy movement.

The mechanical packs in use at the present time differ from Hartz's in various small details. The little wooden wheels are in some cases covered with sandpaper in place of rubber, and in others encircled by little sharp metal points, after the fashion of a spur, those of the latter make probably being the more certain in operation.

Another difference is in the method of starting the movement. The pin at the bottom is replaced by one projecting upward from the top of the pack, and operated by moving it a fraction of an inch from right to left, or vice versa. This arrangement places the mechanism more completely under the control of the operator, who can, by a touch of his finger in the act of removing the card just risen, bring the apparatus to a standstill. The power to do this is useful, as it enables the performer to give a more dramatic form to his *mise en scene.* *L. H.*

Many ingenious rising-card methods are given in Hilliard's *Greater Magic.*

ROBERT-HOUDIN (1805-1871), French magician, widely regarded as the father of modern conjuring. His original name was Jean-Eugene Robert, and (like the original MASKELYNE) he was bred to the watchmaking trade. He first grew interested in magic at the age of eighteen, but did not become a public performer until he was forty. In 1828, while working for a watchmaker at Tours, he had an attack of food poisoning, became delirious, and was picked up on the roadside by TORRINI, who took him along with his wagon show, and nursed him. This was Jean-Eugene Robert's first contact with professional conjuring.

He married the daughter of a celebrated watchmaker named Houdin, and legally added that name to his own. For a number of years, in addition to watchmaking, he repaired the automata that formed a feature of magic shows at the time (see HISTORY). Finally, in 1845, he opened his own theater of magic in the Palais Royal at Paris. After the revolution of 1848 had closed all the Paris theaters, Robert-Houdin went to England, where he had a very successful tour.

In 1850 he turned over his theater and show to an Englishman named Hamilton who became his brother-in-law; in 1852 he formally retired, and devoted his time to mechanical and electrical experiment. In 1856 the French government sent him to Algeria for the purpose of outdoing and discrediting the local magic men, who were supposed to be fomenting revolt.

From that time until his death he continued his studies and wrote his books, which are perhaps his most lasting claim to glory. His autobiography, an entertaining volume, is of very dubious reliability, like the memoirs of most earlier wizards; but his *Les Secrets de la Prestidigitation et de la Magie*, or *Comment on devient Sorcier*, translated by PROFESSOR HOFFMANN under the title of *The Secrets of Conjuring and Magic*, still deserves study by every magician.

The claims to original inventions made in Robert-Houdin's autobiography led HARRY HOUDINI to write *The Unmasking of Robert-Houdin*, in which, with positive proofs, but with more heat than necessary, he sharply reduces Robert-Houdin's stature as an inventor. In later years, however, Houdini himself felt more charitable toward the great Frenchman. Whatever his concrete accomplishments, Robert-Houdin's influence on the art was great and lasting. *B. M.*

ROBIN, HENRI, whose right name was Dunkell, was of Holland birth, and died in Paris in 1874. He was at his prime in about 1839-40, when

he toured the Continent. He was popular in London, Paris, and both the English and French provinces. A polished man, famous for the elegance of his speech and manners, he conducted his performances and all his business in a quiet, conservative fashion. In both Paris and London, he had play-houses named temporarily in his honor, Salle de Robin, and at one time in London he also appeared at the Egyptian Hall. He published his own magazine, *L'Almanach de Cagliostro*, an illustrated periodical which was quite pretentious.

ROPES AND RINGS (See under GRANDMOTHER'S NECKLACE)

ROPE TRICKS (See also INDIAN ROPE TRICK) Rope tricks are an elaboration of the centuries-old "cut string restored" (see STRING TRICKS, TURBAN CUT AND RESTORED). When Dr. Harlan Tarbell, the prolific magical writer, thought of doing the trick with a rope instead of a string, the effect suddenly became a prime favorite with audiences, and even more so with magicians.

Very few tricks have had so much ingenuity spent and misspent upon method without notable change of effect. But all the ingenuities are refinements of three principles.

First, and oldest, is the manipulation that leads the spectator to cut an end from the rope when he thinks he is cutting the middle. (See TURBAN CUT AND RESTORED)

Second, and perhaps equally old, is the use of a short extra piece of rope. Either the short piece is substituted for a loop of the real center, and cut, or it is tied in imitation of a knot around the middle of the real rope, to prepare for the third method.

Third, the only innovation in three hundred years, the performer may really do what he pretends—join the cut ends together. This is accomplished either with an adhesive or mechanically, or by a screw or snap-fastener GIMMICK. The rope is usually tied into a loop with the fake, sliding knot of the second principle, while the actual ends are held together by the adhesive or gimmick. The rope is cut at the prepared spot, and the adhesive trimmed away, or a short piece with a gimmick on each end may be cut and removed, leaving the gimmick ends of the actual rope to be joined. The trick is then repeated by sliding the fake knot along, and cutting the rope at its actual center.

Many rope ROUTINES will be found in John Northern Hilliard's *Greater Magic, The Tarbell Course in Magic, Vol. II,* and Abbott's *Encyclopedia of Rope Tricks.* *H. H.*

ROUTINE (See also COMEDY; PATTER; PRACTICE AND REHEARSAL; PRESENTATION; PROGRAMS; PSYCHOLOGY)

A well-rehearsed sequence of moves or small cumulative effects, which may either constitute an impromptu act in itself or make up part of a set program. Certain tricks, particularly those of a cumulative nature, cannot be successfully performed at all until the routine has become second nature. Such are: the CUPS AND BALLS; EGG BAG; GENERAL CARD; LINKING RINGS; and (in a slightly different category) THREE-CARD TRICKS.

In all of these effects and many more, the natural tendency is to let the routine get much too long.

To work up a routine, see that the effects build up from small to big; don't let the same thing seem to happen twice unless the essence of your trick is repetition (see COMEDY); make each overt act and each secret move blend smoothly into the next; vary your method when the effect is unvarying; and keep it short.

Technically, a most important part of a successful routine is in the way that the timing of STEALS and LOADS is varied. It goes without saying that the secret move is almost never performed at the moment when the trick is supposed to be accomplished. Further than that, however, the dislocation of time should be varied. In the CARDS UP THE SLEEVE, for instance, the PALMING takes place now before, now after a suspicious onlooker would expect it. A good routine will usually not repeat the same timing, any more than the same sleight, twice in direct succession. The variation is even more desirable in apparently "repeating" effects than in varied ones. *B. M.*

S

SALTING The process of secreting small objects in unlikely places about a room where the audience supposes you have never been before. Coins may be put on clocks, cards under the rug, predictions dropped into vases, and so forth. This is a very valuable recourse, which has been too largely forgotten in recent years. It can be particularly effective in PUBLICITY tricks.

SAWING A WOMAN IN TWO Probably the most sensational popular illusion of modern times. Although TORRINI did an effect somewhat like it, it really dates from 1921, when SELBIT, GOLDIN, and another American performer named Leon all devised independent versions.

The effect is that a girl is laid full length in a box that stands on trestles. Sometimes her head, hands, and feet protrude through holes in the ends of the box; sometimes her wrists and ankles are fastened with ropes that come through the sides; sometimes sheets of glass are put through slots in the top and bottom of the box. In any case, the box is sawn in half, either with a two-man crosscut saw or with a rotary power saw. Sheets of metal are slid down to close off the open, cut ends of the box, and the two halves are slid apart. They are then slid together again, the metal sheets removed, and the girl is restored.

The method perhaps most frequently seen involves two girls. The box rests on a table whose edges are beveled so that it seems to have a thin top, but actually there is space for one girl. As the girl who appears before the audience is getting into the box, the hidden girl comes up through a trap in the table, pokes her feet through the holes in the end of the box, and puts her head forward between her knees. The other girl, at the same time, draws her knees up under her chin, leaving the entire center of box and table clear to be sawn through. The hands and feet are frequently held by members of the audience; in this case the man who holds the feet must be a PLANT.

H. H.

SECOND SIGHT (See under MIND-READING)

SELBIT, P. T. Stage name of Percy Thomas Tibbles (died 1938), English magician, inventor, and builder of ILLUSIONS. He was a journalist before 1900, and then took up magic as a profession, touring Europe and America. Selbit devised many of the illusions now widely used, notably the first version of SAWING A WOMAN IN TWO. He constructed tricks and illusions to order for many prominent performers, and had a long-standing connection with the MASKELYNES and St. George's Hall. Although a good performer, he will be remembered in magic wholly for his inventions.

FIG. 1

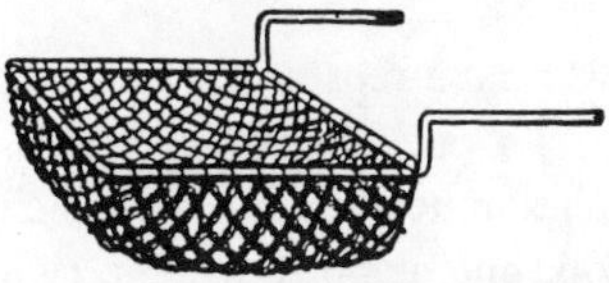

FIG. 3

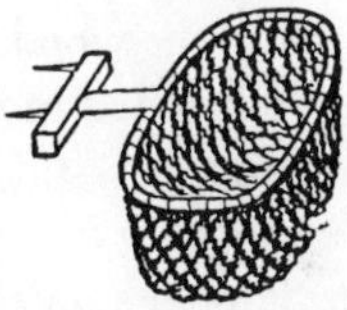

FIG. 5

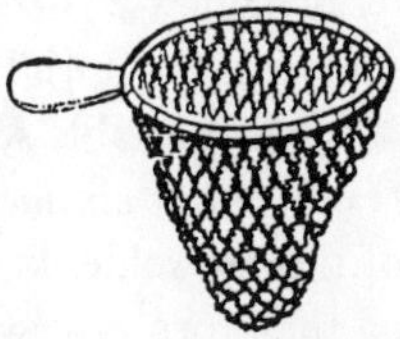

FIG. 2

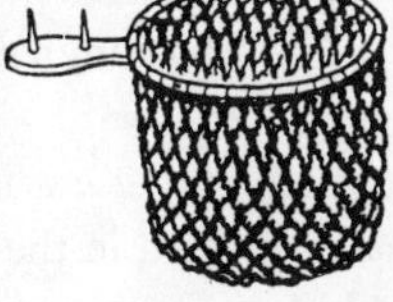

FIG. 4

FIG. 6

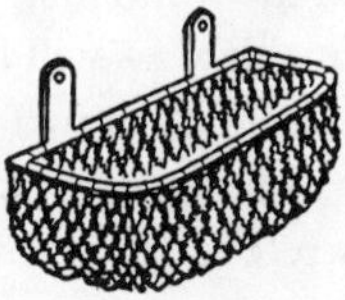

FIG. 7

SERVANTE A hidden shelf or receptacle for LOADS and STEALS.

The *bag* or *net servante* has been developed to a remarkable extent. This class of servante is produced in a host of different forms, as may be gathered from the illustrations, which show only a few of its varieties. Fig. 1 is designed to receive small articles only, and is placed in position by thrusting the wire arms into small screw-eyes, fixed in the under side of the table top. As the screw-eyes have to be fixed beforehand, and as the average householder is apt to object to having gimlet-holes bored in his furniture, this method of fastening is practically restricted to tables belonging to the performer himself, or to very accommodating friends. Fig. 2, which has a gimlet-pointed screw of its own, is open to the same objection. A couple of needle-points, however, may be pressed into any hidden part of even the handsomest table without injuring it, and this is the method of fastening adopted in the servantes shown in Figs. 3 and 4. (These needle-points are of plain steel, eyeless, about two inches in length, and the thickness of a carpet needle. Their normal function—apart from conjuring—is the attachment of moldings of wood or composition to picture frames and the like. A hole is first bored, with a fine awl, in the object to be affixed, and the needle-point is then driven through the hole until it projects on the opposite side as far as need be for the specific purpose. The butt end of the needle is then broken off flush with the surface of the wood. Needle-points are procurable in small packets at any hardware store.)

Fig. 5 is provided with a flat tongue, which may be thrust into the opening of a table drawer. Nos. 6 and 7 are adapted for attachment to the back of a chair, the former by means of hooks going over the back rail, the latter by pressing two needle-points or good-sized drawing-pins through the holes shown in the upright slips into the wood.

In the portable servante illustrated in Fig. 8, *a a a a* represent an oblong frame about six inches by four, of stiff wire. To one of the larger sides of this are soldered two uprights, *b b*, two inches in height, and from each of these project two needle-points, one at top, one at bottom. The two upper points should slope *very slightly downward* and should be inserted in the wood first, the lower points being then pressed in. A servante fastened in this way will bear considerable weight. To remove it the lower points should be drawn out first.

The open space between the four corners *a a a a* is filled by a tightly stretched piece of black calico. (This is omitted in the diagram so that the manner of fastening the servante could be shown more clearly.)

Fig. 9 represents a chair servante especially adapted for SWITCHING a pack of cards. The prepared pack is held, as shown, in a spring clip. In the act of moving the chair backward or forward, the performer rests his hand for a moment on the back. In that moment he drops the pack he has been using into the circular bag, and grasps in its place the prepared pack. A recent improvement consists in hinging the ring of the bag to the clip, so that they may be folded together when not in use.

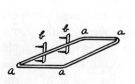

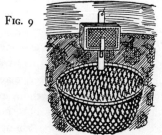

FIG. 8

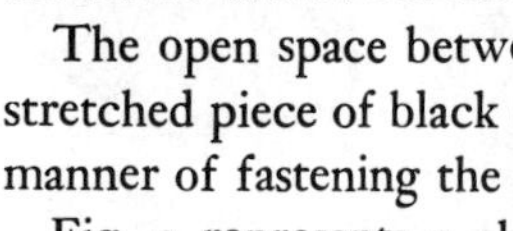

FIG. 9

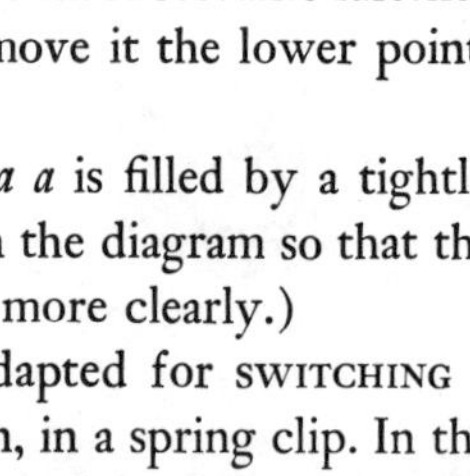

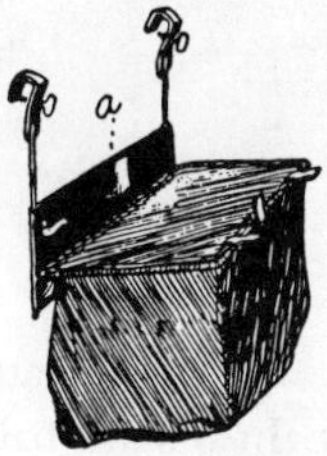

FIG. 10

FIG. 11

FIG. 12

Figs. 10, 11, and 12 illustrate an ingenious form of chair servante which has sundry special recommendations. It is of the bag variety, oblong in shape, and made of black cloth stretched on a wire frame. Its most striking feature is that the bag has a lid, also of cloth tightly stretched, which may be raised or lowered at pleasure. When lowered, as in Fig. 11 (thereby closing the bag), its upper surface in itself forms a flat servante, on which any article may be placed. When an object is to be got rid of by dropping, the lid is raised (Fig. 11), a catch keeping it from falling again, and so giving access to the bag portion. This servante can be raised or lowered relatively to the height of the back of the chair, and when not in use can be folded flat for packing, in which condition it takes the shape shown in Fig. 12.

Where the chair used has an open back, it would seem impossible to adapt a servante to it, but by throwing a shawl or large handkerchief over the back of the chair, the presence of the servante is effectually masked.

Aside from the screw and hook arrangements, there is another way of attaching a servante which seems to have special recommendations: the "sucker" arrangement so frequently used for suspending light articles from the inside of shop windows. This is a little rubber cup, with a hook attached to the outside. The rubber is moistened and pressed against the glass so as to force out the air from within, when it remains firmly attached. The same thing happens if it is pressed against any highly polished surface, such as the back of a chair or the frame of a table. Two of them could be fixed into a little wooden slab, measuring about three by one and one-half inches by an inch thick. The servante could then be attached to this, one or more of these slabs being used, and so placed as might be most suitable for the particular purpose.

Where a glass of water has to be got rid of, the bag is made of waterproof material, while in other cases the bag portion of the servante is dispensed with altogether, as, for instance, where the object to be sup-

FIG. 13

ported is a billiard ball or cannon-ball. In the latter case a ring servante (*A* in Fig. 13) of appropriate size is all that is necessary. In billiard-ball tricks an open ring, as *B* in the same figure, is preferable, the ball being more easily got hold of. To ensure noiselessness in use, the ring should be covered with some soft material.

In some cases the object needs only to be suspended, in which case a hook, preferably of the kind known as a cup-hook, may answer the purpose. Two of these hooks fixed at an appropriate distance will serve to support an object of considerable length, ranging from a wand to a sunshade or umbrella. In place of hooks, the article may be supported on a straight pin or pins, fixed so as to slope slightly upward. The outer end of the pin may be sharp or blunt, according to the purpose for which it is to be used. If it is desired to impale on it an orange, or a handkerchief rolled into a ball, the sharper it is the better; if merely intended to hang something on by a loop, the point may be blunt.

The pin or hook may either be fixed on a wooden base, from the opposite side of which project a couple of needle-points, to be pressed against the wood of a table or chair (Fig. 14), or the base may be of tin or thin brass with a couple of small holes in it (Fig. 15). A couple of good-sized drawing-pins are pressed through these holes into the wood, and all is secure. Two converging pins, one above the other, as *A* in Fig. 14, make a still more substantial fixture.

Where a light object is to be suspended by a loop of thread or wire, a drawing-pin, driven half way in, will be all that is necessary to support it.

The growing desire of performers to be independent of any special table, and at the same time the obvious objections to a too frequent recourse to pockets, almost naturally suggest the vest servante.

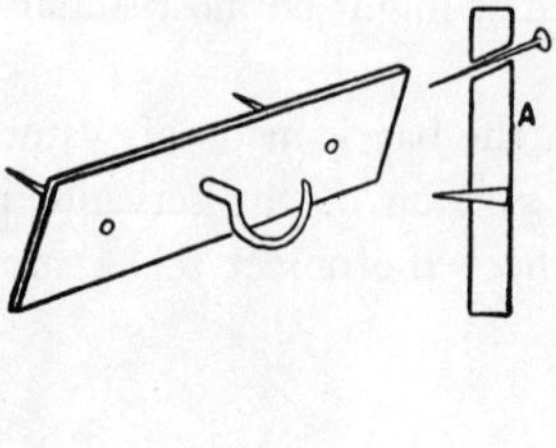

FIG. 14

FIG. 15

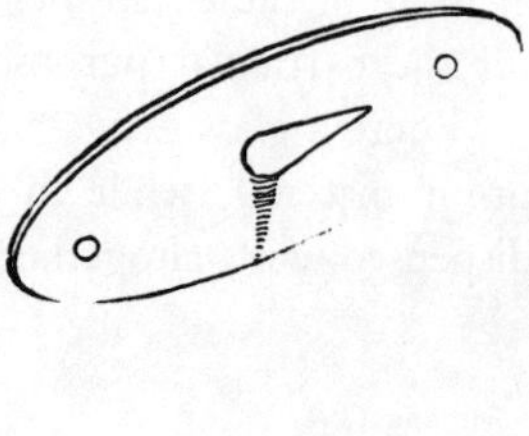

This contrivance consists of an oblong plate of zinc, ten inches by seven, covered with cloth, and a tube of sheet-iron or gunmetal, four and one half inches long, pressed into an oval form, its longer diameter being four inches and its shorter two and one-half inches. This is covered in like manner, and the cloth is continued below the tube to a depth of three inches and closed at the bottom, forming a bag wherein articles may fall noiselessly.

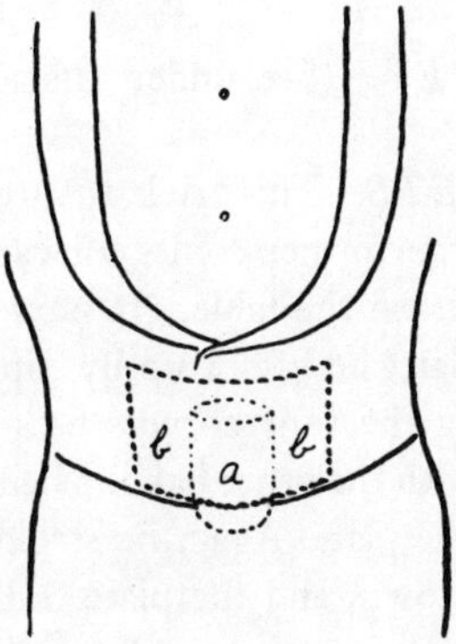

FIG. 16

The plate is first placed in position, across the lower part of the shirt-front within the vest. This indeed may be worn all the evening without inconvenience. The tube is then inserted between this and the shirt-front, the lower part passing inside the waistband of the trousers. (In Fig. 16 the dotted lines show the apparatus in position, *a* representing the tube, and *b b* the covered zinc plate. The slight abnormal projection of the vest attracts no inconvenient notice.)

The appliance may be used in connection with SILK TRICKS (to receive the false finger or a rolled-up handkerchief), or for vanishing small balls, cards, or other articles of appropriate size. *L. H.*

SHELL A hollow or half dummy, a FAKE used to simulate an object such as a BALL or WAND that is actually elsewhere. (See also COINS, SHELL)

SHELL GAME A carnival and outdoor gamblers' variation of the CUPS AND BALLS, known in England as "thimblerigging."

It is performed with three empty half walnut shells and a "pea." The game is for the spectator to pick the shell under which the pea is at a given moment. The pea is actually cut to size from a piece of rubber, which is the essential secret of the trick.

If the shell with the pea under it is pushed forward by the forefinger, the rubber pea imperceptibly crawls out from under the shell, and is nipped between the operator's thumb and second finger. This of course leaves all three shells empty. The pea is introduced under a shell by reversing the process, pressing it with the second fingertip against the rear edge of the shell, and drawing the shell backward.

A variety of moves is explained in Jack Chanin's *Hello Sucker!*

SHOWER OF MONEY (See under MISER'S DREAM)

SHOWER OF SWEETS This trick is sure to be well received by a juvenile audience. The performer comes forward with an ordinary plate or salver, which he places on the table. He next borrows a handkerchief. Laying it flat over the plate, he lifts it up by nipping the middle with his finger and thumb, letting the four corners hang down. He then strokes down the handkerchief with the other hand, when a shower of nuts, candy, etc., pours down upon the plate. Again he strokes the handkerchief, and again the shower pours down; and the plate, full by this time, is handed around to the audience to prove that in the quality of the sweets, at any rate, there is no deception.

The secret lies in the use of a small bag, of cambric or fine calico, shaped like an inverted letter V, in the form shown in Fig. 1. No springs are used, but the bag, when filled, is closed by folding down the flap, and hooking the little ring over the hook, the bag thereby assuming the appearance shown in Fig. 2. It is picked up within the handkerchief, but when it is desired to produce the sweets, a slight inclination of the hook to the left

FIG. 1

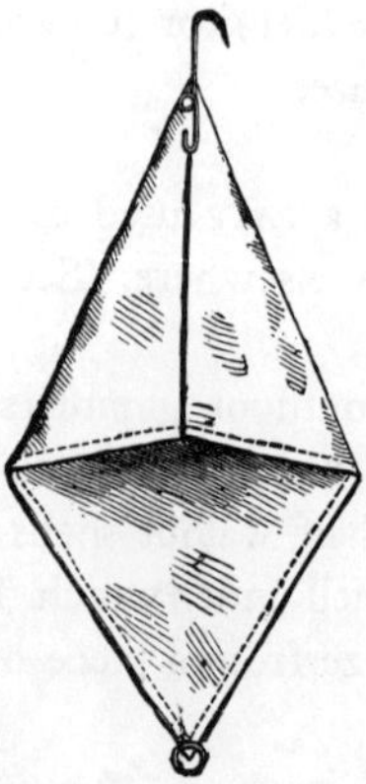

FIG. 2

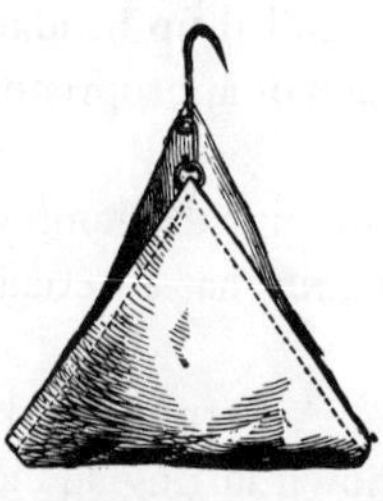

(effected by a barely perceptible movement of the thumb and finger) causes the ring to slip off and the flap to fall down, as in Fig. 1, releasing the whole contents of the bag.

The trick may be still further improved by having two similar bags stitched back to back, each with its own ring and hook. In this case an inclination to the left releases one hook, and an inclination to the right another. The two bags may be filled with bonbons of different colors or descriptions, or one may be filled with bonbons and the other with gray peas. A handkerchief is borrowed, and a lady and gentleman are requested each to hold a plate. The lady is requested to breathe on the handkerchief, and a shower of bonbons falls on her plate. The gentleman breathes in his turn, and retires, amid derisive applause, with a plate of peas. *L. H.*

SILENT ACTS (See also MUSIC; PANTOMIME; PATTER) Acts in which the performer dispenses with all PATTER, relying wholly on PANTOMIME for his PRESENTATION. They make a greater demand on the technical skill of the SLEIGHT-OF-HAND performer than a talking act does, because the methods of MISDIRECTION are more limited, and imperfect manipulation will not escape notice.

Every performer should work up at least one silent ROUTINE, for the sake of the training it will give him in pantomime and manipulation.

Certain types of manipulation—THIMBLES, billiard BALLS, card FLOURISHES—are almost traditionally worked in silence; for them, most patter is a mere encumbrance. At the other end of the scale are fast-moving ILLUSIONS—transpositions, productions, vanishes—, where the effect of speed and dash is more important than any explanation.

Silent work also has value in quieting a restless, but not unmanageable, crowd. Noise from the audience in CHILDREN'S SHOWS can often be stopped by working in silence. It is hard, also, to do an Oriental act any way but silent without shattering the Chinese or East Indian illusion by fluent English chatter.

SILK TRICKS (See also DANCING HANDKERCHIEF; SUN AND MOON TRICK; THREAD; TUMBLERS)

The primary effects to be produced with handkerchiefs (apart from knot tricks, which come under a special category) are four: magical production, change of color, magical disappearance, and magical reproduction.

One of the most ingenious methods of producing a handkerchief from the apparently empty hand is by means of a *false finger*, made in imitation of the extended middle finger. It is of very thin brass, or better, celluloid,

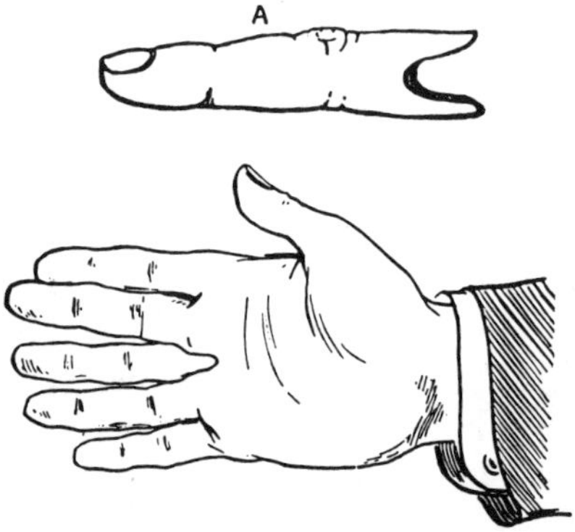

FIG. 1

colored to match the hand, and inserted when in use between the second and third fingers of the right or left hand, as in Fig. 1. On inspection of the detail drawing *A* in the diagram, it will be observed that the finger is not chopped off square, but the metal is cut away on each side, so that it tapers both at back and front to a rounded point. The fork thereby formed acts as a sort of clip to hold the finger in position; strange to say, the hand thus supplemented may even be shown full front, so long as it is not absolutely at rest, without anyone noticing that it has an extra finger. With the hand held horizontally, the false finger is absolutely invisible.

For production purposes the handkerchief is previously loaded into the finger, the corner last inserted being left just within reach, at the bottom of the fork. The performer usually either comes forward with the finger already in place on the hand, or carries it in the trouser pocket, at the right moment carelessly putting his hand in, and bringing it out again with the finger in position.

The actual production of the handkerchief is usually effected by bringing the hands together and working it out between the fingertips. It can be produced with only one hand: under cover of a wave of the arm, bend the sham finger over toward the ball of the thumb, when its open end will naturally be between the thumb and first finger. The remaining fingers grip the FAKE, while the thumb and forefinger work the handkerchief out of it.

A very simple expedient is to place the handkerchief, neatly folded, within the bend of the left elbow. On coming forward, the performer draws up his sleeves and bares his arms, incidentally showing the hands empty. The right sleeve is first drawn up, and then the left, the act of drawing up the latter bringing the handkerchief quite naturally into the right hand.

Two or three forms of wand have been devised for the magical production of a small silk handkerchief, to be used subsequently in the performance of some other trick.

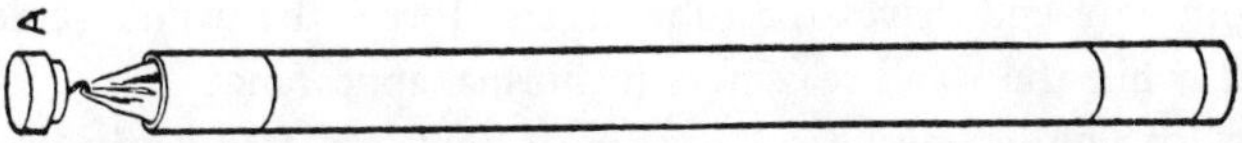

FIG. 2

One such wand consists of a thin metal tube, japanned or otherwise ornamented to match the wand in ordinary use. One end is permanently closed; to the other is adapted a metal plug (*A* in Fig. 2), on the under side of which is fixed a tiny hook. The handkerchief to be produced is worked carefully into the wand, corners first. When the center is reached, this is attached to the little hook, and the stopper replaced. By secretly withdrawing it at the proper moment, the performer gets the handkerchief into the hand without difficulty.

Another and better pattern only differs from the above in the fact that a minute eyelet is substituted for the little hook, and the handkerchief is attached to it by a loop of thread, which is broken after the handkerchief has been produced.

The method of using wands of these makes is as follows: the performer borrows a handkerchief and receives it (or places it) with its center on the prepared end of the wand, which is held upright in, say, the right hand. With the left hand he nips the center of the borrowed handkerchief and draws it off the wand, carrying off within it the little plug and the handkerchief attached to it, which now hangs down inside the borrowed one. The wand, with its open end to the rear, is tucked under the right arm. The borrowed handkerchief is shaken a little, and then turned over, revealing the silken one within it. The two are now displayed one in each hand, after which it is an easy matter to detach the plug and to restore it to its normal position in the end of the wand.

A third wand is constructed on the "pop-gun" principle, as illustrated in Fig. 3. Here *a* is a short tube, open throughout, and fitting on to one end of the wand, which is at that part turned thinner, as *b*, in order to receive it. The wand is prepared for use by drawing this little tube half way off the wand, and loading the handkerchief into it; the performer

FIG. 3

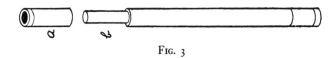

conceals the temporarily altered appearance of the wand by keeping that end in the hand. When it is desired to produce the handkerchief, pressure on the opposite end drives the tube in, and forces the handkerchief into the hand, while the wand reassumes its normal appearance.

Wands of one or another of the above kinds are frequently used in a modern version of the old trick of "the handkerchief burned and destroyed," to supply the performer with the little bit of cambric which is required for the illusion.

A fourth wand for similar purposes consists of a metal tube (*a*, in Fig. 4) duly japanned and nickeled, in one end of which is inserted, for the reception of the handkerchief, a smaller tube *b*, about two and one half inches in length, open at its inner end, but closed at its outer end by a disk of metal a shade larger in diameter than the wand itself, the projecting edge enabling it to be withdrawn instantly, say under cover of passing the wand from one hand to the other. A slot, half an inch wide, is cut in the side of *b*, to facilitate the extraction of the handkerchief.

When *b* is withdrawn, the end of *a* naturally remains open, for the time being; but a little caution will prevent this from being noticed.

The same wand is also used for the purpose of vanishing a handkerchief, which is in such case coaxed into the tube *b* under cover of rubbing it between the hands. The handkerchief is placed, say, apparently in the left hand, and the wand taken in the right, in which the loaded tube remains. A wave of the wand, and the handkerchief has disappeared, after which a very small amount of dexterity suffices to return the tube into the wand, when both hands can be shown empty.

Where the wand is to be used for this latter purpose only, the slot in the side of *b* is not necessary.

Such appliances are useful in their way, particularly to performers who fear to trust to the subtler magic of their own fingers, but the expert will find it just as easy, with a little skill, to produce the handkerchief from the

FIG. 4

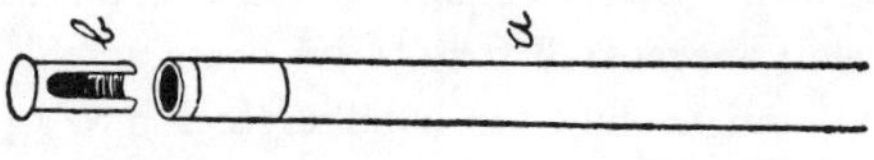

wand in ordinary use. To accomplish this, the handkerchief, first twisted ropewise, should be wound as tightly as possible around one end of the wand, the final end being tucked in, with the aid of a small paper-knife or other convenient instrument, behind the inner folds, in which condition the handkerchief forms a compact little ball.

The performer comes forward with the wand (handkerchief end) in his right hand. In the course of his PATTER he transfers this end to a temporary resting-place under his left arm, while he pulls up his sleeves, incidentally showing both hands empty. He then grasps the projecting end with the left hand, and instantly transfers the opposite end to the right, which moves to meet it, thereby masking the presence of the rolled-up handkerchief. This he slides, still covered by the hand, to the center of the wand. For the final production, he has only to slip the handkerchief off the wand, and shake it out.

Production from a Match-Box. For this clever little expedient the conjurer is indebted to the inventive genius of BUATIER DE KOLTA. The sliding portion of an ordinary match-box is pushed out to the extent of about half an inch, and a handkerchief is packed in the space left vacant at the opposite end. The performer, under the pretext of lighting a candle, takes a match out of the box, which he holds with the open end away from him. Having obtained the match, he closes the box; the act of doing so squeezes the handkerchief out into his hand, to be produced according to his fancy.

There is considerable art in folding a handkerchief for magical production, the requirements being that it shall pack closely, and yet unfold spontaneously and rapidly. To ensure this a good plan is to fold it backward and forward in accordion-pleats one and one-half inches in width, and when the whole length is taken up as a strip, to fold it in the same manner. A handkerchief thus dealt with unfolds instantly on being released.

FIG. 5

The *Multiplying Tube* is a glass tube (Fig. 5) divided into two compartments, *a* and *b*, vertically, by two slips of mirror cemented together, back to back. Around each end of the tube is a band of brass or white metal; between these bands, at equal distances, are four upright strips of the same material. Two of these coincide in position with the edges of the mirror partition. The other two occupy positions midway between these, each exactly facing the medial line of one of the mirrors, and being reflected therein. The effect, to the eye of the spectator, is that he sees right through the tube, the reflection of the forward strip being taken for the rear strip, which is actually hidden from him by the mirror between. (See TUMBLERS)

To prepare the tube for use, one of the compartments is packed with silk handkerchiefs (all of one color), of which half a dozen or more can be inserted without difficulty. In this condition, with the loaded compartment to the rear, the tube may stand on the performer's table, or be brought forward held horizontally between his hands, apparently empty.

In the course of his patter, he places in the empty compartment a single handkerchief of the same color as those to be produced, spreading it well in the tube, so as to occupy as much space as possible. The tube may now be shown on either side, for both look alike. The performer turns the side with the single handkerchief to the rear, and produces first, two or three handkerchiefs in succession from the front compartment; then the single one from the rear compartment, and finally the remainder from the front.

The above order is adopted because, if the production of the single handkerchief were left till last, it would have to be produced from an apparently empty tube. The performer may, however, by way of variety, produce it in this manner: he blows upon the (supposedly) empty tube, at the same moment giving it a half-turn; this brings the single handkerchief to the front, after which it may be produced in the usual way.

The ease with which a handkerchief can be produced, apparently from nowhere, and the really magical effect of such production, if neatly executed, have induced some performers to enlarge upon the idea, producing not just one or two handkerchiefs, but a score, or even a larger number.

This surprising effect is usually produced by the aid of a hollow *Stillwell ball.* This may be of celluloid, aluminum, or thin brass, about one and three-quarters inches in diameter, and should have a hole in its side of about three-quarters of an inch. A ball of the above dimensions will hold, closely packed, about half a dozen fine silk handkerchiefs of the size usually affected by conjurers (twelve to fourteen inches square), but by the use of a very simple artifice, it may be made available, so far as the eye of the spectator is concerned, to produce just double that number.

The plan adopted in this case is to cut each square in half diagonally from corner to corner, hemming the raw edge. A half-handkerchief of this kind, held up by either of the two divided corners, and allowed to hang straight down, will drape itself so as to represent, to casual observation, a complete handkerchief, and count accordingly.

The method adopted for packing the handkerchiefs into the ball is as follows. The first is pushed in pretty much anyhow, until it comes to the last corner. This is folded back three quarters of an inch. The *first* corner of the handkerchief to be inserted next is then folded in like manner, and one hooked, so to speak, into the other. The second handkerchief is then worked into the ball, care being taken not to disturb the above-mentioned arrangement; and the last corner of this is then linked in like manner with the first corner of the next handkerchief, and so on until the ball is full. The final corner of the last handkerchief is allowed to project about half an inch.

The operator, after getting the ball into his hands and showing by the familiar CHANGEOVER PALM that both are empty, leaves it finally PALMED in the right hand. With this hand he makes a grab in the air, and professedly catches a handkerchief, which, however, remains invisible until it is transferred, still invisibly, to the left hand, when it at once materializes. The thumb and finger of the left hand produce this effect by nipping the projecting corner of the handkerchief as the hands come together, and, as they separate, drawing it out of the ball. The remaining handkerchiefs are caught one after another in the same manner, not becoming visible until they are placed in the left hand.

One very elegant little ACQUITMENT, on which the effect of the trick largely depends, will convince the spectators that the hands, except for the handkerchiefs already produced, are entirely empty throughout.

FIG. 6

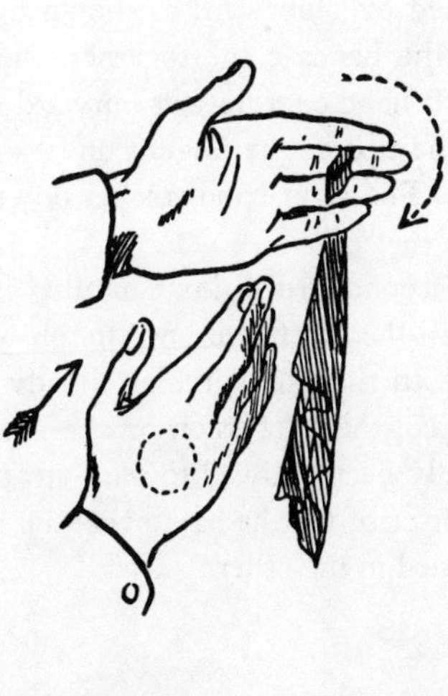

FIG. 7

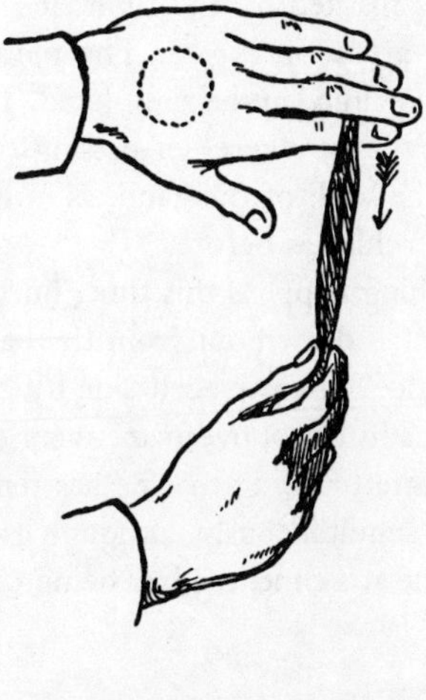

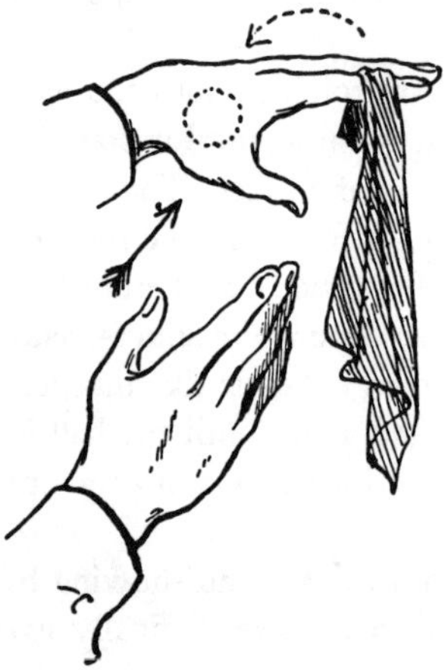

FIG. 8

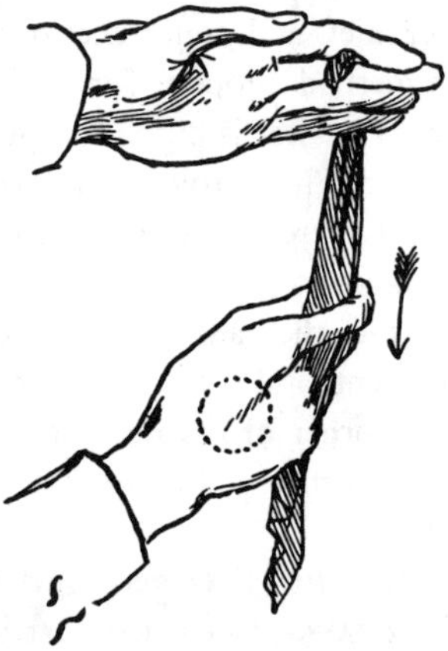

FIG. 9

Suppose the first handkerchief has been produced by the aid of the hollow ball, as above mentioned. It is then taken by one corner between the first and second fingers of the performer's left hand, as shown in Fig. 6, the palm being toward the spectators. The right hand is now brought up to the left, and transfers the ball from the palm of the former to that of the latter. The moment the ball reaches the left hand, this is turned over toward the body (as shown by the dotted arrow) and the right hand strokes down the handkerchief, the two hands assuming the position shown in Fig. 7. The ball is at this stage palmed in the left hand.

The right hand is now empty, and is carelessly shown to be so. The performer then brings it once more up to the left hand. As soon as the left hand is masked by the right, it is turned over outward as shown by the dotted arrow in Fig. 8. The moment the hands come together, the ball is again palmed in the right hand. The left hand continues its outward revolution, the handkerchief passing over the tips of the fingers, and hanging from the back of the hand, as in Fig. 9. The right hand strokes down the handkerchief as before.

Nothing happens this time; but on a second stroke-down another handkerchief is drawn out from the ball with the forefinger and thumb of the left hand. This is placed side by side with the handkerchief already produced, and the above maneuvers repeated, the impression on the mind of the spectator being that he has repeatedly been allowed to see both palms empty simultaneously, although as a matter of fact he has never seen more than one at a time, the ball being concealed in the other.

By having half a dozen balls, duly loaded and distributed in various places, the performer may amplify the trick to any extent he pleases. He may even carry two or three balls under his vest, but where more than that are bestowed in this manner, they should be supported by wire clips.

L. H.

Color-changing is usually performed with some form of *dye tube*, of which there are two kinds in common use. The small, or hand, dye tube is used for changing the color of a single silk by passing it through the fist. The small tube is metal, an inch in diameter and two inches long. Fastened by opposite ends at the center inside is a piece of webbing with enough slack so that its middle can be pushed to either end of the tube. The tube is loaded beforehand with a silk of one color. It is palmed in the right hand, which also holds a silk of another color. In drawing this silk through the left hand, the performer leaves the tube behind, with the end that is momentarily closed by the webbing upward. The silk is poked through the fist from the top, displacing the previously loaded one little by little, and the latter is tugged out of the bottom of the fist. During a final poke at the top of the fist, the right hand steals the tube, and then draws the visible silk away from the bottom of the fist.

The large dye tube (Fig. 10) is a tube of thin brass *a b*, about four inches in length by one and a half in diameter, open at each end, but with the edges turned in about one-sixteenth of an inch. Within this is a smaller tube, not quite an inch deep, open at the top but closed at the bottom, forming a cylindrical cup. This fits the outer tube accurately, sliding up and down it, and can be shifted to either end at pleasure, but it cannot be removed because of the turned-in edges of the tube.

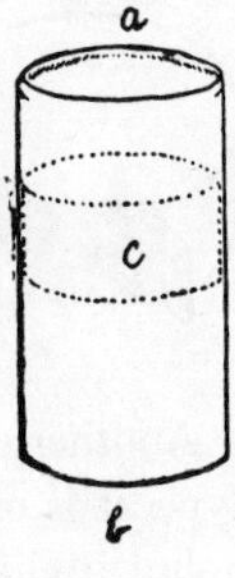

FIG. 10

The cup is pushed to the top of the tube, leaving it mouth outward; the tube is then reversed, and loaded from the other end with three different colored handkerchiefs.

By any one of several methods, a sheet of fairly stiff paper about twelve by eighteen is shown empty, then rolled up into a tube with the dye tube inside, at the bottom. Three white silks are poked through in succession from the bottom, and removed from the top "dyed" a different color. The dye tube is stolen with the colored silks or dropped down a BLACK ART well, and the paper is unrolled, empty.

A special color-changing silk that changes automatically with one sweep of the empty hand is credited to Dr. Harlan Tarbell. It is much more difficult to describe than to operate, but consists basically of two silks of different colors laid one over the other, with a corner of each sewn over a three-quarter-inch metal ring. The silks are stitched together for about two inches just above the center. The corner of the upper silk opposite the ring is folded back and passed through the ring. Then the two opposite free corners of the lower silk are brought together, and stitched from the ring downward in a curve for about two thirds of the distance to the projecting bottom corner of the lower (now the outer) silk. The corner of the inner silk that protrudes through the ring is now replaced by the corresponding corner of the outer silk, and the process of stitching repeated. The final result of this construction is that the silks form a sort of bag with the ring at the mouth, and by holding the projecting corner in one hand, and drawing the ring downward with the other, you turn this bag inside out, and so change its visible color. *H. H.*

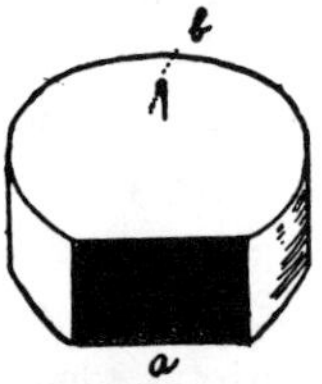

FIG. 11

FIG. 12

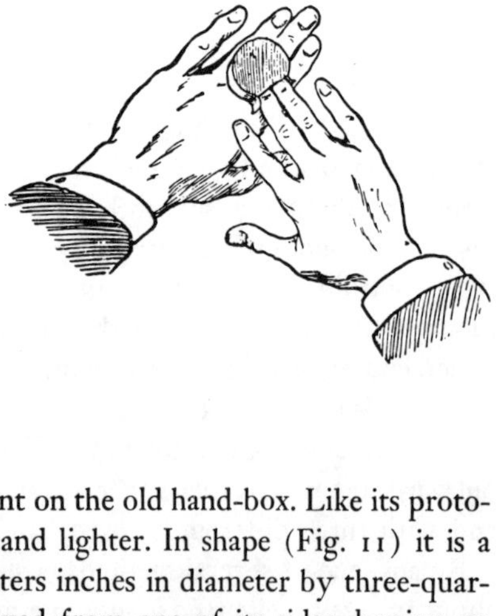

FIG. 13

Another vanisher is an improvement on the old hand-box. Like its prototype, it is of tin, but much smaller and lighter. In shape (Fig. 11) it is a hollow cylinder, one and three quarters inches in diameter by three-quarters in depth, with a segment removed from one of its sides, leaving an opening *a*. The clip which formed part of the original hand-box is lacking, but on each face, at the side farthest from the opening, is soldered a portion of a needle bent into a little hook, *b*. The handkerchief to be got rid of is worked into the vanisher in the same manner as was done with the hand-box.

The special merit of this form of the appliance lies in the little hooks, by means of which the vanisher may not only be attached to the hand, but may also be hitched on to the back of a chair, a hanging table cover, or any portion of the performer's garments. The object of having a hook on each side is to avoid the necessity of turning it around before fixing it in any new position.

The ingenious Mr. Roterberg (an American dealer and writer) improved upon the pattern above described in one or two particulars. In the case of his vanisher, the flat sides project a sixteenth of an inch or so beyond the curved portion, the resulting edge all around giving a capital grip for palming, and the metal on each side of the mouth is continued in an outward curve for three-eighths of an inch, as in Fig. 12, forming a sort of lip. (Fig. 13)

FIG. 14

The Nickel Tube, with Pull. This is a plain nickel tube, *a* (Fig. 14) about four inches long by one and one-quarter in diameter, with two caps, *b b*, one for each end. To a casual view both ends of the tube are alike, but a minute inspection would show that the edge of one end, which we will call the top, is turned over inward all around. The edge of the opposite end is left plain.

The above is the whole of the visible apparatus, but there is another item, of which the spectators know nothing. This is a cup, *c*, of such a size at its upper and open end as to pass easily within *a*. Its opposite end tapers to a point, to which is attached the end of a PULL, arranged so that the cup shall lie until needed just within the left sleeve.

The tube and caps having been handed out for examination, separately, to three different persons, the performer takes back the tube, and in turning to his table to get the handkerchief, inserts the cup into its lower end, and pushes it home. The turned-in upper edge prevents it from going too far. He then loads one or more handkerchiefs, according to the intended *denouement* of the trick, into the tube, pressing them into the cup.

Taking back one of the caps, he closes the upper end of the tube; the moment he has done so, he turns it so as to lie in a straight line with his arm, and works the pull. The cup and handkerchiefs fly up the sleeve. Now taking back the second cap, he closes the other end of the tube, and hands it to someone for safe-keeping, ultimately showing that the handkerchiefs have disappeared, and reproducing them (actually duplicates) elsewhere.

Vanish From a Paper Cylinder, in good hands, is very pretty and effective. The performer is furnished with an ordinary sleeve pull. Getting this down into the left hand, and having in the other a small piece of fairly stiff paper, he forms this into a cylinder around the pull; then, with the aid of the wand, he packs into it a handkerchief (which of course passes into the latter). The moment he relaxes the pressure of his hand on the paper cylinder, the vanisher flies up his sleeve. He blows through the cylinder toward the quarter where the handkerchief is intended to reappear, after which he unrolls the paper and shows it empty. *L. H.*

Another popular vanishing device is the *plunger wand*, used to make a silk disappear from a paper cone. The wand is hollow, and one end, while fitting snugly to the nickeled ferrule, can be pulled out. Fixed to the center of this loose end is a plunger somewhat more than half the length of the wand. In performance, a sheet of paper is rolled into a cone around the wand, and the plunger end, nipped through the paper, is left inside the cone. The performer picks up a silk on the (now open) end of the wand, and pushes it into the cone, but takes care in the process to slide the plunger back into the wand. The handkerchief is thus driven into the wand, which picks up and carries away the plunger end, so that actually the performer folds down the top of a perfectly empty cone.

Handkerchief knots are another class of effect, usually shown as flourishes during a bigger trick.

An instantaneous knot is produced as follows. The handkerchief is twisted ropewise and the middle laid across the outstretched fingers of the right hand (palm up), the two ends hanging down equally on each side of the hand. Close the fingers over the handkerchief, and at the same time turn the hand over with a generous sweep of the arm so that the force of the movement will cause the right tip of the handkerchief (the end protruding from the heel of the hand) to fly up and fall over the top of the hand. The handkerchief should fall across the knuckles, when it will be found that by slightly revolving the hand to the right the tip may be clipped between the second and third fingers (Fig. 15). Clutch this end of the handkerchief and with a smart downward movement of the arm allow the handkerchief to drop off the hand, which forms a single loose knot. Snap the handkerchief by the end clipped between the second and third fingers, and the knot is tightened. The instant this is done the handkerchief is tossed into the air.

The *dissolving knot* is the reverse of this effect: an overhand knot is tied in the center of a silk, and dissolved visibly in an instant. Twist the silk ropewise, and hold it up with about two-thirds of its length hanging down from the crotch of your left thumb across your palm, and the remaining third hanging down the back of your hand. Seizing the lower corner with

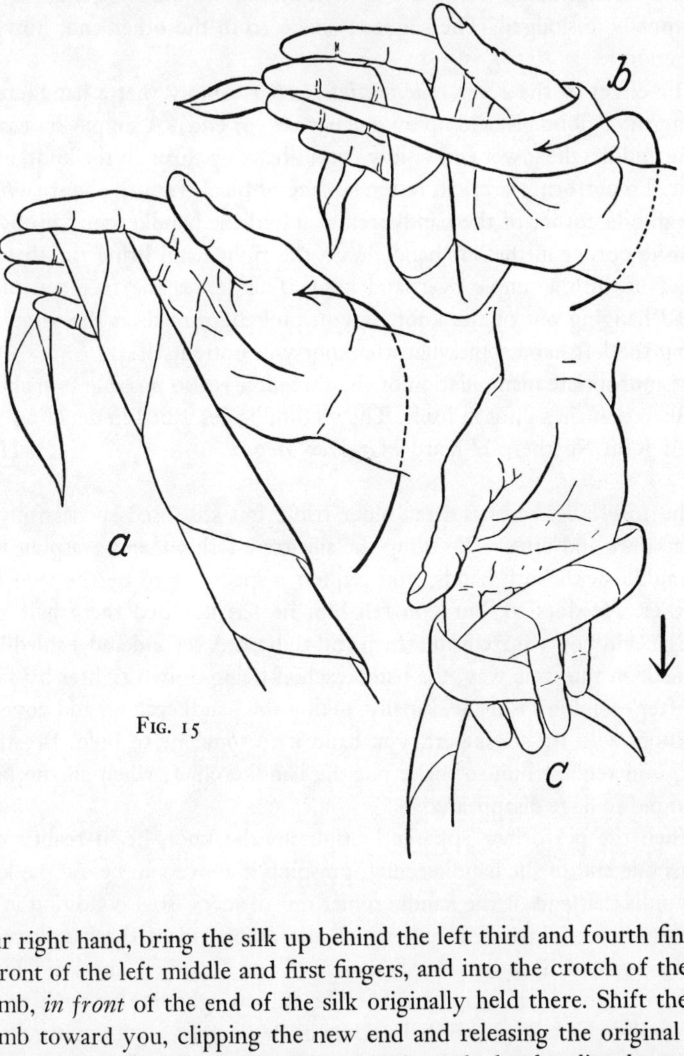

FIG. 15

your right hand, bring the silk up behind the left third and fourth fingers, in front of the left middle and first fingers, and into the crotch of the left thumb, *in front* of the end of the silk originally held there. Shift the left thumb toward you, clipping the new end and releasing the original end. Let go with your right hand, and put it through the dangling loop from front to rear. A part near the middle of the silk is already clipped between your left middle fingers. With your right hand, grab the original upper end of the silk, which is now lying loose because you have shifted your left thumb, and pull this end back through the loop. You cannot see why unless you carry out the instructions with a silk, but the result of this move is to tie a knot around a kink formed in the silk by your left middle fingers. As long as the right hand continues to hold the silk by the same end, the knot will not be dislodged. The slightest shake from the other end, however, will undo it.

The effect of the *Knot that Unties Itself* is simply that a handkerchief or length of ribbon is held up by one corner (or end). A simple knot is tied in the middle; the lower end visibly creeps back up through the knot, undoing it. To perform the trick, fasten a piece of black THREAD about two feet long to one corner of the handkerchief. Hold the handkerchief up by the opposite corner in the left hand. With the right hand bring the threaded corner up into a simple overhand knot. This leaves the free end of the thread hanging out of the knot. If you pull the thread, at the same time raising the left hand somewhat, the knot will untie itself.

By appropriate manipulation of the thread, it is also possible to make the handkerchief tie a knot in itself. The method is described in detail on page 612 of John Northern Hilliard's *Greater Magic*. *H. H.*

The *vanishing knots* is a far older trick, but still used successfully by BLACKSTONE and others. Twisting the silk rope-fashion, and grasping it by the middle with both hands, you request a spectator to tie the two ends together. He does so, but you tell him he has not tied them half tight enough, and you yourself pull them still tighter. A second and a third knot are made in the same way, the handkerchief being drawn tighter by yourself after each knot is made. Finally, taking the handkerchief, and covering the knots with the loose part, you hand it to someone to hold. Breathing on it, you request him to shake out the handkerchief, when all the knots are found to have disappeared.

When the performer apparently tightens the knot, he in reality only strains one end of the handkerchief, grasping it above and below the knot. This pulls that end of the handkerchief out of its twisted condition in the knot into a straight line, round which the other end of the handkerchief remains twisted; in other words, converts (or "upsets") the knot into a slip knot. After each successive knot he still straightens this same end of the handkerchief. This end, being thus made straight, would naturally be left longer than the other which is twisted round and round it. This tendency the performer counteracts by drawing it partially back through the slip knot at each pretended tightening. When he finally covers over the knots, which he does with his left hand, he holds the straightened portion of the handkerchief, immediately behind the knots, between the first finger and thumb of the right hand, and therewith, in the act of covering over the knots, draws this straightened portion completely out of the slip knot.

The student must be on guard against one particular kind of knot, which cannot be upset—the method of tying in which the two ends are placed side by side, and tied simultaneously in a single knot. This may generally be avoided by holding the two ends to be tied at a wide angle, so that they cannot very well be drawn parallel. *L. H.*

Another method is as follows. Hold an end of the handkerchief between the thumb and first finger of each hand, about three inches from the tip—the natural position for tying an ordinary knot. Now lay the right end across the left, and apparently tie the two ends together. Really, when the two ends are crossed, the right over the left, the two ends are clipped at the point of intersection between the tip of the right thumb and the first finger. A sweeping movement of the right end back and down, when it is grasped by the tips of the left first and second fingers and brought up *in front*. The movement is simply the reverse of actually tying the right end around the left. Holding the handkerchief tightly at the point where the ends are apparently entwined, the performer requests one of the spectators to tie the second part of the knot, telling him to pull the ends as tight as possible. In fact, of course, you have in the end only one half of a square knot, which will fall apart almost of its own weight.

This knot (completed by the performer instead of a spectator) is often used in the popular trick next described.

The *sympathetic silks* is an effect performed with great success by GOLDIN, MULHOLLAND, and many other fine conjurers. Three white silks are shown separate, and piled or held by a VOLUNTEER at one side of the stage. Three other silks are tied corner to corner, and piled or held at the other side of the stage. The performer makes the knots pass from the second set of silks, which are now separate, to the first, which prove to be tied corner to corner. No detailed ROUTINE will be given here; the principle of all is the same. Three of the silks are tied together by opposite corners to begin with. They are then picked up and allowed to hang down from the free corners; the two knots are completely hidden in the folds of the bulkiest part of the silks. All six silks are then bundled together and held near the top corners. They can be counted from the left hand into the right, which lifts each silk a little in the act of counting, but does not move far from the left hand, without exposing the knots. The three tied silks are casually dropped or handed over on one side of the stage. The remaining three are knotted together (which may, if preferred, be done by the audience), and the knots are either upset or of the trick variety described above. The working from here on will be obvious.

The *Twentieth-Century Handkerchief Trick* is a remotely similar effect. Two silks are tied corner to corner, rolled up, and put in a glass. A third silk, usually of a contrasting color, is vanished, and reappears tied between the two in the glass.

The method of the original inventor, a dealer named Frank Ducrot, was to have a pocket sewed in the corner of a silk. A duplicate of the vanishing silk was tied to the corner at this pocket, and then worked into the pocket, leaving the opposite, free corner exposed. This was the corner actually tied to the second silk before the two were rolled up. In unrolling the bundle after the third silk was vanished, the performer gave a yank to the two silks, which brought the third one out, tied between.

The effect can be performed quite as well by a simple SWITCH of the rolled-up bundle, either by SLEIGHT-OF-HAND or with a mirror glass (see TUMBLERS).

The *lamp-chimney vanish*, one of the most truly magical-looking tricks in existence, is often combined with the Twentieth-Century Handkerchief trick. In effect, the performer puts a silk into a cylindrical glass lamp chimney (nowadays more usually a highball glass), and holds the chimney horizontal with a palm over each end. The silk vanishes instantaneously without cover. The secret is a PULL, either double- or single-action, anchored or (if double-action) with its pulley near the left elbow. The pull passes down the right sleeve, and terminates in a loop of catgut or strong black thread. When the trick is to be shown, the loop is got down into the right hand, and the silk is doubled and drawn half way through it. The folds of the silk in the glass conceal the loop of the pull. A quick spreading and extension of the performer's arms snatches the silk up the right sleeve too fast for the eye to follow. There is a detailed description in Lang Neil's *The Modern Conjurer*.

H. H.

Still another class of handkerchief tricks is exemplified by the *handkerchief cut and restored*, one of the oldest of conjuring tricks. Every schoolboy knows that the handkerchief is not cut at all, and that if the performer were to spread it out, it would be seen to be uninjured.

Such *was* the case, no doubt, but the conjurer of today *does* spread out the handkerchief. It is not changed, but is the genuine borrowed article. In the middle of it is a huge hole, through which may be seen the coat sleeve, or the trouser leg, over which it is outspread. And yet, "Presto!" the damage is repaired and the handkerchief is whole as at first.

The secret lies in the use of a very simple little appliance. Two small pieces of cambric, about five inches square, are lightly tacked together at the edges, forming a sort of little bag. Between them lies a piece of thin black cloth, a shade smaller. This is VESTED, and at the proper moment got into the right hand, on the palm of which it lies flat, with the center of the borrowed handkerchief laid over it. The hand closes on them and turns them over, then transfers them to the left hand. The little cambric bag is now uppermost.

The performer draws up a portion of the center of this, and cuts it. He then throws the handkerchief loosely over the left coat sleeve, the little bag lying upon it, with the cut side uppermost. The black cloth, visible through the hole just made, appears to be the coat sleeve, seen through the handkerchief. A little gentle friction applied to the hole enables the performer to palm off the little bag and to restore the handkerchief, uninjured, to its anxious owner. *L. H.*

For the fullest development of this effect, see the SUN AND MOON TRICK.

Silk tricks are covered at length in Jean Hugard's *Silken Sorcery*, Rice and Van Zandt, *Thru the Dye Tube*, *The Tarbell Course in Magic*, *Vol. III*, and Professor Hoffmann's *Later Magic*.

SLATE TESTS The production of writing on blank school slates is one of the most popular SPIRIT EFFECTS used by fake mediums, many of whose methods conjurers have borrowed.

Fundamentally there are three methods of getting messages on a slate. The easiest and most familiar depends on the "flap"—a sheet of silicate that fits exactly inside the wooden frame of a school slate. It is indistinguishable from the surface of the slate itself. Generally the performer has two slates, one with a message written on it beforehand, and covered with the flap. The inside of the flap may also bear writing. The unprepared slate is laid over the flap side of the prepared slate. If the two are turned over, the flap drops into the unprepared slate, revealing the writing.

Various spring catches have been devised to hold the flap in place, allowing the slate to be examined. A more radical development is Al Baker's Folding-flap Slate, in which the flap is loose for only half the length of the slate. It is hinged at the center, and normally locked in place by the frame of the slate, which can, however, be slid endwise enough to release the flap. The more elementary working of the slate will now be obvious; it is intended here to leave the inventor in possession of his own ingenious refinements.

The second basic principle is a SWITCH of slates. Naturally the methods of accomplishing this are endless—by tables, hidden assistants, double bags, under cover of a larger slate, book, newspaper. There is no room here even to list them. The made-to-order conditions under which fake mediums work render many of their methods useless to the stage magician.

A different method, which may perhaps be called a sort of switch, is to use two normal slates, one of which, here called No. 1, has a message written on it. Apparently the performer shows both sides of both slates blank, and numbers all four sides in chalk, and then the message is revealed. Write the figure 1 in the lower right-hand corner of the message side of No. 1. Put slate No. 2 on No. 1. To begin with, you hold the two slates together, and turn them over endways toward you, showing that both outer surfaces are blank. Have a spectator write a 2 in the upper left corner of the upper surface, which is the back of slate No. 1. As he does so, your fingers underneath rub off the figure 1 that you have just chalked on slate No. 2. Put slate No. 1 under No. 2, and write a 3 in the upper left corner of No. 2. Turn slate No. 2 over sidewise to the right. Write "4" in the upper left corner; then slide the top slate, No. 2, underneath. Turn the two slates together over again, and fan them slightly to the right. This exposes the figure 1 on the face of slate No. 1 next to the figure 3 on slate No. 2. Turn the two over still again, showing only the figure 2; slide off slate No. 2, turning it both ways to show the 3 and 4, and finally put it back under slate No. 1.

The last method of getting a message on a slate is by writing it there during the trick. One way is with a THUMB WRITER or forefinger writer. Another is to put a piece of chalk on a slate, and hold the slate against the under side of a table. In carrying the slate under the table, the performer tilts it, rolling the chalk into his right palm, then wedges the slate between the table and his wrist, while the fingers write the message on the lower surface with the chalk. The slate is turned over in bringing it back from under the table, thus leaving the piece of chalk on the message on the upper surface.

Chemical methods of slate writing have been discovered, but the whole idea is too obvious and too messy to be much used.

The standard reference on slate tests is David P. Abbott's *Behind the Scenes with the Mediums;* a later valuable book is Peter Warlock, *The Best Tricks with Slates.* *H. H.*

SLEEVE, UP HIS This favorite cry of the eager spectator is, as even the youngest magician knows, mistaken ninety-nine times out of a hundred. Because of it many earlier magicians (especially BACK-PALM experts) used to go through their entire act with their sleeves rolled up to the elbow.

The sleeve can nevertheless do occasional good service. Many PULLS work in the sleeve, but the particular reference here is to the dodge or sleight of sleeving, which will be found covered under COIN MANIPULATION.

SLEIGHT-OF-HAND (See also BALL MANIPULATION; CARD MANIPULATION; CIGARETTE MANIPULATION; CIGAR MANIPULATION; COIN MANIPULATION; CUPS AND BALLS; THIMBLE TRICKS)

In the public mind, *sleight-of-hand* has been extended to cover any sort of magic, even ILLUSIONS. For the magician, however, it retains its original meaning: pure manual dexterity, or tricks produced by pure manual dexterity, and not relying chiefly on apparatus, preparation, or prearrangement. Many small tricks, especially card tricks, require neither apparatus nor sleight-of-hand; much apparatus of the GIMMICK type does require sleight-of-hand. Illusions, because they deal with objects too big to hold in the hand, are the one class of magic that seldom requires sleight-of-hand —though even here, sleight-of-hand FORCING may be called into play. There are successful illusionists and "apparatus conjurers" who can do no sleight-of-hand at all, but their difficulties and restrictions deserve our sympathy rather than our scorn. As entertainers they are far ahead of those incredibly skilful sleight-of-hand students who can do tricks but no magic.

ALEXANDER HERRMANN and HOUDINI were among the stage magicians whose skill at sleight-of-hand equalled their showmanship; HARRY BLACKSTONE is another. NELSON DOWNS and NATE LEIPZIG were probably the finest pure sleight-of-hand artists magic has ever known; CARDINI is the most famous living sleight-of-hand showman. *B. M.*

SPELLING MASTER (See also: CARD MANIPULATION)

The name for two of the most popular modern card effects. In one, a number of cards are shown, and the names of the different values—ace, two, three, and so on—are spelled out, the performer passing one card from the top of the pile to the bottom for each letter. The next card after the last letter is the one spelled out. To do this with all the cards of one suit, arrange them as follows: 3, 8, 7, ace, queen, 6, 4, 2, jack, king, 10, 9, 5. The method of working out the formula for any such spelling trick is given in Hugard's *Encyclopedia of Card Tricks*.

In the other type of spelling effect, a card is drawn, or merely thought of. The spectator spells out the full name of the card (or sometimes, by way of variety, his own name), dealing off a card for each letter, and the chosen card turns up at the end.

Various sleight-of-hand methods will be obvious to every magician. The simplest way is to use the GLIMPSE, then let the pack be shuffled. "To show that you haven't removed the card" you run over the pack face upward, warning the spectator not to stop you, and to notice that you do not watch his eyes. Actually, the moment you see the sighted card you start spelling to yourself as you run the cards from your left hand into your right. When you have run enough cards, you break the fan, make some appropriate remark, and put the remainder at the front.

Another group of methods depends on the fact that in English all the names of cards have ten, eleven, twelve, thirteen, fourteen, or fifteen letters. Thirteen, which is a frequent number, is exactly one-fourth of the pack. For instance, if the pack is cut exactly in half, and one half exactly in half again, the bottom card of the last cut will spell out exactly if it is a thirteen-letter card. Variations in length can be adjusted for by the SHIFT or SLIP, or by varying the spelling—adding *the* to the ten-letter cards, omitting *of* for the fifteens, turning up the next following card for the fourteens, etc. The accuracy of the spectator's cut may be estimated and allowed for, or assisted by the CRIMP.

The versions in which the spectator merely thinks of a card are among the best in all card magic. They depend on prearrangement, coupled with a fairly easy thought FORCE. Six cards can be so prearranged—a fifteen-letter card on the bottom, then a fourteen, and so on up to ten—that by merely adding nine indifferent cards on top, you can spell out any one of the six. Five more cards can be added by the variations in spelling procedure already mentioned. In running the cards over, face up, before the spectator, it is fairly easy to confine his actual choice to the prearranged cards. You add the necessary number of indifferent cards on top, and to all intents and purposes the trick is done.

A chapter of Hilliard's *Greater Magic* is devoted to what he calls "The Spelling Bee." *B. M.*

SPIDER A mechanical device to facilitate BACK-PALMING.

SPIRIT EFFECTS (See also BILLET- AND MESSAGE-READING; BLINDFOLDS; ESCAPES AND RELEASES; SLATE TESTS)

Spirit effects are those that reproduce the "manifestations" obtained by spirit mediums. Spirit seances are conducted under circumstances that make trickery much easier than it is on any stage. This has led uninformed magicians to despise the skill of fraudulent mediums; but on the word of the late Elmer P. Ransom, who once managed Margaret Fox, the co-founder of modern spiritualism, and was a magician for fifty years, the mediums are usually much the better performers.

Readers who are interested in the history and serious pretensions of modern spiritualism must turn to JOHN MULHOLLAND's *Beware Familiar Spirits.* The actual methods of the mediums are described in great detail in David P. Abbott's *Behind the Scenes with the Mediums.*

The Fox sisters, Margaret and Katie, launched spiritualism with the "Rochester rappings"–mysterious rapping noises heard apparently all over the room. In her old age, Margaret Fox publicly confessed and demonstrated that the raps were made by cracking the toe joints, as some people can crack their knuckles. The next improvement was made by the Davenport Brothers, Ira Erastus (1839-1911) and William Henry Harrison (1841-1877), who toured the world producing manifestations inside a cabinet where they were securely bound. They were the first to go systematically into rope releases (see ESCAPES AND RELEASES); HARRY KELLAR once worked as an assistant to the brothers, and HOUDINI made friends with Ira Erastus Davenport when the latter was an old man.

Table-tipping and BILLET-READING were the next popular classes of manifestation. Magicians have since devised various GIMMICKS to perform table-tipping, but the best mediums managed without. A table will actually turn without trickery if a group of people sit around it and put their palms flat on the table-top. That is, it will if they all expect it to turn in the same direction, and if nobody resists the unconscious impulse that makes him exert pressure. Some mediums let their "sitters" unconsciously press on the table until it tips, and then the medium can get a foot under the table leg, push down with his hand, and so float the table two feet in the air.

Billet tests and "pellet tests" were first performed by Charles Foster (*ca.* 1835-1885), whose trick was thus described and explained by an English conjurer: "He gave long, narrow slips of paper to each of his visitors, requesting them to write the names of their deceased friends on them, one under the other, and leave a space between each name. He then tore the names off separately, crumpling up each between his finger and thumb into small pellets, which he threw on the table at which he and his dupes were seated. After a while he would pick up one of these pellets, and, holding it against his forehead, would say, 'The spirit of Mr. So-and-so, whose name is written on this piece of paper, is present, and wishes to communicate with you.' He would throw one of his visitors a pellet, which, on being unfolded, really bore the name mentioned. He repeated this process with all the other pellets except one, which he would hold against his forehead, and then say, 'This spirit says it will write the initials of his name on my arm.' Foster would then pull up his sleeve, and showing his forearm, on which nothing was visible, would rub it vigorously, and blood-red letters representing the initials of the name in the pellet would appear.

"Between the two middle fingers of his right hand, close to the palm, he had concealed a pellet which corresponded in appearance and size with those on the table. He would, before touching the latter, request that they be counted, and then, picking up one with his right hand, he appeared to drop it in his left, instead of which he dropped the palmed pellet, which he then held between his thumb and finger against his forehead, shading his eyes with the same hand. Carrying his right hand under the table, he leisurely unrolled the other pellet, and read the name on it, rolled it up again, and, after again 'ringing the changes' with the pellet against his forehead, called out the name of the 'spirit in waiting,' and threw the pellet to the visitor whose writing was on it. When he had decided which name should appear on his arm, he laid the pellet containing the name on the table, and gazing at it intently he slipped both hands under the table, and with a small, sharp-pointed stick traced the initials with some force and very rapidly just above the front of his wrist. Pulling up his cuff no letters were visible; but, closing his fist tightly and straining the muscles of his arm, the blood showed through the skin where the latter had been scraped by the sharp point, and the appearance of the letters was, of course, also assisted by the energetic rubbing of the right hand."

SLATE TESTS were made popular by Dr. Henry Slade. Slade's favorite method was apparently a THUMB WRITER.

Certain "spirit effects" used by conjurers are at once better and weaker than those shown by mediums, who could not, for instance, get away with the *Talking Skull*, although a magician can show it on a brightly lighted stage. The talking skull is made of papier mache, and answers questions by moving its jaws. The oldest method, and still a good one, is to stretch a black THREAD horizontally across the stage. It is attached to the skull in some way, and lifts it on being tightened. In a more recent method, the skull is mounted on a small board, and is made to talk by poking into a slot in the board a wire GIMMICK that actuates the jaw mechanism of the skull.

The *Rapping Hand* is a first cousin to the talking skull. A wax hand, cut off at the wrist, rests on a sheet of glass, table, or board. Without being approached, it tips up and raps out the answers to questions with its middle finger. The earliest method involved an electro-magnet in the table, and a piece of iron in the wrist of the hand. Next came the horizontal-thread method; and finally an American vaudeville performer devised a mahogany board with a movable batten or a screw underneath, which operated a minute pin that rose and sank through a hole in the surface of the board. The hand (which was carefully balanced) had only to be put in the right spot over the pin, and it would rap away merrily. Only a very careful examination of the board would reveal anything at all out of the way.

H. H.

SPONGE BALLS (See also COMEDY; CUPS AND BALLS; ROUTINES) A comparative novelty in BALL MANIPULATION, and treated separately here because the principles involved are different. The principal sponge-ball effects are due to the compressibility of sponge, and the one special sponge-ball sleight is used to show two balls squeezed to the size of one.

Sponge balls are cut with sharp scissors or a razor blade either from rubber sponge or, perhaps better, from a very soft, fluffy natural sponge. The most popular sizes are about three-quarters of an inch in diameter and two inches in diameter, depending on the performer's particular ROUTINE. The balls should be trimmed as nearly round as possible, but need not be perfect spheres. All those of one set, however, should be as nearly the same size as possible.

The sleights required are few and simple. The regular PALM and FINGER PALM (see BALL MANIPULATION) will serve for most purposes. Sponge balls can also be THUMB-PALMED by catching a bit of sponge in about the same position as you would a THIMBLE. The special sponge-ball sleight referred to above consists of adding a palmed ball to one on the table. The palmed ball is simply brought to the finger palm, clapped down on the exposed ball, and the thumb mashes the two together so that when the hand is turned palm upward, the two balls look like one. This sleight enables the performer to multiply a ball by "tearing it in two." Perhaps most effective of all, he apparently can put a single ball into a spectator's hand, have it clutched tightly, and then pass another ball into the spectator's own hand, for when the victim opens his fingers, he can actually feel the ball growing into two.

It will be unnecessary to detail individual routines. A good COMEDY series, requiring one extra ball palmed at the start, is apparently to put one ball in the trouser pocket, and two in the left hand. When the hand is opened, three balls roll out, and the pocket (though not actually shown to be so) is empty. This is repeated as long as the comedy effect continues to build up.

Many modern CUP AND BALL routines are performed with sponge balls. Sometimes the traditional cups are used, sometimes coffee cups. *H. H.*

STACKED DECKS (See under CARD SETUPS)

STAGE SETTINGS In the drama the well-designed stage setting reflects the atmosphere of the play without distracting the spectator's attention from the actor.

Although a magician's performance is not a play, the above rule can be applied just as well in the field of magic. In the first place, the modern magician is an actor portraying the role of a sorcerer. Then, though it may not have the plot of a play, all magic does have a theme: "Let's escape from reality. Let's believe in miraculous powers that make every wish come true"—a theme that so easily could, and should, be reflected in the setting, yet so seldom is.

The Vaudeville House and Legitimate Theater. The design of most settings for the professional magician of today seems to be influenced by one of two sources: the gaudy carnival, and the ornate Victorian era.

The cheap garishness of the carnival might be called fantastic—fantastically bad. Blue, red, gold, and black vibrating in all their obviousness may be needed to pep up the strip-teaser's act (since she's usually of Civil War vintage anyway) but they merely distract from the subtlety, grace, and beauty of legerdemain.

The Victorian era is notorious for having the most atrocious taste of its own century or any other. It still appears in many of the settings because a good deal of equipment for the large stage illusions shown today was manufactured during the '80s and '90s, and of course is decorated after the Victorian fashion. This explains but certainly does not excuse the over-elaborate folds of the drapes, the fringe, the ornate design of cabinets, lamps, tables, vases, and other equipment, which give off the musty odor of their Victorian origin. The heavy, stodgy realism of such a setting automatically prevents the spectator from feeling "I've escaped reality; I'm in a pleasant dream." He may feel he's dreaming, but it will surely have the atmosphere of a nightmare.

Both these sources of stage design have been defended on the ground that they put the spectator in a whirl of confusion (the former by the profusion of color, the latter by profusion of detail) that aids the magician in his MISDIRECTION. Actually, a setting that distracts takes the attention of the spectator completely out of the performer's control, and a magician who loses control of his audience need not bother with misdirection.

There is a third influence, Oriental design, which has been used by many magicians. It could be well adapted, but seldom is. The result usually turns out like chop suey—a strictly western dish that was never even heard of in the East. Oriental art is extremely subtle, and should be used as a source only by someone who has made a careful study of it.

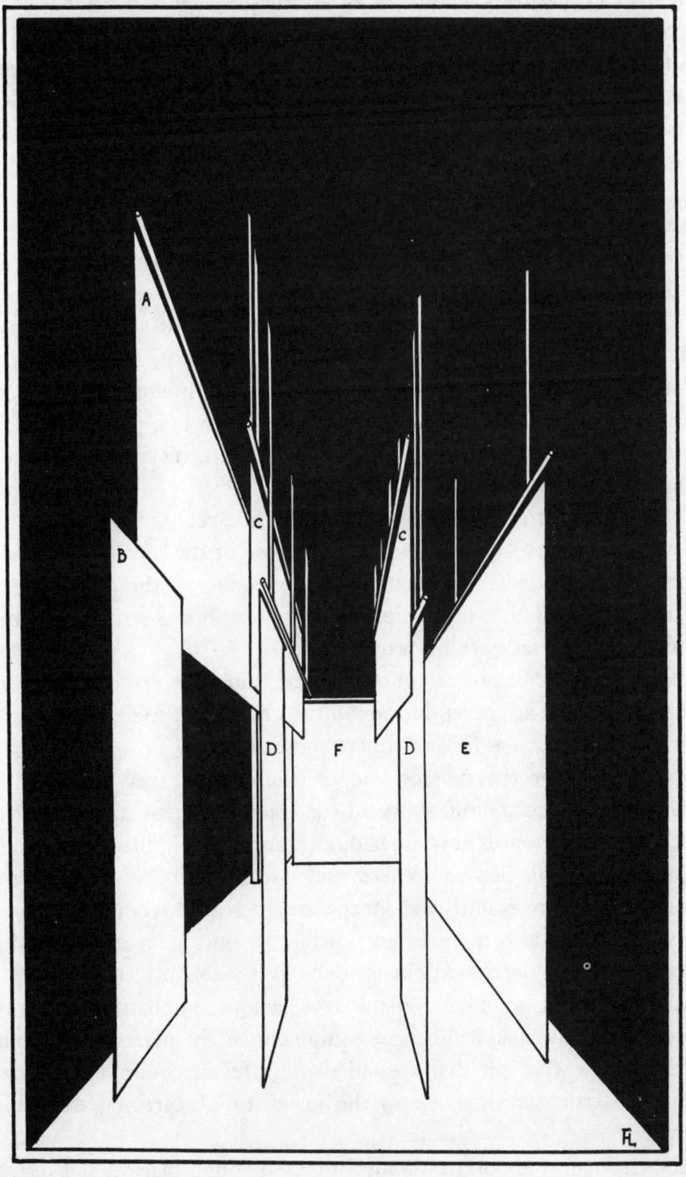

FIG. 1

Magicians refer to their profession as the "art of magic" and many have a talent deserving to be classed as an art. Yet how few dress that art in a correspondingly artistic setting!

Before making suggestions, however, it would be well to treat the technical aspects of the settings found today in the vaudeville house and legitimate theater. On the whole they are very practical. The average set consists of a backdrop, two or three border drops, and several pairs of leg drops hung either as wings or as side-tabs. These may all be of painted canvas, or they may be drapes with the design appliqued on. In either case the complete setting can be folded into trunks and transported in a comparatively small space at minimum expense. (Fig. 1)

This type of setting may also be adjusted easily to the various dimensions of different houses. Further, it can be shifted quickly, and this is an important requirement–especially in the vaudeville house. Lastly, it is an excellent foundation, to which can be added set pieces, plastic units, platforms, etc. Unfortunately, though, very few performers seem to take advantage of this possibility.

To sum up all that has been said so far: the average stage-setting used today by magicians is poorly designed because of the sources from which the design originated and because it is distracting without creating any atmosphere except that of confusion. It is a practical setting, but many technical possibilities have been overlooked.

Finally, it should be pointed out that these comments refer to the *average* setting only; there are exceptions to all the criticisms listed. It is necessary, in such a compilation as this, to adhere to generalities.

Suggestions. For the slender budget, the simplest way to avoid bad scenery is to fall back on the old stand-by, black velour. A stage completely dressed in black velour is never in bad taste, and a set of "blacks" is standard equipment in many houses. Where they are not part of the permanent equipment they are readily and inexpensively rented from any theatrical supply firm. It is also quite often possible to find a set of second-hand drapes that can be purchased outright at a reasonable price.

Besides being in good taste, black as a backing emphasizes rather than distracts from the face, hands, and equipment of the performer. A minor consideration is the fact that a good many effects require a black background, and this setting obviates the necessity of carrying extra black screens.

Blacks have two important disadvantages. Though black is not distracting, its neutrality prevents it from creating a positive atmosphere. Further, the idea is anything but original. It has been, still is, and will continue to be used by many.

For the large budget, the wisest procedure would be to commission a professional scenic designer to create a suitable setting. It would be expensive, but worth it, and has seldom, if ever, been done.

The reason magicians have not approached professional artists is probably because they think of the setting as part of the apparatus of their show, rather than as a backing whose purpose should be to create the proper atmosphere. Occasionally, of course, the setting actually is part of the *modus operandi;* a good example being THURSTON's vanishing horse. However, that is the exception rather than the rule, and even for this type of effect a scenic artist could enhance the stage picture.

Any magician playing the vaudeville circuits or legitimate houses has already made a name for himself, and to have a well-known designer's name on his program as the creator of the settings would be a definite asset.

The majority of the well-known designers are in New York and Hollywood, but since at least one of these places is on most circuits, accessibility should not be a problem.

It is not possible to go into details about procedure with the designer, since every show will have different requirements. Probably, in most cases, it would be best to let the designer see a performance. One last suggestion: if any of the apparatus is of ornate Victorian design (or worse), see if the designer can devise some redecoration that will bring it up to date.

Suggestions have been made so far for the slimmest and fattest purses. It would be well now to make a few for the much larger group that falls between the two extremes.

There is probably no need for these magicians to change the present source from which they obtain scenery, whether it be a theatrical storage warehouse, a theatrical draperies firm, a second-hand setting from some musical show just closed, or from elsewhere. But the next time a new dressing for the show is required, consider the following before ordering it.

As stated earlier, a set of hangings as a foundation is technically the most practical unit of scenery for the road. However, instead of having the backdrop of canvas, with some distracting scene painted on it, use drapes (hung in at least 50% fullness) of velour, rep, monk's-cloth or some other durable material that is obtainable in colors adaptable to the purpose. Permit no design to be appliqued on these drapes, and use no fringe.

In selection of colors try to avoid the primaries, red, yellow, and blue. In fact, avoid the use of any brilliant colors. For a dignified, formal performance rich dark colors would probably be best. For gay comedy presentations, light pastel tints might be adaptable. (One drawback of light-colored drapes is the difficulty of keeping them clean.) But whatever colors are selected, make sure that they are subdued, and will set off rather than distract from the costumes and apparatus.

To use drapes in color may be sufficient for a complete setting for some presentations, but there are many other productions that would be enhanced by creating a positive atmosphere of unreality or fantasy. Set pieces, such as decorative screens, cut-outs, and plastic pieces can be used in conjunction with drapes for this purpose, if the pitfalls mentioned above are kept in mind.

A "Set piece" is a rather loose term applied to *any* piece of scenery used in conjunction with drapes, such as pillars, rocks, trees, steps, platforms, screens, etc. A *plastic piece* is any unit built in three dimensions; a *cut-out* has only two dimensions.

To illustrate their use: Suppose an atmosphere of magnificence, spaciousness, depth, and grandeur is desired. Two or three pairs of columns or pillars might be used to create this effect. A great number of combinations can be made by their placement. The addition of two or three platforms and some steps would further increase the possibilities. For a few of the many possible combinations, see Fig. 2.

The pillars may be plastic—that is, made of a solid wooden framework; but they will then add to transportation difficulties. A much simpler method is to use leg drops hung in 400 or 500% fullness. The heavy folds appear as flutes in the column, and as material hung in that much fullness naturally flares out at the bottom it makes the column wider at its base and adds to the effect of solidity.

Another simple but very effective pillar may be created by hanging a cylinder of silk (or any similar material that is translucent) from a wire ring, either in fullness to give the fluted effect or plain. The base of the column should be made to fit down around a large, circular, metallic container (a most effective container has been made from a large garbage pail or ash can) equipped with a lighting unit that will throw light up the interior of the column. In addition to being a light source, this container acts as an anchor for the base of the column, and as a container for the whole unit in transportation.

(Warning: Should it be necessary to "fly" this pillar, three or four thin wires should extend from the ring at the top to the container at the bottom. The silk alone is not sufficient to carry the weight of the container when it is lifted clear of the floor.)

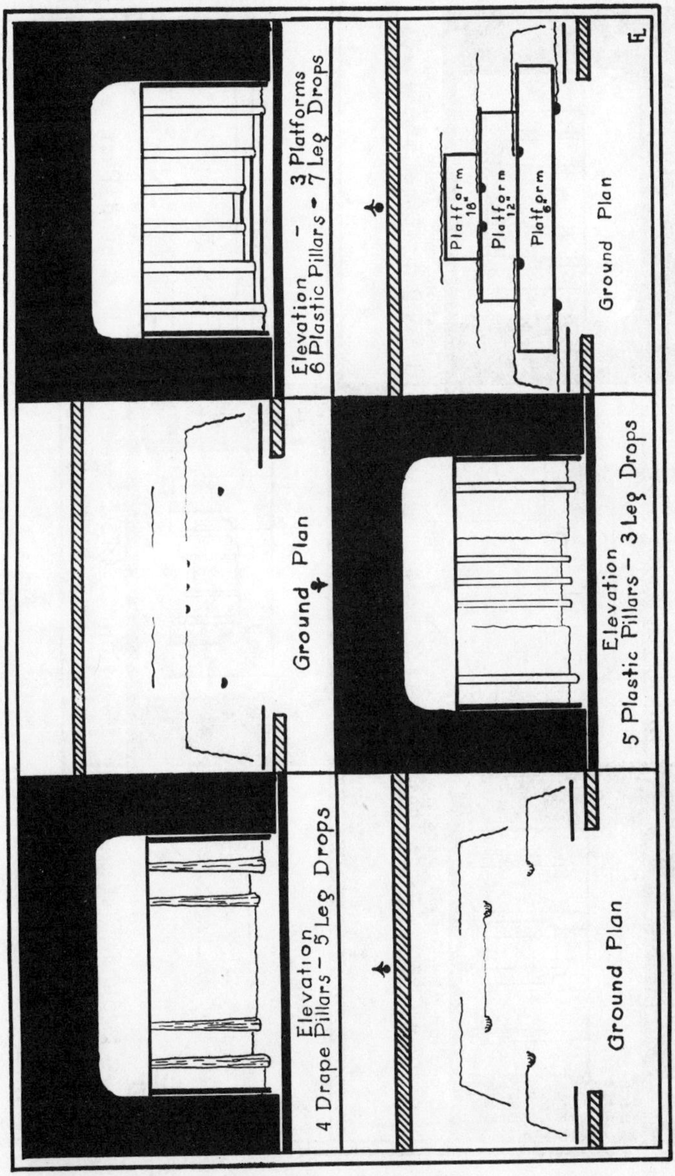
Elevation
4 Drape Pillars - 5 Leg Drops
Ground Plan
Ground Plan
Elevation
5 Plastic Pillars - 3 Leg Drops
Elevation - 3 Platforms
6 Plastic Pillars - 7 Leg Drops
Platform 18"
Platform 12"
Platform 6"
Ground Plan
FL

FIG. 2

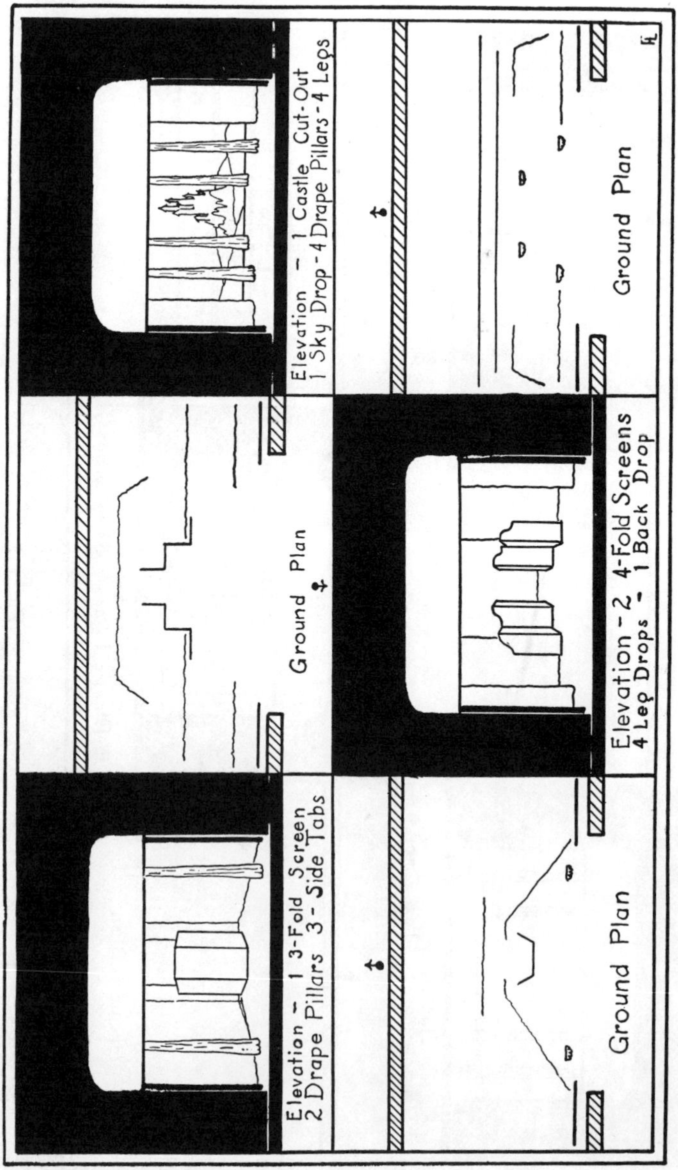
Elevation – 1 3-Fold Screen
2 Drape Pillars 3 - Side Tabs
Ground Plan
Ground Plan
Elevation - 2 4-Fold Screens
4 Leg Drops - 1 Back Drop
Elevation – 1 Castle Cut-Out
1 Sky Drop - 4 Drape Pillars - 4 Legs
Ground Plan

FIG. 3

Platforms for the stage are usually in the form of "parallels." A parallel, in stage parlance, is a folding platform, with a removable top. Thus they are not too expensive to build, and they take little space in transportation. For a more detailed description of a parallel, refer to any of the books mentioned below.

Steps for stage use are either small platforms, or a flight may be built as one unit. In the latter case the supports under the upper end of a flight are collapsible so the unit is not bulky in transportation.

Generally speaking, pillars are not adaptable to comedy design, but screens, cut-outs, and platforms can be used to create an infinite number of moods and effects.

A few sets of three- or four-fold screens are most valuable. Depending upon the decor, they can represent anything from hovel to palace, from sea to woodlands, or from Valhalla to the land "Through the Looking Glass." When folded they take up little space, and if each panel is constructed like a professionally built wing (for details on this construction refer to bibliography) the weight will be negligible. They are technically practical because they stand alone without additional bracing and because they can be set up or cleared quickly and easily. If a platform on casters is used as a base for a screen, the whole may be wheeled on and off stage as a single unit, thus further speeding up the shift. (See Fig. 3 for designs making use of screens.)

In decorating screens, it is again necessary to keep in mind the fact that the setting as a background of atmosphere must not distract from the performer.

Finally it might be well to mention two other units of scenery that can be useful to the magician.

The first of these is the sky-drop. This is an exception to the suggestion condemning the use of painted drops. A well painted sky-drop, however, is essential to most settings that suggests the out-of-doors. It is a canvas drop with nothing on it except blue sky. One that is well painted (a base coat of pale sky blue with pastel stipples over it of red, yellow, and blue) and properly lighted seems to have the depth and spaciousness of the sky. It does not look like a wall painted blue.

The second is a "scrim" drop. This is a drop that can appear as solid as a wall if all lighting is downstage of it. If the source of lighting is changed so that most of the light is upstage of it, however, it will be nearly transparent, and can readily be seen through. Scrim when examined close at hand looks much like mosquito netting. It can be used for special effects, or an ethereal atmosphere can be given to a whole sequence by performing behind it.

Church, School, and Club. Most of the foregoing can be applied to magicians playing in the non-professional auditoriums. However, there are a few comments that should be added. There are many ways for a magician playing this field to help himself.

Some carry their complete show in a suitcase, and have no transportation facilities for scenery. However, a great many of the modern high school and college theaters are well equipped with drapes, scenery, and lighting. Further, in most cases, they are eager to have this equipment used. Thus, if time can be spared for a visit to the client prior to the performance date, much may be done to create a suitable atmosphere without further expenditure.

The magician who uses large stage effects and has transportation facilities can, so long as he does not appear in union houses, build his own settings. To build scenery one need not be a skilled cabinet-maker. Space does not permit a discussion of scenic construction here, but several excellent textbooks on the subject are listed at the end of this article. Having carefully read one of these books on stagecraft, you need only workshop space, a hammer, screwdriver, saw, and paint-brush.

A useful ally in starting such a project might be the head of the dramatics department in the nearest local high school or college. Most instructors in this activity have received some professional training in stagecraft, and few could resist the temptation offered by such a stimulating problem as would be posed by scenery for a magician.

Unfortunately the facilities of the church and club auditoriums are often too limited to follow the suggestions mentioned here. However, a visit prior to performance date is still advisable. This way the most can be made of limited space and equipment.

To the Amateur. All that has so far been said applies as well to the amateur as to the professional magician, but the amateur is likely not to think so.

Many an amateur has a small stage in the playroom, barn or garage. It offers many intriguing possibilities, but too often is enclosed with a set of drapes of the cheapest material available, and no further thought is given to atmosphere.

The amateur having his own stage can build more than one setting. Or once having built a set of screens he may redecorate them from time to time. Creating new settings could become as interesting a part of the hobby as mastering a new trick.

Lighting. Too many performers have ignored the vast aid offered by modern lighting equipment, both in the professional house and in the auditoriums of the schools. It can serve in a dual capacity. The setting can be painted with light as well as by pigment, and a careful use of the equipment will greatly aid in creating the desired atmosphere. Changes in lighting may also help to punctuate the performance. Thus, if spot lighting is used for the MISER'S DREAM, the LINKING RINGS, etc., where all of the attention is to be on the performer; and general lighting is used for a big silk PRODUCTION, where a large display is desired, the changes will greatly assist in pointing up each separate effect.

It is recommended that an immediate knowledge be acquired of the various types of stage lighting equipment, and of their uses. Note that all types of lighting units are equipped with frames for holding color filters. Also, note the large variety of colors available for these frames.

Finally: should you wish to have scenery or improve that which you already have, keep in mind the axiom at the beginning of this article as you refer to the books listed below.

Frederick H. Little
Technical Director, Department of Drama, Columbia University

BIBLIOGRAPHY

The Book of Play Production for Little Theaters, Schools and Colleges
By Milton M. Smith. New York, D. Appleton-Century Co., 1926
This thoroughly practical book on stagecraft is by far the best reference for those who have no previous knowledge of the subject.

Stage Scenery and Lighting; a Handbook for the Non-Professional
By Samuel Selden and Hunton D. Sellman. New York, F. S. Crofts & Co., 1930
A more detailed treatise on the same subject.

The Equipment of the School Theater
By Milton M. Smith. New York, Bureau of Publications, Teachers College, Columbia University, 1930
The magician playing the schools will find this most useful as a guide of what to expect in the way of equipment on the average school stage.

A Method of Lighting the Stage
By Stanley R. McCandless. New York, Theater Arts, Inc., 1932
Though this was written for the drama and is quite technical, many useful pointers on good lighting may be obtained from it.

STEAL To remove an object, the removal being unseen or unnoticed by the audience. A steal is the reverse of a LOAD. Most steals need to be covered by some sort of MISDIRECTION.

STODARE, COLONEL ALFRED Stage name of John English (1831-1866), British conjurer who began by acting as jack-of-all-trades to showmen, occasionally getting an engagement to exhibit magic and ventriloquism, sometimes alone. He showed in Dublin as early as 1859. After J. H. ANDERSON's last season in London (1865), he was engaged as "opposition." He appeared in Egyptian Hall in the guise of a Frenchman.

He featured a bastard version of the INDIAN BASKET TRICK and a flower growth (likewise not Indian). Later he featured the Sphinx illusion and BULLET-CATCHING. He was taken up by Queen Victoria and the Prince of Wales.

He died of consumption (*aet.* 35) at the height of his success. A younger brother, and others, took his name, and performed for some years thereafter.

J. M.

STOOGES (See PLANTS)

STRING TRICKS Cutting and restoring a piece of string is a trick as venerable as the CUPS AND BALLS. It is the ancestor of all the cut ROPE TRICKS. The latter are so much more effective than mere string-cutting that the reader is referred to that article for all the cutting effects.

Several effective string tricks are half trick and half puzzle. One, the *Perambulating String*, can be shown with two fingers, two pencils, or two canes. The string is hung over one cane, its ends hanging down equally. Pick up the two dangling strands, and wind them around both canes together, winding away from yourself, and keeping one strand (call it A) always to the right. In making one of the several turns of string around the two canes, leave strand A behind, and carry only strand B around. You can let someone else unwind the string from the canes; it will have traveled from the cane it was originally on to the other.

The identical principle is used in the "Garter" gambling trick. A string is folded in two, with one end perhaps two inches longer than the other. The central loop is laid flat on the table, and the two strands of string are coiled evenly around it, the longer end being the inner of the two strands. The challenge is, Can the spectator (or the sucker) put down his finger in the right loop to catch the string when the performer draws the two ends away? It is usually not very hard for the spectator to spot the actual center loop, around which the spiral has been laid. If he puts his finger in that loop, the performer picks up the long end of the string, and carries it another half-turn around the spiral before picking up the short end along with it. This action transfers the center of the spiral from the loop the spectator is holding to the next one, and the string comes away clear. If the spectator picks the other loop, the performer picks up the short end of the string, carries it to the long end, and again pulls the string away clear.

The *Snare* is another gambling dodge, worked with about a yard of string whose ends are tied together. The performer holds the string up in his fist, so that the loop forms a sort of oblong as wide as the fist. He lays the lower end of the loop out on the table, keeping it fairly open, and then brings his hand around so that the parallel upper ends of the oblong cross the parallel lower ends at right angles, forming a central square of the four strands. A spectator is told to put his finger down inside this square, and is defied to say whether the finger will or will not catch the string when the performer pulls it away.

The string can be laid out so that it will or will not catch the finger, whichever the performer decides. In crossing the upper end of the loop over the lower end, the performer may keep his knuckles downward throughout the motion; this twists the loop before forming the square. The twist catches the spectator's finger. Or the performer may turn his hand palm downward as he crosses the ends, in which case there is no twist, and the string does not catch on the finger.

Another puzzle release is done with two canes or pencils. Wind a piece of string three times around one stick; put the second stick on top, and wind the other end of the string three times around both sticks in the opposite direction. Tie the ends of the string together. Both sticks seem to be tightly caught, but if you pull out either one, the string comes off the other as well.

"Threading the needle" is a familiar but still effective little string trick. Let about two feet of string hang down through the crotch of your left thumb. Take the upper end, coming back toward yourself, under the thumb, and up, and so make several turns of string around your left thumb. Let the string pass from the last turn around your thumb into a loop perhaps an inch high, which you hold upright between your left thumb and forefinger. Take the original dangling two-foot end in your right hand. You make a sudden pass at the loop with your right hand, and the string is seen to be instantly threaded through the "eye." In stabbing at the loop, you carry your right hand away from you to the full extent of the string, which is thus yanked through between your left thumb and forefinger, and so into the loop. Each time that you "thread the needle," you unwind one more turn from around your left thumb. *B. M.*

SUCKER GAG (See also CHINESE WANDS; COMEDY; DUCK VANISH; DIE BOX, SLIDING; EGG AND HANDKERCHIEF; EGG BAG; EXPOSURES; ROUTINE; THREE-CARD TRICKS; TORN AND RESTORED PAPER)

A trick in which the audience are led to think they have detected or embarrassed the magician, but in the end are embarrassed and doubly confused themselves.

Sucker gags can be devised by the individual performer, and inserted in many sleight-of-hand routines. CARDINI follows the color change of a billiard ball with the "unwitting disclosure" that he has another ball; this suddenly leads into his version of the MULTIPLYING BILLIARD BALLS. In doing the color change with cards (see CARD MANIPULATION), the performer may steal two cards, and leave the outer one awkwardly palmed as if he had carried it away from the pack when he passes his hand over the front; it then proves to be the wrong card altogether.

SUN AND MOON TRICK A white handkerchief is borrowed from a spectator, and a pair of scissors or a knife is handed to someone, who is asked to mark the borrowed article by snipping a piece out of the center. A colored handkerchief is treated in the same manner. The two handkerchiefs with centers cut out are rolled together, and given to one of the audience to hold. The missing pieces are then magically restored, but it is found that the colored piece has gone into the white handkerchief and the white piece into the colored handkerchief. The two are next wrapped up in a sheet of newspaper, and the pieces return to their proper handkerchiefs.

For this trick are required a small white handkerchief; two colored ones, exactly alike; another similar colored one, from the center of which a round piece has been neatly cut, and a piece of white cambric sewed in its place; a white handkerchief, from the center of which a slightly smaller piece has been cut, and the space filled with the colored piece; a newspaper with the top edges of its first two sheets pasted together, and also the edges down one side as far as the middle, and a strip right across the middle.

One of the colored handkerchiefs is folded four times and placed flat in this pocket, allowing the newspaper to be displayed without showing that it is prepared in any way. A pair of scissors, or a sharp knife, and a pistol are also needed.

The white unprepared handkerchief is concealed under the edge of the waistcoat, a little to the left side. One of the colored ones is on the table. The colored with white center and white with colored center are folded together as compactly as possible, and placed in the right coattail pocket.

The newspaper with the concealed colored handkerchief is on the table, as are the pistol and scissors.

The performer begins by borrowing the handkerchief. Should a lace one, or one with a colored border, or distinctly different from the performer's white VESTED handkerchief be offered, some excuse must be made, and a plainer one obtained.

Take the proffered handkerchief in the right hand, and place it in the left, bunching it together as much as possible without seeming to do so; turn to go back to the table, and as soon as the audience are all behind you, take your own handkerchief from your vest with the right hand, and vest the borrowed one from the left. In doing this, care must be taken to keep the elbows close to the body, and to move the forearm only.

Turn around immediately you reach the table, with the handkerchief in your right hand, and ask someone sitting at your right to mark the handkerchief by cutting it with the scissors. Hold the handkerchief by the center in the right hand, and grasp all four corners with the left, so that he must cut out the middle.

Shake out the handkerchief by two corners so that the hole is well displayed. Pick up the colored one from the table, have a piece cut out as before, and show the hole.

Now place both handkerchiefs together and fold them up. Pick up the pieces and fold them together, handing them to your assistant. "Please hold them in your left hand, and close your fingers over them."

The mutilated handkerchiefs are in the performer's left hand. The right hand picks up the wand and gives it to the assistant; in so doing, the performer turns with his left side to the audience, and says, "Take my magic wand and strike your knuckles three times, and the pieces will disappear." Under cover of the body the right hand takes the two rolled-up handkerchiefs from the right pocket.

Bring the left hand down and leave the handkerchiefs on top of those in the right hand; it will appear to hold only the two damaged ones, although actually there are four. This movement must be made quite naturally, as though placing the two handkerchiefs in the right hand to release your left, which is immediately raised to show the assistant how to hold his hand with the pieces in it.

"Now, sir"–place the two bundles of handkerchiefs in your left hand, so that the two just obtained from the pocket are on top–"one, two, three! Have the pieces gone? No? Well, I will ask someone over here to hold these handkerchiefs." Walk to the left, and in handing them to a spectator on the left, take the top packet in the right hand to give to him, the left hand dropping the others into the coattail pocket.

Walk back to the first spectator. "Now, if you will hand me the pieces and my wand."

Place the wand under the left arm; pretend to place the pieces in the left hand, retaining them in the right, and taking the wand at once from under the arm into the right hand. Strike the knuckles of the left hand gently with the wand.

Turning to the spectator holding the handkerchiefs, have him undo them. He does so, and discovers the handkerchiefs with the wrong centers. "My dear sir, you must have held them upside down." Take the handkerchiefs and walk to the table. "You see the result. I must apologize for this gentleman's mistake. I am sorry, but perhaps if I give you both of these handkerchiefs it will make up for it."

Pick up the newspaper and show it carelessly. Tear off the two front pages which contain the colored handkerchief and wrap the two handkerchiefs in it. "Will you hold this package, sir?"–to the first assistant. "Hold it just above your head."

Pick up the pistol and fire. Take the packet and break it open, bursting the paper with a sharp bend, but not undoing it. This discloses the handkerchief, which was concealed between the sheets.

Pull it out and throw the paper, which of course contains two handkerchiefs with wrong centers, carelessly on to the floor near your screen, or out of reach on the table. Open out the handkerchief, and under cover of it take the borrowed handkerchief with the second and third fingers of the right hand from beneath the waistcoat. Raising the right hand sharply, release the hold of the left on the colored handkerchief, shake them out together, and return the borrowed handkerchief. *C. L. N.*

SVENGALI PACK (See under MECHANICAL DECKS)

SWITCH A secret substitution. Switching was formerly often called ringing. The card, coin, billet, handkerchief, and other switches that have been devised are almost innumerable. As an instance, Floyd D. Brown has issued a pamphlet devoted wholly to *Twenty-five Methods for Switching Decks.*

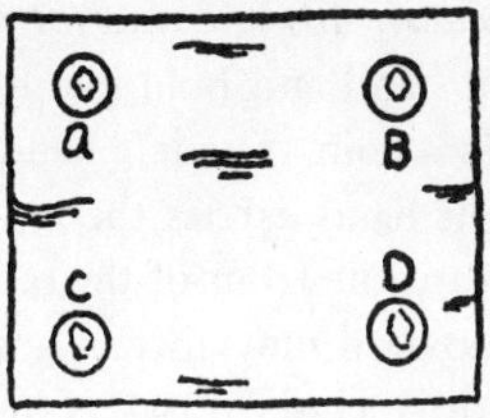

Fig. 1

SYMPATHETIC COINS A borrowed handkerchief or napkin is spread over the table. Four half-dollars are laid on a dark-colored handkerchief so as to form the corners of a square. Two of the coins are covered with small squares of fairly stiff paper, about four inches by four. The four coins eventually come together under one of the papers.

The four coins are placed on the handkerchief in the manner shown in Fig. 1. *A*, *B*, *C*, and *D* are the four coins.

Standing behind the table and holding a square of paper in each hand, revealing the hand otherwise empty, the magician covers coin *A* with the paper in the left hand and *B* with the paper in the right hand.

Observing that this leaves the other two coins visible, he quickly shifts papers so as to cover coins *C* and *D*, observing at the same time that the two front coins are visible. He now covers *C* and *B*, calling attention to the fact that *A* and *D* are visible, and then quickly covers *A* with the left-hand paper, *D* with the right-hand paper.

While the left hand holds the paper over *A*, the right hand shifts its paper from *D* to *B*; while the performer is talking to and looking straight at the audience, the fingers of his right hand (under cover of the paper) pick up coin *B*. This must be done without showing any movement of the paper or the hand. The right thumb should press down on the left edge of the coin, tilting the right edge into the fingertips.

Now comes the crucial move of the trick. While the right hand holds coin *B* under the paper, the left hand removes the paper from coin *A*, and holds it squarely in front of the right hand. Under cover of this paper, the right hand carries paper and coin away; the paper in the left hand is allowed to fall on the table, where coin *B* is supposed to lie. The right hand moves over to the left side of the table, and in the act of covering coin *A* with paper, the coin in the right hand is laid on the table near *A*. All these moves must be made quickly and silently, to the accompaniment of lively

PATTER.

Now grasp the lower left-hand corner of the handkerchief with the left hand, the *fingers well underneath* and the *thumb over*. Take the coin *C* in the fingers of the right hand and hold it up high so that everyone can see that you actually hold a coin. The left hand lifts up the corner of the handkerchief and the right hand carries the coin under the handkerchief, apparently pushing it toward the front of the table until it is directly under the paper at *A*. A slight upward movement is made with the fingers of the right hand; there is an audible clink of two coins coming together; removing his right hand from beneath the handkerchief and showing it unmistakably empty, back and front, the performer picks up the paper at *A*, and exhibits the two coins.

When the performer passes his right hand under the handkerchief, he leaves the coin between the first and second fingers of the left hand. Without pausing, the right hand transfers the coin to the left hand; the fingers of the right hand, held as though they contained the coin, push slowly forward until they are under the paper at *A*. An upward movement is made with the fingers, causing the coins to clink together.

The right hand is then withdrawn; it lifts the paper, and at the same moment the left hand, holding the coin between the first and second fingers, releases the handkerchief and takes the paper cover from the right hand. The coin is now concealed under the paper in the left hand, which replaces the paper cover over the two coins, being careful not to let the coins clink as it is released.

As there are now three coins under the paper at *A*, the process is repeated with coin *D*. When the paper in the left hand is again placed over the coins at *A*, there are four coins under the cover, although the audience is convinced that there are only three.

In order to pass the coin *B* (apparently) under the paper at *A* the performer varies the procedure by blowing briskly under the paper at *B*. The effect is as if he blew the coin from *B* under the paper at *A*. Then he lifts up this paper and exhibits the assembled coins.

In another version of this trick the magician uses five coins instead of four, but the audience is unaware of the existence of the fifth coin, which the performer conceals in his left hand, arranging the four coins as before.

In laying the papers over *A* and *B* he does not take away *B*, as in the first method, but allows the extra coin in the left hand to join the coin at *A*. The trick now proceeds as before, except that after passing the last coin, *B*, under the handkerchief, he must get rid of it in some way. It is easy enough to slip the coin into the pocket while lifting up the paper at *A*, because all eyes are attracted to this part of the table. *T. N. D.*

T

TABLES (See under BLACK ART; SERVANTES)

TABLE TRICKS (See also NIGHT-CLUB SHOWS; ROUTINE) The average table trick—an effect performed at the dinner table—is likely to be a mere transparent laugh-provoker, like "swallowing" a table knife by sliding it into the lap, or something bordering on a puzzle, as described under STRING TRICKS. Really good table tricks are almost as scarce as really good table performers, because their requirements are very severe. Except for the special cover afforded by the table-top, they must be ANGLE-PROOF. The performer has no freedom of movement to disguise LOADS and SWITCHES. His manipulation must be as perfect as that of a GAMBLER; even the best MISDIRECTION cannot take the eyes of the spectators far from his hands. Unlike the table worker in a night-club, he cannot convincingly use properties (such as the LOTA, otherwise an ideal table effect) that will not go in his pockets. To top it all, the performer trying to build a good table routine must not lean heavily on CARD MANIPULATION, which somehow tends to be out of place at dinner.

A good many VEST-POCKET effects can be used at table. So can tricks performed with the THUMB TIP and THUMB WRITER. Some SILK TRICKS, especially the knots, fill the requirements. Clean-working BILLET-READING and MIND-READING are excellent. TORN AND RESTORED PAPER can be done at table, as can SHELL COINS and the JUMPING PEG. Perhaps the king of table tricks is the SYMPATHETIC COINS.

Table tricks, good and not so good, can be found in David Devant's *Magic Made Easy*, John Northern Hilliard's *Greater Magic*, and Barrows Mussey's *Magic*. *H. H.*

TALK Of an object, to make a telltale sound. PALMED coins and cards talk unless handled very skilfully. THREAD and a good many pieces of apparatus sometimes talk, and have to be drowned out by a musical accompaniment.

TALKING SKULL (See under SPIRIT EFFECTS)

TAMBOURINE A small tambourine is improvised by pressing a sheet of paper between two metal rings, and trimming to shape. The performer taps with his wand on the center of the tambourine, breaking a hole in the paper, through which is drawn an apparently endless strip of colored paper. Finally from this bundle of paper are produced flowers, a rabbit, a dove, a doll, or bonbons, as the case may be.

The requisites are two metal rings which fit exactly one over the other so that when a piece of paper is placed between them and they are pressed together the paper is firmly gripped and stretched; a coil of rolled paper known to magical dealers as a tambourine coil; a sheet of white paper; flowers, or whatever it is desired to produce from the paper at the finish; a pair of scissors.

The rings, paper, and scissors are laid upon the table.The coil is slipped beneath the cloth of the table with its edge about one-eighth to a quarter of an inch beyond the table edge, the cloth being previously turned under at the back so as to be flush with the table edge.

Whatever is to be produced from the paper is placed upon a SERVANTE at the back of a chair or the table.

The rings and paper are exhibited with the remark, "Out of these two simple metal rings I shall improvise a tambourine." Lay one ring on the table, and over it the paper. Press the second ring down over the first until the paper is gripped tightly, and show it to the audience.

Lay the rings and paper carelessly on the table over the spot where the coil is concealed. Pick up the scissors with right hand, the left hand taking up the untrimmed tambourine. In doing so the fingers grasp the coil, and pressing it against the tambourine, bring it up held flat against the inside.

While trimming the paper care must be taken to keep the tambourine in a perpendicular position. Taking up the wand, tap sharply in the center of the paper, making a little hole. Put down the wand and draw out a piece of the coil.

Pick up the wand again, striking with it the piece just drawn out, and continue quickly turning the wand round and round in a circle of about a foot from left to right; this will bring the rest of the coil racing out, the end of the wand being gradually loaded with more and more of the seemingly endless strip of paper. The fingers at the back which hold the coil in the tambourine can tell when almost all the paper has run out.

Throw the bundle of paper over the chair-back (or the table if the servante is there) where whatever is to be produced is concealed, and look into the now torn and empty tambourine.

Take up the paper from the chair-back, bringing up whatever is to be produced behind it. If bonbons or flowers are produced they may be showered out among the audience.

If a large number of presents are to be produced, they should be made into a parcel with thin paper and stood upon the floor just out of sight behind the edge of a screen, or other opaque object; instead of throwing the paper over the chair-back, it is thrown down to the floor at the edge of the screen near the parcel, the paper is then picked up with the parcel behind it, and the presents are discovered through the paper, and distributed. *C. L. N.*

TELEPHONE TRICK An effect in which one or several spectators choose cards, and are then invited by the performer to call up a telephone number that he gives them. The person on the other end of the line promptly names the chosen cards.

The simplest method is by FORCING.

Another is to signal the chosen card by the different code names that the spectator may be invited to ask for—Arthur Allen for ace of spades, Billy Allen for deuce of spades, and so forth.

Yet another method, apparently invented by Bill McCaffrey, is for the performer to call up his wife. She picks up the phone, and starts counting aloud. When she reaches the correct value of the card, the performer says "Hello." She then names the suits aloud until he says "Wait," and turns the phone over to the spectator.

THIMBLE TRICKS The simple passage of an ordinary sewing thimble from the forefinger of one hand to that of the other, or elsewhere may have a surprising amount of diversity introduced into it.

As a preliminary, the performer must learn to thumb-palm the thimble. The thimble being first placed on the tip of the forefinger, this latter is rapidly bent into the fork of the thumb, which closes upon it. (Fig. 1) The finger being again extended, the thimble is left palmed. (Fig. 2) A reverse movement brings the thimble from the fork to the thumb to the tip of the finger again. This little sleight is by no means difficult and, if performed with the arm in motion, the smaller movement of the finger is quite invisible.

For the performance of the complete trick *two* thimbles are used, but as it is important that the spectators should not suspect this, it is as well to begin with a few passes in which it can be seen clearly that one thimble

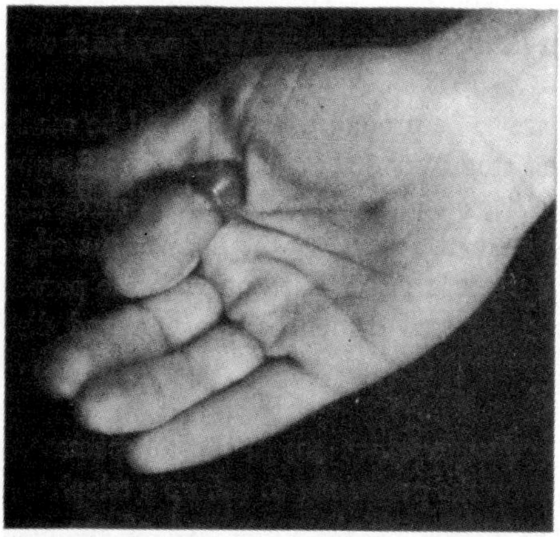

FIG. 1

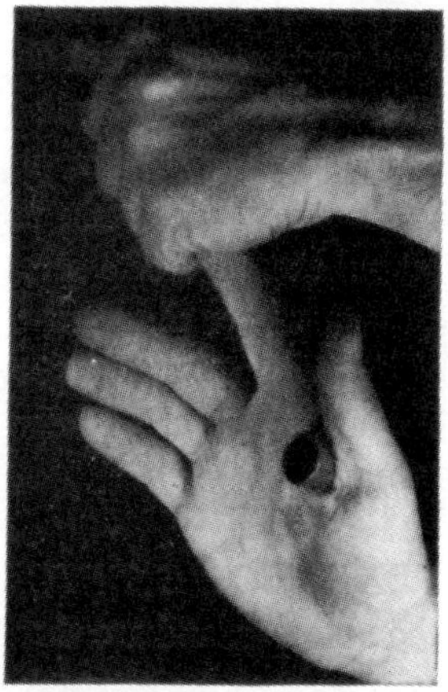

FIG. 2

only is employed. The second thimble may either be VESTED, mouth downward, or placed, mouth upward, in the left-hand waistcoat pocket—anywhere, in fact, where the performer can get secret possession of it at a moment's notice.

For the moment, suppose that he is working with one thimble only. Placing this on the tip of his right forefinger, he makes the motion of transferring it to the left hand, which immediately closes as if containing it, though as a matter of fact it is thumb-palmed in transit, and it is only the bare forefinger which comes into contact with the left hand. With this same hand the performer pats himself on top of the head, and after a momentary pretense of trying to swallow something that won't go down, produces the thimble from his mouth. This sleight is merely the former reversed, the thimble being transferred from the thumb-palm to the fingertip just as the latter reaches the mouth.

The performer may now apparently place the thimble in his mouth (thumb-palming it as he does so), and reproduce it from under his chin. He may with the left hand pick up a lighted candle, blow it out as if blowing the thimble into the candle, and with the right hand reproduce the thimble from underneath the candlestick. If the sleight is neatly worked, the illusion is in each case complete.

Having done as much as he cares to do with the one thimble, he secretly gets the second into his left hand, and proceeds to work with the two.

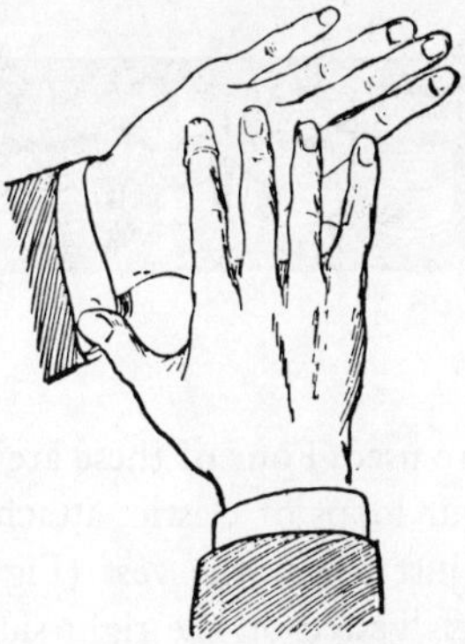

FIG. 3

The two-thimble work may be begun by holding the hands as shown in Fig. 3, the right hand having at this stage a thimble on the forefinger, and the left a second concealed in the fork of the thumb. The performer waves the right hand backward and forward alternately before and behind the other. As the fingers of the right hand pass out of sight behind the left, the visible thimble is palmed. At the same moment the forefinger of the left hand is bent and again extended with a thimble on it, the effect to the spectators being that it has flown from one forefinger to the other.

Some of the passes exhibited with one thimble may be executed still more effectively with two. Thus the thimble may be placed in the mouth, and reproduced with the other hand from the back of the head. It may then be inserted in one ear and brought out of the other.

Another pretty effect may be produced with the performer in a seated position. He brings his hands down three times with a slap upon the knees, at the same time saying, "One, two, three!" At the word "three" the thimble passes from the forefinger on which it was first seen to the other.

The effect of the *Multiplying Thimble* trick is, briefly, as follows: After showing the right hand empty, the performer catches from the air a thimble, which lands on the top of his right forefinger. After one or two of the customary thimble passes, this vanishes, and is reproduced from under the left elbow. Other passes follow, both hands remaining constantly in view, but at a given moment each finger of the right hand is seen to be capped by a thimble. Before the spectators have had time to recover from their astonishment, the left hand is also shown, and on this, too, every finger wears a thimble.

Fig. 4

Eight thimbles in all are used. Four of these are accommodated in a row, mouth downward, in four loops of elastic, attached to a little metal plate stitched to the trousers just below the vest (Fig. 4). The other four are disposed as follows: one is vested on the right side, another is inserted between two of the vest-buttons, and a third between the neck and the shirt-collar on the right side, the mouth being in each case outward. The fourth is thumb-palmed in the right hand.

After a few remarks, accompanied by a certain amount of gesture, designed to convey the impression that there is nothing in either hand, the performer makes a grab at the air, at the same moment transferring the thimble from the thumb-palm to the tip of the forefinger, where it is duly exhibited. Laying this finger on the palm of the left hand and closing the latter, the performer withdraws the finger and shows it bare. The spectators naturally expect to find that the thimble has somehow vanished from the left hand, but they are mistaken. With a "wouldn't-deceive-you-for-the-world" expression, the performer opens his hand and shows that the thimble is there.

He repeats the movement of placing it in the left hand, but this time thumb-palms it, and reproduces it *on the third finger* from under the left elbow. Again he ostensibly places it in his left hand, but this time palms it, not in the fork of the thumb, but in the palm itself, and crooks the left elbow as if again about to produce it from there. While the general attention is thus attracted in this direction, he inserts the tip of the little finger into the thimble, allowing this finger to remain slightly bent into the hand.

Then he inserts the right forefinger under the vest, and brings out on it a thimble, professedly the one which had just previously disappeared.

For the next pass, he holds up the left hand, with fingers extended, and the back of the hand turned to the spectators; the right hand is held up behind the left, with the thimble last obtained visible above it on the tip of the forefinger. He draws the right hand slowly down behind the other, and at the moment when the thimble has passed out of sight thumb-palms it, closing the left hand on the forefinger, which is then slowly drawn out below. The spectators naturally believe that the thimble has been left in the hand. Meanwhile, the performer gets it out of the thumb-palm on to the tip of the third finger, bending this finger also somewhat inward to the palm.

After showing that the thimble has somehow vanished from the left hand, he pokes the forefinger of the right hand into thimble No. 3 (the one that was tucked in between the vest buttons), and exhibits this as being the one missing.

Showing this thimble on the forefinger, he apparently puts it into his mouth; actually, he thumb-palms it in transit. While calling attention to his mouth by an apparent endeavor to swallow the thimble, he transfers it from the thumb-palm to the tip of the middle finger, which he bends, like the others, into the palm. Seeming to find that he cannot get the thimble down, he shakes his head, and a moment later produces it on the tip of the forefinger from inside the collar.

He now has a thimble on each finger of the right hand; if the trick has been well executed, however, the audience believe him to be working with only one throughout. The fact that three fingers are curled into the hand, which would under most circumstances look suspicious, is not so in this case, because the tip of the forefinger is the most appropriate place for a thimble, and on the assumption of only one thimble being used, this is the natural manner in which to show it.

It would, however, be inartistic to exhibit the four thimbles immediately at this stage. Once more the performer apparently places the one thimble only (that on the forefinger) in the left hand, thumb-palming it and showing the hand empty. He then replaces it on the finger and produces all four from under the left elbow.

While the general attention is called to this new development, he makes a half-turn to the left, and, inserting the fingers of the other hand under the vest, gets a thimble on each. He does not, however, produce them at once, but thumb-palms the one on the forefinger and bends the other three fingers into the palm. With the outstretched forefinger he indicates the right hand; then slowly moves the right hand around the left. Just as the latter passes behind the left hand, he again brings the thimble on to the left forefinger, and, spreading the hands apart, shows that each finger is duly capped. *L. H.*

Thimble Passes. The thimble is placed on the first finger of the right hand. The left hand is held horizontally, with the palm toward the au-

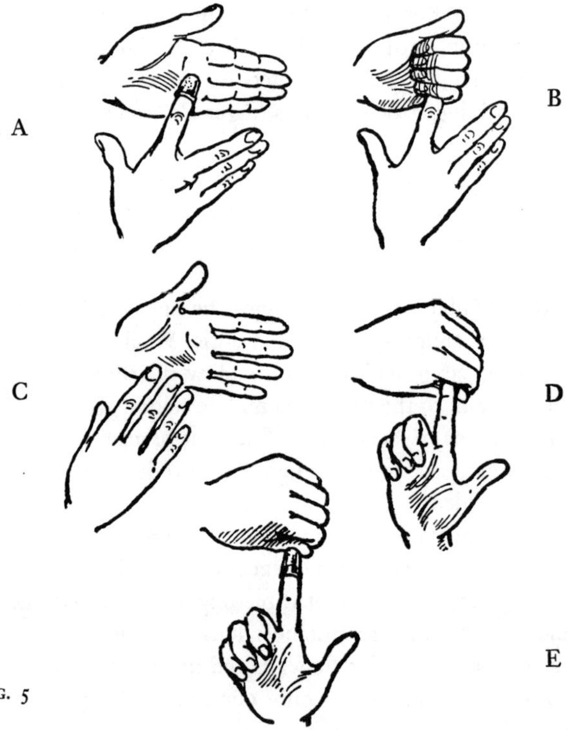

FIG. 5

dience (Fig. 5-A). The right first finger is laid on the left palm and the left fingers close over the thimble (5-B). The finger is withdrawn from the left hand, and apparently the thimble has been left behind in the hand.

The left hand is opened and shown empty (5-C); it is then turned around, the back being shown, and the right hand makes a few passes over it. The right hand is obviously empty. The left hand is closed and the right first finger is pushed into it (5-D) and withdrawn with the thimble on it. (5-E)

Fig. 5 shows the effect of this sleight, and Fig. 6 shows the part which the audience does not see. When the left fingers close over the thimble, the right first finger is bent inward, and the thimble is palmed at the fork of the thumb (Fig. 6-A). After the left hand has been shown to be empty, it is turned around, and while its back is toward the audience the left thumb dips into the thimble (6-C) under cover of the right hand, and gets the thimble away. The thumb carries the thimble into the left hand (6-D), the fingers close over it, and the sleight is practically done.

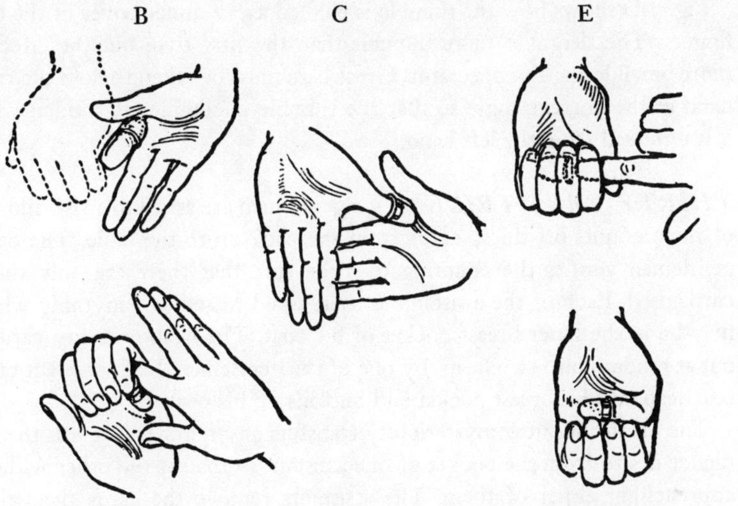

Fig. 6

For another pass, the thimble is placed on the top of the two middle fingers of the left hand (Fig. 7-A), and the fingers close over the thimble, which is then caused to vanish. (7-B) The thimble is eventually recovered as in the first method (7-C).

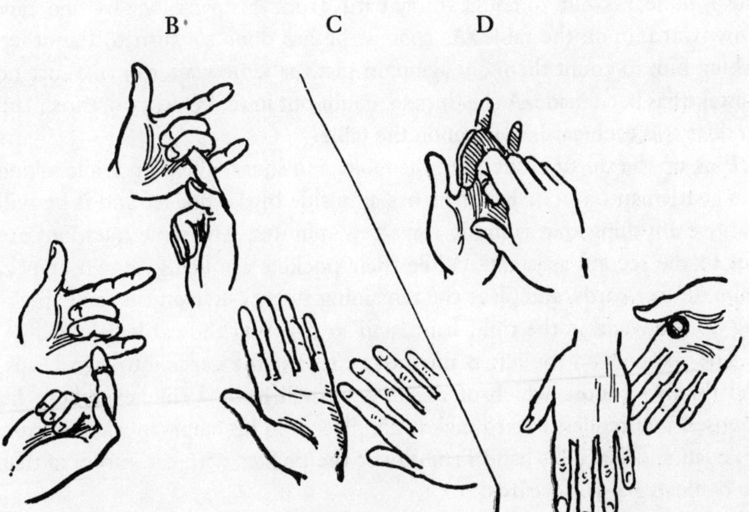

Fig. 7

Fig. 7-D shows how the thimble is palmed away under cover of the two fingers. The sleight is more difficult than the first two, but the effect is more bewildering to a spectator. Great care must be taken to hold the right hand at the correct angle so that the thimble is completely hidden when it is removed from the left hand. *Okito*

THIRTY-CARD TRICK Two gentlemen are asked to assist, and one of them counts off thirty cards from the pack on to the table. The other gentleman verifies the counting to make sure that there are only thirty cards used. Each of the assistants is then asked to remove anything which may be in the inner breast pocket of his coat. The heap of thirty cards is cut at random into two heaps by one of the gentlemen. Each assistant takes one heap into his breast pocket and buttons up his coat.

The performer now mysteriously transfers any number of cards the audience desire from the pocket of one assistant to that of the other without approaching either of them. The assistants remove the cards themselves from their pockets, and count them one by one upon the table, when the exact number decided upon are missing from one man's pocket and that many extra found in that of the other.

Having asked and secured any two gentlemen in the audience who may be interested in card tricks to assist you, request them to stand one at each side of you. Hand the pack to the assistant on your left to shuffle; when this is done, ask him to count thirty cards from this pack, one by one, face downward, upon the table. As soon as he has done so, turn to the other, asking him to count them out again, in just the same way, to make sure no mistake has been made. As he does so, count out loud, "One, two, three," up to thirty, as each card is laid upon the table.

Pick up the thirty cards from the table, and square them up while asking the gentleman on your left if he has an inside breast pocket and if he will remove anything that is inside for a few minutes. The same questions are put to the second assistant. While their pockets are being shown empty, palm off five cards, and place the remaining twenty-five on the table, picking up the wand in the right hand, and so covering the cards palmed.

The assistant on the left is now asked to cut the cards into two heaps, and then to choose which of the two he will have. Whichever heap he chooses, you request him to pick it up, place it in his empty pocket, button his coat, and place his hand firmly over the pocket with the cards, so that no one can get at the cards.

Ask the other assistant to count the cards in the remaining heap, which he does as before, one by one, on to the table–say, twelve. Looking to the audience, say, "How many cards has this gentleman?" (pointing to the assistant who has the other cards in his pocket).

"Now, twelve from thirty leaves—how many?" "Eighteen," the assistant answers. At the instant that you say, "Now, twelve from thirty leaves how many?" bring down the hand with the five palmed cards on to those on the table and square them up, and request the assistant to place them in his pocket as the other gentleman has done, placing his hands over the pocket, adding, "Be sure not to let anyone take anything from you."

Turn to the audience and say, "Now this gentleman on my left has eighteen cards, the gentleman on my right has twelve. I propose to take a few cards from the pocket of the gentleman upon my left and pass them, invisibly, into the pocket of the gentleman on my right. Now the spirits work with three numbers—three, four, or five. How many cards shall I take from this gentleman" (on left) "and give to this gentleman" (on right), "three, four, or FIVE?" The emphasis is on the five, and in all probability several will say "five," in which event you say, "Certainly, you wish me to take five cards from this gentleman's pocket to this gentleman's."

Should some say three, some four, and some five, you ignore those who said three and four and, turning in the direction where "five" was asked for, proceed as above. If three be most distinctly called for you may say, "Certainly, you wish me to take three for you; with pleasure." Turn to someone else and say, "And how many would you like?" Probably they will say "two." In that case say, "Certainly; three for you, sir, and two for you, madam."

"Now here is the first card." Make a pretended grab in the air near the pocket of the gentleman on the left as though you caught a card, and go through the motions of throwing it into the pocket of the other. "The second on the tip of my wand, and so into your pocket," passing while speaking the tip of the wand from one to the other's pocket. "Now the third." Again grab near the pocket of the left assistant, and pretend to throw the card down to the audience; with the right hand point down after it as though following its flight with the wand and your eye.

"Now the fourth. One, two, three, go!" (Make a quick movement across in front of you.) "Now you have four more cards. The fifth you will not see pass; they go so quickly. This one with my wand again."

Turning to the left assistant, say, "You have now only thirteen cards and the gentleman on my right has seventeen. Now take out all the cards yourself, and count them as before, one by one, upon the table, so that everyone may see. You had eighteen cards; you now have thirteen."

As he throws them down you count with him, and when you come to thirteen add, "You see you have lost five cards; so you, sir" (turning to the other), "must have the five extra. Will you take out your cards and count them?" He counts "One, two, three," up to twelve, when you join in counting with him, "thirteen, fourteen, fifteen, sixteen, seventeen."

C. L. N.

THREAD, BLACK The favorite invisible support and motive power in magic. Number ooo silk thread should be used for light work. The thinnest black fish line will usually do where a stronger pull is required. Human hair, frequently called for by the writers of magic books, is not so thin as ooo thread, and rather harder to manage, but often nothing else is available. (See also BLACK ART; CLOCK DIAL; DANCING HANDKERCHIEF; LEVITATIONS; PULLS; RISING CARDS; SILK TRICKS; SPIRIT EFFECTS)

THREE-CARD TRICKS The archetype of gambling tricks. Only three cards are used, but the more players the merrier. The banker, or dealer, shows the faces of any three cards, generally using one ace, and deals or throws them face down in a row on the table. Now he lays even money or perhaps two to one, that no player can pick out the ace. In appearance it is the simplest and easiest proposition a bettor could desire. In reality it is pure chance or accident if he calls the turn. The cards are thrown so slowly, and apparently so openly, that it seems like robbing the dealer to cover his odds.

This is really one of the most subtle and ingenious gambling games ever devised to win money honestly with cards—"honestly" in the sense that it may be applied to any procedure in a game of chance, which gives the player a known percentage for or against him. In this instance it is two to one in favor of the dealer; but as the dealer lays the odds of two to one, and the player keeps his eyes open, it would indicate that the player has the better chance of winning.

The dealer lays out the three cards, and the player takes his choice. One of them is the ace, and there is no hocus-pocus after the deal. Should the player select the ace he wins the money, but his chances are lessened just because he watches the deal. Were he to make the selection at haphazard, his chances of one to two, against the dealer's odds of two to one, would make it an even break.

The banker's advantage lies in his ability to make the deal or throw. The cards are usually CRIMPED lengthwise, the faces being concave, so the dealer may pick them up easily by the ends. There is no other advantage in the crimp, and the game is sometimes dealt with straight cards. When being crimped the cards are placed together, so that all will be bent alike. The deal or throw is performed as follows:

Lay the three crimped cards in a row on the table face down. Pick up one of the indifferent cards, by the ends, near the right side corners, with the right-hand thumb and second finger, and show the face of this card to the players. Now place this card fairly over the ace, letting the left sides of the two cards touch, and pick up the ace with the thumb and the third finger. Now the right hand holds the two cards, with their left side edges touching, and about half an inch of space between the opposite sides; the top card is held by the second finger and thumb, and the bottom card, or ace, by the third finger and thumb. Show the ace to the company, keeping the right hand suspended about six inches from the table; pick up the third card with the left hand, and show it to the company (Fig. 1).

FIG. 1

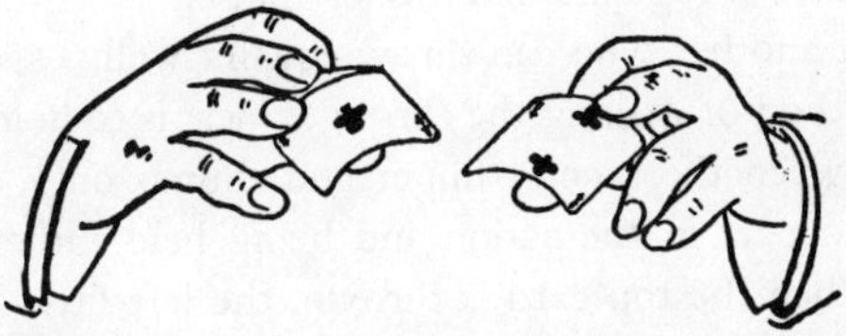

Now turn the faces down, move the right hand over toward the left, and with a slight downward swing release the upper card, letting it drop flatly on the left side of the table by quickly withdrawing the right hand to its former position; the rapid withdrawal gets the lower card out of the way. As the right second finger releases the top card it instantly seizes the lower card and the third finger is straightened out, so when the right hand is again stationary at its first position over the table, the players may see that the finger that held the upper card is still doing duty, and the finger which held the lower card is now idle. Now move the left hand over toward the right, and drop its card there; then again move the right hand over and drop the last card between the other two.

As described above, the blind takes place in the first movement or throw. The right hand apparently drops the bottom card first, but in reality the top is thrown. The action is neither hurried nor slow, and especially not jerky. There is no hesitation after the faces are turned down, and the movements of both hands are made uniformly and gracefully while the three cards are being laid out.

There is very little difficulty in acquiring the ability to throw the top card first, or in changing the positions of the second and third fingers as the top card falls, and a little practice at the game enables an amateur to afford endless amusement or entertainment to his friends with this cunning play.

The proper way to introduce it is to make the throw several times in the natural order, that is, by dropping the under card first, while explaining the game to the company. The ace should be picked up by either hand in the order it happens to fall, and be held at either the top or bottom position in the right hand, and the faces shown before each throw. Then the blind throw is made and the guessing and fun begin. When the deal is performed by a finished artist, it is absolutely impossible for the keenest eye to detect the ruse. Even when the process, or nature of the blind is understood, the player has no greater advantage save that he knows enough not to bet. The particular card cannot be followed with the eye, and if the knowing player were to bet on a blind throw once, the dealer can make his next throw regular. The dealer himself is as hopelessly lost, if guessing against another who can throw equally well.

A second method of making the throw or deal is to hold the two right-hand cards between the second finger and thumb only, the right third finger taking no part in the action and being held rather ostentatiously straight out. When the top card is thrown, the left little finger is moved in under the end of the third finger, and the tip catches and holds the corner of the lower card, while the second finger releases both, so as to let the top card fall. Then the second finger instantly retakes its original position, and the little finger is released. The action of the little finger is completely covered by the position of the third finger. This method is perhaps more subtle, as it appears quite impossible to throw the top card without dropping both.

An addition to the game is made by putting in a crimp or upturn in a corner of the ace. Then several throws are made, and a player finds he can locate the ace "just for fun" every time. When perfect confidence is inspired, and the cupidity of the player tempts him to cover the odds, a throw is made, the player selects the card with the corner turned, and is amazed to find he is mistaken. In a confidence game, the corner of the ace is turned by a "capper," who seizes an opportunity when the careless (?) dealer neglects his game for a moment on any pretext. But the crimp can be put in, taken out, and again put in the corner of another card during the procedure of the throw.

To crimp the corner, pick up the ace with the second finger and thumb of the right hand, second finger at middle of end, and let the third fingertip rest on top of the card close to the second finger. Then catch the corner with the little finger and squeeze it in, pressing down with the third fingertip, and the corner is crimped upward. The corner is turned down again by slipping the third fingertip over the end, and pulling up, pressing down on the corner with the little fingertip. Either action can be performed in an instant as the card is picked up.

To make the corner throw the ace is picked up, shown, and crimped, then the second card is picked up with the third finger and thumb and shown, the left hand picks up and shows the third card, and a natural throw is made which leaves the ace in the middle. Then the right hand picks up the right-hand card, shows it, crimps the corner, picks up the ace, shows it, and the left hand picks up the last card. Now the right hand holds the two turned corner cards, but the fact that the upper one is crimped cannot be seen because of the positions of the fingers, even when the face of the under one, which is the ace, is shown. This time a blind throw is made, the right hand dropping the top card first with its corner turned, and the left-hand card is thrown; long before this the right hand has turned down the corner of the ace and it is dropped innocently in the middle.

The process of turning and reversing the corners requires as much skill and cleverness as making the throw. All details of the game should be perfected before it is attempted in company, and nothing but careful practice before a mirror will enable an amateur to perform the action in anything like a satisfactory manner. But no other single card feat will give as good returns for the amount of practice required, or will mystify as greatly, or cause as much amusement, or bear so much repetition, as this little game.

Mexican Three-Card Monte. When Three-Card Monte is played in the following manner, the bettor has no possible chance to win, and yet it appears simpler and easier than any other.

The three cards are left perfectly flat. Sometimes the four corners are turned the very least upwards, merely enough to allow one card to be slipped under the other when lying face down on the table, but the bend is not necessary.

The dealer now shows the faces of the three cards, and slowly lays them in a row. Then he makes a pretense of confusing the company by changing their places on the table. Now in explaining the game, he shows the faces of the cards by picking up one, and with it turning over the others, by slipping it under them and tilting them over face up. Then he turns them down again in the same manner and lays down the third card. This procedure is continued until the company understands the game, and the manner of showing the cards has grown customary, as it were.

When the bet is made and the player indicates his choice, the dealer at once proclaims that the player has lost, and to prove it he picks one of the other cards and with it rapidly turns over the player's card, and then the third card, and the third card proves to be the ace.

Of course the bettor can really select the ace every time, but he is not permitted to turn the cards himself, or touch them at all. The dealer exchanges the card he picks up for the player's card, and again exchanges that for the third card, when apparently turning them over. The exchange is made by the MEXICAN TURNOVER (see CARD MANIPULATION).

S. W. E.

Slow-Motion Method. The performer holds to view in one hand three cards, of which the undermost is a queen. These he places on the table without disarranging their order.

With the tip of his first finger he draws the top card to the right and the second card to the left, leaving the bottom card in the center. The spectators are asked to pick out the queen, and of course select the center card, which they saw at the bottom. The queen is, however, found to be the card on the performer's right or left.

Any two number-cards and two duplicate queens should be arranged as follows: queen, number-card, number-card, queen.

The performer takes the four cards in his right hand and fans them, taking care only to show three, the bottom one of which is a queen, the duplicate queen being exactly behind the top card.

With the left hand he presses the cards together from the back. This is done from the back to convey to the spectators that they see the faces of the cards with the queen at bottom the whole time. This and every movement in the sleight must be slow and deliberate; the sudden semblance of hurry will completely spoil the effect.

At this moment, without speaking, he pretends to see something upon the surface of the table, and holding his left hand out, with the flat palm visible to the spectators, lays the cards downward on it the long way for an instant, ostentatiously showing (without verbally calling attention to it) that he does not disarrange them in any way, while his right hand makes a movement across the surface of the table, as though flicking away some dust.

The right hand now takes the cards from the left, the bottom one being palmed in the left hand, and lays them face downward upon the table.

This is a very difficult palm to make neatly, and needs considerable practice. It will be found of great assistance if, when exhibiting the queen, the thumb of the right hand just separates that card from the others. The sleight depends entirely upon the way in which the right hand naturally takes the cards and lays them upon the table, and the left falls naturally to the side. It must be done in the steady, deliberate way in which each movement in this trick is made.

The cards are now moved with the tip of the first finger of the right hand, the top one (the duplicate queen) to the right. The next to the left, and spectators are invited to pick the queen.

They naturally choose the center card, which they have seen at the bottom all along. The performer then turns up the center card, which of course proves to be one of the other two, the queen being on the performer's right or left as he desires. *C. L. N.*

The basic effect of the three-card trick has been extended to other objects (see also SHELL GAME), notably the *Rattle Bars*. These are three small metal bars, one of which has inside a slug that rattles to and fro when shaken. The other two are mute. The audience is defied to keep track of the rattling bar. The secret lies in a duplicate rattling bar, which is palmed. Either of the mute bars can be picked up and rattled by using the hand in which the duplicate is palmed.

The identical trick can be done with three small matchboxes, two empty and one containing matches. A further refinement in this case is to SWITCH the original box of matches, which was only partly full, and so would rattle, for another that is packed tightly full, and is silent.

THUMB PALM (See under CIGARETTE MANIPULATION; COIN MANIPULATION; SPONGE BALLS; THIMBLE TRICKS)

THUMB TIE A release (see ESCAPES AND RELEASES) introduced by the Japanese conjurer Ten Ichi. There have been several imitation methods, but none better than the original.

The performer's thumbs are crossed, forming an X, and tied together tightly with a cord that bisects the X perpendicularly. The two sides of this cord are drawn together by another wound around them at right angles, and tied tight. Although the tie is tight enough to stop the circulation, the performer can instantly separate and rejoin his thumbs, catching on one arm a large ring that is thrown at him, etc.

The cords are specially made by the performer out of strong tissue paper; Ten Ichi naturally used Japanese rice paper. The first cord is about eighteen inches long, and tapers to pointed ends from a central diameter of a quarter inch. The other cord is half as thick, and about fourteen inches long. The cords are made by cutting the paper into one-inch strips, and twisting a strip into a spiral, like a spill, with each turn overlapping half of the previous turn. About three inches from the end of the first strip, another strip is laid underneath, and the twisting continued; the overlapping ends should be moistened. On reaching the required length, tear off the paper, and start twisting a new strip in the opposite direction, back toward the other end of the cord. The finished cord will be stiff (hence the necessity of making it specially) and too strong to break.

When the thumbs are offered to be tied, they cross at the base, the large knuckle of one over the large knuckle of the other. The longer cord is laid over, brought down underneath, back up on the opposite sides, and tied hard on top of the upper thumb, usually the right thumb. As the tie is being made, however, the left thumb is withdrawn until its smallest part is in the loop, and pulled downward to conceal the slack. The right thumb, on the other hand, is driven into the loop as far as it can be forced. The second cord bisects the X of the thumbs horizontally. During this tie the left thumb is driven in, and the right thumb withdrawn to bring its smallest diameter into the loop. Both ties must be tight. Finally, one end of the long cord is knotted hard to one end of the short cord.

If the performer now brings his fingertips together, and lowers his thumbs into the palms, the left thumb will slip easily out of the tie, and back in. The fingertips are kept together to mask this withdrawal. *H. H.*

THUMB TIP (See also TORN AND RESTORED PAPER) A sort of thimble, made of thin metal, and arranged to fit over the end of the thumb, which it is modeled and colored to resemble exactly. This invaluable general-utility FAKE was invented, according to PROFESSOR HOFFMANN, by the ingenious J. M. Hartz, for the purpose of producing a silk. It is now much more generally used as a vanisher. A burning cigarette butt can be poked into the thumb tip, which is hidden in the left fist, the tip STOLEN on the right thumb, and the cigarette thus caused to disappear. Small SPONGE BALLS, salt, loose tobacco, and BILLETS are among the many articles that can be stolen or SWITCHED with the thumb tip.

The thumb tip as a device has become quite well known to the lay public, and it must therefore not be depended on as a trick in itself, but must be employed with discretion and subtlety. Hilliard's *Greater Magic* includes several ingenious uses.

Furthermore, the learner must remember that the thumb tip is not invisible, but merely inconspicuous. In use, it must invariably be kept out of sight, or at least moving. *H. H.*

THUMB WRITER A flesh-colored metal cap, similar to a THUMB TIP, bearing on the end a short piece of pencil lead, or, for SLATE TESTS, slate pencil or chalk. By its aid words and figures can be written on a blank card held either out of sight or up in plain view, the performer's fingers remaining motionless and visible to the audience. In MIND-READING the thumb writer is invaluable; see Annemann's *Practical Mental Effects.* Its usefulness in card tricks is explained by Charles H. Hopkins in *"Outs" Precautions and Challenges.*

THURSTON, HOWARD (1869-1936) American card manipulator and illusionist. His vaudeville card act was the outstanding one in the heyday of BACK-PALMING, and he got a good deal of publicity for his adoption or revival of the horizontal-thread version of the RISING CARDS. In 1908, when HARRY KELLAR retired, Thurston bought his show. For the rest of his life he occupied the place in American public favor that had been held by HERRMANN and Kellar before him. He took his full-evening show all over the world with uniform success.

TORN AND RESTORED PAPER This trick is of the simplest kind, both in effect and in execution, consisting merely of tearing a strip of paper into small pieces, rolling them between the fingers, and reproducing in a single strip as at first. But its very simplicity constitutes its charm, and it has achieved extraordinary popularity, both with the public and among performers.

There is a little drawing-room trick precisely the same in general effect, except that a needleful of red cotton takes the place of the strip of paper. The performer takes this by one end, between the forefinger and the thumb of the right hand. With the other hand he picks up the opposite end, and brings the two together so as to form a hanging loop. Someone is invited to snip this loop at its lowest point with a pair of scissors. The two hanging ends are picked up as before, now forming a double loop, and the thread is again cut, the cutting being repeated as long as the length of the fragments permits their being doubled at all.

When this point is reached, the performer rolls the snippets, now only about an inch long, between the forefinger and the thumb. Presently, catching hold of a loose end, he begins to draw it out, and the thread appears whole as at first.

The secret lies in the fact that the performer has a second piece of thread of the same length rolled into a ball, concealed from the outset between the finger and thumb, or between the top joints of the first and second fingers of the right hand. The act of holding the thread to be cut between the same fingers and thumb completely masks the presence of this second piece. The cut pieces, when rolled together, form a similar ball, and at the right moment one ball is rolled over the other, bringing the whole thread into view, and concealing the fragments.

The only drawback to the trick in this form is that the thread is visible only at close quarters. Hence, doubtless, the substitution of paper. This should be thin tissue paper, two strips being used, twenty to thirty inches long and not quite half an inch wide. The general routine of the trick is the same as where the thread is used, but there are two or three differences. The paper is torn instead of cut, and this is done by the performer himself. It is not looped up like the thread, but torn across the middle. The two fragments are then laid one on the other, and these torn simultaneously across the middle, and so on till the pieces become too short to tear.

The method of reproduction, or rather of retaining the unbroken strip till it is needed for reproduction, varies. One method (said to have been that used by CHING LING FOO himself) is to conceal it in a special little FAKE, consisting of an oval-shaped piece of tin, bent nearly double, and colored to match the hand. This, with the piece of paper rolled up tightly within it, is inserted between the roots of the second and third fingers, as shown in the diagram. With a little caution, and at stage distance, this little addition to the hand is not perceptible to the spectators. Others, again, adapt a similar appliance to the fork of the thumb.

Neither of these arrangements is, however, entirely satisfactory. If mechanical aid is employed at all, the most perfect form it can take is a THUMB TIP. The strip of paper for the restoration is packed inside this, against the ball of the thumb.

The performer takes the strip of paper intended to be torn between the thumb and first finger of the right hand, showing the left hand empty. He then transfers the strip to the thumb and forefinger of the left hand, and shows the right hand empty. If the hand is held so that the thumb tip is pointed at the spectators, the keenest eye cannot detect its presence.

The paper is then torn into pieces as already described. These are placed in the left hand, which at the same time draws off the false thumb, and thereby releases the unbroken strip. The fragments are packed into the thumb, and this is replaced in position, after which the restored strip is drawn out between the thumbs and fingers of the two hands.

It is a good plan to roll half the strip of paper from one end and the other half from the opposite end. This makes a flatter roll for insertion in the thumb, and the strip can be unrolled from both ends simultaneously.

It is, however, quite possible to dispense with extraneous aid altogether. It will be found by experiment that a strip of tissue paper, such as is used for the trick, can be rolled so as to form a cylinder only a quarter of an inch in diameter, and in this condition can be perfectly well concealed between the roots of the second and third fingers, without being covered in any way. If the outer surface is rubbed with a little drawing chalk, so as to make it match the color of the flesh, it will be still less likely to attract attention.

The chief difficulty is to roll the paper tightly. A handy little tool for this purpose may be fashioned as follows: take a large-sized darning-needle, and with a pair of cutting-pliers snip off the portion above the eye. This will transform the upper end of the needle into a miniature fork. The point should be thrust into a two-inch length cut from a wooden skewer or penholder, to form a handle, and the appliance is complete. To use it, pass the extreme end of the paper strip through the little fork, so that about a third of an inch projects on the other side. By turning the needle, the strip may now be wound up as tightly as you please, being secured, when wound up, by tying a bit of cotton of the same color around it, after which the little fork may be withdrawn.

In unwinding the strip, the little roll should be kept well under cover of the fingers, for if the roll is once caught sight of, a substitution will naturally be suspected.

In order to leave the hands of the performer free until the little roll is actually needed, it may be temporarily impaled on the point of a black pin, thrust downward through the cloth of the performer's vest from the outside, near the bottom button. *L. H.*

If the paper ribbon is Dennison crepe paper, no duplicate is necessary: the ribbon is torn in half, and one half is left intact, while the other half is torn into small pieces. By a series of tugs at the remaining half, the paper can be uncrinkled, and so stretched out to the full length of the original piece.

A popular SUCKER GAG in this trick is to explain that two pieces of paper are necessary. One is rolled up into a ball, and held in the hand (see EXPOSURES). The other is torn up. The pieces are rolled up, and the whole ball is substituted for the ball of pieces. In case anyone should ask about the pieces, though, says the magician, you simply unroll the ball of pieces, and they have joined together too. Of course the performer merely makes a SWITCH, palming the ball of pieces, and putting a duplicate whole ball in the hand that holds the other ball ready to explain the "substitution."

Torn Cigarette Paper. The conjurer asks a friend to lend him a cigarette paper, and having taken one, he proceeds to tear it up. He rolls the small pieces up in a ball, blows on it, and then, unrolling it, shows that the paper has been magically mended.

To do this trick, you have a whole cigarette paper rolled up in a ball. When you have said that you will show a little trick with a cigarette paper, you put your fingers in your pocket to get a paper out, and in so doing take out the little ball formed by the whole paper, keeping it concealed between the tips of the first and second fingers. The ball is kept there until the other paper has been torn up, and then, while rolling the ball up, you roll the whole paper to the tips of your fingers, and let the ball of torn paper take its place.

In rolling the ball, you put your fingers, in a natural movement, to your lips to moisten them, and in so doing get the ball of torn paper in your mouth. This movement can be done quickly and openly, and in such a way that the audience will never suspect what you have done. You can then unroll the ball of the whole cigarette paper, and afterward give it for inspection. This is much better than the old method of rolling up the ball of torn paper with the ball made of the whole paper, and flicking both away.

The most effective part of the trick comes when you have rolled the torn paper in a ball. At the same time you can press the whole paper ball against the other, and hold them up between the first finger and thumb. The audience see that your hands are empty, and never suspect that the ball of paper is really made up of two balls of paper.

A still more effective way of doing this trick is to have a specially prepared strip of paper. In the middle of the strip is the whole strip rolled up, and fastened in with a small piece of paper gummed over it. Then, when the strip is torn up, the roll can be got out of this little pocket. If the trick is performed in this way, the best plan is to have a large piece of paper, and to tear off a strip before the audience, who will not then suspect that the strip has been prepared. The special advantage of doing the trick with the whole strip fastened on to the strip that is torn is that the hands can be shown perfectly empty before the trick is begun. *D. D.*

TORRINI Stage name of Count Edmond de Grisy (17? -18?), a French nobleman who was first a physician, then a conjurer. He fled the French Revolution to Italy, and while there, as the result of a quarrel with

PINETTI, exchanged medicine for magic. He had an adventurous and intermittently successful career all over Europe, but is best remembered now as the itinerant wagon showman who picked up young Jean-Eugene Robert while he was wandering delirious by the roadside in 1828, and gave him the start in magic that carried him to everlasting fame as ROBERT-HOUDIN.

TOURNIQUET The most familiar and probably the easiest pass to vanish any small object. (See COIN MANIPULATION)

TRANSFIXED PACK (See also CARD MANIPULATION) The name for two different card tricks. In the first, two cards are selected from a shuffled pack, and returned to the deck, which is again shuffled by the spectators. The pack is now wrapped in a sheet of paper and the packet held securely by a rubber band. The performer thrusts a paper knife through the packet of cards, and, upon investigation, the knife blade is found between the chosen cards.

For this trick you need a pack of ordinary cards; a paper knife; a sheet of plain paper or newspaper, about 8 by 6 inches; a pencil and a rubber band.

Hand an unprepared pack of cards to one of the spectators with the request that the cards be thoroughly shuffled and cut. While the deck is in the spectator's possession, allow him to draw a card, and while he is marking it take the deck and request a second spectator to select a card, which should also be marked.

The drawn cards are returned to the pack, brought to the top by the SHIFT, PALMED, and the deck offered for shuffling. You may prefer to shuffle the pack yourself, taking good care, of course, to keep the two drawn cards on the top. Whichever method is adopted, it is necessary that when this preliminary part of the trick is over, one of the selected cards shall be at the bottom of the pack and the other on top.

Lay the pack on the table and bring forward the sheet of plain paper and the pencil. Allow the audience to examine the paper and request a spectator to write his or her name on it, or mark it in such a manner that it may readily be identified. There is, of course, no preparation about the paper, but the writing of the name is an excellent bit of MISDIRECTION; for while this is being done, you pick up the cards, bend the whole pack downward over the first finger of your left hand, and as quickly bend the top half of the deck upward. By doing this, the deck will be CRIMPED, and the chosen cards which were originally at the top and bottom of the pack will now be the first cards of the upper and lower halves of the crimp. To prevent the audience from seeing this very noticeable bridge, hold the pack between the first finger and thumb of the right hand, near the center, and squeeze the cards so that the bridge is obliterated.

Hold the pack in the air and call attention to the fact that it is impossible for anyone to know the location of the drawn cards. Wrap the pack in the marked paper and, when the cards are concealed in the folds, release the pressure of finger and thumb, which allows the bridge to spring back into shape. Turn down the ends of the paper and snap a rubber band lengthwise over the package.

Call attention to the apparent fairness of the proceeding and remark that even if you knew in the first place what cards were drawn, it would be impossible to locate the cards now. While you are speaking, hold the package in the right hand, and, running the left thumbnail lightly along the side, locate the bridge, marking the location by slightly pressing on the paper.

Then plunge the blade through the side of the package, at the point where it was marked by the thumbnail. The knife naturally enters the opening of the crimp and passes between the drawn cards. Bend the bundle sharply upward, which takes the crimp out of the cards, and hand the package to a spectator with the request that he remove the paper. While he is doing this, ask for the names of the drawn cards. When the paper is removed, the knife is found between the two marked cards. *T. N. D.*

In the other trick, you are BLINDFOLDED by a member of the audience, whom you invite to shuffle a pack of cards, and take any one card and show it to the spectators. The card is then shuffled into the pack, and the pack placed face downward on the table. With the assistance of the man who chose the card, mix all the cards, face downward, upon the table, first with the point of a knife, and then with your hands. Touch the wrist of the assistant with one hand, and with the other throw the knife among the cards, at the same instant giving the name of the chosen card. The knife is raised, and the bandage pulled off, showing the identical card transfixed on the knife blade.

A pack of cards, a large white pocket-handkerchief for a blindfold, and a penknife are needed.

Invite a gentleman to assist you, and ask him to bandage your eyes so that it will be impossible for you to see. Take up the handkerchief folded to make a bandage, and holding the center of it against your forehead and covering your eyes, ask the gentleman to tie the ends together at the back of your head.

As he does this, with the hand which is holding the center of the handkerchief in front of the eyes, pretend to pull it well down over the eyes;

in reality, take care that it comes only low enough to allow a downward glance. Ask him whether it is now quite impossible for you to see through the folded handkerchief, to which he will reply that you are certainly fairly blindfolded.

As he hands you the pack of cards, put out your right hand toward him, and move it as though groping in the air to find his hand with the pack. If this is not overdone, the effect of its being a perfect blindfold is emphasized. Next ask him to take a penknife, which he will find on the table, and open one blade of it, replacing it on the table.

There are three ways of proceeding, all of which should be practised. One way is, while the assistant opens the knife, to palm off the top card with the right hand, and give him the pack with the same hand to shuffle. having yourself knowledge of the top card before beginning the trick. When he returns the shuffled pack, grasp it with the same hand, slipping on top the palmed card as you take the pack, and after making the TWO-HANDED SHIFT, invite him to choose a card, FORCING this one upon him, and asking him to show it to the audience while you turn your back for an instant.

The second method is to make the two-handed shift immediately after the assistant gives you the pack from the table, force the top card, which you know, and let him show it to the audience.

The third and best of all, though a little more difficult, is to hand the assistant the pack. Let him shuffle the cards and retain one, returning the rest of the pack to you. After he has held it up for the audience to see, ask him to replace it in the middle of the pack.

Hold half the cards in the left hand, and the other half in the right, just a few inches away. He places the card on top of those in the left hand, and you immediately bring down the remainder from the right hand on top, thus apparently losing the card in the center of the pack. In reality, as he places the card on those in the left hand, you slip the little finger on top of the corner of his card and as soon as the other half of the pack is placed on top of it, you have only to make the shift and his card comes to the top. Under the cover of asking whether your wand is on the table, you instantaneously obtain sight of the top card.

Now hold up the pack in the right hand, so that assistant and audience can see the bottom card, saying, "Is your card at the bottom of the pack?"

"No," he replies, and you take the pack in your left hand, taking off the *two* top cards, but appearing only to have the top one, saying, "Then is it at the top of the pack?" He will again reply, "No."

Replace on top of the pack, and ask the assistant to guide your hand with pack to the table. Grope with your hand until you find the left-hand side of the table, and then place the pack down near the edge. Lift off about three-quarters of the cards, and place them next to the heap left. Repeat the process several times until you have, say, five heaps, and the chosen card is, of course, on top of the fifth heap.

"Now, sir, please give me the knife which should be on the table." He does so. "And now direct my hand, so that the point of the knife touches the first of the heaps." You now flip the cards about the table with the point of the knife, taking care as you come to the fifth heap to send the top card a little to one side, so as not to lose sight of it. Place both hands, palm downward, on the cards, and move them about, mixing all the cards, and invite the assistant to do likewise. You, of course, keep the chosen card under the fingers of the right hand during all the mixing up. Stop the mixing and say, "Now my trick is this. I shall take the knife and throw it among the cards, and if I am successful it will find your card. Let me take your hand, and concentrate all your thoughts for a moment upon the card selected."

Take the assistant's right hand with your left, and place it against your forehead, as though reading his thoughts, saying, "Yes, your card was the ———." At the same instant release his hand, and throwing the knife sharply, point downward, on to the card, quickly pull off the bandage from your eyes with the left hand, while the right hand raises the knife, which comes up with the face of the card sticking on its point toward the audience.

C. L. N.

TRAPS Concealed, flush doors or flaps in the surface of the magician's stage or table. They are still occasionally used in ILLUSIONS, but must be concealed by the MIRROR PRINCIPLE or in some other completely effective way, since they are among the first things a modern audience suspects. Table traps are no longer used, their place being taken when absolutely necessary by BLACK ART wells.

TRUNK TRICK, SUBSTITUTION A lady is put into a bag and locked in a trunk, on top of which a gentleman takes a seat. Two assistants hold a cloth in front of the trunk for a few seconds. When the cloth is taken away, the lady is seen sitting on the trunk; after unlocking the trunk, the gentleman is found inside, tied up in the bag.

The actors in this illusion have to work with extreme quickness.

The bag in which the lady is tied has at the bottom a false seam, made of wide stitches, so that when one end of the thread is pulled the whole comes out easily, leaving the bottom of the bag open.

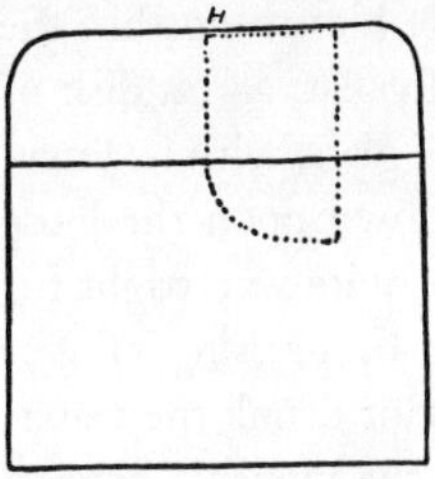

FIG. 1

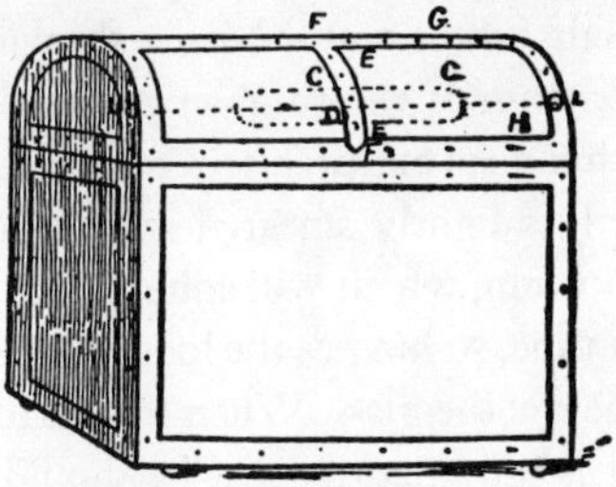

FIG. 2

In this way the lady escapes from the bag without injuring the ties in any way. The lid of the trunk is prepared so that one section of it opens inward (Fig. 1H). The frame (Fig. 2) is solid, whereas the strip *F* which runs across the top can be pushed sideways. To open the trunk the strip *F* is pushed aside, which releases a concealed mechanism that keeps the false panel shut.

The gentleman opens the panel, in the manner described above, and the lady gets out of the trunk. She assists him to get into the bag, and closing the panel, takes her seat on top of the trunk. *E. S.*

TUMBLERS (See also BLACK ART; EGG AND HANDKERCHIEF; SILK TRICKS)

The *bottomless tumbler* is an ordinary glass tumbler, from which the bottom has been cut out.

To give an elementary example of its use: the glass may be held in the hand, either resting on the palm, or with a finger crossing the lower opening. A billiard-ball, say, is dropped into it, plainly in view. A borrowed handkerchief is then thrown over it, and the glass (with the other hand) placed on a table; the ball, ostensibly safe within, is left comfortably PALMED in the hand which first held the glass, to be disposed of at pleasure. An egg or a folded handkerchief may be dealt with in like manner.

There is a modification which appears to be an improvement for certain purposes: instead of removing the whole bottom of the glass, remove the central portion only, leaving a rim half an inch or so wide, all around. This reduction in size of the opening makes it possible to place an egg lengthwise in the tumbler, and show it around without placing the hand underneath. As long as it is kept horizontal, the ends of the egg rest on the edges of the opening, but the moment the glass is tilted ever so slightly, the egg falls through as readily as though the whole bottom of the glass were missing. A gentle shake, professedly to show by the sound that the egg is still in the glass, will dislodge it instantly.

The glass may even be so arranged as to enable the performer to fill it half full of water before showing the trick. To enable him to do this, the bottom of the tumbler must be ground mathematically flat, and a disk of thin glass cut precisely to the shape of the bottom. The glass, with its lower edges lightly smeared with vaseline, is then pressed down upon the loose bottom, which will adhere to it. The glass will then be quite watertight for a time, so long as the loose bottom is kept from shifting by pressing a finger below the glass. When the performer has poured away or drunk the water, it is only natural that he should wipe the glass, when the movable bottom may be left in the cloth used for drying it.

Its greatest value is in connection with the BLACK ART table; indeed, one may almost be said to be the complement of the other, from the extraordinary facility the two combined afford for the vanishing of small objects. An egg or billiard-ball, say, is placed in the glass as it rests on the table beside one of the pockets, and the glass is covered with a handkerchief. (In such cases it heightens the effect to secure the handkerchief by stretching a rubber band over it, around the rim of the glass.) The glass has then only to be moved an inch or so in the direction of the pocket; the article goes "down trap," and the glass is empty.

The Mirror Glass. Among appliances of general utility, the glass with a mirror partition merits a place of special honor, for few pieces of apparatus have a wider range of employment.

The credit of the original idea belongs to the veteran wizard Hartz, to whom the conjurer of today is indebted for some of the most effective weapons in his magical armory.

FIG. 1

The apparatus, in its simplest form, consists of a glass tumbler (preferably on a foot and having straight sides, as shown in Fig. 1), divided vertically into two compartments by a movable partition of thin mirror glass, protected on the silvered side by a coating of colored varnish. To use it, the tumbler, with the plate in position, is placed on the table so that the mirror side of the partition shall be directly facing the spectators, in which condition the glass appears to be empty, though the space behind the partition may contain anything the performer pleases, say bonbons. When he desires to produce these, he shows a handkerchief, first on one side, then on the other, to prove it unprepared; then throws it over the glass. He nips it in the center, between finger and thumb, and so lifts it off again, at the same time lifting out the partition with it. This remains within the handkerchief, and may be removed at leisure;

meanwhile the glass, previously shown empty, is now seen to be half full, any doubt on the subject being removed by an immediate distribution of the bonbons.

The tumbler thus prepared is, however, merely the germ of the complete contrivance, which enables the performer to show both sides of the goblet, and so an empty and a full compartment, or two different sets of contents, in succession.

To this end, the mirror partition is made to consist of two mirrors glued back to back, with a piece of cotton velvet between them. The velvet should be a shade larger than the plates themselves, and when all is dry the margin should be trimmed down to a width of about an eighth of an inch; this arrangement makes the partition fit more exactly in its place, and at the same time prevents any rattling against the sides of the glass.

Thus arranged, the glass looks the same, whichever side of it is presented to the spectators. The rear compartment is loaded with, say, a blue silk handkerchief; at the outset the front compartment is empty. In the front compartment a *red* silk handkerchief is now openly placed. If the glass is reversed, the compartment now at the front will be occupied by the blue handkerchief, one having apparently changed into the other. When the blue handkerchief is removed, the glass is again apparently empty.

The only difficulty is to give the glass the necessary half-turn without the knowledge of the spectators, and this may be done in three or four different ways. In the case of a small glass, the simplest plan is to hold the glass in one hand, and with the other throw a handkerchief over it. The operator a moment later decides to perform the trick without cover, and so at once removes the handkerchief, but meanwhile the glass has received the necessary half-turn, and the trick is done.

Another plan is to borrow a lady's fan, and with it to fan the glass and its contents, the half-turn being made under cover of the fanning movement. If the contents of the two sides are to a casual view alike, as for instance if a white silk handkerchief enveloped in a blue one is to be changed for a red one similarly enveloped, even this amount of cover is not necessary. The performer, standing beside his table, lifts the glass with the hand nearest to it, and transfers it across his body to the other. In this case the semicircle described by the arm automatically produces the half-turn of the glass.

For stage use, the MIRROR PRINCIPLE is applied to glasses large enough in some cases to accommodate a dove or small rabbit in the rear compartment. For the semi-revolution of glasses of this size it is necessary to make special provision, which usually takes one of two forms. The first plan is to have a circular disk, a little larger than the foot of the glass, let into the top of the performer's table. A wooden bar is fixed just below the opening; on this bar the disk revolves on a metal pin through its center. A THREAD, led away behind the scenes to the hands of the assistant, moves the disk, and a stop at a given point on either side prevents the disk from making more than the desired half-turn.

A vase is placed on the disk, and the performer covers it with a handkerchief. This he does in a leisurely way, holding the handkerchief in the first instance well to the front, before dropping it on the top. During the instant thus occupied, the assistant pulls the thread, and the trick is done. If a double pull, traveling around the spindle in opposite directions, is attached, the vase may be brought back to its original position, but this is rarely necessary.

Another plan, preferable in some respects, is to place the vase on a heavy circular stand made of ebony or ebonized wood, about two inches in height. The upper part of this, which is covered with black velvet, is movable, and works exactly the same way as the disk in the table top, the thread being led away in the same fashion. If it is necessary to bring in the stand after the performance has begun, the assistant should take up his position with the thread in his hand, and pay it out gently until the performer has placed the stand in the desired position.

Besides the immense variety of changes which a glass of this kind places within the reach of the performer, it has another use. The glass, say, is standing on the table empty, having been used for some trick and being apparently done with for the time being. The performer rests his wand upon it, lying from back to front. Presently he has occasion to get rid of some article, say a glove, which is PALMED in his right hand. With the same hand he picks up the wand, and the glove drops silently into the rear compartment. A moment later the glass is carried off by the assistant, who extracts the hidden article, and disposes of it as may be necessary for the purpose of the trick.

Where it is proposed to utilize the glass in this exceptional way, and not for its ordinary purpose, the rear compartment is sometimes lined with tinfoil, making no difference in its external appearance as long as this compartment remains at the back. The space thus enclosed is then half filled with cotton wool (preferably black) on which a watch or other delicate article may be dropped without injury. Of course in this case there is no revolution of the glass.

Two cautions may be given here: first, the pattern of the glass should not be entirely plain on the outside, but of a cut or molded pattern, which helps to mask the presence of the mirror partition. The other point to be noted is that any object placed in the foremost compartment, and not entirely filling it, is reflected by the mirror; thus an egg appears as two eggs, and so on. This may be got over by professing to put two eggs in the glass, while actually putting in only one. Some performers meet the difficulty by using a half egg, cut lengthwise, and laying the flat side close to the mirror. In either case, however, it must be remembered that the performer's hand is also reflected so long as it is in the glass, and it is therefore necessary to stand so as to screen it from the view of the spectators at the critical moment. *L. H.*

The Center-well Glass. A tumbler is filled with wine, or milk, or any other opaque liquid, and placed on a table. A silk handkerchief is caused to disappear; it is then produced, perfectly dry, from the liquid in the glass.

The tumbler has a tapered glass tube in the center. These glasses, which can be purchased from any reliable dealer, are made from a single piece, and to mask the tube the glass is either frosted so that it is practically non-transparent, or made of cut glass.

The liquid is really poured in at the side of the glass, and the tube protrudes above it. The dark color of the liquid makes the tube invisible.

A handkerchief is vanished—in the magician's favorite manner—and extracted from the liquid; in reality it is pushed through the glass and taken from the tube. *Okito*

The *coin-vanishing tumbler* has a horizontal slit cut in the side, level with the bottom, through which the coin will slide out at a shake. To show the glass unprepared, the performer first fills it with water, simply keeping a finger pressed over the slit.

TURBAN CUT AND RESTORED (See also ROPE TRICKS) The current version of the ancient cut string restored. The "turban" is a piece of cheesecloth ten feet long and a foot wide. The performer has a spectator cut it through the center with a pair of scissors; he ties the cut ends together, and either trims or burns off the knot, whereupon the turban is found restored.

The secret lies in the position of the turban and one hidden move just before the spectator wields the scissors. The two ends of the turban are held, pointing upward, in the forks of the magician's thumbs. He picks up a short piece of the center, holding it taut between the right middle fingers at one end and the left middle fingers at the other. This taut piece of center is what the spectator thinks he is going to cut. With a swinging motion of both hands, the performer spreads his left second and third fingers, dropping that part of the turban, and with his left forefinger hooks the turban just below the right-hand end; with the same motion he closes both hands. The result is that the piece of turban now held taut between right and left fists is actually the right-hand end. This the spectator cuts off, and the performer ties the short end around the middle of the turban, simulating a square knot. This knot is then trimmed off bit by bit, and thrown away.

H. H.

V

VAN HOVEN, FRANK (18? -19?), comedy magician, the first to poke fun at magic itself. He began as a serious performer, and the story is told that he had an act painstakingly accumulated of self-working APPARATUS, relying heavily on push-buttons and THREADS. During one performance before a rough and disorderly audience, he grew confused and began operating all the apparatus at once, prematurely. Cards were rising and production boxes overflowing in every direction. The whole twenty-minute act was over in a minute and a half, but it was such a hilarious success that he built it back to its full length, with all the tricks exposing themselves or backfiring.

VANISHING PERFORMER An effect that is in its way the essence of true magic.

Various methods generally used for vanishing a person in ILLUSIONS may be employed. There is one principle that seems to be reserved largely for this particular effect: disappearing in a crowd of assistants. The performer wears some distinctive costume, while five or six assistants all wear one, conspicuously different, uniform. The performer, hidden for a moment behind a curtain, fan, or other concealment, strips off his own costume, revealing a uniform like what the assistants have on. The performer slips out and mingles with the crowd, and one assistant more is never noticed.

In another method, the performer steps up on a stool, holds a large shawl in front of himself, and vanishes when the shawl falls to the stage at a pistol shot. The shawl is held up by a horizontal THREAD across the stage at the proper height for a man's hands above his head, while the performer makes his escape through a swinging spring door in the center panel of a three-fold screen that serves as a background behind the stool. An assistant then fires a pistol and breaks the thread, dumping the shawl.

VESTING (See under COSTUME)

VEST-POCKET MAGIC The generic name usually given to close-up tricks with APPARATUS (usually shown "IMPROMPTU," the necessary preparation being simple), as distinguished from pure SLEIGHT-OF-HAND.

Many vest-pocket effects are useful as TABLE TRICKS. A number of good ones are described in *Blackstone's Secrets of Magic.* Others are constantly being invented and marketed through magic dealers. (See CIGARETTE MANIPULATION; COIN BOX; COIN IN HANDKERCHIEF; COINS, FOLDING; COINS, SHELL; DICE; DIVINATIONS; GRANDMOTHER'S NECKLACE; JUMPING PEG; LEVITATIONS; SHELL GAME; SILK TRICKS; THREE-CARD TRICKS)

VOLUNTEERS The successful use of assistants and committees from the audience is an art in itself. The close-up performer and the NIGHT-CLUB table worker are at such close quarters with their audience that every spectator is a potential volunteer, and to this extent close work is good training for stage and platform acts.

The cardinal rule is, never genuinely embarrass a volunteer; if you cannot help it, then redeem his dismay (see COMEDY).

The stage performer must learn the trick of talking without moving his lips much, in an undertone that will not carry across the footlights. When the magician talks this way, he must not be furtive or hurried, and he positively must not whisper; he simply does not try to make himself heard at any distance. Private remarks to volunteers are made in this tone. For instance, if you invite on the stage a volunteer for the SUN AND MOON TRICK, who is going to look ridiculous, shake hands with him as he comes up. Say in your undertone, "Let's have some fun with them." This at once makes him a conspirator on your side, and reassures him that whatever happens *is* only in fun. The same undertone is used to take the sting out of any PATTER at the volunteer's expense.

The late E. V. Lucas, most charming of essayists, gave a warning that should be taken to heart: "Conjurers, it is true, can . . . be amusing, but too often there is in their humour an element of cruelty which cannot be defended. I can remember how angry that dexterous magician, the late Dr. Byrd Page, could make the victims invited to assist him . . ."

Which volunteers to pick is another question that can be answered only by experience. The general opinion seems to be that people who are too eager often make trouble or try to hog the stage, and people who are too shy may be scared speechless. The occasional drunk who wanders on to the stage can usually be handled by an effusive show of pleasure and gratitude at his assistance. Volunteers who come up intending to crab the act can usually also be handled under pressure of embarrassment, because the audience have paid for the privilege of enjoying the show, and are naturally on the performer's side.

Men make better volunteers than women, because they are less likely to be self-conscious.

Whether to use volunteers at all in a stage show is a fertile subject for argument among conjurers. Certainly they should not be used often, because the process of recruiting and dealing with them slows up the act. ESCAPES are almost the only class of stage effect where the choice and supervision of a volunteer committee are vital elements of success. The audience must realize that the performer has really been tied up by people who put their heart into it, or else the escape can be no surprise.

In IMPROMPTU work with volunteers—having cards chosen, and the like—don't expect too much of your assistant. He is not there to perform feats of memory and mental agility; that is your part. First explain to everyone what you are going to have him do. Then explain to him what he is to do; and after he has done it, remind everyone what he has done. If he must remember a card, try to have two or three other people see it as well.

Victor Farelli, the British conjurer, says he can pick people on whom to FORCE cards by the expression in their eyes, and warns that anyone who watches the magician's hands too closely, either knows something or is naturally suspicious. He also passes on the word of an experienced performer that anyone in a theater audience who seems very anxious to draw a card should be avoided.

You will discover by experience that certain turns of phrase have an irrational tendency to mislead people. For instance, if a chosen card is at a chosen number, and you ask the volunteer, "What was your number?", perhaps two times out of five he will name the card instead of the number. If you put down two coins, and ask somebody to choose one, John Mulholland points out that he will pick one up instead of indicating it. To avoid this, Mulholland always said, "Please name one," until he tackled the late Alexander Woollcott. Woollcott retorted briskly, "Certainly. I name this one Elmer."

To sum up the handling of volunteers, treat them as you would like casual acquaintances to treat you; and don't expect too much from them.

H. H.

W

WALKING THROUGH A BRICK WALL The performer asks for a number of VOLUNTEERS to come on the stage to act as a committee from the audience. The more that avail themselves of this opportunity, the better. A large sheet is shown, and laid on the floor of the stage, to do away with the idea that any stage traps are used. A brick wall, about one foot thick, and running on wheels, is then brought on, and is thoroughly examined and tapped by the committee to prove that it is solid.

A lady is introduced to the audience, and placed on the right-hand side of the wall, a screen being placed around her. A screen is also placed on the other side of the wall. The committee are requested to form a circle around the wall, but after the lapse of a few seconds, the screens are removed and the lady is seen to be on the opposite side of the wall to that on which she was placed, having apparently gone through the solid bricks. Everything can be examined again, without any fear of the *modus operandi* being discovered.

Although the most elaborate precautions are apparently taken to eliminate the possibility of a stage TRAP, this is the secret of the whole illusion. A trap is cut in the stage in the most convenient place—usually in the center. This is not noticeable to the committee, as the carpet is also cut to correspond with the trap. A sheet is brought on, thoroughly examined by the committee, and laid down on the stage with the trap somewhere near the center. When laying this sheet, do not stretch it tightly, but allow it to lie on the floor fairly loosely.

The wall is then brought on and thoroughly examined; it is brought on to the stage end-on, and adjusted so that it comes over the stage trap. The audience can see on either side of it. The lady stands close up to the wall, right over the trap; a screen is placed around her, and another screen put on the opposite side of the wall. The committee are then asked to form a circle around the wall.

As soon as the screens have been adjusted, an assistant releases the trapdoor. This allows the sheet to sag where the trap is opened, leaving room for the lady to get underneath the wall and emerge on the other side under cover of the screens. The trap is immediately closed, and both the wall and the sheet can be examined further. Obviously it is necessary to have a lady slim enough to get through the small space allowed, and the more spectators you have on the stage and on the sheet, the better the working of the trick.

H. & A. W.

WANDS (See also COIN MANIPULATION (PASS); CUPS AND BALLS; LEVITATIONS; SILK TRICKS)

The wand is a light rod from twelve to fifteen inches long and about three-quarters of an inch in diameter. It may be of any material, and decorated in any manner which the owner's fancy may dictate. To the uninitiated its use may appear a mere affectation, but such is not the case. Apart from the prestige derived from the traditional properties of the wand, and its use by the wizards of all ages, it affords a plausible pretext for many necessary movements, which would otherwise appear awkward and unnatural, and would thereby arouse the vigilance of the audience at possibly the most critical period of the trick.

Thus, if the performer desires to hold anything concealed in his hand, by holding the wand in the same hand he can keep it closed without exciting suspicion. If it is necessary to turn his back on the audience for an instant, the momentary turn to the table, in order to take up or lay down the wand, affords the opportunity.

Even when the use of a wand is not absolutely necessary for the purpose of a trick, its use is in strict accordance with the character the conjurer professes to fill, and the touch of the wand for the supposed purpose of causing a magical transformation assists materially in leading the audience to believe that such transformation actually did take place at that particular moment, instead of having been (as is really the case) secretly effected at an earlier period.

Production. Since the wand is the symbol, and professedly the instrument, of the wizard's power, he cannot begin his performance more appropriately than by some feat which appears to prove its magical qualities. One of the most effective "manifestations" of this kind is to come forward empty-handed and make the wand appear from nowhere. ROBERT-HOUDIN had a very simple method for producing this effect.

At one end of the wand is a minute metal ring, to which is attached a black THREAD, a trifle longer than the wand itself. The other end of the thread is fastened to the right sleeve of the coat, just inside the cuff. Thus attached, the wand rests (ring end upward) within the sleeve, the performer of course taking care not to slope the arm downward until the right moment. When he desires to make the wand appear, he has only to extend the arm with a quick outward sweep, when centrifugal force at once shoots it into his hand.

In place of the ring, a minute hole may be bored from side to side through one end of the wand. The thread (which in this case should be double the length of the wand) is passed through this hole, and its two ends, tied together, secured to the sleeve. When the loop thus formed is broken the wand will come away clear.

Another effective way of producing the wand is for the performer to draw it out of his purse, explaining that being in company with the silver tends to keep up its magnetic force, or giving any other sham-scientific reason for adopting so peculiar a method of safe-keeping.

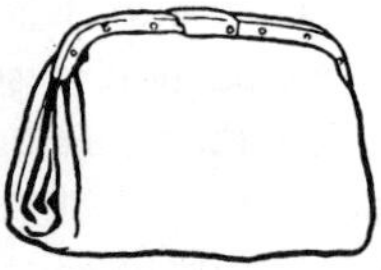

FIG. 1

To produce the desired effect, all that is needed is a small purse of the "bag" kind (Fig. 1), the lower seam of which has been ripped open. The wand lies till needed in the left sleeve, kept from falling out by slightly bending the second and third fingers. The purse is placed in the trouser-pocket on the same side, with the open seam upward. In the act of placing the hand in the pocket to take out the purse, the end of the wand is introduced into the opening. The purse then is opened in the ordinary way, and the wand taken out of it, actually being drawn through it. If the performer stands with his left side toward the spectators, and uses due care as to his position, the arm masks the wand, and no one can possibly see that it comes from the sleeve.

Another arrangement which may be adopted for magically producing the wand is to place it in a clear glass decanter on the performer's table, its upper end projecting above the neck. The wizard finds that he has somewhat mislaid the talisman without which he is powerless. He looks about on all sides, but in vain, till the wand itself calls attention to its presence by rising and falling an inch or so and rapping inside the decanter.

Delighted to regain the instrument of his power, the performer holds his hand ten or twelve inches above the decanter, simply saying "Come." The wand obeys, rising spontaneously into his hand.

The thread in this instance is attached to the lower end of the wand, the remainder of the silk being led away over the neck of the decanter, through an eyelet on the table top, to the hand of an assistant behind the scenes, who pulls as may be required. (Fig. 2)

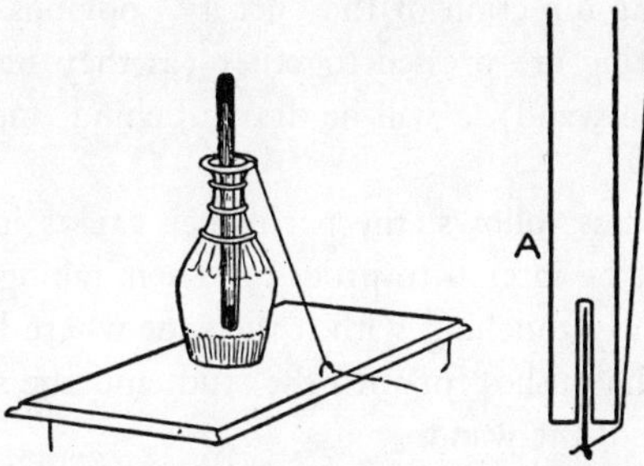

FIG. 2

The best method of attaching the thread is to pass it through the eye of a stout needle, making a knot on the opposite side. The needle, broken off to half its length, is then inserted into a hole, just large enough to receive it loosely, bored in the lower end of the wand in the center of its circular section (*A*, Fig. 2). While the thread is in operation this is perfectly secure, but the moment the wand is taken hold of by the performer, the needle drops out by its own weight, and is drawn away with the thread.

The *Coin Wand* is apparently of ebony, but really of brass, japanned black. It is about twelve inches in length and five-eighths of an inch in diameter. On one side of it, and so placed as to be just under the ball of the thumb when the wand is held in the hand, is a little stud, which moves backward and forward for a short distance (about an inch and a quarter). When this stud is pressed forward, a half-dollar appears on the opposite end of the wand (Fig. 3), retiring within it when the stud is again drawn back.

The half-dollar is a genuine one, but is cut into three portions, as indicated in Fig. 4, which represents a cross-section of it at right angles to the actual cuts. Each of the three segments is attached to a piece of watch-

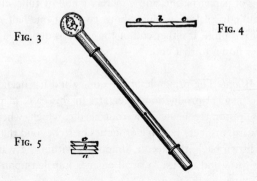

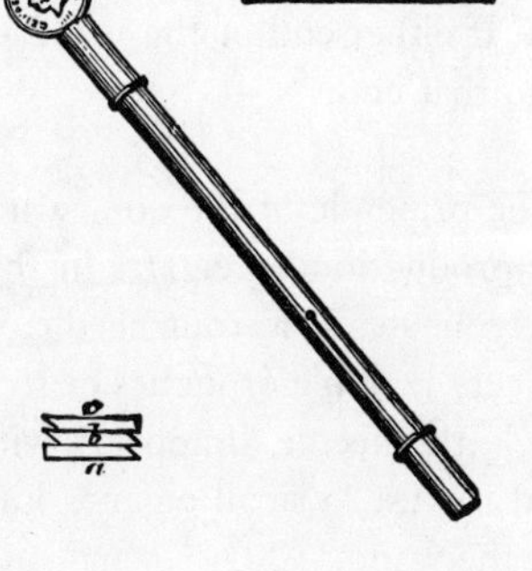

FIG. 3

FIG. 4

FIG. 5

spring, and from the direction of the cuts it is obvious that, when these pieces of watch-spring are pressed together (as they naturally are when drawn back into the wand), *c* will be drawn behind, and *a* in front of *b*. (Fig. 5).

The wand is used as follows: the performer PALMS in his left hand as many half-dollars as he intends to produce. Then, taking the wand in the right hand, and lightly touching with it the spot where he desires to produce a half-dollar, he pushes forward the stud, and the split coin appears on the opposite end of the wand.

He now draws the upper part of the wand through the left hand, at the same moment pressing back the stud, and causing the split coin to retire within the wand, immediately handing for examination with the left hand one of the half-dollars already placed there, and which by this gesture he appears to have just taken from the top of the wand. This is again repeated, and another half-dollar exhibited, until the stock in the left hand is exhausted.

It is desirable, on each occasion of pressing forward or withdrawing the stud, to place the opposite end of the wand in such a position as to be a little shielded from the eyes of the spectators, so that they may not see the actual appearance or disappearance of the coin. A very slight cover is sufficient. The end of the wand may be placed within a person's open mouth (and withdrawn with the half-dollar thereon), within a pocket, or the like. Where no such cover is available, a quick semi-circular sweep should be made with the wand as the coin is protruded or withdrawn.

The Auto-Gravity Wand. A curious effect may be produced by laying down the wand with its loaded end on a table or chair, three parts of its length projecting beyond the edge, in impudent defiance of the law of gravitation.

The wand is of papier mache, and is merely a hollow tube, closed at each end, with a cylindrical leaden plug, about two and one-half inches long, fitting loosely within it. If either end of the wand is depressed, the weight naturally slides down to that end.

The Cigar Wand. The principle of the coin wand has been ingeniously applied to the magical production of cigars. In this case, in place of the half-dollar, the piston terminates in a stout needle, which, when the piston is pushed forward, projects a couple of inches or so beyond the end. When the piston is drawn back, the needle disappears within the wand.

To prepare the wand for use, a small cigar is impaled upon the needle, and drawn back within the wand.

FIG. 6

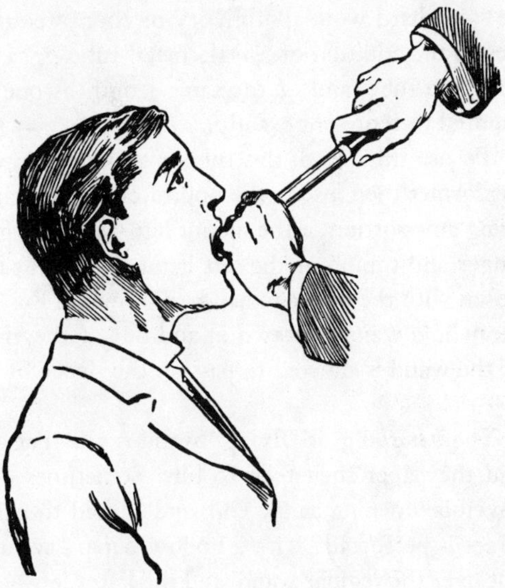

FIG. 7

The Swallowing Wand derives its rather curious title from the fact that it is apparently made to pass, to the extent of two-thirds of its length, down the throat of some young gentleman selected from the audience.

FIG. 8

The wand is in fact the one ordinarily held by the performer, made, say, of some hard wood, with ivory or ebony mounts, as *a* in Fig. 6. The secret lies in the addition of a little metal tube *b*, of such a size as to pass easily over the tube, and of the same length as one of the mounts, which it is painted to represent exactly.

To use this wand, this tube is secretly slipped over one end of it. The performer then inserts the opposite end into the mouth of his victim, covering any portion of the mount left visible by grasping it between the forefinger and thumb of the left hand. He then slides the false mount up and down with the opposite hand, as shown in Fig. 7, producing the effect that the whole wand is drawn in and out of the victim's mouth. The free end of the wand is allowed to pass up the sleeve of the performer. (Fig. 8)

The *vanishing* or "flying" wand is one that can be wrapped up in paper, and the paper then torn to bits. Sometimes the wand is slid into a long envelope opening at the end, and caused to pass to another envelope. The effect is performed with a hollow paper "wand SHELL." Either the shell is put over the regular wand, and the latter left behind in the envelope during the performer's "demonstration" of what is going to happen, or it may be a shell representing only the black body of the wand, with solid tips stuck into the ends. This type of wand shell can be tapped on the table to show it is still there after it is wrapped up.

Yet another variety is made in segments, held together by an elastic through the center, and so constructed that a half-turn of the tip will lock the segments solidly together. Released, the wand will fold down to perhaps four inches long when the paper is crumpled up.

WATCH TRICKS (See also DIVINATIONS; HOOKS; PULLS) The great majority of effects with watches are of two kinds: simple manipulation, as with coins, and smashed-and-restored tricks.

The only special watch sleight of any importance is the SELBIT thumb palm. The watch lies flat on the two middle fingers of the open hand, the bow projecting above and slightly outward from the forefinger (Fig. 1).

FIG. 1

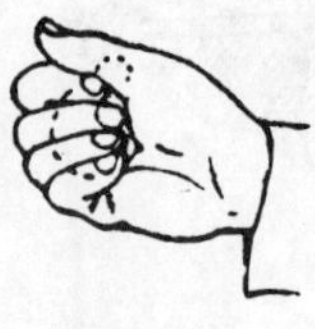

FIG. 2

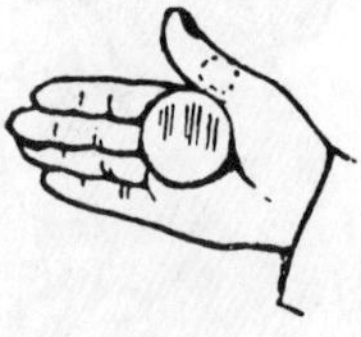

FIG. 3

A momentary closing of the fingers, in the pretended act of putting the watch in the other hand, turns the watch over, and throws the bow into the fork of the thumb. (Fig. 2) The thumb clips the bow, and the palm is complete. (Fig. 3)

Most watch manipulation is performed with dummy watches, lighter, less fragile, and thinner than the real thing; they also often have milled edges to make palming easy.

The dummies are frequently fitted with a HOOK. Small ones can also be BACK-PALMED.

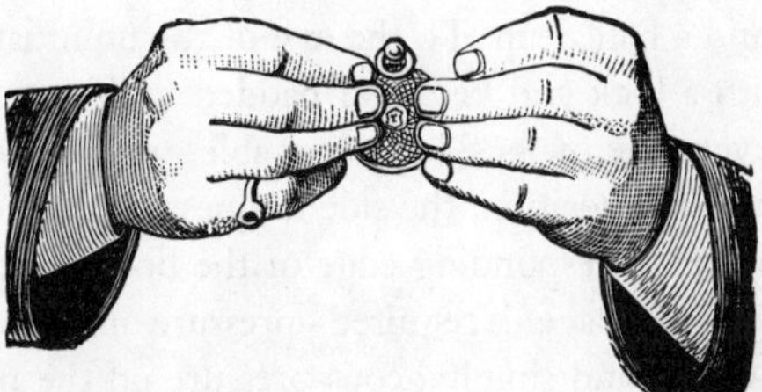

FIG. 4

Bending a borrowed watch backward and forward can hardly be called a conjuring trick, but it may be introduced with good effect in the course of any trick for which a watch has been borrowed. Looking intently at the watch as though you noticed something peculiar about it, you remark to the owner, "This is a very curious watch; it is quite soft." Then taking it (as shown in Fig. 4), with the dial inward toward your own body, and holding it between two fingers of each hand on the back and the thumb of each hand on the face, you bend the hands outward, at the same time bringing the points of the fingers nearer together, immediately bringing them back to their former position. This motion may be repeated any number of times.

By a curious optical illusion, probably produced in some way by the varying shadow of the fingers on the polished surface of the metal, the watch appears, from a distance, to be bent nearly double by each outward movement of the hands.

The first requirement, in the case of most watch tricks, is to obtain secret possession or control of the borrowed article, so as to be able, unknown to the spectators, to deal with it as may be necessary for the purpose of the trick. The use of the *watch box* (with or without the ticking movement) is familiar to all conjurers; it is an oblong mahogany box, four inches by

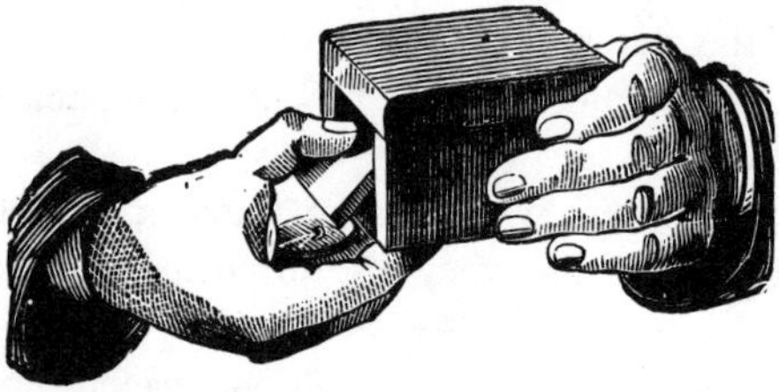

FIG. 5

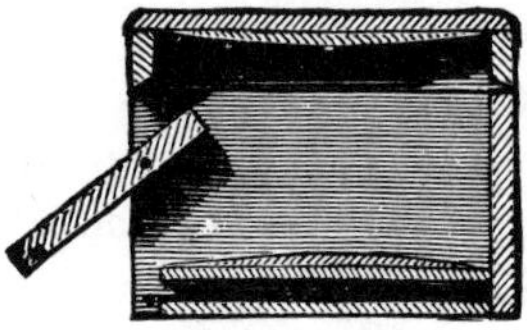

FIG. 6

three, and two and a half deep. To the eye of the uninitiated, it is a simple wooden box, with a lock and key, and padded within at top and bottom. In reality, however, one of its sides is movable, working on a pivot (Figs. 5 and 6). In its normal position, the side in question is held fast by a catch projecting from the corresponding edge of the bottom of the box. To release it, pressure in two places is required—pressure on the bottom of the box so as to lift the catch, and simultaneous pressure on the upper part of the movable side of the box, thus forcing the lower part outward, and allowing the watch or other article placed in the box to fall into the performer's hand. For this purpose the box is held as shown in Fig. 5.

The manner of using the box is as follows: a borrowed watch is placed in it, the owner being requested, in order to ensure its safe-keeping, to lock it up and keep the key. The performer places the box on his table, in full view, but avails himself of the moment during which his back is turned to the audience to extract the watch, as shown in Fig. 5, and to again close the secret opening. Having thus gained possession of the watch, he can conclude the trick by causing it to reappear in any way that he thinks proper.

An improved watch-box, the invention of ROBERT-HOUDIN, contains concealed in the lid, a mechanical arrangement producing a ticking sound, which may be set in motion and stopped at the performer's pleasure. By using this box, the watch may be heard apparently ticking inside until the very moment when it is commanded by the operator to pass to some other apparatus.

The *watch mortar* is an apparatus in the form of an ordinary mortar and pestle. Suggesting to the owner of the borrowed timepiece that it needs regulating, you offer to undertake that duty for him. He probably declines, but you take no notice of his remonstrances, and, placing his watch in the mortar, bring down the pestle with a heavy thump upon it. A smash, as of broken glass, is heard, and, after sufficient pounding you empty the fragments of the watch into your hand.

You promise to return the watch in its original condition, saying that you can only do so through the use of a pistol. Getting a loaf of bread, you place it on the table in view of the audience. Then wrapping the fragments of the watch in paper, you place them in a PISTOL, and, aiming at the loaf, request the owner of the watch to give the signal to fire. The word is given, "One, two, three–Bang!"

Stepping up to the loaf, you bring it forward to the spectators, and tearing it apart, exhibit in its center the borrowed watch, completely restored, and as bright as when it first left the maker's hands.

The seeming mystery is easily explained. The mortar has a movable bottom, which allows the watch to fall through into the performer's hand. There is a hollow space in the thick end of the pestle, closed by a round piece of wood lightly screwed in, which, fitting tightly in the bottom part of the mortar, unscrews itself as the performer apparently grinds away at the ill-fated watch. The fragments of a watch are placed in the cavity beforehand; these fall into the mortar and are poured out by the performer into his hand.

When the performer goes to get the bread, he has already obtained possession of the watch; after giving it a rub on his sleeve to brighten it, he pushes it into a slit already made in the side of the loaf. When the loaf is torn apart (which the performer takes care to do from the side opposite to the slit), the watch is found inside.

The mortar may be of the construction indicated in Fig. 7, which is just the reverse of the ordinary construction. The mortar in this case has no trap; its only speciality is a hemispherical cavity at the bottom, where the fragments of a watch are placed beforehand, and concealed by a loose piece

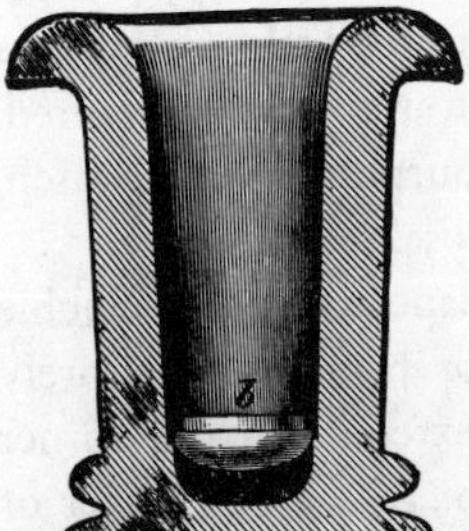

FIG. 7

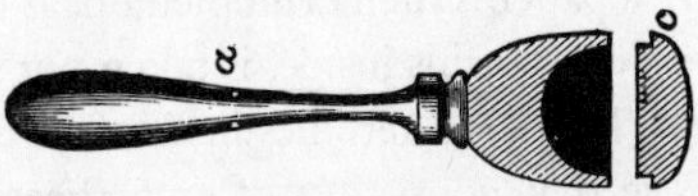

FIG. 8

of boxwood, *b*, which is shaped so as to fit into the lower portion of the pestle.

The pestle is, as shown in Fig. 8, in two portions, *a*, and *c*; *c* is a duplicate of *b*, but fits loosely within *a*, whereas *b* fits it comparatively tightly. When either *c* or *b* is in position, there is a considerable cavity in the head of the pestle; this cavity, the interior of which is padded with some soft material, is utilized to carry off the watch.

The mortar is brought on prepared as described, the pestle empty, but with *c* in position. Having reached the stage of the trick already mentioned, the performer, shaking the fragments of glass on to the outspread paper bag, lowers the watch carefully (with its back toward the audience) into the mortar, where it rests on the top of *b*. He takes the pestle in his right hand with a flourish, then grasps the head with his left, while he peers into the mortar, as if to see that the watch is in the proper position.

This perfectly natural gesture enables him to PALM off *c*, and when he later begins to grind away with the pestle, it is *a* alone that is introduced. A slight rotary motion causes *a* to pick up *b*, and with it the borrowed watch. The grinding motion is continued for a moment or two.

The performer lifts the pestle, and gazes into the mortar; then, as if dissatisfied with his progress, says to his assistant, "This won't do; it would take a week at this rate. Bring me the kitchen poker." A poker is brought, the larger and heavier the better. "Ah! that is something like," says the performer, handing his assistant the pestle in exchange. "Now we shall get on faster."

He pounds away vigorously with the handle of the poker, finally showing the loose watch-works at the bottom of the mortar, and pouring them on to the paper bag, whereon the fragments of glass are already lying. These are now rolled up together, placed in the pistol, and fired in any desired direction. The assistant meanwhile removes the watch from the pestle, and disposes of it as may be required.

Another plan is to form a cone-shaped paper bag, in view of the spectators, drop in the watch (or its substitute), and after a little appropriate PATTER to open out the paper and show that the watch has disappeared. The paper is then crumpled up, as having served its purpose, and the watch, which remains inside, is taken out at leisure for disposal.

The secret here lies in the fact that the sheet of paper is actually double (Fig. 9), consisting of two sheets of newspaper or plain paper entirely pasted together except for a kite-shaped portion extending from corner to corner as indicated by *d*, *e*, *b*, *f*, *d* in the diagram. The loose corner of the upper sheet is cut off, so that the line *e*, *f* forms the mouth of a triangular pocket.

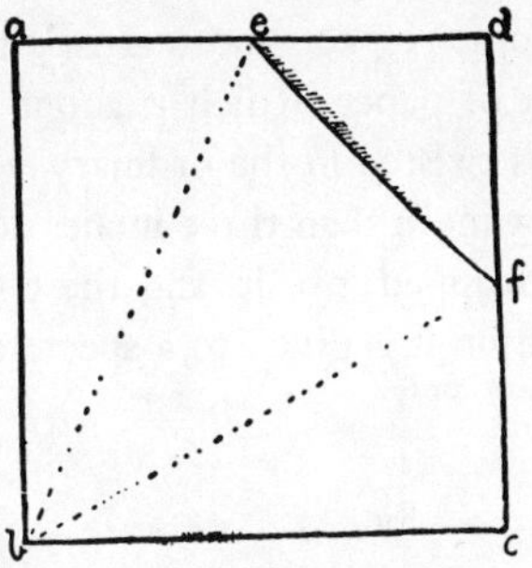

FIG. 9

In the act of twisting the sheet of paper into a bag, the mouth of this pocket (which is kept on the inner side) is opened, and the watch is dropped inside. When the paper is again spread out, and held by the corners *a* and *d*, or *d* and *c*, the watch has disappeared, but does not fall, being held in the angle *b*.

Another method of forming the bag is to take a four-page sheet of some periodical of convenient size, as shown in Fig. 10, and to prepare it by pasting a duplicate (by the edges only) over the upper page. The portion pasted (half an inch wide) extends from *a* to *b*, *b* to *c*, and *c* to *d*; *a* to *d* being left open, and forming the mouth of a square pocket, nearly the size of the page.

In use, the paper is twisted as shown in Fig. 11, the inner edge of the pocket being laid over against the opposite side of the bag. As in the former case, any article dropped into the bag actually goes into the pocket, and

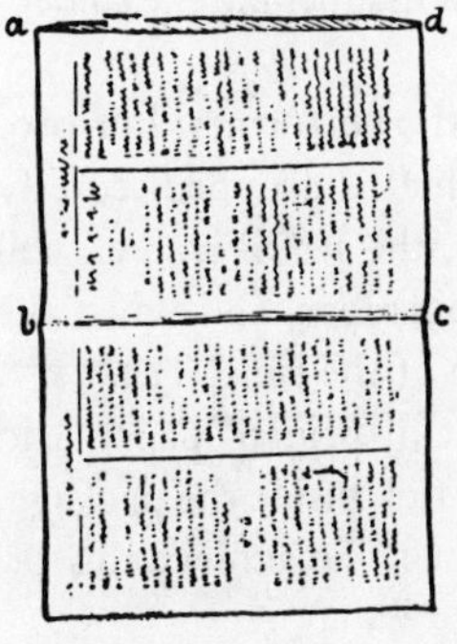

FIG. 10

FIG. 11

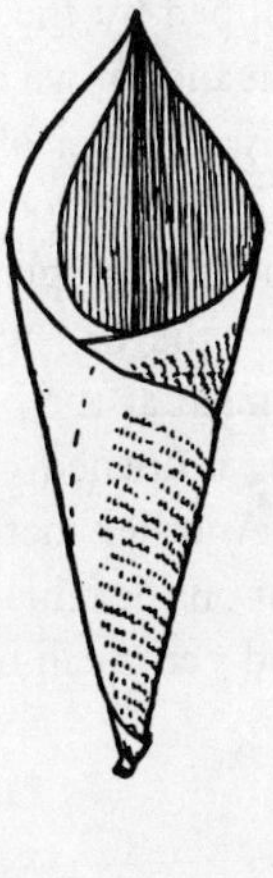

when the paper is unrolled and held by the corners *a*, *d*, or either of them, is found to have disappeared.

For another, and in some respects more artistic method of working this disappearance, the sheet of paper, which is about fourteen inches square, is quite unprepared. It is twisted in the ordinary way into a cone of comparatively small size, not more than three inches across at its widest point (Fig. 12). A watch is dropped into it, and the corner *a* turned down as in Fig. 13. In this condition it is given to a spectator to hold.

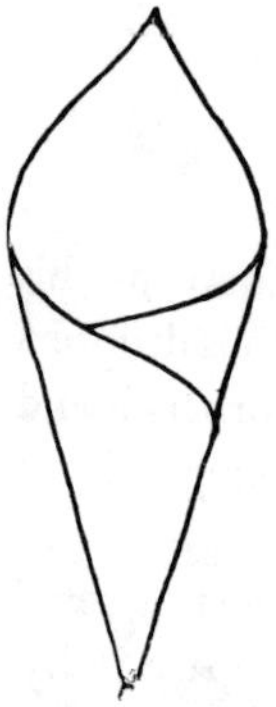

FIG. 12

FIG. 13

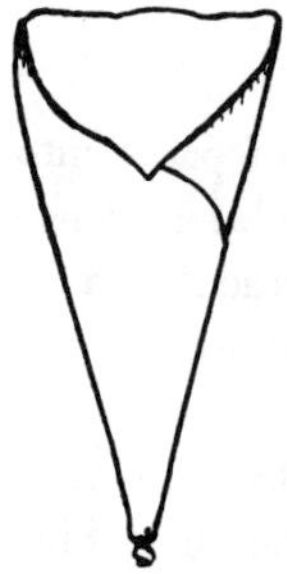

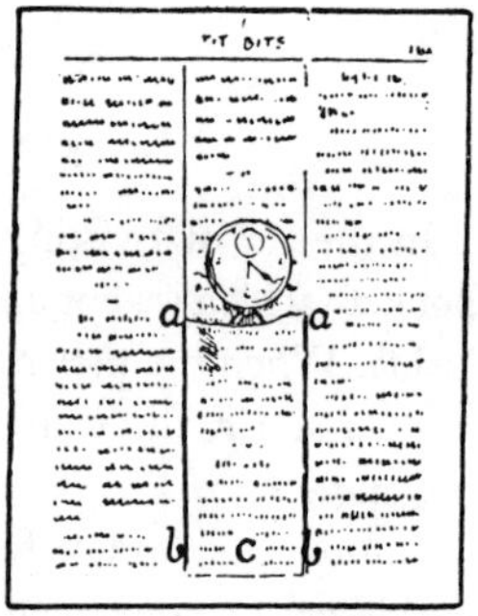

FIG. 14

After a little by-play, the performer takes it from him, grasping it by the upper end, with the fingers in front and thumb behind. He holds it to the spectator's ear, asking if he hears the watch still ticking. In so doing, however, he lowers the bag to a horizontal position, so that the watch runs to the larger end, where it is secured by light pressure with the fingers. The cone is then restored to its normal position, smaller end downward.

The bag may now be transferred from hand to hand, the watch being clipped by the thumb and fingers of each in turn. The bag is then opened out and shown empty, the watch remaining hidden at first behind the folded-down corner of the paper and afterwards palmed.

This method demands some skill on the part of the performer, but produces a complete illusion. If a folded silk handkerchief is dropped secretly into the bag with the watch (the watch on top), the handkerchief will remain at the bottom during the subsequent manipulations, and when the bag is opened will be found to have taken the place of the timepiece.

Another method is to wrap the watch in a sheet of printed paper, laid flat on the table. The watch can be felt and heard to tick inside the package, and yet it can be extracted instantly by the performer. To achieve this result, the paper is again faked, but in a different manner. The paper should be one which has three columns of print, such as that shown in Fig. 14.

A half-column cut from a similar paper is gummed or pasted by its edges along the lines *a b*, *a b*; the ends *a a* and *b b* are left open. The intervening space forms a sort of tunnel across the surface of the paper.

Spreading the sheet on the table, the performer, standing at the side marked *b b*, places the watch in the center, and wraps it up by folding the paper over once or twice toward himself; first, however, he slips the bow of the watch inside the opening *a a*.

If the folding is properly done, the watch will slide along the paper tunnel toward the performer. When it has reached the position indicated by the letter *c*, he turns down the sides from left and right. The watch is now apparently wrapped securely in the middle of the paper, though actually it is resting only in an outward fold, from which the performer can allow it to drop into his hand at pleasure.

The same effect may also be obtained with a piece of unprepared paper, which in this case should be about six inches square, of stout substance, but not harsh or brittle. The performer, taking this in his left hand, lays the watch in the center, and folds down first the right, then the left side over it, not too closely, but leaving a clear half-inch of space on each side of the watch. In folding down the paper, he molds it a little to the shape of the watch.

Having turned down the sides, he next folds down the upper end in the same way. Before making the final fold, he tilts the paper slightly toward him, with the result that the watch runs down to the lower end of the paper, the left little finger, held beneath, preventing it from coming too far. The lower end of the paper is then folded back *with the watch in it.* The watch is, as in the last case, resting in an outer fold, where it may be heard to tick, but from which it can be slipped out instantly when desired.

A next expedient is to use a piece of FLASH PAPER, five inches square, prepared by cutting a cross, an inch and a half long, in its center. If this is done on a flat surface with a sharp knife, the paper may be shown at a short distance without the cut's being noticeable.

Having exhibited it in a casual way, the performer lays it on his left hand, with a small borrowed watch on it. He then gathers up the corners, and twists them together. He holds the packet, still on his hand, to the ear of some spectator, who is satisfied by the ticking that the watch is still there.

With his right hand he picks up the packet by the screwed-up corners, and immediately flashes it off over the candle on his table. At the same time he drops the watch, which has slipped through the cut into his left hand, into his PROFONDE, to be dealt with as the nature of the intended *denouement* may require.

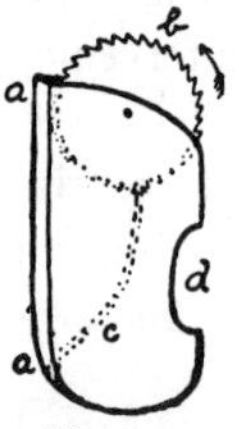

FIG. 15

The *Noisy Watch-Winder* consists of a little flat metal case, *a a* (Fig. 15), about two inches long by one wide, and three-eighths of an inch deep. One end is closed. Projecting from the opposite end is a little cog-wheel *b*, taking up its whole width. Within the case is a steel spring, *c*, whose free end is engaged in the cogs of the wheel.

When the wheel is moved in the direction shown by the arrow in the diagram, a sharp metallic sound, like the winding of a large clock, is produced.

To use the winder, it is held in the right hand, across the second and third joints of the fingers, with the wheel end pointing toward the forefinger. A borrowed watch is taken in the other hand, and a pretense made of winding it (after the usual stem-winding fashion). The performer at the same time runs the ball of the right thumb over the cogwheel, causing it to revolve and producing a sound horrifying to the owner of the watch. The noise may be made greater or less accordingly as the soundhole *d* is left open or covered by the lower part of the thumb.

Watch it! The performer must provide himself, to begin with, with four watches, of the cheap nickeled kind, exactly alike in appearance. To the bezel of one of them, just above the 12, is soldered a needle-point about a quarter of an inch long, pointing downward. This forms a little hook, by means of which the watch is hooked into the performer's coat, behind his back, but within reach of his hand.

The other three watches, which are not prepared, are disposed of as follows: two of them are placed in the vest pocket, one attached to the swivel of the watch chain, the other loose; the third is placed, bow downward, under the front of the vest. The watch attached to the chain will be referred to as No. 1; the one under the vest, No. 2; the one on the back, No. 3; and the one loose in the pocket, No. 4.

Prepared in this way, the performer comes forward to the audience, and takes out watch No. 1, as if to see the time. The sight of the watch suggests that he might do a little conjuring with it. He accordingly takes off the chain, the end of which he tucks under the front of his vest, hooking the swivel into the bow of No. 2 as he does so.

Apparently transferring No. 1 to the left hand (actually palming it in his right), he carries his left hand with the (supposed) watch to his mouth, and makes believe to swallow the watch. After some facial distortion, as if he found it difficult to get down, he draws in the pit of the stomach, when No. 2, released, drops to the full extent of the chain. This is caught by the left hand, the right hand meanwhile dropping No. 1 into a POCHETTE or the PROFONDE.

No. 2 is then unhooked from the chain, and taken in the right hand, while the empty swivel is put back with the left hand into the vest pocket and is hooked into the bow of No. 4. No. 2 is next apparently transferred by any of the familiar passes from one hand to the other, and the hand in which it is ostensibly left is rubbed lightly against the pit of the stomach.

The performer exhibits this hand empty and then turns around to show that the watch has passed through his body and is hanging on his back. This is of course really No. 3, which has been there from the beginning. While he thus turns away from the audience, he has ample opportunity to get rid of No. 2.

With some pretense of difficulty, he gets No. 3 from off his back and holds it in his right hand, with the face toward the spectators. Turning his right side away a little, he counts "One, two, three!" dropping the hand each time, and making believe at the word "three" to throw the watch in the air. The hand rises empty, having at the third downward movement left the watch hooked against the clothing.

After showing the hands empty, the performer places the left hand on the watch-chain and slowly draws out No. 4, the surprise occasioned by its unexpected appearance giving him ample opportunity to palm No. 3 again and transfer it to safer quarters.

The hooking of the swivel into the bow of the watch, using the fingers of only one hand, will require some practice.

The performer, taking a watch in one hand and a pencil in the other, proposes to give a specimen of his powers of DIVINATION. For this purpose he requests anyone present to write down, or, if preferred, merely to think of, any hour he pleases. This having been done, the performer, without asking any questions, proceeds to tap with the pencil different hours on the dial of the watch, requesting the person who has thought of the hour to count the taps mentally, *beginning from the number of the hour he thought of*. (Thus, if he thought of the hour "nine," he must count the first tap as "ten," the second as "eleven," and so on.) When, according to this method of counting, he reaches the number "twenty," he is to say "Stop," when the performer's pencil will be found resting precisely upon the hour of the dial which he thought of.

This capital little trick depends upon a simple arithmetical principle;

but the secret is so well disguised that it is very rarely discovered. All that the performer has to do is to count in his own mind the taps he gives, calling the first "one," the second "two," and so on. The first seven taps may be given upon any figures of the dial indifferently; indeed, they might equally well be given on the back of the watch, or anywhere else, without affecting the ultimate result. But the eighth tap must be given invariably on the figure "twelve" of the dial, and from then on the pencil must travel through the figures one after another, but in reverse order, "eleven," "ten," "nine," and so on.

By following this process it will be found that at the tap which, counting from the number the spectator thought of, will make twenty, the pencil will have traveled back to that very number.

Suppose, for instance, that the hour the spectator thought of was twelve. In this case he will count the first tap of the pencil as thirteen, the second as fourteen, and so on. The eighth tap will complete the twenty. The performer always lets his pencil fall on number twelve at the eighth tap; so when the spectator, having mentally reached the number twenty, cries, "Stop," the pencil will be pointing to that number.

Suppose, again, the number was eleven. The first tap will be counted as twelve, and the ninth (at which, according to the rule, the pencil will be resting on eleven) will make the twenty.

Taking again the smallest number that can be thought of, one, the first tap will be counted by the spectator as two, and the eighth, at which the pencil reaches twelve, will count as nine. From here on the pencil will travel regularly backward around the dial, and at the nineteenth tap (completing the twenty, as counted by the spectator) will have just reached the figure one.

L. H.

A thorough treatment of the whole subject will be found in Samuel Berland's *Tricks with Watches.*

WAX Beeswax is an article of frequent use in magical operations; if, as sometimes happens, the pure wax is found to be too hard, or not adhesive enough, the addition of a small quantity (say an eighth part) of turpentine, mixed with the melted wax, will soften it.

The best wax for magic purposes may be purchased at any drugstore. It is called "Diachylon Plaster" (or lead plaster). Its usual form is a round bar about one inch in diameter.

Cut out from the center a small piece, and work it between the fingers a few moments, when it will become tacky; it will come off clean and in one piece from the card or other object with which it is used.

WILLIAMS, OSWALD (ca. 1881-1937) outstanding English conjurer and illusionist, long connected with the third generation of the MASKELYNE family at St. George's Hall.

WINE AND WATER In effect, this venerable trick is related to the INEXHAUSTIBLE BOTTLE, but the methods are entirely different. The performer has a clear glass pitcher of water, from which he pours either water or red wine at will; the wine can be changed to water and back.

The chemical method of doing the trick has even found its way into the official high school curriculum of New Jersey, and is entirely worn out. The nearest approach to it that would be tolerated by a present-day audience is the distribution of various drinks by means of essences in the bottom of the glasses, as in the modern inexhaustible bottle methods.

A stage method calls for the use of translucent colored plastic FAKES, sheets of celluloid or plexiglas cut to fit loosely upright in the glasses, and just tall enough to reach the proposed water line. The fakes must be dropped into the glasses under cover of a handkerchief or piece of paper, and the water diffuses the color quite deceptively.

An older, related method is to use a cylindrical silk bag that fits inside the glass. A black one makes a fine imitation of ink, and other colors can also be used. In order to prove the quality of the ink, the performer may dip in a card, withdrawing it with the lower half stained black. One side of the card has one half inked; a half-turn while dipping the card brings the stained side to the front. A ladle with a hollow handle, on the principle of the FUNNEL, enables the conjurer to dip out ink for inspection, which is seldom a good idea (see PSYCHOLOGY).

WYMAN, JOHN (1816-1881), the first American-born magician to give a full evening's show. He first launched himself as a ventriloquist, then branched out into magic. He was one of the first performers to expose spiritualism in his act. Although not so well remembered, Wyman was the contemporary, competitor, and apparently pretty much the equal in public esteem of ANDERSON, BLITZ, HELLER, and CARL HERRMANN.

Y

YOU DO AS I DO The name for a class of card tricks performed with two decks, usually a red-backed one and a blue-backed one. A VOLUNTEER chooses one pack, and shuffles it, while the performer shuffles his. The volunteer is told to copy every move the performer makes. In basic effect, the performer chooses a card from his pack, the volunteer does likewise, and both cards prove to be the same. Sometimes the two participants look at their cards to begin with, more often they do not. The simpler methods of doing the trick are good enough to support its popularity, but many of the elaborations are confusing and poor entertainment.

Perhaps the simplest method is to STEAL beforehand one card of the volunteer's pack, catch a glimpse of it, and then cut it to a position about a third of the way down in your own deck. Then run through (taking care not to disclose the stolen card) and get the corresponding card of your own pack to the top.

The volunteer removes one card from his own pack without looking at it, and puts it face down on the table. You do likewise, taking the known top card from your pack. You then thrust your card into his pack, and put his into your pack, fairly well down. This brings it below the card you originally stole.

"Wait, we should have left the cards sticking out," you say. You then run through your pack as far as the upper, or stolen card, which you pull part way out. The volunteer pulls your card part way out of his pack, and when turned over, the two cards prove to coincide.

By giving the spectator a SET-UP deck, you can learn immediately what card he has drawn (in this case he may look at it), and find the corresponding card in an unprepared pack.

Many versions of the trick will be found in Hilliard's *Greater Magic* and Hugard's *Encyclopedia of Card Tricks.*

A CATALOGUE OF SELECTED DOVER BOOKS IN ALL FIELDS OF INTEREST

VISUAL ILLUSIONS: THEIR CAUSES, CHARACTERISTICS, AND APPLICATIONS, Matthew Luckiesh. Thorough description and discussion of optical illusion, geometric and perspective, particularly; size and shape distortions, illusions of color, of motion; natural illusions; use of illusion in art and magic, industry, etc. Most useful today with op art, also for classical art. Scores of effects illustrated. Introduction by William H. Ittleson. 100 illustrations. xxi + 252pp.
21530-X Paperbound $2.00

A HANDBOOK OF ANATOMY FOR ART STUDENTS, Arthur Thomson. Thorough, virtually exhaustive coverage of skeletal structure, musculature, etc. Full text, supplemented by anatomical diagrams and drawings and by photographs of undraped figures. Unique in its comparison of male and female forms, pointing out differences of contour, texture, form. 211 figures, 40 drawings, 86 photographs. xx + 459pp. 5⅜ x 8⅜.
21163-0 Paperbound $3.50

150 MASTERPIECES OF DRAWING, Selected by Anthony Toney. Full page reproductions of drawings from the early 16th to the end of the 18th century, all beautifully reproduced: Rembrandt, Michelangelo, Dürer, Fragonard, Urs, Graf, Wouwerman, many others. First-rate browsing book, model book for artists. xviii + 150pp. 8⅜ x 11¼.
21032-4 Paperbound $2.50

THE LATER WORK OF AUBREY BEARDSLEY, Aubrey Beardsley. Exotic, erotic, ironic masterpieces in full maturity: Comedy Ballet, Venus and Tannhauser, Pierrot, Lysistrata, Rape of the Lock, Savoy material, Ali Baba, Volpone, etc. This material revolutionized the art world, and is still powerful, fresh, brilliant. With *The Early Work,* all Beardsley's finest work. 174 plates, 2 in color. xiv + 176pp. 8⅛ x 11.
21817-1 Paperbound $3.75

DRAWINGS OF REMBRANDT, Rembrandt van Rijn. Complete reproduction of fabulously rare edition by Lippmann and Hofstede de Groot, completely reedited, updated, improved by Prof. Seymour Slive, Fogg Museum. Portraits, Biblical sketches, landscapes, Oriental types, nudes, episodes from classical mythology—All Rembrandt's fertile genius. Also selection of drawings by his pupils and followers. "Stunning volumes," *Saturday Review.* 550 illustrations. lxxviii + 552pp. 9⅛ x 12¼.
21485-0, 21486-9 Two volumes, Paperbound $10.00

THE DISASTERS OF WAR, Francisco Goya. One of the masterpieces of Western civilization—83 etchings that record Goya's shattering, bitter reaction to the Napoleonic war that swept through Spain after the insurrection of 1808 and to war in general. Reprint of the first edition, with three additional plates from Boston's Museum of Fine Arts. All plates facsimile size. Introduction by Philip Hofer, Fogg Museum. v + 97pp. 9⅜ x 8¼.
21872-4 Paperbound $2.50

GRAPHIC WORKS OF ODILON REDON. Largest collection of Redon's graphic works ever assembled: 172 lithographs, 28 etchings and engravings, 9 drawings. These include some of his most famous works. All the plates from *Odilon Redon: oeuvre graphique complet,* plus additional plates. New introduction and caption translations by Alfred Werner. 209 illustrations. xxvii + 209pp. 9⅛ x 12¼.
21966-8 Paperbound $4.50

DESIGN BY ACCIDENT; A BOOK OF "ACCIDENTAL EFFECTS" FOR ARTISTS AND DESIGNERS, James F. O'Brien. Create your own unique, striking, imaginative effects by "controlled accident" interaction of materials: paints and lacquers, oil and water based paints, splatter, crackling materials, shatter, similar items. Everything you do will be different; first book on this limitless art, so useful to both fine artist and commercial artist. Full instructions. 192 plates showing "accidents," 8 in color. viii + 215pp. 8⅜ x 11¼. 21942-9 Paperbound $3.75

THE BOOK OF SIGNS, Rudolf Koch. Famed German type designer draws 493 beautiful symbols: religious, mystical, alchemical, imperial, property marks, runes, etc. Remarkable fusion of traditional and modern. Good for suggestions of timelessness, smartness, modernity. Text. vi + 104pp. 6⅛ x 9¼.
20162-7 Paperbound $1.50

HISTORY OF INDIAN AND INDONESIAN ART, Ananda K. Coomaraswamy. An unabridged republication of one of the finest books by a great scholar in Eastern art. Rich in descriptive material, history, social backgrounds; Sunga reliefs, Rajput paintings, Gupta temples, Burmese frescoes, textiles, jewelry, sculpture, etc. 400 photos. viii + 423pp. 6⅜ x 9¾. 21436-2 Paperbound $5.00

PRIMITIVE ART, Franz Boas. America's foremost anthropologist surveys textiles, ceramics, woodcarving, basketry, metalwork, etc.; patterns, technology, creation of symbols, style origins. All areas of world, but very full on Northwest Coast Indians. More than 350 illustrations of baskets, boxes, totem poles, weapons, etc. 378 pp.
20025-6 Paperbound $3.00

THE GENTLEMAN AND CABINET MAKER'S DIRECTOR, Thomas Chippendale. Full reprint (third edition, 1762) of most influential furniture book of all time, by master cabinetmaker. 200 plates, illustrating chairs, sofas, mirrors, tables, cabinets, plus 24 photographs of surviving pieces. Biographical introduction by N. Bienenstock. vi + 249pp. 9⅞ x 12¾. 21601-2 Paperbound $5.00

AMERICAN ANTIQUE FURNITURE, Edgar G. Miller, Jr. The basic coverage of all American furniture before 1840. Individual chapters cover type of furniture—clocks, tables, sideboards, etc.—chronologically, with inexhaustible wealth of data. More than 2100 photographs, all identified, commented on. Essential to all early American collectors. Introduction by H. E. Keyes. vi + 1106pp. 7⅞ x 10¾.
21599-7, 21600-4 Two volumes, Paperbound $11.00

PENNSYLVANIA DUTCH AMERICAN FOLK ART, Henry J. Kauffman. 279 photos, 28 drawings of tulipware, Fraktur script, painted tinware, toys, flowered furniture, quilts, samplers, hex signs, house interiors, etc. Full descriptive text. Excellent for tourist, rewarding for designer, collector. Map. 146pp. 7⅞ x 10¾.
21205-X Paperbound $3.00

EARLY NEW ENGLAND GRAVESTONE RUBBINGS, Edmund V. Gillon, Jr. 43 photographs, 226 carefully reproduced rubbings show heavily symbolic, sometimes macabre early gravestones, up to early 19th century. Remarkable early American primitive art, occasionally strikingly beautiful; always powerful. Text. xxvi + 207pp. 8⅜ x 11¼. 21380-3 Paperbound $4.00

ALPHABETS AND ORNAMENTS, Ernst Lehner. Well-known pictorial source for decorative alphabets, script examples, cartouches, frames, decorative title pages, calligraphic initials, borders, similar material. 14th to 19th century, mostly European. Useful in almost any graphic arts designing, varied styles. 750 illustrations. 256pp. 7 x 10. 21905-4 Paperbound $4.00

PAINTING: A CREATIVE APPROACH, Norman Colquhoun. For the beginner simple guide provides an instructive approach to painting: major stumbling blocks for beginner; overcoming them, technical points; paints and pigments; oil painting; watercolor and other media and color. New section on "plastic" paints. Glossary. Formerly *Paint Your Own Pictures.* 221pp. 22000-1 Paperbound $1.75

THE ENJOYMENT AND USE OF COLOR, Walter Sargent. Explanation of the relations between colors themselves and between colors in nature and art, including hundreds of little-known facts about color values, intensities, effects of high and low illumination, complementary colors. Many practical hints for painters, references to great masters. 7 color plates, 29 illustrations. x + 274pp.
20944-X Paperbound $3.00

THE NOTEBOOKS OF LEONARDO DA VINCI, compiled and edited by Jean Paul Richter. 1566 extracts from original manuscripts reveal the full range of Leonardo's versatile genius: all his writings on painting, sculpture, architecture, anatomy, astronomy, geography, topography, physiology, mining, music, etc., in both Italian and English, with 186 plates of manuscript pages and more than 500 additional drawings. Includes studies for the Last Supper, the lost Sforza monument, and other works. Total of xlvii + 866pp. 7⅞ x 10¾.
22572-0, 22573-9 Two volumes, Paperbound $12.00

MONTGOMERY WARD CATALOGUE OF 1895. Tea gowns, yards of flannel and pillow-case lace, stereoscopes, books of gospel hymns, the New Improved Singer Sewing Machine, side saddles, milk skimmers, straight-edged razors, high-button shoes, spittoons, and on and on . . . listing some 25,000 items, practically all illustrated. Essential to the shoppers of the 1890's, it is our truest record of the spirit of the period. Unaltered reprint of Issue No. 57, Spring and Summer 1895. Introduction by Boris Emmet. Innumerable illustrations. xiii + 624pp. 8½ x 11⅝.
22377-9 Paperbound $8.50

THE CRYSTAL PALACE EXHIBITION ILLUSTRATED CATALOGUE (LONDON, 1851). One of the wonders of the modern world—the Crystal Palace Exhibition in which all the nations of the civilized world exhibited their achievements in the arts and sciences—presented in an equally important illustrated catalogue. More than 1700 items pictured with accompanying text—ceramics, textiles, cast-iron work, carpets, pianos, sleds, razors, wall-papers, billiard tables, beehives, silverware and hundreds of other artifacts—represent the focal point of Victorian culture in the Western World. Probably the largest collection of Victorian decorative art ever assembled—indispensable for antiquarians and designers. Unabridged republication of the Art-Journal Catalogue of the Great Exhibition of 1851, with all terminal essays. New introduction by John Gloag, F.S.A. xxxiv + 426pp. 9 x 12.
22503-8 Paperbound $5.00

THE ARCHITECTURE OF COUNTRY HOUSES, Andrew J. Downing. Together with Vaux's *Villas and Cottages* this is the basic book for Hudson River Gothic architecture of the middle Victorian period. Full, sound discussions of general aspects of housing, architecture, style, decoration, furnishing, together with scores of detailed house plans, illustrations of specific buildings, accompanied by full text. Perhaps the most influential single American architectural book. 1850 edition. Introduction by J. Stewart Johnson. 321 figures, 34 architectural designs. xvi + 560pp.
22003-6 Paperbound $5.00

LOST EXAMPLES OF COLONIAL ARCHITECTURE, John Mead Howells. Full-page photographs of buildings that have disappeared or been so altered as to be denatured, including many designed by major early American architects. 245 plates. xvii + 248pp. 7⅞ x 10¾. 21143-6 Paperbound $3.50

DOMESTIC ARCHITECTURE OF THE AMERICAN COLONIES AND OF THE EARLY REPUBLIC, Fiske Kimball. Foremost architect and restorer of Williamsburg and Monticello covers nearly 200 homes between 1620-1825. Architectural details, construction, style features, special fixtures, floor plans, etc. Generally considered finest work in its area. 219 illustrations of houses, doorways, windows, capital mantels. xx + 314pp. 7⅞ x 10¾. 21743-4 Paperbound $4.00

EARLY AMERICAN ROOMS: 1650-1858, edited by Russell Hawes Kettell. Tour of 12 rooms, each representative of a different era in American history and each furnished, decorated, designed and occupied in the style of the era. 72 plans and elevations, 8-page color section, etc., show fabrics, wall papers, arrangements, etc. Full descriptive text. xvii + 200pp. of text. 8⅜ x 11¼.
21633-0 Paperbound $5.00

THE FITZWILLIAM VIRGINAL BOOK, edited by J. Fuller Maitland and W. B. Squire. Full modern printing of famous early 17th-century ms. volume of 300 works by Morley, Byrd, Bull, Gibbons, etc. For piano or other modern keyboard instrument; easy to read format. xxxvi + 938pp. 8⅜ x 11.
21068-5, 21069-3 Two volumes, Paperbound $12.00

KEYBOARD MUSIC, Johann Sebastian Bach. Bach Gesellschaft edition. A rich selection of Bach's masterpieces for the harpsichord: the six English Suites, six French Suites, the six Partitas (Clavierübung part I), the Goldberg Variations (Clavierübung part IV), the fifteen Two-Part Inventions and the fifteen Three-Part Sinfonias. Clearly reproduced on large sheets with ample margins; eminently playable. vi + 312pp. 8⅛ x 11. 22360-4 Paperbound $5.00

THE MUSIC OF BACH: AN INTRODUCTION, Charles Sanford Terry. A fine, nontechnical introduction to Bach's music, both instrumental and vocal. Covers organ music, chamber music, passion music, other types. Analyzes themes, developments, innovations. x + 114pp. 21075-8 Paperbound $1.95

BEETHOVEN AND HIS NINE SYMPHONIES, Sir George Grove. Noted British musicologist provides best history, analysis, commentary on symphonies. Very thorough, rigorously accurate; necessary to both advanced student and amateur music lover. 436 musical passages. vii + 407 pp. 20334-4 Paperbound $4.00

MATHEMATICAL PUZZLES FOR BEGINNERS AND ENTHUSIASTS, Geoffrey Mott-Smith. 189 puzzles from easy to difficult—involving arithmetic, logic, algebra, properties of digits, probability, etc.—for enjoyment and mental stimulus. Explanation of mathematical principles behind the puzzles. 135 illustrations. viii + 248pp.
20198-8 Paperbound $2.00

PAPER FOLDING FOR BEGINNERS, William D. Murray and Francis J. Rigney. Easiest book on the market, clearest instructions on making interesting, beautiful origami. Sail boats, cups, roosters, frogs that move legs, bonbon boxes, standing birds, etc. 40 projects; more than 275 diagrams and photographs. 94pp.
20713-7 Paperbound $1.00

TRICKS AND GAMES ON THE POOL TABLE, Fred Herrmann. 79 tricks and games—some solitaires, some for two or more players, some competitive games—to entertain you between formal games. Mystifying shots and throws, unusual caroms, tricks involving such props as cork, coins, a hat, etc. Formerly *Fun on the Pool Table.* 77 figures. 95pp. 21814-7 Paperbound $1.25

HAND SHADOWS TO BE THROWN UPON THE WALL: A SERIES OF NOVEL AND AMUSING FIGURES FORMED BY THE HAND, Henry Bursill. Delightful picturebook from great-grandfather's day shows how to make 18 different hand shadows: a bird that flies, duck that quacks, dog that wags his tail, camel, goose, deer, boy, turtle, etc. Only book of its sort. vi + 33pp. 6½ x 9¼. 21779-5 Paperbound $1.00

WHITTLING AND WOODCARVING, E. J. Tangerman. 18th printing of best book on market. "If you can cut a potato you can carve" toys and puzzles, chains, chessmen, caricatures, masks, frames, woodcut blocks, surface patterns, much more. Information on tools, woods, techniques. Also goes into serious wood sculpture from Middle Ages to present, East and West. 464 photos, figures. x + 293pp.
20965-2 Paperbound $2.50

HISTORY OF PHILOSOPHY, Julián Marias. Possibly the clearest, most easily followed, best planned, most useful one-volume history of philosophy on the market; neither skimpy nor overfull. Full details on system of every major philosopher and dozens of less important thinkers from pre-Socratics up to Existentialism and later. Strong on many European figures usually omitted. Has gone through dozens of editions in Europe. 1966 edition, translated by Stanley Appelbaum and Clarence Strowbridge. xviii + 505pp. 21739-6 Paperbound $3.50

YOGA: A SCIENTIFIC EVALUATION, Kovoor T. Behanan. Scientific but non-technical study of physiological results of yoga exercises; done under auspices of Yale U. Relations to Indian thought, to psychoanalysis, etc. 16 photos. xxiii + 270pp.
20505-3 Paperbound $2.50

Prices subject to change without notice.
Available at your book dealer or write for free catalogue to Dept. GI, Dover Publications, Inc., 180 Varick St., N. Y., N. Y. 10014. Dover publishes more than 150 books each year on science, elementary and advanced mathematics, biology, music, art, literary history, social sciences and other areas.

Bob + Pam Mulholland